ENEMY ORDER OF BATTLE IN WEST NORMANDY
AS AT 30 JUNE 44

7/11

81 CORPS

16 GAF

10 SS Pz

2 SS

Normandy '44

NORMANDY '44

D-Day and the Battle
for France

A New History

James Holland

BANTAM PRESS

TRANSWORLD PUBLISHERS
61–63 Uxbridge Road, London W5 5SA
www.penguin.co.uk

Transworld is part of the Penguin Random House group of companies
whose addresses can be found at global.penguinrandomhouse.com

Penguin
Random House
UK

First published in Great Britain in 2019 by Bantam Press
an imprint of Transworld Publishers

A CIP catalogue record for this book
is available from the British Library.

ISBNs 9781787631274 (cased)
9781787631281 (tpb)

Typeset in 11.25/14 pt Minion Pro by Jouve (UK), Milton Keynes
Printed and bound in Great Britain by Clays Ltd, Elcograf S.p.A.

Penguin Random House is committed to a sustainable
future for our business, our readers and our planet. This book
is made from Forest Stewardship Council® certified paper.

MIX
Paper from
responsible sources
FSC
www.fsc.org   FSC® C018179

1 3 5 7 9 10 8 6 4 2

For Bill Scott-Kerr

Contents

List of Maps

Map Key

ALLIED UNITS

▢	Static division
⊠	Infantry division
▽	Parachute division
◣	Armoured division

GERMAN UNITS

▪	Static division
⊠	Infantry division
▽	*Fallschirmjäger* (paratrooper) division
◣	Panzer division
⊠	Panzergrenadier division
●	Artillery division

STANDARD MILITARY SYMBOLS

I = Company
II = Battalion
III = Regiment

X = Brigade
XX = Division
XXX = Corps
XXXX = Army
XXXXX = Army group

Aerial photo: Gold Beach.

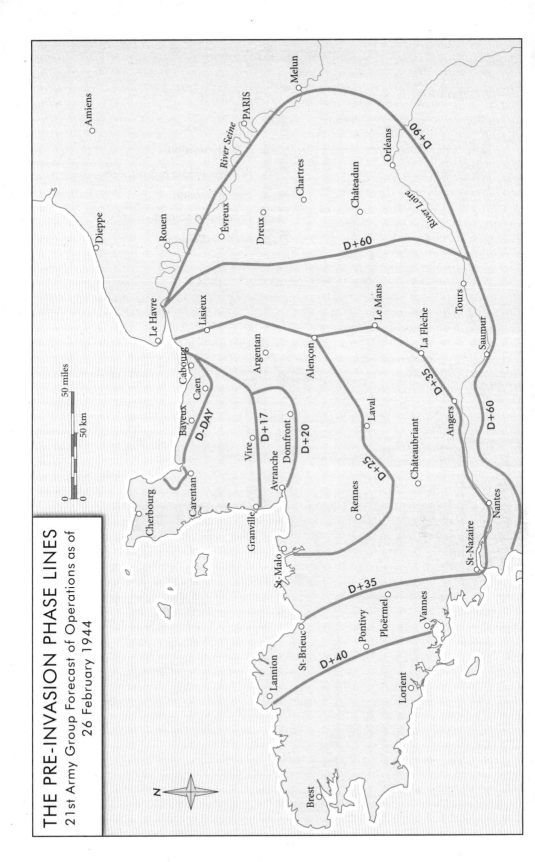

THE PRE-INVASION PHASE LINES
21st Army Group Forecast of Operations as of
26 February 1944

50 miles
50 km

N

Amiens

Dieppe

River Seine

PARIS

Melun

Orléans

D+90

Chartres

Châteadun

Rouen

Evreux

Dreux

River Loire

D+60

Le Havre

Lisieux

Le Mans

Tours

Cabourg

Argentan

Alençon

La Flèche

Saumur

Caen

Bayeux

D-DAY

D+17

Domfront

D+20

Laval

Angers

D+35

D+60

Vire

Avranche

Châteaubriant

Cherbourg

Carentan

Granville

Rennes

D+25

St-Malo

Nantes

St-Nazaire

D+35

Pontivy

Ploërmel

Vannes

St-Brieuc

D+40

Lannion

Lorient

Brest

ALLIED BOMBING TARGETS IN NORTHERN FRANCE BEFORE D-DAY

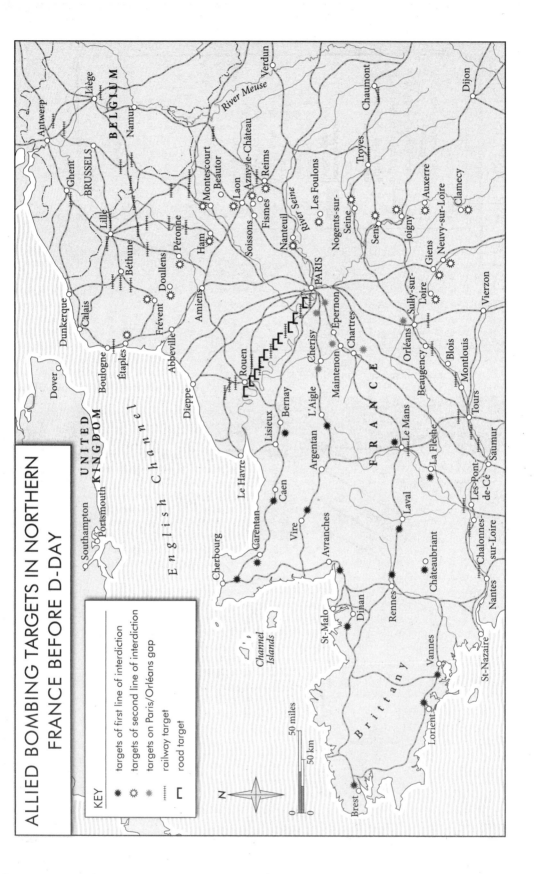

KEY

🟎 targets of first line of interdiction
✸ targets of second line of interdiction
✶ targets on Paris/Orléans gap
╟╫╢ railway target
⌐ road target

50 miles
50 km

N

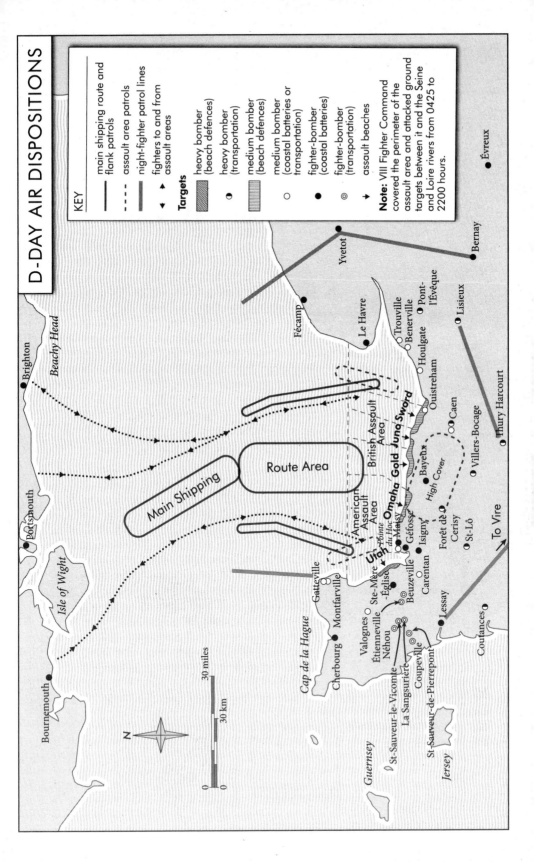

D-DAY AIR DISPOSITIONS

KEY

- main shipping route and flank patrols
- assault area patrols
- night-fighter patrol lines
- fighters to and from assault areas

Targets

- heavy bomber (beach defences)
- heavy bomber (transportation)
- medium bomber (beach defences)
- medium bomber (coastal batteries or transportation)
- fighter-bomber (coastal batteries)
- fighter-bomber (transportation)
- assault beaches

Note: VIII Fighter Command covered the perimeter of the assault area and attacked ground targets between it and the Seine and Loire rivers from 0425 to 2200 hours.

Brighton
Beachy Head
Bournemouth
Portsmouth
Isle of Wight
Guernsey
Jersey
Cap de la Hague
Cherbourg
Montfarville
Gatteville
Valognes
Étienneville
Néhou
St-Sauveur-le-Vicomte
La Sangsurière
Coupeville
St-Sauveur-de-Pierrepont
Coutances
Lessay
Carentan
Beuzeville
Ste-Mère-Église
Pointe du Hoc
Maisy
Géfosse
Isigny
St-Lô
Cerisy
Forêt de
To Vire
Villers-Bocage
Thury Harcourt
Lisieux
Caen
High Cover
Bayeux
Ouistreham
Houlgate
Benerville
Pont-l'Évêque
Trouville
Le Havre
Fécamp
Yvetot
Bernay
Évreux

Main Shipping
Route Area
British Assault Area
American Assault Area
Utah Omaha Gold June Sword

N
30 miles
30 km
0

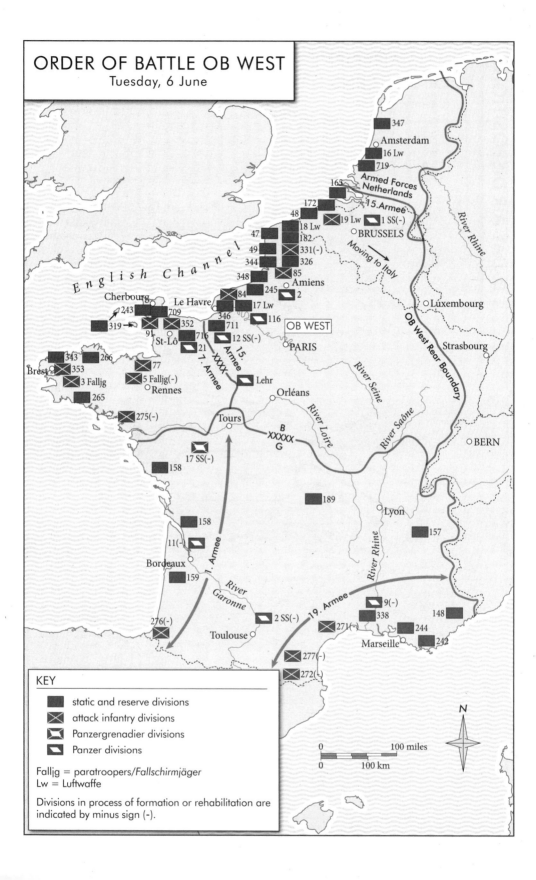

ORDER OF BATTLE OB WEST
Tuesday, 6 June

347

Amsterdam

16 Lw

719

Armed Forces
Netherlands

165

172

48

15.Armee

18 Lw

19 Lw

1 SS(-)

182

BRUSSELS

47

331(-)

49

326

344

85

Moving to Italy

348

245

Amiens

84

2

Luxembourg

17 Lw

346

Cherbourg

709

Le Havre

116

OB WEST

243

711

319

12 SS(-)

Strasbourg

91

352

St-Lô

716

PARIS

OB West Rear Boundary

21

343

266

77

15.
Armee

River Seine

Brest

353

7. Armee XXXX

3 Falljg

5 Falljg(-)

Rennes

Lehr

Orléans

River Saône

265

River Loire

BERN

275(-)

Tours

B
XXXXX
G

17 SS(-)

158

189

Lyon

158

11(-)

River Rhine

157

Bordeaux

1. Armee

159

River
Garonne

276(-)

2 SS(-)

19. Armee

9(-)

338

148

Toulouse

271(-)

244

242

Marseille

277(-)

272(-)

KEY

- ■ static and reserve divisions
- ⊠ attack infantry divisions
- ▱ Panzergrenadier divisions
- ▰ Panzer divisions

Falljg = paratroopers/*Fallschirmjäger*
Lw = Luftwaffe

Divisions in process of formation or rehabilitation are
indicated by minus sign (-).

English Channel

N

0   100 miles

0   100 km

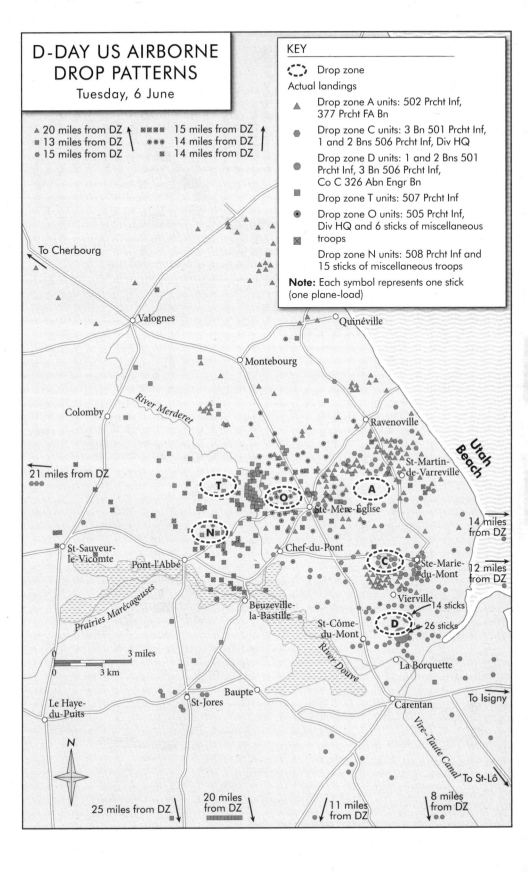

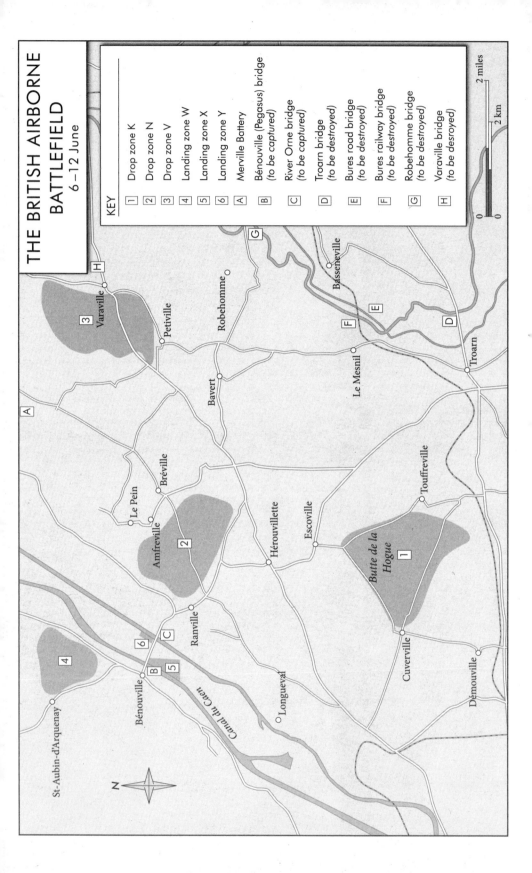

THE BRITISH AIRBORNE BATTLEFIELD
6–12 June

KEY

1. Drop zone K
2. Drop zone N
3. Drop zone V
4. Landing zone W
5. Landing zone X
6. Landing zone Y
A. Merville Battery
B. Bénouville (Pegasus) bridge (to be captured)
C. River Orne bridge (to be captured)
D. Troarn bridge (to be destroyed)
E. Bures road bridge (to be destroyed)
F. Bures railway bridge (to be destroyed)
G. Robehomme bridge (to be destroyed)
H. Varaville bridge (to be destroyed)

0   2 km
0   2 miles

N

St-Aubin-d'Arquenay
Bénouville
Canal du Caen
Longueval
Cuverville
Démouville
Ranville
Hérouvillette
Escoville
Butte de la Hogue
Touffreville
Amfreville
Le Pein
Bréville
Bavert
Le Mesnil
Troarn
Petiville
Robehomme
Basseneville
Varaville

Troops of the 6th Airborne Division meet up with Commandos in Bénouville.

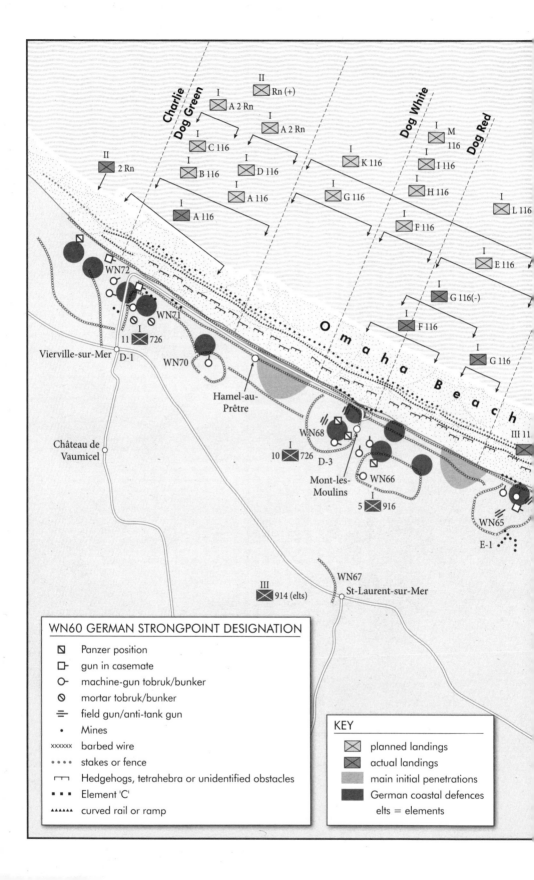

Charlie
Dog Green
Dog White
Dog Red

II ⊠ Rn (+)

I ⊠ A 2 Rn

I ⊠ A 2 Rn

I ⊠ C 116

I ⊠ M 116

I ⊠ I 116

II ⊠ 2 Rn

I ⊠ B 116

I ⊠ D 116

I ⊠ K 116

I ⊠ H 116

I ⊠ A 116

I ⊠ G 116

I ⊠ L 116

I ⊠ A 116

I ⊠ F 116

I ⊠ E 116

WN72

WN71

I
11 ⊠ 726

Vierville-sur-Mer D-1

WN70

Hamel-au-Prêtre

Château de Vaumicel

O m a h a   B e a c h

I ⊠ G 116(-)

I ⊠ F 116

I ⊠ G 116

III 11

WN68

I
10 ⊠ 726   D-3

Mont-les-Moulins

O WN66

I
5 ⊠ 916

WN65

E-1

III
⊠ 914 (elts)

WN67
St-Laurent-sur-Mer

WN60 GERMAN STRONGPOINT DESIGNATION

- ◩ Panzer position
- ⬚ gun in casemate
- o– machine-gun tobruk/bunker
- ⊘ mortar tobruk/bunker
- = field gun/anti-tank gun
- • Mines
- xxxxxx barbed wire
- •••• stakes or fence
- ⊓ Hedgehogs, tetrahebra or unidentified obstacles
- ▪ ▪ ▪ Element 'C'
- ▲▲▲▲▲ curved rail or ramp

KEY

- ⊠ planned landings
- ⊠ actual landings
- ▨ main initial penetrations
- ● German coastal defences
- elts = elements

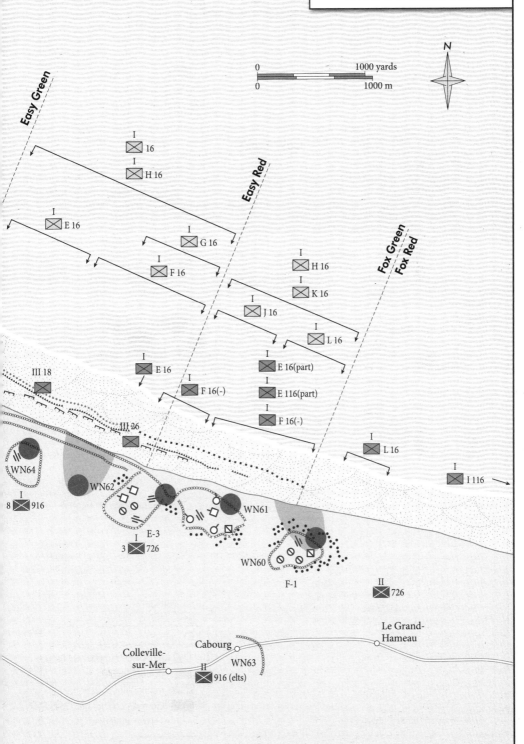

D-DAY ASSAULT ON OMAHA BEACH

0 — 1000 yards
0 — 1000 m

N

Easy Green

Easy Red

Fox Green
Fox Red

I ⊠ 16
I ⊠ H 16
I ⊠ E 16
I ⊠ G 16
I ⊠ F 16
I ⊠ H 16
I ⊠ K 16
I ⊠ J 16
I ⊠ L 16
I ⊠ E 16(part)
I ⊠ E 116(part)
I ⊠ F 16(-)
I ⊠ L 16
I ⊠ I 116

III 18 ⊠
I ⊠ E 16
I ⊠ F 16(-)
III 26 ⊠

WN64
I ⊠ 8 916
WN62
WN61
I ⊠ E-3
3 ⊠ 726
WN60
F-1
II ⊠ 726

Le Grand-
Hameau

Colleville-
sur-Mer
Cabourg
WN63
II ⊠ 916 (elts)

D-DAY ASSAULT ON THE BRITISH AND CANADIAN BEACHES

0 _____ 2 miles

0 _____ 2 km

Gold Beach

XX
⊠ 50(Br.)

X
⊠ 8(Br.) **King**

X
⊠ 56

X
⊠ 231

X
⊠ 151

X
⊠ 69

Love

X
7(Can) ⊠

Jig

II
⊠ 47 Cdo

II
⊠ 1 Hants

II
⊠ 1 Dorset

II
⊠ 6GH

II
⊠ 5 EY

II
RWR ⊠

Item

Mike

Putot-en-Bessin

Arromanches

Le Hamel

La Rivière

Courseulles-sur-Mer

Longues-sur-Mer

Tracy-sur-Mer

Mont Fleury

Meuvaines

River de Provence

III
726 (elts)

La Rosière

River la Gronde

III
915 (elts)

Ryes

Crépon

Ste-Croix-sur-Mer

III
736 (elts)

Banville

River Drôme

Magny-en-Bessin

Poligny

Bazenville

XX
352

Sommervieu

Villiers-le-Sec

Creully

Bayeux

Esquay-sur-Seulles

River Seulles

St-Gabriel-Brécy

Le-Fresne-Camilly

Coulombs

River Mue

River Aure

Nonant-le-Pin

St-Léger

Ste-Croix-Grand-Tonne

Loucelles

Brouay

Port-en-Bessin

Audrieu

XXX
⊠ LXXXIV

La Villeneuve

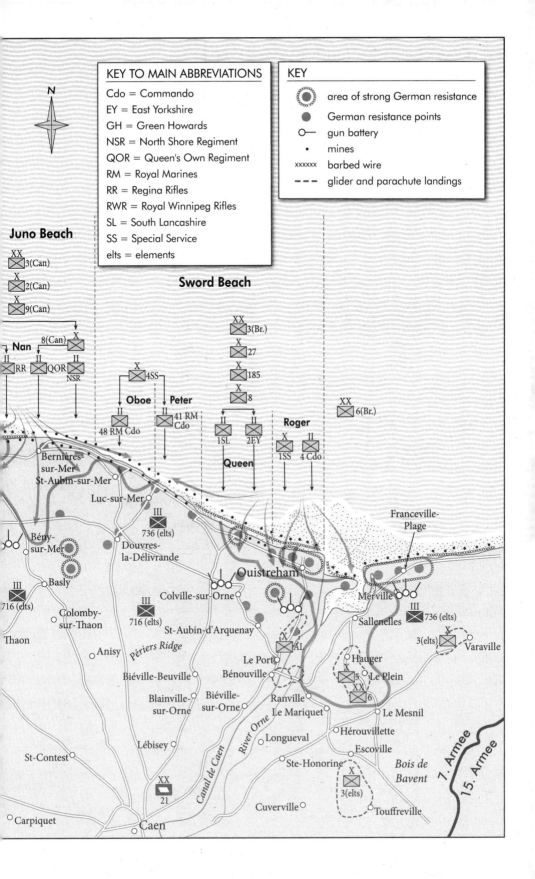

N

KEY TO MAIN ABBREVIATIONS

Cdo = Commando
EY = East Yorkshire
GH = Green Howards
NSR = North Shore Regiment
QOR = Queen's Own Regiment
RM = Royal Marines
RR = Regina Rifles
RWR = Royal Winnipeg Rifles
SL = South Lancashire
SS = Special Service
elts = elements

KEY

- area of strong German resistance
- German resistance points
○— gun battery
· mines
xxxxxx barbed wire
– – – glider and parachute landings

Juno Beach

XX 3(Can)
X 2(Can)
X 9(Can)

Sword Beach

XX 3(Br.)
X 27
X 185
X 8
XX 6(Br.)

Nan

8(Can) X
II RR II QOR II NSR

X 4SS

Oboe | **Peter**
II 48 RM Cdo | II 41 RM Cdo

II 1SL II 2EY

Queen

Roger
X 1SS II 4 Cdo

Bernières-sur-Mer
St-Aubin-sur-Mer
Luc-sur-Mer

Franceville-Plage

III 736 (elts)

Bény-sur-Mer
Douvres-la-Délivrande

Ouistreham

Merville

III 736 (elts)

III 716 (elts)
Basly

III 716 (elts)

Colville-sur-Orne
St-Aubin-d'Arquenay

Sallenelles

Colomby-sur-Thaon

X 3(elts) Varaville

Thaon

Anisy   Périers Ridge

Le Port X AL

Hauger

Biéville-Beuville
Bénouville

X 5 Le Plein

Blainville-sur-Orne Biéville-sur-Orne
Ranville
Le Mariquet

XX 6

Le Mesnil

St-Contest

Lébisey

Longueval Hérouvillette
Escoville

Ste-Honorine
Bois de Bavent

X 3(elts)

XX 21

Carpiquet Caen   Cuverville

Touffreville

7. Armee

15. Armee

River Orne

Canal de Caen

D-DAY BRITISH AND CANADIAN BEACHES AT MIDNIGHT

Canadians landing at Juno Beach.

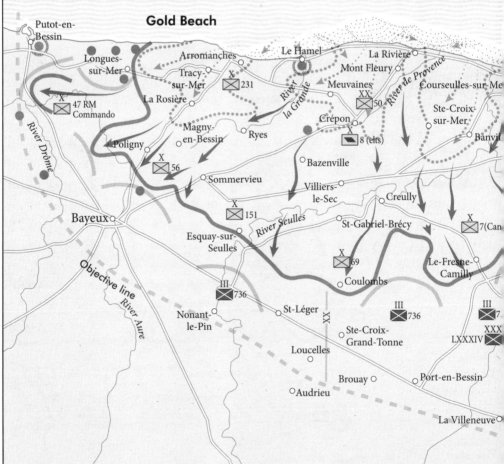

Gold Beach

Putot-en-Bessin

Longues-sur-Mer

Arromanches

Le Hamel

La Rivière

Mont Fleury

Tracy-sur-Mer

X 231

Meuvaines

Courseulles-sur-Mer

X 47 RM Commando

La Rosière

XX 50

Ste-Croix-sur-Mer

River la Gronte

River de Provence

Crépon

X 8 (elts)

Banvil

Magny-en-Bessin

Ryes

Poligny

X 56

Bazenville

Sommervieu

Villiers-le-Sec

Creully

Bayeux

X 151

River Seulles

St-Gabriel-Brécy

X 7(Can

Esquay-sur-Seulles

Le-Fresne-Camilly

X 69

Objective line

River Aure

III 736

Coulombs

Nonant-le-Pin

St-Léger

III 736

III 7.

Ste-Croix-Grand-Tonne

XXX LXXXIV

Loucelles

River Drôme

XX

Brouay

Port-en-Bessin

Audrieu

La Villeneuve

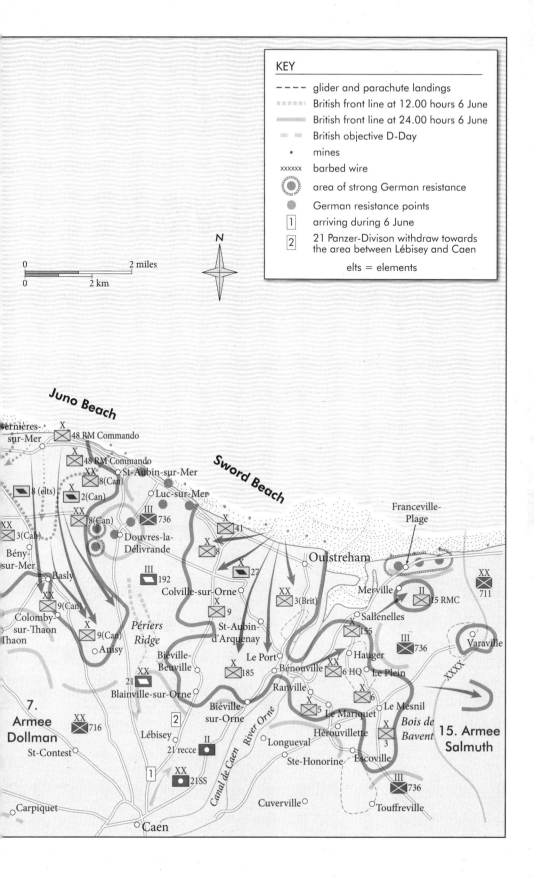

KEY

- - - - glider and parachute landings

British front line at 12.00 hours 6 June

British front line at 24.00 hours 6 June

British objective D-Day

• mines

xxxxxx barbed wire

area of strong German resistance

German resistance points

1 arriving during 6 June

2 21 Panzer-Divison withdraw towards the area between Lébisey and Caen

elts = elements

N

0   2 miles
0   2 km

Juno Beach

Sword Beach

Bernières-sur-Mer

X 48 RM Commando

X 48 RM Commando

XX 8(Can)   St-Aubin-sur-Mer

X 2(Can)

8 (elts)

XX 8(Can)

Luc-sur-Mer

III 736

XX 3(Can)

Douvres-la-Délivrande

X 41

X 8

Franceville-Plage

Bény-sur-Mer

Basly

III 192

Colville-sur-Orne

X 27

Ouistreham

XX 711

XX 9(Can)

Colomby-sur-Thaon

Thaon

X 9(Can)

Anisy

Périers Ridge

X 9

St-Aubin-d'Arquenay

XX 3(Brit)

Merville

II 15 RMC

Sallenelles

X 155

III 736

Varaville

Bréville-Beuville

XX 21

Blainville-sur-Orne

X 185

Le Port

Bénouville

XX 6 HQ

Le Plein

Hauger

Ranville

Le Mesnil

7. Armee Dollman

XX 716

2

Lébisey

21 recce II

1

XX 21SS

Biéville-sur-Orne

Bréville-sur-Orne

X 5

Le Mariquet

Longueval

Hérouvillette

Ste-Honorine

Escoville

X 6

X 3

Bois de Bavent

15. Armee Salmuth

St-Contest

Carpiquet

Caen

Cuverville

Touffreville

III 736

Canal de Caen   River Orne

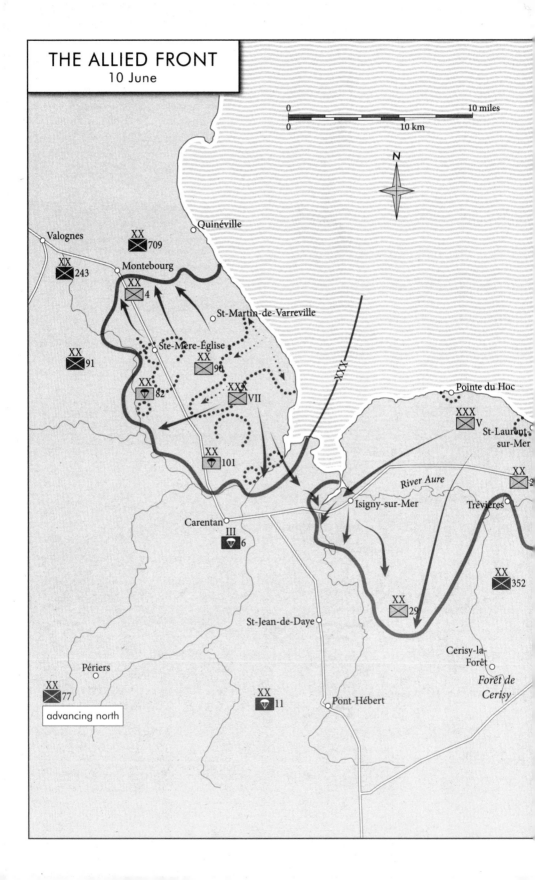

THE ALLIED FRONT
10 June

0   10 miles
0   10 km

N

Valognes

XX 709

Quinéville

XX 243

Montebourg

XX 4

St-Martin-de-Varreville

Ste-Mère-Église

XX 90

XX 91

XX 82

XXX VII

Pointe du Hoc

XXX V

St-Laurent-sur-Mer

XX 101

XX 2

River Aure

Isigny-sur-Mer

Trévières

Carentan

III 6

XX 352

XX 29

St-Jean-de-Daye

Cerisy-la-Forêt

Forêt de Cerisy

Périers

XX 77

advancing north

XX 11

Pont-Hébert

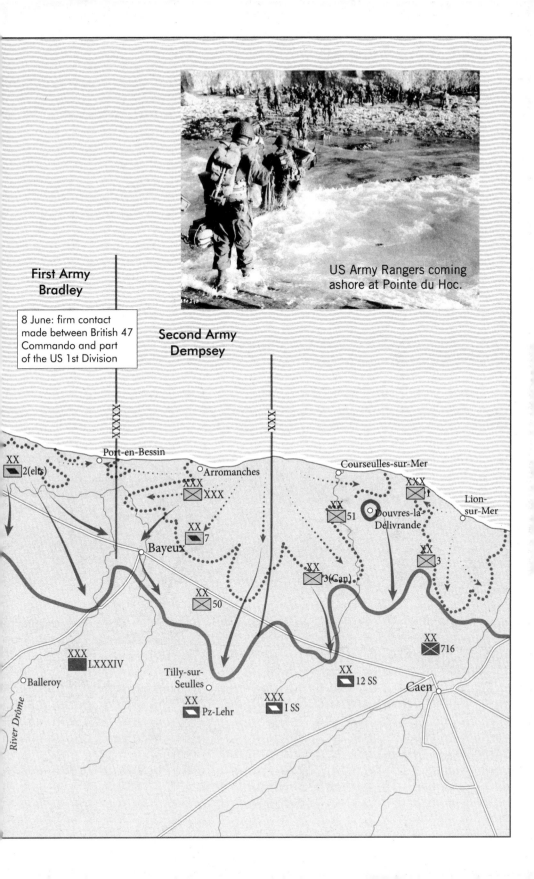

US Army Rangers coming ashore at Pointe du Hoc.

First Army
Bradley

Second Army
Dempsey

8 June: firm contact made between British 47 Commando and part of the US 1st Division

XX 2(elts)

Port-en-Bessin

Arromanches

Courseulles-sur-Mer

XXX 1

Lion-sur-Mer

XXX XXX

XX 51

Douvres-la-Délivrande

XX 7

Bayeux

XX 3(Can)

XX 3

XX 50

XX 716

XXX LXXXIV

Tilly-sur-Seulles

XX 12 SS

Caen

Balleroy

XX Pz-Lehr

XXX I SS

River Drôme

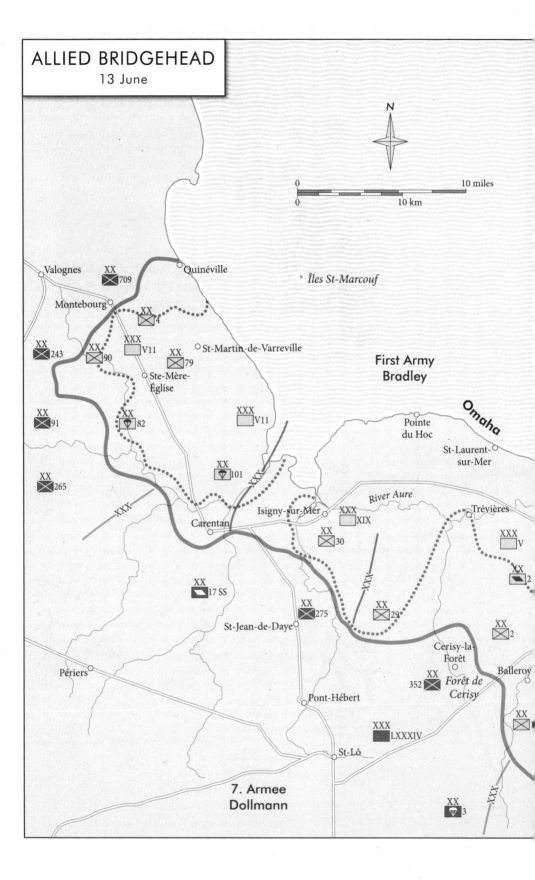

ALLIED BRIDGEHEAD
13 June

N

0 ——————— 10 miles
0 ——————— 10 km

Valognes
XX 709
Quinéville
Îles St-Marcouf

Montebourg
XX 4
XX 243
XX 90
XXX V11
XX 79
St-Martin-de-Varreville

**First Army
Bradley**

Ste-Mère-
Église
XX 91
XX 82
XXX V11
Omaha
Pointe
du Hoc
St-Laurent-
sur-Mer

XX 265
XX 101
Isigny-sur-Mer
River Aure
Trévières
XXX
XXX XIX
XXX V
Carentan
XX 30
XX 2
XX 17 SS
XX 275
XX 29
XX 2
St-Jean-de-Daye
Cerisy-la-
Forêt
Balleroy
Périers
XX 352 *Forêt de
Cerisy*
XX
Pont-Hébert
XXX LXXXIV
St-Lô
**7. Armee
Dollmann**
XX 3

KEY
━━━ front line 13 June
••••• front line 10 June

British troops advancing.

Second Army
Dempsey

Baie de la Seine

Gold   Juno   Courseulles-sur-Mer

Port-en-Bessin   Arromanches   Douvres-la-Déliverande   Sword

Lion-sur-Mer

XX 11

XXX I

Bayeux   XX 15 (elts)

XX 3

XX 346

XXX   XXX   XX 3 (Can)   XX 6

River Drôme   XX 50   XX 49   XX 716   XX 51

XX 7   XX 21

Tilly-sur-Seulles   XX 12 SS   Caen

XX Pz-Lehr   Operation PERCH – British 49th Army Division tries to cut off Panzer-Lehr

XXX   XXX I SS

XX 2

15. Armee Salmuth

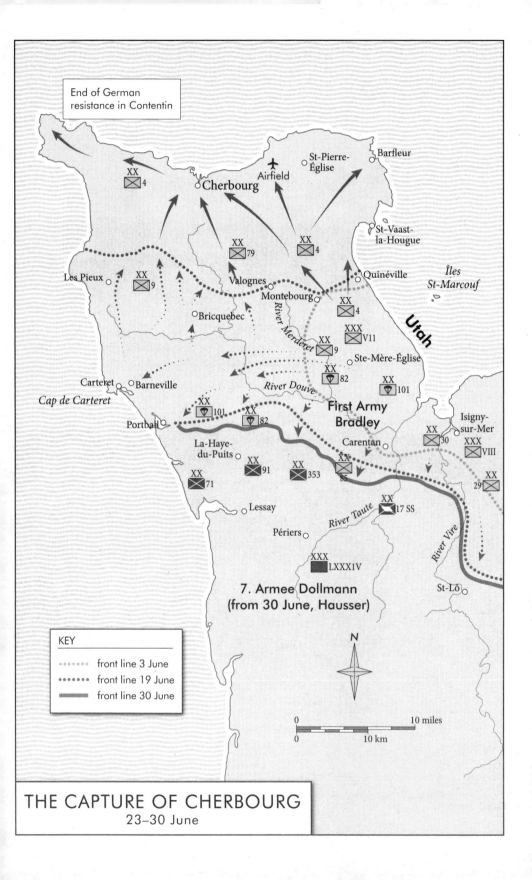

End of German
resistance in Contentin

Barfleur

St-Pierre-
Église

Airfield

Cherbourg

XX 4

St-Vaast-
la-Hougue

XX 79

XX 4

Îles
St-Marcouf

Quinéville

Les Pieux

XX 9

Valognes

Montebourg

River Merderet

XX 4

Utah

Bricquebec

XXX V11

XX 9

Ste-Mère-Église

Carteret

Barneville

River Douve

XX 82

XX 101

Cap de Carteret

XX 101

XX 82

First Army
Bradley

Portbail

La-Haye-
du-Puits

Carentan

XX 30

Isigny-
sur-Mer

XXX VIII

XX 71

XX 91

XX 353

XX 85

XX 29

Lessay

XX 17 SS

Périers

River Taute

River Vire

XXX LXXXIV

St-Lô

7. Armee Dollmann
(from 30 June, Hausser)

KEY

········ front line 3 June
•••••••• front line 19 June
━━━━━━ front line 30 June

N

0 _____ 10 miles
0 _____ 10 km

THE CAPTURE OF CHERBOURG
23–30 June

Shermans assembling
for Operation EPSOM.

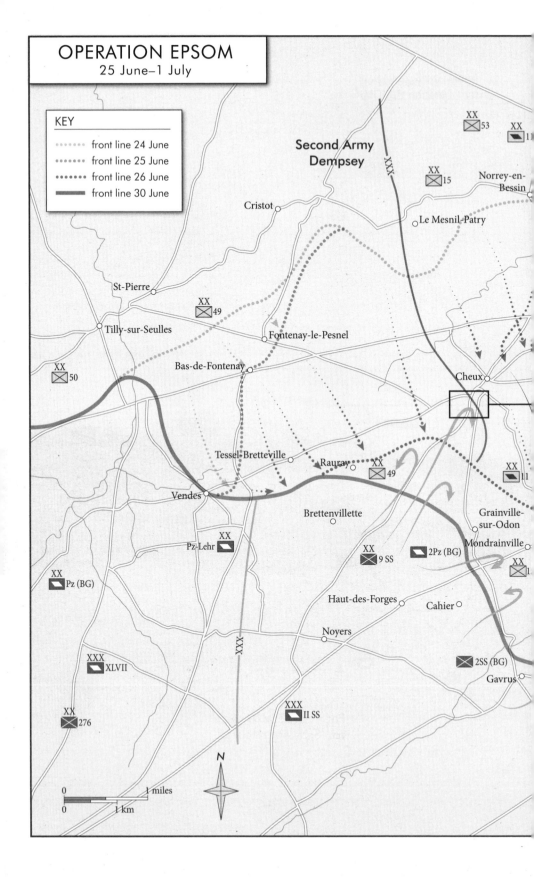

OPERATION EPSOM
25 June–1 July

KEY
- .... front line 24 June
- ●●●●● front line 25 June
- ●●●●● front line 26 June
- —— front line 30 June

Second Army
Dempsey

XX 53
XX 11
XX 15
Norrey-en-Bessin

Cristot

Le Mesnil-Patry

St-Pierre

XX 49

Tilly-sur-Seulles

Fontenay-le-Pesnel

XX 50

Bas-de-Fontenay

Cheux

Tessel-Bretteville

Rauray

XX 49

XX 11

Vendes

Brettenvillette

Grainville-sur-Odon

Mondrainville

XX 1

Pz-Lehr

XX 9 SS

2Pz (BG)

XX Pz (BG)

Haut-des-Forges

Cahier

Noyers

XXX XLVII

2SS (BG)

Gavrus

XXX II SS

XX 276

N

0   1 miles
0   1 km

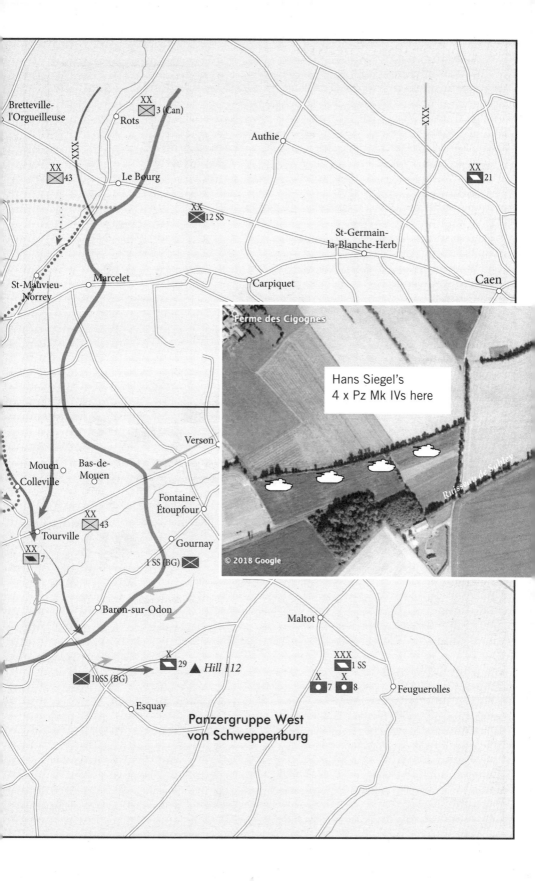

Bretteville-
l'Orgueilleuse

Rots

XX
3 (Can)

Authie

XXX

XX
21

XX
43

Le Bourg

XX
12 SS

St-Germain-
la-Blanche-Herb

Caen

St-Mauvieu-
Norrey

Marcelet

Carpiquet

Ferme des Cigognes

Hans Siegel's
4 x Pz Mk IVs here

Verson

Mouen

Bas-de-
Mouen

Colleville

Fontaine-
Étoupfour

Ruisseau de Sublev

XX
43

Tourville

Gournay

XX
7

1 SS (BG)

© 2018 Google

Baron-sur-Odon

Maltot

X
29 ▲ *Hill 112*

XXX
1 SS

10SS (BG)

X
7

X
8

Feuguerolles

Esquay

**Panzergruppe West
von Schweppenburg**

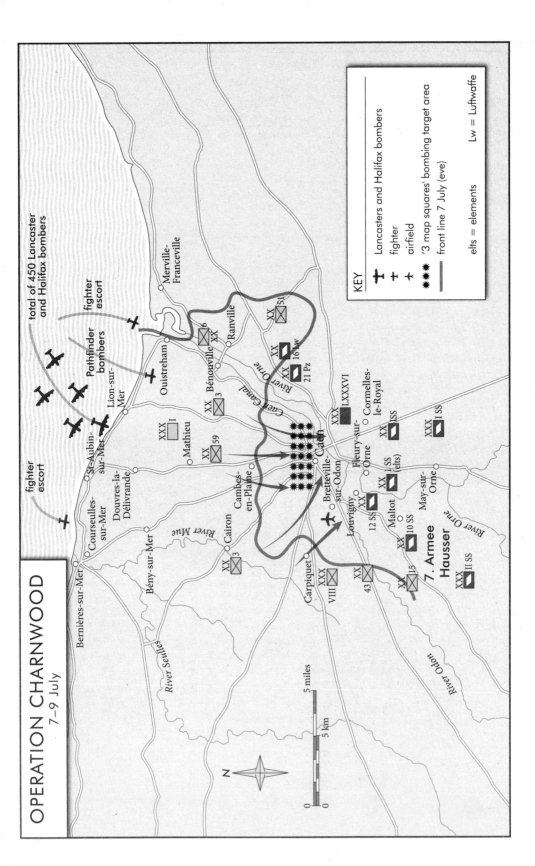

OPERATION CHARNWOOD
7–9 July

KEY

✠	Lancasters and Halifax bombers
✝	fighter
✛	airfield
✶✶✶	'3 map squares' bombing target area
──	front line 7 July (eve)

elts = elements   Lw = Luftwaffe

total of 450 Lancaster and Halifax bombers

fighter escort

Pathfinder bombers

fighter escort

fighter escort

Merville-Franceville

Ranville

Ouistreham

Lion-sur-Mer

St-Aubin-sur-Mer

Courseulles-sur-Mer

Bernières-sur-Mer

Douvres-la-Délivrande

Bény-sur-Mer

River Seulles

River Mue

Cairon

Carpiquet

Mathieu

Cambes-en-Plaine

Bénouville

River Orne

Caen Canal

Bretteville-sur-Odon

Louvigny

Fleury-sur-Orne

Cormelles-le-Royal

Maltot

May-sur-Orne

River Orne

River Odon

XXX I — Mathieu

XX 59

XX 3

XXX VIII

XX 3

XX 43

XX 15

XX 6 — Bénouville

XX 51 — Ranville

161 Lw

21 Pz

XXX LXXXVI

I SS

I SS

II SS

12 SS

I SS (elts)

10 SS

7. Armee Hausser

N

0   5 miles
0   5 km

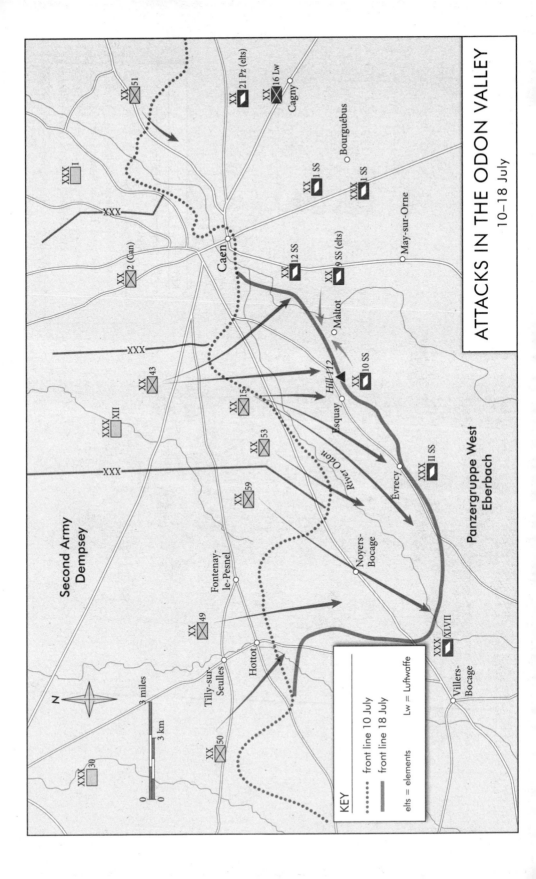

ATTACKS IN THE ODON VALLEY

10–18 July

KEY

⸺⸺⸺	front line 10 July
▬▬▬▬	front line 18 July
	elts = elements
	Lw = Luftwaffe

Second Army
Dempsey

Panzergruppe West
Eberbach

Caen

Cagny

Bourguébus

May-sur-Orne

Maltot

Hill-112

Esquay

Evrecy

Noyers-Bocage

River Odon

Fontenay-le-Pesnel

Tilly-sur-Seulles

Hottot

Villers-Bocage

30

50

49

59

53

XII

15

43

1

2 (Can)

51

21 Pz (elts)

16 Lw

1 SS

1 SS

12 SS

9 SS (elts)

10 SS

II SS

XLVII

N

3 miles

3 km

0

0

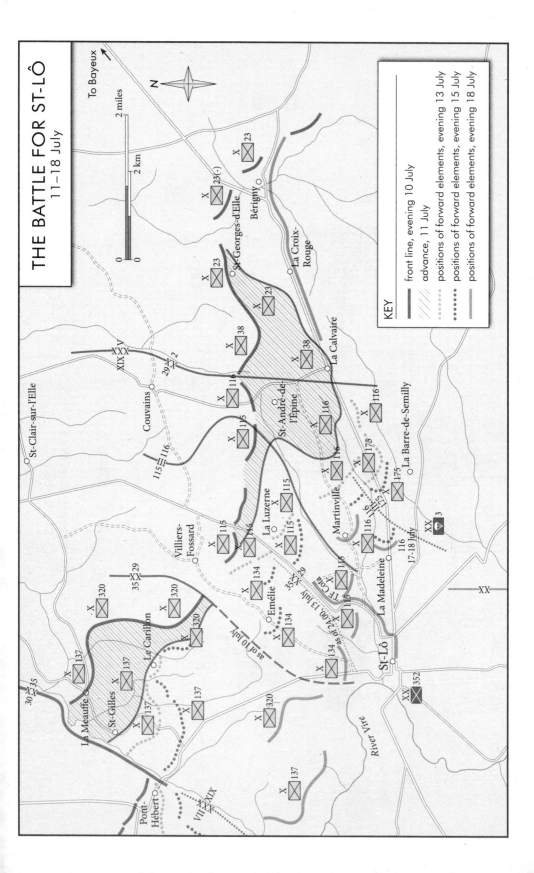

THE BATTLE FOR ST-LÔ
11–18 July

To Bayeux

N

2 miles

2 km

St-Clair-sur-l'Elle

Couvains

XXX

29 XX 2

115 116

115

Villiers-Fossard

St-Georges-d'Elle

Bérigny

La Croix-Rouge

X 23

X 23(-)

X 23

23

38

X 38

La Calvaire

X 116

St-André-de-l'Épine

116

116

X 116

175

La Barre-de-Semilly

X 116

X 175

175

XX 3

Martinville

116

X 116

17-18 July

116

La Madeleine

115

X 115

La Luzerne

X 115

35 29

XX

TF Cota

X 115

115

X 115

X 134

Emélie

X 134

St-Gilles

La Meauffe

35 29

XX

320

X 320

Le Carillon

X 320

X 320

X 137

X 137

X 137

X 137

as of 10 July

13 July 21:00 as of

134

X 134

X 320

X 137

St-Lô

XX 352

River Vire

30 XX 35

35

VII XXX XIX

Pont-Hébert

XX

The Battle for Saint-Lô: a Sherman Firefly and crew before Operation GOODWOOD.

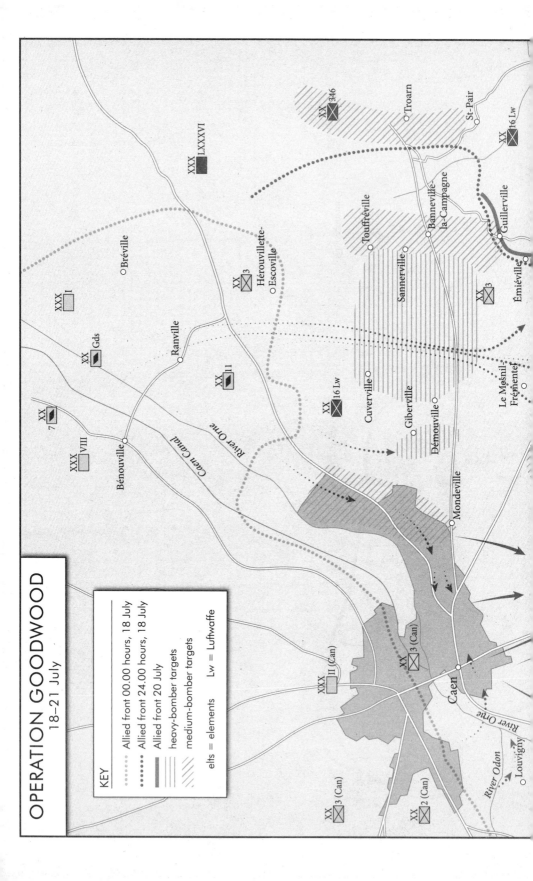

OPERATION GOODWOOD
18–21 July

KEY

········· Allied front 00.00 hours, 18 July

•••••••• Allied front 24.00 hours, 18 July

••••••• Allied front 20 July

▮ heavy-bomber targets

▥ medium-bomber targets

elts = elements   Lw = Luftwaffe

XXX LXXXVI

XX 346

○ Troarn

○ St-Pair

XX 16 Lw

XX 3
Hérouvillette-
○ Escoville

○ Bréville

XXX I

○ Touffréville

Banneville-
la-Campagne

○ Guillerville
○ Guillerville

XX Gds

○ Ranville

○ Sannerville

XX 3

○ Émiéville

XX 11

XX 16 Lw

○ Cuverville

○ Giberville

○ Le Mesnil-
Frémentel
○

XX 7

River Orne

○ Démouville

XXX VIII

○ Bénouville

Caen Canal

○ Mondeville

XXX II (Can)

XX 3 (Can)

○ Caen

River Orne

○ Louvigny

XX 3 (Can)

XX 2 (Can)

River Odon

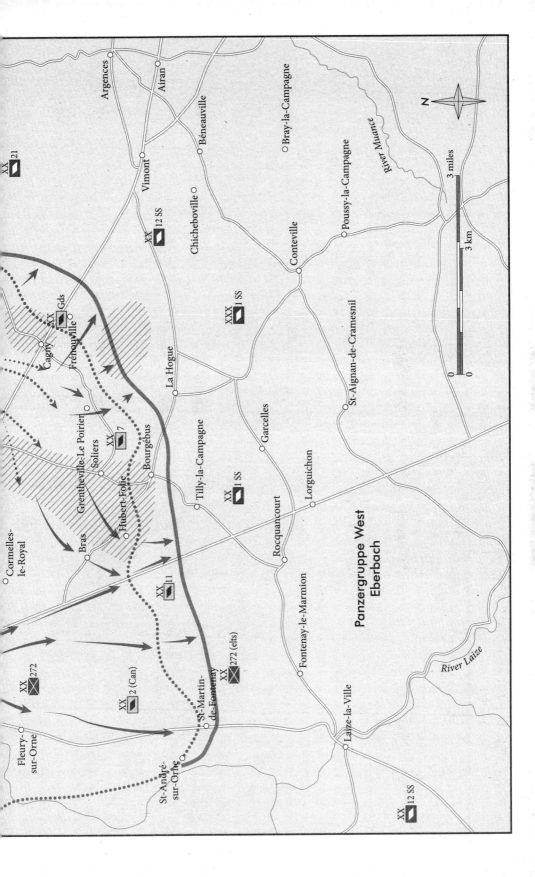

XX 21

Argences

Airan

Vimont

Béneauville

Bray-la-Campagne

N

XX 12 SS

Chicheboville

Poussy-la-Campagne

River Muance

3 miles

3 km

Conteville

XXX 1 SS

Gds

Cagny

Frénouville

La Hogue

St-Aignan-de-Cramesnil

Grentheville-Le Poirier
Soliers
XX 7

Bourgébus

Garcelles

Tilly-la-Campagne

XX 1 SS

Cormelles-
le-Royal

Hubert-Folie

Bras

Lorguichon

Rocquancourt

XX 11

Fontenay-le-Marmion

Panzergruppe West
Eberbach

XX 272 (elts)

XX 272

XX 2 (Can)

St-Martin-
de-Fontenay

River Laize

Fleury-
sur-Orne

St-André-
sur-Orne

Laize-la-Ville

XX 12 SS

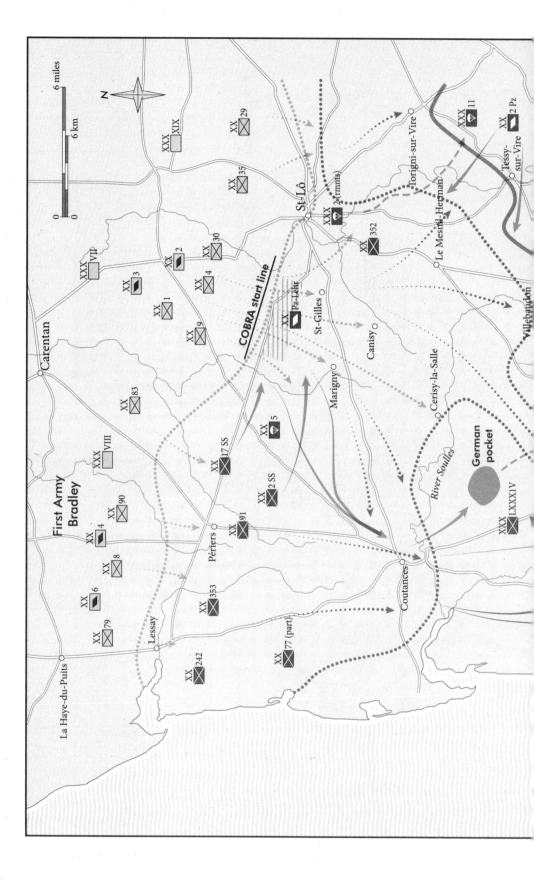

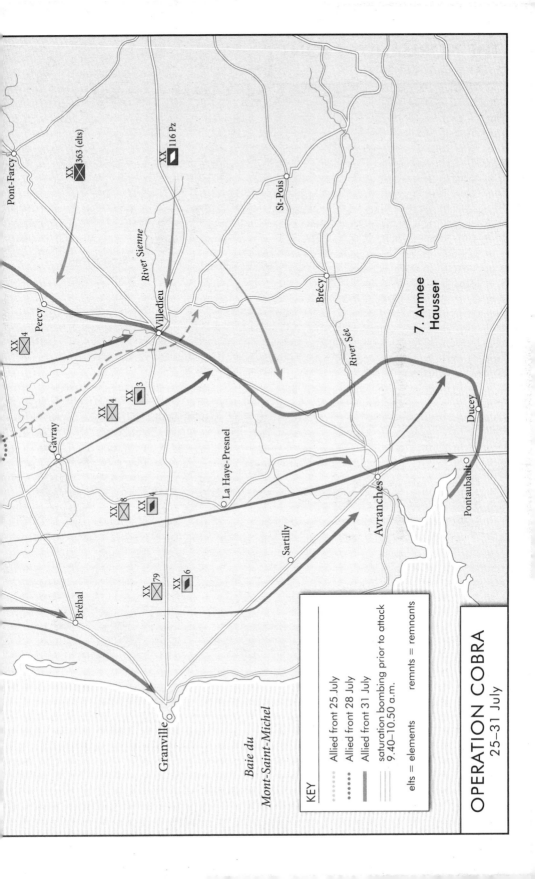

Pont-Farcy

XX 363 (elts)

XX 116 Pz

St-Pois

River Sienne

Brécy

Villedieu

Percy

XX 4

River Sée

7. Armee
Hausser

XX 4   XX 3

Gavray

La Haye-Presnel

Ducey

XX 8   XX 4

Avranches

Pontaubault

Sartilly

XX 79   XX 6

Bréhal

Granville

*Baie du
Mont-Saint-Michel*

KEY

Allied front 25 July
Allied front 28 July
Allied front 31 July
saturation bombing prior to attack
9.40–10.50 a.m.

elts = elements   remnts = remnants

OPERATION COBRA
25–31 July

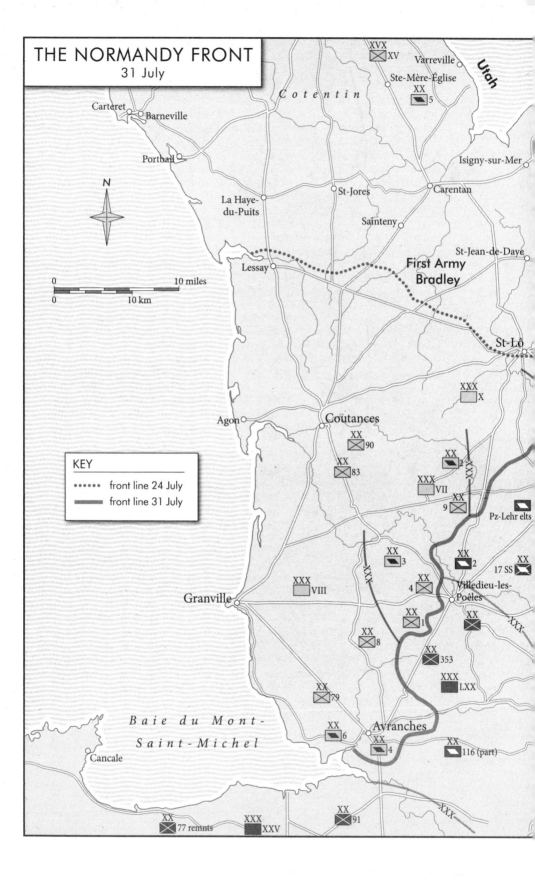

THE NORMANDY FRONT
31 July

C o t e n t i n

Varreville

XVX
XV

Ste-Mère-Église

XX
5

Utah

Carteret

Barneville

Portbail

Isigny-sur-Mer

St-Jores

Carentan

La Haye-
du-Puits

Sainteny

St-Jean-de-Daye

Lessay

**First Army
Bradley**

St-Lô

N

0   10 miles

0   10 km

Agon

Coutances

XXX
X

XX
90

XX
83

XX
2

XXX

KEY

••••• front line 24 July

front line 31 July

XXX
VII

XX
9

XX

Pz-Lehr elts

XX
3

XX
2

XX
17 SS

XXX
VIII

XX
4

Villedieu-les-
Poêles

Granville

XX
1

XX

XXX

XX
8

XX
353

XXX
LXX

XX
79

B a i e   d u   M o n t -

S a i n t - M i c h e l

XX
6

Avranches

XX
4

XX
116 (part)

Cancale

XX
77 remnts

XXX
XXV

XX
91

XXX

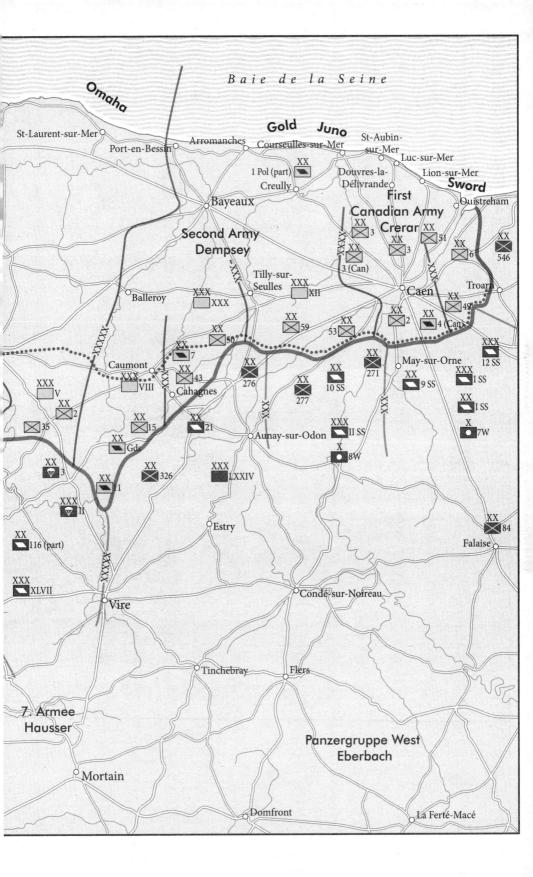

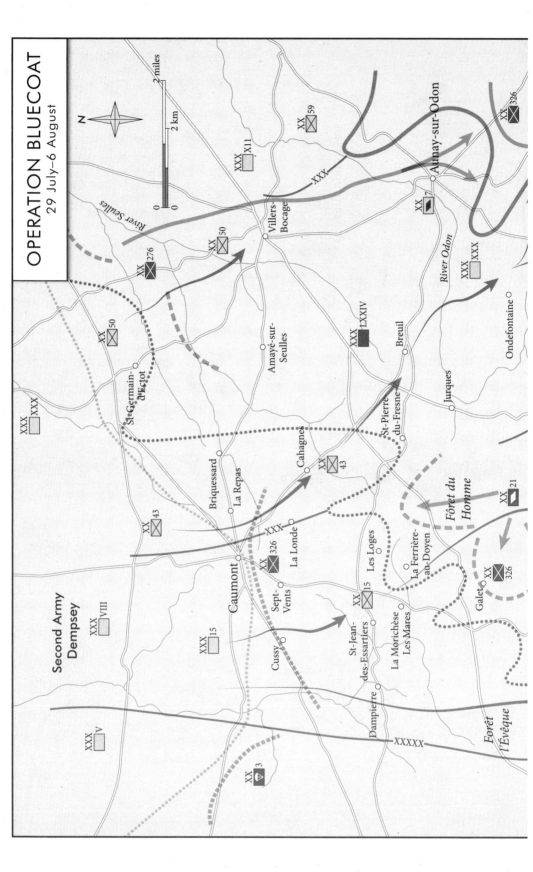

OPERATION BLUECOAT
29 July–6 August

N

River Seulles

2 miles
2 km

Second Army
Dempsey

XXX V

XXX VIII

XXX 15

XXX 43

XXX XXX

St-Germain-d'Ectot

XX 50

XX 276

XX 50

Villers-Bocage

XXX X11

XX 59

Amayé-sur-Seulles

XXX

River Odon

Aunay-sur-Odon

XX 7

XX 326

XXX XXX

Ondefontaine

Breuil

Jurques

XXX LXXIV

St-Pierre-du-Fresne

XX 43

Cahagnes

Briquessard

La Repas

La Londe

XXX 326

XX 326

Sept-Vents

Cussy

La Ferrière-au-Doyen

Les Loges

Forêt du Homme

XX 21

XX 326

Galet

St-Jean-des-Essartiers

XX 15

La Morichèse
Les Mares

Dampierre

Caumont

XX 3

Forêt
l'Évêque

XXXXX

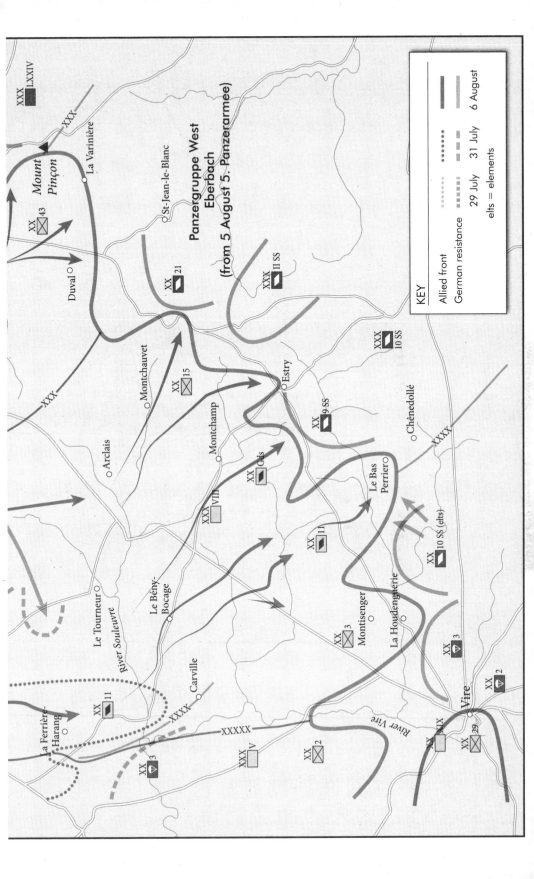

KEY

Allied front

German resistance

29 July   31 July   6 August

elts = elements

Panzergruppe West
Eberbach
(from 5 August 5. Panzerarmee)

XXX LXXIV

La Varinière

Mount
Pinçon

St-Jean-le-Blanc

XX 43

Duval

XX 21

XXX 11 SS

XXX 10 SS

Montchauvet

XX 15

Montchamp

Estry

XX 9 SS

Chênedollé

XXXX

Arclais

XXX VIII

XX Gds

Le Bény-
Bocage

XX 1

Le Bas
Perrier

XX 10 SS (elts)

Le Tourneur

River Souleuvre

Montisenger

La Houdengterie

XX 3

XX 3

Carville

XXXX

XX 11

La Ferrière-
Harang

XXXXX

River Vire

Vire

XIX

XX 29

XX 2

XX 3

XXX V

XX 2

XX 3

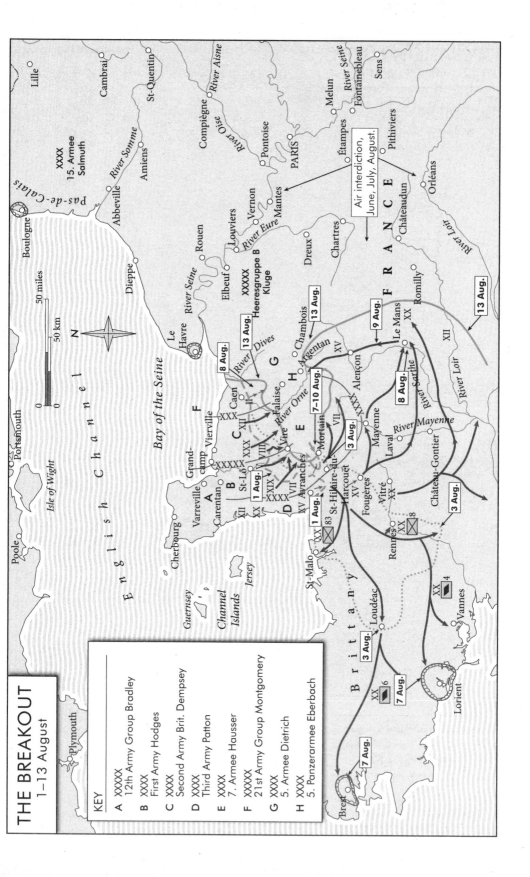

THE BREAKOUT
1–13 August

KEY

A	XXXXX	12th Army Group Bradley
B	XXXX	First Army Hodges
C	XXXX	Second Army Brit. Dempsey
D	XXXX	Third Army Patton
E	XXXX	7. Armee Hausser
F	XXXXX	21st Army Group Montgomery
G	XXXX	5. Armee Dietrich
H	XXXX	5. Panzerarmee Eberbach

Air interdiction, June, July, August.

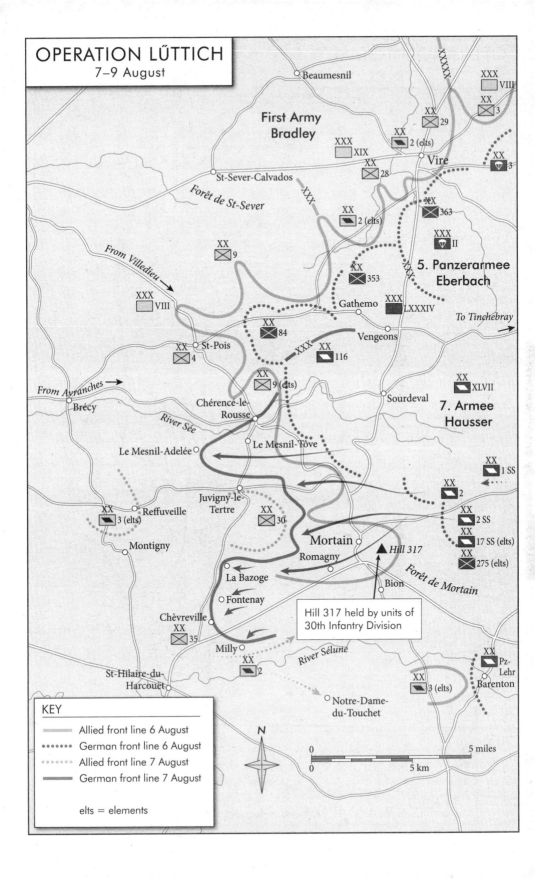

OPERATION LÜTTICH
7–9 August

Beaumesnil

XXX VIII

XX 3

First Army Bradley

XX 29

XX 2 (elts)

Vire

XX 3

XXX XIX

XX 28

XX 363

St-Sever-Calvados

Forêt de St-Sever

XX 2 (elts)

XXX II

XX 9

XX 353

5. Panzerarmee Eberbach

From Villedieu →

XXX VIII

Gathemo

XXX LXXXIV

To Tinchebray →

XX 84

Vengeons

XX 4 St-Pois

XX 116

XX XLVII

From Avranches →

XX 9 (elts)

Sourdeval

7. Armee Hausser

Brécy

River Sée

Chérencé-le-Rousse

Le Mesnil-Tôve

Le Mesnil-Adelée

XX 1 SS

XX 2

Juvigny-le-Tertre

XX 3 (elts) Reffuveille

XX 30

XX 2 SS

XX 17 SS (elts)

Montigny

Mortain

Romagny

▲ Hill 317

XX 275 (elts)

Bion

Forêt de Mortain

La Bazoge

Fontenay

Hill 317 held by units of 30th Infantry Division

Chèvreville

XX 35

Milly

XX 2

River Sélune

St-Hilaire-du-Harcouët

XX 3 (elts)

XX Pz-Lehr

Barenton

Notre-Dame-du-Touchet

KEY

— Allied front line 6 August

••••••• German front line 6 August

••••••• Allied front line 7 August

— German front line 7 August

elts = elements

N

0 ___ 5 miles

0 ___ 5 km

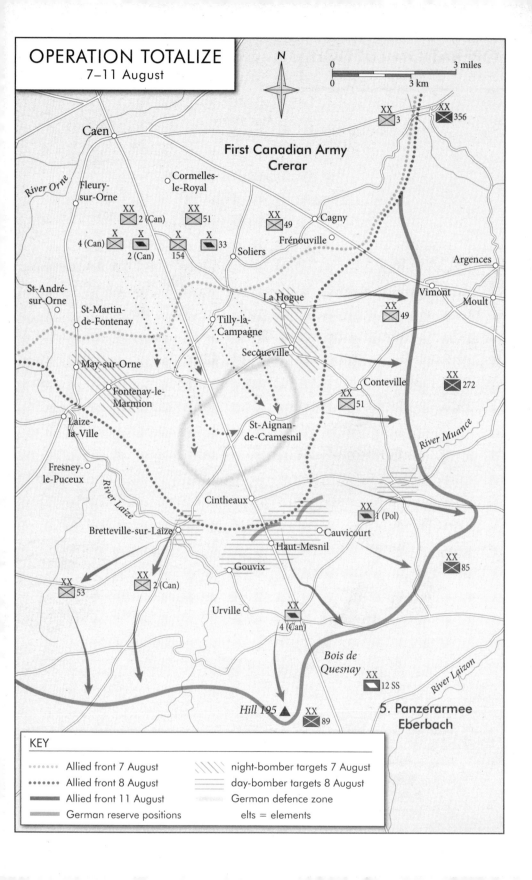

OPERATION TOTALIZE
7–11 August

N

0 ____ 3 miles
0 ____ 3 km

Caen

First Canadian Army
Crerar

River Orne

Fleury-sur-Orne

Cormelles-le-Royal

XX 3

XX 356

XX 2 (Can)

XX 51

XX 49

Cagny

Frénouville

X 4 (Can) X 2 (Can) X 154 X 33

Soliers

Argences

St-André-sur-Orne

St-Martin-de-Fontenay

La Hogue

Vimont

Moult

XX 49

May-sur-Orne

Tilly-la-Campagne

Secqueville

Conteville

XX 272

Fontenay-le-Marmion

XX 51

Laize-la-Ville

St-Aignan-de-Cramesnil

River Muance

Fresney-le-Puceux

River Laize

Cintheaux

XX 1 (Pol)

Bretteville-sur-Laize

Cauvicourt

Haut-Mesnil

XX 85

XX 53

XX 2 (Can)

Gouvix

Urville

XX 4 (Can)

Bois de Quesnay

XX 12 SS

River Laizon

Hill 195

XX 89

5. Panzerarmee
Eberbach

KEY

· · · · · Allied front 7 August

••••• Allied front 8 August

▬▬▬ Allied front 11 August

▒▒▒ German reserve positions

\\\\\ night-bomber targets 7 August

═══ day-bomber targets 8 August

· · · German defence zone

elts = elements

Heavy bombing during
Operation TOTALIZE.

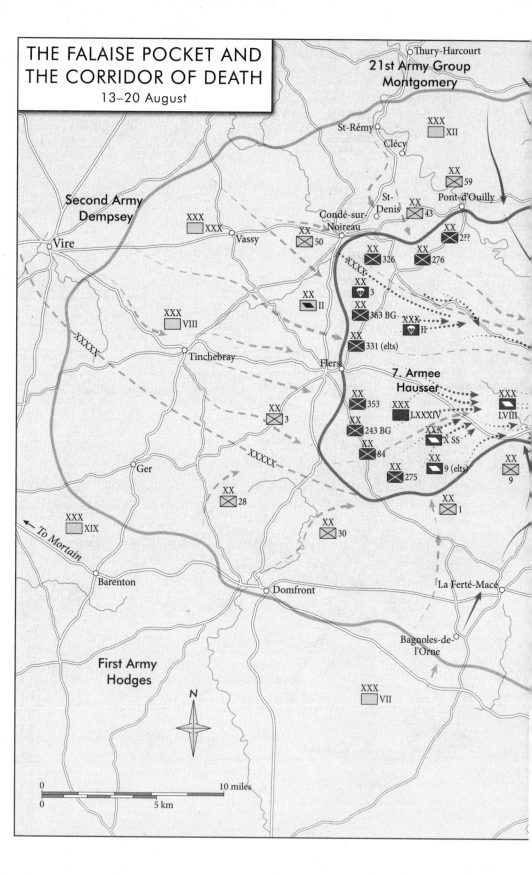

THE FALAISE POCKET AND THE CORRIDOR OF DEATH
13–20 August

21st Army Group
Montgomery

Thury-Harcourt

St-Rémy

XXX
XII

Clécy

XX
59

Pont-d'Ouilly

St-
Denis

XX
43

Second Army
Dempsey

Condé-sur-
Noireau

XX
2??

Vassy

XX
50

XX
326

XX
276

Vire

XXXX

XX
3

XXX
VIII

XX
II

XXX
II

Tinchebray

XX
363 BG

Flers

XX
331 (elts)

7. Armee
Hausser

XX
353

XXX
LXXXIV

XXX
LVIII

XX
3

XX
243 BG

XXX
X SS

Ger

XXXXX

XX
84

XX
9 (elts)

XX
9

XX
275

XX
28

XX
1

XXX
XIX

To Mortain

XX
30

La Ferté-Macé

Barenton

Domfront

Bagnoles-de-
l'Orne

First Army
Hodges

N

XXX
VII

0   10 miles
0   5 km

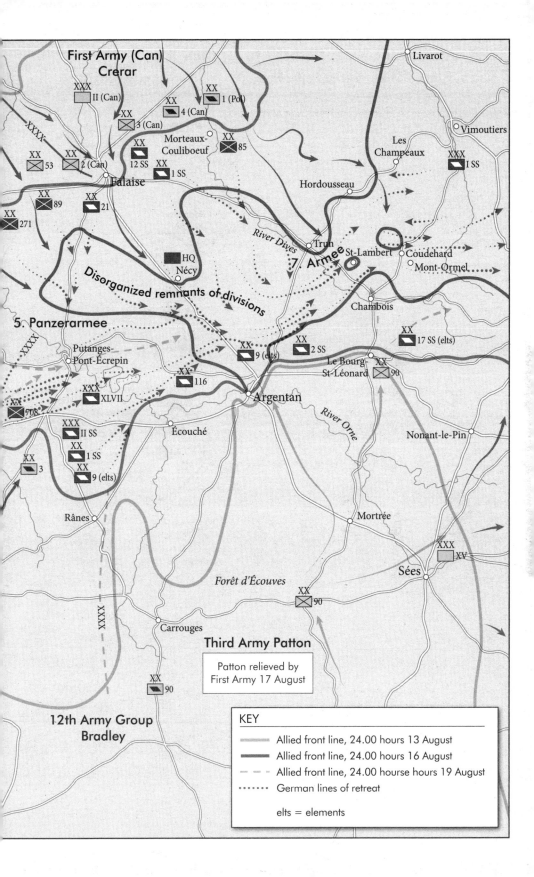

First Army (Can)
Crerar

XXX [ ] II (Can)
XX [ ] 4 (Can)
XX [ ] 1 (Pol)
XX [X] 3 (Can)
XX [X] 53
XX [X] 2 (Can)
XX [ ] 12 SS
XX [ ] 1 SS
Falaise
XX [X] 89
XX [ ] 21
XX [X] 271
Morteaux-Couliboeuf
XX [X] 85
Livarot
Vimoutiers
Les Champéaux
XXX [ ] I SS
Hordousseau

XXXX

HQ [■]
Nécy

River Dives
Trun
St-Lambert
7. Armee
Coudehard
Mont-Ormel

Disorganized remnants of divisions

5. Panzerarmee
Chambois

Putanges-Pont-Écrepin
XX [ ] 9 (elts)
XX [ ] 2 SS
XX [ ] 17 SS (elts)
XXX [ ] XLVII
XX [ ] 116
Le Bourg-St-Léonard
XX [X] 90
XX [X] 708
Argentan
River Orne
Nonant-le-Pin

XXX [ ] II SS
Écouché
XX [ ] 1 SS
XX [ ] 9 (elts)
XX [ ] 3
Rânes

Mortrée
XXX [ ] XV
Sées

Forêt d'Écouves
XX [X] 90

XXXX
Carrouges

Third Army Patton

Patton relieved by
First Army 17 August

12th Army Group
Bradley
XX [ ] 90

KEY
─────────── Allied front line, 24.00 hours 13 August
─────────── Allied front line, 24.00 hours 16 August
- - - - - - Allied front line, 24.00 hourse hours 19 August
· · · · · · · German lines of retreat

elts = elements

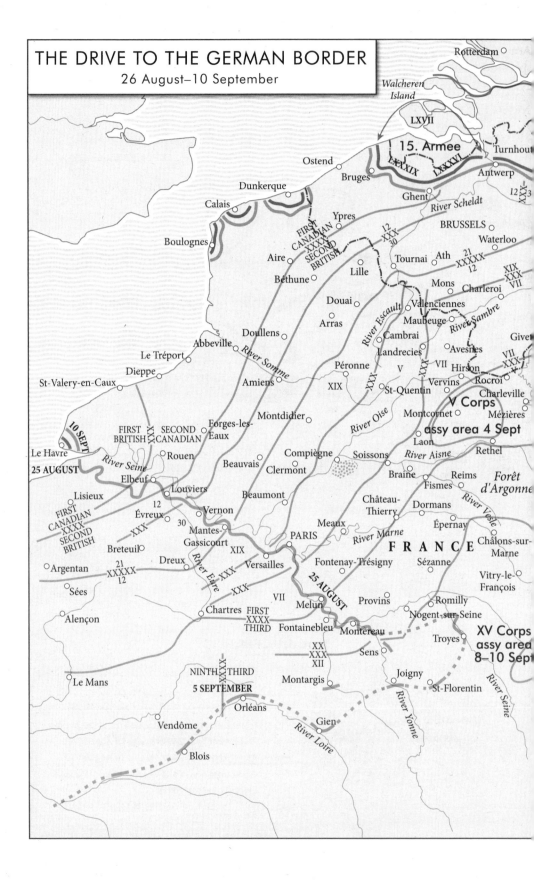

THE DRIVE TO THE GERMAN BORDER
26 August–10 September

Rotterdam

Walcheren Island

LXVII

15. Armee

Turnhout

Ostend

Dunkerque

Bruges

Ghent

Antwerp

LXXXIX LXXXVI

12 3

Calais

Ypres

River Scheldt

BRUSSELS

Boulognes

FIRST CANADIAN XXXX SECOND BRITISH

12 XXX 30

Waterloo

Aire

Lille

Tournai

Ath

21 XXXXX 12

Béthune

Mons

Charleroi

XIX XXX VII

Douai

Valenciennes

Arras

River Escaut

Maubeuge

River Sambre

Cambrai

Landrecies

Avesnes

Givet

Doullens

Péronne

V

VII

Hirson

VII XXX

Abbeville

River Somme

St-Quentin

Vervins

Rocroi

Le Tréport

Dieppe

Amiens

XIX

XXX

Montcornet

Charleville

Mézières

St-Valery-en-Caux

Montdidier

River Oise

V Corps

assy area 4 Sept

Laon

10 SEPT

FIRST BRITISH XXX SECOND CANADIAN

Forges-les-Eaux

Compiègne

Soissons

River Aisne

Rethel

Le Havre

25 AUGUST

River Seine

Rouen

Beauvais

Clermont

Braine

Fismes

Reims

Forêt d'Argonne

Elbeuf

Lisieux

Louviers

Beaumont

Château-Thierry

Dormans

River Vesle

FIRST CANADIAN XXXX SECOND BRITISH

12

Évreux

30

Vernon

Meaux

River Marne

Épernay

Châlons-sur-Marne

Breteuil

Mantes-Gassicourt

XIX

PARIS

Fontenay-Trésigny

Sézanne

FRANCE

Argentan

21 XXXXX 12

Dreux

River Eure

XXX

Versailles

XXX

Vitry-le-François

Sées

VII

Melun

Provins

Romilly

Nogent-sur-Seine

Troyes

XV Corps

assy area 8–10 Sept

Alençon

Chartres

FIRST XXXX THIRD

Fontainebleu

Montereau

Sens

XX XXX XII

Joigny

River Seine

St-Florentin

Le Mans

NINTH XXX THIRD

5 SEPTEMBER

Montargis

Montargis

River Yonne

Orléans

Gien

Vendôme

River Loire

Blois

Armed Forces Netherlands

Nijmegen

Cleve

Wesel

Paderborn

Hamm

XXXX
FIFTH FRONT

NETHERLANDS

Maashees

Mörs

Nuttlar

Eindhoven

LXXXVIII Korps and elts of misc units

München-Gladbach

Düsseldorf

Note: symbol indicates part of the front where German troops were withdrawing on night of 10–11 September

Roermond

River Ruhr

River Rhine

Cologne

Siegen

Hasselt

Maastricht

1. FALLJG
XXXX
7.

BELGIUM

Aachen

Düren

Bonn

Remagen

Giessen

Liège

Verviers

LXXXI

GERMANY

River Meuse

Huy

Malmédy

River Ahr

Sinzig

Koblenz

Dinant

March

St-Vith

LXXIV

I SS-Pz

B
XXXXX
G

Mayen

Wiesbaden

Frankfurt-am-Main

Prüm

Troisvierges

Wittlich

River Moselle

Bad Kreuznach

Oppenheim

Bastogne

Bitburg

Mainz

Trier

LXXX

10 SEPTEMBER

Sedan

Arlon

Luxembourg

River Saar

Worms

Mannheim

Kaiserslautern

Heidelberg

FIRST
XXXX
THIRD

Thionville

LXXXII

SAAR

Saarlautern

Saarbrücken

Karlsruhe

River Meuse

Verdun

Metz

Conflans

Sarreguemines

XIII SS

Wissembourg

Pforzheim

XX
XXX
XII

St-Mihiel

Pont-à-Mousson

XLVII Pz

River Sarre

Haguenau

River Moder

Commercy

Toul

Nancy

Sarrebourg

Bar-le-Duc

Rhine Canal

Vaucouleurs

Saverne

Strasbourg

St-Dizier

Joinville

Neufchâteau

Charmes

Rhine Canal

River Meurthe

N

Mirecourt

Épinal

St-Dié

River Mosel

Chaumont

LXVI

Colmar

0   50 miles
0   50 km

19. Armee

Langres

Luxeuil

Mulhouse

KEY

LXIV

IV Lw–Feldkorps

Saône

LXXXV

Vesoul

Belfort

Altkirch

River

7. Armee

Allied front line, date indicated
German front line, evening 25 September
West Wall
National border

assy = assembly   elts = elements
Falljg = *Fallschirmjäger* (paratroopers)
Lw = Luftwaffe

Principal Personalities

American

Lieutenant-Colonel Mark Alexander
Executive Officer, 505th Parachute Infantry Regiment, then XO 508th Parachute Infantry Regiment, 82nd Airborne Division.

Private William Biehler
Company K, 3rd Battalion, 357th Infantry Regiment, 90th Infantry Division.

2nd Lieutenant Richard Blackburn
Company A, 121st Regiment, 8th Infantry Division.

Pfc Henry 'Dee' Bowles
18th Infantry Regiment, 1st Infantry Division.

Pfc Tom Bowles
18th Infantry Regiment, 1st Infantry Division.

Lieutenant Joe Boylan
B-26 Marauder pilot, 573rd Squadron, 391st Bomb Group, Ninth Air Force.

Corporal Walter Halloran
165th Signal Photographic Company.

Major Chester B. Hansen
Aide to General Omar Bradley, US First Army.

Lieutenant Archie Maltbie
P-47 Thunderbolt pilot, 388th Fighter Squadron, 365th Fighter Group, Ninth Air Force.

Ernie Pyle
Journalist, Scripps-Howard Newspapers.

Brigadier-General Elwood 'Pete' Quesada
CO IX Fighter Command, Ninth Air Force.

Captain John Raaen
CO HQ Company, 5th Ranger Battalion.

Sergeant Carl Rambo
Company B, 70th Tank Battalion.

Captain John Rogers
CO Company E, 2nd Armored Division.

Lieutenant Orion Shockley
Company B, 1st Battalion, 47th Infantry Regiment, 9th Infantry Division.

Sergeant Bob Slaughter
Company D, 1st Battalion, 116th Infantry, 29th Infantry Division.

Lieutenant Bert Stiles
401st Bomb Squadron, 91st Bomb
Group, Eighth Air Force.

Major Dick Turner
CO 356th Fighter Squadron, 354th
Fighter Group, IX Fighter
Command, Ninth Air Force.

Lieutenant Dick Winters
CO Easy Company, 506th Parachute
Infantry Regiment, 101st Airborne
Division.

British

**Flight Sergeant Klaus 'Ken' Adam
(German)**
609 Squadron, 123 Wing, Second
Tactical Air Force.

Corporal Arthur Blizzard
Pioneer Platoon, 1st Battalion,
Suffolk Regiment, 8th Brigade, 3rd
Infantry Division.

Sergeant Walter Caines
Signals Company, 4th Battalion,
Dorset Regiment, 130th Brigade,
43rd Wessex Division.

**Lieutenant-Colonel Stanley
Christopherson**
CO Nottingham Sherwood Rangers
Yeomanry, 8th Armoured Brigade.

Private Denis Edwards
D Company, 2nd Battalion,
Oxfordshire and Buckinghamshire
Light Infantry, 6th Airlanding
Brigade, 6th Airborne Division.

Flight Sergeant Ken Handley
Flight Engineer, 466 Squadron,
Royal Australian Air Force, 4
Group, Bomber Command.

Captain Carol Mather
Liaison Officer, 21st Army Group
Tactical Headquarters.

**Lieutenant-General Dick
O'Connor**
Commander, VIII Corps.

Corporal Reg Spittles
2 Troop, A Squadron, 2nd
Northamptonshire Yeomanry, 11th
Armoured Division.

Captain Richard Todd
7th Battalion, 5th Parachute
Brigade, 6th Airborne Division.

Lance Corporal Ken Tout
1st Battalion, Northamptonshire
Yeomanry, 33rd (Independent)
Armoured Brigade.

Captain Robert Woollcombe
7 Platoon, A Company, 6th King's
Own Scottish Borderers, 44th
(Lowland) Brigade, 15th (Scottish)
Division.

Lance Corporal Frank Wright
X Troop, 47 Marine Commando.

Canadian

**Lieutenant Latham B. 'Yogi'
Jenson, RCN**
1st Lieutenant, HMCS *Algonquin*,
Force J.

Sergeant-Major Charlie Martin
A Company, Queen's Own Rifles,
8th Infantry Brigade, 3rd Division.

Corporal Eldon 'Bob' Roberts
B Company, North Shore New
Brunswick Regiment, 8th Infantry
Brigade, 3rd Division.

French

**Flight Lieutenant Pierre
Clostermann**
602 Squadron, Second Tactical Air
Force.

Geneviève Dubosq
Civilian.

Lieutenant Hubert Fauré
Kieffer Commandos, 4 Commando.

Robert Leblanc
Commander, Maquis Surcouf.

German

Generalleutnant Fritz Bayerlein
Commander, Panzer-Lehr Division.

Kanonier Eberhard Beck
10. Batterie, Artillerie-Regiment
277, 277. Infanterie-Division.

Jäger Johannes Börner
15. Kompanie, III. Bataillon,
Fallschirmjäger-Regiment 5, 3.
Fallschirmjäger.

Grenadier Martin Eineg
Infanterie-Regiment 726, 716.
Infanterie-Division.

Leutnant Wolfgang Fischer
Fighter pilot flying with 3./
Jagdgeschwader 2.

Gefreiter Franz Gockel
3. Kompanie, I. Bataillon,
Grenadier-Regiment 726, 716.
Infanterie-Division.

Leutnant Hans Heinze
Ordnanz Offizier, 5. Kompanie, II.
Bataillon, Grenadier-Regiment 916,
352. Infanterie-Division.

Major Hans von Luck
Commander, Panzergrenadier-
Regiment 125, 21.
Division.

SS-Oberführer Kurt Meyer
Commander, 12. SS-Panzer-
Division 'Hitlerjugend'.

Willi Müller
Pioneer-Bataillon 2, 17. SS-
Panzergrenadier-Division 'Götz von
Berlichingen'.

Oberleutnant Martin Pöppel
12. Kompanie, III. Bataillon,
Fallschirmjäger-Regiment 6.

Hauptmann Helmut Ritgen
Commander, II. Bataillon, Panzer-
Lehr-Regiment 130.

**Leutnant Richard Freiherr von
Rosen**
Bataillon HQ, Schwere
Panzerabteilung 503, 21.
Panzer-Division.

Vizeadmiral Friedrich Ruge
Naval advisor to Rommel,
Headquarters, Heeresgruppe B.

Obersturmführer Hans Siegel
Commander, 8. Kompanie, II.
Bataillon, SS-Panzer-Regiment 12,
12. SS-Panzer-Division.

Oberleutnant Cornelius Tauber
Pioneer-Kompanie, II. Grenadier-
Regiment 736, 736. Infanterie-
Division.

Obergrenadier Karl Wegner
3. Kompanie, Panzergrenadier-
Regiment 914, 352. Infanterie-
Division.

Irish

Lieutenant Mary Mulry
Nurse, 101st British General
Hospital.

New Zealand

**Air Marshal Sir Arthur 'Mary'
Coningham**
Commander, Second Tactical Air
Force, RAF.

Flight Sergeant Ken
Adam

Lieutenant-Colonel
Mark Alexander

Tom *(bottom left)* and
Henry *(top right)* Bowles

Lieutenant-Colonel
Stanley Christopherson

Winston Churchill

Flight Lieutenant
Pierre Clostermann

Air Marshal Sir Arthur
'Mary' Coningham *(right)*
and Air Vice-Marshal
Harry Broadhurst

Lieutenant-General
Miles Dempsey

Oberstgruf. Sepp
Dietrich *(left)*, Feldm.
Günther von Kluge
(centre) and Gen.
Hans Eberbach

Gefreiter Franz Gockel

Corporal Walter
Halloran

Major Chester Hansen
(left) and Lieutenant-
General Omar Bradley

Robert Leblanc

Major Hans von Luck

Oberführer Kurt Meyer

General Sir Bernard Montgomery

Brigadier-General Elwood 'Pete' Quesada

Hauptmann Helmut Ritgen

Feldmarschall Erwin Rommel

Leutnant Richard Freiherr von Rosen

Lieutenant Orion Shockley

Obersturmführer Hans Siegel

Lance Corporal Ken Tout

Major Dick Turner

Foreword

D-Day and the Allied invasion of France is probably the best-known episode of the entire Second World War, certainly in the consciousness of most in the West. It has been the subject of countless books and television documentaries, as well as major movies and internationally successful television dramas. Each year, millions go on pilgrimage to Normandy to see the invasion beaches and the war cemeteries where so many of those who fought now lie. It is the scene where the Allies began their liberation of north-west Europe and where Nazi Germany finally lost its grip on the lands it had taken with such brilliance back in 1940.

Paradoxically, it is the very popularity of the place and the subject, as well as the repeated retelling, that has prompted me to tackle the campaign in this new narrative history. Distortions have crept into the story, while a number of assumptions, accepted as fact, have also taken root when even cursory research suggests that, at best, the truth is more nuanced and, at worst, the supposition completely wrong. For too long, the subject has also been told largely at the higher level of command and from the perspective of those at the coal-face of battle; as John 'JJ' Witmeyer, a soldier in the US 79th Infantry Division, quite rightly pointed out, most young men like himself knew very little indeed about their enemy or what was going on around them. Far less, on the other hand, has been told about the mechanics of war – the level that allows warring sides to operate and maintain their overall objectives – their strategy – and to fight at the tactical level in a way best suited to their war aims. This is the nuts and bolts of war: the ability to produce arms and weapons, to make technological advancements, the ability to supply millions of men in the field, or in the air or at sea. It is the economics and logistics of war, and while that might sound boring, it most certainly is not, not least because, ultimately, it is also, at its basic level, about human drama, just as generalship and fighting in a tank or a fighter plane is also about extraordinary human endeavour. What's more, by understanding this operational level and reinserting it into the narrative, a quite different and more exciting picture emerges about what really happened in Normandy in the summer of 1944. A picture that deserves to be understood and accepted far more widely than is currently the case.

Interestingly, over the past fifteen years or so a quiet revolution has been taking place in academic circles about the way in which we understand the Second World War. My own research and conclusions have been building upon this, and I believe it is vitally important that these academic shifts – possible only recently now that archives, primary sources and our ability to access them is so much greater – become more fully absorbed into the accepted narrative. My hope is that this book, a history not of D-Day but of the entire 77-day Normandy campaign, will help with that.

For such a vast subject, this is, though, designed to be an overview. There is much to say, but inevitably there is also a lot of detail that it has not been possible to include. Rather, I have chosen to demonstrate the incredible drama of this brutal battle through the eyes of a handful of people from both sides and to concentrate on the primary events that occurred, alongside fresh analysis of why events unfolded in the way that they did.

Prologue

MONDAY, 15 MAY 1944. Down by the River Thames at Hammersmith in west London, field marshals, generals, air chief marshals, admirals as well as the British king and prime minister had gathered at St Paul's School for Boys for what the Supreme Allied Commander, General Dwight D. Eisenhower, called the 'final review' of plans for the cross-Channel invasion of France. It was a warm, sunny day that seemed to augur well as grand staff cars gently purred up to the entrance of the Victorian red-brick main school building. Guards clicked to attention as staff officers greeted the dignitaries and ushered them into an assembly room, at the end of which stood a low stage. At the front a couple of comfortable armchairs had been set, and it was to these that the British prime minister, Winston Churchill, and King George VI had been directed. Behind, on rather narrow, curved and somewhat inappropriate school benches, were the service chiefs and army and force commanders for this giant enterprise, as well as other war leaders, including a South African field marshal, Jan Smuts, who had once been Britain's enemy but was now a trusted friend and advisor.

The pupils had long since been moved elsewhere – back in 1940 when it was Britain that had been facing the prospect of invasion – but since January the school had been headquarters of 21st Army Group commanded by General Sir Bernard Montgomery, an old boy of the school and the man who would be in overall command of all Allied land forces for the landings and for the immediate weeks that followed.

Both the king and Churchill were smoking, the former a cigarette, the latter one of his cigars; this was a rarity, as Montgomery was a non-smoker and had strict rules that no one was allowed to smoke in his presence on his turf – that had even included General Dwight D. Eisenhower, who had been sharply reprimanded for doing so when the two had first met in the spring of 1942. But even Monty could hardly tell the prime minister to stub out his cigar and it was certainly not his place to admonish the king. What's more, despite the somewhat unexceptional setting, with notices on the walls announcing that the sons of clergymen could apply for scholarships, this was a rather exceptional gathering. Rules could be bent on this occasion.

On the stage was set a giant map that Montgomery had been using since taking over command of the main planning for Operation OVERLORD, as the invasion was code-named. The present form of the plan had taken shape from the moment the current team had been appointed in December 1943, and although Monty took the lead, it was very much a collaborative effort. The principles had first been discussed at the St George's Hotel in Algiers, Allied Forces Headquarters in the Mediterranean, between Montgomery, then still British Eighth Army commander in Italy, Eisenhower, then newly appointed Supreme Allied Commander, and his chief of staff, Lieutenant-General Walter Bedell Smith. Back in England, Monty's joint Anglo-US planning team had then got to work adjusting and refining earlier, more restricted plans for OVERLORD. These had quickly taken shape and on 21 January had been shared with Bedell Smith, who had then presented them to his boss, who had in turn shared them with the British and American chiefs of staff.

When these plans had been broadly approved, they began to develop in detail, with the staffs of the various component parts all working on their own specific areas. Numerous conferences had been held to resolve the inevitable concerns and difficulties that had arisen. The Allies now commanded vast air forces and navies as well as land forces – coordinating these was a fraught and extremely difficult enterprise and often tempers flared. However, by 7 April a strategy for the ground forces had been agreed and confirmed, allowing detailed planning to continue in other areas. Those preparing the naval plan, Operation NEPTUNE, had two months in which to master the unbelievably complex shipping requirements.

On 15 May, the invasion was now just three weeks away. The day of judgement was almost upon them. In the school assembly room, the atmosphere was palpably tense. So much rested on this enormous enterprise to which they were all committed. Failure was inconceivable, yet transporting armies across more than 80 miles of sea, through waters peppered with enemy mines and landing on beaches defended by armed forces that had cowed much of Europe just a few years earlier, and with secrecy of paramount importance, seemed a Herculean task. And so it was. Much could go wrong.

The headquarters in which they were assembled might have been Montgomery's, but Eisenhower, the Supreme Commander, had called the meeting and it was he who opened proceedings. Eisenhower, known to his friends and colleagues simply as 'Ike', was a 53-year-old career soldier. Bald, with a kindly face and an air of imperturbability, he was, in many ways, an unlikely candidate for this most testing of jobs. Born in Texas, he had been raised in Abilene, Kansas, a small town in the middle of the flat plains of the Midwest. Despite these somewhat humble beginnings, he had gained a place at West Point, the United States Army's officer academy, and had repeatedly proved himself as a highly able staff officer. Affable but resolute, clear-thinking and with rare skills of diplomacy, he had taken command of all US troops in Britain following America's entry into the war in December 1941, had then been given overall command of Allied forces for the invasion of north-west Africa in November 1942, and a few months later had been elevated to the first Allied Supreme Commander in the Mediterranean. In this role he had overseen victory in North Africa, then Sicily and after that the invasion of southern Italy. His subordinate commanders, both American and British, all liked and respected him, he had proven theatre experience, and he had continued to show good judgement while also working valiantly to create an atmosphere of close partnership between the Allies.

This was a term that sounded closer and more official than was the reality, because the 'Allies' weren't actually allies at all. They might be fighting alongside one another, and agreeing strategy and even sharing arms and war materiel, but they were coalition partners, united in the desire to defeat the Axis powers yet not bound by a formal alliance. Directly under Eisenhower were unquestionably experienced, skilled and talented men, but most were strong characters with very different personalities. There were cultural divergences too, but more often than not tensions arose less on national lines than through differing levels of understanding of the complexities of modern warfare and all its rapid changes – changes that had been dramatically accelerated by the necessity of winning this current and catastrophic global conflict. These were men prepared to fight their corner, the strength of their convictions often driven by personal experience and by the knowledge that on their actions and decisions the lives of thousands, if not millions, might depend. That was a terrible burden. Keeping these disparate men on an even keel and unified in purpose was no easy matter. Tensions simmered. Personalities clashed. Suspicions and mistrust were easily aroused.

They were, however, all largely singing from the same hymn sheet that morning in the assembly hall at St Paul's School, and Eisenhower wanted to keep it that way, especially once the invasion got under way. All had been repeatedly consulted about the plan and there had been plenty of opportunities for each to say his piece, and this was what Eisenhower wanted to underline now. None of the men assembled there was born yesterday; they all knew the old adage that the first thing to go awry in battle was the plan, but clarity and a singleness of purpose were still needed and that was what was being delivered.

The Supreme Commander stood before them, wearing his immaculate special short 'Ike' jacket based on the British battledress. Before he spoke he looked around at the men assembled in front of him and smiled – a smile of warmth and quiet confidence.

'Here we are,' he said, 'on the eve of a great battle to deliver to you the various plans made by the different force commanders. I would emphasize but one thing: that I consider it to be the duty of anyone who sees a flaw in the plan not to hesitate to say so.' This was the crux of the meeting. 'I have no sympathy with anyone,' he continued, 'whatever his station, who will not brook criticism. We are here to get the best possible results and you must make a really cooperative effort.'

All those assembled knew these plans intimately already and had had ample opportunity to question and challenge what was being proposed, but to emphasize the point, the force commanders then briefly went through the separate land, naval and air plans once again: Montgomery in battledress and trousers with cut-glass creases, then Admiral Bertram Ramsay, commander-in-chief of the Allied Naval Expeditionary Force for the invasion, and then Air Marshal Sir Trafford Leigh-Mallory, his opposite number for the air forces. Two further commanders stood up and spoke: Lieutenant-General Carl 'Tooey' Spaatz, commander of all US European Strategic Air Forces – the heavy bomber force – and Air Chief Marshal Sir Arthur Harris, his counterpart at RAF Bomber Command. Occasionally the prime minister interjected to clarify a point, but otherwise not one person there quibbled with the plans that had been drawn up.

Later, after lunch, Churchill made a brief speech. It was no secret that he had had doubts about the invasion and the terrible cost in lives it might cause. But now his rallying cry was one of optimism and growing confidence. 'Gentlemen,' he told them, 'I am *hardening* to this enterprise.'

No one there, however, was under any illusions. The task before them was a monumental one and their plan based on assumptions and variables over which they had little control. It was no wonder they were feeling the heat that warm early-summer day in London.

PART I

The Battle Before D-Day

CHAPTER 1

The Atlantic Wall

THERE WERE FEW PLACES lovelier in Nazi-occupied Europe that May than Normandy in north-west France. It had not been fought over during the Battle for France four years earlier, and although it had always remained within the territory directly controlled by Nazi Germany rather than that of Vichy France under Maréchal Philippe Pétain, this coastal region had avoided the worst hardships of occupation, and that applied to both the occupied and the occupiers. Normandy had always been a largely agricultural area with its rich, loamy soils, lush fields and orchards; here, the harsh rationing that affected city dwellers was felt far less keenly. Normandy, even in the fifth year of war, was a land of plenty: the patchwork small fields – the *bocage* – were full of dairy cows; the more open land around its major city, Caen, still shimmered with corn, oats and barley; and its orchards continued to produce plentiful amounts of fruit. Now, in May, it looked as fecund as ever. Pink and white blossom filled the orchards, hedgerows bursting with leaf and life lined the network of roads and tracks. It looked, in some ways, a kind of Eden, with centuries-old farmsteads and quiet villages dotting the landscape, while beyond its coastline of rugged cliffs and long, golden beaches, the English Channel twinkled invitingly in the sunshine.

For all this loveliness, however, the war was getting closer. Normandy that May was also now a scene of intense military activity as the beleaguered German defenders braced themselves for the Allied invasion they knew must surely come soon. To this end, a race against time was going on, because only since January had action really got under way to turn the Germans' much-vaunted Atlantic Wall from a mere concept of propaganda into an effective defence against enemy invasion. Certainly, when Feldmarschall Erwin Rommel had begun his inspection of the north-west Europe coastal defences in December the previous year, he had been shocked by what he discovered. There were coastal batteries and defences around the major cities and in the Pas de Calais; parts of Denmark were well defended too; but there were far too many gaps for his liking and especially so in Normandy and Brittany.

Nor had the troops manning these areas been much cause for confidence. The German Army had always had more than its fair share of poorly equipped and under-trained troops, even back in the glory years of the Blitzkrieg, but this part of north-west France seemed to have an excess of the very old and very young, and of ill-trained and unmotivated foreign troops in the Ost-Bataillone – eastern battalions – and of veterans recovering from wounds by eating way too much cheese and drinking far too much cider and calvados.

One of those unimpressed by what he had seen so far was 24-year-old Leutnant Hans Heinze, recently posted to join the newly formed 352. Infanterie-Division. Heinze was a veteran of the Eastern Front and one of the few to have escaped the hell of Stalingrad, where he'd served as an NCO. Wounded three times before even being sent to an aid station, he had even then refused to leave his men. Only when slipping into unconsciousness had he been evacuated. That had been Christmas Eve 1942, only five weeks before the German Sixth Army's surrender; most of those he had left behind at Stalingrad had since perished either in the fighting or in captivity.

Having recovered from his wounds, Heinze was considered suitable officer material and so posted to *Waffenschule* – weapons school – and given a commission. In the pre-war and early war years, officers had to serve in the ranks as a *Fahnenjunker* – officer cadet – and only after nine months to a year would they then be sent for an intense and lengthy stint at a *Kriegsschule*, or war school. This process had been abolished, though, as manpower had dwindled along with everything else and standards had to be cut out of necessity. Heinze, however, was as good a bet to become a decent officer as any: he certainly had the experience and had already proved himself a leader, albeit a non-commissioned one. So it was that he now found himself in Normandy and posted to the Grenadier-Regiment 916, one of the 352.'s new infantry units.

Although the division had its headquarters at Saint-Lô, some 20 miles south from the coast, Heinze had wasted no time in visiting the coastal defences in his sector. On arrival, he and his colleague could not find much evidence of the Atlantic Wall until eventually they spotted some bunkers surrounded by wire. Leaving their vehicle, they stepped through the wire with ease and without once snagging their trousers, and met a *Landser*, an ordinary soldier, who cheerily told them he had been based in Normandy since 1940. If the Tommies decided to invade, he said, they would soon roll out their guns and teach them how to feel scared. 'We found no cheer or solace in this remark,' noted Heinze. 'It was clear that much work was ahead of us.'

Soon after, Heinze was given 5. Kompanie and briefed to lick them into shape. The 352. had been given a good number of experienced officers and NCOs – some 75 per cent had been in combat, mainly on the Eastern Front – but only 10 per cent of the rest had any front-line experience at all. The first troop train delivering new recruits, for example, unloaded several thousand mostly 17-year-olds: *Grünschnabel* – greenhorns – fresh from a mere three weeks' training in Slaný in the former Czechoslovakia. By contrast, barely a single Allied soldier waiting to cross the Channel had had less than two years' training. A further 30 per cent of German troops were newly drafted conscripts from the Alsace region, or from Poland and various parts of the Soviet Union. Other infantry divisions in Normandy had an even higher number of foreign troops. Language barriers were a major issue, but so too was an inherent lack of trust; many German officers and NCOs worried that when the fighting began they might well find themselves with a bullet in the back rather than the chest.

What's more, these soldiers were hardly well equipped, and wore a variety of uniforms that had been cobbled together from stocks left over from the North African campaign, many of which were dark green denim as well as the more normal woollen field grey. They had barely enough weapons and certainly not enough transport. The artillery could not train to begin with, for example, because there were neither sights for their guns nor the correct harnesses for the horses who were to tow them.

Another problem for the newly formed 352. Division was malnourishment. Rationing in Germany, and especially further east, was harsh, with a notable lack of fruit, meat and dairy products. One of the challenges for the division's staff was not only training them properly but also feeding them up. Requests to 7. Armee for an increased dairy ration were refused, so Generalleutnant Dietrich Kraiss, the division commander, had authorized his staff to buy or barter for extra supplies of milk, butter, cheese and meat locally. It certainly helped, but standards of food supplied to the men, even in Normandy, were poor and most were dependent on buying eggs and other luxuries to supplement rations. Gefreiter Franz Gockel was a young recruit serving in I. Bataillon of Grenadier-Regiment 726, part of the 716. Infanterie-Division. One day he helped bring a pot of soup from the field kitchen to their coastal bunker. His comrades all lined up in anticipation as he took a ladle and gave the soup a good stir. Feeling something substantial move at the bottom, he pulled out the ladle to discover the remains of a dead rat. They then found another in the second canister. 'How is this possible?' he wondered.

The 716. Division was even more poorly equipped than the 352. and, unlike the core of NCOs and officers in the latter, had no combat experience at all, having been based in northern France since its formation in May 1941. Infantry divisions had already been reduced from the 16,000 men that had been standard at the start of the war to just over 12,000, but the 716. was just 8,000 strong and until the deployment of the 352. had been holding the entire Normandy coastline from Carentan to the River Orne, a stretch of around 60 miles. The 716. had no vehicles of any note; its infantry were issued with bicycles and, like most infantry divisions in Normandy, it was largely dependent on horses and carts to bring forward supplies.

The inherent weakness of the 716. Division along this stretch of coastline meant that the 352., considered to be of much higher quality despite its own obvious shortcomings, was given more to do than perhaps it should have been. On 15 March, orders had reached Generalleutnant Kraiss direct from Rommel. They were now to take over much of the 716.'s part of the coast, while that division would instead cover the stretch north of Caen. They were rapidly to improve the coastal defences, but also to build and maintain defensive positions further inland, all the way to Saint-Lô. In between all this construction work the 352. was also to continue training.

This was expecting a lot, particularly since the division still had to be on permanent standby to be moved elsewhere, which Kraiss and his staff assumed would be the Eastern Front. This in turn meant they could keep on hand only what they could easily transport should the division be suddenly redeployed. However, because the area they were covering was far greater than it had been, it meant a lot of time, manpower and fuel were being wasted in never-ending trips to the supply depots of the LXXXIV. Korps, to which they were attached.

Clearly, the standby alert should have been taken off the division; that it wasn't was typical of the mess in which the German Army now found itself. Quite simply, the Germans no longer had enough of anything with which they could realistically turn around the fortunes of the war. They didn't have enough food, fuel, ammunition, guns, armour, men, medical supplies or anything needed to fight a rapidly modernizing war. They knew the Allies would attempt a cross-Channel invasion, although where, when and in what manner remained the subject of fevered debate. The Atlantic Wall, protecting Fortress Europe, was thousands of miles long: Germany had been building coastal gun positions, bunkers and defences all the way from the Arctic Circle in northern Norway to the southern Atlantic coast of France. It was no wonder Normandy and Brittany had looked a bit light on defences; there was only so much manpower, steel and concrete.

Supply shortages were one thing, but there was no doubt that Germany was making life even harder for its put-upon commanders by the convoluted and muddle-headed command structures that had blighted the army ever since Hitler had taken direct command back in December 1941. The Führer remained utterly convinced of his own military genius, but a key feature of his leadership, first of the German people, then for the past two and a half years of the army, was his iron control. Naturally lazy, he none the less had a gift for absorbing detail and, while he left much of the day-to-day running of the Reich to others, he would, conversely, often stick his nose into the kind of minutiae of military operations that simply should not have concerned him. He also liked to operate through a policy of divide and rule, creating parallel command structures that tended to pit subordinates against one another, while also making predictions and command decisions that defied military logic but from which he could rarely, if ever, be dissuaded.

The German Army of the early years of the war had achieved its successes largely because it had created a way of operating in which both speed of manoeuvre and striking with immense concentrated, coordinated force were the key components. Tied in with this had been the freedom of commanders on the spot to make swift decisions without recourse to higher authorities. That had all gone as Germany's armed forces found themselves horrendously stretched and with almost all major decisions now requiring consultation with the Führer. The *Oberkommando der Wehrmacht* – OKW, the combined General Staff of the Armed Forces – was merely his mouthpiece and neither Feldmarschall Wilhelm Keitel, the head of the OKW, nor General Alfred Jodl, the chief of staff, was willing to play any role other than lackey to Hitler's megalomania.

To say that the Führer himself was a handicap to Germany's war aspirations was, on so many levels, a massive understatement.

Battling the endless supply challenges, as well as a particularly counter-productive command chain, was Feldmarschall Erwin Rommel, now fifty-two and, as of 15 January 1944, the commander of Heeresgruppe B – Army Group B. Rommel's war had so far been one of extraordinary highs but, like many of the Wehrmacht's senior commanders, of lows as well. He had rampaged across France in 1940 as a panzer division commander, and had then been feted by Hitler and become a pin-up back home for his dash and flair in North Africa. Awards and promotions had followed in swift succession, so that by the summer of 1942 he was the Wehrmacht's youngest field marshal – despite not commanding enough men for such a rank, nor having achieved enough to warrant such an accolade.

Then things began to go wrong, as British generalship improved along with their supply situation and dramatically more effective Allied air power. At Alamein in Egypt, Rommel was twice defeated, the second time decisively enough to send his Panzerarmee Afrika all the way back across Egypt and Libya into Tunisia. There he made one last striking attack in February 1943, forcing the bewildered and still-green US forces back down the Kasserine Pass. But Rommel pushed too far, just as he had done before Alamein, over-extending his supply lines and running out of steam as American and British opposition stiffened. Ill and disillusioned, he left Africa in early March 1943, never to return.

By the autumn, recovered but increasingly convinced the war was now lost, he had been put in charge of German forces in northern Italy. However, whereas in North Africa Rommel's cut and dash had overshadowed Feldmarschall Albert Kesselring, the German theatre commander, it was Kesselring who now outdid Rommel, throwing up a vigorous and determined defence against the Anglo-US invasion of southern Italy in September 1943 and causing Hitler to overturn early plans to retreat well to the north of Rome. Suddenly, Rommel's role there had become redundant. It had been a shattering blow for him, flinging him into depression. He was, however, about to be thrown a lifeline.

Overall military commander of the West was Feldmarschall Gerd von Rundstedt, who had entered the German Army eight months before Rommel was born and was the Wehrmacht's oldest active field marshal while Rommel was its youngest. He had commanded the main strike force of Army Group A during the invasion of France and another army group for BARBAROSSA, the invasion of the Soviet Union. Since then he had been sacked then reinstated as commander of Oberbefehl – High Command – West. In October 1943 he had submitted a report on the state of the Atlantic Wall, making it clear it was far from fit for purpose – a report that had jolted Hitler and the OKW into action, because, as they were well aware, at some point in the not-too-distant future the Allies would launch an invasion of the Continent.

General Jodl at the OKW suggested to Hitler that he appoint the humiliated Rommel to carry out an inspection tour of the Atlantic Wall. Reinvigorated, Rommel began at the start of December, heading first to Denmark and then south towards the Pas de Calais, where the Channel was at its narrowest and the defences strongest. His renewed energy and swift grip of the situation encouraged von Rundstedt to suggest making Rommel commander of the Channel coastal areas, where logic suggested the invasion was most likely to come. Von Rundstedt, ageing, patrician and disillusioned, was not prepared to rock the boat. He remained superficially loyal to Hitler, but was happy to hand over military command to Rommel; he might have been commander of OB West, but, as he quipped bitterly, in reality he only commanded the guards outside his Paris headquarters.

So, on 15 January 1944, Rommel had become commander of Heeresgruppe B, charged with defending northern France and the Low Countries and throwing any Allied invasion back into the sea. The task, he had known, was a stiff one. The defences of the Atlantic Wall and the state of the forces under his command were far worse than had been suggested by von Rundstedt; Rommel had been horrified. Since then, he had been tireless: more defences had to be built, training intensified, red tape cut, more supplies diverted. He toured the front constantly, encouraging his subordinates, urging his men, and laying out his vision for the defence of the Continent. In between, he pleaded, cajoled, bartered and bullied staff officers, bean-counters and his superiors. It was why the 352. Infanterie-Division found themselves holding a lengthy strip of the coast while also preparing defences in depth and carrying out training as the mixed bag of veterans tried desperately to turn their raw young recruits and eastern 'volunteers' into a half-decent infantry division capable of blunting any Allied attack from across the sea. It was a tall order, but there was no alternative. Not if disaster was to be averted.

In the second week of March, Rommel had moved his headquarters south to the small town of La Roche-Guyon on the banks of a big loop in the River Seine. Rommel's was a large command, geographically, and La Roche-Guyon was about as well placed as he could reasonably hope for – tucked away from prying enemy aircraft, but only 45 miles west of Paris and the headquarters of von Rundstedt as well as those of General Carl-Heinrich von Stülpnagel, both the military commander of occupied France and also the head of the *Reichssicherheitshauptamt*, RSHA, the SS security forces in the country. To the north, Calais was 160 miles away, while Caen was around 100 and Rennes, the main city of Brittany, about 180. Rommel rather eschewed luxury, but even so, in basing himself in the elegant renaissance chateau that stood beneath the ruined medieval castle, he was hardly slumming it. He was enchanted by the lovely, elegant library and large drawing room with its terrace beyond and views across the Seine. Even better, tunnels linking the renaissance and nineteenth-century chateau to the old castle above made ideal and easily expanded bunkers and a communication hub.

Here, Rommel kept a tight team. Generalleutnant Hans Speidel was his new chief of staff, having arrived in April from the Eastern Front at Rommel's request; his former CoS, Generalleutnant Alfred Gause, had served under Rommel in North Africa and the two were old friends, but Gause had upset Lucie, Rommel's wife, and she had demanded he go. Speidel and Rommel were both from Swabia, in south-west Germany, which stood them apart from the Prussian aristocratic elite that dominated the army high command. They had served together briefly during the last war and Speidel had an outstanding reputation as a highly intelligent and efficient staff officer – indeed, back in the twenties he had earned a PhD in political and military history.

There were a few other trusted colleagues, such as 36-year-old Oberst Hans-Georg von Tempelhoff, Rommel's chief operations officer, who had an English wife. The bushy-browed Generalleutnant Wilhelm Meise, his chief engineer, was playing an increasingly vital role in the construction of coastal defences; Hauptmann Hellmuth Lang was his aide-de-camp, another Swabian and a Knight's Cross-winning panzer commander; while a fourth member of his inner circle was yet another from Swabia, Vizeadmiral Friedrich Ruge, his naval advisor. 'In our circle we spoke quite frankly and openly,' noted Ruge, 'since we trusted each other implicitly. The trust was never misused.' And while there was no doubting who was the boss, Rommel was not a man to dominate the dinner conversation and was always interested in what others had to say. 'He had a good sense of humour,' noted Ruge, 'even when he was the butt of the joke.'

Ruge was forty-seven, a career naval officer, jovial and good company, and until joining Rommel's staff in Italy he had been in charge of naval coastal defences in France. The two got on well, and in evenings back at La Roche-Guyon they would often go for walks in the grounds and the woods beyond, where Rommel would talk quite candidly about his thoughts, plans and the future. Certainly, Rommel increasingly thought Normandy was a likely place for the invasion; his hunch told him it would come either side of the Seine estuary, even though in March OB West and the OKW had accepted the Pas de Calais as the most probable location.

As a senior commander, Rommel was unusual in having never fought on the Eastern Front, but he had experience of battling both the British and the Americans and understood how debilitating their air power could be; combatting overwhelming enemy air forces was something with which veterans of the Eastern Front had far less experience. 'Our friends from the East cannot imagine what they're in for here,' he told his old friend from North Africa, Generalleutnant Fritz Bayerlein, now commanding the Panzer-Lehr-Division. 'It's not a matter of fanatical hordes to be driven forward in masses against our line, with no regard for casualties and little recourse to tactical craft; here we are facing an enemy who applies all his native intelligence to the use of his many technical resources . . . Dash and doggedness alone no longer make a soldier, Bayerlein.'

His mission to repel an Allied invasion had unquestionably given him renewed self-confidence and he was tackling the challenge with a sense of grim determination, despite the shortages and supply issues being exacerbated by never-ending Allied air attacks. 'I have to be satisfied with what little I've got,' he told Hauptmann Lang, 'and try and defeat the enemy with only the most modest means. And defeated they must be, if Bolshevism is not to triumph over us.' The fear of a westward spread of communism was very real to many Germans and was certainly one of the reasons they continued to fight. 'Even then,' Rommel added, 'when we have defeated Britain and the United States, the war with Russia won't be over because she has enormous resources of men and raw materials. Perhaps then a united Europe will come forward to fight this enemy.' This, then, was Rommel's motivation. Despite the reverses, despite the defeats, and despite the chronic shortages and the overwhelming material advantage of both the Allies and the Soviet Union, in May 1944 he still believed that the battle was worth fighting and that there was some hope.

Rommel was certain that if the Allies were allowed to make a landing and create a firm foothold, all would be lost. The key, then, was to fight them at the coast, at the crust. The infantry and the coastal fortifications would be the first line of defence and would, with the help of minefields, booby traps and the thousand fighter aircraft that the Luftwaffe had promised, hold the Allies at bay. Then would come the coordinated counter-attack by the mobile armoured divisions now in France. These were the best equipped, only fully armed and generally best trained available in the West; crucially, for the most part they were also the most motivated. These units were bursting with half-tracks, assault guns, Panzer Mk IVs, as well as Panthers and even Tigers – monsters both with their heavy armour and powerful high-velocity guns. The full force of these divisions – ten in all in the West – would, Rommel believed, be enough to push the enemy back. This would buy Germany vital time, because clearly there could then be no second Allied invasion attempt for a long while after.

There was, however, a snag with this theory. Because of Allied air power, moving these mobile divisions swiftly into a massed counter-attack – and Rommel was talking about within a day or two – would mean holding all of them very close to the coast where the invasion was likely to happen. This was a huge gamble, because for all the soothsaying from Hitler's headquarters, no one was really certain where the invasion would land. For Rommel, this was an all-or-nothing gamble that simply had to be taken. A punt, yes, but, frankly, not a bad one. He had a point, and the old Hitler of 1940 – then the gambler to beat all gamblers – might have agreed. But this was 1944 and Hitler was no longer the same man.

Had Rommel been able to convince von Rundstedt, things might have been different, but the old field marshal had never had much cut and dash and, in any case, these days preferred to hedge his bets. So too did General Leo Freiherr Geyr von Schweppenburg, who, shortly after Rommel had been given Heeresgruppe B, had been appointed commander of Panzergruppe West with the brief to train up and coordinate the actions of the panzer divisions. Geyr – as he tended to be known – was a highly cultured and decorated panzer commander. He had been military atta-ché in London in the 1930s, spoke fluent English, had repeatedly proved himself on the Eastern Front and was a protégé of Generaloberst Heinz Guderian, in many ways the father of Blitzkrieg and now commander of Germany's armoured troops. That Geyr was a highly able panzer general was not in doubt, but for all his knowledge of the British he had never yet fought against them and unquestionably was underestimating the effect of Allied air power. As far as he was concerned, the panzer divisions could be held further back and still quickly brought together in a swift and successful counter-attack.

These differences of opinion had surfaced early and, no matter how much they discussed the matter, neither Rommel nor Geyr – or von Rundstedt for that matter – was prepared to shift their stance. Rommel demanded that Geyr and his panzer divisions should be subordinated to him and their deployment be his decision. Geyr, busily training his panzers against air attack and on night exercises, was convinced this tactic was a mistake; he was against being put under Rommel's command and had the influential Guderian to support him.

Back in March, Rommel had believed the debate had finally been resolved by Hitler himself. Having summoned Rommel on the 19th to the Berghof, his mountain home near Berchtesgaden in Bavaria, the Führer had first expounded his belief that Normandy and Brittany were the most likely invasion locations and then, the following day, and confidentially during a one-to-one, had agreed to consider giving Rommel full control of the panzers. Rommel, who had openly boasted to the Führer that the Allies would be kicked straight back into the sea on the first day, had believed this was as good as a promise. However, in the days and weeks that followed, there was still no formal order from Hitler putting the vital panzer divisions under his command. Rommel continued to lobby hard. 'Provided we succeed in bringing our mechanised divisions into action in the very first hours,' he told Jodl on 23 April, 'then I'm convinced that the enemy assault on our coast will be defeated on the very first day.'

But still no confirmation had come and so Rommel had simply gone over the head of von Rundstedt and Geyr and ordered 2. Panzer-Division towards the coast at Abbeville. Furious, on 28 April Geyr arrived at La Roche-Guyon, followed shortly by Guderian. 'Subject:' noted Ruge in his diary, 'fundamental questions of tactical employment, especially the use of the panzer divisions.' Whatever the disagreements, however, Ruge enjoyed the subsequent dinner, when Guderian, especially, appeared to be on lively form and there was no sign of the tactical disagreement that had dogged invasion preparations since January. 'It was to be hoped,' wrote Ruge later that evening, 'that the commitment of the panzer units would soon be decided in Rommel's favour.'

Such hopes were swiftly dashed, however. On Thursday, 8 May, Hitler finally presented OB West with a horrible fudge. Rommel was to have tactical command of 2. Panzer, 116. Panzer and 21. Panzer, this last the only mobile division already in Normandy. A new grouping, Army Group G, was to be formed in the south of France and would be allocated 2. SS-Panzer and the newly formed 9. and 11. Panzer. Geyr kept hold of four: the 1. and 12. SS-Panzer-Divisions of I. SS-Panzerkorps, as well as Panzer-Lehr and the 17. SS-Panzergrenadier-Division. No one, not even Rommel with his allocated three divisions, was authorized to move them into a concentrated counter-attack without the direct say-so of Hitler himself. In an ill-considered stroke, this meant kissing goodbye to any rapid concentration of force or flexibility of command. With this order, Hitler, once so ready to throw caution to the wind and back the dash of the gambler, had nullified both. Having repeatedly told his audiences that Brittany and Normandy were where the Allies would most likely land, he was no longer willing to back his hunch or, with it, Rommel. To all intents and purposes, the ten mobile divisions – the only possible key to repelling the Allies, for all the mines and hastily built defences – were to remain flung to the four winds.

Rommel intended to lobby hard to have this carving up of the panzer divisions overturned, but the following day, 9 May, as he and Ruge set off for another two-day inspection tour of Normandy, he was still grumbling to his companion. He had two armies under his command, the Fifteenth and the Seventh, but they both contained badly equipped and mostly low-grade infantry divisions, although there were some Luftwaffe *Fallschirmjäger* – paratrooper – units as well, who generally were cut from a better cloth. The 15. Armee had nineteen divisions, covering the coastal regions of northern France and the Low Countries, and had a very competent and experienced commander in Generaloberst Hans von Salmuth. He did, however, have blood on his hands, like so many Eastern Front commanders, having assisted the *Einsatzgruppen* – the Action Groups – to round up and execute Soviet Jews. He had later broken his 2. Armee out of Stalingrad against Hitler's wishes, for which he was sacked and demoted, but was soon after promoted again and given 15. Armee. He now loathed Hitler and the OKW, and was clearly disillusioned. Rommel thought he had become a little lazy.

The 7. Armee covered Normandy and Brittany, and now had fourteen divisions. It was commanded by Generaloberst Friedrich Dollmann, a man who exemplified the wildly varying skills and experience levels of both commanders and units under Rommel's charge. Although a career soldier and artilleryman, Dollmann had been an early enthusiast for both Hitler and the Nazis, had correctly read which way the wind was blowing and, by actively promoting National Socialism within the army, had been quickly promoted. Given command of 7. Armee in 1940, he had remained in post ever since, mostly sitting on his backside and gaining an ever-widening girth as he enjoyed the full delights of the countryside in which he was based. Fat and indolent, he made absolutely no effort to learn about or understand modern warfare. Consequently, he was hopelessly out of touch and a woefully ineffective army commander.

On the other hand, the commander of LXXXIV. Korps in Normandy, General Erich Marcks, thin-faced and bespectacled, was every bit as cultured and intellectual as he looked and brought with him considerable experience of high-level staff work and combat command. He had even lost a leg during Operation BARBAROSSA, but had overcome his disability with a determination and courage that had earned him great respect. Rommel had wanted him as 7. Armee commander, but Hitler insisted on keeping Dollmann in post. It paid to be a good Nazi.

It was to see Marcks that Rommel and Ruge were now heading, as he was far more able to give an accurate and intelligent report than Dollmann; in effect, Rommel was simply cutting his army commander out of the loop. En route they stopped to inspect coastal defences south of the Seine. With Meise's help, Rommel had supplemented concrete with vast numbers of offshore obstacles that ran the depth of the beach at low tide. There were steel tetrahedrons, as well as logs covered with mines, and poles that could jag on to any vessel – some of them tipped with further mines. Each beach was due to have four belts of obstacles, each at a different depth of the beach. Rommel assumed the Allies would land close to full tide in order to let troops get off the beach quickly, but the third and fourth belts were to provide lines of obstacles at low tide too.

While they were looking at this array of obstacles the tide began to rise swiftly. 'On this beach,' noted Ruge, 'it rises three metres in an hour, so we had to leave the beach in a hurry.' Off the beach, thick belts of wire and more minefields covered the coastline, while yet more mines continued to be laid inland – these, Rommel knew from his experiences in North Africa, could be very effective in slowing and breaking up attacks, especially by armour, and giving his poorly equipped infantry more time to fight back. The previous October, some 2 million mines had been laid in Normandy. Now that figure had risen to 6.5 million. Rommel understood such weapons were effective force multipliers, but he and Meise had reckoned 20 million were needed to protect the coast to the level he intended – and they were still a long way from achieving that.

After pausing for an air raid to pass over, they drove on through Caen. Large areas of land around the River Dives to the east and the various river valleys that ran from the River Douve estuary at Carentan had all been flooded on Rommel's orders by shutting a number of sluice gates so that the water built up behind them. This was designed both to hinder any planned Allied airborne drop and to channel any attempted advance inland towards roads that were now mined and blocked. Over larger areas, there were signs that further anti-invasion work was going on – in bigger fields, posts had been driven into the ground and strung together with wire to prevent gliders from landing.

They met Marcks in fields near Caen. The sun was shining as the one-legged corps commander made his report. There had been plenty of enemy aerial reconnaissance, he told Rommel, over both the Cotentin Peninsula and either side of the River Orne. Air attacks had been targeting coastal artillery positions as well as crossroads and main thoroughfares. Reinforcements had arrived into the Cotentin – the 91. Luftlande-Division – Air Landing Division – who were now digging across its 20-mile width and making the most of the dense hedgerows to hide themselves from prying enemy eyes in the air. He was confident they could respond to any attack on either the east or west coast of the peninsula. Marcks also reported that 50 miles of offshore obstacles had now been completed, as well as 170,000 stakes against airborne landings.

After briefings from the commander of the Cherbourg fortress and Generalmajor Edgar Feuchtinger of the 21. Panzer-Division, they drove on, pausing by the four 150mm coastal guns at Longues-sur-Mer, and then on along the coast to the tiny ports of Grandcamp and Isigny, before finishing for the day at General Marcks's headquarters at the Château de la Meauffe near Saint-Lô.

More inspections followed the next day, while at La Roche-Guyon a message from OKW arrived warning of an invasion around 18 May. 'Irrefutable documentary proof is, of course, not available,' ran the signal. 'Point of concentration first and foremost: Normandy; secondly: Brittany.' But really, it was still anyone's guess.

CHAPTER 2

Command of the Skies

Monday, 22 May 1944. Sixteen P-47 Thunderbolt fighter planes of the 61st Fighter Squadron were speeding towards the northern German city of Bremen led by the imperturbable Lieutenant-Colonel Francis 'Gabby' Gabreski. Shortly before, the 61st, part of Colonel 'Hub' Zemke's 56th Fighter Group, had helped escort almost 300 B-17 Flying Fortress heavy bombers on an attack on the Baltic port of Kiel, but, their escort duty over, their role now was to maraud the skies of northern Germany shooting down any enemy planes they might see and, especially, destroying locomotives on the ground. The intensive train-smashing operation, begun the previous day, had been given the code name CHATTANOOGA CHOO CHOO, after the famous song. A jaunty and jolly jingle it may have been, but the business of shooting up railway engines was a deadly serious one. The German rail network, the Reichsbahn, really was the glue that kept the German war effort together. Almost everything travelled the shrinking Reich by rail: raw materials, weapons, labour, troops, food, Jews being sent to death camps. The more marshalling yards that were smashed, the more locomotives shot up, the more railway bridges destroyed and lines cut, the harder it would be for the Germans to move. The Allies' greatest fear before the invasion was a concentrated counter-attack by the mass of ten panzer divisions known to be in the West. The aim of the 'Transportation Plan', as it was called, was to make it as difficult as possible for the Germans to move those all-important troops, as well as other reinforcements, to Normandy.

Hub Zemke had introduced a new tactic that day, which the men quickly named the 'Zemke Fan'. There were three squadrons in the group, each flying sixteen planes in flights of four, and to make max-imum use of them on the return leg he ordered them to maraud over three distinct areas rather than all flying together back to base. So, the 62nd FS had been sent to hunt over the Paderborn area, the 63rd FS to Hanover, while Gabreski's bunch had sped south-west towards Bremen.

They were around 20 miles east of the city when a couple of locomotives were spotted. With their clouds of white steam, they were easy enough to spy on such a lovely clear day, so Gabreski ordered Evan McMinn's Yellow Flight down to shoot them up, while the remaining twelve Thunderbolts circled as cover at around 15,000 feet. They had barely begun circling, however, when Gabreski spotted a not very well camouflaged air base below. Moments later, McMinn's voice crackled over the radio saying he could see some Focke-Wulf 190 fighters taking off.

Gabreski felt the now familiar surge of excitement as he led the squad-ron down in a dive. The Thunderbolt was a big fighter and unrivalled in a dive. Armed with .50-calibre machine guns, it could pack a big punch, take a lot of punishment itself and was highly manoeuvrable. More to the point, American fighter pilots were in a different league to those in the Luftwaffe in terms of flying skill. Most new pilots joined their squad-rons with more than three times the flying hours of their German opposite numbers, and because of the plentiful quantities of fuel and the large pilot overlap in each squadron – usually over fifty to keep sixteen planes flying per mission – there was a lot of time to practise further and hone skills alongside those who had more experience. Because of the chronic shortages of fuel, new Luftwaffe fighter pilots tended to fly on missions only. Most were promptly shot down.

That was about to be the fate of a number of FW190s now. As Gabreski and his men hurtled towards them, he saw around sixteen of them spread out in line abreast. The enemy fighters were now at a height where they could have turned and fought, but they seemed oblivious to what was happening and instead flew on in steady formation, presenting them-selves as juicy targets for the P-47s. Picking out one, Gabreski opened fire and saw his bullets flash all over the German's fuselage and wing. It turned and fell away, then burst into flames. Now Gabreski got behind a second and, closing in, opened fire a second time. This time the canopy flew off and, moments later, the pilot bailed out. Looking over his shoul-der, he saw two 190s homing in on him. He managed to climb, turn and shake them off, but then saw one of his men going down in flames and another trailing smoke, which was a big blow. Climbing back up to

12,000 feet, Gabreski ordered his men to regroup on him over the enemy airfield. Soon he had six Thunderbolts together and they spotted some twenty Focke-Wulfs down below. Suddenly, though, the German fighter's own anti-aircraft gunners opened up on them. Someone fired a green recognition flare, but the enemy formation had scattered.

Without hesitating further, Gabreski led his men back down, speeding in behind a formation of six German fighters. Moments later, he had shot down his third of the day, but then caught sight of a further Focke-Wulf sneaking up on him on his left. Yanking back the control column into his stomach and cutting the throttle, his Thunderbolt climbed and slowed to a near stall so that his pursuer had no choice but to hop over him. Suddenly, Gabreski was behind him, but with his ammunition low and five more Messerschmitt 109s behind, he reckoned it was time to cut and run. He ordered his men home and they sped west, only to run into a lone Focke-Wulf flitting in and out of cloud. Speeding in behind and using the last of his ammunition, Gabreski shot him out of the sky too, giving him three confirmed kills and one probable for the day.

In all, Gabreski and his men shot down thirteen confirmed, one probable and two damaged that day for the loss of two of their own. A further pilot, Joel Popplewell, managed to get his Thunderbolt back home to England despite counting over a hundred bullet holes on his ship. Gabreski, now one of the leading aces in the US Eighth Air Force, reckoned it had been one of the toughest missions he had ever been on, but it demonstrated the absolute dominance the American day-fighters now had over the Luftwaffe in the West. A little over two weeks before the invasion, that was good news. Just as good was the hunting that day by Zemke's fighter group: six locomotives destroyed, seven damaged, as well as eighteen river barges shot up. CHATTANOOGA CHOO CHOO was going well.

And there was further cause for cheer just under a week later, on Sunday 28 May, a day that saw the culmination of what had been in effect a five-month battle in the skies for air superiority over north-west Europe. This was a non-negotiable precondition for the invasion that had been uppermost in the Allied war leaders' minds since the previous summer.

All through the summer and autumn of 1943, the US Eighth Air Force, along with the RAF's home commands, had struggled to make much headway, despite their growing numbers, experience and improving navigational aids. Air Chief Marshal Sir Arthur Harris, the C-in-C of RAF Bomber Command, had stubbornly insisted that night bombing of

German cities by growing numbers of heavy bombers would be enough to bring not only the Luftwaffe but all of Nazi Germany to its knees. As the months passed, that claim had become an increasingly misguided one for a number of reasons. First, the Luftwaffe had finally put together an increasingly efficient and coordinated air defence system. Second, they had brought much of the Luftwaffe home to defend the Reich, while at the same time dramatically increasing aircraft production. There had been many more night-fighters in the skies to meet Harris's bomber streams than ever before and, what's more, they were now being expertly directed towards the British bombers by a combination of well-organized intelligence, ground control and radar. Bomber Command was still causing lots of damage, but not enough to hustle Germany into surrendering, and bomber crews were being slaughtered in the process.

The Americans had begun bombing Germany by day in the belief that this would enable them to bomb targets with greater precision and therefore more efficiently and effectively. To do this, they had developed very heavily armed four-engine bombers flying in tight defensive formations, but soon learned the hard way that bombers flying alone could not protect themselves effectively. Like Bomber Command, they were getting hammered.

Over the crisis months of the second half of 1943, the Americans, especially, had recognized they needed to rethink how to achieve air superiority, which was their priority for strategic bombing. This had been agreed as early as January 1943 and more formally in early June that year in a directive called POINTBLANK. The reason for prioritizing the Luftwaffe as a target was twofold: strategic bombing would be considerably more effective if there were no longer any enemy fighters intercepting them along the way; and gaining air superiority over not just the invasion beaches but the skies of all of western Europe was an unequivocally agreed prerequisite before the Allies launched a cross-Channel invasion. Air power was both absolutely vital to the planning of OVERLORD and rightly seen as key to victory on the ground.

In fact, even Hitler had understood the importance of air superiority over the invasion front; it was why his Luftwaffe had been trying to destroy the RAF before he even considered launching troops across the Channel back in 1940. For OVERLORD, however, air superiority was essential over the invasion front so that troops could land without interference from the air, but was also needed much further inland as well. This was because it was recognized that, for all the millions of men and gargantuan amounts of weaponry and supplies being built up in Britain, shipping and port restrictions limited the number of men and amount of materiel that could be landed in Normandy on D-Day, as the day of the invasion was known, and the days immediately after. If the Germans were to have any chance of throwing them back into the sea, they would need to launch a coordinated counter-attack with all their mobile forces as quickly as they possibly could. Intelligence had shown there were ten German panzer and mobile divisions in the West, so it was critical for the Allies that these units should be slowed, delayed and obstructed as much as possible in their efforts to reach Normandy. In this, the French Résistance had a crucial role, but the hard yards were to be performed by the air forces, who would strike bridges, locomotives, railways and any vehicle that moved during the nine weeks leading up to D-Day and in the days – and weeks – that followed. For the most part, these operations would be carried out by the tactical air forces – that is, those created specially to support ground operations. The bombers were faster, smaller, two-engined varieties that operated at lower levels with the support of fighters and ground-attack aircraft. To fly effectively at lower altitudes, however, it was essential that the skies were largely clear of enemy air-craft. This was why winning air superiority was so important to the Allies. Without it, OVERLORD was a non-starter.

Until very recently, however, it had seemed like a very distant goal. The dilemma back in the autumn of 1943 had been just how to destroy the Luftwaffe, because bombing alone was clearly not cutting the mus-tard, not least because most of the enemy factories were deep in the Reich where the daylight bombers and even Bomber Command at night could not effectively reach. What was needed, urgently and in large numbers, was a long-range fighter. Only in the nick of time, however, did they real-ize the solution was, in fact, right under their very noses.

The RAF had had the opportunity to make Spitfires long range, but – largely because of Bomber Command's continuation with night bombing, and the insouciance and lack of vision of men like Leigh-Mallory and even Sir Charles Portal, chief of the Air Staff – had not thought it necessary. However, the previous year a US-built P-51 Mustang had been equipped with a Rolls-Royce Merlin 61 rather than its original Allison engine, and its performance and fuel economy had improved astonishingly. Extra fuel tanks had been added and had made little difference to its speed or manoeuvrability, then so too had discardable drop tanks. Suddenly, the Allies had a fighter capable of nearly 1,500 miles and able to fly to Berlin and back with ease. That was a game-changer. Unfortunately, however, the American air chiefs had only woken up to the potential of the P-51 in the summer of 1943.

The question that autumn was whether there would be enough Mustangs to make a decisive difference quickly enough. By November 1943, the first complete P-51B Mustang fighter group, the 354th, was in England and the following month they began flying their first missions. By January, a second Mustang fighter group had arrived, while a third, the already legendary 4th Fighter Group, was due to switch from Thunderbolts at the end of February. In March and April more had followed.

At the end of November, the height of the autumn crisis, a new directive, ARGUMENT, had been issued. This was an all-out concentrated offensive against the Luftwaffe and the enemy aircraft industry, but it was held back by the poor weather that descended over Britain and Europe like a shroud for much of the winter. For ARGUMENT to have any chance of success, a spell of high pressure was essential, but not until the third week of February 1944 was there any sign of such a break in the weather.

In what became known simply as 'Big Week', the Allies repeatedly bombed key Luftwaffe factories and did their best to draw the German fighter force into the air. It was the biggest air battle ever witnessed and, although damage to the German aircraft industry was not as great as had been originally hoped, the real victory of Big Week was the blow to German pilots. Losses of aircraft of all types amounted to a staggering 2,605 for February 1944 alone. Such attrition was totally unsustainable; experienced pilots were being chipped away while the new boys were arriving with decreasing amounts of training and were being slaughtered. Yet more were shot down in March and April. Germany was still churning out thousands of fighter aircraft each month, but the ability of its pilots to fly and fight effectively was diminishing further with every passing week. Like the rest of Nazi Germany, the Luftwaffe was in terminal decline.

Meanwhile, the Eighth Air Force was being protected by an increasingly large cadre of highly experienced pilots like Gabby Gabreski. From Oil City, Pennsylvania, he was the son of Polish immigrants and after the invasion of Poland in September 1939 was determined to join what was then the Air Corps. He soon discovered, however, that he was far from being a natural pilot and very nearly flunked out. Given a reprieve, he scraped through and was posted to Pearl Harbor. He was still there when the Japanese attacked in December 1941, but later managed to get approval to transfer to England and the RAF, where he briefly joined 315 Polish Squadron flying Spitfires. Only once the Eighth began arriving in England in early 1942 did he switch back to the United States Army Air Forces, USAAF, and join the 56th Fighter Group. Since then, incredibly, he had become one of the Eighth's leading aces, developing into not only a fine fighter pilot but a natural leader too. It was around men such as Gabreski that VIII Fighter Command was rapidly growing in strength, confidence and skill.

With the end of Big Week, however, and the rapid approach of OVER-LORD, there had been much discussion about, and even consternation over, exactly how the Eighth Air Force in England and RAF Bomber Command should be used in the weeks and months to come. Both were 'strategic' air forces – created, set up and trained to operate independently of any other force. Ever since Eisenhower had been appointed Supreme Allied Commander for OVERLORD in December 1943, however, it had been accepted that by April 1944 the strategic air forces would have to start operating in direct support of OVERLORD. This had prompted deep concerns from the strategic air force commanders, not least General Tooey Spaatz, the C-in-C of US Strategic Air Forces, and Air Chief Marshal Sir Arthur Harris, the C-in-C of Bomber Command. Both men were deeply committed to strategic bombing and were considerable personalities wielding equally considerable influence. Since taking over Bomber Command in early 1942, Harris had run his force with almost complete autonomy and did not appreciate being told what, where and when to bomb by either his peers or his superiors. Rather, he preferred to listen to the suggestions of others and then make his own judgement on targets based on a series of considerations about which he felt he and his staff were best placed to decide.

Spaatz was second only to General Henry 'Hap' Arnold in the USAAF and was, by early 1944, hugely experienced, highly regarded and a deep thinker about air power. He carried about him an easy air of sagacity and authority, and commanded a great deal of respect after being the first senior American airman to visit Britain back in 1940, then taking command of the Eighth Air Force before being given key commands in the Mediterranean during the campaigns in North Africa, Sicily and Italy. He had returned to Britain in January as the most senior US airman in the European theatre, with overall command of the Eighth and the Fifteenth Air Forces.

Harris and Spaatz disagreed about how best to use the strategic air forces in support of OVERLORD. Harris believed his ongoing policy of hammering German cities was the most effective use of his force, while Spaatz thought that focusing on hitting German fuel sources was most likely to bring the German war effort to a standstill and so, in turn, help the invasion. With the so-called 'Oil Plan', Spaatz intended to target synthetic-fuel plants as well as Ploesti in Romania, the one real oil well to which the Germans had access. Spaatz reckoned this sustained attack would account for 80 per cent of production and 60 per cent of refining capacity. What was less clear was the time frame within which this might be achieved.

The Deputy Supreme Commander, on the other hand, Air Chief Marshal Sir Arthur Tedder, favoured the Transportation Plan, in which railways, marshalling yards and bridges would be hit. A lot of the work outlined in this plan would be left to the tactical air forces, who, with their smaller and faster medium twin-engine bombers and fighter-bombers, could fly in at lower levels and hit smaller targets. Where the heavies came in was in attacking the large marshalling yards in major cities in France and Germany particularly. Harris protested that his bomber force could not be expected to hit targets with the kind of accuracy that would be needed. Even a year earlier this might have been the case, but by the spring of 1944 improved navigational technology and better marking tactics meant that it no longer was. In this, squadrons like 617, which had destroyed the German dams in May 1943, were taking a pioneering lead, using very fast Mosquitoes to drop target-marker flares at low level.

Much has been made of the dispute over how best to use the Allied heavy bomber forces, but in fact the differences of opinion over the priority of targets was secondary to the issues of the chain of command. Really, it was all about control, and more specifically the unwillingness of Harris and, especially, Spaatz to serve under the direct command of Air Marshal Sir Trafford Leigh-Mallory, a man whom neither liked very much and whom they respected as an air commander even less.

Leigh-Mallory had been one of the first of the key command appointments for OVERLORD the previous summer. Much had changed since then and a number of those singled out early on had been replaced, but Leigh-Mallory, the Commander-in-Chief, Allied Expeditionary Air Force (AEAF), was still very much in place. Younger brother of the famous George Mallory, lost heroically in his attempt to reach the summit of Everest in 1924, he was a career RAF officer, who at the end of the First

World War had commanded 8 Squadron, then the first dedicated to army cooperation. In the interwar years he had also commanded the RAF's School of Army Co-operation.

In 1940, however, Leigh-Mallory was commanding 12 Group of RAF Fighter Command during the Battle of Britain, and then later held the all-important command of 11 Group, in the south-east of England, before being promoted to become C-in-C of Fighter Command itself. While in this role he began lobbying to take command of a unified Allied air force for the forthcoming invasion. In the spring of 1943, Air Chief Marshal Sir Charles Portal, a member of the Combined Chiefs of Staff, believed that the most important air aspect of D-Day and the subsequent establishment of the beachheads would be the maintenance of air superiority overhead. Both the British and Americans accepted that the air C-in-C should therefore be a fighter commander, so there was some logic, especially given his army cooperation background, in giving that role to Leigh-Mallory.

There is little doubt, however, that Leigh-Mallory's ego, ambition and ability to ingratiate himself with superiors also played a part in his appointment. As head of Fighter Command, with an HQ on the edge of London, he was a stone's throw from Downing Street, the Air Ministry and the War Office. What's more, Portal, who had been based in London ever since becoming chief of the Air Staff in October 1940, had less experience or understanding of how rapidly tactical air power had been developing in North Africa and the Mediterranean. Leigh-Mallory, the commander of the British-based fighter force, was on his doorstep, lobbying hard and saying all the right things.

At the time of his appointment, he had been cooperating with the Americans well enough and providing short-range fighter escorts for the Eighth's bombers. By early 1944, however, with Spaatz now in place in England as overall commander of US Strategic Air Forces, serious doubts were starting to emerge about Leigh-Mallory's abilities. He was perceived to be not much of a team player, had a somewhat aggressive temperament, especially to peers and subordinates, and was as stubborn as a mule. Close examination of his wartime career should also have raised some serious concerns. It was he who had introduced the 'Big Wing' theory of massing four or five fighter squadrons together towards the end of the Battle of Britain. Although they had some psychological value, they were tactically extremely questionable because it took them longer to form up than for the Luftwaffe to reach London and so the aim of intercepting the enemy before they reached their target was scuppered. He oversaw outrageous claims he knew to be false and repeatedly undermined the authority of Air Chief Marshal Hugh Dowding, the first CO of Fighter Command, and schemed against Air Vice-Marshal Keith Park, commander of the RAF's 11 Fighter Group. Both were sacked to Leigh-Mallory's career advancement. Subsequently, as 11 Group commander and then C-in-C of Fighter Command, he hoarded seventy-five fighter squadrons for ineffective fighter operations over France and north-west Europe. Only very reluctantly did he finally agree to release Spitfires to Malta and North Africa in the spring of 1942, where they swiftly proved decisive; they could quite conceivably have made a significant difference had they been sent in 1941. Even then, he still stubbornly refused to release new Typhoon and Tempest fighters overseas, so there were none operating in Italy, for example.

Nor had he pushed to give Spitfires long-range capabilities, something that could and should have been easily resolved and provided, had he had the inclination and foresight. Instead, masses of Spitfires were flying short-range missions to France and achieving very little as, for the most part, the Luftwaffe quite sensibly refused to play ball. Both Britain and America were blessed with some truly talented and dynamic air commanders, men who had repeatedly proved themselves to be tactically acute, charismatic and wonderful coalition players. Sadly, Leigh-Mallory did not fall into that category.

Over the summer of 1943, Leigh-Mallory had gradually begun to assume the role of Allied Air Commander for OVERLORD and, in August, was the first of the key appointments to be formally approved. It was proving to have been a premature appointment to say the very least. In December, Air Chief Marshal Sir Arthur Tedder had been made Deputy Supreme Allied Commander directly under Eisenhower. This was a smart move and, of course, reflected the vital importance air power was to play in the invasion. Tedder had been Allied Air Forces C-in-C in the Mediterranean, where he had repeatedly proved his skill, vision, operational competence and astuteness. What's more, he worked effectively with Eisenhower and the two got on well; OVERLORD was not the time to be forging new relationships but rather to be building on those already established. It was also accepted that since Eisenhower was an American, his deputy should be British. No one quibbled over Tedder's appointment.

There were now two tactical air forces for the invasion and they were, on paper at any rate, now directly under Leigh-Mallory's control. The first was the USAAF Ninth Air Force under Lieutenant-General Lewis Brereton, who also had experience of command in the Mediterranean. There were question marks about his overall competence, but none over Brigadier-General Elwood 'Pete' Quesada, the young, dynamic commander of IX Fighter Command. The second was the RAF's newly formed Second Tactical Air Force, and it made perfect sense to give this command to Air Marshal Sir Arthur Coningham, a tough and equally charismatic New Zealander nicknamed 'Mary', supposedly a derivation of 'Maori'. It is hard to imagine a more macho figure with a less appropriate name, but Coningham rather liked it; certainly, it was the name by which he was known to most.

Coningham had played a huge part in the Allies' development of tactical air power. Taking command of the RAF's Desert Air Force in North Africa the autumn of 1941, he had – with the active support of Tedder, then C-in-C RAF Middle East – spent much time and effort developing concepts of close air support for Eighth Army as they battled back and forth across the desert below, arguing that his forces should support ground operations but should never come under the direct control of the army. He suggested his HQ and the Tactical Headquarters of Eighth Army should be side by side and they should work in the closest of harmony, but while the army could put in specific requests for targets, ultimately such decisions should remain with the air force commanders. In this he had the backing of both Tedder and Churchill.

In partnership with his right-hand man and administrative chief, Air Commodore Tommy Elmhirst, Coningham also honed the operational performance of the Desert Air Force with incredibly effective results. Maintenance was streamlined, while his squadrons were able to move forward or backwards to operate from different airfields with astonishing efficiency and flexibility. Arguably, it was the Desert Air Force that saved Eighth Army from annihilation after the terrible defeat at Gazala and the loss of Tobruk on 21 June 1942. As the battered remnants of Eighth Army streamed back into Egypt and the Alamein Line, the Desert Air Force never let up on their pursuers, Rommel's Panzerarmee Afrika. Round-the-clock attacks checked the Germans' progress, not only allowing Eighth Army to escape but buying them time to shore up defences at Alamein.

Techniques were further honed during the ground victories at Alam Halfa and Alamein and as Eighth Army chased Rommel's forces in turn all the way to Tunisia. There Coningham was made commander of the newly created North African Tactical Air Force, with the American Brigadier-General Larry Kuter as his deputy. Together, and in perfect harmony, Coningham and Kuter began to establish the tactical air doctrine that holds for close air support even to this day. Training pilots and aircrew in low-level and dive-bombing techniques was part of it, but most important was the method of communication between air and ground forces, which, in essence, involved army forward observers operating in a vehicle on the ground alongside an RAF ground controller and radio operators.

In Tunisia, over Sicily and in Italy, tactical air power became an integral part of offensive ground operations, taken forward not only by Coningham, Elmhirst and Kuter but by other enlightened air commanders such as Jimmy Doolittle, Pete Quesada and more. Operationally and tactically, close air support was constantly being honed, principally by improving the speed with which impromptu requests for strikes from ground troops could be passed on to air forces in the skies above.

It therefore made perfect sense that Mary Coningham should take over command of Second Tactical Air Force with his pioneering understanding, experience and his long collaboration with Tedder. 'Mary Coningham was the logical person,' said General Pete Quesada, 'and his was the easiest selection of all the selections that had to be made.' General Brereton, too, was well known to Tedder and had enough experience in the Middle East to warrant retaining his position in charge of the Ninth Air Force, especially with Quesada in charge of the Ninth's fighters, which, with their speed, agility and increased fire-power, were by 1944 a crucial part of the ground-attack support role and of keeping any potential enemy fighters – the primary defensive aircraft – at bay.

While that meant the tactical air forces had firm and strong leadership, there remained a massive question mark over the role and chain of command of the strategic air forces, and precisely what role they would play in support. Matters had come to a head on 25 March at a bombing policy conference in which it was agreed that Tedder would coordinate the operations of the strategic forces, while Leigh-Mallory would coordinate the tactical plan, both under the 'direction' of Eisenhower – wording that was eventually ratified by the Combined Chiefs of Staff on 7 April.

Eisenhower had been so fed up with the to-ing and fro-ing and differing arguments about both the role of the strategic bombers and the chain of air command that he had privately threatened to resign if a solution could not be found. That day, 25 March, both issues were finally resolved, albeit subject to final approval from the Chiefs of Staff. Eisenhower came down in favour of the Transportation Plan over Spaatz's Oil Plan, because it quite clearly offered more immediate help to his invasion forces. Spaatz had admitted that attacking synthetic-fuel plants would require longer to show results, and in any case there was no reason why, within the broader POINTBLANK directive which still demanded the continued hammering of the Luftwaffe, Spaatz could not order his daylight bombing force to attack such targets as well as marshalling yards. In other words, the Oil Plan could, to a certain extent, sit alongside the Transportation Plan. In fact, Spaatz was delighted by the outcome. Lieutenant-General Ira Eaker, C-in-C of the Mediterranean Allied Air Forces, who dined with him after the 25 March conference, reckoned he had never seen his old friend and colleague so jubilant. 'The strategic British and American Air Forces were not to be put under Leigh-Mallory,' Eaker reported to Hap Arnold. 'The communication plan had won out over the oil plan, but Tooey was not too displeased about this, since all had firmly agreed that the German Air Force was to be an all-consuming first priority.'

However, while there now seemed to be a way forward for the strategic air forces, strong concerns remained, because although sound reasons could be found for using heavies against marshalling yards, their proximity to city centres meant that civilians – including French citizens whom the Allies were planning to liberate – would inevitably be killed and wounded in the process. Bombing had become considerably more accurate in recent months, but it was still not precise enough to avoid collateral damage. Bombing Frenchmen did not sit easily with a number of Allied war leaders, especially not Churchill and his Cabinet, who took a very grave view of the plan. 'Considering that they are all our friends,' the prime minister wrote to Eisenhower on 3 April, 'this might be held to be an act of very great severity, bringing much hatred on the Allied Air Forces.'

After discussions with Tedder, Eisenhower replied two days later, pointing out that one of the prime factors in the decision to launch the invasion was the use of overwhelming air power. 'I and my military advisors have become convinced that the bombing of these centers will increase our chances for success in the critical battle,' he wrote, adding that he believed estimates of civilian casualties, some as high as 160,000, had been massively exaggerated. 'The French people are now slaves,' he told Churchill. 'Only a successful OVERLORD can free them. No one has a greater stake in the success of that operation than have the French.' Everything would be done to avoid loss of life, but he felt very strongly that it would be 'sheer folly' to overlook any operation that would dramatically improve the chances of the invasion's success. And at the beginning of April 1944, despite the huge materiel superiority of the Allies, the cross-Channel invasion, all the way from southern England to Normandy, still looked an immensely difficult and fraught operation. For Eisenhower, the most senior military officer for the entire operation, OVERLORD was in no regard a foregone conclusion. It is hard to imagine the oppressive burden of responsibility resting on his shoulders.

On 19 April, Eisenhower gave Spaatz direct authority to bomb oil targets, while bombers from the Eighth and Bomber Command struck at marshalling yards and even bridges over the Seine and Meuse rivers. At the same time, bombers and fighters from the tactical air forces continued to destroy further bridges, railway lines and any sign of enemy movement all across France and the Low Countries. Any targets in this large swathe of western Europe were potentially useful to OVERLORD, while at the same time helping to keep the enemy guessing where the invasion would actually come.

Eisenhower had also agreed on 19 April to give greater priority to targeting V-1 flying bomb and V-2 rocket sites. These were so-called *Vergeltungswaffen* – 'vengeance' weapons – that had been developed by Nazi scientists. The Allies had been aware of them for some time and had targeted Peenemünde, the testing site on the Baltic coast, for precisely that reason. Since the previous May they had also been monitoring the launch sites being built in northern France for both V-1 bombs and V-2 rockets. Operation CROSSBOW had begun that November specifically to target these sites, which appeared to be being built with the aim of directly attacking Britain. That was potentially bad enough, but the concern, of course, was that once the invasion began they would be turned towards Normandy too. The British had been sufficiently worried about the devastation they might cause to ask Eisenhower to give their destruction priority over all other air attacks apart from those urgent requirements for OVERLORD. This he had now agreed to do.

Meanwhile, Bomber Command were also doing a very good job of disproving Harris's earlier concerns about a lack of accuracy. On the night of 19/20 May, for example, Bomber Command simultaneously hit the railway yards at Boulogne, Orléans, Amiens, Tours and Le Mans with considerable success. Orly, Reims, Liège and Brussels were all plastered by the Eighth on the 20th. On the 21st, the first day of CHATTANOOGA CHOO CHOO, the Eighth claimed ninety-one locomotives destroyed. Le Mans and Orléans were hit again by Bomber Command on 22/23 May. The Eighth struck at bridges along the Seine and enemy airfields in France on 25 May. Aachen was hit heavily by Bomber Command on 27/28 May, its marshalling yards severely damaged and all traffic through this major thoroughfare halted. So it had gone on, night after night, day after day.

For the Luftwaffe, these were dark days indeed. Once the spearhead of the dazzling Blitzkrieg victories, it had become a depository for huge numbers of increasingly under-par fighter aircraft for which there was no longer enough fuel nor sufficiently trained pilots. Reichsmarschall Hermann Göring was still commander-in-chief, but his star had long been on the wane and his influence over Hitler had plummeted. He had always been a far better businessman and Machiavellian politician than air commander in any case; like Hitler, he chopped and changed his plans and tactics continually.

For the most part, the Luftwaffe was run by Göring's number two, Feldmarschall Erhard Milch, and the Luftwaffe General Staff, although day-to-day operations were left in the hands of a number of much younger and highly capable commanders desperately trying to salvage some kind of order from the mounting mayhem and increasingly impossible demands from Hitler. At a meeting about supply and procurement on 21 April, General der Flieger Adolf Galland, still only thirty-two and a highly decorated fighter ace in his own right, warned that the Allies had already gained not only superiority but almost supremacy. 'The ratio in which we fight today is about one to seven. The standard of the Americans is extraordinarily high,' he reported. 'During each enemy raid we lose about fifty fighters. Things have gone so far that the danger of a collapse of our arm exists.' Something had to be done, and he urged Milch and the procurement teams to hurry up and bring the exciting Messerschmitt 262 jet fighter into service at the earliest available opportunity. Only this miracle weapon, he suggested, could turn the tide in the air war.

Galland's fighter pilots were simply being swamped by the growing number of American day-fighters: Thunderbolts with drop tanks flying over north-west Europe and Mustangs penetrating deep into the Reich. One of those battling against the massed formations of the enemy was

22-year-old Leutnant Wolfgang Fischer, a Focke-Wulf 190 fighter pilot of 3./Jagdgeschwader 2 (JG2). From the tiny town of Waldthurn in the ancient Upper Palatinate Forest in Bavaria, he had joined the Luftwaffe in late 1939 although he had not initially been chosen for flying training, instead becoming an 'airmen/general duties', which to Fischer had meant the lowest of the low. In fact, he had worked in the *Wetterzentrale* – the meteorological office – deciphering Allied weather reports, but continued to try to get posted for pilot training, a dream that had finally come true in February 1942. It was not until more than two years later, however, that he had at last been posted to a front-line fighter squadron, having first retrained as a night-fighter and then been assigned as a temporary instructor. 'It had been a long and at times incomprehensible road,' he wrote. 'But now that road was finally behind me.' No matter how frustrating it had been, however, such a long apprenticeship would certainly give him a much greater chance than the vast majority of fighter pilots being newly sent to the front. Very few now had a blind-flying certificate or anything like the number of hours in their logbooks that Fischer had.

Initially, he had joined 4./JG2 in Italy, where the last few Luftwaffe units were still based. Flying a Messerschmitt 109G-6, he and his fellows had almost immediately been told to fly to southern France, but en route they had run into some American P-39 Aircobras and Fischer had been shot down. Bailing out safely, he had then been forced to complete the journey to Aix-en-Provence by train. There he had been reassigned to 3./JG2, which flew Focke-Wulfs rather than 109s, and on 1 May the I. Gruppe had been posted up to Cormeilles, north-west of Paris. With this as their new base, they would operate daily from forward airfields further to the west, usually flying two or three sorties each a day, mostly against marauding fighter-bombers, or '*Jabos*' as the Germans called them, from *Jagdbomber*.

After a week, 2. and 3. Staffeln had been moved again, this time to Boissy-le-Bois, near Beauvais to the north-west of Paris, and were quartered in a luxurious small chateau. Fischer might have enjoyed it had it not been for the permanent air of tension and fear. Every morning on the bus taking them to the airfield, he could not help wondering who might still be there the following day. The only time the dead weight of apprehension left him was the moment the airfield loudspeakers ordered them to scramble. Then the ground crew would hurriedly pull back the camouflage netting, push them clear of the trees, and Fischer would clamber up and into the cockpit and get moving. Only then, focusing solely on flying, did his mind start to clear.

Thursday, 25 May, was typical of the daily missions he and his comrades were now flying. Scrambled to intercept a formation of enemy bombers approaching, they climbed until ahead of them they spotted some 120 B-24 Liberators, flying in four distinct boxes and surrounded by at least fifty P-38 Lightnings. There were just five in Fischer's *Staffel*. They pressed on and, still in formation, made a headlong pass over the outer box of B-24s, claiming a *Herausschuss* in the process – a bomber that was damaged and so began falling out of formation. The German fighter pilots flew on, however, before turning to attack some P-38s that seemed not to have noticed them. Leutnant Walterscheid, the *Staffelkapitän*, shot down two and Fischer hit a third. 'Its pilot,' noted Fischer, 'immediately bailed out and tumbled past beneath my wings like a badly wrapped parcel.'

One of Fischer's colleagues was in trouble, however. 'Start travelling!' Fischer yelled at him over the radio. 'Start travelling!' But it made no difference. By now, more P-38s were swarming around them and, with tracers hurtling past his cockpit, he pushed the stick forward and dived, almost vertically. To his great relief, none of the American pilots followed. Heading for home, he safely touched back down, but was joined by only two others; two more dead pilots were found in the burning wreckage of their Focke-Wulfs a couple of hours later.

Recognizing that operating in such small formations could achieve very little, General Galland and Generalmajor 'Beppo' Schmid, commander of I. Jagddivision, had begun, by the second half of May, sending up massed formations of 50–150 of their fighters to intercept the bombers. It meant they could attack only one formation at a time, but it was the only way to confront the hordes of American fighters; VIII Fighter Command was now regularly sending out as many as 600 fighters with every bomber raid.

On Sunday, 28 May, a little over a week before D-Day, more than 850 of Eighth Air Force's bombers were sent out on two separate raids against mainly oil targets, principally around Magdeburg and Leuna in eastern Germany. Among the 697 fighter aircraft dispatched to escort them were fifty-six P-51 Mustangs of the 354th Fighter Group. The 354th, although flying with the Eighth, were actually only on loan from the Ninth Air Force and were due to rejoin IX Fighter Command once the invasion got under way. For the past few months, however, they had been racking up scores against the Luftwaffe and making aces out of an increasing number of their pilots.

Among them was 24-year-old Dick Turner, commander of the 356th Fighter Squadron, newly promoted to major and now leading the entire group. Adopting a similar approach to Colonel Zemke, Turner split his three squadrons as they escorted the 3rd Bomb Division's Flying Fortresses on their mission to bomb the Brabag synthetic-fuel complex at Magdeburg-Rothensee, so that two were covering the north of the bomber formation while his squadron was to the south. It was now around 2 p.m., and Turner took his own Red Section up to 30,000 feet flying top cover, while the other three sections remained lower down at about 22,000 feet. Glancing out, Turner could see the bomber formation glinting in the afternoon sun below, stretching across the sky, their contrails following.

Of the enemy there was no sign, but then suddenly he heard excited chatter over his radio as a large number of German fighters attacked from the north directly into the other two squadrons of the 354th. Knowing he and his own squadron could not abandon their southern sector, on they flew, listening as one after another of their colleagues excitedly made their claims over the airwaves. 'There is no torture,' he noted later, 'comparable to that suffered by a fighter pilot forced to listen to a nearby aerial action which he cannot join.'

Eventually the battle died away and the bombers hit their target, but then, just as Turner was about to turn for home, his wingman spotted a 'bogie' – an enemy aircraft heading towards them. Turner now ordered his squadron to try to intercept. As they got closer, he wondered at its odd shape – it was certainly unlike any fighter plane he had seen before. It was probably one of the Luftwaffe's new jet or rocket planes, and possibly the Me262 jet, which was entering service that April. At any rate, his four different flights were converging on this peculiar aircraft when it suddenly dived at incredible speed, then pulled away, disappearing before they had a chance to pursue and despite the Mustangs flying at a true airspeed of over 400 m.p.h. themselves.

Back safely on the ground in England, and still wondering what he had seen up there in the skies over Magdeburg, Turner discovered that not only the 354th but the Eighth as a whole had had a very successful day. For the loss of just nine aircraft, the Americans had shot down and heavily damaged seventy-eight enemy planes, with eighteen German pilots killed or missing. What's more, the last week of flying had shown that every aircraft shot up on the ground had been at least 500 miles from the Normandy beaches. This meant the majority of the Luftwaffe's fighter force had been successfully pushed back into the Reich – from where they could not interfere with the D-Day landings. The battle in the air was very much a part of the wider battle that was about to begin on the beaches and in the hedgerows of Normandy. A vital stepping stone to Allied victory had already been achieved.

For the Luftwaffe, 28 May had been a dark day. Those losses were devastating. Then came even more shattering news. Fighter leaders like Galland and Schmid knew they were losing, and understood they were reaching a stage where losses in pilots could no longer be made up. Their one hope lay in the development of dazzling new aircraft, and especially the Me262 jet. Even this, it seemed, was now being taken away from them. At a meeting on 23 May at the Berghof, the Führer had discovered that Milch had been developing the Me262 as a jet fighter. Hitler had earlier demanded it be a bomber. When he learned he had been duped, he was apoplectic. So too was Milch, but he wasn't the Führer. The news reached Galland and Schmid that evening of Sunday, 28 May: the Me262, on which so much of their future hopes had been resting, was being taken away from their jurisdiction. 'The fighter arm and the defence of the Reich, which had seen in the jet fighter the saviour from an untenable situation,' noted Galland, 'now had to bury all hopes.'

CHAPTER 3

Understanding Montgomery and the Master Plan

ARRIVING AT BROOMFIELD HOUSE, General Montgomery's new 21st Army Group Headquarters near Portsmouth on the south coast of England, on Saturday, 20 May was Captain Carol Mather. Mather was twenty-five years old and originally from Manchester, where his father was the head of a successful engineering company. Mather Senior was also an avid adventurer and naturalist, a member of the Royal Geographical Society and had known the explorer Ernest Shackleton well. This spirit of inquisitiveness and adventure had rubbed off on his son, who during the 'long vac' from Cambridge University in the summer of 1939 had headed off on his own to explore the Yukon and Alaska. He had been on his way back when war was declared.

There had been no question of returning to Cambridge; instead he had headed to the Royal Military Academy at Sandhurst, trained as an officer and joined the Welsh Guards. Unsurprisingly for such an adventurous spirit, he had been swiftly seduced by the Commandos and, having been posted to the Middle East, then joined the fledgling SAS. Mather had been part of the core team during the summer of 1942 when its founder David Stirling's men had wreaked havoc behind Rommel's lines in North Africa, but had briefly joined Montgomery's staff, which included his older brother, for the Battle of Alamein; Monty was an old family friend. Returning to the SAS, Mather had been captured by the Italians and spent the next nine months in a POW camp in Italy before escaping and walking 600 miles south through the mountains. After arriving home in December 1943, he had rejoined the Welsh Guards, now in tanks and training in Yorkshire for the invasion. Out of the blue that spring, Mather was summoned to London to dine with Monty at Claridge's hotel near Grosvenor Square. The general wanted him to join his Tactical Headquarters as a liaison officer.

'This is going to be quite a party!' Montgomery told him across their dining table, then added ruefully, 'If you come with me, your chances of survival are not very good.' Mather was loath to leave his fellows in the regiment, but knew it was an invitation he could not turn down. So it was that on that Saturday, 20 May, he arrived at Monty's encampment at Broomfield House.

As always, Montgomery had established himself in a series of caravans, tents and Nissen huts in the grounds rather than using the house itself; that would have been too reminiscent of First World War generals. Monty preferred a military aesthetic where minds could be concentrated on the job in hand. Conditions were comfortable but in no way luxurious. No one was to become soft. None the less, he had taken over the study in the main house as his temporary office and it was here that Mather presented himself.

'Sit down or remain standing,' said Montgomery crisply, so Mather stood. Around were a number of framed photographs of Monty with his fellow commanders and also a large colour picture of Rommel. Mather remembered that after the Battle of Alamein Montgomery had invited the captured General Wilhelm Ritter von Thoma to dinner.

'Perhaps,' Mather suggested, looking at the picture of Rommel, 'you will have him to dine one night as you did von Thoma?'

'I hope so,' Monty replied, eyeing Mather sharply with those narrow, pale eyes of his.

It is easy to understand why Mather so willingly returned to Montgomery's staff. The chance to see great world events from the perspective of the land forces commander was irresistible. Mather would be exposed to all the senior commanders at close quarters, but it also meant joining a bevy of British and American ADCs and other liaison officers, all of whom were of similar age and of like-minded disposition. And as far as Mather was concerned, Monty was a great boss and an inspiring, brilliant general.

History has not been kind to Montgomery, particularly not over the last fifty years as one historian after another has lined up to crucify both his character and his military reputation. To a certain extent, he brought it upon himself through his monstrous ego, the crass way in which he spoke to his peers and superiors, and the very large chip that remained planted on his shoulder. Montgomery was the son of a vicar, had been refused entry into the Indian Army and had never had the easy charm of many of his contemporaries. This lack of breeding, the perceived early setbacks to his military career and his social gaucheness, in a pre-war British Army in which breeding and ready charm counted for so much, all contributed to his social inferiority complex, which he masked with haughtiness and arrogance – an arrogance that was supported by a grow-ing self-belief. Discipline, clear thinking, preparation and sound, solid training were his watchwords, all of which had much merit. He liked to impose himself by giving the impression of absolute self-assurance. Insisting no one could smoke in his presence was another means of imposing not just his personality but his authority. His physical appear-ance hardly helped: he was only 5 feet 7 inches tall, had a sharp beaky nose, pale darting eyes and a clipped nasal voice, and was unable to pro-nounce his 'Rs' properly. He never particularly worried about what others thought of him, although, paradoxically, he unquestionably enjoyed the high standing in which he was held by the British public and the popularity that went with it. From comparatively humble beginnings he had risen to the top. He had shown all those who had dismissed him out of hand early in his career. On the other hand, Eisenhower had had even humbler beginnings and had managed to retain a sense of humility. Montgomery had not.

It has to be admitted, though, that most senior commanders had risen to the top with the help of ruthless ambition and had considerable egos to boot. There were exceptions, but not many. Montgomery's great failing was his social awkwardness. He simply did not know how to interact with others. He compensated for his lack of charm by talking entirely on his own terms, regardless of what offence he might be causing. Once, in the late 1920s, this apparently confirmed bachelor had fallen in love, married and had even had a son, David. By all accounts, Monty had adored his wife, Betty, and had she lived perhaps she would have blunted some of his worst character traits and proved a gentle, caring critic rather as Clementine Churchill faithfully was to Winston. Tragically, Betty died of septicaemia in 1937, leaving Monty with a nine-year-old son and two stepsons. Her death unquestionably changed him: from then on, he dedi-cated his life entirely to soldiering. It has been claimed that Montgomery was autistic, a condition undiagnosed in the 1940s. Perhaps he was what is today termed 'on the spectrum'. He certainly lacked the ability to read the emotions of others very clearly. This would cause him all manner of trouble in the weeks and months to come.

None the less, these failings of character did not mean he was a bad general and all too often since the end of the war successive historians have put their personal distaste towards his character ahead of sound historical judgement. Monty has been presented as a 'Marmite' character, after the British yeast-based spread which people tend to either love or hate. The reality is, of course, a lot more nuanced. Montgomery could be spectacularly rude and discourteous, and tactically he was arguably not the most imaginative. But at this stage of the war sound strategic vision and operational skill were very possibly more important for the Allied armies. Montgomery understood that, although most of the men under his command were now well trained, most were reluctant soldiers, conscripts who were in uniform only because of a global war in which they had had no choice but to participate. He also understood the Allied mantra of 'steel not flesh', a strategy Britain had been determined to pursue long before war had been declared and one to which the United States had been equally wedded. This meant using their global muscle and reach, their modernity and technological know-how to the greatest possible effect, allowing industrialized mass-production and mechanization to do as much of the hard work as possible and limiting the number of those in the firing line to an absolute minimum.

For the most part, this had been incredibly successful and was why, despite fighting on multiple fronts all around the world and on land, sea and in the air, the number of British and American fighting men was far, far smaller than that of the Germans, the Japanese and especially the Soviet Union. Germany and Japan had vast armies because they had neither the global reach nor industrial muscle to fight any other way. Boots on the ground had to compensate for a shortage in mechanization. It was, however, a deeply inefficient way to fight a war in the 1940s and cost them millions of lives.

However, because of this global effort in the war, because Britain had been fighting since 1939 and because her war leaders, rightly, insisted on maintaining industrial output and fighting an industrialized, mechanized war, British manpower was getting short by the summer of 1944. The British population in 1939 had been half that of Germany and could be stretched only so far, yet Britain's war leaders had never once lost sight of their pre-war mantra, something that was very much to their credit.

Up until the autumn of 1943, for example, it was not any of the armed services that had priority for manpower but actually the Ministry of Aircraft Production. Of course, Britain could have pulled men out of the factories and sent them to the front, and could have reduced the vast number of service corps supplying the front line, but that would have been to follow Germany's lead – and look where it had got the Nazis: millions already dead and factories manned by emaciated, inefficient slave workers. That was no way to win a modern, industrialized and technologically driven war.

Britain was a democracy – perhaps not the liberal democracy of the early twenty-first century, but a freedom-loving nation all the same – and the thought of slaughtering a generation of young men for the second time in half a century was utterly repugnant to all. Those conscripts now making up around 75 per cent of Montgomery's forces would no longer be shot at dawn for running away. They might be court-martialled and put in prison, but that might easily be considered a better option than getting oneself maimed or killed.

This was where conveying a clear sense of purpose came in and why maintaining morale was so important. The British people were weary of war, but one way to keep men fighting at the front as the endgame finally began to draw near was to make sure those men knew their generals were not callously throwing away their lives and were supporting them as well as they possibly could with arms, weapons, guns, food and medical supplies. Montgomery understood this very well, something that has to be taken into account when considering his reputation.

He also recognized that both the British and Americans had now developed a way of war that could destroy the German armies they faced. In 1918, Britain had the world's finest and largest navy, air force and artillery. Now the Americans had a larger navy as well as air force, and, furthermore, waiting in the wings was a larger army with more guns. However, the Royal Air Force was now vast, with thousands of heavy bombers, fighters, ground-attack aircraft, multi-role aircraft and medium bombers; the Royal Navy was, by a margin of 3:1, to take the lead in numbers of both warships and landing craft for the invasion; and the British Army's artillery was as good and proficient as it had been back in 1918, when, arguably, it had proved decisive in winning the war.

Montgomery intended to bludgeon his way through the German opposition. What he had learned in North Africa, in Sicily and in southern Italy was that the Germans always counter-attacked. It was almost

Pavlovian. He would soften up the enemy with a barrage of artillery, then send forward his infantry and tanks, which would invariably get stuck against the dogged defence of the Germans. As the forward troops began to overreach themselves, so the German forces would rise up out of their foxholes and what cover they had and expose themselves. And at that point, the full weight of fire-power would be brought down upon them.

Thus weakened, the Germans would invariably fall back, leaving in their retreat roads laid with innumerable mines, bridges blown, booby traps, as well as machine-gun crews and snipers. This would slow the Allies down, as they were not willing to bulldoze their way forward through sacrificing their men in the manner in which the Red Army had proved very willing to do. While the Allies cautiously advanced, the Germans would prepare their next position and the whole procedure would start all over again.

From Monty's perspective, it was methodical, it took time, but it was within the realms of what could realistically be expected from the armies under his command. Central to this approach was the fire-power he could bring to bear, both from the air and from the artillery, to grind the enemy into the dust. It was no use trying to ape the small-scale tactical versatility of the Germans, because both the British and Americans were bringing large-scale industrialization to their *modus operandi*. This meant that the bigger the operation and the greater the number of component parts, the harder it was to operate with tactical agility. Any forward-attacking operation had to be carried out in collusion with the artillery, with the tactical air forces, with engineers, infantry and armour. Timings had to be coordinated to ensure advancing troops were not hit with friendly fire. Ammunition, reserves, fuel all had to be brought forward to maintain the necessary weight of fire. It was the constraints of wealth against the freedom of poverty; the Germans could organize themselves more quickly because they had so much less to organize.

All of this Monty understood very clearly and these considerations, as well as the Allies' experience of being on the offensive against German forces since the autumn of 1942, were what shaped his own views on the OVERLORD plan and those of the Allied staff officers, American, British and Canadian, who were helping both to shape it and to prepare the detail.

The whole point of Operation OVERLORD was to get a foothold in France, build up sufficient weight of forces and then drive the German armies out of the country, back into Germany and force them to surrender. No one expected them to roll over. In the last war, Germany had eventually signed an armistice because they had run out of cash and had no hope of winning. That moment had passed once again in the autumn of 1941 when the German invasion of the Soviet Union, Operation BARBAROSSA, had failed, but two and a half years on, with the Germans in retreat and materially with no hope of ever regaining the initiative, they were still fighting on. The Allies knew enough about Hitler and his monstrous regime to accept that Germany would most likely slug it out to the bitter end. Some hoped that the German people might rise up and the regime implode, but few were betting on it.

The Allies also recognized that, despite their decline, Germany still posed a major threat and that a successful invasion of France was filled with a large number of stumbling blocks. What was understood totally by Allied planners was that if a cross-Channel invasion took place, then it could not, under any circumstances, fail. Ensuring enough men and materiel were landed quickly enough to secure a lodgement – a connected bridgehead – before any concentrated enemy counter-attack could be mounted was the absolute number-one priority. This didn't just mean a success on D-Day itself, when, if deception plans worked, they would achieve tactical surprise, but also on D plus 1, D plus 2, D plus 3 and D plus 4. Those were the most critical days. Ambitious further objectives could be contemplated, but the invasion plan had to be the very best that would be likely to secure that essential lodgement. This trumped absolutely everything.

To achieve it, a terrible juggling act had to be performed and it was almost entirely down to the availability of shipping. Britain in the build-up to the invasion was awash with overwhelming numbers of troops, weapons and war materiel, but because of the limited amounts of shipping only a very small fraction of it could be delivered on D-Day itself and the days that followed. After shipping, a second major constraint was port facilities. Cherbourg was in enemy hands; so too was the much smaller Ouistreham, 10 miles north of Normandy's largest city, Caen. Normandy did, however, have wide, deep beaches on which landing craft and larger landing ships could deposit men and materiel. But again, the numbers of these were a constraint. Landing craft and landing ships were in use in the Mediterranean – in the Battle for Italy – and especially in the Pacific, where US forces were island-hopping in the war against Japan. American – and British – industrial might was impressive, but there were tanks to build, aircraft to build, trucks, weapons, ammunition, warships, submarines and much more to be constructed and then shipped across oceans. Getting enough LSTs – landing ships, tanks – and LSIs – landing ships, infantry – especially was not just a matter of manufacture; it was also about distribution. A previously unscheduled amphibious outflanking manoeuvre at Anzio in southern Italy had kept landing craft in the Mediterranean longer than planned, then OVER-LORD itself had been expanded, while a conundrum had arisen over an intended Allied landing in southern France, code-named ANVIL. Eisenhower wanted this to take place at the same time as OVERLORD, to draw enemy troops away from Normandy and to open up both ports and a further toehold in France. This, however, would impose a further strain on shipping.

From the moment that Montgomery had arrived back in England on the morning of 2 January 1944, a logistical battle had begun between what he and his planners considered necessary to achieve a successful landing and shipping production and requirements elsewhere. It is important to understand, though, that the final plan for OVERLORD was a compromise. Every single man in those planning teams wanted more.

The plan that was developed involved large numbers of people, endless conferences with air and naval chiefs and planning teams, and drew on a huge amount of source material. Among those working round the clock, for example, was Colonel Charles 'Tick' Bonesteel. From a family of career soldiers, Bonesteel had passed out ninth from his class at West Point, had later studied at Oxford as a Rhodes Scholar and since arriving in the European Theater of Operations, or ETO, had become a highly regarded operational planner. He had originally arrived in Britain at the height of the Blitz in early 1941 as an observer for the US Army Engineer Board, but had then joined the Combined Operations staff under Admiral Lord Louis Mountbatten when Normandy had first been mooted for what was then called Operation ROUNDUP. As a result, Bonesteel had begun to study the terrain and topography of Normandy back in 1942 before helping with the planning of TORCH, the invasion of north-west Africa in November that same year. He had then joined the staff of Force 141, the planning team for the invasion of Sicily in July 1943, before returning to Britain to be acting head of plans for the US First Army under Lieutenant-General Jacob Devers. After Eisenhower's appointment as Supreme Allied Commander, Devers had been moved and First Army given to Lieutenant-General Omar Bradley instead, an old and trusted friend and colleague of Ike's.

Bradley had been in England only a week when Bonesteel was temporarily transferred to the planning team of 21st Army Group, where his earlier study of Normandy proved invaluable. The original draft plan for OVERLORD, for example, had called for landings on three beaches and only on the northern Normandy coast. Bonesteel, however, had earlier pinpointed a further landing on the eastern flank of the base of the Cotentin Peninsula. This was immediately insisted upon by Montgomery's planning team the moment they arrived in London.

This beach had, by 7 April, become Utah, one of five landing beaches rather than the original three put forward by the planning team early the previous year. Known as COSSAC – Chief of Staff Supreme Allied Commander – the team had been under-resourced and inevitably those early plans had been developed further since the start of the year. The point is, the eventual plan proposed by Monty had the hands of a number of others on it. With his immediate team, he outlined the basic concept, then left the army commanders – Bradley in the American western sector and Lieutenant-General Miles Dempsey in the eastern British and Canadian half – to work out their own plans. The army commanders in turn developed more detailed objectives and plans in consultation with the corps then divisional commanders, all of which had to be worked into what was feasible with the navy and air forces.

On Friday, 7 April the plans for OVERLORD and the naval operation, NEPTUNE, as well as the air plans, were first formally presented in what was dramatically called Exercise THUNDERCLAP. All the senior commanders were present at Montgomery's headquarters at St Paul's School. 'This exercise,' Monty began, 'is being held for the purpose of putting all general officers of the field armies in possession of the whole outline plan for OVERLORD, so as to ensure mutual understanding and confidence.' He spoke from experience of fighting against Rommel. 'Some of us here know Rommel well. He is a determined commander and likes to hurl his armour into the battle.' Intelligence suggested they could expect to come up against sixty enemy divisions, of which as many as ten would be mobile with tanks, assault guns and so on. These were the best equipped, best trained and most experienced, as well as being the only mobile all-arms units, and, without question, they posed the greatest threat. They could also count on the enemy knowing by dusk on D plus 1 that Normandy was the main invasion front. By D plus 5, Montgomery assumed Rommel would have at least six panzer divisions near the front with which to counter-attack if he chose and that there would be considerable enemy forces in the area from D plus 4.

Since ensuring the invasion did not fail was the prime priority, securing the flanks of the lodgement area was essential. In the eastern end of the invasion front were the Caen Canal and River Orne, running almost perfectly north–south. There was then an area to the east around 6 miles wide before the valley of another river, the Dives, which also ran north–south. Although not particularly high, the Bréville Ridge dominated the eastern flank of the main assault area. If the British could capture intact the bridges over the Orne and the Caen Canal, and destroy the four bridges over the Dives and hold the high ground in between, that would stop any enemy forces attacking the flanks, which in turn would leave the British and Canadians to push directly south to Caen and beyond.

Initially, there were thoughts of possibly extending the invasion to the coast immediately to the east of the mouth of the River Orne – it was even given the code name 'Band' Beach – but lack of shipping and the strength of enemy guns further east dissuaded planners. Instead, back in February the task of capturing this area had been given to the 6th Airborne Division. Meanwhile, at the western end American airborne forces supporting the Utah Beach landings could sever the Cotentin Peninsula and isolate all German forces there. This would not only protect the western flank but help with the swift subsequent capture of Cherbourg. For this, one, and then eventually two, US airborne divisions would be used.

The intention was for British troops from Sword, the easternmost beach, to hurry inland and capture the key city of Caen on D-Day itself. The British and Canadians would then push on and capture the higher ground to the south and south-east of the city. This was open countryside, ideal for airfields but also a point from which the Allies could eventually pivot eastwards. It was assumed that most of the panzer divisions and reinforcements would arrive in Normandy from the east and south-east, so the British and Canadians were expected to hold them there while the American First Army, and later General George Patton's Third Army, would swing south then east.

With the shipping and resources available, this was a good plan and no one attending THUNDERCLAP quibbled with the essence of what was being proposed. What was vital was, first, establishing the lodgement, and then building up forces quickly enough not only to defend against a concentrated counter-attack, but also to go on to the offensive as quickly as possible. Hand in hand with the build-up of ground forces was the establishment of forward air bases. Air power was critical: as extra fire-power, for taking out key targets, and especially for slowing down the enemy's movement and ability to concentrate its forces.

Where there was some dissent, however, was over Montgomery's large map on which had been drawn prospective phase lines. By D plus 17 – that is, two and a half weeks after the invasion – Montgomery reckoned they could realistically expect to have secured Cherbourg and the Cotentin Peninsula and be around 50 miles south of the coast; twenty-five days on, 100 miles south; and south of the River Loire and at the gates of Paris by D plus 90. General Bradley had objected to Monty showing such phase lines: he felt it made the plan seem too rigid and did not take into account the unexpected. 'If projected phase lines were not met,' noted Bradley, 'it might appear that we were "failing".' He certainly had a point, although, as he admitted, Montgomery's briefing made a 'profoundly favourable' impression on all those attending, including Eisenhower and even Bradley himself, despite the phase lines.

Perhaps those lines should have been left off as Bradley suggested. On the other hand, from experience in North Africa, in Sicily and in southern Italy, advancing in stages, or rather expecting the enemy to retreat in stages, was an entirely valid assumption. And it was just that: an assumption. After all, no one was openly admitting to any doubts about the success of the invasion – and yet it was in those first few days, not at D plus 17 or D plus 30, where unquestionably the greatest risk lay. Furthermore, seeing a large map with phase lines and arrows of advancement helped give a picture of optimism and success. This was such a gargantuan exercise; the stakes could not have been higher and everyone was nervous, twitchy, even slightly overwhelmed by what lay before them. In their private thoughts, the spectre of failure loomed heavily, and yet here was a map that made the entire operation seem feasible. Montgomery was standing before them without betraying even the slightest hint of doubt. He might have been a difficult, cussed, obnoxious, arrogant, overly-controlling SOB, but he had lifted everyone in that room and they had all begun to believe. This *was* winnable. Paris in ninety days. What a great achievement that would be!

CHAPTER 4

Countdown

IN NORMANDY, AND ALL along the Atlantic Wall, the construction work continued: more bunkers, more mines, more offshore obstacles. For the most part, the work was carried out by the German labour service, the Organisation Todt, and specifically the *Oberbauleitung Cherbourg* – OBL, the Chief Construction Directorate, Cherbourg – which was mainly responsible for the fixed positions and which employed, amongst others, nearly 70,000 Frenchmen. By May, some 913 concrete emplacements of various kinds had been built in Normandy alone, although along the entire length of the Atlantic Wall a staggering 9,671 permanent concrete structures had been constructed, using a mind-boggling 13 million cubic metres of concrete as well as 5 per cent of Germany's total steel production. It cost 3.7 billion Reichsmarks – around $45 billion today.

As Rommel was well aware, however, even this increased building fell some way short of what had been planned. The 380mm gun batteries at Cherbourg, for example, had not been put in place, nor had the major defensive complex covering Utah Beach been constructed. Also frustrating were shortages of concrete and other supplies as the Allied air forces continued to hit locomotives, blow up railways and bridges, and generally interrupt the flow of traffic. The result was increasingly low-grade concrete, with insufficient binder and additives for the amount of concrete. This meant it was more likely to crumble and so would be less able to withstand bombs and shells. But what was the alternative? A kind of manic fury had gripped not only Rommel and Meise but many of the engineers now employed along the continental coast.

In between these structures, yet more obstacles and mines were being laid. Meise had even reckoned a dense minefield of at least a kilometre was needed all the way from Holland and round the northern French coast, which would mean not 20 million mines but 200 million. Of course, this was pie in the sky. As May drew to a close only two of the four belts of offshore obstacles had been laid along the Normandy coast, for example, and gaps still remained in the more open areas where no anti-glider stakes had been installed.

While much of this feverish construction activity was in the hands of the Organisation Todt, an increased number of army engineers had been sent to swell the ranks of the coastal infantry divisions and they were now overseeing the building of a number of strongpoints and other defences using the sweat of their own troops. Near Colleville, for example, a few miles west of Ouistreham, a series of *Widerstandsnester* – WNs, or strongpoints – had been hastily built on the rising high ground that sloped gently for a couple of miles from the sea. These had been designed by the chief engineer of the 716. Infanterie-Division, Oberst Ludwig Krug, and was now the headquarters of Infanterie-Regiment 736, of which Krug had been handed command, and around 150 men. A series of bunkers and gun casements stood on the lower slopes, while on the crest had been built an elaborate series of gun positions, tank turrets – known as 'Tobruks' – ammunition stores, a water reservoir, medical facilities, food stores and command bunkers, each dug-in casement connected by an elaborate and reverted trench system, a mass of wire entanglements and, of course, a dense minefield. *Widerstandsnester* stretched all along the Normandy coast, numbered chronologically from the eastern end of 7. Armee's boundary, with WN1 on the far eastern side of the River Orne. WN17 and the gun casements on the lower slopes – WN16 – were perfectly sited. Eight miles to the south lay the city of Caen, while to the north the position commanded views across miles of coastline. From here, the radar station Finkelstein could clearly be seen, as could the tiny city of Douvres with its twin-spired cathedral. Even if the enemy did manage to get ashore here, they would not be heading very far inland unless they neutralized this position. That would be no easy task.

Krug was not the only engineer assigned to his regiment. Another was Oberleutnant Cornelius Tauber, now based at Courseulles, where WN20 was sited, some 10 miles westwards along the coastline from WN17. Tauber had been given a quite specific task: to construct a series of beach defences that could then be exploited using 'Goliaths', mini-tracked vehicles about the size of a wheelbarrow that were controlled electrically by wires and packed with explosives. The idea was to build a series of bunkers in which the controllers could be protected but still see enough to send the Goliaths on to the beaches towards a tank, landing craft or concentration of troops, and then detonate them. Tauber had a store of some twenty-five of these weapons. He and his men had built quite a complex defensive network along the sea front at Courseulles, with the cellars and lower levels of villas strengthened and connected to bunkers built between. There were also casements armed with anti-tank guns firing not out to sea but down along the stretch of the beach.

Tauber was yet another young officer who had been transferred from the Eastern Front. All his colleagues in Russia had slapped him on the back and called him a lucky swine when he received his transfer orders. 'And, you know, when I joined the 716th Infantry Division in France,' he recalled, 'I realised what a lucky swine I was.' Compared with just about everywhere else in the Reich, the food was excellent, he could buy pretty much anything on the black market, the weather was mild and his barracks comfortable as it was a requisitioned house with proper beds and running water; he had never had such luxuries in Russia. 'Every morning I thought of my brother in combat in Russia,' he added, 'and I felt extremely guilty.' Tauber knew the invasion was coming – they all did – but tried simply to get on with his tasks. As May gave way to June, he was still overseeing the construction work. 'The Atlantic Wall,' he said, 'was still unfinished.'

On 30 May, Rommel paid a visit to 21. Panzer-Division at Saint-Pierre-sur-Dives on the Caen–Falaise road. He still hoped to persuade the Führer to give him tactical control of the panzer divisions in the west, but as matters stood 21. Panzer was still the only one in Normandy, with its headquarters at Falaise. Among those he visited that day was Major Hans von Luck. The two went back a long way, as von Luck had been in Rommel's reconnaissance battalion when he commanded 7. Panzer for the invasion of France back in 1940. Von Luck had then been posted to the Eastern Front before rejoining Rommel in North Africa. Since the previous autumn, the 32-year-old had been based in Paris, where he had managed to bring his fiancée, Dagmar. He'd been happy enough there, although he was frustrated that, because of Dagmar's one-eighth Jewish heritage, they were not allowed to marry. Then in May he had been posted to General Bayerlein's Panzer-Lehr before at the last minute being transferred to 21. Panzer instead and given command of Panzergrenadier-Regiment 125. The division had been part of the Afri-kakorps, but had been destroyed in Tunisia and since reconstituted. Its leadership and make-up once again revealed the extremes of the German Army in 1944. Composed mainly of veterans from the Eastern Front but also with plenty of new recruits, its commanding officer, Generalmajor Edgar Feuchtinger, was another good Nazi but had absolutely no experience of armoured operations nor any combat experience whatsoever. In fact, he had risen up the ranks through organizing the military aspects of the Nazi rallies back in the 1930s. It is hard to think of anyone less suitable to command a mobile all-arms division such as 21. Panzer.

On the other hand, his new commander of Panzergrenadier-Regiment 125 had bucketloads of combat experience, in multiple theatres; unit commanders like von Luck made up for a lot of Feuchtinger's shortcomings. 'Feuchtinger,' noted von Luck, 'had to delegate most things, that is, leave the execution of orders to us experienced commanders.' And von Luck wasn't the only one with experience; men like Oberstleutnant Hermann Oppeln-Bronikowski, for example, the commander of Panzer-Regiment 22, was also a huge asset to the division. An Olympic gold medal-winning equestrian, he had been awarded a Knight's Cross in Russia and had repeatedly proved himself to be a commander of high calibre. In terms of equipment, the division had been forced to scrape the barrel somewhat to make up the shortfall from Germany. One officer, Major Becker, a skilled engineer, had gathered a number of old French tanks and converted them into better-armoured and more effective assault guns – that is, tracked vehicles but with fixed heavy guns on them rather than a tank turret.

Now, on 30 May, Rommel was up near the coast at Lion-sur-Mer to inspect the division and some of Becker's newly fashioned weapons. Several times they had to take cover from Allied aircraft roaring overhead. 'Gentlemen,' he told the assembled commanders and troops from both 21. Panzer and the 716. Infanterie-Division, 'I know the English from Africa and Italy and I tell you they will choose a landing site where they think we do not expect them to land. And that will be right here, on this spot.' Rommel then predicted the invasion would not happen for another three weeks, but General Marcks told those assembled he thought it would come sooner than that. 'From my knowledge of the English,' he said, 'they will go to church again next Sunday and then come on Monday.' That would be Monday, 5 June.

Further along the coast, Gefreiter Franz Gockel, part of the 716.

Division now attached to the 352., was one of just over forty men occupying WN62, near Colleville. There were thirteen such positions along this stretch of the coast, which differed from elsewhere because, while there was a long, 5-mile and slightly concave stretch of sand here, roughly between the two villages of Colleville and Vierville, the beach – which would become known to the Allies as Omaha – was overlooked by bluffs, some 70 feet high, which curved downwards offering the defenders clear views out to sea. Along this stretch there were five possible exit points, or draws, off the beach, with the two most developed tracks running off them pretty much at either end, with tracks running up to the two villages, which stood about three-quarters of a mile inland. These were the obvious weak spots for the defenders, as well as being the focus for any invaders trying to get inland from the beach, so a proportionally higher number of strongpoints had been built here. In between these exits, the defences overlooking the sea were quite light – in terms of fixed positions at any rate. All along the beach, though, offshore obstacles were in place, thick tanglements of wire, mines and an anti-tank ditch that ran its entire length.

At WN62, Franz Gockel and his comrades were now very alive to the rumours of a vast invasion fleet lying just across the sea. Would it come here? No one was sure. There had been more low-level passes by enemy reconnaissance aircraft recently, but Oberleutnant Bernhard Frerking, the officer in charge of the 1. Batterie, Artillerie-Regiment 352, felt sure their particular stretch of coastline was too formidable. Any troops landing here, he said, would be cut to pieces. It would be too costly for the enemy. Most of the older men, however, disagreed. In the meantime, there was more defence work to be done. Gockel was exhausted by it all, but his sergeant was insistent they finish a trench that connected their underground quarters to the forward bunkers; without it, they would have to cross open ground in full view of any enemy below or out to sea.

All things considered, by the start of June the 352. Division was in reasonable order. Its commander, Generalleutnant Dietrich Kraiss, reckoned his men were at last combat ready, although training had been necessarily hurried and ammunition remained short – so much so that the artillery and anti-tank units had been limited to just five rounds per month per crew. Other cracks had also been papered over. Many of the guns and vehicles they had been given were of different kinds, for example, salvaged from the four winds; this, of course, made obtaining spare parts difficult. They were all right when they worked, but the moment they broke down – perhaps during the stress of battle – they could become a major problem. Finally, the battle area given them, from the coast to the ridge either side of Saint-Lô, was now prepared for defence – not enough to withstand a major attack, but much improved since March. History has been generous to the calibre of the 352. They are often referred to as an 'elite' division. This was far from the truth. They had some experienced men, some good and capable commanders, and some half-decent weaponry, but they were far from elite.

On the Normandy coast there were now 130 guns of 100mm calibre or bigger. That sounded like quite a lot, but there were some 15,000 anti-aircraft guns, for example, in the Reich itself; what Rommel would have done for just a fraction of those. Nor were all the guns embalmed within casements – that work was still going on and, in any case, most of the coastal batteries had been so heavily bombed by the Allies already that on 17 May Rommel's headquarters had recommended those not in casements should be moved to concealed positions a little further inland.

There were, however, still some very different opinions from Rommel's subordinate commanders on how best to defeat the enemy – and not just over the use of mobile troops. On his tours of the front, Rommel always repeated the same message: that the coast was the main line of defence and that the enemy had to be destroyed before getting a firm foothold. Dollmann, by contrast, told troops he visited that this would be next to impossible. 'In view of the thin line of coastal defence,' he told senior staff of Fallschirmjäger-Regiment 6, 'we will scarcely be able to prevent the enemy from establishing a beachhead.' Their task, Dollmann told them, was to bring forces into the fray as quickly as possible and then push them back.

Nor was Oberst Friedrich Freiherr von der Heydte, the commander of Fallschirmjäger 6, much impressed by what he had seen of other troops or by the equipment available in Normandy. It was deplorable. 'Weapons from all over the world and all periods of the twentieth century seemed to have been accumulated,' he noted, 'in order to convey the impression of a mighty force.' Within his heavy weapons companies he had German, French, Italian and Russian mortars and seven different types of light machine gun. Von der Heydte had only reached Normandy at the beginning of May, but during a subsequent exercise near Cherbourg, General Marcks had been most scathing about his corps. 'Emplacements without guns,' he had told von der Heydte, 'ammunition depots without ammunition, mine fields without mines, and a large number of men in uniform with hardly a soldier among them.' In 325. Division's sector,

Leutnant Hans Heinze was not much impressed either. 'A large percentage of the machine guns in the bunkers were captured weapons that did not fit our standard ammunition,' he said, which created further difficulties for both the quartermasters and the troops using them. 'At several points the barbed wire and trenches were not complete or manned properly.'

On 4 June, Heinze had accompanied a staff officer from Marcks's LXXXIV. Korps Headquarters on an inspection tour, going from strongpoint to strongpoint. At one stage, a sergeant stepped forward and said, 'Herr Major, we have enough ammunition to stop the first, second, third, fourth and maybe even fifth wave of Tommies. But after that they're going to kick the door in on top of us then all is lost.'

Rommel was still working hard to rectify this and to wrest back control of the all-important panzer units. On 3 June, he visited von Rundstedt in Paris to tell him of his intention to drive to the Berghof to see Hitler and ask for more armour, more anti-aircraft guns and to try to persuade the Führer to give him tactical command of the panzer divisions. 'The weakest point in the overall defence structure,' noted Admiral Ruge in his diary on Sunday, 4 June, 'was still the fact that the panzer divisions had not pulled up close enough to the "Rommelbelt" to allow them to participate immediately in the attack, thereby giving the infantry the urgently needed support.'

Across the sea in England, the countdown to invasion was on. By the third week of May, training was largely complete and the 155,000 men earmarked to be dropped or landed had been moved to camps close to the coast from where they would march to embark. Training had been thorough. Men had practised jumping from landing craft, operating with live ammunition, training with other arms, and every effort had been made to make it as realistic as possible. Inevitably, there were accidents, with soldiers getting both badly wounded and killed. The 1st Battalion, Suffolk Regiment, for example, had been training up on the west coast of Scotland, with the Royal Navy, with tanks and with explosives. Corporal Arthur Blizzard of the Pioneer Platoon was among the men firing machine guns at the rest of the infantry and setting off explosives as they practised seaborne landings. On one occasion, an explosive was detonated by mistake before one of the men, a Royal Engineer corporal, had got clear. 'The corporal was lying with his arm off,' said Blizzard, 'and I lay there all day with him . . . It shows what war is. He was just watching with his officers to see how things go.' The injured corporal died in hospital.

Now, however, the regiment was in one of the 'sausages', as the concentration areas were known, at Havant, near Portsmouth, the port from which they would be heading to France, and confined there with guards to make sure they stayed put. A few of Blizzard's mates thought about absconding, but he wasn't interested and told them not to be fools. After all, they would be sent over eventually, even if they managed to avoid it this time. Blizzard reckoned it was far better to go with your mates than with strangers.

Not far from Havant, the Sherwood Rangers Yeomanry were also now confined to camp at Sway in the New Forest. The Sherwood Rangers were a Territorial regiment, who, like the American National Guard, only trained part time in peacetime. Mostly made up of country farmers and local Nottinghamshire men, they had been posted to Palestine in September 1939 and had headed overseas with their horses. Early in 1940, they had taken part in a cavalry charge with sabres drawn against Arab insurrectionists, before an embarrassing stampede had led to them being ordered to send their chargers home. To compound their hurt and humiliation, they had then begun retraining as gunners, something that was seen as massively demeaning by these proud but hopelessly out-of-date yeomen. They served at the siege of Tobruk and on Crete before being retrained on tanks. Their baptism as an armoured regiment had taken place at the Battle of Alam Halfa in late August 1942, Rommel's last attempt to break the Alamein Line in Egypt, and although they had proved a little impetuous and rough around the edges, they had then performed well at the Battle of Alamein and had remained in Eighth Army until victory in Tunisia in May 1943. By then they had turned themselves into a highly experienced, slick and professional outfit, part of the independent 8th Armoured Brigade. Sent back to England, they had been training for D-Day ever since and were earmarked to land with 50th Division on Gold Beach, the westernmost of the three British and Canadian assault beaches.

One of those who had been with the regiment since the beginning of the war was Major Stanley Christopherson. Now thirty-two and commanding A Squadron, he was bright, well travelled and charming. Christopherson made friends easily and was a gifted sportsman, as well as being socially as smooth as glass. He had also proved himself to be a good man in a crisis, with the kind of courage and phlegmatism that made him ideal officer material. He also had a healthy dose of steely competitiveness and was among a number of officers in the regiment who had always striven to improve. Amateur they might have been at the start of the war, but since then Christopherson and his fellows had trained hard, learned the lessons and honed themselves into one of the best-armoured regiments in the British Army, which was precisely why they were to be among those spearheading the invasion.

Christopherson had drilled his men well, and had insisted on each man, no matter what his role, being expert in both gunnery and radio training. A couple of years earlier, the Sherwood Rangers had adopted a radio code based largely on horse-riding and cricket; that had long gone. 'The success of any tank versus tank battle,' Christopherson had noted, 'depended on accurate and quick fire, and it was quite impossible to fight any kind of battle, either on a troop, squadron, regimental or brigade level, unless wireless communication was good.' As he rightly pointed out, that could only come with training.

On Saturday, 20 May, all the officers in the Sherwood Rangers were informed that the invasion would take place on 5 June and were given the broad outlines of the plan and then very specific details of their own role and objectives, although still not the location. The plan of assault was demonstrated on a sand model with code names for all the villages and towns. 'I lay you 10–1 we shall land in Normandy,' John Bethell-Fox, one of Christopherson's troop commanders, told him. 'I recognize the coastline.'

All along the south coast of England, men were now in 'sausages' roughly in alignment with the beach on which they would be landing. Far to the west, in Devon, were the Americans of the US 4th Division, who would be landing at the eastern base of the Cotentin Peninsula, code-named Utah. Further east, in Dorset, were the men of the US 29th Infantry and 1st Infantry Divisions, who would be landing at the long and potentially most problematic beach along the invasion front, code-named Omaha. The Sherwood Rangers, now in Hampshire, would be coming ashore at Gold Beach along with the 50th Division; the Canadians, who had been based some way east along the coast of England, correspondingly further along at Juno; and Arthur Blizzard and the 1st Suffolks, part of 3rd Infantry Division, who were coming from Kent, at Sword.

Among those scheduled to land with the US 1st Infantry, the 'Big Red One' as it was known, were identical twins Henry 'Dee' and Tom Bowles.

From Russellville, Alabama, the brothers were already combat veterans having fought through the Tunisian campaign and then also in Sicily. Incredibly, Normandy was to be their third amphibious landing. Through it all, they remained remarkably laid-back. They had been in different companies in North Africa and Sicily, but Tom had recently managed to get a transfer to Headquarters Company in the 2nd Battalion, 18th Infantry Regiment of the 1st Division, where he had joined his twin as a wireman. This meant that the moment they moved anywhere, it would be their job to run telephone wire from Battalion HQ to the various companies. 'So, yeah,' said Tom, 'we were now doing the same thing in the same company.'

To all intents and purposes, the brothers were alone in the world. Growing up in the Depression-hit Deep South, in a poor family, they had lost a brother and then their mother when they were just twelve and their father died in 1940, soon after they joined the army. An older sister had married and they hadn't seen her in years. 'I know we had some guys that worried about getting home to their wives and everything,' said Dee Bowles, 'but we didn't have anything to worry about. The 18th Infantry was our home. And we knew we wasn't going to get back until the war was over.'

They were now confined to camp on the edge of the small village of Broadmayne, a few miles east of Dorchester, but on one of their last evenings off they and a couple of their friends visited the New Inn, a pub in neighbouring West Knighton. Tom was a keen amateur photographer and as they sat outside, tankards in hands, he first took some pictures of Dee and their buddies Dotson and John R. Lamm, then the brothers posed for a picture on their own, taken by Lamm. They were a good-looking pair and, despite what lay around the corner, did not appear to have a care in the world. Rather there was a look of insouciance and even confidence on their faces. If they were worried, they certainly weren't showing it.

About 15 miles to the east was Blandford Camp, where the 116th Infantry were finally finishing their training. The 116th was part of the 29th Infantry Division, due to lead the US First Army's invasion at Omaha alongside the Big Red One. Unlike the 1st Division, however, the 29th – and the 116th Infantry – were new to combat and, as yet, completely untested. Sergeant Bob Slaughter was confident enough, though. 'The men were honed, eager and ready to go,' he wrote. 'We were sure that with our training and skill most of us would survive.' Although a sergeant, Slaughter was still only nineteen years old, having joined the National Guard on 3 February 1941, his sixteenth birthday. His motives had been financial rather than patriotic. As for so many families in the US in the 1930s, times had been tough. Slaughter's father, a lumber salesman, had lost his job in Bristol, Tennessee, and the family had moved to Roanoke, Virginia, where eventually he joined the Skyline Lumber Company, albeit in a lesser position and with a cut in pay. His declining health required his four children to pitch in, first with newspaper rounds and then, in Bob's case, by taking a job at a sawmill at 50 cents a day.

When he joined the National Guard his parents were not happy, but young Bob was determined and the money was not to be sniffed at, so they signed for him and he was in, joining Company D, the heavy weapons unit, of 1st Battalion, 116th Infantry. Ten months later, America was at war and another ten months after that the 116th Infantry, along with the rest of the 29th Infantry Division, sailed for England. Ever since then, first in Scotland and then in south-west England, Slaughter and his fellows had been in training for the invasion. Physically, they could hardly be fitter. They were well equipped. Morale was high. Since the start of the year they had practised amphibious assault training intensely. What they hadn't done was train with either tanks or artillery; nor had they learned how to attack the many small, high-hedged fields of Normandy, despite being based in Devon where there were plenty of both small fields and high hedges.

On Thursday, 1 June, the 116th Infantry's command post at Blandford was closed and the assault units moved to transit camps closer to the coast. Just over a month earlier, Eisenhower, General Bradley and other senior commanders had watched the men carry out one of their amphibious assault exercises and afterwards the Supreme Allied Commander had spoken to some of the men. One of them had been Sergeant Bob Slaughter.

'Sergeant,' Eisenhower had asked, 'are you and your men ready to go?'
Slaughter had snapped out his reply. 'Yes, Sir, we are!'

Eisenhower and Bradley were not the only senior commanders inspecting the men and giving pep talks. General Montgomery had been touring much of the country in a final visit to his troops that had begun on 23 May and was finishing on the morning of Friday, 2 June, at Broomfield House, 21st Army Group Headquarters.

Now it was the turn of his immediate staff, who sat cross-legged like schoolboys on green tarpaulins on what had formerly been a grass tennis court. There was a palpable sense of expectancy while they waited for him to arrive. In front of them was a Jeep with a set of mounting steps up to the bonnet, while behind this makeshift podium was a wood of chestnut trees, already in full leaf. It was sunny and fresh – England at its early-summer best.

Monty's car drew up behind them and, accompanied by one of his aides, he walked round to the front, at which point everyone, generals and captains alike, stood. He ushered them to sit down again, then climbed on to the bonnet of the Jeep. In addition to this last tour, Montgomery had spent much time travelling the country speaking to the men who would be fighting under him in the coming battle. This has since drawn much criticism, which has suggested Monty should have been concentrating on the details of the plan rather than gadding about pandering to his own ego. However, it was important that army commanders were visible, honest, and gave their men a clear picture of what was going on and their part in the battles to come; certainly, it had proved very successful in South-East Asia, where both British General Bill Slim and the new Allied Supreme Commander, Admiral Lord Louis Mountbatten, had managed to get around all their troops with a palpable rise in morale as a result. Leigh-Mallory and Ramsay sometimes found it frustrating that Montgomery was not always available, but after presenting the plan on 7 April his part in the process was largely complete. Detailed planning was not down to him and, in any case, the complexity of the naval operation meant the land plan had to be set in stone by then; there could be no major tinkering after that point, so boosting the morale and confidence of his armies was a very good use of his time.

Monty now gave a brief overview of what had already happened in the war, what was happening right now, and how he envisaged the endgame playing out. 'The essence of his technique,' noted Carol Mather, one of those listening to his clipped no-nonsense words, 'was clarity. Everyone knew exactly where they stood, where they were going and their part in the proceedings. The "fog of war" was for a moment dispelled and the curtain lifted on future events.' Montgomery concluded with five key points. The first was the importance of unity with their allies. Second, they all needed to remember to keep fit in body and mind and to believe in the rightness of the cause. Third, they should all feel confident: they were highly trained, well equipped and ready. Fourth, they should be enthusiastic about the cause for which they were fighting. Finally, it was essential they threw everything into the all-out battle, especially in the initial, most vital, stages of the landing.

He then paused and a deep silence descended. Carol Mather felt as though time was briefly standing still as he dwelt on the enormity of the task before them.

'He either fears his fate too much,' continued Montgomery, intoning the soldier-poet James Graham, Marquis of Montrose, 'or his deserts are small, that will not put it to the touch, to win or lose it all.' He looked up at them. 'Good luck to each one of you. And good hunting on the mainland of Europe.'

'Then everyone burst out cheering,' wrote Mather, 'and we knew we were going to win.'

CHAPTER 5

The Winds of War

To the east of the planned invasion front, south of Le Havre and the Seine estuary and some 50 miles from Caen, stood the small village of Saint-Étienne-l'Allier in the Eure Valley. Like most of the villages in Normandy, it was surrounded by lush farmland, had centuries-old stone houses and a church, and was, to all intents and purposes, entirely unremarkable. It was, though, now the headquarters of the Maquis Surcouf, a Résistance group that had swollen considerably in the past year, and because of its location – in the path of many of the German reinforcements that could be sent to Normandy – it seemed likely to play an important role in the battle to come.

The undisputed leader of the Maquis Surcouf was Robert Leblanc, the owner of the village café and grocery, a handsome 34-year-old with thick, dark hair swept back from his brow. Leblanc had had tuberculosis and so had avoided military service at the start of the war, remaining in the village with his wife, Denize, and their four young children. A fierce patriot, from the outset he had been outraged by the German occupation and was determined not to stand by idly. With the village priest, the Abbé Meulan, and the carpenter, Robert Samson, he began carrying out small acts of defiance, such as painting V for Victory signs on doors and tearing down German posters. Leblanc refused to sell newspapers that were pro-German and pro-Vichy. The three also hid downed Allied airmen and helped them escape. By the spring of 1943, others had begun to visit them and join their movement. Most were young men trying to avoid the Service du travail obligatoire, introduced in February 1943, in which all men aged 18–25 were compelled to work in Germany for two years, where they could expect minimum pay, minimal rations, brutal conditions and to have to work like slaves – which is pretty much what they were. The first 250,000 had been called up within days of the law being passed. Needless to say, a lot of young Frenchmen fled to the hills. Very quickly, a new word spread through France, from the mountains of the Alps and the Pyrenees to the remote valleys of Normandy: *maquis* is the Corsican word for mountainous scrubland, but it came to describe the groups of young men escaping forced labour in Germany and instead organizing themselves into groups of resistance.

Since November 1942, all of France had been occupied by German troops, but the day-to-day running of the country was left to the French government based in Vichy under the ageing dictator Maréchal Pétain and his prime minister, Pierre Laval. Resistance in France had been disorganized, isolated and disjointed until Jean Moulin, a former regional official, had managed to make his way to England to meet Général Charles de Gaulle, the leader of the Free French and the self-proclaimed head of the French government-in-exile in London. Although Moulin was left-wing, he decided the best course of action was for all resistance to follow the banner of the right-wing de Gaulle and he returned to France to try to bring these disparate movements into a more organized and coordinated whole. In this quest, Moulin was incredibly successful, until he was betrayed, captured, tortured and killed in July 1943. Since then, the Résistance had begun to splinter again, especially because of the increasingly brutal measures taken by both the Germans and Vichy to try to stamp it out. In addition to the 200,000 German occupying troops, the Vichy government had, by the start of 1944, more than 50,000 gendarmes, 25,000 Gardes Mobiles de Réserve and some 30,000 Milice française, a new paramilitary fascist militia whose members were ill-trained, often ill-disciplined but dedicated to a campaign of brutal repression. In the first half of 1944, France was, in many respects, gripped by civil war.

Controlling and coordinating outlawed young men, as well as agreeing how resistance should be carried out among extreme and differing political motivations, egos and expectations, was no easy matter, especially with many leaders already dead and with others abroad in London or Free French North Africa. However, by the spring of 1944 matters were improving. The Commission militaire d'action (COMAC) had been set up to help unify but not control armed resistance and then formed a common command structure called the Forces françaises de l' intérieur – the FFI – which soon took hold in public consciousness. FFI armbands were widely worn and the initials were daubed liberally on buildings, leaflets and even vehicles. Nominal leadership of the FFI was given to Général Pierre Koenig, a Free French commander who in 1942 had led their heroic stand against Rommel's forces at Bir Hacheim in Libya and who had later fought at Alamein. His appointment had been an enlightened decision, even though in practical terms it accounted for little, as Koenig was in England, not France. None the less, by May 1944 both COMAC and the creation of the FFI had done much to give the Résistance movements a sense of unified purpose, even if political aims remained wildly divergent.

To be head of any resistance organization remained, though, an incredibly challenging and dangerous task, as Robert Leblanc, the unchallenged leader of the Maquis Surcouf, had discovered. He now had some 2,000 men under his direct command, was under constant threat of betrayal, never had enough arms or ammunition and only a tentative link to higher authorities and British supply drops via third parties. Yet in the coming invasion, he and his men were expected to do all in their power to halt the flow of German forces. Much was anticipated from very little and with the prospect, if caught, not of a POW camp, but of torture and death.

Across the sea in Britain, just what to do with the French was one of many conundrums and challenges facing the Allies on the eve of the invasion. The British had housed and supported de Gaulle ever since his arrival in London in June 1940, and in July 1942 both the British and Americans had given cautious acknowledgement of the Comité français de libération nationale – or CFLN – and de Gaulle's political organization, but refused to accept it as the provisional government. While de Gaulle was unquestionably brave, dedicated and a natural leader, he did little to endear himself to those helping him and his country in these dark days of war. Haughty, touchy and quick to flare up, and in possession of a pride and ego the size of Paris, he rarely showed any gratitude for the help given him and instead projected a spectacular sense of entitlement.

Churchill and the British were broadly tolerant, but the Americans, and President Roosevelt in particular, were deeply mistrustful. Roosevelt's greatest concern was that the liberated French should choose their new political leader democratically and he was not convinced that the CFLN had a mandate, nor that de Gaulle was the leader to whom the liberated

French wanted to flock. He had a point. Moulin might have believed resistance should follow de Gaulle's flag, but since his death plenty of Résistance leaders had thought otherwise. In fact, even in March 1944, the Conseil national de la résistance (Committee of National Resistance), set up by Moulin on Gaullist lines, had dismissed out of hand de Gaulle's claim that COMAC and the FFI should be controlled by him from his headquarters in Algiers.

Eisenhower had asked permission to open negotiations with the CFLN, which had eventually been granted by Roosevelt, but only for help in restoring law and order in France. Liberated areas, however, would be administered by the Allied Military Government for Occupied Territories, AMGOT, which had run civil affairs in Italy. There was to be no recognition of the CFLN as the provisional government and no sharing of any of the details of OVERLORD. The CFLN's cipher system was also ludicrously easy to crack – which added to the concerns over a potential intelligence leak. To add fuel to the fire, the British had quite sensibly imposed a travel and uncensored communications ban on all diplomatic representatives of any neutral or allied country except those from the British Dominions, the United States and the Soviet Union. The security risk was simply too great. Because de Gaulle's CFLN was not included in those exempt, it could no longer freely communicate from Algiers with its own forces now in England. These were not insignificant – French aircrew were flying with the RAF; French naval vessels were operating with the Allied navies; and an entire armoured division under Général Philippe Leclerc was training in England and attached to General George S. Patton's US Third Army. That, however, was not due to be sent to France until much of Normandy had already fallen.

All this spelled out a humiliating reality for de Gaulle: that he would have no part in the invasion, nor could he hope to return to his country as the head of a liberated France. He responded angrily, forbidding Koenig to have any more communications with Eisenhower or his staff at Supreme Headquarters Allied Expeditionary Force (SHAEF). For Eisenhower, the growing breakdown of relations with de Gaulle and the CFLN was an added headache. He needed the cooperation of Koenig because of the role of the Résistance and, of course, other French forces in OVERLORD. Koenig was also in an invidious situation. 'If our planning does not get ahead,' wrote Eisenhower to his friend General Joe McNarney, 'we are going to be sadly embarrassed. Moreover, if we had somewhat closer relationships with the French, I think they could do much to alleviate the resentment that is undoubtedly growing up in France against our bombing operations.'

Eisenhower's suggestion was to bring de Gaulle to London for a meeting with Churchill, who was far more sympathetic than Roosevelt. Whether de Gaulle could be persuaded to go was another matter, however, and in the meantime he had provocatively announced the CFLN was to be renamed the Gouvernement provisoire de la République française – the Provisional Government of the French Republic. Roosevelt was not impressed. The impasse continued.

While de Gaulle was being sidelined, the Allies had begun to take the Résistance more seriously. After a series of meetings with its leaders, first Churchill and then Eisenhower decided in favour of arming the Résistance in France, which had previously had low priority compared with the support given to partisans in Italy and the Balkans. Arms drops over France were increased considerably, both through de Gaulle's organizations and through the Special Operations Executive – SOE – the British sabotage and resistance organization, which was now also brought under the control of Eisenhower. Between February and May 1944, more than 76,000 Sten sub-machine guns, nearly 28,000 pistols, almost 17,000 rifles, 3,400 Bren machine guns and hundreds of mortars and bazookas were dropped to the Résistance. Robert Leblanc's Maquis Surcouf benefited from this, though the aid was nothing like enough to create the kind of mass insurrection the Résistance were dreaming about.

However, the last thing the Allies wanted was either the mass of French people out of control and erupting into full-scale civil war or any group trying to take political control of the country – not, at least, until the battle for France was won. Instead, Eisenhower wanted to use the Résistance for a surge of activity in which primarily they supported the work of the Allied air forces in stemming the flow of German men and materiel to the front. A series of plans had been put forward by the FFI and endorsed first by Général Koenig and his team in London and then accepted by Eisenhower: Plan Vert to sabotage the railways; Plan Tortue, the main roads; and Plan Violet, communications. Instructions about when to activate these plans would be delivered by coded messages broadcast by the BBC, the details of which had been passed on by Allied agents dropped into France. In addition, three-man teams, known as 'Jedburghs', would be parachuted into France, each containing one British SOE agent, one American OSS agent and one Frenchman, and equipped with a radio. Jedburghs would act as training and liaison teams with the various Maquis and as the point of contact for the Allies. In addition, the SAS would also be sent deep behind enemy lines to further help and organize the FFI. In this way, the Allies would be better able to coordinate and, more importantly, maintain some control over resistance activities.

The leaders of the Maquis Surcouf, meanwhile, were holed up in a small room at the Château de la Bivellerie in Tourville-sur-Pont-Audemer, just 8 miles from Saint-Étienne-l'Allier. Robert Leblanc and his most trusted men were on standby, glued to their radio set waiting for the signal to activate the plans. Leblanc's men had already won the respect and thanks of the Allies for responding to a request from Koenig's staff to find and execute Violette Morris, a former gold-medal-winning French athlete who had become a particularly effective and sadistic agent for the Gestapo. On 26 April, Leblanc's men had ambushed her and two collaborator colleagues on a country road near Épaignes. All had been killed and her car, a Citroën, taken as a highly sought-after prize.

Now, though, Leblanc and his comrades were sure the invasion was close; on 1 June they received a series of coded messages via Radio Londres warning them that they needed to remain alert. Finally, the day for which they had been waiting so long was almost upon them.

If one of the Allies' headaches was relations with the French, another was the continual fear of an intelligence leak by which the Germans would learn when and where the invasion was to be launched. This was why only those with special clearance were in the know. In an effort to keep the Germans guessing, an elaborate deception plan had been put into action, known collectively as Plan FORTITUDE. Every German agent attempting to infiltrate Britain had been caught, imprisoned and either turned or executed, but German intelligence was not aware of that. Double agents, overseen by the XX Committee of MI5, were busily spinning large amounts of false information in amongst the real but unimportant intelligence. One of the ways the Allies knew this was hitting home was because 'Axis Sally', an American radio broadcaster working for the Nazis, would mention much of the information that had been fed by the Double Cross operation. It was unnerving for the Allied troops who heard the broadcasts, but reassuring to those managing Allied intelligence.

In the field of wartime intelligence, it unquestionably helped that the western Allies were democracies. In Nazi Germany, intelligence organizations tended to operate independently of one another, generally mistrusted each other and rarely pooled their resources. Intelligence was power and so all too often jealously guarded. The only time it came together was at the very top. The SS, for example, increasingly had a grip on much of the internal intelligence within the Reich that came under the control of the RSHA, the Reich Security Office. The Abwehr was the Wehrmacht's intelligence organization, but was already embroiled in plots to overthrow the regime and was loathed by the RSHA. Each of the services had intelligence units but they tended not to cooperate much. Incredibly, Göring also had his own private intelligence system, the Forschungsamt, but this was primarily for keeping him one step ahead of his enemies – and those were within the Nazi hierarchy, not outside it.

The British and Americans, on the other hand, pooled their intelligence very effectively. Much, rightly, has been made of the code-breakers of Bletchley Park cracking the German Enigma machines used to send coded Morse messages; but the cryptanalysts at Bletchley had also broken the Lorenz cipher machines attached to teleprinters, which the Germans used between Berlin and major headquarters and commanders in the field. In the run-up to OVERLORD, this decoded traffic, known as 'Fish', gave the Allies a pretty clear picture of troop dispositions in Normandy and throughout OB West. In addition to the British cryptanalysts, US code-breakers had also cracked the codes used by the Japanese ambassador in Berlin, while a host of other agencies contributed to the intelligence picture, such as the Y Service (a radio-listening organization), photo reconnaissance, the various British military intelligence services such as MI5, MI6 and MI14, plus divisions within those like MI5's XX Committee and also agents in the field, whether MI6, SOE or the American Office of Strategic Service (OSS). All this intelligence was swiftly and effectively pulled together and collectively it added up to considerably more than the sum of its individual parts. Via the BBC, British civilians had also been asked to send in any postcards and photographs people might have kept from France before the war. Millions poured in and those from Normandy were carefully put to one side and analysed to help create a clearer picture of the cities, towns, villages, beaches and countryside from the ground.

Another part of FORTITUDE was the creation of a fictitious US First Army Group and various other fake units, divisions and corps headquarters. Dummy airfields and tank parks were created too. Had the Germans stopped to think about it, they might have realized FORTITUDE was too clever for its own good. After all, there was simply not the space in Britain for the number of units being suggested. The need for secrecy, however, also worked against the Allies. For every photo reconnaissance mission flown over the invasion front, for example, two others were flown elsewhere over France, when tactically it would have been far more helpful to have done it the other way around; but quite rightly, strategic secrecy trumped tactical intelligence. Planners had a very good picture of what enemy units were where, though little understanding of their quality or precise size, and they continued to monitor changes and troop movements up to the last moment. In fact, the final intelligence picture before D-Day came on 4 June, but before that the Allies were aware of considerable enemy reinforcements in Normandy, with the arrival of divisions such as the 91. Luftlande in the Cotentin Peninsula.

By this stage, though, little could have been changed, since the plan had been largely set in stone since 7 April in order to give the naval planners the chance to organize NEPTUNE. Furthermore, the number of beach obstacles and defences had grown exponentially since Montgomery had presented the first outline of the plan back in January. The commanders preparing for OVERLORD simply had to gulp and hope for the best. Montgomery's steadfast confidence, regardless of whether it was misplaced or not, was crucial to morale.

These German reinforcements were certainly causing Air Marshal Leigh-Mallory sleepless nights. Not only had the 91. Luftlande-Division been moved up into the Cotentin, so too had Fallschirmjäger-Regiment 6, the highest-quality infantry unit in Normandy. It was also known that the 352. was now very near the coast. Leigh-Mallory couldn't shake from his mind the conviction that these reinforcements spelled disaster for the airborne drop. The plan was for the 82nd and 101st Airborne to be dropped quite far apart, with the 82nd on the west side of the Cotentin and the 101st protecting Utah, but with the knowledge of these reinforcements, the plan was scrapped on 26 May and instead it was agreed that the 82nd would be dropped around the town of Sainte-Mère-Église and, at the request of VII Corps (to which they were attached), also on the western side of the Merderet Valley, from where they could establish bridgeheads across the river. This way, they would be dropped apart, but at a distance from which they could still be mutually supporting.

Leigh-Mallory, though, wanted the entire airborne operation scrapped. The American paratroopers did not fall under his command, but the IX Troop Carrier Command, part of US Ninth Air Force, did. The plan was for the 915 transport planes involved to cross the peninsula from west to east at just 1,000 feet directly over where there were now concentrations of enemy troops. The airborne drop would take about three hours in total, plenty of time for the enemy to adjust his aim. With neither armour plating nor self-sealing fuel tanks, the C-47 Skytrains transporting the airborne troops – or Dakotas, as the British called them – were certainly vulnerable, and Leigh-Mallory foresaw carnage: burning planes plunging to the ground, formations scattering and what troops were dropped being so badly spread as to be unable to fulfil their mission.

He put his concerns to Bradley, but the US First Army commander was having no truck with this; nor was either Major-General Matthew Ridgway, commander of the 82nd, or Major-General Maxwell Taylor of the 101st. And so Leigh-Mallory turned to Ike. 'I hesitate to increase your problems at the present difficult time,' he wrote to Eisenhower on Monday, 29 May, 'but I feel I should be failing in my duty to you if I did not let you know that I was very unhappy about the US Airborne Operations as now planned.'

Eisenhower replied with the kind of firm but diplomatic rebuttal that made him such an ideal Supreme Commander. Leigh-Mallory was quite right to express his concerns; he was worried about the risks himself. 'However,' he added, 'a strong airborne attack in the region indicated is essential to the whole operation and it must go on.' All concerned must do everything possible to diminish the hazards, he added, and then firmly warned Leigh-Mallory to spread no more negative talk. 'It is particularly important that air and ground troops involved in the operation be not needlessly depressed,' he wrote. 'Like all of the rest of the soldiers, they must understand that they have a tough job to do but be fired with determination to get it done.' The American airborne drop would go ahead.

No matter how riled Bradley had been by Leigh-Mallory, his senior aide, Captain Chester 'Chet' Hansen, thought he had rarely seen him in a better mood than he was over dinner on Friday, 2 June. Earlier that afternoon, they had driven to an airfield near their headquarters in Bristol to bid farewell to General Patton, who had been Bradley's guest.

'Brad, the best of luck to you,' Patton had said to him, clenching both Bradley's hands. 'We'll be meeting again – soon, I hope.' When they did, Third Army would be joining the battle from Brittany and Bradley would assume command of the US 12th Army Group on the Continent.

Travelling back to Bristol, Hansen thought England had never looked prettier or greener. A former journalist from New Jersey, he had been working in public relations in New York before being drafted and sent to Officer Candidate School, where he graduated seventh in his class. From there he had been recruited directly to Bradley's staff, and shortly after found himself bidding his wife, Marjorie, farewell and heading overseas with the general to North Africa. Nearly two years later, they were about to embark on one of the greatest military operations ever mounted and, as Hansen was keenly aware, he would have a grandstand view of the US Army's part in it. 'We are done with the heavy, earnest days of planning,' he noted in his diary that night, 'the long and endless conferences, the changes, the disappointments. The invasion has been tied up in a package. There is nothing to do now but to climb aboard a ship and sail on our way to France.'

The following day, Saturday, 3 June, they drove to Plymouth on the south Devon coast, passing fields crammed with tanks and tens of thousands of other vehicles, then met up with Bradley's deputy, Lieutenant-General Courtney Hodges, and Major-General 'Lightning' Joe' Collins, VII Corps commander, before reaching the ancient port from which the Pilgrim Fathers had set sail for America. From there, a launch conveyed them to USS *Augusta*, the cruiser that would take Bradley to Normandy and the flag of Rear-Admiral Alan Kirk, the US Naval Commander. Later, they transferred again, to USS *Achernar*, an old freighter converted into a command ship, in the lower centre section of which was the First Army Command Post. A large air-locator map covered a table in the centre of the room, while further maps were fixed to the walls. Next door was a filter room for radar intercepts of enemy aircraft, belying the nervousness everyone felt at the prospect of Luftwaffe attack during the invasion.

Later that afternoon, Hansen settled down to write up his diary in the much smaller operations room they had been allocated on *Augusta*. Maps once again lined the walls, while the sound of typewriters chattered incessantly. Coffee mugs littered every surface. Hansen learned there were other concerns than the threat of the Luftwaffe, not least whether there were enough cleared sea lanes through the minefields. Then there was the weather. While it was horribly hot and fetid on board, weather reports reaching them were not encouraging. Winds were on their way, with low cloud and reduced visibility. It was a worry . . .

Weather forecasting in the summer of 1944 was an imprecise science. Weather stations were dotted all over the United Kingdom and others on the west coast of Ireland could be drawn upon by Allied meteorologists despite Ireland's neutrality. Beyond the British Isles, though, sources diminished woefully: a few weather ships and that was all. Each was equipped with barometers, anemometers, wind vanes, hygrometers and thermometers, and the meteorologists aboard could read cloud heights, bases, sea swell as well as wind speeds, but the Atlantic was a big place, the variables were massive and, ultimately, predicting weather became harder with every passing day.

There were also different schools of thought about how best to forecast. One of the senior American weathermen attached to US Strategic Air Forces, Dr Irving Krick, was a fervent believer in using historic patterns and weather cycles to supplement what could be learned from weather stations: what was known as analogue forecasting. Krick was considered something of a smug self-promoter within American meteorological circles, but he had the backing of General Hap Arnold, the commander of the US Army Air Forces, and now led the US team based at Widewing, the code name for Eisenhower's main SHAEF HQ at London's Bushy Park. The British Air Ministry meteorological team, on the other hand, was led by Dr Sverre Petterssen, a Norwegian, and Charles Douglas, who took a more strictly scientific approach. The Admiralty's weather team also offered forecasts and their collected predictions were forwarded to Group Captain James Stagg, a geophysicist by training but now chief meteorologist to Eisenhower, and Colonel Donald Yates, Stagg's deputy. It was Stagg, a thin-faced 39-year-old Scot, who had the unenviable task of drawing the various weather forecasts together and reaching some kind of conclusion.

The trouble began brewing on a gloriously sunny Thursday, 1 June, when at an evening weather conference the Air Ministry team of Petterssen and Douglas painted a gloomy outlook for D-Day, which had been set as Monday, 5 June. Krick and the Widewing team, in contrast, were far more optimistic. By the following day, the Air Ministry men were even more pessimistic, and Stagg felt compelled to relay this to Eisenhower and his commanders. By the evening, Petterssen was predicting ten-tenths cloud and a risk of a Force 5 wind on the Monday.

Reports from the weather stations arrived every few hours and the charts were updated by hand. By the evening of Saturday, 3 June, even Krick and the team at Widewing were agreeing with Petterssen's view, as were the Admiralty's weathermen. For Stagg, it was time to confront the commanders of the invasion once more, which he did in the library at

Southwick House in Portsmouth at 9.30 p.m. Full of largely forlorn and empty bookshelves, the library was now Southwick House's mess room.

'Gentlemen,' said Stagg, 'the fears which I hoped you realised we had yesterday, Friday morning . . . are confirmed.' A low pressure area was sweeping in bringing low cloud, gales and rain. 'Those details apply for Sunday to Tuesday and at first on Wednesday.'

Questions were asked. Leigh-Mallory wanted to know what cloud cover they could expect over the French coast. Ten-tenths. Admiral Ramsay asked whether the Force 5 winds were likely to continue on Monday and Tuesday. Yes. And Wednesday? Not settling immediately but getting brighter. For a moment no one spoke. A gloom had descended over the room. As Stagg and Yates left, they heard Eisenhower say, 'Are we prepared to take a gamble on this?' Their discussions continued until around 11 p.m., when Stagg was told to return for another briefing at 4.15 the next morning, Sunday, 4 June.

'Pleasant dreams, Stagg,' said Tedder as he passed him.

The hours passed quickly, with no dream time for Stagg or any of the weather teams. Krick and the Widewing team now felt certain a ridge of high pressure from the Azores would keep the worst of the cloud away from the Normandy coast. Petterssen strongly disagreed. On the other hand, following a cold front – such as the one due to be passing through – would come a few hours of lighter winds and clearer weather regardless of how the Azores high behaved. If the front passed across the Cotentin Peninsula around midnight, then, in theory, there would be an opportunity for the US airborne drop to go ahead almost on schedule with the British one a few hours later. The bombers would most likely have the visibility they needed.

Stagg, though, felt he should side with Petterssen, who was sure there would still be too much cloud cover to make the airborne drops and bombing feasible; instinctively, Stagg trusted Petterssen more than Krick, even if, deep down, it was for cultural reasons rather than anything else. Back in the library, he advised the assembled commanders that there was no real change: the forecast still looked bad.

Once again, Stagg was thanked and asked to leave while the commanders discussed the matter. Monty was for pressing on regardless, but Tedder disagreed and opted for postponement. Ike had always been worried that they would be attacking initially on D-Day with a significantly smaller force than that available to the enemy and pointed out they had always felt such an operation was possible only because of air power. If they were unable to bring that to bear, however, then he too felt they should postpone. 'Are there any dissenting voices?' he asked. There were none. It was a terrible decision to have to make: Forces S and J – those invasion forces heading for Sword and Juno Beaches – were already on their way and had to be recalled; the entire amphibious invasion force was already loaded on to their ships, where they would have to stay, cramped, uncomfortable, their morale and spirits draining with every passing hour. And what if the weather didn't improve?

Outside, Stagg looked up at the still, almost cloudless sky and felt the enormity of the decision resting on their shoulders. He headed back to the SHAEF command post and to his tent to try to get some rest. Eisenhower also headed to his caravan, where he was surrounded by Westerns, newspapers and a plentiful supply of cigarettes; he had begun chain-smoking these past few days.

4.30 p.m., Southwick House, Sunday, 4 June. Stagg called a conference with all his weather teams. Everyone agreed there was a small ridge of high pressure that looked as if it might follow in behind the current low, which, if it remained on track, should last until Tuesday morning, 6 June. The weather from Wednesday to Friday still looked unsettled. It was, however, quite a big 'if'. This small ridge of high pressure was being reported from the few weather ships out in the Atlantic; there was a pattern, definitely, but whether it would stay on course and develop into the clearer skies they hoped for was far from certain. The danger, though, was that in clutching at this potential lifeline they were resting too much upon it. Such a ridge could easily be pinched, squeezed out, pushed off course. Then there would be no high coming in at all. The low cloud would continue along with the wind and rain. 'The fair interval from early hours Monday to Tuesday is confirmed,' noted Stagg in his diary after the next meeting with his teams at 7.30 that night. This was still not quite as certain as he was making out, however. The small high was still off the west coast of Ireland and only limited weather stations were tracking its progress. There remained a distinct possibility it could still be pushed north over central England rather than over the Channel.

At 9 p.m. Stagg once more spoke to the assembled D-Day commanders and reported the improved picture. After being thoroughly grilled, he left them to their discussions. Monty was emphatically for going. So too was Bedell Smith. 'It's a helluva gamble,' said Ike's chief of staff, 'but it's the best possible gamble.'

'The question,' said Eisenhower, 'is just how long can you hang this operation on the end of a limb and let it hang there?' Because of tides and moons, the next opportunity would be 19 June. That was two weeks away. A fortnight in which the Germans further strengthened their defences, and in which there was a huge dip in the morale of the invasion force, and potential security leaks. It was unthinkable. They *had* to go.

Around twenty minutes later, Eisenhower emerged from the library.

'Stagg, we've put it on again,' he told him. 'For heaven's sake hold the weather to what you have forecast for us. Don't you bring any more bad news.' He smiled, then stepped back inside. Shortly after that, it was agreed they would reconvene once again at 4.15 a.m. on Monday, 5 June for the final, irreversible decision.

Stagg returned to his tent around 10.30 p.m. and tried to get some rest, but sleep eluded him. Outside, the rain was slashing down against the canvas, the wind testing the guy ropes to the full. 'Lay and thought of what it all meant,' he noted, 'and hoped and hoped that our story would come through.' His choice of words could not have been more apt.

At 3 a.m. he was up again and meeting his weather teams. By this time the front had already passed through – the skies were largely clear and the winds had dropped; if it was clear in Portsmouth, it was clear on the Cotentin Peninsula and probably rapidly clearing across the rest of Normandy as well, so had they stuck to the original D-Day it would hardly have been the disaster that had been feared. No one mentioned that, however. The decision had been made. How the weather was going to behave the following night was what mattered now.

After a further meeting with his teams, at 4.15 a.m. Stagg was back in the library to face the Supreme Commander and the commanders-in-chief. Montgomery was there, looking spry in corduroy trousers and a high-necked grey pullover. They all sat informally in armchairs as Stagg began his forecast. If anything, he told them, there were grounds for greater optimism. Once again a detailed grilling followed, then he was dismissed. It was decision time. Monty, Bedell Smith and Ramsay were for going. So too was Tedder. Leigh-Mallory had major doubts. Ultimately, though, the decision rested with Eisenhower. The burden was his.

The Supreme Commander sat in his chair, rubbed his face in his hands, then looked up. 'OK,' he said. 'Let's go.'

CHAPTER 6

Big War

THERE IS A TEMPTATION, when considering D-Day, to take much of its planning, organization and scale for granted. After all, who cares about logistics and the hundreds of thousands of office staff, stevedores, merchant sailors and bean-counters? Usually, the D-Day story begins in the landing craft with the cold sea spray lashing across the seasick and scared young men about to assault the beaches. Yet they were the spearhead only. It was their terrible misfortune that they were the age and physique to have to do the actual fighting, but they were the minority in the 'big war' that the United States and Britain had developed over the previous couple of years. Historians, journalists and commentators can argue all they like about the tactical merits or otherwise of the Allied war machine, but it is important to remember that by D-Day the Allies were fighting a totally industrialized and highly technological war so gargantuan that today it almost makes one's head hurt trying to absorb its scale and complexity.

The level of detailed planning involved, and the many different strands that all needed to be pulled together by men and women of different nationalities is quite astonishing. It was not just a matter of training enough men and making enough rifles and machine guns, but of keeping them fed, supporting them with the right amount of medical assistance, fuel, clothing, ammunition. Between January and June 1944, for example, Britain alone produced 7 million 5-gallon jerry fuel cans. They then had to be stored, transported and filled. It was also estimated that the Allies would need a staggering 8,000 tons of fuel every single day. Oil terminals, largely out of reach of the Luftwaffe by this stage of the war, were specially built around Liverpool and Bristol, but the fuel had to come from the US and the Caribbean in the first place and could only do so by ship across the Atlantic. Some 1,720,900 tons of fuel had reached Britain in the first five months of the year, three times the amount already used by Germany.

Once fully operational ports were established on the Continent, tankers would be able to sail straight to France, but until then, for the Allies to be able to bring their vast material superiority to bear, the oil for the initial phase of the campaign would have to come direct from Britain. Shipping would play a part, but the huge burden could be lessened by using new piping technology, and so from these new terminals pipelines were constructed across England and under the Solent to Sandown on the Isle of Wight; from there, once the invasion had succeeded, the plan was to lay a fuel pipeline all the way under the Channel to Normandy. This was not a straightforward operation. First, a pipeline had to be created that was strong and big enough to take the quantity of fuel requiring to be constantly pumped. Second, it had to be robust enough to withstand the pressure of lying at the bottom of the Channel. The result was a flexible, 76mm-diameter pipe made from a combination of lead lining, steel mesh and reinforced rubber. The plan was to lay it using a 'Conundrum' – a giant floating spool from which this extraordinary bit of special piping, weighing 55 tons per mile, would be laid. The logistics were considerable. Before the pipeline – code-named PLUTO: pipeline under the ocean – could be laid, the invasion forces would be dependent on what they could carry with them, which was where the fuel tankers and the millions of jerry cans came in.

Vast depots of munitions and food also had to be established. Enormous numbers of warehouses were designed, built and filled to the rafters throughout Britain, but especially around the ports. Every port in southern England was crammed for the invasion, while enormous quantities of shipping continued to cross the Atlantic. The demand on shipping was breathtakingly high. On any given day during the war, at any given hour, on average some 2,000 British merchant vessels were sailing the world's oceans; for US merchant ships the figure was closer to 3,000. For any supply to reach Britain, whether it be wool, cotton, rubber, timber, bauxite or any number of other goods, it all had to pass through the Atlantic, arrive in British ports – usually on the west coast and mostly at Greenock in Scotland, Liverpool, Cardiff and Bristol – and then be unloaded and moved on. Meanwhile, the Allies were fighting the war elsewhere – in

Italy, in South-East Asia, in the Pacific – and were still sending supplies through the Arctic to the Soviet Union. Incredibly, US shipping to the Pacific had also increased by 62 per cent since 1943 – in all, some 5,552,000 tons of supplies would be shipped to the Pacific in 1944. In fact, as OVER-LORD was about to be launched, in the Pacific the Americans were preparing to assault the Marianas, while in South-East Asia British Four-teenth Army was just beginning to turn the screws against the largest single land force the Japanese had yet assembled, around Imphal in north-east India. These joint operations all required scarcely comprehensible amounts of shipping and it was still barely enough.

Arguably the most important vessels for the invasion of Normandy were the landing ships (LSTs), which, at 4,800 tons each, over 100 metres long, flat-bottomed with a draught of just 4 feet 7 inches when fully loaded, were big enough to deliver the huge amounts of war materiel on which the Allies depended. They could carry eighteen 30-ton tanks and 350 troops, or 2,100 tons of supplies, and sail pretty much straight on to a beach. Giant doors in the bows then opened up, a ramp was lowered straight on to the sand and the tanks and vehicles simply drove straight off.

Colonel Tick Bonesteel had been among those pleading with Don Nelson, the head of the American War Production Board, for more of these precious vessels. During a visit by Nelson to London, Bonesteel had spent almost two days with him in a hotel suite at Claridge's, con-vincing him of the urgent need to somehow increase production. Nelson listened. 'Damn, he did unbelievable things,' said Bonesteel. 'He almost doubled the production of landing craft.'

Even so, the shortfall of required landing ships and landing craft of all kinds had been the prime reason for moving the original invasion date of early May by a month. Shipping issues had also caused the postpone-ment of the planned invasion of southern France, Operation ANVIL, on 19 April – possibly indefinitely. There was still a shortfall of the all-important LSTs – 236 instead of the 277 reckoned to be needed. This meant calling upon British coasters, smaller freighters that plied their trade around the British Isles. In turn, this put a greater strain on Brit-ain's inland transport system and came at the discomfort of the British people: OVERLORD had to be the priority. In all, some 1,260 merchant vessels were earmarked for the invasion, including ocean-going vessels, colliers, tankers and personnel vessels.

A staggering array of other landing craft had been designed and built by both Britain and America during the past three years. The evacuation of Dunkirk back in 1940, when there had been none available, and the realization that future offensive operations would require such vessels, had kick-started this new wave of landing craft design and construction. It included other landing ships for infantry, for emergency repairs, for delivering headquarters and even from where fighter aircraft control could be provided. There were barges called 'Rhinos' and smaller British-designed LCAs (Landing Craft, Assault) and US LCVPs (Landing Craft, Vehicle and Personnel), designed by Andrew Higgins in New Orleans and more commonly known simply as 'Higgins Boats'. There was even an LBB (Landing Barge, Bakery) and an LCT(R) – a floating rocket launcher equipped with a Type 970 radar set, which could fire salvoes of up to a thousand 60lb warheads designed to saturate enemy beaches from 3,500 yards. In all, there were thirty different landing ships and craft, including DUKWs – pronounced 'ducks' – amphibious trucks that could carry 3 tons of supplies and travel 6.4 m.p.h. in the water and over 50 m.p.h. on land.

Assembled under Admiral Ramsay's command for Operation NEP-TUNE were a jaw-dropping 7,000 vessels. The Allied invasion fleet included 138 bombarding warships, 279 escort ships, 287 minelayers and 495 gunboats, torpedo boats and other launches. The total number of naval warships was 1,213. Because of the US Navy's heavy involvement in the Pacific, most of these – some 892 – were Royal Navy, but there were a number of Royal Canadian Navy, French, Dutch, Belgian, Norwegian and Polish vessels as well. In contrast, at the time, the Kriegsmarine, the German Navy, had just three warships larger than a destroyer. In addition to these Allied warships were 4,127 landing craft of all thirty varieties, all of which had to be manned, coordinated and fulfil their allotted tasks where and when they were needed, and, it now seemed, in conditions that would be far from ideal.

It was the largest armada ever mounted. Just organizing it into five different invasion forces and one support force was a phenomenal logistical headache, but to then sail it without being picked up by the enemy and, more importantly, to pass through an English Channel heavily laid with enemy mines and a dense mine barrier 7–10 miles from the coast was a further challenge of unprecedented proportions. How to mine-sweep enough safe channels effectively was a constant worry during the planning phase. 'It is a most complicated operation,' Admiral Ramsay had noted in his diary on 24 March, 'and however we looked at it we could find no satisfactory solution of how best to sweep the channels for the faster groups & bombarding ships.'

The answer was to plan for the largest minesweeping operation of the war, with the creation of two clear channels for each of the assault forces which would be marked with Danbuoys – buoys with flags extended on a pole above the surface – spaced a mile apart throughout. Specialist minesweeper ships were dedicated to clearing mines, using what was called the 'Oropesa sweep' – a wire with angled blades known as 'kites' and 'otters' that streamed out either side of the vessel and was kept below the surface by a series of weights and floats. Mines were held in position by cables and weights and floated below the surface; the aim was to sever the cable so the mine would rise to the surface where it would be destroyed by gunfire. Minesweepers could work individually or in formation, which was best for clearing a specific channel. Clearing the invasion channels would necessarily be a highly complex undertaking, involving some 255 minesweepers – an astonishing number – all of which would have to change sweeps at key moments to avoid an unfavourable tide and ensure the swept channels were straight.

Such were the challenges facing Operation NEPTUNE. Meanwhile, in its support, Operation MAPLE had begun forty-five days earlier, with minelayers at work all along the Channel coast. Mines were laid at key points, including off the ports of Cherbourg, Le Havre, Brest and all around the Brittany coast.

All this and so much more had to be planned in minute detail: from the allocation of each ship and landing craft, to the numerous training exercises in the lead-up to D-Day, and then to NEPTUNE itself. The mooring of every ship and landing craft had to be worked out, as well as which troops, which trucks, which tanks and so on were going where. The invasion consisted of five assault forces named after the first letter of the beach to which they were heading, plus a bombarding force and a support force for each beach, preceded by a fleet of minesweepers. The combined forces would head initially for an area south-east of the Isle of Wight – Area Z, known as 'Piccadilly Circus' – then the separate forces would head south along their two swept channels, each of which was numbered between 1 and 10.

Planning was in the hands of the staff officers working under Ramsay and the staffs of the Western Task Force under Rear-Admiral Alan Kirk, and the Eastern Task Force under British Rear-Admiral Philip Vian. For all this planning, there were now over a thousand staff in Fort

Southwick, the Victorian naval fort built on the 400-foot-high chalk ridge overlooking Portsmouth, while for the control and coordination of the invasion forces – the naval traffic controllers – a further 700 staff occupied Underground Headquarters, an enormous bombproof complex of tunnels and command and control rooms consisting of five 110-yard tunnels and fourteen cross-tunnels of around 55 yards each. Work on it had begun in early 1942 specifically for the future cross-Channel invasion. UGHQ remained a top-secret facility known to very few, with access down a series of steps from inside Fort Southwick.

Much thought had been given to the port facilities, or rather the lack of them, on the other side of the Channel. A key part in the success of the invasion rested on how quickly large quantities of supplies could be delivered to a part of northern France in which the two major ports – Cherbourg and Le Havre – were in enemy hands. Cherbourg was a priority objective, but there was no knowing what state it would be in once captured. While supplies could be taken directly on to the beach, no one thought anything like enough could be delivered there. This would have been even more difficult to achieve back in 1942 when Admiral Lord Louis Mountbatten's Combined Operations organization was first considering Normandy for any future Allied invasion. In a memo to Mountbatten on 30 May that year, Churchill had suggested it might be possible to build floating piers for use from open beaches. 'They *must* float up and down on the tide,' he told him, then added, 'Don't argue the matter. The difficulties will argue for themselves.'

A little over a year later, Commander John Hughes-Hallett, then working at COSSAC, had suggested that if no harbour was available in Normandy then perhaps they should take one with them. Initially scoffed at, he pursued the point, found an ally in the prime minister and so began one of the most outrageous engineering projects of the war: two giant makeshift harbours that could be floated across the Channel and put in place wherever they liked. The ambition for these was extraordinary. A breakwater would be created initially by steaming or towing obsolescent ships to the spot then sinking them. Then huge concrete and steel caissons, hollow so that they could float, would be towed across the Channel, the air removed and then sunk, one next to the other, until a series of harbour walls had been created. Floating piers would stretch out from the coast inside this artificial harbour and be attached to equally floating quaysides that would, as Churchill had suggested, rise up and down on the tide. The design was ingenious, the ambition and vision astonishing, and remarkably, despite quite phenomenal challenges, by the beginning of June they were ready.

Some of Britain's biggest engineering firms, such as Balfour Beatty, Wimpey and Sir Robert McAlpine, were involved, but as many as 300 different firms were employed for this gargantuan project. In a little over six months, a workforce of 55,000 managed to construct two floatable harbours, each the size of the port of Dover. The largest component parts were the 200-foot-long caissons, code-named 'Phoenixes' – these alone used 542,000 cubic yards of concrete and 39,000 tons of steel. Although built all around the country, most of the Phoenixes were constructed along the River Clyde and the Thames, then trialled in Scotland, far from prying eyes; secrecy was, of course, paramount, because should the Germans get wind of what was afoot then it would become increasingly obvious the Allies were planning an invasion where no port existed. On the other hand, the 'Mulberries', as the two harbours were code-named, needed to be taken over to France and got up and running just as soon as humanly possible.

The man in charge of this monumental task was Rear-Admiral Bill Tennant, who had been senior naval officer at Dunkirk during the evacuation and who, along with General Harold Alexander, had been the last British serviceman to leave the shattered port in June 1940. He had been serving under Ramsay then, and now the naval C-in-C had brought him in to become RAMP – Rear-Admiral Mulberries and Pluto.

One of those on Tennant's team was 32-year-old Lieutenant-Commander Ambrose Lampen, a career naval officer who had joined the Royal Navy in 1924 at the modest age of thirteen. So far in the war, he had served in the Mediterranean and the Arctic before being posted in March to Dover with a 'top secret' classification. For several days, he hadn't had the faintest idea what he was to be doing until finally he was presented to Ramsay and given a black book in which were the plans for OVERLORD. 'Every detail was there,' noted Lampen, 'and I felt slightly hot under the collar as I realized the responsibility with which I was now entrusted.' Ramsay then told him he was to set up 'TURCO' – Turn Around Control – an organization for refuelling and reloading ships returning from the first wave of the assault.

No sooner had he set this up than in early April Lampen was told his team would now be in charge of 'parking' the Phoenixes near the coast at Dungeness and Selsey Bill as they arrived from the shipyards. 'It's been decided to "park" them – as the saying is,' Ramsay's chief of staff told him, 'before they are towed to the French coast.' Before Lampen could reply, he was also told he would be getting an admiral above him whom they needed to employ: Rear-Admiral Menzies, taken off the retirement list. 'However,' Lampen was told, 'there's no point telling him that TURCO is just a cover, and that he really won't have anything to do.'

Throughout much of the rest of April and May, Lampen was at sea for long hours planting the Phoenixes as they reached the south coast. Sometimes several arrived together, which added to the pressure as they had to be planted at high tide; this meant carefully opening valves, letting in water and making sure they sank on to the seabed and were then securely anchored. The principle of lowering them was much the same as for a diving submarine. 'I became familiar with their idiosyncrasies,' noted Lampen, 'and came to regard them not so much as tough concrete castles as delicate half-incubated egg-shells, which would then crack at the least mishandling.' In any kind of wind and swell, the difficulties massively multiplied.

With the task successfully finished, he was summoned to Portsmouth to see Admiral Tennant, en route passing by verges crammed with army vehicles in long, unbroken lines. At Portsmouth he was told he would be travelling to Normandy, not to plant more Phoenixes but rather as 'berthing officer' for the handling and planting of the blockships – the 'Corncobs'. These were the old, obsolescent ships that were to be sunk to form a breakwater – or 'Gooseberry'. Lampen was most put out. He had spent two months becoming something of an expert at the difficult task of planting the enormous Phoenixes and now would have a different role in the creation of Mulberry B, the planned British harbour. It made little sense, but there was nothing he could do about it. Instead, he had to acquaint himself with his new team: a mixed force of two British and six American tugs and their crews. They would be towing the blockships unable to cross the Channel under their own steam. No one, it seemed, had thought to provide them with any towing ropes. Time was running out. It was now 2 June and they were due to set sail in two days' time. A frantic trip to the USN supply officer in Southampton and then to the American naval stores brought Lampen his rope, as well as extra radios and other stores. The invasion might have involved spectacular levels of planning, but right up to the wire some things had been overlooked.

As Lampen had discovered when he drove through Sussex and Hampshire from Dover, there were few corners of southern England that were not filled with troops, Nissen huts, stores, vast numbers of trucks, tanks and artillery pieces. Crammed into the southern shires were millions of American, British and Canadian troops, and those of many other nationalities besides.

At the start of the war, in the dark, distant days of September 1939, the United States had had an army of a mere 189,000 and just 72 fighter planes in what was then the Army Air Corps. In 1939, the US had built a mere 18 tanks of all types. Eighteen! Since then, the growth had been exponential: nearly 60,000 tanks, including 26,608 in 1943 alone. Four million Americans were now in uniform, and nearly 85,000 aircraft were built just in 1943 – considerably more than Germany had produced in the entire war to date. That record looked set to be smashed in 1944. More than 1.7 million trucks had been built already by the US and more than 150,000 artillery pieces.

British war industry had also been more than pulling its weight, with over 28,000 aircraft in 1943, just over 49,000 tanks and other armoured fighting vehicles (AFVs) and nearly 19,000 guns. Admittedly, this colossal arsenal had to fuel a war now raging globally, but it was the invasion of France and the swift defeat of Nazi Germany that was the priority. The Allies were going to bludgeon the Germans into defeat, but not until a foothold had been established in Normandy could they start to ship these huge numbers of men, guns and tanks across the sea in the kind of numbers that would prove unbeatable.

The nub of the matter was that so much depended on the actual invasion and the days that immediately followed – the time when the Allies would be most vulnerable and when the vast majority of troops, tanks, guns and ammunition would still be in England. One of the side-effects of the big war strategy was the differing requirements of the various facets involved. These came to the fore in the discussion about H-Hour, the moment when the troops would come ashore in Normandy. 'No single question,' wrote Admiral Ramsay, 'was more often discussed during planning than that of H-Hour.'

A number of factors came into play. The naval armada needed to cross the Channel under cover of darkness, which meant the airborne forces would have to be dropped during the night, but to do so effectively they would need moonlight in which to jump and reasonably clear skies. It was agreed the air forces should bomb targets along the coastline before the men landed, but they needed at least forty minutes of daylight to be able to carry that out effectively. Naval guns also had to be able to see their targets, but then again, the earlier H-Hour was, the greater the tactical surprise and hopefully fewer casualties as a result. Then there were the Normandy tides: it made sense to land on a rising tide so that the assault troops would not be exposed for too long on the beaches. Balancing everything, the best landing time appeared to be about 40 minutes before dawn, when the sun was 12 degrees below the horizon – that is, around four in the morning.

This had been agreed, but then came the discovery that many more beach obstacles had been laid by the Germans, which meant the first assault waves needed to touch down short of them and so at lower tide and with greater distance for the troops to cross. Adding to the complications was the realization that the rocky shoals off Juno Beach would cause major landing problems at anything lower than half-tide. 'Further discussions about H-Hour,' noted Ramsay in his diary on 23 May, 'after realisation of impact of reefs.' The final compromise was agreed just days before D-Day. The Americans would land at 6.30 a.m., the British at Sword Beach at 7.25 a.m. and at Gold at 7.30 a.m., and the British and Canadians at 7.45 a.m. at Juno.

The only light relief for Ramsay was a game of cricket between his Mess and the Wrens on Monday, 29 May. 'Made 16,' he noted. 'Very stiff. Very hot playing.'

Another indication of the astonishing weight and energy being thrown behind the Allied planning for OVERLORD was the extraordinary growth of the Ninth Air Force, which, along with Mary Coningham's Second Tactical Air Force, was due to play a pivotal role in the invasion and the campaign that followed. The Ninth had been moved to England the previous September from the Mediterranean, although with only a skeleton staff and almost no assets, as these had been largely left behind in Italy for the air forces there. Overall command lay with General Lewis Brereton, but the man in charge of all the Ninth's fighters in IX Fighter Command was Brigadier-General Elwood 'Pete' Quesada, then still only thirty-nine years old, but already with plenty of command and operational experience in the war, a huge amount of energy and an enquiring mind eager to develop air power. Few had quibbled about his appointment to so lofty a position at such a young age.

From Washington DC, Quesada had joined the army as a private, then switched to the Air Corps, been made an officer, earned his wings, attended the Air Corps Tactical School and, by the time America entered the war, was considered among the brightest and most able of a new cadre of young and dynamic air commanders. Always known as 'Pete' – after one of his fellow recruits had given him the nickname – Quesada had faced a huge challenge on his arrival in England. Setting up his headquarters at RAF Middle Wallop, a former Battle of Britain fighter airfield to the north-east of Salisbury in southern England, he had begun his new job with just a dozen men. Thereafter, some 40,000 personnel a month had arrived to join the Ninth, all of whom needed to be organized, housed, equipped, trained and put into action. By the eve of D-Day, the Ninth had swollen to 35,000 airmen and 1,600 aircraft, a larger number than that of the Mighty Eighth. Directly under Quesada were no fewer than five fighter wings, nineteen fighter groups split into two different tactical air commands, the IXth and XIXth, as well as one tactical reconnaissance group, three night-fighter squadrons, one signal aviation company, four communications squadrons, five fighter control squadrons, eight airfield squadrons, two signal battalions, five detached signal companies, eleven military police companies and eighteen station complement squadrons: all this in just seven months.

As his force grew, so they had been thrown into the air battle, first supporting the strategic bombers and then carrying out the interdiction operations in the run-up to the invasion. Quesada's role was to integrate and coordinate with his peers and superiors, bring around him a staff that was competent and far-sighted, oversee the development and evolution of tactics and, in particular, set up the communications system and network that would allow him to operate with the flexibility and speed that were necessary. He was the first to admit that the support from back home in the US was second to none. New groups were arriving with an incredible level of training and at least 350 hours in their logbooks. They were also reaching their new bases with everything already in place. 'Everybody who was supposed to have equipment had it in their hands,' Quesada recalled. 'In a matter of a few days that was often done and within a week or ten days after arrival, we had these boys flying their airplanes over Normandy.' When technical glitches appeared, they were ironed out. Some of his men, for example, complained of guns jamming in their P-51s after turning tightly in a dog-fight. Quesada demanded this be sorted and ended up speaking to General Hap Arnold himself about it by phone link to Washington. 'Goddam it, Pete,' Arnold told him, 'we are going to get that fixed within forty-eight hours.' Arnold was true to his word. Specialist engineers were immediately sent over from the US and the problem was resolved on every single P-51 within a week. 'You have to have people in your airplanes that have confidence in their leadership, that have confidence in their equipment,' Quesada commented later. 'If you don't have those two things you have poor morale. If you have poor morale, you don't have much to lean on.' Few would argue with that, least of all Montgomery. This was the kind of support, however, about which most German units could only dream.

By June his IX Fighter Command was ready, with stores stacked up, pilots and ground crews primed and engineers poised to hurry across the Channel to create new airfields. The only shortcoming that seriously troubled Quesada was the lack of integrated training with troops on the ground. This, however, was a consequence of the intense air campaign that had been going on and into which his units had been thrust the moment they arrived in England. There simply hadn't been the chance. 'The air forces were fighting,' commented Quesada, 'whereas the ground forces weren't.' This meant air–land integration would have to be worked out once in Normandy. It wasn't ideal, but it was a question of priorities and the most important was to make sure the actual invasion was a success. Winning air superiority and paving the way for invasion was more important than training for something that would not happen if the former had not been assured.

Travelling around England was the American war correspondent Ernie Pyle. Small and wiry, balding and looking considerably older than his forty-three years, Pyle had made a name for himself before the war as a columnist for the Scripps-Howard chain of newspapers. His forte had been recording everyday American life in a beautifully observed, informal and affectionate style that made him seem like a personal friend to the millions who followed his travels and musings across the States. Since the start of the war, he had continued to write about what he had seen and the ordinary folk caught up in this extraordinary conflict that he had met along the way, whether it be in London in the Blitz, or North Africa, or Sicily or southern Italy. His dispatches from the front line had won him ever greater legions of fans, so that he was now one of the most well-known names in America.

He was, however, neurotic, prone to bouts of depression and had a fractious relationship with his wife. Ernie Pyle was a troubled soul, but he was an unquestionably brilliant writer and observer of life, so it was only natural that the US army brass would want him to be one of the 28 out of 450 journalists lined up to cover the coming campaign to take part in the assault phase. While there was no way Pyle was going to refuse the opportunity, he was certainly feeling deeply apprehensive. As he travelled around southern England it had seemed as though every soldier in the land was busy waterproofing vehicles for the landings. He also noticed that much of the equipment was stacked high in wooden crates, which gave him an idea. 'I stayed up for a couple of nights with a hammer and saw,' he wrote, 'preparing a large box for myself, with horseshoes tacked all over it.' By this time he knew the invasion was imminent; everyone did. Bouts of despair started sweeping over him and he was having bad dreams. He and the other chosen few journalists had been told they would be given twenty-four hours' notice before depart-ure, and then, at the very end of May, that warning had been issued and they were ordered to a specific assembly area – a 'sausage' – on the south coast. Pyle's heart was heavy with dread.

On the morning of 3 June, he was woken at four along with his com-panions, a number of officers from US First Army Headquarters. Blearily, they loaded up their kit, which seemed woefully excessive. 'The Germans will have to come to us,' said one of the officers. 'We can never get to them with all this load.' From there, they were told they would be joining an LST in Falmouth. As they motored south, the English roads were cleared of normal traffic, with civil and military police at every crossing. As they drew near to Falmouth, more and more people lined the route, with children signalling the American OK symbol of a finger and thumb together in an 'O'. Then they were on the quayside and loading on to the LST and, before Pyle knew it, ropes were being cast off and they were setting sail. 'From a vague anticipatory dread,' he wrote, 'the invasion now turned into a horrible reality for me. In a matter of hours the holo-caust of our own planning would swirl over us. No man could guarantee his own fate. It was almost too much for me. A feeling of utter depression obsessed me through the night.'

As the Sherwood Rangers left Hursley Camp, Stanley Christopherson was rather surprised to see so many people lining the streets down to the Southampton docks; each time their column paused, people plied them with tea and cakes, much to the consternation of the military police, who had been told to ensure there was no contact between civilian and soldier. The regiment eventually was boarded on Landing Craft, Tank Flotillas 15 and 43, and on 4 June they finally moved away from the quayside only to anchor out in Southampton Water. The invasion fleet certainly impressed Christopherson. 'I tried to visualise other invasion fleets which had left England over the years,' he noted, 'and vaguely wondered whether the invader of bygone days had the same rats-in-the-stomach feeling which I had then and experienced before going into bat, or ride in a steeple chase.' Most alongside him were probably feeling a little more apprehensive than they were before a game of cricket.

The plan, as explained before they left Hursley, left him in no doubt about the scale of the operation. They would be landing on Gold Beach, Jig sector. They had also been issued with maps – some 17 million had been printed – as well as aerial photographs of extraordinarily sharp detail on to which had been marked every German position down to the last machine gun. Bunkers, minefields, wire – all were plotted. Each company of each battalion was told its objective, the distance the men had to go and what obstacles they could expect along the way. Above them would be continual aerial cover and support. Some 12,000 Allied aircraft were ready and waiting to fly. On Battle of Britain Day, in September 1940, the Luftwaffe's largest raid had amounted to 300 aircraft, which at the time had seemed like a lot. By June 1944, the Allies had turned the scales of the early years of the war on their head. Germany might still have many more infantry divisions than the US and the British, but that was because they had no alternative. The Allies did have a choice about how they used their manpower and their enormous global clout, and as a result had created the most modern and technologically advanced war machine the world had ever known.

The following day, the camp emptied and they trundled towards the Southampton docks. They headed out into the Solent, but then came news of the delay, which did nothing to improve morale. By the time they finally set sail, at around 4 p.m. on Monday, 5 June, there was still a heavy swell. Christopherson and his fellow tank commanders were now given a case of maps of their invasion area. 'I immediately set about sorting out my set of maps,' he noted, 'and endeavoured to identify from coded maps the various place names and objectives, a somewhat awkward undertaking on a flat-bottomed craft on a choppy sea.' It made him feel rather seasick.

Further west, sailing from Plymouth with Force O, was the USS *Augusta*, with its mighty guns ready for the naval bombardment. Aboard was not only General Omar Bradley, commander of First Army, but his aide, Captain Chet Hansen, who was conscious of being part of something so immense, but so unknowable too. 'This was the invasion,' he wrote in his diary. 'This is what we waited for through three years of war. The ships carry a grim, throbbing atmosphere about them, but there were no demonstrations, no cheering. We are sailing off to the continent, but no one seemed unduly excited about it.'

Through the night, the largest invasion armada the world had ever witnessed ploughed on through the rising swell and into the unknown.

CHAPTER 7

Air Power

'CONSTANT ENEMY AIR ATTACKS concentrated on bridges over the Seine, Oise, and to a certain extent over the Aisne,' noted a weekly situation report by the staff at Heeresgruppe B, 'also coastal defences in the Dunkirk–Dieppe sector and on the northern sides of the Cotentin. Attempts to cripple rail transport continue, with raids on marshalling yards . . . and on locomotives.'

Air Chief Marshal Tedder and his fellow Allied air force commanders had good reason to be pleased with the past nine weeks' efforts. Some 197,000 tons of bombs had been dropped on French targets alone – by contrast, just 18,000 tons of bombs had been dropped by the Luftwaffe on London during the entire seven-month Blitz. For all the debates that had raged over the Transportation or Oil Plans, in fact the Allied air forces had hammered a multitude of different targets, including marshalling yards, oil plants, Luftwaffe airfields, coastal radar sites, V-1 and V-2 launch and command sites, and coastal batteries, and with a combination of heavy strategic forces, tactical medium bombers and fighter aircraft. More than 200,000 individual sorties had been flown. 'Paris has been systematically cut off from long distance traffic,' ran a Luftwaffe report on 3 June, 'and the most important bridges over the Lower Seine have been destroyed one after another.' Only by the greatest of efforts, it continued, could purely military and essential traffic be kept moving. 'Large-scale strategic movement of German troops by rail is practically impossible at the present time, and must remain so while attacks are maintained at the present intensity.' There would certainly be no let-up once the invasion began. Rather, the bombardment would intensify, especially when the Allied air forces were freed from the restrictions of keeping the invasion location secret.

It had not been without cost. Some 712 French civilians were killed in March 1944 as a consequence of Allied air attacks, 5,144 in April and 9,893 in May – not as many as some had feared, but still a terrible and tragic number. From 1 April to 5 June, the Allies had lost 12,000 aircrew dead and missing, as well as some 2,000 aircraft. Without doubt, it was the strategic air forces that had borne the brunt of the losses – 763 bombers from the Eighth Air Force and 523 from RAF Bomber Command. Among those becoming increasingly fatalistic about his chances was Lieutenant Truman 'Smitty' Smith, co-pilot of a B-17 Flying Fortress in the 550th Bomb Squadron, part of the 385th Bomb Group based at Great Ashfield, to the east of the Suffolk town of Bury St Edmunds.

Smith and the rest of Lieutenant Ernest 'Moon' Baumann's crew had arrived at Great Ashfield on April Fool's Day, which they had all hoped signified nothing. The ten-man crew was, Smith reckoned, an eclectic yet homogeneous pack that he hoped would be more than the sum of its parts as they battled to stay alive over the course of their tour of duty. From Ponca City, Oklahoma, Smith had always been interested in flying and as a boy had saved up $4 for his first flying lesson. At sixteen he had even soloed, and spent the next few years hanging out at the Ponca City airfield, soaking up the atmosphere, cleaning planes and bumming rides; later, he managed to help out when the local Civil Air Patrol was formed in 1941. After graduating from high school the following year, he naturally decided it was to be the air force for him. He won a coveted place, began training and won his wings in October 1943. He had then been posted as a 'pick-up' co-pilot – on standby to join a crew – on B-25 medium bombers before being packed off to Tampa in Florida, where he joined Moon Baumann's crew. From Florida they collected a brand-new Fortress and flew it across the Atlantic. Although the B-17 had seemed uncomfortably large compared to the B-25, Smith soon adjusted, not least because of Baumann's relaxed attitude. 'In fact,' noted Smith, 'the whole crew was very casual, had a great sense of humour and was the most non-military group I had encountered in service.'

Somehow, they had survived their first ten missions, then two more to reach their thirteenth, an attack on the marshalling yards at Aachen on 20 May. Smith had been convinced it would be his last: the odds had just seemed so stacked against them. Some crews referred to the thirteenth as '12-B', but that hadn't worked for Smith. 'There was an overpowering feeling that Mission #13 was really to be my last,' he wrote. 'It had to happen sometime. That was common knowledge. That was the business we were in. We knew that up front. That's why nobody had "graduated" for over a month that I knew of.' He tried to be fatalistic – at least he had been to London and had some sex – but before that mission there had been nothing to shake the conviction that he was doomed. He had even initially refused to get up that morning. 'I'm not going,' he told the others, before reluctantly changing his mind.

All too often such premonitions ended up being self-fulfilling prophecies, but Smith and the rest of the crew made it back and by 2 June had completed another four missions in a row: a railway marshalling yard at Königsborn in west Germany, then the Leipzig aircraft plants on 29 May, an operation against V-1 sites – known as a 'NO BALL' mission – at Watten-Stracourt in France on the 30th, and then the major marshalling yards at Hamm in Germany's Ruhr Valley on the 31st. 'This was the fourth mission in a row,' Smith noted, 'and a diet that did not agree with me.' He had worked out he was getting $10.67 a mission, and that the USAAF were more than getting their money's worth. Again, though, the crew made it back, which meant he had just seven missions left to complete his combat tour. Two days later they were off on Mission Number 19, targeting more marshalling yards, this time at Équihen, just south of Boulogne in northern France, one of 805 B-17s and B-24 Liberator heavy bombers hitting the Pas de Calais, including 64 NO BALL targets as well as marshalling yards. It was utterly, overwhelmingly relentless.

In terms of numbers of missions, things were even more intense for the medium bomber crews of the Ninth Air Force, who, for the most part, were flying more frequent, shorter-range missions. The 391st Bomb Group, for example, flew two missions on 27 May and an incredible four on the 28th. Such was the urgency to hit targets before D-Day that extreme numbers of sorties were now expected.

Among those flying with the 391st was Lieutenant Joe Boylan and his crew. Twenty-two-year-old Boylan was from the town of Waterbury, Connecticut. He had had a tough childhood: money had been tight and his mother had died of cancer when he was twelve. His father, struggling to cope, had hit the bottle. Despite this, he had wisely pushed his son to get into a good high school in New York, which allowed him to sit and pass the exams for air force pilot training, something for which young Joe had long harboured high hopes. He subsequently did well and hoped to fly multi-engine fighters like the P-38, but although he had been posted to train on multi-engines, when he was finally awarded his wings and granted a commission his orders were to report to the 573rd Bomb Squadron, part of the 391st Bomb Group, now forming at MacDill Field in Tampa, Florida, where he would be flying B-26 Marauders.

Boylan had heard bad things about the Marauder, which had the reputation of being something of a 'widow maker' because of the high rate of accidents on take-off or landing. By 1944, however, most of these early issues had been resolved and it had become a highly reliable, robust medium bomber, capable of nearly 300 m.p.h. and agile. Unlike the B-17, it had a tricycle undercarriage so that pilot visibility was good on the ground, and it proved very easy to fly once properly initiated. 'Once the pilots and crew learned to fly it,' noted Boylan, 'it was hard to knock down.' Casualty rates amongst B-26 groups were so far proving incredibly low and, having reached England and heard about the losses amongst heavy bomber crews, Boylan thanked his lucky stars he was flying in the Ninth and on B-26s.

Even so, they were not immune, as Boylan had seen with his own eyes on 28 May, his first mission after a spell of leave in London. Their target that morning had been a bridge over the River Risle, which flowed roughly parallel to the Seine just south-east of Le Havre. The weather was not great, so they were guided by pathfinders and, although they had been warned to expect some flak, generally the anti-aircraft guns dotted about the French villages did not have gun-laying radar and so were pretty inaccurate. Boylan and the other six men in his crew were fully expecting it to be a 'milk run'.

The stone bridge was at the small village of Grosley-sur-Risle and most of the thirty-one Marauders attacking this target were carrying a single 1,000lb bomb. Safely crossing the coastline, they flew on, the cloud thinning so they could see patches of the east Normandy countryside. Not far from the target, flak started to rock them, peppering the sky with smoke as shell fragments clattered around them. Positioned in the high flight formation, Boylan had a bird's-eye view of the Normandy landscape and the flight below him.

'One of our planes got it!' shouted the bombardier from the nose, Lieutenant Billy Rose.

'Who?' Boylan asked.

Rose wasn't certain, but the aircraft had taken a direct hit and was plummeting, an engine on fire. Then the starboard wing tore off. Rose counted the parachutes. 'There's one chute! There's another one!'

They flew on, and, directed by the flares of the pathfinder, spotted the bridge and hit it as planned. There had been no flak at all over the target.

Only once safely back at their base at Matching Green, near Harlow in Essex, did they learn that the downed aircraft had been Lieutenant Bob Goodson's plane. Boylan was quite choked up when he heard the news. The co-pilot, Bob Clark, and the bombardier, Ross Taylor, were both good pals of his and had been his companions during their leave in London just a few days earlier.

Another vital target was the German radar stations. A raft of intelligence sources, including specialist organizations such as the Noise Investigation Bureau and Telecommunications Research Establishment, had collaborated to create a clear picture of ninety-two radar installations between Calais and Cherbourg. Some were to be jammed, while the long-range radars would be bombed. The campaign against them had started on 10 May, four years to the day after the Germans had launched their attack on the West. For the most part, these air attacks were to be carried out not by the bomber forces but instead by ground-attack single-engine aircraft armed with bombs, cannons and also rockets, as it was felt that the best way to knock out radar installations was to strike obliquely from a low level – and this could only be done with forward-firing missiles.

The best-suited Allied machine for such a task was the Hawker Typhoon, a brute of an aircraft that could fly at over 400 m.p.h. and was armed to the teeth with four 20mm cannons, as well as being able to carry two 500lb bombs; it could also be equipped with four RP-3 air-to-ground rockets under each wing. It had a wingspan of over 41 feet, a Napier Sabre 24-piston, 2,200 h.p. engine and a massive bulbous and menacing air intake under the engine cowling that somehow made it look like an angry Spanish bull about to charge. The Hawker Typhoon, originally designed to replace the Hurricane, looked like exactly what it was: a big, mean, incredibly fast and powerful ground-attack fighter.

There were eighteen squadrons of Typhoons in Coningham's Second Tactical Air Force, among them 609 Squadron of 123 Wing. This had been a pre-war auxiliary squadron based in the West Riding of Yorkshire – the 'weekend fliers', as they were known – and had been mostly young, well-to-do gentlemen, but since the start of the war they had evolved into a highly professional, multinational outfit. The first squadron to score one hundred victories in the Battle of Britain, even then they had attracted Americans, Poles and others, and by 1944 were a magnet for Belgian pilots too. They were also home to three New Zealanders, three Canadians, one Argentinian, and to Flight Sergeant Klaus 'Ken' Adam, a German Jew from Berlin who had fled Germany with his family in 1934.

They had escaped in the nick of time. Adam's father had run an upmarket sports store in the capital and had been a decorated cavalry officer in the First World War. Refusing to accept the threat of the Nazis, Herr Adam had been devastated when he was arrested in 1933. Through contacts, he was released forty-eight hours later, but his eldest son, Peter, already studying in Paris, had urged the family to leave. 'Living outside Germany,' said Adam, 'where the press was hostile to the Nazis, he could see what was happening.'

The children were sent ahead to Britain, then their parents followed. Klaus went first to St Paul's School – Montgomery's old *alma mater* – and then to University College, London, to study architecture. By this time he had worked hard to embrace England and Englishness, and despite his accent had changed his name from Klaus to Ken. He was also very keen to do his bit once war arrived and repeatedly tried to join the RAF. Eventually accepted in late 1941, he trained in Canada and was finally posted to 609 Squadron in October 1943. Almost inevitably, no one called him Ken; in the squadron, he was always known as 'Heinie'. Despite the nickname, he was made to feel at home immediately and was struck by the camaraderie and team spirit that pervaded the squadron. New pilots were welcomed and carefully nurtured until their fighting skills were sufficiently honed.

By the spring of 1944, Adam had become a fully established part of the 609 team. The squadron had been operating independently in a fighter role, but at the end of February they had begun retraining as a rocket-firing unit. They were then attached to Second Tactical Air Force and assigned to 123 Wing, part of 84 Group. Now based at Thorney Island, near Portsmouth, they had become primarily aerial artillery, given the task of carrying out regular ground-attack 'shows' on targets in northern France. Early May had begun with a flurry of missions: an attack on a road bridge near Cherbourg on the 2nd; the following day, nearly a hundred rockets were fired by the squadron at railway sheds near Amiens. On 7 May targets included a shipping canal and another bridge.

Four days later – 11 May – they began their part in neutralizing the enemy radar, attacking the station at Fécamp, near Le Havre. It was a big operation and their attack was preceded not only by American bombers, but by other Typhoon squadrons as well. 'We were the last in,' said Adam. 'The German flak was trained on us by the time our wave of Typhoons came in.' Moreover, they had been ordered to attack from inland and out to sea. The first four of 609's planes attacked in line astern, one behind the other; two were promptly shot down and a third badly hit. Flying behind, Adam watched in horror as Flight Lieutenant Wood's Typhoon burst into flames, hit Flight Sergeant Keith Adams's Typhoon, ripping 2 foot 6 inches from the latter's port wing, and then plunged to the ground. Realizing what sitting targets they were, Adam immediately fell out of the line-astern formation and made his attack from a different angle. This decision probably saved his life. 'Junior Soesman hit and bailed out but didn't get into dinghy,' Adam noted in his logbook. 'Woody was also hit. Caught fire, collided with Adams and crashed into houses, exploding. Damned tough luck.' To lose three aircraft – and two pilots – out of eight was, as Adam pointed out, 'a big hit'.

Twelve days later, they were hitting the Normandy coast and three radar stations: at Pointe de la Percée; Distelfink, the largest radar base along the Normandy coast at Douvres; and also at Saint-Valéry, north of Le Havre. The next day it was another radar station at Cap de la Hague, on the north-west tip of the Cotentin Peninsula. Just four, Adam included, hit that one. 'Target well pranged,' was the comment in the squadron records book.

The Typhoons were certainly causing considerable damage, but by 3 June it was agreed that the strategic air forces should hammer the key installations as well. Later that day, and again on 4 and 5 June, heavy bombers pummelled radar sites on the northern French coast, including Distelfink. By D-Day, 76 out of 92 radar stations along the coast had been put out of action, including all those containing the particularly accurate Mammut and Wassermann radars. Along the planned invasion front not a single radar station was still working. With the addition of jamming measures, the entire German radar chain along the Channel coast was operating at just 5 per cent effectiveness. Allied air power and radio technology had turned out many of Germany's defensive lights.

Conflicting intelligence and interpretations dogged the defenders in these final days before the invasion. The relentless bombing, strafing and drone of overhead aero-engines took their toll, while the bad weather prevented them building much of a clear picture of Allied intentions. German weather forecasters had very few weather stations out in the west, so, although they had plenty to draw from all along the Atlantic coast and right up into the Arctic Circle, they had even fewer reports from the Atlantic than the Allies. They had picked up the low front sweeping across Britain and heading towards the Continent, though, and general unsettled weather that looked to be sweeping in that first full week of June. General Marcks had also repeatedly studied previous Allied invasions and realized that the confluence of moon and tides was paramount. He now reckoned the next time the moon and tides were suitable for an invasion was around 20 June. According to Marcks the weather outlook, the rising winds, the moon and the tides all suggested any invasion was at least a fortnight away.

Largely for this reason, Feldmarschall Erwin Rommel had felt able to leave La Roche-Guyon on Sunday, 4 June and head to the Berghof to see Hitler in person, to ask that two more panzer divisions be sent to France and to implore, one further time, that he be given tactical control of the panzer divisions. He still believed the Allies could be halted, but he also remained utterly convinced that it could happen only if the panzer divisions were congregated close to the front in the Normandy–Pas de Calais area, although his hunch remained that the invasion would come in Fifteenth Army's sector, from the Seine estuary up to the Pas de Calais and the Belgian and Dutch coasts. Without his direct control – without the freedom to manoeuvre the panzers with speed and decisiveness – he feared all would soon be lost. And there was another reason for going now: en route to the Berghof lay his own family home at Herrlingen, near Ulm, and Tuesday, 6 June would be his beloved wife Lucie's fiftieth birthday. He had even gone to Paris the previous day to buy her a pair of new shoes.

Elsewhere, however, different intelligence sources were picking up different signals. On 1 June, a French Maquis commander had been caught by men of the 352. Division and during his interrogation had told them the invasion would be coming any day. No member of the Résistance knew exactly when it would be, but they had been picking up the BBC's alerts. For General Kraiss, this was enough to warrant putting the division on full alert, but this being 1944 and not 1940, he could not do so without higher authority. Nor could General Marcks, who agreed with Kraiss that it would be the most sensible course of action. Their request, however, was turned down. Kraiss was able to get around this because of the war games that had been scheduled for that week; he would put his division on full alert, but if questioned by his superiors would tell them they were carrying out practice operations as part of the week's exercises. As a result, on Monday, 5 June, the 352. Division was the only one in all Normandy on full alert.

The truth was, though, that none of the Germans really knew Allied intentions. Thanks to a German spy in Turkey, Elyesa Bazna, or 'Cicero', who was working as a valet to the British ambassador in Ankara, they knew the invasion code name was OVERLORD, but that didn't count for very much. On 27 May, Hitler confidently told the Japanese ambassador that the Allies had completed their preparations. After diversionary operations in Norway, Denmark, south-west France and on the French Mediterranean, they would establish a bridgehead in Normandy, or possibly Brittany, and then would launch the real second front across the Pas de Calais. This, of course, was just waffle. Hitler was hedging his bets and displaying his woeful ignorance of military planning and operations. After all, how could the Allies conceivably mount all these amphibious operations?

On the afternoon of Monday, 5 June, OB West released its latest intelligence summary, suggesting the most likely place for invasion was somewhere between the Scheldt Estuary in Holland and Normandy. '*Where* within this entire sector the enemy will attempt a landing is still obscure,' ran the report. 'As yet,' it concluded, 'there is no immediate prospect of the invasion.'

Certainly at La Roche-Guyon no one was braced for imminent invasion. In Rommel's absence, General Hans Speidel was in charge. Admiral Ruge had spent the day driving through the rain to see Marinegruppe West and give them a dressing down. The 2nd Minesweeper Flotilla had been in Brittany, had been sent to Le Havre and en route had been heavily attacked by Allied air forces and all but one had been lost. Their movement was, as far as Ruge was concerned, inexplicable, as there were already plenty of S-boats – very fast torpedo boats – as well as motor minesweepers, both of which were small vessels with low silhouettes. Also, because these were made of wood they were less susceptible to British radar.

Having given them what for, Ruge was back at La Roche-Guyon for dinner, which he found a highly convivial affair. Among others, Speidel had invited his brother-in-law, Dr Horst, and the writer Ernst Jünger.

What Ruge didn't know was that all were conspirators, plotting against both Hitler and the regime. Speidel was under specific instructions to try to recruit Rommel, although so far this had not gone well. Reinvigorated, Rommel was somewhat in thrall to the Führer once more and full of fight; on 13 May, he had even asked Hitler to begin the V-1 flying bomb campaign against Britain early in an effort to disrupt Allied invasion plans. The forthcoming battle was one he still had every intention of winning.

In fact, Jünger had even drafted a peace proclamation, which would be put into mass circulation the moment the Hitler regime was eliminated. It declared that they believed in a united and Christian Europe in which notions of democracy, tolerance and social justice would be thrust to the forefront. However, such things were not discussed at the dinner table, although there was, as always when Rommel was not there, plenty of badinage about 'the arsehole from the Berghof'. Ruge thought the discussions were 'highly animated'. Much wine was drunk.

Unbeknown to them, the invasion armada was already sailing across the Channel and by the time the party broke up after midnight, the first of nearly 25,000 Allied airborne troops were poised to land on French soil.

The hour had come. It was Tuesday, 6 June 1944. D-Day.

Landing craft of the US 18th Infantry and
115th Infantry approaching Omaha Beach.

PART II

Invasion

CHAPTER 8

D-Day Minus One

O N FRIDAY, 2 JUNE, Lieutenant-Colonel Mark Alexander wrote to his parents in Lawrence, Kansas, for what he knew might well be the last time. At thirty-two, he was older than most of the men he was serving alongside, and married too, and both his age and his position as executive officer of the 505th Parachute Infantry Regiment allowed him to see a somewhat bigger picture than most of the young men under his command. He also had experience behind him, including combat jumps into Sicily and southern Italy and the bitter and tough fighting that had followed.

'Well, here it is,' he wrote, 'the day before we take off again and I'm about to jump into the roughest one of the lot. We paratroopers are going in ahead of everyone else as usual, to try and soften it up a bit for the beachheads. And I'd much rather be going in this way than coming in with the amphibious forces. Yes, I still feel pretty lucky and shall of course take very good care.' At the bottom he signed, 'Remember that I love you always, your son, Mark.'

An athletic and artistic young man from the Midwest, Alexander had left high school and then travelled around America, bumming rides and doing a number of different jobs, before, with a bit of money in his pocket, he had enrolled at the University of Kansas and undertaken a degree in art, which he gained in 1940. Intending to pursue a masters, once war began he instead joined the local National Guard in Lawrence. Encouraged to sit exams for officer training, Alexander passed with flying colours, becoming 2nd lieutenant on 1 January 1941 and a platoon commander in the 35th Infantry Division. As he was older than most, smart and with a worldliness the majority of his fellows lacked, Alexander soon stood out. He had learned enough on his travels around America about what made good and bad leadership – lessons he swiftly applied to being an infantry officer. He was also physically fit, a decent marksman from his childhood days with a .22 rifle, confident and able to lead by example.

By the spring of 1942, he had been promoted captain and, after a whirlwind romance, had married an Irish nurse called Mary Collins, although since their hurried wedding there had been little time to spend together. Alexander had decided to volunteer for the airborne branch; he wanted to push himself and certainly did so during the rigorous four-week jump-school course. With five completed jumps and the course behind him, he was posted first to the 504th Parachute Infantry Regiment and then to the newly formed 505th PIR. Almost a year after first heading off to jump school, he was heading to North Africa. In July 1943, by then commanding the 2nd Battalion of the 505th, he jumped into Sicily.

The 505th PIR had been pulled out of Italy that November, sailed to Northern Ireland and had been training for OVERLORD ever since. Alexander, now decorated with a British Distinguished Service Cross as well as a Silver Star for actions in Italy, was made executive officer – deputy commander – of the 505th, but would be dropping into Normandy as a fighting man, just like the rest of the US Airborne Forces. Also jumping was the divisional commander, Major-General Matthew Ridgway. 'I want to be there on the ground right from the start,' he told Alexander. 'And I want you to pick a plane for me where I'll have the best chance of landing on the drop zone.' It was understandable that Ridgway had chosen the 505th – they were the only regiment in the two airborne divisions to have combat jump experience. For the general, Alexander selected a C-47 taking men from the 505th's Headquarters Company, while he opted to go with an experienced jump master and a plane that would be on the right side of the flying formation; he intended to stand by the door and watch for the beacons on the ground marked out by the pathfinders, sent in thirty minutes ahead and specially trained to set up configurations of giant letters in lights and to operate Eureka homing beacons.

Now, on the evening of Monday, 5 June, Alexander was preparing to jump into France. Orders were that every paratrooper was to jump – not one of them was to be brought back to England. It didn't matter how well trained or experienced one might be; at this stage each paratrooper, from private to general, was placing his life in the hands of the aircrew delivering them to their intended drop zone – DZ – and trusting in Lady Luck.

At least it seemed likely they would be flying over the Cotentin with the benefit of tactical surprise. 'There has been no intelligence during the last week,' concluded the Joint Intelligence Committee on Saturday, 3 June, 'to suggest that the enemy has accurately assessed the area in which our main assault is to be made.' That was a huge relief, but there had been potentially catastrophic intelligence breaches on the 5th, first when an Associated Press report announced that the invasion was under way and then when a fighter pilot from the Eighth looked down on the huge invasion fleet and shared his amazement over his radio. Furthermore, the latest intelligence picture about German strength in Normandy was sobering; unquestionably, the month's postponement from early May had cost the Allies. Some 59 German divisions were in the West, including 10 panzer and panzer-grenadier, with a possible further 13 divisions arriving within two months. These were of varying sizes; infantry divisions by this stage of the war were only around 12,000 men full strength, while the panzer divisions were more like 20,000. Immediately facing the invasion, the Joint Intelligence Committee predicted, were 7 divisions, which might well rise to 10 by the end of D-Day. By D plus 2, that figure could well be 16 or 17 and by D plus 8 as many as 24. The moment the first Allied troops landed, the race would begin to see which side could build up sufficient strength and weight of arms first. That was what it boiled down to: which side could build up weight of arms quickest in the Normandy coastal bridgehead. Shipping vast armies methodically across the sea was one thing; shipping them very quickly was quite another.

The first troops in, though, had no need of shipping. They would be airborne forces, dropped with the specific task of securing the all-important flanks and so enabling the Allies to isolate the battle zone immediately to their front. Their role could not have been more important and it was quite absurd that Leigh-Mallory should have even considered cancelling them, no matter the risk; that he had implored first Bradley then Eisenhower to do so demonstrated his lack of understanding about how OVERLORD was planned and expected to work. Those flanks had to be protected if the seaborne landings were going to have a realistic hope of success. At the western end of the invasion front, that meant severing the vital arteries that led to Cherbourg and protecting the Utah landings, and in the east, destroying the crucial bridges over the River Dives and securing intact those crossing the Orne and Caen Canal.

Ever since 10 May 1940, when the Germans had dropped glider-borne troops on to the Belgian fort of Eben Emael and paratroopers had captured key bridges, both Britain and America had become rather dazzled by the potential of airborne troops. They had, however, absorbed all the benefits but filtered out – or not properly analysed – the many drawbacks of such operations. For example, in May 1940, when the Germans had launched their assault in the West using large numbers of airborne troops, some 353 aircraft had been destroyed, most of them transports; it was the worst single day of losses in the air for the Luftwaffe in the war to date. The airborne operation at Dombås in Norway in April 1940 had been a spectacular failure, as was their airborne drop on The Hague the following month; they captured only two of three bridges over the Albert Canal in Belgium; and on Crete secured only one of three objectives and over half their number were slaughtered. Where they had proved more successful was that those who survived their jump fought superbly on the ground.

Churchill had been among the first to insist the British Army create an airborne arm of 5,000 men. One or two brigades, however, had soon ballooned. In October 1941 the War Office decided to create the 1st Airborne Division, followed by a second division in the spring of 1943. The SAS also grew quickly in 1943, as did a British-funded Independent Polish Brigade. A similar story was unfolding in the United States: a paratroop test platoon formed in June 1940 evolved into the 501st Parachute Infantry Unit. A parachute school was established at Fort Benning and then in March 1942 the 82nd Airborne Division was activated, swiftly followed by the 101st in August the same year. Two more divisions were then created: the 11th and 17th in May 1943. Glider troops were added, requiring yet more special equipment and further training, and absorbing yet more assets.

There had been no shortage of applicants, and from the outset paratroopers, especially, had been perceived as elite, and very much special forces. They were expected to train harder and be physically fitter than most other units, and, crucially, they were all volunteers and were consequently more motivated. The large majority of conscripted troops – and both armies were around 75 per cent conscripts – did not want to fight in the war, would never have entered the military were it not for the global conflict now raging, and simply hoped to keep their heads down and get through it. Most also wanted to be led and told what to do. In theory, the Americans still had capital punishment for desertion, though there was no appetite for enacting it, while the British had abolished it altogether. Unlike the Germans, Allied servicemen were not going to be shot for desertion. It was why maintaining morale was so important: there was nothing, really, to stop them throwing down their weapons and walking away. The best troops were those that could think on their feet and, crucially, use their initiative. This was linked to motivation, and the combination of motivation, a desire to be the best, and physical fitness made the airborne troops stand out.

Not quite the same thought had been devoted to how these excellent troops might be delivered to the battlefield, or in what format and conditions. The British had no specifically designed troop-carrying aircraft, nor did they attempt to create one. Instead, bombers were refitted with hatches built into their bellies. Bombers, however, were designed to carry bombs, not troops. Wing spars, a lack of seats and badly positioned jump hatches all mitigated against using them for dropping paratroopers. Instead, Britain turned to the United States, which was using slightly adapted Douglas DC3s. These aircraft would be the means of dropping most Allied paratroopers, American and British. The US military classified them as C-47s while the British called them Dakotas, but they had not been given self-sealing fuel tanks, something that massively reduced the chances of fire spreading or an aircraft blowing up and had become standard on most other combat aircraft; nor had they been given defensive guns or armour plating. By June 1944, none of the 1,176 transport aircraft earmarked for the American airborne drop had been updated. Each one remained as vulnerable as ever, and their aircrew knew it. Rumours circulated that they were considered expendable and that high casualties were assured. It did nothing for the already fragile morale amongst the transport wings.

Training was intense for the transport crews once they reached Britain – collectively, they logged some 30,000 hours in the lead-up to D-Day. Allocations were made early on, so the divisions could train together with the troops they would be carrying, but with the exception of Exercise EAGLE, the last big joint training exercise in May, the 101st Airborne, for example, carried out no further drops after 18 April. Although the brief history of airborne operations clearly showed the drop was the most problematic part, for the next seven weeks General Maxwell Taylor felt his men were better served carrying out further training on the ground.

In fact, previous Allied airborne operations had demonstrated the difficulties of such missions with vivid clarity. Drops in north-west Africa had been an utter fiasco, and not much better on Sicily, where fewer than one in six American paratroopers had landed close to the drop zone and some as far away as 65 miles. A subsequent airlift had been badly shot up by the Allies' own naval guns. British glider troops had also been spread to the winds over Sicily, where just four out of 144 had landed in the correct DZ. Sixty-nine had landed in the sea.

Over North Africa and again over Sicily, the troops that landed had fought brilliantly. The problems had all lain with the airlift – the delivery to the battlefield. Since Sicily, both the Americans and British had given much further thought to this issue. General Ridgway had delivered a report in autumn 1943 in which he outlined his own views. 'Airborne troops,' he had written, 'are weapons of opportunity.' In this he was correct, but he then went on to insist it was no use using such troops piecemeal; instead they should be sent into the fray en masse – that is, in divisions. Again, he had a point, but still he was focusing more on what airborne troops might achieve once on the ground rather than how they might get there in the first place. The more paratroopers dropped, the more transports needed, but the number, status and quality of those had not improved very much since the fiascos in the Mediterranean.

This was the problem in a nutshell: while American airborne troops were among the best in the US Army, they were being delivered to the battle zone by the least well trained aircrew. Few in the USAAF aspired to become pilots or navigators on transport aircraft, so it was those of lower ability and charisma who tended to be posted to them. The conundrum had, if anything, been made worse when, late the previous year, General George Marshall, the US chief of staff of the army, and General Hap Arnold had together encouraged a greater use of airborne troops for OVERLORD and so had made available considerably more transport aircraft. Now ready and waiting in England were three wings and fourteen transport groups – some 1,176 in all. It was a mighty fleet, except it had been achieved only by hurrying pilots and, especially, navigators through their training. As Sicily had shown, the combination of inadequate training and unexpected winds was not conducive to successful airborne operations. Now, even if the meteorologists got lucky and the small ridge of high pressure did come into play, there were still going to be some strong gusts – stronger than they had been for the invasion of Sicily the previous July.

At least, though, the new American plan, enforced by the sudden arrival of Germany's 91. Division and Fallschirmjäger-Regiment 6 into the area, was a better one, in which the two US divisions – the 82nd and 101st Airborne – would be more obviously mutually supporting. It could, however, have possibly been even better, because the final plan had settled for two regiments of the 101st to protect the four exits from Utah Beach and just one – of three battalions – to be dropped further south towards Carentan. For the planned link-up between the invasion troops at Utah and those at Omaha Beach, the town of Carentan, with its bridges and locks over the canal and the River Douve, was a key target. This was the area in which Fallschirmjäger-Regiment 6, unquestionably the best-trained and -led enemy infantry in Normandy, were based. With two regiments of the 82nd now scheduled to be dropped around Sainte-Mère-Église – around 2,600 men – there would be potentially twelve paratroop battalions in an area that, until the switch of plans, had been allocated to just six.

While the new plan was unquestionably a more sensible one, regardless of German reinforcements, it seemed the planners had become so fixated with the protection of Utah that they had taken their eye off Carentan. The gap between Omaha and Utah, within which were the significant waterways of Carentan, was around 20 miles, by some margin the biggest gap between the five invasion beaches – a gap into which a wedge of enemy troops might well be driven and at a time when expanding and linking the bridgehead as quickly as possible was vital. There was no other possible landing beach in between, but dropping a second regiment of the 101st towards Carentan might have been a more judicious option. Certainly they could have been spared from Utah with the configuration as planned.

The British plan was no less demanding. Although using just one division rather than two, they were to blow up bridges across the Dives at four separate places, destroy a potentially dangerous coastal battery at Merville, and also secure intact vital bridges across the Caen Canal and River Orne. It was asking a lot, but at least with a smaller airlift the transport crew were not being suddenly and dramatically increased in size and so had more time to train.

The operation to capture the two bridges intact had been given to the 2nd Battalion of the Oxfordshire and Buckinghamshire Light Infantry, who, despite their heritage as a local regiment from the provincial shires of England, had been absorbed into the 6th Airlanding Brigade of the 6th Airborne Division along with the 12th Devons and 1st Royal Ulster Rifles. Major-General Richard 'Windy' Gale, the division commander, gave his senior brigade commander, Brigadier James Hill, the task of drawing up the initial plan. Still only thirty-two at the time, the tall, lean-faced Hill quickly proposed the bridges over the Caen Canal and River Orne be captured by glider troops, reasoning that the Germans would be bound to have prepared them for demolition and that the only way to take them intact, before the enemy destroyed them, was if they could arrive like a bolt from the blue. They would have one chance to capture them in the brief moment of indecision by the enemy and that, Hill reckoned, could be achieved only by glider-borne troops arriving accurately and en masse, rather than paratroopers, who by their very nature would land over a wider area. Gale agreed completely and allocated two lots of three gliders for each bridge. These would spearhead the entire invasion and, because speed and surprise would be so important, would have to arrive silently and ahead of the rest of the airborne drop.

Each Horsa glider could carry twenty-eight men, of whom twenty-three would be airborne infantry and five engineers; this meant just one company and two extra platoons from 6th Airlanding Brigade would be needed to spearhead the invasion and the assault on the bridges. D Company, the Ox and Bucks, had particularly impressed during a key training exercise at the end of March and so had been given this job, along with two platoons from B Company. Everyone, from the company commander Major John Howard, to the ordinary rank and file, were keenly aware that this was both a considerable honour and also a hugely important but high-risk task.

One of those getting ready for the glider assault that night was Denis Edwards, a month short of his twentieth birthday and attached to 25 Platoon, D Company, scheduled to be the first glider to touch down at the swing bridge across the Caen Canal, now code-named 'PEGASUS'. Edwards had been brought up by very well-to-do and eccentric parents. His father had had a business building airfields, but had lost much of his money during the Crash and so, from once employing a chauffeur and servants, the family had become much reduced in circumstance. It hadn't bothered Edwards much; he was a phlegmatic soul who tended to take life's obstacles in his stride, and by the age of sixteen he was working in stables near his home in Kent. After leaving school he began a milk round for the Co-op Dairy and, although a member of his local Home Guard, only after a horse had bolted and injured itself on his watch had he joined the army; he had been too mortified to face his employers at the dairy.

Having been posted to the 70th (Young Soldiers) Battalion of the Ox and Bucks, he responded to a notice for volunteers for the 2nd Battalion, who were being retrained as glider-borne troops. He was accepted into D Company under Major Howard, a former Oxford City policeman, who, like Mark Alexander, had worked his way up the ranks from being a private. 'In D Company we had the hardest of taskmasters,' wrote Edwards. 'His company had to be the best at everything, be it sport, marches, field exercises or physical endurance training.' Training had been rigorous, including exercises and tests in which troops were expected to think on their feet and use their initiative. 'Apart from flying training,' noted Edwards, 'we were continuously undergoing every other type of training for the skills that we should need when, eventually, we had to face a real enemy.' That included numerous training assaults on bridges, so that by the time they were posted from Bulford Camp to a mysterious airfield location in southern England on 4 June, Edwards felt confident in their skills and abilities.

They were now at Tarrant Rushton Airfield near Blandford in Dorset, although Edwards never learned the name. Howard had been briefed on the invasion in early May, but now the rest of his men were finally let in on the secret. The plan, as drawn up by Howard, was studied in minute detail, with each glider platoon and each seven-man section considering and analyzing their given tasks. Detailed photographs were pored over and all key features memorized. A large-scale model had also been built, with every building, tree and bush accurately recorded. Everything had to run like clockwork.

The night of the 4th, Edwards struggled to sleep. He and his mates all thought they were being sent on a suicide mission: 180 men were going to crash-land into enemy territory without any heavy weapons, capture two bridges and then, crucially, hold on to them until reinforcements arrived, first from the airborne drop and then Commandos, who, they were told, would arrive by sea some 5 miles away and work their way towards them. Edwards thought the prospect of being able to hold the bridges, even if they took them intact, was little more than a pipe-dream. 'I smoked a great many cigarettes on the night after the first briefing,' he wrote, 'just about the longest night I can ever remember.'

Monday, 5 June passed slowly. Latest intelligence suggested 21. Panzer- and 12. SS-Panzer-Divisions were now in the area around Caen. Just their bloody luck, Edwards and his pals moaned to one another. Weapons were checked and re-checked. A film was shown, then they were given a last pint of beer. Finally, they were told to get dressed. Fully laden, with extra bandoliers of ammunition and grenades, each man averaged 231 lb; Edwards thought they all looked like pack mules. At 2200 – 10 p.m. – they were ordered to emplane and clambered aboard the waiting gliders. The men were joking and singing, but Edwards was conscious of feeling increasingly scared. Both Major Howard and Lieutenant Hubert 'Den' Brotheridge, his platoon commander, were aboard the lead glider. Their pilot was Jim Wallwork, a Sicily veteran and now highly trained for the role he had been given; British glider pilots were also fighting men and considered themselves elite troops. At four minutes to eleven the roar of engines from their Halifax bomber tow-planes increased as the throttles were opened prior to take off. 'My muscles tightened,' noted Edwards, 'a cold shiver ran up my spine, I went hot and cold, and sang all the louder to stop my teeth from chattering.' Suddenly there was a jerk as the tow-rope tightened and they began to roll forward. 'You've had it chum,' Edwards told himself. 'It's no use worrying any more.' And after that, as they left English soil and rose up into the sky, he began to feel a bit better.

While the airborne troops were waiting to load up on to their transport planes, the invasion fleet was stuck in harbour and on the waters off the south coast of England. At anchor off the Isle of Wight was HMCS *Algonquin*, a Royal Canadian Navy destroyer that was part of the 25th Flotilla attached to Force J, which, as the letter indicated, was to support the Canadian landings at Juno Beach. The Canadians had shown extraordinary commitment to the war and had so far punched massively above their weight. Every serviceman was a volunteer. The 1st Canadian Division had reached Britain in 1940 and Canadian divisions were fighting in Italy, as well as an entire army readying for battle on the Continent. RAF Bomber Command had an entire group – 6 Group – that was Canadian and the rest of the RAF was sprinkled with Canadian fighter wings and Canadian pilots, aircrew and ground crew. The RCN, for its part, had played a vital role in the all-important Battle of the Atlantic. Back in 1939 it had been tiny, but it had grown exponentially, battling swiftly, taking stiff lessons on the chin and turning itself into an exceptionally successful navy that had contributed to what was arguably the most crucial campaign of the entire conflict – for in this war of supplies, the Atlantic was the most important thoroughfare of them all.

First Lieutenant Latham 'Yogi' Jenson was typical of the tough, committed Canadians who were very much the backbone of the RCN. Born in Calgary in 1921, he had nursed a boyhood desire to escape the vast, flat, dusty prairies of central Canada and head to sea. At seventeen, he had left home and joined the navy as an officer cadet, then had later been posted to Britain to train with the Royal Navy. He had served on the mighty HMS *Renown*, hunting for the *Graf Spee*, and had fought in the naval Battle of Norway. Later, he had been posted to the famous British heavy cruiser HMS *Hood*, leaving the ship in 1941, only a couple of weeks before it had been sunk, to return to the Canadian Navy. His next ship was sunk from under him and he was lucky to be among the few who were rescued from the bitter grey waters of the Atlantic. Now he was executive officer – second-in-command – on *Algonquin*, having only just turned twenty-three.

All these adventures Jenson had taken in his stride. He was a phlegmatic fellow – as well as a talented artist – and believed strongly that a happy ship was a successful ship. So too did the skipper, Lieutenant Commander Desmond 'Debby' Piers, DSC. The entire flotilla had been based at Scapa Flow in the Orkney islands, but had moved south ready for the invasion on 25 May. Up until then they had been training intensively – up to fifteen hours a day – and covering every conceivable type of gunnery practice; standards were kept very high. There had also been plenty of opportunity for fun: they had beard-growing competitions, music was played out loud across the ship whenever possible, games were organized, including bingo and poker nights and wrestling competitions. 'In my opinion,' noted Jenson, 'there was no destroyer in our navy that was as contented and efficient as *Algonquin*.'

At 3 p.m. on Monday, 5 June, the bo'sun's mate blew the whistle for all hands to fall in aft of the torpedo tubes to hear a message from the captain. 'I have just been informed that tomorrow, June 6,' Piers told them, 'is D-Day, and we have been chosen to be in the spearhead of the invasion.' He then went on to tell them that they had also been picked to be the point of the spear. 'A spear sometimes gets blunted,' he continued. 'If our ship gets hit near the shore, we will run the ship right up on the shore and keep firing our guns, until the last shell is gone.' It was fighting talk and, after the low groans about the cancelled shore leave that night, it seemed to lift the pride and spirits of them all, no matter the potential danger.

Later, Jenson and Piers were walking the deck when they spotted half a dozen rats scurry across it and jump into the sea. Neither man said a word, but it was hardly the kind of omen either wished to see. A few hours later, after they had had supper, they weighed anchor and set sail for Normandy.

CHAPTER 9

D-Day: The First Hours

At 9.15 p.m. on 5 June, Robert Leblanc and five of his most trusted lieutenants in the Maquis Surcouf were once again gathered around their radio in a back room of the Château de la Bivellerie in Pont-Audemer. Earlier that evening they had heard a message, 'the time of fights will come', their pre-arranged code to stand by for further instruction. They had the volume low and it was the turn of René, the head of their group's 2nd Section, to listen. He was bent over, his ear glued to the radio set.

'Here we go!' he exclaimed suddenly. 'They said, "the dice are on the mat".'

Leblanc felt his heart almost leap. Was that it? Their message was supposed to be 'the dice are *thrown* on the mat'. Was this correct? Or not the message at all? Or a trick? For some minutes they argued the matter. There were, however, others in the group listening to other radios and at 10 p.m. another of their number, Beslier, turned up, short of breath and sweating. He too had heard the message and also the next one, which was to signal the landings beginning: *Il fait chaud en Suez* – 'It is hot in Suez'. Leblanc was still stricken by doubt – could this really be the moment they had all been waiting for? – when Madame Lefèvre hurried in and confirmed that she, too, had heard both messages.

'This time, no more hesitation,' noted Leblanc in his diary. 'The hour we've been waiting so long for, the hour my lads have been expecting for fifteen months has come: the landings!!' He looked around and could see the joy in the eyes of his men, then ordered them to pack their belongings and equipment quickly. Leblanc issued other orders to his men.

Arazo was to pick up Paul, who was at the village of Routot. Serpent and Bezo were to collect the Citroën they had taken after killing Violette Morris from its hideaway on a nearby farm and bring it to La Pilvédière, their prepared headquarters in the grounds of the Château de Launay a few miles away, where a supply drop was due later that night. Normally, they were safer if they kept well spread out, but now was the time for action and Leblanc needed his men gathered around him. Alert messages were also sent out – all the sector commanders needed to be told within a maximum of two hours that the time had come and that they should get their men ready. Another man, Prosper, was to requisition carts and vans, while Roger was to collect a truck and also call at the grocer, Bosquet, to pick up supplies of food.

This all took a couple of hours, as Leblanc had anticipated, but by midnight they were almost ready. Beslier had cut the telephone lines as ordered, and now it was time to attack the local Feldgendarmerie, the Wehrmacht occupation police force. 'I make the most of the minutes before the lorries arrive,' scribbled Leblanc, 'to go and say goodbye to my wife. I kiss my kids.' He was worried about his young daughter, Claudine, who had a fever, but duty called. That night he had to go into battle and fight for France.

Meanwhile, the gliders carrying the men of the 2nd Battalion Ox and Bucks were approaching the Normandy coast at around 6,000 feet. It was just a few minutes past midnight, British double summertime. In the cockpit of the first glider, Chalk 91, pilot Jim Wallwork and co-pilot John Ainsworth were getting ready.

'Two minutes from cast-off,' Wallwork said to Ainsworth, then from the Halifax tug that was towing them he was given details of wind speed, height and their heading.

'Prepare for cast-off!' he called back to the men behind him. Immediately, Major Howard told the men to stop talking and singing, then came a 'twang' and a slight jolt as the tow-rope was cast off, followed by almost complete silence as they went into a steep descent. Once the glider began to level out at about 1,000 feet, Lieutenant Den Brotheridge, the platoon commander sitting next to Howard, undid his safety belt, handed his equipment to the major and leaned carefully forward to open the door, which lifted up into the roof. Another of the men did the same at the back. As the air came whistling through the wooden Horsa, the men could look out and see the French landscape passing beneath them, all of it looking reassuringly familiar. The cool air was suffused with the sweet smell of the nighttime countryside and a streak of silver below told them they were on course.

A sharp right turn, then a second, and Wallwork called out, 'Link arms!' Crossing their arms and gripping the hands of their neighbours, the men braced themselves. This was it. Heart-stopping moments, but then Denis Edwards felt a slight bump, a small jerk, then a much heavier crunch and the glider bounced lightly, landed again, bumped over the rough surface and sped forward, scraping and grinding, filling the darkness with sparks as it lost its right wheel. A loud ripping sound and Edwards felt as though his body was being sent in several directions at once. His vision greyed and when it cleared he found the glider had stopped. There was momentary silence. It was sixteen minutes past midnight. For an instant he wondered whether they were all dead, but then they began to stir, unstrap themselves and clamber out of the dark interior. Edwards looked at the twisted, shattered remains of the exit door next to him, then joined the others in using the butts of weapons to smash their way out.

Moments later, he was outside, as were a number of his comrades. Glancing up, he saw the giant super-structure of a swing bridge silvery against the sky. This was the Bénouville Bridge, code-named PEGASUS, across the Caen Canal. Miraculously, they had landed almost perfectly, the glider's nose no more than 40 yards from the bridge and just to the right of a line of trees on the canal's bank and touching the edge of the wire fence. An officer shouted, 'Come on, boys, this is it!' and Edwards was charging forward along with others, firing his rifle, hurling grenades and shouting. A cannon and bunker by the bridge were knocked out with phosphorus grenades, then an enemy machine gun opened fire from the far side. The men immediately returned fire and in a moment were on to the bridge itself. Edwards was following Brotheridge as another burst of machine-gun fire hissed and whizzed towards them. Suddenly, Brotheridge fell, but Edwards and the others kept charging forwards, shouting, firing and lobbing grenades, although he saw his fall into the canal. 'Probably the only thing they killed,' he said, 'were a few fish but they went off with quite a good bang. And the Germans literally ran. They scattered.' They had captured the bridge intact, as planned, and in a matter of a minute or two. After the fiascos of Sicily the previous July, so far it could hardly have gone better. 'Relief, exhilaration, incredulity – I experienced all these feelings upon realizing that we had taken the bridge.'

There had been just eleven bridge guards – one corporal and ten men – from Infanterie-Regiment 736 and all were killed or fled. Lieutenant Brotheridge had been fatally hit in the neck; tragically, he had a heavily pregnant wife back at home in England. Meanwhile, the other two gliders, Chalk 92 and Chalk 93, had also landed with equally impressive precision, despite the strong breeze, and the men had swarmed out and over to the bridge. Engineers swiftly found demolition chambers on the bridge but they were empty. After a quick search of the area, the charges themselves were found in a nearby shed; the Germans had not placed them on the bridge because the language barriers of the Ost troops – Poles and former Soviets – meant that in the past bridges had been blown prematurely because orders had been misunderstood. And, of course, they had not been expecting an attack that night.

Meanwhile, Major Howard and his wireless operator, Lance Corporal Ted Tappenden, were trying to make contact with the men attacking the Orne bridge, code-named HORSA. The first two gliders had landed at about thirty-five minutes after midnight, while the third had missed completely and was currently unaccounted for. Despite this, the bridge had been even more swiftly secured and the empty demolition chambers removed by Sapper Cyril Larkin and his twin brother, Claude.

By this time, six twin-engine Albermales had dropped sixty pathfinders of the 22nd Independent Parachute Company. Equipped with lights and Eureka beacons, their task was to pick out the DZs for the main airborne force that would begin arriving just before midnight. This, however, had not gone as well as hoped, as the men were too heavily laden; this had slowed their jump from the aircraft and they had floated down in a far more dispersed fashion than planned. Furthermore, the pathfinders for DZ K had been dropped on N instead and began transmitting the wrong signal. It did not bode particularly well and underlined the extreme difficulty of carrying out airborne drops at night with only limited navigational equipment and a particularly stiff breeze.

In England, American bomber crews of the US Eighth Air Force, normally used to operating by day, were being roused from their beds. RAF Bomber Command was due to bomb strongpoints and gun batteries along the French coast in the early hours, but would then be followed by waves of further bombers, beginning at first light and continuing up to ten minutes before H-Hour. In the interests of safety, and with Eisenhower's full approval, the bombardiers were told to delay the release of their bombs by up to thirty seconds to make sure they didn't hit the assault forces out at sea.

At Bassingbourn in Cambridgeshire, home to the 91st Bomb Group, the crews were woken at half past midnight.

'Breakfast at one, briefing at two,' the waker-upper announced in a tired voice.

'Jesusgod,' muttered Lieutenant Bert Stiles. He was already utterly sick of the war and had only been in bed half an hour. Stiles was twenty-three, but looked younger, and was co-pilot of a Flying Fortress called *Times A'Wastin*. First pilot and captain was Lieutenant Sam Newton, also twenty-three and a former fraternity brother of Stiles at Colorado College. By pure chance, they had bumped into each other at the USAAF training base at Wendover, Salt Lake City, and had managed to talk their way into being in the same crew. Both were still very good friends on the ground, but once in the air Stiles worried they somehow didn't quite gel, and actually rather grated on one another. Their first mission had been on 19 April, four days after reaching Bassingbourn, and the target had been Luftwaffe assembly plants at Eschwege in Germany.

'Are you scared?' Stiles had asked Newton before they set off.

'I'm Sam,' Newton had replied, and certainly he had seemed to keep his composure on that trip and on the ones that had followed. They might have lacked chemistry as a crew, but collectively they had managed to keep their cool and keep going.

On this morning of 6 June, the officers in their crew were all grumbling and grousing as they wrenched themselves out of bed.

'Maybe this is D-Day,' said Stiles, but nobody laughed or even replied. It had been said so often and had never turned out to be true. Once they were in the mess hall, however, Mac, the public relations officer, told Stiles this was it and suddenly it began to seem real.

'D-Day,' Stiles replied. 'Honest to God.'

Unbeknown to Stiles and his fellows at Bassingbourn, across the western side of Normandy the American pathfinders were now dropping over what were supposed to be the three planned DZs for the 101st Airborne, with those of the 82nd Airborne due to arrive an hour later at 1.21 a.m. Three aircraft were heading to each DZ, which in the case of the 101st were code-named A, C and D, the first two behind Utah Beach and the third, D, 3 miles north of Carentan. Each plane carried two Eureka radio beacons, Holophane lights and thirteen pathfinders. None had any difficulty finding the Cotentin Peninsula, although one had engine trouble and had to ditch. The rest then hit a bank of low cloud that ran from the west coast almost to the drop zone, causing formation cohesion to dissolve, and it was made worse by sporadic flak. Using the Gee navigation system, however, they reached their DZs and the first pathfinders parachuted down at sixteen minutes past midnight. At A they were a mile to the north of target, at D they landed reasonably accurately and at C they were a couple of miles off course. They now had a race on to get to the right place and set up the lights and Eureka in time.

Back at the bridges, on the eastern flank, the men of the Ox and Bucks had moved forward to their planned positions and were now awaiting the promised reinforcements from the 7th Parachute Battalion, due to head towards them the moment they dropped. The following morning, the Special Service Brigade of Commandos was to land on the eastern edge of Sword Beach and hurry towards them too. First, though, they were to make radio contact with the pathfinders. The code word for capturing the Caen Canal bridge was 'Ham' and that for the Orne bridge 'Jam'. Over and over, Tappenden repeated 'Hello Four Dog, Hello Four Dog, Ham and Jam, Ham and Jam'. Eventually, losing patience, he said, 'Ham and bloody Jam!' into his radio. But there was no reply. Unbeknown to Tappenden, the pathfinders' radio operator had been killed in the jump; his signals had been going out to a dead man.

At 1.50 a.m., the drone of aircraft could be heard and flares were lit along the drop zones a mile away. To the east of the Orne lay the village of Ranville; beyond was a large area of open farmland before the rise of the Bréville Ridge. It was an ideal DZ, so much so that Rommel, visiting the ridge in May, had ordered that his 'asparagus' – anti-airborne poles – be immediately sown across the entire strip. Now, paratroopers were falling there, in the light of the flares their chutes quite visible to the men at the bridges. German tracer was also stabbing into the air.

The first man to jump was a young platoon commander, just five days shy of his twenty-fifth birthday. Lieutenant Richard Todd had been an aspiring actor when war was declared, but on his call-up in the spring of 1940 he had left the Dundee Repertory Theatre and been posted to the King's Own Yorkshire Light Infantry. Officer training had followed, then Battle School, in which he was training with live ammunition, and then a spell of Arctic training in Iceland. His so far safe passage through the war had eventually taken him back to England as a liaison officer for 42nd Division. Increasingly bored, he had been looking for an escape route, but his repeated attempts to join the Commandos or Parachute Regiment had led nowhere. While delivering a message to General Windy Gale on Salisbury Plain one day in 1943, however, he was recruited to join 6th Airborne Division instead. Todd was delighted. Then, by chance, he had been accosted by a colonel in the 6th Airborne who said he was looking for some officers. 'Fate,' noted Todd, 'had led me straight to the one man who was responsible for all officer-postings to 6th Airborne Division.' Now, just under a year later, he was commanding a stick of paratroopers in the lead transport aircraft, which made him the first man in the main drop to make the jump.

For much of the journey from Fairford in Gloucestershire, southern England, to Normandy Todd had been asleep, and had only woken when shaken by the despatcher a few minutes before he was due to jump. Like everyone else, he was heavily laden and heaved himself to his feet unsteadily, hooking himself on to the static line, the device that pulled the cord on the parachute once out of the plane. The hatch was opened and Todd stood over it, looking down at white-crested waves which then gave way to the coastline. As the red light came on, he saw yellow and orange stabs of light arcing upwards like leisurely shooting stars. This, he realized, was tracer. A minute later, the green light went on and, heaving an extra dinghy bag towards him, he jumped, from around only 600 feet above ground. He had about ten seconds to land and as soon as the canopy of his chute opened, he pulled the ripcord to release his leg-bag and held on to its rope with his other hand. This slipped, burning and tearing his skin as it dropped.

'Bugger!' he called out in pain. The noise around him was immense: aircraft droned overhead, machine guns chattered, guns boomed. Moments later he landed heavily in a cornfield. Quickly discarding his harness and the leg-bag cord, he crouched down to take stock. There was no one around and he couldn't see Ranville church, a given marker, which made him think he had probably dropped a little early. Suddenly, an aircraft descended in flames, burning brightly across the sky, but there wasn't time to think much about that; he needed to get moving. Heading for a wood, to his relief he soon heard English voices and in a clearing found Lieutenant-Colonel Richard Pine-Coffin, the improbably named commander of Todd's own 7th Parachute Battalion and part of 5th Parachute Brigade. Their task was to head to the bridges and reinforce Major Howard's men, while the other two battalions took Ranville and secured the approaches and the areas of the DZs. The battalions of Brigadier

James Hill's 3rd Brigade would destroy the bridges over the Dives and take out the German battery at Merville.

That was the plan but, as ever with airborne operations, it was unravelling somewhat, and quickly too. Overall, 5th Brigade had landed pretty successfully: Drop Zone N, next to Ranville, was inland a few miles, which allowed the aircrew and troops aboard to get their bearings; it was also close to the canal and river for guidance, and the pathfinders had done a good job. Over 2,000 men and 702 containers were successfully dropped. The bulk of Brigadier Hill's 3rd Brigade, however, which arrived at much the same time, was considerably more scattered. Confusion was caused by the pathfinders of DZ K landing on N and not realizing their mistake until too late, while at DZ V the pathfinders ran into the hundred Lancasters of Bomber Command, who were due to bomb the Merville Battery at half past midnight. For strategic bombers operating at night with limited visibility and a stiff wind with which to contend, this was a small target and a very tall order, and perhaps not unsurprisingly they overshot by 2,400 yards and almost wiped out the DZ V pathfinder force in the process. They also smashed the Eureka beacon, the radio-direction finding set that would send directional pulses to the lead transport plane heading for this DZ. To make matters worse, smoke from the accident then drifted right across the entire area, largely obscuring it. Only 17 out of 71 aircraft carrying the 9th Parachute and 1st Canadian Parachute Battalions were dropped with any kind of accuracy. What's more, the area just to the east of DZ V had been flooded and too many landed in waterlogged ground. 'Gentlemen, in spite of your excellent training and orders, do not be daunted if chaos reigns,' Brigadier Hill had warned his men. 'It undoubtedly will.' He had not been wrong, but their challenge now was swiftly to make sense out of the chaos and get on with the considerable tasks they had been given.

Just inland from Courseulles, some 10 miles to the west of the Caen Canal, Oberleutnant Cornelius Tauber had returned to his barracks from a site inspection of a new bunker at around midnight and had immediately heard the sound of aircraft overhead, most of them flying low. It didn't feel to him like an air raid. There was drizzle in the air, clouds were flitting across the moon and, now that he paused to look closely, he could actually see the shapes of the aircraft. Flak guns were firing, tracer streaking up into the sky. Was this the invasion? Neither Tauber nor his colleagues were sure, but if it was their last peaceful night, they thought they might as well make the most of it, so they opened a bottle of brandy to share.

Sitting in a sparsely furnished house in Bellengreville, a village just to the south-east of Caen and only a few miles to the south of the British drop zones, Major Hans von Luck heard low-flying aircraft coming over twenty minutes or so after midnight. He was generally not in the best of moods; a man of action, he yearned for the old days when they had charged through France and then North Africa. Sitting around waiting for an invasion was not to his taste. He was still up and about because he was waiting for a report from his II. Bataillon that their night exercise around Troarn had ended. Now, large numbers of Allied aircraft were flying over – they could be nothing else – and minutes later his adjutant was on the field telephone telling him paratroopers and gliders were dropping.

'All units are to be put on alert immediately,' von Luck ordered without hesitation, 'and division informed.' Despite orders from higher up the chain to the contrary, he also told his adjutant that II. Bataillon was to go straight into action wherever necessary and prisoners brought straight to him. He then headed to his command post, where he learned that some of II. Bataillon were already in action, but that 5. Kompanie had been training without live ammunition, which worried him. He was further annoyed to discover Generalmajor Feuchtinger was away in Paris.

It really was incredible how often senior German commanders were absent at the launch of major Allied attacks. Rommel had been in Germany when the Battle of Alamein began and was absent again now; before the Allies had launched DIADEM, the battle for Rome in May 1944, the German 10. Armee commander, Generaloberst Heinrich von Vietinghoff, and senior corps commander, Generalleutnant Fridolin von Senger und Etterlin, had also been back in Germany; Oberst Wilhelm Meyer-Detring, the chief of intelligence at OB West HQ, was also now away. This was careless to say the least.

Elsewhere, the Germans were only slowly waking up to what was happening. The Allies had hoped to achieve complete tactical surprise at every level and so far that had proved to be the case. There had, of course, been various signals and a gathering intelligence picture that something was afoot – von Rundstedt's intelligence men had cracked the BBC's codes to the Résistance, for example – but this counted for little if the senior headquarters at Heeresgruppe B and OB West chose to ignore them. Since the intelligence picture issued by the OKW had stated that the Allies were likely to mount diversionary raids and landings first, senior commanders were reluctant to respond too quickly in case they made the wrong call; they were all keenly aware that whatever was issued by the OKW was, in effect, Hitler's own take on the situation.

However, Generalmajor Josef Reichert, commander of the 711. Infanterie-Division, soon recognized this was no diversion when one of the scattered British paratroopers from 3rd Brigade landed right on top of his headquarters as he and his senior staff officers played a late-night game of cards. Although Reichert and his division were part of Generaloberst Hans von Salmuth's 15. Armee, he immediately telephoned General Marcks. It was then 1.11 a.m. Generaloberst Friedrich Dollmann, the 7. Armee commander, was then informed and at 1.30 a.m. ordered a general alert. Reports of paratroopers now landing in the Cotentin Peninsula were also passed on to Heeresgruppe B at La Roche-Guyon at 1.35 a.m.

Speidel, Rommel's chief of staff, however, hesitated and did not immediately tell the OKW, or even Rommel, most likely because he was drunk or at the very least half-cut. Certainly, drinking large amounts of wine and spirits and then acting with clear-headed decisiveness did not really go hand in hand. However, any senior German commander should have known after nearly five years of war that airborne troops were, by their very nature, lightly armed and best used for short, sharp *coup de main* operations. After only a brief time they would need to be supported by considerably more troops – in this case troops that could only realistically arrive by sea. Even if this was a diversionary operation – and if the Germans had thought this through sensibly they would have realized it was unlikely to be so – the odds were that troops would be landing on the Normandy beaches very soon. Swift, decisive action was needed, just as Rommel had rammed into the minds of all, but none of the panzer divisions could be ordered up without the express authority of the Führer. This being so, the sooner Hitler knew and issued orders, the better. Speidel, however, remained silent. He did not even ring his boss, Rommel, at home in Herrlingen.

In Paris, however, Konteradmiral – Rear Admiral – Karl Hoffmann, commander of the Marinegruppe West, had no such doubts and at 1.50 a.m. signalled to the OKW that the invasion had begun. Ten minutes after this, von Rundstedt was informed and tentatively placed 21. Panzer-Division – and only 21. Panzer – on Level 2 alert, which meant they needed to be ready to move within ninety minutes. This was, to put it mildly, a half-hearted response. On the other hand, both General Marcks and Generalmajor Max Pemsel, the 7. Armee chief of staff, did recognize the airborne assaults for what they were. Over the past weeks, Pemsel had become increasingly convinced that Normandy would be the location for the Allied invasion: in his view, the intelligence picture clearly pointed that way. War games for how to deal with an airborne assault on the Cotentin had been planned for 6 June and the commanders were due to meet at Rennes in Brittany. Pemsel, however, had issued a strict order for them not to start their journeys until after dawn – just in case the Allies arrived. Not all had obeyed him, including Generalleutnant Wilhelm Falley, the highly experienced commander of the 91. Luftlande-Division. He was still en route to Rennes when he was stopped and ordered to return.

Across Normandy, the US airborne assault was now under way. Ironically, had they gone the previous night, the sky would have been clearer over the Cotentin, although cloudier over the eastern flank; the rain had run across Normandy and cleared from the eastern parts by around 3 a.m. on the 5th. With timings adjusted to the British airborne drop, it would possibly have been better to have stuck to the 5th rather than risk a small ridge of high pressure that could well have dissipated. In fact, that night the ridge had developed into something that would provide a longer window than had first been anticipated.

Be that as it may, the decision to postpone had certainly not helped the American airborne assault. Some 6,900 paratroopers of the 101st Airborne were approaching the Cotentin coast just a little after 1 a.m. in a massive armada of 433 C-47s, each in giant vics – V-formations of three flying together in 'serials' of thirty-six aircraft. Following up were a further fifty-two gliders, primarily carrying Jeeps, anti-tank guns and other weapons. This large force was to cross the coast at 1,500 feet, then throttle back to just 110 m.p.h. and drop to some 600 feet, the optimum speed and height for an airborne drop. Much higher and the paratroopers would spend too long in the air, where they were very exposed and vulnerable; too low and their chutes would not have the chance to open; too fast and they would be swept off course and the drop would dramatically lose accuracy. Yet for all the intricate planning, no one had thought to send a reconnaissance plane ahead to see what the weather situation actually was over the Cotentin – nor had the British for their drop, though they had largely got away with it. Neither had there been any specific nighttime training in adverse weather; and apart from the dress rehearsal in May, the 101st hadn't made any practice drops for more than seven weeks.

The 2nd Battalion, 506th PIR was flying in Serial 12, numbers 46–81, and up front near the hatch of Number 67 was Lieutenant Dick Winters, 1st Platoon commander in Company E, nicknamed Easy Company. Twenty-six years old and from Lancaster, Pennsylvania, he was a college business graduate with a high-class degree, an excellent work ethic and a natural athleticism. Having volunteered to take part in a war he had absolutely no desire to join, so far he had shown natural aptitude as a soldier and leader of men – albeit one who, like all of those in the 101st, had yet to taste combat.

Twenty minutes before they were due to jump, the pilot called back to the crew chief, who then took off the door. Winters stood up from his seat and glanced out. The full moon, although low, gave off sufficient light for him to see clearly enough. It seemed as though the entire sky was filled with aircraft, but this calm and awe-inspiring scene was quickly shattered as they crossed the coast and hit a wall of cloud that had not dispersed since the pathfinders had come over. Suddenly, the pilots could see nothing. They were still supposed to be in tight formation, however, so the risk of collision was enormous. Most of the aircraft in each serial were dependent on the leader for navigation, but now they could not see them and were flying blind. Some pilots panicked, climbing higher or lower, speeding up and slowing down.

Between 10 and 12 miles inland, the cloud became progressively thinner and more broken. Winters, who had been surprised to encounter little flak as they crossed the coast, now saw the entire sky lit with criss-crosses of red, blue and green tracers hurtling up towards them. Some aircraft were still in vague formation, but the serene cohesion of the crossing had gone. Suddenly, the C-47 next to them was hit: Winters saw tracers go right through it and out the roof. A further bank of cloud hid it from his view. Unbeknown to Winters, the stricken aircraft turned over on its wing and fell away, crashing to the ground below and exploding, killing all on board, including Lieutenant Thomas Meehan, the Easy Company commander.

On Number 67, the pilot now accelerated to avoid enemy fire and Winters looked down, adrenalin coursing through him, searching the ground for landmarks and for signs of the DZ. Ordering everyone to their feet, they hooked their static lines and then he glanced out of the open doorway once more. The tracer was getting closer, until finally it hit their tail, rocking the aircraft and causing some of the men to topple over. Winters glanced back at the despatcher and then, when the green light flashed on, he yelled, 'Go!' just as a 20mm cannon shell hit the aircraft. He jumped, but by this time the plane was travelling closer to 150 m.p.h. than 110, and in the initial shock of jumping at such speed his leg-bag was torn off along with most of his other equipment.

In moments, he was down, landing heavily and badly bruising his shoulders and legs. But he was alive. None the less, his situation was hardly ideal. He had missed the DZ, he knew, but wasn't quite sure where he was. Nor did he have his weapon, which was also lost in the jump. Strangely, he didn't feel at all scared. He knew he needed to think clearly and calmly and found he was able to do so. 'Though I had been apprehensive whether or not I would measure up,' he wrote, 'the long months of training now kicked in.'

Winters was soon joined by another trooper, although from HQ Company, not Easy. After skirting round a German machine-gun team, they pushed on and by using the dime-store cricket clickers with which they had been issued, managed to link up with others from his platoon. After a cautious examination of the map, Winters realized they were close to Sainte-Mère-Église – in fact, they could see the town lit up by a fire blazing in one of the houses. They were about 4 miles north-west of their DZ, which wasn't great but, on the face of it, not too disastrous either.

At 2 a.m., at his 12. Kompanie Headquarters in a farmhouse not far from Carentan, Oberleutnant Martin Pöppel was roused and told that the entire Fallschirmjäger-Regiment 6 was now on full alert. The only *Fallschirmjäger* regiment in the area, its three battalions had been split up – the I. to Sainte-Marie-du-Mont, the II. to Sainte-Mère-Église, and the III. to Carentan. They had spent several weeks making a thorough investigation of the surrounding countryside, which was largely reclaimed marshland criss-crossed with a close network of hedgerows, or *bocages*. These, they realized, were high earthen walls, thickly woven with tree and dense bush roots. And so they had trained hard, carrying out regular exercises that made the most of these natural defences, and waiting for the day the Allied armada arrived off the coast of France – as they knew it surely would.

Fallschirmjäger-Regiment 6 had been recently formed from a cadre of experienced officers and NCOs, and about a third of their number were combat-experienced paratroopers. The rest were all fanatically keen volunteers with an average age of just seventeen and a half, who had had a mere four months' training. Despite its short duration, their training had been intense and their discipline, combined with a backbone of immense experience, ensured they were certainly among the very best German troops in Normandy. They were also among the best equipped, with each rifle *Gruppe* of ten men given two MG42 machine guns rather than the normal one, and with heavy weapons companies that had twelve heavy mortars and heavy machine guns – more than was normal in equivalent army companies. Light on vehicles, they had just seventy trucks for the entire regiment of 4,600 men, and these were a mixture of German, British, French and Italian manufacture, scrounged during the war and a nightmare to maintain because of lack of spares and the huge range of parts needed. 'The regiment is completely fit for ground combat,' Oberst Friedrich von der Heydte had reported at the end of May, 'but only conditionally fit for ground combat because it does not have enough heavy anti-tank weapons and motor transport.'

Pöppel had fought just about everywhere the *Fallschirmjäger* had been in action, from Norway and the Low Countries to the carnage of Crete, from the Eastern Front to Sicily and southern Italy. Along the way he had won the Iron Cross 1st and 2nd Class, been promoted early to *Oberjäger* and then to *Leutnant*, and now finally, having been brought over from 1. Fallschirmjäger-Division, had been given his own company. Still only twenty-four, he was exactly the kind of battle-experienced, highly disciplined young officer on which the Wehrmacht was increasingly dependent.

Now, he hurried to his observation post with his Kompanie HQ personnel, the safety catches off their weapons as they waited to try to learn more. He gazed out into the night. The wind was getting stronger, but now and then the moon appeared and lit up the countryside. Occasionally, single rifle shots cracked out, but so far there was no massed attack. More Allied paratroopers were, however, on their way: another 6,420 men of the 82nd Airborne.

The 'All American' Division, as the 82nd was known, began arriving around half an hour after the first of the 101st started their drop, at 1.51 a.m. Whatever problems the 101st had faced were even worse for the 82nd because the Germans on the ground were now very much alert to what was going on. The hornet's nest had been thoroughly stirred. Nor had the cloud bank dispersed. Lieutenant-Colonel Mark Alexander was aboard a lead serial C-47, seated by the open doorway at the rear of the plane. Looking down as they crossed the Channel, he had seen the awe-inspiring sight of hundreds of ships below, lit up by the creamy light of the moon. Then they hit the Normandy coast and remained in cloud until the red light came on. Pretty sure his plane had climbed, he worried about jumping into the path of C-47s that were lower than them. With the red light on and everyone standing up and hooked on to the static line, some of the men were now getting twitchy and Alexander felt certain they must have overshot the DZ. Suddenly the light went green and he jumped. Because of the excessive speed, the shock of the parachute opening was severe, but he was on the ground quickly in a small clearing in a wood, unhurt apart from the stock of his carbine hitting him in the jaw. Amazingly, the entire stick landed quite close together and within a short time all eighteen had gathered their equipment and joined Alexander. The 505th PIR's drop zone had been to the north-west of Sainte-Mère-Église, but Alexander reckoned they had landed about 2½ miles north. It could have been a lot worse – and for many of the 82nd it was.

The other two drop zones were to the west and south-west on the far side of the River Merderet and the area Rommel had ordered flooded. Because the reaction of so many of the C-47 pilots to the cloud and flak was to speed up, this meant a lot had overshot. DZ T, closest to the Merderet, was where the 507th PIR were to drop, but far too many had come down in the flooded area. Although only a foot or two deep in most places, this was enough for a number of men, weighed down by excessive equipment, to drown.

Meanwhile, away to the east, Denis Edwards and his seven-man section at the western side of the Pegasus Bridge had taken up positions alongside a single-track tramway that ran beside the canal. Somewhere not far away, an air-raid siren began to wail. Others had now liberated the Buffet du Tramway, a café on the same Bénouville side of the bridge; it was the first French building to be liberated from the Nazi yoke. The owner, Georges Gondrée, promptly dug up ninety-nine bottles of champagne he had kept hidden in his garden and offered them to Major Howard and his men. While a much-appreciated gesture, it was important the men ensured that M. Gondrée and his family remained liberated.

Not far away on the Ranville side of the River Orne, about fifty men,

Lieutenant Richard Todd included, had gathered around Lieutenant-Colonel Pine-Coffin at the pre-arranged rendezvous on the slight escarpment above the river. A bugler repeatedly sounded his clarion call, and more and more men began to appear. Back at the bridge, Howard had been blowing his own penny whistle in notes that corresponded to 'V for Victory' in Morse code. Soon enough, Brigadier Nigel Poett, the 5th Parachute Brigade commander, appeared, told Howard to hold firm, assured him that help was on its way, then melted away again to continue rounding up his men.

A defensive perimeter had been set up at both ends of the two bridges, with Howard bringing some of the men from Horsa Bridge back to the canal side. Lieutenant Brotheridge, Howard's great friend in the company, had been taken to the makeshift casualty command post set up in the remains of a glider between the two, but he died soon after. He was a big loss.* Firing could now be heard from the direction of Ranville and soon after a German patrol reached the Horsa Bridge and opened fire. They were immediately cut down, only for the defenders to discover they had also killed three of their own paratroopers who had been taken prisoner earlier.

Soon after that, a German staff car sped towards them from the same direction, through the outer defences and across the bridge, at which point it was raked with fire and slewed off the road. Three men jumped out and were killed, but the other, hit in the legs, was wounded. It turned out he was Major Hans Schmidt, the local commander of Infanterie-Regiment 736, and had been with a local French lady rather than supervising his men. Bleeding and distraught at the dishonour of losing the bridge, he pleaded to be shot. Instead, he was given a shot of morphine, which prompted him to pipe down and take a more sanguine view of the situation.

---

* Den Brotheridge's military death certificate has recently come to light and curiously states that he died of 'Multiple Injuries, Aircraft (Glider crash.)'. It also says that his body was received at the mortuary in Portsmouth at 2.50 p.m. on 8 June. His grave, however, is in Ranville churchyard. The only conceivable explanation for this strange anomaly is that while still alive he was taken to the CCP, set up in a glider, and his bruised and badly wounded face was mistakenly believed to be a result of the crash rather than of a bullet. The reception of his 'body' must refer to his personal belongings rather than his mortal remains. It is inconceivable that the countless eyewitness accounts of his fatal wounding have been wrong. In war, many administrative mistakes occurred.

Just after 2 a.m., tanks could be heard rumbling from the village of Bénouville on the western side. From the Panzerjäger-Kompanie of the 716. Infanterie, they came clanking and squeaking towards the canal bridge. Denis Edwards, who had been furiously trying to dig in, stopped what he was doing and looked, spellbound. The first tank stopped and several crew got out to converse with some of the infantry following behind, as though unsure of where they were. At this point, Sergeant 'Wagger' Thornton, who had come over from the Horsa Bridge, ran forward and, when close enough, coolly fired his PIAT, a portable anti-tank weapon and generally not much liked for being too unwieldy. It did the job this time, however. There was a crack, followed a moment or two later by a huge explosion. 'It burned very nicely,' noted Edwards, 'illuminating the bridge structure with a huge blaze of orange, red and yellow.' Hastily, the Germans pulled back. That single shot by Thornton had probably not only saved the bridges from being overrun, it had also bought them precious time.

Lieutenant Todd and more than 150 paratroopers from 7 Para finally reached the bridges at around 3 a.m. As they crossed the causeway between the two, Todd spotted his first dead German. The body was legless, but Todd could hear a groaning sound. Internal gases, he supposed, and passed on by, surprised by how little it had upset him. Although he was the battalion assistant adjutant, at the Gondrées' bar he was directed north along the canal to the tiny hamlet of Le Port and told to set up a defensive outpost. Gathering a dozen men, he led them about half a mile to a small conical hill beside the canal, overlooking a chalk quarry. The hope was that more men from 7 Para would join the makeshift positions around the ends of both bridges as the night wore on, but for the time being Todd and his men were rather isolated and cut off from the rest.

The defenders of the bridges could do nothing but wait – for the enemy, for the Commandos, for whatever fate had in store.

Meanwhile, away to the east, at 2 a.m. Robert Leblanc had finally left Pont-Audemer in the lorries and headed to La Pilvédière, their prepared HQ. So far the news was mixed: the Feldgendarmerie had been successfully attacked and three Germans killed, but the rest had been out when the attack took place. En route to their new HQ, Leblanc picked up more food and, crucially, 25 litres of fuel. Finally, at La Pilvédière, he met up with three gendarmes, now working for him, and waited for the sound of aircraft overhead. It wasn't long before they heard one circling nearby – and at the agreed time. 'No mistake,' wrote Leblanc, 'quick, quick, let's do the signals!' Grabbing their electric lamps, he and the three gendarmes hurried outside, ran to the drop zone and switched on the lamps. Everyone was excited – this was it! They could barely contain themselves – yet Serpent and Bezo had not yet arrived back with the Citroën and that worried him. Then, at 3.15 a.m., instead of seeing canisters floating down, they heard a whistle and explosions. Instead of weapons, they had been on the receiving end of four bombs. 'Nobody is killed or hurt,' scribbled Leblanc, 'but it's not a good start!' But whether an enemy bomber or friendly fire, they could no longer risk using La Pilvédière and so had to move again, this time to a small farm on the edge of some nearby woods.

By now, the German troops all along the Normandy coast were being brought to full alert. At his billet inland, Leutnant Hans Heinze had only recently got to bed and had been fast asleep when he was roused and hurried to an observation post near Colleville, above the eastern end of Omaha Beach. Personally, he was not convinced this was anything more than a false alarm, so he was not unduly concerned. The men on the ground, however, were definitely alarmed. Gefreiter Franz Gockel had also been fast asleep in his bunker at WN62 after being on watch for the first half of the night. He and his companions had beds that folded down on chains from the walls in rows of three. Above him was a 35-year-old who had recently had all his teeth taken out and been given a false set, which, when sleeping, he kept in a glass of water. Below was another 18-year-old, who had lost an eye as a child and had been given a glass replacement.

'Highest Alarm Status,' shouted one of their comrades standing in the bunker entrance, 'and you'd better damn hurry!' As Gockel and the others rubbed their eyes and quickly roused themselves, an *Unteroffizier* yelled, 'Boys, it's for real!' In a matter of minutes, Gockel and his fellows were at their posts, machine guns and rifles ready. But as they stared out into the inky darkness they could see nothing and wondered whether it was another false alarm. 'In our lightweight uniforms,' noted Gockel, 'we stood shivering at our weapons.' The cook came around and gave them some hot red wine, what they called 'the spirit of life'.

Further east along the coast, Oberleutnant Tauber had hurriedly made the thirty-minute walk from his barracks to the bunkers at Courseulles. The PAK gunners were ready and so were his five men in the

Goliath bunker, with three Goliath machines, small remote-controlled tracked vehicles, loaded with explosives and enough petrol to travel about a kilometre. At the right moment, each would be sent down a camouflaged concrete tunnel and out on to the beach. Visibility was through a slit in the bunker and a periscope that could be extended up out of the slit. It was now 3 a.m., and all he and his men could do was wait anxiously in this cold bunker in the dark. They had started up the Goliaths to test their engines and now the fumes hung heavy in the air, stinging his eyes. He tried to keep calm, but he couldn't help thinking about what would happen if there was a landing. It was also important to try to keep up the spirits of his men, who were either older fellows in their forties or still teenagers.

A little later, standing at his observation post on the bluffs and roughly halfway along Omaha Beach, Leutnant Hans Heinze was by now thinking it really must be just another false alarm. Mist rose off the sea and far to the east the very first grey streaks of dawn could be seen. Putting his field glasses to his eyes for one more sweep before making a report to his immediate superior, Hauptmann Grimme, he saw something far out on the horizon: a masthead. Then he spotted another. And another, until in just a matter of minutes the horizon appeared to be full of them. Heinze cleaned the lenses and looked again. There could be no doubting it: out at sea and approaching the coast was a truly vast armada. Quickly, he scribbled a message and gave it to his orderly. 'Thousands of ships in front of us,' he had written, 'the invasion is at our doorstep.'

CHAPTER 10

D-Day: Dawn

A LONG WITH THE AMERICAN and British airborne divisions dropping from the sky that night were around 400 dummy paratroopers, known as 'Ruperts' and equipped with 'Pintails' – crackers to simulate the sound of rifle fire. This was Operation TITANIC, part of the deception plan and split between four different locations to simulate an airborne drop around the Seine, to the east of the River Dives, to the west of Saint-Lô, and also near the Odon River south of Caen. Two six-man SAS teams were also dropped near Saint-Lô, landing around twenty past midnight, and immediately set up recordings of men shouting, small arms and mortar fire broadcast through loudspeakers. A number of 'Jedburghs' were parachuted into France as well – the three-man teams consisting of one Frenchman, one British and one American agent with the specific task of helping Maquis groups and ensuring the French Résistance did its best to restrict German movement to the front.

Out in the English Channel, meanwhile, the invasion armada was getting ever closer to Normandy. Among the American assault forces was Captain John Raaen, the commander of Headquarters Company of the 5th Ranger Battalion. Tall, fair-haired and stocky, Raaen was the son of a career army officer, and also bright, athletic and in possession of a sharp analytical mind. He had decided early on that he wanted to go to West Point and, despite short-sightedness and a perforated ear drum – which he managed to keep quiet – he won a place, entering in July 1939, just before Germany marched into Poland.

As a young officer, he joined the engineers and was then posted to the 55th Armored Engineer Battalion in the 10th Armored Division, but on the Tennessee Maneuvers decided he would rather be in the infantry. Soon after, he saw a recruiting advertisement for the 5th Ranger Battalion, applied and was accepted. They were, they told him, looking for an officer with engineering knowledge. So far, however, he had not done one minute's work as an engineer. 'They immediately made me a platoon leader,' he said, 'and I was in the infantry, which is what I loved.'

The US Army Rangers had been formed in Britain in early 1942 from a cadre of the first troops to arrive in the country following America's entry into the war. They were the brainchild of Captain William Darby and modelled on much the same lines as the British Commandos: they were volunteers and were highly trained for dashing hit-and-run raiding operations. Darby had intended his Rangers to be elite, special forces, and so they had become. Now a colonel, he had, until April, led the Rangers in Tunisia, in Sicily and in southern Italy, but new battalions had since been formed, including the 2nd and 5th, both of which had been specially created, trained and sent to England for the invasion of France.

John Raaen had arrived in England with the rest of the battalion on 19 January and training had continued with increased intensity. 'We trained hard,' he said, 'I mean, the training was *hard*.' There had been Commando training in Scotland, then amphibious training in Devon. In between, he had enjoyed travelling all round southern England; as HQ Company commander he had accompanied the battalion S4 – supply – staff officer visiting various depots for equipment, weapons and other necessary material for the invasion. Seeing the fields crammed with tanks, trucks, artillery, tents and millions of men, he wondered how it was that England hadn't begun to sink.

Along the Normandy coastline a number of German gun batteries were considered particularly threatening. All had come in for attention from the heavy bombers prior to D-Day and were being targeted in the early hours before the landings as well. Those considered especially troublesome had been allocated to forces whose mission it was to destroy them manually in case the bombing failed either prior to the landings or soon after. Among these was the Merville Battery, east of the River Orne, which had been given to 9 Para to destroy. Another was at Pointe du Hoc, about 4 miles west of Omaha Beach, where the concave shoreline curved to a sharp point with sheer 100-foot cliffs either side. Reconnaissance photographs had revealed a battery of what appeared to be six 155mm guns atop Pointe du Hoc in what also looked like a well-prepared position with a number of concrete casements, linking trenches and a concrete observation post at the cliff's edge.

The site, like many of the Normandy coastal defences, had been improved, with two of the guns under cover of concrete by mid-April. A few days later, on 25 April, it had been pummelled by bombers, then again at the end of May and beginning of June; subsequent photo reconnaissance suggested the site had been given a thorough going-over, but the planners were not prepared to take any chances. Its destruction early on D-Day had been given to the Rangers and was exactly the kind of special force operation they had originally been conceived to undertake.

On paper, the mission to scale the cliffs and destroy the guns looked suicidal, but actually there was some encouraging precedent for such an operation. The previous July, the SAS,* led by Major Paddy Mayne, had landed by sea at a very similar cliff-faced promontory, the Capo Murro di Porco in Sicily, and had scaled the sheer rocks and destroyed several batteries of coastal guns. Admittedly, the batteries had been manned by poorly trained Italian troops, but there was nothing to suggest the guns at Pointe du Hoc were manned by much better; being German was no longer the stamp of quality it might once have been. Such a *coup de main* could be very successful – and in Sicily had proved considerably more so than any of the airborne operations; it had cost the SAS one dead and two wounded. What's more, Pointe du Hoc was to receive further treatment both from the air and from naval guns off the coast. The raid in Sicily had had no such support.

The D-Day plan for Pointe du Hoc was to send three companies of the 2nd Battalion – Force A – at H-Hour, 6.30 a.m., and under direct command of Lieutenant-Colonel James Rudder, the overall Provisional Ranger Group commander. Using rocket-fired ropes and London Fire Brigade extendable ladders, the men would scale both sides of the cliffs, just as Mayne's men had done in Sicily, and then methodically take out the batteries and the entire site, which also included two anti-aircraft casements. Both surprise and speed were key, so only half an hour was allocated for this. Assuming all went well, they would send a signal by radio to that effect, and two of the remaining 2nd Battalion companies and those of the 5th Battalion – Force C – would then follow, moving to

---

* The SAS had been briefly renamed the Special Raiding Squadron, and it was under this name that the attack in Sicily had been mounted. They had been renamed 1 SAS early in 1944.

clear the coast road, which lay 1,000 yards inland and parallel to the coast, and then continuing to Grandcamp and a second gun position at Maisy, a couple of miles to the west. The Maisy Battery was too far away to threaten Omaha, but could cause problems for Utah, so was an important objective, although not such a priority as Pointe du Hoc.

There was a caveat in the plan, however. If Force A did not send a success signal by 7 a.m., Force C would land at the extreme western, or right-hand, edge of Omaha and, with men from the 116th Infantry Regiment, would then head towards Pointe du Hoc and Maisy. That left just one company, C, from the 2nd Battalion, and as Force B they were given the separate objective of the enemy emplacements at Pointe de la Percée, halfway between the edge of Omaha and Pointe du Hoc.

Captain John Raaen would be landing on Omaha Beach, however, and the prospect of what was to come early that morning was keeping him from sleep. On watch since 10 p.m., he had already let his first relief sleep on and then, at 2 a.m., decided he would stick it for a couple of hours more. Then at 3.34 a.m. their transport ship, HMS *Prince Baudouin*, dropped anchor and Raaen set off to collect his equipment. It was time to get into their landing craft and make the final journey to the beaches of Normandy.

The US airborne drop had not been the apocalyptic massacre the fretful Leigh-Mallory had feared. Some 13,100 paratroopers had been dropped and only 21 out of 821 aircraft had been shot down or lost in the two operations. Some 389 tons of supplies had also been parachuted out over the Cotentin, along with fourteen anti-tank guns. Among those who had jumped were the two divisional commanding generals, Matthew Ridgway and Maxwell Taylor, and both had landed safely. Historians have repeatedly painted a picture of paratroopers being spread to the four winds in a hopelessly disastrous air drop, and yet 50 per cent had landed within 1–2 miles of their DZ and 75 per cent within 5 miles. This meant that three-quarters of those who landed had between 1 and 5 miles to go to reach their D-Day objectives and between five and three hours in which to do this – something that, on paper at any rate, might be considered perfectly achievable for highly motivated troops specifically trained to think on their feet and use their initiative.

Only 10 per cent had landed more than 10 miles away or were completely unaccounted for, so, considering the weather, the lack of navigator training and the intensity of the flak, IX Troop Carrier Command had done very well indeed. Of the comparatively few who were far-flung, one stick inexplicably had been given the green light to jump 3 miles to the north of Caen, which was 45 miles away; it is hard to see how the pilot and navigator could have been so far off track. The best drop was that of the 501st PIR in the 101st, nearly all of whom landed in their DZ to the north of Carentan; the worst was that of the 82nd's 507th, most of whom floated down into the flooded area of the Merderet.

Fortunately, help was at hand for many of those, and from a rather unexpected quarter. Running across this area on a raised embankment was the railway line. Just to the north of the small hamlet of La Fière was a farm and a railway level crossing, PN 104, just a little over 2 miles to the west of Sainte-Mère-Église. The gatekeeper was Maurice Dubosq, who lived there with his wife and two children, an 11-year-old daughter, Geneviève, and a nine-year-old son, Claude. Dubosq was an abusive father and a wastrel, who spent much of his meagre wages on alcohol and would then return from the bar and beat his children for the slightest misdemeanor. They were terrified of him, but recently the Germans had ordered him to guard the railway bridge a few hundred yards to the south by night, which had put a temporary end to his drinking. Geneviève had found him a much nicer person since then.

In the early hours of 6 June her father had returned to the house in a state of great excitement, accompanied by Gaby, a young man also guarding the bridge. 'The Allies are landing! This time it's true, they are coming!' He explained that he had tried to persuade the other railway workers to come with them and discard their swastika armbands as he and Gaby had done, but they had refused. He was still telling his family what was going on when an American paratrooper burst in, his face blackened, clasping a Tommy gun. Dubosq assured him he and his family were friends and then showed him where the Germans were on a map – circling the villages all around. Dubosq also quickly realized the Americans would be landing in the flooded areas and so asked the paratrooper how to call out 'Venez ici, les gars!' in English.

'Come here, guys!' the American replied.

Dubosq then left the house, taking Gaby with him, and headed out on to the water in his wooden rowing boat. Over the next few hours, they returned time and again with more and more paratroopers rescued from the flooded area. For Geneviève, it was all rather overwhelming; the house was full of soldiers, who were giving her and her brother chocolate. 'Suddenly,' she wrote, 'I am overflowing with admiration and even affection for my father.'

The house was so full of paratroopers there was barely room to move, but just before dawn they decided they should move out. Geneviève now spoke up and warned them not to head north along the railway – it was very exposed and the Germans on the far side of the *Grand Marais* – the big swamp – would be able to see them. Her father agreed. Far better was to guide them to La Fière – the route along the railway was lined with trees, which would keep them from view. Geneviève watched her father lead the men away. 'We are extremely sad and worried,' she wrote, 'to see the Americans leave in a silent file.'

All over the southern Cotentin, paratroopers were slowly but surely getting themselves into groups and trying to make their way towards their objectives. Lieutenant Malcolm Brannen, an officer in 3rd Battalion Headquarters Company in the 508th PIR, had landed slightly south-west of the planned DZ and with a handful of others was heading north-east when, at around 4.30 a.m., the glider force began arriving with the planned guns, Jeeps, radio equipment, medical supplies and many of the two divisions' staff. Around an hour later, Brannen and his companions banged on the door of a farmhouse, got directions from the frightened inhabitants, then, using their maps, realized they were halfway between Étienville and Picauville, two villages to the west of the Merderet flooding. They were still outside the farmhouse when Brannen heard the sound of a vehicle.

'Here comes a car,' he said to the others. 'Stop it.' Stepping out into the road, Brannen put up his arm to stop the vehicle, but when it sped up as it neared them they all opened fire. As the driver ducked to avoid the shots, the car swerved and crashed into a stone wall. The driver was thrown out, but was alive and trying to hide in a cellar window at the farmhouse, while another officer was slumped, dead, half in and half out of the vehicle. A third man had been thrown clear and was crawling across the road trying to reach his Luger pistol. Brannen was about 15 yards from him, standing on raised ground by the hedge on the opposite side of the road.

'Don't kill, don't kill!' the German shouted, but he was still moving towards his pistol. Brannen paused. He didn't think of himself as a cold-hearted killer, but if the German reached the Luger he risked being shot. 'So I shot,' he confessed. 'He was hit in the forehead and never knew it.'

He watched blood spurt from the dead man's head about 6 feet into the air then subside. They then grabbed the driver, along with two briefcases of official papers, and Brannen also took the cap off the officer he had killed, examining it for some kind of identification. He could find just a single word: FALLEY. Unbeknown to him at the time, he had just put a bullet into the brain of the commander of the 91. Luftlande-Division. It was good news for the US airborne forces, but bad news for the Germans as they tried to fight back amidst the mayhem and confusion. If General Falley had obeyed Pemsel's orders not to head early to Rennes, he would have avoided this chance and, as it turned out, fatal encounter.

Across the far side of the Merderet, Lieutenant Dick Winters and his companion from Company A had been making their way south-east from Sainte-Mère-Église and soon joined a group of around fifty men from the 502nd PIR. Along the way, they ran into a small column of German horse-drawn wagons. In the brief firefight, the Germans were all killed or fled. Soon after that, with the first streaks of dawn starting to light the sky, Winters was able to pick up a replacement M1 Garand rifle, revolver and lots of ammo. He felt much better now that he was armed. He felt ready to fight.

At either end of the invasion front, the airborne operations continued with vicious fighting. More gliders carrying anti-tank guns, Jeeps, ammunition and medical supplies began landing, with varying degrees of success, from around 3.30 a.m. in both the American and British sectors. Of 68 British Horsa gliders and four larger Hamilcars, 55 made it to France, most of them coming down in the DZ near Ranville as planned. Fifty-two Waco gliders supporting the 101st Airborne also landed, although the executive officer of the division, Brigadier-General Don Pratt, broke his neck on landing and was killed. By 4.30 a.m. the same number had landed to support the 82nd Airborne, although 22 of them lost their cargoes on crash-landing, including 26 men, 8 anti-tank guns, the division's main radio equipment, 11 Jeeps and vital medical supplies.

Despite the mayhem and the excessive number of paratroopers skulking along Normandy hedgerows, there were some notable successes. Sainte-Mère-Église fell to the Americans at around 4 a.m., while by this time every one of the targeted bridges across the Dives in the British airborne sector had been successfully blown. The 1st Canadian Parachute Battalion had lost their demolition charges in the jump, but had improvised and still managed to blow up the bridge at Robehomme. At Troarn, using a Royal Army Medical Corps Jeep that had been brought in by glider, a handful of men simply drove straight through the village, right under the noses of the enemy, and, having safely reached the bridge a mile to the east, blew it up.

Even the Merville Battery had been captured, although 9 Para had had just 150 men for the operation. Time had been of the essence because RAF Bomber Command was due to strike it once more before the landings and no later than 5.30 a.m., so it was imperative the hastily cobbled together 9 Para force reached the battery and were well clear again before the bombers arrived. Two gliders were also due to land right on to the battery, rather as the Germans had done at Eben Emael in Belgium back in 1940. In the event, they overshot and achieved little. Despite this and a ferocious defence by the enemy in which the paratroopers lost half their number, after a 25-minute firefight the battery was successfully captured at around 5 a.m. Only then, however, did they discover that it was equipped not with invasion-threatening 155mm guns, but with anti-quated Czech First World War-vintage 100mm field howitzers. It was still a major strongpoint, however, and because 9 Para was so dimin-ished and did not have enough explosive charges, they were able to spike the guns but not destroy the casements. They had successfully neutral-ized Merville in time for the landings – which was their main objective – but the survivors then withdrew, only for German troops to reoccupy it soon after.

The heavy bombing of Merville prior to D-Day might have fallen well short of destroying the battery, but the heavies of RAF Bomber Com-mand were not so wide of the mark elsewhere. In 1940, during the Blitz, the Luftwaffe rarely sent over more than 100 bombers on one night and those were all twin-engine types with comparatively small payloads. On this early morning of D-Day, RAF Bomber Command alone dispatched 1,012 aircraft: 551 Lancasters and 412 Halifax heavy bombers, as well as 49 of the remarkable Mosquitoes. The targets were ten coastal batteries, including Merville and Pointe du Hoc.

Among those attacking the Maisy Battery just a few miles west of Pointe du Hoc were fourteen Halifaxes of 466 Squadron Royal Austra-lian Air Force, part of Bomber Command's 4 Group. By this stage of the war there were no specific Australian divisions operating in the West, but there were plenty of Aussies sprinkled throughout the RAF and even entire squadrons, such as the 466th. Based at RAF Leconfield near the old East Riding town of Beverley in Yorkshire, they had flown south over England, then out across the sea. It was, for these long-range heavy bombers, a short mission. In Flight Sergeant Jack Scott's crew, the only Englishman was 20-year-old Flight Sergeant Ken Handley, the flight engineer, whose station on the Halifax was a fold-down dickie seat on the right-hand side of the pilot. It didn't bother him at all that he was the only 'pom' among the seven of them – like the majority of crews, they were young, reasonably like-minded, all in it together and had gelled quickly and well.

Handley and the rest of Scott's crew had begun their operational careers in February that year with a trip to Berlin – one of the toughest first missions a crew could be given – and had then been plunged into Big Week. They had also taken part in an ill-fated raid on Nuremberg on 30 March, in which ninety-five bombers were shot down, nearly 12 per cent of the entire force. It had been the worst night for Bomber Command so far in the war. Scott's crew had repeatedly taken dramatic evasive action that night, suffering not inconsiderable damage themselves, but had made it back in one piece.

Now they were on their twenty-fourth mission, fast approaching the thirty needed to complete a first tour. Loaded with 11,000 lb of bombs – 5½ tons – they came in low for heavy bombers, at just 11,500 feet. All around was ten-tenths cloud, but it was much thinner over the target – hazy at most – and the Mosquitoes had done their work, marking the battery accurately. 'We saw the red and green T.I.s go down,' noted Handley in his diary, 'and running up, pranged them good and proper.' There was some light flak, but nothing much to worry about – as trips went, it was a cakewalk. They took photographs as they bombed Maisy on what was written up as an entirely 'successful' trip.

Heading back, Handley saw the invasion convoys out in the Channel, although no one had told them at the squadron that this Tuesday was D-Day. As they flew on up to Yorkshire, they saw masses of fighters and bombers heading south. 'Coming in over base,' noted Handley, 'we clipped short the circuit and pipped the Wing Commander for 1st place on landing. A nice, pleasant trip.' Their 'trip' had not been quite so pleasant for the unfortunate German soldiers cowering in the bunkers and dugouts below. Collectively, Bomber Command's early-morning raid had been the heaviest of the war so far: some 5,000 tons of bombs had been dropped on the Normandy coastline, churning earth, rock, the entire landscape, hurling millions of fragments into the air and creating shock waves so intense they could have been registered in the strato-sphere. And there were now more bombers on their way.

Bombers of the Ninth Air Force and the Second Tactical Air Force would be over soon enough, along with hordes of fighters, fighter-bombers and rocket-firing Typhoons. In all, nearly 11,600 aircraft were scheduled to fly on this day of days. Gabby Gabreski and the boys of the 56th Fighter Group were up early too, at 3 a.m., helping crews to hastily paint inva-sion stripes on the wings. One of the problems the Allied air forces had faced over Sicily and in southern Italy had been being hit by friendly fire. The idea of painting large black and white stripes on the wings and even fuselage would, it was hoped, make them easier to distinguish and so reduce the number of such incidents. Better, it was thought, to lose potential camouflage – never that effective in daytime in any case – than to be shot down, but the decision to add these stripes had literally been made at the eleventh hour. Ground and aircrews were all hurriedly issued with paint and brushes and told to get on with it.

Gabreski led the group's first mission of the day, taking off in the dark at 3.36 a.m. and heading towards Dunkirk before patrolling all the way down the French coast to the invasion area. With thick cloud, however, they saw little and were blown off course; they were heading towards Abbeville when they were vectored back via the radar controller on a ship below. As they crossed back over the Normandy coast, the cloud cleared, revealing an English Channel covered almost as far as they could see by the invasion fleet. 'It was,' noted Gabreski, 'one of the most spectacular sights that I have ever seen, a massive demonstration of power.'

Also heading out early that morning was the 365th Fighter Group, part of General Pete Quesada's IX Fighter Command in the Ninth Air Force. The 'Hell Hawks', as they were known, were equipped with P-47 Thunderbolts, just like Gabreski's 56th FG in the Eighth. These radial-engine, elliptical-winged fighters were quick, manoeuvrable and rugged, able to take considerable punishment. They were powerful, too, capable of carrying two 1,000lb bombs – 1 ton each – an immense load for a single-engine fighter, but which made them ideal fighter-bombers. Like the rest of the Allied air forces, the Hell Hawks had been flying flat-out pretty much ever since their arrival in England the previous December. Now they were based at the hastily built airfield at Beaulieu in the New Forest, not far from the south coast.

Lieutenant Archie 'Lin' Maltbie was twenty years old and part of the Hell

Hawks' 388th Fighter Squadron. From California, he had wanted to fly ever since seeing a tri-motor Ford delivering mail when he was a boy. After leaving school, he had a job with the Douglas Aircraft Company, helping to make SBD dive-bombers for the navy. He kept expecting his draft, but after turning nineteen with no sign of the official letter, he decided to volunteer for the air force. Accepted, he was singled out for pilot training and got his wings in December 1943. After transitioning to the P-47, he was posted to Britain, crossing the Atlantic on the *Queen Mary* and reaching Scotland in April 1944. Ten days later, he was joining the Hell Hawks. After six weeks of shooting up locomotives and bridges, suddenly the invasion was on and, like the fighter boys of the 56th, they were hastily painting invasion stripes one minute and the next flying right over the invasion force.

They passed over Utah Beach ahead of the B-26 Marauders, then attacked a railway bridge and an embankment at Saint-Sauveur-le-Vicomte on the western side of the Cotentin. It was a low-level raid, for which they had each been given a 1,000lb bomb under either wing. As well as dodging flak, they also had to keep craning their necks to look for enemy fighter planes. 'We got flak,' said Maltbie. 'We got a lot of flak, but there were no German planes at all.'

Next up were the heavy bombers of the Eighth Air Force. Some 659 B-17 Flying Fortresses and 418 B-24 Liberators set off towards the invasion beaches. First, though, it was the turn of the naval guns with their opening salvoes.

As dawn spread over the Normandy coast, there was no longer any mistaking the scale of the invasion force out at sea. 'I'm not ashamed to say,' admitted Obergrenadier Karl Wegner, 'that I was never so scared in my life.' One of the newly recruited 17-year-old soldiers that had helped to form the 352. Division, he had been posted to 3. Kompanie, Grenadier-Regiment 914 and was now manning a machine gun at a strongpoint overlooking the track running off the beach towards the village of Vierville. Having never been in action before, he was terrified about what he was about to face, yet could not help but gaze in amazement at what was appearing before his eyes. A few miles down the coast, Franz Gockel, at WN62, was also staring at the scene emerging before him. A terrible, forbidding silence had descended and for him and his comrades the tension grew palpably.

At 5.10 a.m., the first Allied naval guns opened fire, targeting the German coastal batteries, including the four Kriegsmarine guns at Longues-sur-Mer, halfway along the coast between Omaha and Gold

Beaches. This battery, perched on cliffs, had come under immense aerial bombardment three times already, including by the RAF a couple of hours earlier, but the guns and observer post were protected by thick roofs of concrete, so the guns were still intact and now opened fire in turn. Suddenly the silence was riven by the sound of screaming shells being lobbed back and forth over the sea.

At 5.50 a.m. the battleship USS *Texas* opened fire for the first time, with her ten immense 14-inch heavy guns directed on to the Omaha sector. At WN62, Franz Gockel watched mesmerized as the big naval shells hurtled into the ground all around them, throwing up vast columns of dirt, stone and dust. 'It was,' he noted, 'only the beginning of hell.' A few minutes later, the first wave of the Eighth's bombers hove into view. Gockel was standing in his concrete bunker behind his machine gun, which was positioned on a table pointing out to sea through the viewing slit. As the bombs began falling he immediately ducked down under the table, trying to make himself as small as he possibly could. The sound was thunderous and in moments their bunker was full of dust and smoke. 'The earth trembled,' he wrote. 'Eyes and noses were full of dust. Sand gritted between our teeth. We had no hope of help, our planes stayed away and we had no flak. Unhindered, the bombers could drop their deadly cargoes.' Within minutes, debris had buried much of the strongpoint. Daring to glance up, he saw a bomb land directly on top of another casement and watched as dirt, bits of concrete and wire were flung into the air.

In fact, Gockel was more alone than he might have realized, because already decisions had been made higher up the chain that would have a devastating bearing on the defenders' chances in the hours to come. Not only had General Hans Speidel still not contacted Rommel, but General Erich Marcks at LXXXIV. Korps Headquarters appeared to have completely lost his head. It was the Germans who had invented airborne operations and, although they were part of the Luftwaffe rather than the army, someone of Marcks's calibre and experience should have known perfectly well that not only would the airborne troops quickly need support from follow-up troops arriving by sea, but the airborne troops now falling from the sky were doing so at night, over quite a wide area, and would be landing on unfamiliar territory. They would be as disorientated as the defenders on to whom they were falling and would inevitably take a number of hours to achieve any kind of meaningful attack. In other words, Marcks could have afforded to keep a cool head and wait to see how matters developed in the ensuing hours before committing his reserve. In any case, there were plenty of German troops already in situ in the Cotentin to deal with the invaders.

Despite all this, at 2 a.m. Marcks's staff immediately ordered the corps reserve to move west from its central position behind the Normandy coastline in the direction of the Cotentin and the area to the south of Carentan. The corps reserve had been drawn from the 352. Division and consisted of Grenadier-Regiment 915, commanded by Oberstleutnant Karl Meyer, and Fusilier-Bataillon 352. Meyer had been given overall command of this force, and at 3 a.m. they had set off, two battalions moving by bicycle and the rest being transported by French drivers in requisitioned trucks. As if that wasn't enough, Grenadier-Regiment 914 was also ordered to send troops to investigate reports of Allied airborne troops in the Vire Valley south of Carentan – these were the dummy paratroopers of Operation TITANIC, a plan that was inexpensive and cost nothing in human life but which was already proving a very effective 'force multiplier'. As a consequence, Marcks had sent his entire corps reserve towards the American airborne drop and some dummy paratroopers hours before they would be needed to help repulse the landings.

The same mistake was being made in the east. Although Major Hans von Luck had committed one company from his regiment to battle with the British airborne forces, he had held back the rest of his troops, keenly aware of the orders for 21. Panzer not to be committed without express permission from Heeresgruppe B. Not only was General Feuchtinger, the divisional commander, in Paris, so too was his chief of operations, Oberstleutnant Wolf Freiherr von Berlichingen, who was the only member of the divisional staff with panzer experience. This had meant the division was effectively rudderless. After a breakneck journey from the French capital, Feuchtinger arrived at the divisional command post at Saint-Pierre-sur-Dives at 5.20 a.m. and von Berlichingen shortly after. They then ordered the rest of the division not already in the Caen area to move straight away to the area around Bellengreville, to the south-east of Caen and on the eastern side of the River Orne, even though that ran directly against orders from on high. Their intention was to throw their troops immediately against the British airborne forces. At 6 a.m. they implored Speidel to let them go into the attack. Around the same time, Marcks's headquarters was demanding that Speidel subordinate 21. Panzer to LXXXIV. Korps so that it could be fully committed to attacking the British airborne forces east of the Orne. Speidel finally agreed at 6.45 a.m., and at 7 a.m. 21. Panzer was put under the command of General Marcks. Minutes later, Feuchtinger was given orders to advance his division east of the River Orne.

Within half an hour, thousands of British troops would be landing on the beaches to the west of the Orne, and fifteen minutes after that the Canadians would be landing too. But 21. Panzer was already advancing some way to the east. This meant that neither the only panzer division close to the coast nor the main corps reserve were where they needed to be for a swift counter-attack against the seaborne assault. All too frequently over the intervening years, it has been the Allied command that has been picked over and criticized, but in these first crucial hours of D-Day it was General Erich Marcks, usually seen as one of the very best German commanders in the West, who was responsible for the biggest blunders of the day.

CHAPTER 11

D-Day: The American Landings

W HEN LIEUTENANT YOGI JENSON went on watch at 4 a.m., the coast of France was already visible, lit up by bombs falling and exploding from the RAF's heavy bombers. It reminded him of watching from Falmouth, back in 1940, the night bombing of Plymouth further up the coast. Above him, gliders were being towed across the sky. Then an hour or so later, as first light crept over the sea, he looked back and saw the entire invasion fleet behind them. 'What a stupendous sight it was!' he wrote. 'Thousands of fighting ships and transports all on the same course bound for the Continent.'

A little further to the west, Captain Chet Hansen was on the deck of USS *Augusta* with the US First Army commander, General Omar Bradley. On a ship this large, armed and armoured, Hansen had had a comfortable feeling of security, so much so that as they crossed the Channel he found it hard to believe this was it – the invasion at long last. Nor did the swell seem too bad, although that was because he was on a 48,000-ton battleship rather than in a flat-bottomed landing craft. Then suddenly they could see the coast – there were fires ashore, and the noise of anti-aircraft guns reverberated above the sound of aero-engines. Above, the moon was obscure, only occasionally and briefly flitting out from behind the cloud. They were approaching Omaha Beach.

Just before 5 a.m., Hansen saw a B-25 bomber suddenly catch fire away to their port side. Trailing a long tail of flame and dropping lower and lower, it banked around *Augusta* before erupting completely into a vivid, angry ball of fire. Two men could be seen bailing out, then the nose dropped and the stricken bomber crashed into the sea, a ball of flame quickly extinguished and gone for ever. 'The invasion has now suddenly become alive,' noted Hansen, 'and the plan on paper is real.'

Not far from *Augusta*, on board *Prince Baudouin*, were Captain John Raaen and the 5th Rangers, and at 5 a.m. the ship's crew were ordered to their stations. Then came a second announcement over the claxon: 'Attention on deck! Attention on deck! United States Rangers, embarkation stations!' Raaen moved up on to the boat deck, then counted his men and counted them again, and checked his equipment once more: bandoliers, grenades, three-days' rations, Tommy gun, Colt 45. Then he checked his men's equipment. Now they were climbing into the assault boats hanging from davits on the side of *Prince Baudouin*, all British LCAs, thirty-six fully equipped men and four crew to a boat. Ahead, the dark looming shape of the coast could be seen dimly silhouetted against the slowly lightening sky.

After circling until all seven LCAs of the 507th Assault Flotilla were loaded, they began heading in towards the coast, bursting through the swell in their flat-bottomed craft at around 5 knots. The swell was actually worse, now, in the early hours of 6 June, than it had been twenty-four hours earlier, and waves of 6–8 feet smacked into them and showered them with sea water. In no time they were all drenched and the volume of water coming in meant they had to begin bailing out with their helmets. At 5.50 a.m. they had already passed many of the great warships when suddenly there was a terrific eruption of noise.

'Sirs,' said the naval officer commanding their LCA, 'that is the battleship *Texas* opening the bombardment of the coast.' Now every other warship opened fire along the invasion front: 9 battleships, 23 cruisers, 104 destroyers and 71 corvettes, an enormous force of staggering firepower, the destroyers closing up to within 1,000 yards in places, the battleships and cruisers further out.

Like Raaen and his fellows, 19-year-old Sergeant Bob Slaughter and the men of Company D, 116th Infantry, were also now on the water, having clambered into their British LCAs and been lowered by davits from the parent LSI (large), SS *Empire Javelin*. With so much of the US Navy in the Pacific, the naval part of the invasion was predominantly in the hands of the British. The US contribution was not insubstantial – 200 warships and 865 landing craft – but of the 1,213 warships in total, 892 were Royal Navy and of the 4,126 landing craft of various types, 3,216 were British and manned by British crews. It was mostly British, not American, vessels and crews now leading the assault forces at Omaha.

For a while Slaughter and the rest of the platoon in his LCA circled round and round waiting for the entire assault wave to be ready. The swell continued to smack against them, soaking them completely within a few seconds. The roar of the engines, the wind and the sea made it hard for the men to hear one another – not that anyone felt much like talking. Bob Slaughter was cold, sodden and shivering. They had all been given 'puke' bags and Dramamine anti-seasickness tablets, but Slaughter didn't feel at all sick until he put his gas cape over his head for warmth; in moments he was pulling off his helmet and vomiting into it. Throwing the contents over the side, he rinsed it out with the water already sloshing around the bottom of their vessel.

All the invasion beaches had been divided into sections and subsections, with code names that ran across the phonetic alphabet, and also colours. Omaha had been divided, from west to east, into four main sectors: Charlie, Dog, Easy and Fox; Dog was then divided again into Green, White and Red, and Easy and Fox into Green and Red sectors. The 116th Regiment of the 29th Division, as well as the Rangers, would be landing on the western side of the beach, between Charlie and Easy Green, and the 16th Infantry of the 1st Division would be landing between Easy Red and Fox Green. Also due to land were two tank battalions equipped with 'DD' – Duplex Drive – Sherman tanks. These rather improbable machines, each weighing over 30 tons fully loaded, were protected by a waterproof canvas covering and equipped with a propeller drive that enabled them to 'swim' through the water. In training, they had worked far better than might be imagined. No one, however, had tried launching them into a heavy swell such as the one now coursing across the approach to the beach. What's more, the plan was to launch them some 6,000 yards from the beach. That was 3½ miles, and anyone with an ounce of common sense would have realized it was ludicrously over-ambitious in the current circumstances. Fortunately, the US Navy lieutenant in charge of the 743rd Tank Battalion recognized this and instead made the sensible and correct decision to forge ahead in the landing craft and take them directly on to the beach in the 116th Infantry's sector. The same could not be said for the officer in charge of launching the 741st Tank Battalion towards Easy Red and Fox Green. The DD Shermans were ordered into the rolling sea at 5.40 a.m. Unsurprisingly, several sank almost immediately.

Also now heading towards Easy Red was 20-year-old Corporal Walter

Halloran of the 165th Signal Photographic Company. Equipped with a Bell & Howell fixed-focus single-lens Eyemo movie camera wrapped in protective plastic, a musette bag holding ten cans of film and orange Signals Corps bags in which to send the footage back to England, he was armed only with .45 Colt pistol. He also carried his rations and personal items, along with a basket containing two carrier pigeons strapped to his back, which had been given to him at the last minute. Part of a two-man team that included stills photographer Pfc Wes Karalin, Halloran had been attached to the 16th Infantry and was due to be among the first wave of assault troops, there to capture the historic Allied invasion of Normandy for the tens of millions of Americans waiting back home and also for posterity. Normally, the company was split into teams of three, but the third in this case was a Jeep driver and there wasn't space for him in the initial assault. 'So we agreed I'd meet him in an apple orchard,' said Halloran. 'We did some map work and I said, "If I make it, I'll meet you in a couple of days."' Whether he would make it, however, was a moot point; it was bad enough clambering down rope nets into the Higgins boat that was bobbing up and down far too much for comfort. Somehow, he got on board without breaking anything, but since then had been as sick as a dog. He was no longer afraid, however; he just wanted to get off the damned boat.

Sherman DD tanks were also to be part of the 4th Infantry Division's assault on Utah Beach on the eastern foot of the Cotentin Peninsula. The task had been given to three companies of the 70th Tank Battalion, fifty-four tanks in all, of which five were dozer Shermans, with bulldozers attached to the front. Utah, like the other beaches in Normandy, was long and deep, but the high tide was edged by dunes. The plan was for engineers to blast paths through with explosives and then the bulldozers would clear the sand and debris out of the way.

Company B were aboard four LCTs of four DDs each, and among the crews was Sergeant Carl Rambo. From the Deep South, he had been born and raised in Tennessee, although at the time of his drafting he was working as a caterpillar driver in a construction firm in Pennsylvania. Of his draft in Pittsburgh, only seventy-five were sent to the 70th, every one of them a high-school graduate with a trade and most with experience of working heavy equipment. This was certainly a logical selection process for tank crews, who not only needed to know how to operate large vehicles but also how to keep them working. Mechanical knowledge was a huge advantage, and in this the United States had a head start over every other warring nation because it was, by some margin, the most automotive nation in the world. At the start of the war, one in four Americans had some kind of motorized vehicle; in Germany, by contrast, that figure was closer to one in fifty.

Rambo had been drafted in 1941 and was serving in North Africa during the joint Anglo-US invasion in November 1942. 'On the ship going to North Africa,' said Rambo, 'I tried to figure out how I could fight this war honourably and stay alive. I thought about this a lot on that trip.' He had so far managed to do both, surviving Tunisia and Sicily, and was, by now, commanding his own tank. The 70th had become a battle-hardened and experienced armoured unit and, with men like Rambo among their number and two amphibious invasions already under their belt, they were the ideal support for a division such as the 4th, which had yet to see proper combat in the war. They had, however, had a taste of it on 28 April when, during a practice nighttime amphibious assault, they had been attacked by German S-boats. Two LSTs had been sunk, two more damaged, 746 men killed and a further 200 wounded. It had been a disaster.

The 70th Tank Battalion, however, had been untouched, and had carried out their part of Exercise TIGER without a glitch. Now, on the morning of 6 June, Rambo and his fellows in Company B felt quietly confident. Around 6 a.m., they were about to launch when 276 B-26 Marauders came over and pasted the beaches, flying parallel rather than at 90 degrees to the beach as had the heavy bombers of the Eighth along the rest of the invasion coast. There, plenty of bombs had still fallen on and around beaches, but they had not destroyed the thick casements and, because of the drop delay to avoid hitting their own forces, even more bombs had landed inland, beyond the immediate crust of the German defences. At Omaha, for example, where 329 B-24s had dropped their loads, there simply was neither the room nor the time for them to fly parallel to the coast, because Eighth Air Force heavy bombers were not trained for night operations. Their window of attack had been short, and so there had been no alternative but to attack in normal formation, across the front rather than alongside it. As a result, the damage to the defences had been considerably less than had been hoped for.

At Utah, on the other hand, there had been fewer and smaller medium bombers and so more air space in which they could operate. And very effective they were too. 'They really saturated that beach,' recalled Carl Rambo. 'Germans were shooting at them and then one plane must have been hit in the gas tank as fire was belching out of the bomb bay before it blew apart.' Bits of debris fluttered down all around their LCTs, nearly a mile out. Further drama happened moments later when one of the four Company A LCTs hit a mine. Rambo and his LCT were only 100 yards away and he watched as a couple of the tanks were blown 50 feet into the air like matchboxes. The LCT was broken in two, but one half was still floating. One of the men on board had been hurled 75 yards away, but miraculously survived and swam back to the wreckage, only for it to capsize, flinging him into the water again. This time he was picked up by an LCA, but the rest of the tank crews on that LCT had been killed.

Just after six, the rest of the 70th Battalion DDs launched into the sea. Only the driver was actually inside; the rest were on top, the waterproof canvas screen around them, ready to swim for it should the worst happen, but Rambo's crew slipped in 'nice and easy', and at just 1,500 yards rather than the 6,000 yards at Omaha. Here, the waters were sheltered from the worst of the westerly winds by the Cotentin and so the swell, although still choppy, was nothing like as severe as that running across the northern Normandy coast. Rambo and his crew, with the rest of 70th Tank Battalion, were on their way.

From their positions on the bluffs overlooking the beach, the defenders waited with mounting fear and anxiety. For both Karl Wegner and Franz Gockel, this would be their first taste of action; both had been in the army for less than nine months. What was happening before them was a scene of utter and overwhelming intensity for which they could not possibly have been prepared. The barrage of the naval guns was devastating: collectively the Omaha Bombardment Group could bring to bear 183 guns of 90mm or more plus a large number of quick-firing cannons. By contrast, the Germans didn't have a single gun of that calibre.

The mined stakes in front of WN62 were blown to smithereens as the shells crept up the beach and towards the bluffs. 'A rolling pin of smoke, dust and flames came towards us, cutting down everything in its path with howls, whistling and hissing,' wrote Gockel. 'We sat small and helpless at our weapons, here we prayed and took refuge.' Shells were landing all about them, shrapnel and grit and stone clattering around their casement, splinters hurtling through the viewing slits. For all this, not one of the six men in Gockel's bunker had yet been physically injured. Nor had any in Karl Wegner's gun position at the other end of the beach.

Out in the water, the landing craft were getting ever closer to the beach. It was fast approaching 6.30 a.m. Bob Slaughter was still feeling as though his guts had been ripped apart and they were all beginning to sense this wouldn't be the easy ride they had been expected to believe. John Raaen, meanwhile, was waiting off shore, circling and wondering how the assault Rangers at Pointe du Hoc were faring. Opposite Franz Gockel, nearing the shores of Easy Red beneath WN62, Walter Halloran was thinking he didn't care what lay on the beaches – he just wanted to get clear of the sea.

Around Pointe du Hoc and across the bay north of Carentan, at the foot of the Cotentin Peninsula, the lead landing craft of the 2nd Battalion, 8th Regiment of the 4th Infantry Division landed at Utah Beach at 6.31 a.m. behind a naval bombardment. The weather was miserable: wind, low cloud and drizzly rain, although there was so much sea spray it was hard to tell that it was raining. The infantry and tanks were supposed to land between the exits numbered 3 and 4 by the Allies, north of the village of Les-Dunes-de-Varreville, but the wind, strong currents and extremely poor visibility meant they actually hit the beach either side of Exit 2, right next to WN5, which was well over a mile further to the south. This strongpoint was manned by a handful of men from 3. Kompanie, Grenadier-Regiment 919, 709. Division, commanded by Leutnant Arthur Jahnke. He was a 23-year-old Knight's Cross-winning veteran of the Eastern Front and highly capable, but the men under his command weren't up to much.

Along the beach were obstacles and plenty of wire, while at the strongpoint and behind there were minefields and the flooded areas of a couple of miles' depth before the ground gently began to climb. At the strongpoint were a handful of guns encased in bunkers and eight tracked Goliaths, but they had received brutal treatment from both the Ninth Air Force's Marauders and naval fire. By the time the first troops came ashore, the lone 88mm high-velocity gun had been badly damaged, one 75mm and both 50mm guns had been destroyed, as well as all machine-gun nests, an ammunition bunker and the control mechanisms for the Goliaths. Jahnke had been hoping for support from the battery of 122mm guns a couple of miles away at Saint-Martin-de-Varreville, but unbeknown to him that had been bombed and knocked out several days earlier.

Among the first to land was the 4th Division's executive officer, Brigadier-General Teddy Roosevelt Jr, son of the former president, First

World War veteran, former Governor-General of the Philippines, multi-millionaire businessman and Assistant Secretary of the Navy. His had been an extraordinary career and life, and now here he was, fifty-six years old – with a son, Captain Quentin Roosevelt, about to land at Omaha – coming ashore as the first Allied general on D-Day to set foot in Normandy. He was also about to provide the clarity of command needed. Swiftly realizing they had landed at the wrong part of the beach, he made the instant decision to remain where they were and attack from there. 'We'll start the war from right here!' he told the 8th Infantry's battalion commanders. And that was exactly what they did.

The first tanks landed just after the infantry and although Jahnke's lone 88mm fired one shot and knocked out a Sherman, its barrel then blew and it troubled the attackers no more. In the minutes that followed, all the 70th Battalion's DD tanks made it safely to shore. Carl Rambo's Sherman came on to the beach just after that of his company commander. Dropping the canvas screen, they moved towards the dunes and the concrete sea wall, towards which engineers were already carrying blocks of TNT on their backs. Rambo watched them build a pyramid of these blocks then detonate them. When the dust, smoke and sand had settled, there was a big hole and a Company C Sherman dozer was surging forward to clear a path. Suddenly, Rambo spotted a wounded infantryman and immediately clambered down from the turret to help him – and in so doing, broke one of his golden rules, which was to look after his own crew, not stop for others. 'He was nearly dead,' said Rambo, 'and I couldn't do anything for him. I never should have gotten out of my tank.' On this occasion, however, he got away with it. With the route through the dunes already cleared, they rumbled forward, crushing chunks of concrete as they went, and when they were through they made towards the causeway across the flooded marshland beyond and down Exit 2 in the direction of Sainte-Marie-du-Mont. So far, the men at Utah were having a pretty easy time of it.

The same could not be said for those now landing at Omaha. Of the five exit points from the beach, the most heavily defended were those roughly at either end – the Vierville Draw, labelled 'D1', and the Colleville Draw, 'E3' on the attackers' maps. The two other principal draws directly facing the attackers – 'D3' and 'E1' – were also well defended but not as heavily, while in between there were no fixed defences at all. The aim had been to get on to the beach to overwhelm the enemy in quick order, but nearly all the German troops manning the key strongpoints had survived the morning's bombardments. There weren't many of them. Only ten *Widerstandsnester* directly overlooked the beach and there were others further inland at Colleville and at the village of Saint-Laurent-sur-Mer, halfway between Colleville and Vierville. Each was manned by between thirty and fifty men. WN62, where Franz Gockel was stationed, was the strongest, but even so had a permanent complement of just 27 men of Grenadier-Regiment 726 of the 716. Division, plus four others from the 352. Central command of the I. Bataillon lay within WN63, to the east of Colleville. This meant that at the crust there were only around 350 men in total. Along the beach, the strongpoints were designed to be mutually supporting, but the moment one of them was knocked out of action the entire defensive position might quickly unravel. What's more, while it was true that the bunkers and casements had so far survived all that had been thrown at them, they had been hastily built with low-grade materials.

Most of the men, Franz Gockel and Karl Wegner included, were *Grünschnabel*. Wegner worried that the moment the enemy bore down on him, he would freeze. The men on the bluffs facing the Americans coming ashore at Omaha have often been portrayed as hardened combat veterans, fanatical elites of the Wehrmacht. Nothing could have been further from the truth. Most were young men, terrified out of their wits, wishing they could be anywhere but on the coast overlooking the gargantuan invasion force blackening the sea. They had among them, however, some 85 machine guns, each firing at a rate of 1,400 rounds per minute, or 23 bullets per second. From their clear viewing positions on the bluffs, the moment the landing-craft ramps went down and American troops began making their way out, those Germans – so long as they didn't freeze up – could hardly miss. Nor did they. But it was nothing to do with being elite, highly trained, fanatical Nazis and everything to do with being utterly terrified and survival instincts kicking in.

Things were going badly wrong for the 116th Infantry as they headed towards Dog Green near the Vierville, D1, draw. Two LCAs of Company A were destroyed, killing all on board; one received four direct mortar hits. That was sixty men, or a third of the company, gone in a trice. The remaining four landing craft, carrying the other two assault platoons, landed in the smoke, spray and rain, and at 6.31 a.m. the first ramps on Company A's LCAs and LCVP Higgins boats were lowered.

'Fire, Wegner, fire!' yelled Obergefreiter Lang, the corporal in their bunker. Seeing all the Americans pouring out of their landing craft and into the water, Wegner was transfixed, astonished by how vulnerable they looked. Suddenly, Lang brought his pistol butt down on Wegner's helmet. The loud clang jolted him immediately and, bringing the butt of the MG42 tight into his shoulder, he closed one eye and felt his finger squeeze the trigger. Immediately the machine gun burst into life, spewing hundreds of bullets across the 400 yards or so that separated him from the invaders. He saw men fall, saw the sand ripped up, and watched other men dive for cover. 'Now was not the time to think of right or wrong,' he said, 'only of survival.' A further ninety-one men from Company A, 116th Infantry were cut down in a moment. A mere twenty made it across the 350 yards of beach to the sea wall.

At WN62, Franz Gockel was also thinking of survival. He had opened fire as the first wave landed directly in front of him; these were two assault platoons of Company E, 16th Infantry, which had been due to land on Easy Green, further to the west. Other assault parties from Company I landed even further east, some 2,000 yards off course at the edge of Fox Green. Waiting until those landing had made their first tentative steps, Gockel squeezed the trigger. The MG42 had its faults, but there was no question that it could spray a huge number of bullets on to a target very rapidly – bullets that now tore into the young men trying to get clear of the beach. He tried to rationalize what he was doing. So many had died at home, victims of Allied bombing, and they had been unable to fight back. 'Here, we were facing the same opponent,' he wrote, 'but unlike the many defenceless civilians, we could defend ourselves and we wanted to survive.'

Struggling ashore was Walter Halloran, still clinging to his camera and musette bag. Not a tall man, he had jumped off the ramp and into water that was far too deep, but had managed to keep his head above the surface and struggle ashore. Then he ran for it. All around people were screaming and crying out, but he kept going. 'If you stopped to help a guy,' he said, 'then there were two casualties not one. Because the moment you stopped moving you got shot.' Despite this, halfway up the beach he ducked down behind a beach obstacle and, lying flat on his stomach, lined up his camera and began shooting. Some of the footage he took at that moment remains the only live action footage of men advancing – and being cut down – in that first wave of troops moving across Easy Red. 'There's five soldiers coming ashore,' he said, 'and the furthest on the left is shot and killed and falls over. I was lying on my belly – it's a low angle shot.'

Those first fifteen minutes on Omaha were carnage, although mostly only at Vierville and Colleville. Men were drowning, weighed down by too much equipment and dropped too far out; others were being hit on the water and on the beach, by machine guns, by mortars, by rifle fire. Disaster was also unfolding further out at sea. Of the Shermans that had been launched to support the 1st Division, only two out of thirty-one tanks of the 741st Tank Battalion managed to make it ashore – all the rest had sunk, and most of the crews with them, underlining the terrible, tragic folly of the decision to launch them so far out. Some managed as much as 3,000 yards and all, it seems, had been aiming for the church spire of Colleville. Unfortunately, both the swell and the current were running eastwards, pushing them off course. In an effort to keep orientated on the church, they had been moving at an angle and against the flow of both the current and the swell. The waves had smacked against their sides and over the protective covers. And then they had sunk.

At 6.45 a.m., General Bradley joined Captain Chet Hansen in the operations room aboard USS *Augusta*. They were around a mile off shore, and hopeful the Rangers would already be ashore at Pointe du Hoc. They could see rockets being fired, smothering Omaha Beach. From where they were watching, it looked utterly one-sided.

'I don't understand this lack of return fire,' muttered Major-General Bill Kean, Bradley's chief of staff. 'Do we have another Anzio?' The landings at Anzio in Italy, in January, had been initially largely unopposed.

Bradley smiled. 'That's unlikely.'

Captain John Raaen was wondering much the same thing about the progress of the Rangers. He and his men had been circling off shore since about 6.15 a.m. For the most part they had been keeping their heads down. On LCA 1137, the Rangers of HQ Company had an SCR-300 radio and were trying to listen to what on earth was going on above the din of the guns and battle. 'After H-Hour,' said Raaen, 'suddenly the air was just full of messages, so we were listening carefully.' What they were hoping to hear was a signal from Colonel Rudder's Force A that they had successfully climbed Pointe du Hoc and destroyed the guns there. On Raaen's LSA they managed to pick up something about 'Charlie' from Force A, but that was all. Round and round they went. Seven o'clock came and went, then at 7.10 the decision was made to revert to Plan B: the rest of the Rangers would land directly on to Dog Green on Omaha Beach.

The Rangers' Force A had, in fact, been delayed. Just under 2 miles out, the British guide craft mistakenly changed direction and began heading to Pointe de la Percée instead. It was a bad mistake, although the swell, the immense amount of spray, the low cloud and smoke from the naval gunfire no doubt helped cloud judgement. Colonel Rudder, no naval navigator but a man who had studied every detail of his objective in minute detail, suddenly realized what was happening and managed to get the force back on track. It had, however, set them back by half an hour. Consequently, the first Ranger craft touched down just after 7 a.m. – the time at which they were supposed to have completed the mission.

Successive waves were now arriving at Omaha, although the smoke and dust of battle, combined with the misty low cloud, meant the beach was almost completely hidden from the sea and coxswains in the landing craft were becoming confused and landing wherever they could. For the assault troops, this was, in fact, an advantage; poor visibility cut both ways. At the western, Vierville end, Companies B, D and C were following the decimated Company A, but a number were landing further east, driven off course by the currents and wind, where the German defences were not so strong. The first boats from Company B, for example, landed unexpectedly near rocks, which provided some cover from the shooting. Although the men were dropped in water far too deep, with coaxing and goading from Staff Sergeant Odell Padgett and Lieutenant Leo Pingenot, they managed to get out and make a dash for the beach wall. 'They crossed the beach,' ran the After Action Report, 'with a loss of one killed and three wounded.'

Company C also landed off course, about 1,000 yards to the east, at Dog White, and, for the most part, ten minutes early at 7.10 a.m. No German strongpoint sat directly above them, and some of the bushes and vegetation on the bluffs had caught fire, providing a helpful smokescreen. The first assault boat initially lowered the ramp too early, but the coxswain raised it again and pushed forward. 'The enlisted men,' ran the After Action Report, 'reached the shore safely.' The second boat landed well in shallow water and the men poured out and ran fast to the sea wall. 'None of the men were wounded on this run,' it was reported, 'despite the small arms.' The fourth section landed in waist-deep water. 'Small arms was received but there were no casualties between the boat and the sea wall.' Following behind was the fifth assault section, which landed in very shallow water. Because the tide was coming in fast, the distance to the sea wall was now less than 100 yards. 'Only one casualty was incurred en route to the sea wall.' These men – almost the entire company – were now, like Company B, sheltered by the 4-foot-high sea wall, fully armed, with radios and assault engineers, and ready to push on.

From his bunker at WN71, overlooking Dog Green, the Vierville Draw, Karl Wegner had continued to fire. It was strictly *verboten* to fire an MG42 continuously for more than 250 rounds, or 11 seconds, and it was not advisable either. Each bullet was propelled by a charge that exploded in the casing, causing immense heat as it did so. With twenty-three explosions in the breech every second, and with comparatively thin steel barrels that were only air-, not gas-cooled, it took no time at all for an MG42 to become, first, red hot and then white hot. Accuracy was never the MG42's strength at the best of times – hardly surprising at that rate of fire – but very soon the barrels literally began to melt and needed changing. Firing discipline was all very well in practice, and Karl Wegner, for one, was trying hard to fire short, sharp bursts as he had been trained to do, but with hundreds of Americans coming towards him and the sea thick with enemy boats, the bursts were getting longer and the cooling-off periods shorter. Accuracy was becoming wilder and the stoppages and jams more frequent. 'When I pulled back the bolt for what seemed to be the thousandth time,' said Wegner, 'I paused for a good look down the beach.' Americans were lying everywhere, some dead, others alive. Landing craft were at the shore. One boat appeared to hit a mine, sending both men and boat fragments high into the air. But naval guns were also firing back at them, causing Wegner and his fellows to duck for cover. One shell hit their view slit and a chunk of concrete struck Obergefreiter Lang in the face. With every gun jam or barrel change, and every duck-down from Allied naval fire, so the gaps between firing were growing greater and the chances for the American assault troops to get off the beach increased.

The killing ground of Dog Green, overlooked by three strongpoints, was still a horrifically dangerous place to be, however, no matter how overheated Karl Wegner's machine gun was becoming. On board his LCA, Sergeant Bob Slaughter was not only feeling literally sick, he was also feeling increasingly apprehensive about what was unfolding. He and his fellows had been told beforehand they could expect little opposition, but where this idea came from is unclear; Colonel Charles Canham, commander of the 116th, had circulated a memo throughout all three battalions expressly warning of underestimating the enemy and it was read to all the troops before they set sail. 'We expected A and B Companies to have the beach secured by the time we landed,' noted Slaughter.

As they neared the shore, artillery and mortar shells exploded in the water around them. 'I suddenly became very worried about what Jerry could do to us.'

His LCA landed at 7.10, some 300 yards to the east, but still within view of the Vierville cluster of strongpoints. The first man off jumped before the ramp was fully down, the LCA surged forward and he was crushed to death. When it was Slaughter's turn, the craft was still bobbing up and down and it took him a moment to judge the right time to leap into water he knew was far too deep. At 6 feet 5 inches tall, his height was, for the moment, a huge advantage, and he could feel others grabbing on to him as he pushed forward through the surf. Both bullets and water seemed to be killers of equal potency. 'It was demoralizing to hear good men scream as bullets ripped into soft flesh,' wrote Slaughter, 'and others scream as the fierce, flooding tide dragged the non-swimmers under.' He was still in the water when Private Ernest McCanless appeared next to him, struggling with an ammunition box.

'Slaughter, are we going to get through this?' he shouted above the din of artillery and mortars, men's screams and the rattle of small arms.

Slaughter could not answer him; he thought they must surely be killed, a feeling reinforced as a body floated by, the face already turned purple. He struggled on, reaching the cover of a beach stake, only to notice a teller mine tied to its top. Struggling to comprehend what was happening, he looked around, wondering where all the senior non-coms and officers were. Leadership was needed and he was a sergeant, but he was nineteen and he now saw a GI get up and move only to be cut down. Lying there on the beach, his blood pouring on to the sand, the wounded man was screaming. A medic hurried over to him but was shot as well. A couple of minutes later, both were dead.

Slaughter knew he had to get off the beach. He couldn't go back and he couldn't stay where he was, so, summoning all his reserves of courage, he shouted to his depleted squad and urged them to get moving. With his bayonet fixed to the end of his Garand rifle, he got up and ran, although even without his assault jacket he was loaded down with gear and heavy, sodden clothes. Hitting a small tidal pool, he tripped, accidentally loosed off a round, recovered his balance and hurried forward, finally making the comparative safety of the sea wall. He then tried to fire his rifle but it was jammed. Taking off his assault vest, he spread it on the sand so that he could lay down his weapon to clean it, only to notice several bullet holes in his pack. Overwhelmed by a renewed bout of fear, he felt his knees weaken and his hands begin to shake. Breathing deeply, he desperately tried to compose himself.

It was 7.45 a.m. and approaching the shore were Captain John Raaen and the assault craft of the 5th Rangers. The noise was overwhelming. On his LCA, standing next to the coxswain and the British crew, Raaen could see ahead. Away to their front right, an LCM or LCT – he wasn't sure which – was hit by an artillery shell and burst into flames. 'The scene was one from hell,' he wrote, 'smoke from the fires on the face of the bluff, fires from the burning vessels and equipment, black ugly puffs from artillery bursting, dust and flying debris everywhere.' They were nearing the shore, the coxswain weaving through the obstacles. Suddenly, it looked as if they were bearing down on a staked mine, only for a wave to push them off course in the nick of time. Moments later, the LCA ground to a halt, the ramp went down and Raaen jumped off, mercifully into water only boot-deep.

'Headquarters! Over here!' he shouted, then dashed forward, heading to the sea wall now only 50 yards or so ahead and conscious of lots of small arms pinging, zipping and fizzing all around, mostly from the right. Fortunately, they too had landed further east, around the same stretch of Dog White as Company C of the 116th, having been alerted on the run-in to the suicidal situation at Dog Green. Smoke filled the air and blood – there was now lots of blood, on the sand, in little tidal pools – and the sound of artillery shells was absolutely deafening. The assault on the senses was immense and ugly. Behind Raaen, his HQ Company runner was hit in the leg and cried out, but kept going. The beach wall was just 20 yards away now, packed with men. Crouching down, he glanced back to see that his men were still coming. He watched LCI 92 touch down, the ramp drop and men spill out – then suddenly an artillery round hit it. A shard must have struck the man with the flamethrower, because the whole side of the vessel burst into flames. Another shell hit his own LCA, killing the British crew on board, but not before all his men were off. He did a quick head count. All were there. All thirty-three, albeit with one wounded.

Further towards Dog Green, Sergeant Bob Slaughter was working up the courage to lead his depleted squad over the sea wall and to the foot of the bluffs. He might have been terrified and might also have believed the situation to be hopeless, but it was not. Already, by 8 a.m., the tide was literally and metaphorically beginning to turn. Despite the carnage and the slaughter of that first wave, it was the Americans, not the German defenders, who were winning on Omaha.

CHAPTER 12

D-Day: The British and Canadian Landings

JUST BEFORE 5.30 A.M., first light was creeping over the beach at Cour-seulles. Now off shore, having navigated safely through the cleared channels among the dense enemy minefields, HMCS *Algonquin* was in position off Juno Beach, designated for the Canadian landings, and Lieu-tenant Yogi Jenson was overseeing the laying of a Danbuoy with a large metal reflector that was to be their reference mark as they moved up and down the line of bombardment. For now, however, bombing of the coast was left to the cruisers and the air forces. Jenson kept wondering when the enemy might open fire at them, but as the light began to grow there appeared to be very little happening on shore. As far as he could see, he was looking at a quiet Normandy coastal town. 'Any minute now,' he thought, 'we will be surrounded by white columns of water, but all stayed quiet.'

Algonquin was one of eleven destroyers, two cruisers – HMS *Belfast* and HMS *Diadem* – and a number of specially adapted landing craft that made up the bombardment arm of Force J. The combined fire-power of this force alone was impressive: twelve 6-inch guns, eight 5.25-inch, twenty-nine 4.7-inch and sixteen 4-inch – sixty-five guns all firing shells of 100mm in diameter. Along all the Juno defences, the Germans had just four guns of 100mm or larger, and just twenty of 50–88mm. The Canadians also had six Landing Craft, Gun (Large), each with a further two 4.7-inch guns, four Landing Craft, Flak, eight Landing Craft, Rocket, and several of the amazingly named Landing Craft, Assault (Hedgerow), which could fire twenty-four 60lb bombs to saturate wire, mines and obstacles.

Behind this screen of destroyers, the men of the Canadian 3rd Infantry Division were clambering into landing craft and experiencing much the same difficulties and nausea as their American allies further to the west. Company Sergeant-Major Charlie Martin had been up since 3.15 a.m. and was scrambling down nets thrown over the side of their transport, SS *Monowai*, at 5 a.m. Getting into the LCA as it bobbed up and down on the swell had been no easy feat, especially with all the heavy kit they were carrying. Martin had immediately realized that the real invasion was going to be nothing like the training exercises. Originally from Wales and the son of travelling circus performers, he and his family had emigrated to Canada in 1928 when Charlie was nine, settling in the Dixie area to the west of Toronto. In 1940, Martin was working on a dairy farm when the local regiment, the Queen's Own Rifles, mobilized in Toronto. He felt strongly that he ought to do his bit and so, like all other Canadians in the war, volunteered to serve. He was accepted into the Queen's and in July 1941 they set sail for England. They had been training for this moment ever since. In the meantime, Martin had won his corporal's stripes, then his sergeant's, and also the heart of an English girl; he and Vi were married on 30 October 1943. She was now working for the ATS (Auxiliary Territorial Service) as a Royal Artillery gun radar operator and he was now A Company sergeant-major and bracing himself to storm the beaches of Normandy.

The Queen's Own were part of the 8th Infantry Brigade, who would be coming ashore in the Nan sector, which ran across the beach-front towns of Bernières-sur-Mer and Saint-Aubin-sur-Mer. A second assault brigade, the 7th, was to land a little further to the west on Mike sector, either side of the town of Courseulles-sur-Mer. Martin and his fellows had about 5 miles to travel and as they began the journey to the shore, and despite the weight of naval fire-power to support them, they were silent and he couldn't help feeling rather alone. Like Yogi Jenson, Martin was also struck by how quiet it seemed. There were no enemy guns firing as they ploughed forward through the choppy surf. The battalion was being transported by ten assault craft. 'Ten boats stretched out over fifteen hundred yards is not really a whole lot of assault force,' he wrote. 'The boats began to look even tinier as the gaps widened.'

To the west of Omaha, the cliffs became more pronounced before dropping briefly to the small fishing ports of, first, Port-en-Bessin and then Arromanches. They then climbed again before dropping away once more, 12 miles from Omaha, to the beach designated Gold. The long, sandy shoreline ran east from Gold to Juno to Sword Beaches, all the way to the mouth of the Caen Canal. Perched high on the hill between Port-en-Bessin and Arromanches was the Kriegsmarine's four-gun battery of Longues-sur-Mer and these guns and other strongpoints along the British and Canadian section were now coming in for particular attention from the Royal Navy's big battleships and cruisers as the assault forces headed towards the beaches. Longues-sur-Mer alone was hit 179 times by the cruisers HMS *Ajax* and HMS *Argonaut* firing their eight 150mm and ten 133mm guns against the four 150mms of the coastal battery. The massively superior British fire-power was already beginning to count; by 6.30 a.m. the Longues battery had been silenced, as had a key strongpoint in the Gold Beach sector.

There were still *Widerstandsnester* fairly evenly spaced out and mutually supporting all along this stretch of the coast. At La Rivière, a village on the shore near Vers-sur-Mer, WN33 stood right on the beach's edge. There were two high-velocity 88mm dual-purpose anti-tank and anti-aircraft guns, as well as a 50mm Tobruk and all the usual wire entanglements, networks of trenches, mines and machine-gun posts. Martin Eineg was a private in Infanterie-Regiment 726, twenty years old and something of a boxer, despite a chronic lung condition that had technically made him unfit for active service. But this was 1944, and that was not the exemption ticket it had once been in Nazi Germany. After serving with the Luftwaffe as flak crew near Munich, he had been posted west a few months earlier and made an observer and machine-gunner. His position was in a bunker with a slit fitted with an MG34 – the early-war German light machine gun – on a gimbal mount set in the floor. This was part of a larger concrete casement housing the two 88mms 100 yards back from the sea wall, while his billet was several hundred yards further inland in an old farmhouse that had been reinforced with concrete and sandbags.

Eineg had been roused and sent forward at first light. Hurrying to his position, he found two of his comrades already there and manning the MG. Looking through the viewing slit, he was stunned. 'I was struck speechless at this sight,' he said, 'which I had never imagined possible.' Beside him, the machine-gunner, who was a middle-aged man, turned to him and laughed mirthlessly. 'Are we sorry we started this war now?' he said. Soon after, a Typhoon sped towards them, low, fast and spewing cannon shells, which hit the concrete around them. It was so low Eineg could smell its fuel. Then the firing from the ships began, endlessly it seemed, with shells whistling and screaming over and some hitting the casement. The structure shook, dust, smoke and grit filled the air, while the noise was unbearable. The loader began to scream and bang his hands against the wall, then the steel door opened and one of the artillery officers with the 88s came in. As he did so, another shell hit the edge of the viewing embrasure, sending shrapnel and bits of concrete hurtling into the bunker and whirling around, pinging off the walls. Several pieces hit the officer in the face, blinding him and smashing teeth. Flung back against the wall, he slumped to the floor.

Suddenly, the shelling stopped and, slowly, Eineg got himself to his feet. The hands of the machine-gunner were shaking, but he managed to get a grip of himself, although the loader was still on the floor, clutching his head in his hands. Eineg took over as loader. In front of them the ground was on fire, partly obscuring their view, but they could see landing craft reaching the shore.

This was the section of Gold Beach the Allies had named King sector. It was now around 7.30 a.m.; the landings by 50th Northumbrian Division were taking place almost an hour after those on Omaha – a delay necessary because the tide had to be high enough for the assault craft to get over the Calvados Reef that lay off shore. Here, at King sector, the 6th Green Howards and 5th East Yorkshires came ashore alongside DDs and AVREs – Armoured Vehicle, Royal Engineers – including flail tanks and dozers. The infantry, tanks and assault engineers were also arriving more or less where they were supposed to, and all fairly close to each other, with the result that they were able to operate together, straight up the beach and off it again, as Martin Eineg and his fellows at WN33 were about to discover.

First, though, the attackers had to get off the beach and to begin with they came under heavy fire. From WN33, the 88s began firing, tracer flashing across the beach. One shell hit the ramp of a landing craft, which then started sinking, nose down. Eineg's MG began chattering and he watched six or so men cut down as the troops tried to exit a landing craft. Another landing craft was hit by an 88. It was burning from the rear and continued to surge forward, flames rising, as it crashed on to the beach.

The shelling began again from out at sea and soon after the 88s stopped firing. Eineg heard shouting and yelling from the casement and men screaming for fire-fighting equipment. In their own bunker, Eineg and his middle-aged gunner kept firing. 'Our MG was running very hot,' said Eineg. 'The breech was glowing and it was difficult to lift the mechanism to insert fresh belts of ammunition.' Churchill tanks had come ashore and although several had been hit and knocked out, others were now targeting WN33. Blinded by smoke and dust, Eineg and his gunner stopped firing while Eineg hurried back to get some more ammunition. As he reached the corridor, however, he was stopped at pistol-point by an officer. Ordering Eineg back to his position, the officer then yelled at some medics to bring in the ammunition boxes. These arrived soon after and they began firing again, cutting down a column of infantry that had been cautiously moving towards them. It was clear, though, that their position would soon be overrun. A Sherman tank rumbled forward, infantry crouching behind. One of the 88s, functioning once more, fired, hitting the front of the tank and blowing bits off, but it still came forward. In the bunker, the MG was overheating again and Eineg struggled to reload, partly because of the heat but also because his hands were shaking and his eyes were filled with grit.

'Come on, be quick boy,' urged his comrade, 'because those troops will kill us for sure after what we've done. There's no point surrendering, do you see?' Eineg was shocked – that hadn't occurred to him – but now the Sherman was firing again and was being fired at in turn by one of the 88s. A shell knocked the tank off its tracks, slewing it sideways, and a second hit it in the side near the engine. It erupted in flames. Hatches opened and two men clambered out, only to be shot by Eineg's machine-gunner. Eineg saw them tumble off the tank and into the flames. Another shell hit the turret and the tank commander, immobile, stood there, rapidly engulfed by fire. 'I began to understand now,' said Eineg, 'what the gunner meant when he said these English would kill us for sure.' A Churchill emerged and came forward to within a few yards, firing at point-blank range at the 88, destroying both the gun and the inside of the casement.

Briefly blinded by smoke and dust, Eineg heard the Churchill firing over and over. Frantically, he tried to change ammunition belts, but then came face to face with a Tommy, covered in grey concrete dust, charging towards them. The soldier flung in a grenade, which bounced off the wall and exploded in the corridor. Eineg ducked, crouching a split second before the Tommy opened fire with his Sten sub-machine gun. The gunner, however, was not so quick. Eineg saw the bullets punch holes in his chest, then emerge from his back and ricochet wildly around the concrete walls. Several hit Eineg, but their energy was spent and, miraculously, he remained uninjured. Suddenly, the Tommy trod on a mine and bits of him and his uniform flew through the slit. Eineg ran out into the corridor. Mayhem reigned, but despite this, the same officer who had stopped him before now motioned for him to follow him back to the MG post. As the officer stepped inside, first a burst of Sten-gun fire and then another explosion rocked the room. 'I looked into the MG room and the scene was terrible,' said Eineg. 'The officer and my gunner were on fire, with their limbs burned away, and the room full of burning powder which coated the walls and was dripping from the ceiling. I was sickened by the sight.'

Eineg hurried out of the back as a flurry of Allied fighters sped overhead, running towards a number of cooks and clerks who were also fleeing and taking odd pot shots. He glanced back and saw the roof collapsing. One of the men said, 'We should surrender,' then threw away his rifle and put up his hands, only to be shot in the head, his skull fragmenting while he stood there. Tommies were now charging towards them. One German soldier was bayoneted in the stomach. Eineg turned and ran for his life along a sunken path towards his billet, where at last he met some more of their own troops, equipped with MG42s and *Panzerfaust* anti-tank weapons. An officer ordered them into the re-inforced billets. Here, he said, they would make a stand.

A little over half a mile away, the 6th Green Howards had also been charging German strongpoints. Hurrying straight up the track towards Vers-sur-Mer, they had almost passed the forward positions of the Mont Fleury strongpoint when Company Sergeant-Major Stan Hollis, realizing one of the casements was still active and threatening the troops coming off the beach, charged up a track, firing his Sten sub-machine gun. Somehow dodging enemy machine-gun fire, he jumped on top of the first bunker, threw a grenade into the viewing slit then finished off those inside with his Sten. With one bunker knocked out, he jumped into the connecting trench, changing his magazine as he ran, and was about to attack the next bunker when the Germans swiftly emerged with their hands up. Soon after, the entire Mont Fleury strongpoint, an extensive and major position with commanding views over much of Gold Beach, was overrun and out of action for good.

Meanwhile, a couple of miles to the west, at Jig sector, where the Sherwood Rangers were due to land, most of the assault troops had come ashore too far to the east. The 1st Hampshires had had a particularly difficult time of it. Several of their landing craft had hit the offshore reefs and, thinking they had beached, they had lowered the ramps only for the first men to jump out into deep water. Weighed down by their heavy equipment and packs, most of them drowned. When the rest did finally reach the shore, they had drifted some way down the beach. Meanwhile, the Royal Engineer breaching parties had landed more or less where they should and so had started clearing lanes. To reach these, the Hampshires then had to advance sideways and westwards, along the beach, which was exactly where most of the German fixed gun positions from the strongpoint at Le Hamel were pointed. Typhoons carrying 1,000lb bombs had been over and attacked the position shortly before the landings, but had been unable to knock it out. 'Get on the beach and then get off the beach' had been drummed into every man, so despite the lack of tanks and coordination with the engineers, they had pressed forward and moved inland before working their way back towards Le Hamel from behind. They still suffered considerable casualties.

Among the DD tanks supposed to support them had been the Shermans of the Sherwood Rangers Yeomanry. Major Stanley Christopherson's A Squadron was in reserve, so not swimming ashore; that dubious privilege had been given to B and C Squadrons. At H-Hour, 7.30 a.m., Christopherson, still out at sea on his LCT, switched on his own tank's radio set to see how the other two squadrons were faring. Reception was, unsurprisingly, poor and there was continual interference from other stations, but he was able to hear occasional familiar voices, including that of his greatest friend in the regiment, Stephen Mitchell, who was commanding C Squadron. 'He certainly appeared to be most irritated,' noted Christopherson with typical understatement, 'but it was good to hear his voice, which meant he was safe for the time being.'

He was, but in fact they too were drifting off course and badly behind schedule. In all, five DD tanks from C Squadron and three from B sank, but the rest – which amounted to thirty – made it, thanks to the good sense of the navy, who took them in to within 600 yards of the shore rather than releasing them at 7,000 yards as originally planned; so far, only the 741st Tank Battalion had suffered that error of judgement. The first tanks of the Sherwood Rangers came ashore just after 8 a.m., and also too far east, which meant they too had to work their way back up the beach, and under the watch of a 77mm gun in a casement at the western end, part of the Le Hamel strongpoint. Within moments of getting ashore, Lieutenant Monty Horley's B Squadron Sherman was hit. Three of the crew managed to get out, only for two of them, Horley included, to be shot and killed. Horley had been with the regiment since North Africa.

All along the beach, vicious fighting was taking place, while landing craft were struggling against the beach obstacles.

To the east, at Juno Beach, the first destroyer of Force J had opened fire at 6.19 a.m., targeting enemy gun positions inland, but *Algonquin* did not join in until 7 a.m., when she began pasting two strongpoints at Saint-Aubin and Saint-Bernières, WN27 and WN28, both of which had 50mm anti-tank guns as well as machine guns and mortars; these were the *Widerstandsnester* that Bob Roberts, Charlie Martin and their respective regiments had been told to capture. Their landing craft were heading towards Juno, but slightly behind schedule and with almost no interference from the enemy; the contrast with Omaha could not have been greater, as German guns inland were firing at Force J – not that Yogi Jenson noticed – and the guns on the beaches were faced along the beach rather than out to sea. DD Shermans were also heading towards the beach, as were AVREs of the 80th Assault Squadron. AVREs were part of the British 79th Armoured Division, commanded by Major-General Percy Hobart, who, despite being a pioneer of British armoured warfare and a superb trainer of men, had been retired before the war and in 1940 had been serving as a private in the Home Guard. Swiftly brought back into service, he had first raised and trained up the 11th Armoured Division and then the 79th, with a specific brief to expand specialist assault armour. DD tanks had been developed on his watch, as had a number of other 'Hobart's Funnies', as they became known, most of which were based on the Churchill tank, which not only had the thickest armour of any tank in the Allied arsenal but could also climb more steeply than any other. The AVREs were designed to help the infantry get ashore by blasting paths through beach defences. Among these AVREs were ramp carriers, bridge layers, fascine carriers, Churchills with the main gun replaced with a 290mm bunker-buster mortar and also a 'Crab' or flail tank, which rotated chains ahead of a Sherman, whipping up the ground and any potential mines. Then there was 'Crocodile' – a Churchill tank that, in addition to its main gun, was fitted with a flame-thrower that towed a trailer filled with fuel. Using compressed nitrogen as a propellant, it could project a lethal burst of flame as far as 150 yards.

The Canadian troops landed at 7.45 a.m. As soon as the ramp was down, Sergeant Charlie Martin of the Queen's Own Rifles shouted,

'Move! Fast! Don't stop for anything! Go! Go! Go!' Then they were running across the beach, scaling the sea wall and dashing across the railway line. Bullets pinged and zipped all around. A number of men were hit. From his LCA alone, Martin lost four killed and one wounded. One of the platoon commanders was hit twice; two NCOs from 9 Platoon were also wounded; others from the company, men Martin had known since joining the regiment, were cut down and killed. Discipline and training kept them going, however. They were fit and at least 30 per cent of the platoon were first-class marksmen. They quickly cleared one MG post, which gave them some let-up, then hit wire entanglements. With mortars falling worryingly close and the hiss of bullets, they swiftly opened a path with their cutters and pushed on through, only to reach a minefield. There was no choice but to keep going. Martin led, and had gone ten paces when he trod on a Schu-mine – an anti-personnel mine that, the moment the pressure was released, burst in the air at knee height, spreading shrapnel and buckshot over a wide area. The key was not to release the pressure. Waving his men on past, Martin waited until they were all clear and was just leaning forward about to spread himself flat on the ground when a bullet hit a glancing blow on his tin helmet, spinning it round and knocking it off his head. Leaping forward, he dived for the ground, the mine exploded – thankfully above his head – and, having survived two close calls within a matter of moments, he hurried on without his helmet.

While the Queen's Own had been approaching Nan White, on their left had been the North Shore New Brunswick Regiment, due to land at Nan Red, facing the town of Saint-Aubin. One of those now heading towards the sea front was 21-year-old Eldon 'Bob' Roberts, his section's Bren machine-gunner. Unlike the MG42, the Bren was magazine- rather than belt-fed and had a rate of fire of around 500 rounds per minute, the firing speed that had proved so effective in the First World War. While a Bren could not produce the initial weight of fire of the German light machine gun, it was considerably more accurate, far easier to carry and manoeuvre than the MG42, and had a thicker barrel that could fire 250,000 rounds before replacing. The lower rate of fire and a change of magazine after twenty-eight rounds also ensured it suffered none of the overheating issues of the German model. 'It was a great gun,' said Roberts. 'Reliable, accurate, easy to handle.'

Roberts was a fairly laid-back fellow. One of an astonishing fifteen children, he had been brought up on a farm in New Brunswick on the eastern edge of Canada. The nearest town of any note was 30 miles away. 'Right out in the country,' he said. 'Real wild. We had cows, sheep, pigs – all horse power in those days. Man power and horse power.' The tiny local school for the farming families round about was 2 miles away. In summer they walked there, in winter they skied. They were almost entirely self-sufficient and the children were expected to pitch in just as soon as they were old enough. 'When I was eight years old,' said Roberts, 'I was on the end of the old cross-cut saw, sawing down trees with my father.' His parents were strict but loving and devoutly Christian, so Roberts grew up respecting authority and discipline, but was also independent of mind and used to thinking on his feet. It was, in fact, the kind of upbringing that prepared him very well for life in the army.

He joined up in May 1942, reaching England very early in January 1943. Since then he and his mates had been training non-stop: eighteen months preparing for this moment. He felt ready for what was to come and wasn't particularly scared. 'Because you didn't know what you were going to face,' he said. 'You'd done so much training, it had become second nature.'

In his bunker in Courseulles, Oberleutnant Tauber looked out across the long stretch of the beach, then at low tide, and at the belts of defence obstacles silhouetted spectrally against the grey dawn. Turning to his men, he was reminding them of their tasks when suddenly a massive barrage of explosions broke all around them. 'When the explosions began,' he said, 'I realised they were of an enormous calibre, much bigger than any artillery I had heard before.' This was the Eastern Task Force opening fire, which to anyone watching from the coast looked rather like a single flash of orange flame. The ground shook and shock waves pummelled the Germans' ears as they crouched down, hands around their heads. One of the younger lads broke down and began sobbing uncontrollably. Another tried to run, but Tauber's corporal tackled the man before he could escape. 'However great the pressure,' said Tauber, 'we could not tolerate men acting like that.' Looking through the periscope, all he could now see was smoke, dust and debris filling the air.

At Saint-Aubin, Bob Roberts's landing craft was the first to touch down and he was the second man ashore as the ramp came down on to sand rather than in water. It was around 7.50 a.m. There was absolutely no firing at all in those first moments. 'There was nothing,' said Roberts. 'It was absolutely empty because they all had their heads down.' He was following Corporal Cleeve Campbell and several others from his section. They went around the 50mm bunker, then pushed down a road that led from the sea front, wondering where all the Germans were. Campbell now ordered them to start searching the houses, two men to each house. Roberts was with Private Lecroix. They kicked open the house door to find a startled-looking Frenchman. Lecroix, a French speaker, told him they had come to search his house. The man showed them into a room that had a hatch, which, he told them, led down to a tunnel to the sea front and a bunker where the Germans had a machine gun. Roberts hurried out to find Campbell and get permission to investigate, which the corporal granted. He also handed Lecroix a flame-thrower.

Back they went into the house, then through the hatch and down a ladder. It was dark and Roberts wondered if they would ever get back out alive. Feeling their way along a narrow tunnel, they eventually saw a slit of daylight and other tunnels joining theirs. Up ahead a machine gun was chattering – whatever stupor the Germans had been in, they had clearly recovered. The firing of the machine gun masked the sound of Roberts's and Lecroix's approach, however. 'All I could see was two men standing there,' recalled Roberts. 'It was like a semi-circular platform with a four-foot wall and a gun on top.' He now stepped forward and gave them a burst from his Bren gun across their legs; at the same time, Lecroix moved in with the flame-thrower. They stepped back into the shadows as more troops came running to the help of the downed men. 'They thought it was something coming from the sea,' said Roberts, 'and so they come trying to beat the flames out of the burning men.'

Roberts and Lecroix took another step forward and let rip with the Bren and flame-thrower once again. 'Come on,' Roberts now said to Lecroix, 'let's get the hell out of here. And if you hear or see anything on the way out it won't be one of ours, so give them a lick of flame.' But they both got out safely without meeting any more of the enemy. By neutralizing that gun position, Roberts and Lecroix had saved the lives of a lot of their fellows.

A short way up the coast at Courseulles, Oberleutnant Cornelius Tauber was peering through his periscope in his camouflaged bunker, desperately trying to make out what was going on. He had ordered one of the Goliaths to be started and moved to the tunnel towards the beach; the sound had seemed so feeble compared to what was going on outside, it had made them all laugh somewhat manically. Now Tauber saw Sherman tanks moving up across the beach – precisely the targets for which the Goliaths had been intended – and so ordered his men to move out the first Goliath. Through his periscope he watched it advance towards the first Sherman. The nearby 50mm gun was also firing and a shell could be seen ricocheting off the tank's turret. Off shore, the naval guns were continuing to fire, shells hurtling over. One struck the rocks in front of the bunker, the blast wave knocking Tauber over. Recovering, he looked back towards the Goliath and saw it was stationary and had shed a track. It was now effectively useless. A second Goliath was sent out, but 20 yards from the nearest tank it also ground to a halt. Tauber ordered its detonation – what else could he do? – but the explosion did not appear to cause much damage.

Moments later, a number of Canadian troops passed by the viewing slit without noticing them. Unfortunately for Tauber, one of his men fired his rifle, hitting one of the Canadians, who began writhing on the sand while his fellows took cover. Then, before Tauber and his men had a chance to respond, one of the Canadians stepped forward and a second later a shot of flame sped through the viewing slit. Two of the men were hit immediately, their uniforms catching fire. They threw themselves about, thrashing wildly and crashing into the others. 'They screamed as they thrashed about,' recalled Tauber. 'I can still hear those screams in my mind.' Another spurt of flame shot through the slit, setting a waiting Goliath on fire. Those who could leaped for the exit tunnel as the two burning men collapsed on the floor. Tauber and his men ran like rabbits, down the tunnel and towards the main bunker, where he emerged, pistol in hand, straight into a Canadian with a rifle and bayonet fixed. Tauber was stunned to see enemy troops there already. The Canadian yelled out and swung his rifle butt, hitting Tauber in the face. Stunned, in pain and utterly shocked that someone would actually want to kill him, Tauber fired twice, sprays of the man's blood blowing back at him. Half dazed, he looked up, saw a mass of contrails in the sky and then realized the Canadian had fallen. Dazed and confused, he rolled into a trench, landing on two bodies, a German and a Canadian who had apparently killed one another. He crawled over them and tried to escape, his pistol still in his hand, blood from the smash on his face blurring his vision.

Rounding a corner of the trench, he saw three other retreating soldiers and followed them until the trench ran out. They then made a dash for it, running clear of the strongpoint and heading for the next, further inland. As they ran, a mortar shell burst nearby, ripping off the arm of one of the men and tearing half his face away. Grabbing the dead man's MP40 sub-machine gun, Tauber ran on towards the next strongpoint, based around a Tobruk tank turret. The approach, however, was mined and one of the other men with him trod on one. There was a small explosion and the soldier fell forward, gurgling. 'I saw that his legs were blown off below the knee and his trousers were burning,' said Tauber, 'showing his shin bones in the smoke.' The man's whole body was convulsing and as he shook he set off a second mine, which blew away a large piece of his chest. On Tauber went, barely pausing to glance at the dreadful sight, and was himself nearly cut down by one of their own machine-gunners. Bullets had hit the third soldier with him, but Tauber grabbed him and they made the last few yards, dropping down into the temporary safety of the next strongpoint. Of his men in the Goliath bunker, there was no longer any sign.

It was now nearly half past eight. At Gold Beach, the LCTs with British 8th Armoured Brigade Tactical (TAC) Headquarters landed a half-track of the Royal Army Medical Corps (RAMC) attached to the Sherwood Rangers, as well as the brigadier, brigade major and Shermans of the Protections Troop, plus signals trucks and two platoons of 12th/60th King's Royal Rifle Corps – the brigade's motor battalion – with their Jeeps and carriers. Also travelling with this group of LCTs were the brigade's four chaplains, including Padre Leslie Skinner. The son of a hairdresser from York, Skinner was thirty-four years old and, although he had joined his father's business, he had also become a lay Methodist preacher before deciding to join the church. Posted to northern India in 1937, he returned a year later after contracting malaria and otosclerosis, which left him permanently hard of hearing. When war was declared, he joined the Royal Army Chaplains' Service, was finally ordained in 1941 and served in Persia, Iraq and Egypt before returning to England in late 1942. Now he was the senior chaplain of four in the brigade and chaplain to the Sherwood Rangers, where he had become a firm friend, a cheerful presence to all and a much-valued source of spiritual guidance to the young men facing battle.

'Up at 5.00 hours cold, wet, sea rough,' he wrote in his diary. 'Stand to for 08.00. This is it.'* They were running for the beach and under fire by 8.10 a.m. Major Lawrence Biddle, the brigade major, asked for volunteers

---

* There has been some debate over precisely when the Sherwood Rangers landed. Skinner records 'stand to' was at 07.00 and that they beached at 07.25, but this cannot be so. Other sources make it clear he was an hour early in his diary, an

to unroll the coconut matting off the prow of the LCT and Skinner and three others volunteered. Beaching at 8.25 a.m., they hit a mine as they did so. The men either side of Skinner were wounded, one losing a leg, and the padre himself was blown backwards on to a Bren carrier, but still in one piece. The blast also jammed the landing doors. While others were desperately trying to get them open, Skinner attended the wounded men and gave them morphine. Eventually, the doors opened and they rolled out the coconut matting on to water that was about 6 feet deep and still rough. Shelling was heavy, the noise immense. Skinner watched the carriers and Jeeps move off and was then knocked into the water himself. He managed to struggle through to the shore, although his side now hurt like hell from the mine blast. 'Chaos ashore. Germans firing everything they had,' he scribbled in his diary. 'Road mined – great hole. Bulldozers unable to get through because mines. One tried – went up on mine.' Further down the beach, two AVREs were burning fiercely. Wrecked landing craft littered the shoreline. Thick smoke filled the air.

Stanley Christopherson and the rest of A Squadron, meanwhile, came ashore around 9 a.m. Now the tide was so much higher, the beach obstacles were even more of a problem and the LCTs had to be steered around very carefully, no easy task in the wind and swell. Christopherson's LCT did ram a stake, although fortunately it was not mined. The coxswain then had to extricate them – the LCT was put into reverse and made a complete turn, so by the time they got clear they were facing England once more. Christopherson had a 'sneaking desire' to keep going in that direction. Eventually, a little late, the ramps went down and they drove off, into the sea, and made it to shore. The beach was already calmer, not least because the troublesome 77mm had been knocked out by a 25-pounder field gun of the Essex Yeomanry.

Landings had also been made by the British at Sword Beach, on the eastern edge of the main invasion front. Offshore reefs and shipping constraints meant there had been neither the space nor capacity for two complete divisions to be landed on this stretch, although 3rd Division had become substantially swollen for the assault with the addition of the Commandos of 1st Special Service Brigade, as well as No. 41 Royal Marine Commando and the Marines' 5th Independent Armoured

---

entirely justifiable error in the circumstances. I have amended his timings to reflect this.

Support Battery. Nor was the division light on engineers and artillery. In fact, 3rd Division was pretty close to two divisions' worth of fighting men.

However, the two components – infantry and Commandos – had quite different roles. The Commandos were to capture the coastal port of Ouistreham, then hurry to reinforce the airborne forces hopefully still holding Pegasus and Horsa Bridges, and after that to strengthen the crucial left, eastern, flank. The infantry, meanwhile, were to break through the coastal crust and, all things being well, head unchallenged to Caen, 10 miles to the south. It was a big ask, but there was some form for this. Eleven months earlier, in Sicily, XIII Corps had landed 10 miles from Syracuse and had captured it that same day, despite having to take various batteries, strongpoints and vital bridges en route. Commanding XIII Corps then had been Lieutenant-General Miles Dempsey. Now Dempsey was commanding British Second Army.

The first troops ashore at Sword had been DD Shermans at around 7.20 a.m., with the infantry following five minutes later and various AVREs arriving shortly after. Despite the hammering German defences had received in the run-up to D-Day and already that morning, they had still been functioning and as the 'funnies' had come ashore they had run into a storm of fire from guns, mortars and small arms. On the Queen Red sector of the beach, where the 2nd East Yorkshire Regiment landed, more than 200 men had been killed or wounded in a matter of minutes and, as at Omaha, the infantry quickly became pinned down by the sea wall. Progress was being made, however, even if Sword Beach did look chaotic. The biggest challenge for the invading infantry was overcoming the strongpoints WN18 and WN20, code-named COD by the British. These were among the best developed and coordinated defensive positions along the entire coast.

Every bit as formidable, however, was the next line of defences, Oberst Ludwig Krug's strongpoints a mile or so inland, which were code-named MORRIS and HILLMAN by the British, and which were the objective for the 1st Suffolks, the third battalion in 8th Brigade, who were landing at around 8.30 a.m. No matter how nightmarish it might have seemed on the beach, Corporal Arthur Blizzard of the Pioneer Platoon was feeling reasonably confident as his landing craft approached the shore. Like his fellows in the platoon, he was laden with equipment, including a flamethrower, his Sten gun, and what were known as 'beehives' – explosive charges that could blow holes in walls and which weighed 60 lb strapped to his back. He was also carrying a Bangalore torpedo – a long pipe filled with nails, shot and an explosive charge. These could be fed into wire entanglements to blow open a path the size of a small room. It was a lot, but Blizzard felt fit enough for two men, not one. All in all, he was reasonably optimistic and had been buoyed by the sight of the invasion fleet. 'It was terrific when you looked and saw all that was around you,' he said, 'hundreds of ships of all sizes. It was a marvellous do.'

As the ramp was lowered, Blizzard jumped down on to Queen sector of the beach at around 8.30 a.m. The smoke was less than it had been, but there was still plenty of machine-gun fire raking the beach, so he paused by the wreck of a burned-out Sherman to get his bearings. Enemy fire was coming from an old sea-front house ahead of them. 'Jerry was machine-gunning us from there,' said Blizzard, 'so we had to lay there and machine gun back. That's all you could do and then run like anything, as hard as you could.' All the time, offshore naval shells were screaming in and the Shermans and AVREs were also still hammering the strongpoints, so that with the combination of suppressing fire from the Bren as well, Blizzard and his section were able to get off the beach in one piece.

The Commandos had finally begun coming ashore at around 8.20 a.m. The 1st Special Service Brigade was made up of Nos 3, 4 and 6 Commando and 45 Royal Marine Commando, each of 464 men and commanded by Brigadier the Lord Lovat, chief of Clan Fraser of Lovat and a colourful, swashbuckling character who had already won a Distinguished Service Cross (DSC) for his part in the Dieppe Raid in 1942. The assault on Sword Beach seems to have attracted some eccentrics. One company commander in the first wave had spent the run to the shore reciting key passages of *Henry V* through a megaphone, while Lord Lovat insisted on wearing his beret rather than a helmet and was equally adamant that his own personal piper should play the bagpipes as they landed. It all helped with the *esprit de corps*. Like the airborne troops, the Commandos – whether the army or naval version – were volunteers, had undergone special training and were taught to use their initiative and think on their feet. Each man was supremely fit. They thought themselves a cut above the rest and, collectively, they were.

Among Lovat's men were two troops of French Commandos under Capitaine Philippe Kieffer, a 44-year-old naval officer who had joined the Free French following the fall of France in June 1940. In 1941, inspired by the raising of the British Commandos, he asked for permission from his Free French superiors to raise a unit of Fusiliers-Marins Commandos, based on the Royal Marine Commandos, and was duly given it. Kieffer led his men in the failed Dieppe Raid and since then they had taken part in a number of night raids on the French and Dutch coasts. Understandably, Kieffer was desperate to take part in the invasion and so agreed to bring his two troops – now 177 men strong – into 4 Commando and to serve under its commander, Lieutenant-Colonel Robert Dawson, a fluent French speaker.

The *Bérets Verts* – Green Berets – were the only French troops to be part of the seaborne landings. Among them was Lieutenant Hubert Fauré, twenty-nine years old and returning to France with no small amount of hope in his heart. Fauré had joined the French cavalry in 1940 and had fought throughout the Battle for France, before being captured on the day of the armistice that June. He had managed to escape his prison camp and join an embryonic resistance group in the Périgueux region, then crossed into Spain and was promptly arrested and put into a fascist camp. Escaping again, he made his way to Portugal, managing in Lisbon to get on board a flight to Bristol. In late 1942, after being fully debriefed, he joined other Free Frenchmen. There he learned that Kieffer was recruiting for his Commandos. Volunteering with around forty others, he spent four weeks in north Wales undergoing intensive physical and psychological training and was then made a section commander in 1 Troop. By the spring of 1944, they had been training for over a year and the men were chomping at the bit. 'The most difficult challenge as a section leader was to contain the men's impatience,' said Fauré. 'The only way to keep them quiet was to impose ever tougher training on them.'

Finally they were returning to France, not for a quick, dashing raid, but, they hoped, for good. Their two troops were in two LCIs, much larger than LCAs. It was now 8.20 a.m., the tide was rising and, for the landing craft, weaving their way through a mass of Rommel's beach obstacles was difficult and hazardous in equal measure. Avoiding them entirely was next to impossible, and the first hit a stake and became stuck a little too far out, while the second damaged her propellers. Despite this, and mortar shells dropping around them, both beached more or less in the right place at the eastern edge of Queen Red. However, their landing, alongside the LCAs of the rest of 4 Commando, prompted a hail of mortar and machine-gun fire, and as the second lowered its twin ramps they were smashed by a direct hit. Netting was hastily thrown over the sides, while on the first LCI several men were shot and wounded as they clambered down the ramps. Others began to jump off, over the side and into the sea, Fauré included. He was completely submerged when a mortar shell hit the water nearby. 'The shock was so strong I thought I had been hit,' he said. 'The impact on my lungs really affected me.' Gasping for air, he managed to surface and, passing floating dead bodies and wounded men, staggered on to the beach and ran. As elsewhere, they had been told to keep moving and not stop, even to help comrades. Two of his good friends were injured but, having taken their maps, he pressed on.

Mortar fire, especially, was crippling the Frenchmen as they headed through the blown wire and minefield to reach the planned assembly area in the dunes. Of the 177 men in Kieffer's two troops, only 114 made it across the beach, and although fortunately most of those hit were wounded rather than dead, almost a third were now *hors de combat*. Off the beach, among the dunes, it was quieter and calmer, and the French troops were able to rendezvous with the rest of 4 Commando before starting their assault on Ouistreham. Diplomatically, Colonel Dawson agreed that the French should lead the attack and even accepted that Kieffer should remain in command.

It was around 9 a.m. on D-Day, and along the invasion front Allied forces had managed to secure a tentative foothold. So far, Rommel's crust had not proved thick enough. The beach obstacles had not been sufficiently dense to prevent the landings and, one by one, strongpoints were being knocked out. Nor was Rommel himself anywhere near the front, while his senior commanders were frantically trying to respond to what was happening. It was early still, the day was young, and much remained uncertain, unclear and altogether chaotic, yet already the task facing the defenders was growing. The next few hours would be critical.

CHAPTER 13

D-Day: The Turning of the Battle

7.30 A.M. LIEUTENANT DICK Winters had managed to find a number of others from the 2nd Battalion of the 506th PIR, including Captain Clarence Hester, the battalion S3 operations officer, and Captain Lewis Nixon, the S2 intelligence officer. Both were good friends of Winters, so he was relieved to see they had both safely made the jump. They were now holed up in a cluster of farm buildings at a small settlement called, rather inappropriately, Le Grand Chemin, about a mile north of the village of Sainte-Marie-du-Mont and 3 miles south-east of Sainte-Mère-Église. There were now around 200 men at Le Grand Chemin, including as many as eighty from Battalion HQ Company, even more – some ninety – from Company D, six from F and just eight, Winters included, from Easy Company. Nearby, some enemy guns were firing intermittently, the boom sending pulses through the ground that were clearly felt at the cluster of farm buildings.

Winters had been looking for Lieutenant Meehan, unaware that Easy's commander was already dead, when Hester informed him a battery of four 105mm guns was threatening Utah. 'Take care of it,' Hester told him. The reason the small number of Easy men were given the task rather than the larger group from Dog Company was because, minutes before Winters had arrived, a patrol from Company D had been shot up in front of Brécourt. The survivors had returned to Le Grand Chemin and had spooked the other Dog Company men; one lieutenant was shaking uncontrollably. So Winters, a platoon commander in a company that so far had just eight paratroopers, was singled out to destroy this position. He was given no further brief and allocated no men, which was also surprising. A rule of thumb is to attack with a numerical advantage of at least 3:1, which would have made this at the very least a company-size attack of over 120 men.

Instead, Winters gathered his seven men and a couple of others, told them to get rid of everything except ammo, grenades and their weapons, then together they hurried across a couple of fields, hidden by dense hedges. Winters went forward alone until he could peer through into the field where the guns were positioned. The field appeared to be roughly triangular, with four guns dug in behind the longest hedgerow. Trenches had also been dug to connect the guns to each other. A direct assault was clearly out of the question. Instead, Winters decided they should take out the guns one by one. He had two .30-calibre machine guns among his understrength assault platoon. These were accurate, as reliable as anything, and his men knew how to use them. They would provide covering fire. Then he split his men into two teams. He would lead one of three other men, while Lieutenant Buck Compton would take the rest. Moving into the next field, Compton, along with Sergeants Guarnere and Malarkey, now moved along the other side of the hedgerow behind which the guns were firing, until they were almost in line with the first gun.

Winters led his team on the other side, crawling across the open field to close in on the edge of the field near the first gun. The Germans manning the guns were partly hidden by the trenches and busy with firing. The noise was also deafening. As a result, they did not notice Winters and his team crawling through the lush Normandy grass. At the hedge, Winters paused, positioned one of the machine guns, then they moved forward along the hedgerow with Compton and his team on the other side. Winters now spotted a German helmet, fired a couple of shots and the head disappeared from view. Moments later, Compton's team were lobbing grenades and, as they did so, Winters and his team charged the gun position, getting into the trench as the first grenade exploded on the head of one of the Germans manning the gun. Now the enemy was reacting and one of Winters' men, 'Popeye' Wynn, was hit in the backside. 'I'm sorry, Lieutenant, I goofed,' he said to Winters. 'I goofed, I'm sorry.' At the same moment, a German stick grenade flew towards them and landed between Corporal Joe Toye's legs as he lay spreadeagled.

'Move, for Christ's sake, move!' Winters called and Toye rolled, the grenade exploding against his rifle butt without injuring any of them. Quickly, they got up and rushed the gun. Three Germans fled across the open field. Winters hit one, while Guarnere fired with his Tommy gun and missed. A second was hit and the third began to turn back when Winters lay down and shot him clean in the head. 'This entire engagement,' noted Winters, 'must have taken about fifteen or twenty seconds.'

Up ahead, two Germans were now frantically setting up a machine gun but, spotting them, Winters fired, hitting one in the hip and the second in the shoulder. He now sent Wynn back to battalion to get his backside looked at, then got ready to assault the next gun. Clearly, the Germans were now fully alive to what was happening and were probably preparing to counter-attack. At this moment, Compton, who had been fiddling with a grenade, dropped it; they were all in the gun pit, but although it exploded, for some miraculous reason none of them was hurt. Meanwhile, Malarkey now ran out to one of the dead Germans to take what he thought was a Luger pistol. As it turned out, he was mistaken so ran back, Winters yelling at him and bullets pinging around him as he dived back into the cover of the gun pit. Two acts of foolishness had nearly cost them dear.

A frightened German now ran towards them with his hands over his head – their first prisoner – but they needed to disable the first gun. Only Sergeant Carwood Lipton had any TNT, but it was in his musette bag, left where they had started the attack. Winters ordered him to fetch it and they got ready to attack the second gun. Leaving three men with the first gun and to provide cover, Winters led four others on a charge down the trench, lobbing grenades and managing to hit the second gun. The enemy crew fell back and the two men he had wounded earlier were taken prisoner. Six more Germans came forward, hands up, calling out, 'No make me dead!'

That was two guns down. Captain Hester came along the hedge line with extra TNT and an extra man, Private John Hall of HQ Company. Reinforcements were on their way, Hester told him – Lieutenant Ronald Speirs would soon be along with some Company D men – but in the meantime Winters had three of his men charge the third gun. Hall took the lead and was killed, but the gun was captured in much the same way as the others. Meanwhile, Winters had found a map at the second gun on which every gun position on the Cotentin Peninsula was clearly marked; he immediately had it sent back to Battalion. He also spotted a box of wooden machine-gun bullets. 'Perhaps the Germans were short of ammunition,' he noted, 'but that was the least of my concerns.'

Here they paused. The final gun was still firing, though most of the enemy troops had pulled back towards the manor house of Brécourt beyond the far end of the field; none the less, the attackers were still drawing heavy machine-gun fire every time they raised their heads. Eventually, Speirs arrived and they put in an assault on the last gun, charging down the connecting trench, lobbing grenades and firing. Having disabled the fourth gun with TNT down the barrel and the mission accomplished, Winters ordered them all to fall back. He was the last to leave. 'I took a final look down the trench,' he wrote, 'and there was this one wounded Jerry trying to put a machine gun into operation. I drilled him through the head.'

By the time they reached Battalion HQ, three hours had passed: it was 11.30 a.m., and more men had arrived. The next task would be to clear the entire area of enemy troops, but for the moment Winters and his men could afford to take a breather. Just twelve men had destroyed four guns and although the German troops, from Artillerie-Regiment 90, had hardly been the finest in Normandy, it had been a spectacularly audacious and brilliantly executed operation.* Winters neither drank nor smoke, but he did allow himself a swig of cider. 'I was thirsty as hell,' he admitted, 'and I needed a lift.' It had been a very long day already.

While the Allies assaulted the Normandy coastline, the German reaction to what was happening was, frankly, a chaotic mess. Achieving tactical surprise had been such a key objective for the Allied planners and, despite the hints, leaks and signals, that was exactly what had happened. As General Miles Dempsey, the commander of British Second Army, pointed out, assuming surprise was achieved, D-Day would always favour the attacker. 'Everything is in his favour,' he noted. 'Detailed plans, rehearsals, tactical surprise, morale.' It gave them an extraordinary advantage. On the morning of 6 June, German leadership was in disarray to say the very least. At OB West Headquarters in Paris, it had been around 4 a.m. before von Rundstedt had finally agreed with General Günther Blumentritt, his chief of staff, that the invasion was upon them; Blumentritt had contacted the OKW at Berchtesgaden ten minutes earlier, asking permission to release the Panzer-Lehr, which was at Le Mans, and the 12. Waffen-SS-Division 'Hitlerjugend', which was north of Paris. Without waiting for a reply, von Rundstedt ordered both

---

* Oberst von der Heydte of Fallschirmjäger-Regiment 6 later claimed he discovered that the gun battery at Brécourt had been abandoned at around 7 a.m., so had his own men take over. He must have mistaken this battery for another, however, as Winters was certain they were not *Fallschirmjäger*. The quality of the defenders suggests Winters was right.

divisions to send forward one *Kampfgruppe* – battle group – towards Lisieux and Caen respectively. Permission to take control of those divisions was not granted, however, even though during these hours of darkness, before the main invasion force landed and Allied air forces flew over en masse, every minute counted.

Meanwhile, General Max Pemsel at 7. Armee HQ was repeatedly ringing General Speidel at La Roche-Guyon. At 5.15 a.m. he reported that a map of Caen had been discovered on a crashed British glider. Everything that was happening, Pemsel said, pointed to this being a major assault. At 5.40 a.m. Speidel asked whether any troops had actually yet landed from the sea? Pemsel had to admit they had not. Pemsel rang again at 6.15 a.m. A massive naval bombardment had begun and a huge fleet lay off the Normandy coast. Still Speidel refused to accept this was the main invasion; that, he told Pemsel, could still be coming elsewhere. What was Speidel thinking? Was he still drunk? Another member of staff at Rommel's HQ was Admiral Ruge. He had stayed up all night listening to the various reports coming in, although there had been little he could do. Like Speidel, he was not thinking logically or clearly; perhaps he had drunk too much the previous evening as well. At 6.45 a.m., Pemsel had rung von Salmuth's 15. Armee and told him about the naval bombardment, but added that no troops had yet landed. In fact, by then they had. 'So,' replied von Salmuth, 'the enemy invasion has failed already.' He then went back to bed.

Speidel finally rang Rommel at around 6.20 a.m. – 7.20 a.m. in Germany. The field marshal had already been up getting things ready for Lucie's birthday – arranging presents on the drawing-room table, with the shoes he had bought for her in Paris as the centrepiece. The house resembled a hothouse, there were so many flowers. Then he was called to the phone. It was Speidel. Was it the main invasion, Rommel demanded, or some kind of large-scale raid? Speidel wasn't sure. 'Well find out – now!' Rommel told him, slamming down the phone. After hurrying to change and get ready to head straight back to France, Rommel was then kept waiting at least three more hours. Not until 10.15 a.m. did Speidel call back to confirm that what was happening was unquestionably the invasion. Five invasion beaches, the airborne drops, all well established already. Rommel was stunned. 'Normandy! Normandy!' he muttered over and over. 'How stupid of me!' He finally got going for France at around 10.30 a.m. It was a bit like shutting the stable door after the horse had bolted.

With Speidel still inebriated, inert or just having a momentary loss of reason, it had been left to Pemsel and General Marcks to organize what response they could without any armoured-division support except that of 21. Panzer. Conflicting reports and demands were addling Marcks's brain too. At 8 a.m. Oberst Fritz Ziegelmann, the chief of staff of the 352. Division, had telephoned Marcks and implored him to hand back command of Oberst Karl Meyer's reinforced Regiment 915. Yes, it was the corps reserve, but, Ziegelmann argued, it was needed by 352. Division further west and certainly not where Marcks had sent Meyer's *Kampfgruppe* shortly after 3 a.m. Whatever trouble was being caused there by enemy paratroopers was being dealt with by Regiment 914 and Fallschirmjäger-Regiment 6. Instead, Ziegelmann suggested, they should be ordered urgently to head to the Bayeux area to protect the division's right flank. Marcks agreed.

At Pointe du Hoc, the US Army Rangers had achieved their task with ease. Despite wet ropes made overly heavy by the sea spray, and despite the entire force landing on the eastern side of the Pointe rather than on either side, the Rangers had clambered up the cliffs with very little difficulty. Only a few defenders above took pot shots and lobbed grenades, and the Rangers reached the top with just fifteen casualties. At the summit, they encountered a scene of barely imaginable devastation: bomb craters peppered the site, turning it into a lunar landscape, with smashed and broken concrete and debris all around. Of the 155mm guns there was absolutely no sign: the gun positions were all empty, and while a small amount of inaccurate enemy sniping greeted them, the Germans appeared to have either fled or gone to ground. The observation post was quickly neutralized and some prisoners taken, and Colonel Rudder set up his command post by the smashed concrete of the anti-aircraft casement on the western side of the Pointe's cliffs.

Meanwhile, patrols from Companies D and E pushed inland, reached the coastal road 1,000 yards from the tip of the Pointe, then crossed and probed further down a hedge-lined track. Both patrols, moving at different times, came across five guns, heavily camouflaged along a hedgerow in an orchard and pointing towards Utah Beach. Much to their surprise, they were completely abandoned. Sergeant Leonard Lomell of Company D was first to find them.* He had only a couple of incendiary grenades,

---

* This comes from the original after-action report into the actions at Pointe du Hoc, which was later significantly altered. Later in life, Lomell claimed he had

which he used to disable two of the guns, and then bashed the optics on a third before heading back to the rest of his men to get more charges. On his return, he was within 50 yards of the guns when he saw the patrol from Company E, led by Sergeant Frank Rupinski, destroying the rest with thermite grenades down the barrels and setting fire to the enemy powder charges. The Rangers' Force A mission had been accomplished. It was now around 7.50 a.m., a mere forty-five minutes or so since they had first landed at the base of the cliffs.

This action has gone down in folklore as one of the most challenging and heroic of the war, yet it could hardly have been easier. The enemy had quite sensibly moved the guns back 1,500 yards into a camouflaged position and the intense air bombardment and naval fire had understandably driven what troops were there under cover. The Germans manning the position had not expected American troops to then scale the sheer cliffs and so the Rangers had managed to achieve almost complete tactical surprise.

What was unknown to Rudder's men at this stage was what enemy forces remained in the area, and whether and on what scale they might counter-attack. Another unknown was how long it might be before Force A was relieved by the Rangers' Force C, coming from Omaha with a company from the 116th Infantry. The truth was, their mission might have been fulfilled in quick order, but they were now in a potentially precarious situation. Ranger companies were only sixty-five men strong and they had already lost one LSA, which had turned back because of flooding on the way in and had taken those fifteen casualties who reached the top. That didn't leave a lot of men holding the Pointe – not an issue so long as reinforcements from Omaha arrived soon. What the Rangers on the Pointe did not know, however, was that a far tougher battle was raging on the increasingly bloodstained sand 4 miles to the east.

The scene on Omaha Beach was chaotic, yet by 9 a.m. the Americans were most definitely wresting control from the defenders. At WN61, an 88mm gun had been knocked out just after 7 a.m., while at WN62 Franz Gockel and his comrades had been feeling the heat. 'With every casualty we weakened,' Gockel admitted. 'More and more comrades were killed or wounded.' The 75mm gun near him was knocked out by naval gunfire,

---

destroyed all the guns, but I think the original report conveys the most accurate account of events. Why the report was so significantly changed is intriguing.

while smoke, dust and grit were making it ever harder to see clearly what was happening down below. Grit had got into the breech of his machine gun and caused it to jam. Frantically, he cleaned it and had just fired a few rounds when a burst of fire from the beach knocked it from his hands. Miraculously, he was unscathed, but attrition was chipping away at the ability of the defenders – so few in number to begin with – to keep hammering the attackers effectively.

Down on the beach, to the east of the Vierville Draw, Sergeant Bob Slaughter had gathered a number of his men around him and now had a clean weapon that was once more working. He knew they had to keep going, had to move. Having organized his squad as best he could, he ordered them to make a dash for it, over the wall and towards the bluffs. Up they went, running for their lives and, to Slaughter's great relief, to a man they made it to the base of the bluff.

A little further to the east Captain John Raaen and his HQ Company of Rangers were now taking cover by the sea wall, which here was made of wood with groynes stretching at right angles towards the water. Of some 450 men, only four or five had been hit. To his left, some of the Company C men of the 116th Infantry were already climbing up the bluffs and at various points gaps had been blown through the wire. Colonel Max Schneider, the 5th Rangers commander, was by this time also ashore and ordered Raaen and his men to come along the beach and follow him through the wire to the foot of the bluffs. As Raaen was moving out, one of his men said, 'Hey, Captain, look at that crazy guy on the beach there! Raaen looked and beyond the sea wall saw a soldier waving a cigar, walking down the beach towards them, yelling at the men still stuck on the beach.

Raaen hurried towards him. As he got close, he saw the man's collar tabs and realized he was a brigadier-general, and so had to be Brigadier-General Norman 'Dutch' Cota, executive officer of the 29th Division. During the planning of OVERLORD, Cota, fifty-one years old, had pleaded for a nighttime assault, but had been overruled because of the need to tie in both the air and naval bombardments at first light. Now, he was the first general on Omaha Beach and was exhorting his men to get off their backsides and keep moving forward.

Raaen saluted.

'What's the situation here?' Cota asked him.

'Sir, the 5th Ranger Battalion has landed intact over a 200-yard front.'

After asking where Colonel Schneider was, Cota strode along the line of Rangers, shouting, 'You men are Rangers. I know you won't let me down. You gotta lead the way.' In fact, neither Raaen nor any of his men needed much encouraging. 'Our attitude,' said Raaen, 'was let's get on with the job. We'd trained for it, we're fed up with being shot at, let's do some shooting.'

At that part of the beach, though, no Germans were shooting at any of them. Mortars were still falling on to the beach itself, while further along, on either side, men were still being hit, but at no point was there any consistency of enemy fire. Even at Dog Green and Easy Red, enemy fire was lessening. It is not true that all Americans arriving on the beaches faced the same intense fire as had faced Company A of the 116th in the first wave. Weight of numbers, even by 8 a.m., was starting to count. By 8.45, men from Company A, 16th Infantry, down at Easy Red, had even managed to climb the summit of the bluffs that dominated the beach.

For the actual attack, rifle companies had been restructured and split into two assault platoons, and then two assault sections, each of twenty-nine men and one officer, the number determined by the size of the Higgins boats and LCAs. Each assault platoon, which would be carried to the shore in two landing craft, included rifle teams, a wire-cutting team, a bazooka team, a flame-throwing team, a Browning Automatic Rifle (BAR) team, a 60mm mortar team and a demolition team. A third platoon in each company was similarly organized, but with an 81mm rather than a 60mm mortar team. This was quite a bit different to their normal make-up, in which a platoon consisted of two rifle squads of ten men each, a heavy weapons squad and a six-man platoon headquarters. Men were grouped together in new ways, sometimes with different NCOs and even officers. Since officers and NCOs tended to be the first off the landing craft, they were proportionally more likely to be killed or wounded.

One of the consequences of this was that, once on the beach, many of the men found themselves leaderless. Fear certainly played a part, but what was keeping men of the 116th Infantry bunched up behind the sea wall was not decimating enemy fire, but a lack of leadership. General Dutch Cota had realized this; someone needed to get a grip of the situation, show some leadership and get them moving fast. This was what he was doing on the beach. It worked, and, with the men attacking once more, the German defence began to unravel. All those strongpoints were mutually supporting, but the moment one fell, a domino effect was set in motion.

By around 8.30 a.m., Raaen and the men of the 5th Rangers had got through the wire, across the marshy area and were climbing the bluffs, straight up to the top. They encountered no opposition whatsoever. 'Absolutely none,' said Raaen. 'We didn't take any fire at all going up the bluff.' The combination of smoke and the little folds in the terrain had masked their climb, but they also faced few defenders. Glancing back, Raaen saw more boats arriving, men running across the beach, more pushing through the four gaps that had been blasted through the wire. At the top, the Rangers found a trench system and began moving east-wards, clearing it, before reaching an MG post that was still firing. A few carefully lobbed grenades and the position was destroyed, the enemy gunners, part of WN66, killed. By this point, the men from the 2nd Rangers had also climbed the bluffs a few hundred yards to the west and had knocked out WN70 at Hamel-au-Prêtre. By 9 a.m., Colonel Charles Canham, the CO of the 116th, and General Cota were also both at the top of the bluffs. So too was Colonel Schneider, who sent out orders that they would now pause, wait for stragglers to catch up and then attack as a battalion, rather than infiltrate as platoons. Crucially, there were now plenty of men, and leaders, up there and so began the operations to spread along the top of the bluffs, clearing one strongpoint after another. Down below, more men were arriving.

These included, at around 10 a.m., the men of the 18th Infantry Regi-ment of the Big Red One, the US 1st Infantry Division, coming ashore at Easy Red and Fox Green. The identical twins Tom and Dee Bowles were on the same landing craft. Suddenly the ramp was down and out they went on to the sand of Easy Red, just to the east of the E1 draw. With the tide in, the stretch to the sea wall was only 40 yards, but on this section of the beach, below Franz Gockel and the men of WN62, there was still plenty of enemy fire. 'You could see bullets hitting in the sand there,' said Tom Bowles, 'the sand flying up all over the place and mortar shells bursting around, and, of course, in the water, the bodies floating in the water and lying all over the beach.' He paused behind an obstacle but quickly realized the only thing it was good for was getting him killed, so he got up and carried on. Dee Bowles had done the same and both men managed to reach the wall in one piece. There they paused, pinned down by MGs, mortars and 50mm gun emplacements from WN65.

Help, however, was at hand. As elsewhere along the invasion front, the naval fire support was immense. At Omaha, there were two battleships, four cruisers and twelve destroyers. USS *Texas*, one of the two battle-ships, had ten 14-inch guns of 356mm calibre, substantially bigger than any German gun anywhere along the Normandy coastline. In addition it had a further twenty-one 127mm guns. As the Bowles twins crouched beneath the sea wall, they saw a destroyer, USS *Harding*, had already moved in close, to within 1,000 yards of the shore. This ship was now firing vast numbers of broadsides at WN65 and 62 with its four 5-inch guns, four 40mm quick-firing Bofors and six .50-calibre machine guns. This one ship alone was firing more at the defenders than the Germans were at the men on the beaches. 'You could see the shells going in,' said Dee Bowles, 'he was throwing them right at this pillbox.' By 10.30 a.m., WN65 had fallen, which meant the E1 draw was now open.

At Gold Beach, fighting continued around the Le Hamel strongpoint, but the British troops were all off the beach ahead of schedule and by 11 a.m. lead troops of 50th Division were pushing well inland. They had done well against coordinated and organized German defences. Unquestionably, the array of 'funnies' that accompanied them on to the beaches had helped. Subsequent waves of troops and armour had also landed pretty much on time, including 47 Royal Marine Commando, who came ashore around 9.20 a.m. There were 420 of them in all and they had been given an extraordinarily tough challenge: to ignore any beach fighting as far as possible and then head west for 10 miles through enemy-held territory and take some high ground, Hill 72 on their maps, before attacking and capturing Port-en-Bessin to the east of Omaha Beach. This was where the American Mulberry harbour was due to be created, so there was an urgency about taking the village swiftly, but a number of strongpoints and gun positions meant it was far from undefended. The 10 miles from Hill 72 to Port-en-Bessin was the same distance as from Sword Beach to Caen.

Lance Corporal Frank Wright was understandably nervous on the LCA heading to the shore. They all were. No one said much. He was in X Troop, one of six platoons in the Commando, and along with most of his mates he reckoned the chances of them pulling off their mission ranged somewhere between unlikely and downright impossible. As they neared the beach plenty of enemy shelling came their way. Suddenly, he heard an almighty explosion about 30 yards to his right. He could feel the vibration through his boots and saw a huge column of water rise into the air. One of their LCAs had been hit, killing twelve from Q Troop, including the troop commander, and wounding fourteen others. As they were landing, a second LCA hit a mine and sank, killing another eight in Y

The battle for Normandy began well before the invasion with the all-out effort of the Allied air forces to destroy bridges, railways and marshalling yards in France to make it as difficult as possible for German troops to reach the front. **Top left**: A B-17 of the Eighth Air Force heads out over Germany; and (**top right**) a Douglas A-20 Havoc of the Ninth Air Force hits railways on 5 June 1944. **Above left**: A railway bridge on the River Orne is destroyed, while (**above right**) the station at Cherbourg lies in ruins.

Above: The 12. SS-Panzer-Division 'Hitlerjugend' being inspected in April 1944.

Above right and right: Anti-invasion beach obstacles along the Normandy coast. Rommel insisted that the numbers of these were massively increased in the final weeks before the invasion.

Above: US Paratroopers of the 101st Airborne Division aboard a C-47 en route to Normandy.

Right: Nan section of Juno Beach, where Charlie Martin came ashore on D-Day.

Left: Landing craft with the Bowles twins' 18th Infantry Regiment heading towards Omaha Beach on D-Day; behind is USS *Augusta*, on board which was General Omar Bradley.

American 1st Division troops nearing Easy Red on Omaha at around 10.30 a.m. Despite the slaughter of the initial waves of troops and at certain points along the beach, many assault platoons landed and crossed the sand with minimal casualties.

Right: HMS *Warspite* firing in support of the invasion off Sword Beach. Allied naval fire-power was immense and dwarfed the number of German guns opposing the landing.

Left: Sword Beach on D-Day. Unloading became very congested with the higher than expected tide.

Below: Rangers at Pointe du Hoc capture not only low-grade German soldiers but also labourers of the Organisation Todt still working on the Atlantic Wall at the time of the invasion.

Above left: One of the many concrete casements, or *Widerstandsnester*, along the Normandy coastline. This is WN100 at Varreville on Utah Beach, still smoking after being knocked out on D-Day.

Right: British troops just off the beach at Hermanville-sur-Mer, Sword Beach. The house behind is still there today.

Below: DD Sherman tanks pushing inland from Gold Beach.

Above: Troops of the 12. SS-Panzer-Division 'Hitlerjugend' passing through Caen on 7 June.

Below: The first two Allied landing grounds were built and in operation by evening on 7 June – an astonishing achievement. Here, an American machine-gunner scans the skies as rapid construction work continues behind him on A-4 at Deux-Jumeaux.

Above: Commandos digging in next to a Horsa glider near Ranville. The British airborne landings might have been chaotic, but they succeeded brilliantly in achieving their D-Day objectives and securing the eastern flank as planned.

Above: A flame-throwing Churchill tank, known as a Crocodile, fires a 120-metre jet of burning oil and rubber. Germans feared these terrible weapons even more than Allied troops feared the Tiger tank.

Above: Pegasus Bridge on 7 June. On the far – Ranville – side, crashed gliders, landed so perfectly, lie where they came to a halt soon after midnight on D-Day.

Above right: Men of the 101st Airborne. They were not scattered in the drop anything like as widely as the popular narrative has claimed.

Right: Many 'German' troops were not German at all. These are from the Ost-Bataillone – men from the furthest eastern extremes of the Soviet Union captured and forced to fight for Nazi Germany.

Above: A big US 155mm gun in action.

Right: Cromwells and Shermans of the 4th County of London Yeomanry heading inland from Gold Beach on 7 June. These were the tanks that would soon be in Villers-Bocage.

Above: With no sizeable port to use, the British conceived, built and floated across the Channel two portable harbours, each the size of Dover.

Left: Port-en-Bessin, captured by 47 Royal Marine Commando in an often-ignored but vital operation. Mulberry A would be built here.

Omaha Beach a week on from D-Day. In addition to the Mulberries, some 16,000 tons a day were being landed directly on to the beaches (**right**) using Gooseberry breakwaters and landing ships. Although behind schedule because of the weather, the Allies unquestionably won the race to build up the Normandy front.

Allied air power was absolutely vital to Allied success. The Germans' ability to fight effectively was hampered massively by the immense weight of Allied air power. **Above left**: German troops of 12. SS 'Hitlerjugend' look skywards, while (**above right**) another German column hurrying to the front lies burning after being caught by the dreaded *Jabos*.

Above: The amount of rain hindered movement too, as the weight of Allied traffic quickly reduced roads and tracks to quagmires.

Left: The Great Storm of 19–21 June. Here, waves smash into Mulberry A, which was left irreparably damaged.

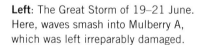

Above: Any German vehicles trying to move by day were invariably hammered by Allied air power. It really was incredibly debilitating, sapped morale and hindered their ability to fight. **Right**: A P-47 Thunderbolt climbs after attacking targets on the ground.

12. SS troops moving through the much-fought-over village of Rauray.

Fallschirmjäger (paratroopers) moving by horse and cart. It was no way to fight a modern, mechanized war.

Left: Robert Capa's photograph of German troops surrendering in Cherbourg, as witnessed and reported by Ernie Pyle on 27 June 1944.

Below: Churchill tanks and men of the 15th (Scottish) Division move forward through the mist and drizzle at the start of Operation EPSOM, 26 June 1944.

Below left: Fontenay-le-Pesnel, the scene of vicious fighting. A knocked-out Pak 40 75mm anti-tank gun alongside its dead gunner, 25 June 1944.

Below right: Shermans of the Sherwood Rangers near Rauray on 30 June 1944. The regiment was rarely out of the action.

THE BOCAGE

Above left: A Panzer IV well camouflaged in the hedgerows. **Above right**: US troops of the 90th Infantry Division cautiously push forward over captured German positions in the Cotentin.

Above: American Shermans line up along a hedgerow. Until they added dozers or hedge-cutters, they struggled to get through the bocage.

Right: Tom Bowles' foxhole near Caumont. This was home for long weeks in June and July.

Below left and right: British and American troops peer apprehensively through the hedgerows. Advancing through the dense bocage was enough to strain the nerves of any man. Danger literally lurked around every corner.

Troop, including the commander, and wounding others. It was not a good start.

As the ramp went down, Wright was thinking, 'I am not ready for this. I AM NOT . . .' but then he was out, his boot into just 2 inches of water and the driest landing he had ever experienced. Nor was anyone shooting at him. Ahead, however, was a burning tank. He ran past, noticing one of the crew dead by its tracks, his crushed head a bloody pulp. By the sea wall they waited, keeping their heads down, while some sappers cleared a path through the minefield away to the right and while the battle around Le Hamel continued to rage. Some seventy-six officers and other ranks were missing, including their commander, Colonel Charles Phillips. The beach looked a mess, but at last they were on their way and, mercifully, the colonel had reappeared as well. Through the minefield they went, as the battle at Le Hamel finally died down. Frank Wright, weighed down by his pack, double bandoliers, extra Bren magazines and a Bangalore torpedo, wondered whether they would ever make it to Port-en-Bessin. It was around midday, and it seemed a very long way to march.

Meanwhile, after de-waterproofing their tanks, Major Stanley Christopherson and the rest of A Squadron, the Sherwood Rangers, were rumbling down the road away from the beach towards the village of Ryes, a couple of miles to the south-west. It fell quickly, without much opposition, but this was the first time since the closing stages of the Tunisian campaign that they had driven tanks through villages and close country. 'It was not altogether pleasant,' noted Christopherson, 'as we found once again that a 30-ton tank with a crew of five is extremely vulnerable to one German infantryman who simply had to conceal himself in a ditch while the tank went past, and then either fire a "bazooka" or throw a sticky bomb on the engine of the tank, which he could write off most easily and then slip away without being seen.'

Further east along the coast at Juno Beach, the Canadians were also doing well. Around 10 a.m., the Canadian 7th Brigade had landed two battalions at Courseulles and all the shoreline enemy defences had been knocked out. Shermans, infantry from the Regina Rifles and AVREs followed behind and were now advancing to attack WN30, a few hundred yards inland at the southern edge of the town. This was where Oberleutnant Cornelius Tauber had fled. There was a Tobruk old French 7mm tank turret, several machine-gun posts and thick belts of wire and mines, and all the positions were linked by trenches. Tauber's blood was up. He was angry, adrenalin was pumping, and he urged the men around him to fight. 'I had a feeling,' he said, 'that I might make a name for myself in this battle.'

Soon after, a Sherman appeared at the edge of the minefield and opened fire, its second shell hitting, but not destroying, the Tobruk. The German gunners in the Tobruk fired back, the first shell deflecting off the front armour. Beginning to reverse, the tank was hit on one of the front tracks, which shattered and flew off. Desperately, the crew tried to pull back, but as they swivelled around they exposed their much more vulnerable and less armoured sides. Another Tobruk shell went straight through, sending the engine covers hurtling into the air with flames erupting behind. Three of the crew managed to jump out as the German machine-gunners opened fire, but as they tried to get away were cut down. The last two then emerged from the tank turret and were immediately shot, their bodies draping over the barrel. 'Our gunners in their enthusiasm kept firing,' recalled Tauber, 'and those two tank men over their gun were ripped to shreds, with their limbs falling off and their bodies exploding with spurts of flame.' He yelled at them to stop – they were wasting valuable ammunition – but then a second tank appeared, a Churchill Tauber did not recognize. It pushed past the Sherman seemingly nonchalantly. The Tobruk fired again, but the shells bounced off the Tommy tank, which now opened fire in turn. High-explosive shells destroyed one machine-gun position, throwing two of the men into the air and on to the wire, where they writhed and cried out for help.

The Tobruk gunners were panicking. Twice they missed completely and then the Churchill fired at them, its shell knocking the turret clear off its concrete base. The gunner remained standing there, stunned, his uniform smoking. Tauber watched this pathetic figure, then saw that the tank had halted. A moment later, a jet of flame burst from below its turret, but it fell short, setting the grass on fire in front of the strongpoint. It took about a quarter of an hour for a Crocodile to reach full operating pressure, but when it fired again it seemed that moment had been reached, because this time a much longer jet of flame burst out, creating a curtain of fire that swallowed up the two wounded men on the wire. The men in the front trench were also enveloped. Tauber could smell it from where he was, about 20 yards away, and could feel the heat burning his skin and hair. He saw the whole front trench saturated with flame; it was so intense he could barely breathe. Panic now gripped the survivors.

Tauber leaped from his trench, as did all the other men around him. Some were cut down by machine-gun fire as they ran. Tauber fled, and only he and two other men made it safely to a sunken lane. On they ran, desperately trying to get to the next position. 'I looked back,' said Tauber, 'and I saw a huge column of smoke rising from the area of the resistance point, which I assumed was burned up completely.'

Further to the east, the infantry were pressing inland from Sword Beach, while Lord Lovat's Commandos moved towards the bridges and the link-up with the airborne forces. No. 4 Commando, meanwhile, with the French taking the lead, were pushing along the back streets and railway line towards Riva Bella, where the old casino had become the focus of an extensive strongpoint, WN18. The casino had been demolished by the Germans and rebuilt as a concrete casement, and a number of the sea-front villas had been reinforced and incorporated into the web of defences. An anti-tank ditch surrounded it, as well as MG posts, sniping positions, and the usual network of wire and mines. This entire sea-front part of Ouistreham was now a ghost town, with the civilians evacuated back behind the lateral road a few hundred yards inland. Although already knocked about by bombing and shelling, winkling out the defenders was never going to be easy, especially since it had to be done so swiftly.

Armed with PIATS (portable anti-tank weapons), grenades and flame-throwers as well as machine guns, Stens and rifles, the Commandos dumped their heavy kit for the attack and then pushed on inland, using the main lateral road and railway line as their axis of advance. To begin with, they simply bypassed a lot of the German forward bunkers, but as they neared the casino they came under heavy fire and began suffering casualties once more. Capitaine Philippe Kieffer was wounded in the thigh and had to be taken to get treatment. How exactly to reach the casino and mount an attack was a conundrum: they had no idea which houses were empty and which were occupied. Hubert Fauré now met an old Frenchman, M. Lefèbvre, a civilian living to the south of the lateral in the still civilian-occupied part of the town, who offered to guide them. He led Fauré and a few others to within sight of the casino. On the concrete top was a 37mm cannon. Fauré ordered one of his marksmen to climb on to a nearby garage and snipe the gunners. 'He missed the gunner,' said Fauré, 'but the gunner didn't miss him. He was shot dead.'

Kieffer rejoined his men, his thigh bandaged. German snipers were hitting men every time they got close. One of the younger Commandos,

Rollin, was hit. Dr Lion went to help him, but was shot too and collapsed, his brains seeping from his skull, though Fauré could see he was not yet dead. They could hear Allied tanks not far away and Fauré suggested to Kieffer that he try to get them to come and help. Shortly after, Kieffer returned, riding on the turret of a Sherman. The gun atop the casino was swiftly knocked out, but the French captain was hit a second time. 'Kieffer was not very prudent,' admitted Fauré. The arrival of the tanks had changed the course of the battle, however. Charges blasted a route through the wire and mines, and the Commandos were able to work their way into the trenches and bunkers of the strongpoint. By late morning it was over, the casino captured, and it was time for the Frenchmen and their comrades in 4 Commando to move on towards Bénouville to help the airborne forces at the bridges.

Only at 9 a.m. did 352. Division Headquarters manage to make contact with Oberst Meyer. He and his men had already travelled over 30 miles, many of them on bicycles and without either rest or rations. Now they were being told to cut back eastwards and be ready to counter-attack from Crépon, where the 6th Green Howards were headed. Off they set once more, but it was now daylight and, despite low cloud, there were plenty of Allied *Jabos* about. All too frequently, his men had to ditch their bicycles and take cover. What's more, the weather was improving; by mid-morning, the cloud was starting to thin. *Jabos* now seemed to be overhead incessantly, and none of them was from the Luftwaffe. Still 15 miles from their destination, Meyer ordered his men to ditch their bicycles. They would continue on foot, although whether any of them would be in a fit state to fight if and when they did finally reach their objective was a moot point.

But was counter-attacking the British at Gold Beach the best use of Meyer's men, or should they have been sent to Omaha? After all, it was closer. When Ziegelmann eventually spoke to Oberst Ernst Goth, commander of Grenadier-Regiment 916 at Omaha, he was given a description of utter mayhem on the beach – dead Americans everywhere, burned-out tanks and landing craft. To begin with, Goth's report made it sound as if they had the situation in hand and so sending Meyer's *Kampfgruppe* to Crépon had been the logical decision. But then came a more sobering part to the report. 'Some of our battle positions have ceased firing,' Goth told Ziegelmann. 'They do not answer any longer when rung up on the telephone.'

In truth, Meyer's men were needed everywhere, because at every inva-sion beach the Allies had successfully got ashore. Even at Omaha, where the blood of young Americans could be clearly seen upon the sand, the German defenders had nothing to compare with the awesome fire-power of the Allied naval forces, or with their sheer weight of numbers. By 10 a.m., the defence at Omaha was already rapidly unravelling and the out-come was not seriously in doubt. Would some exhausted men on bicycles have been able to compete with the fire-power and fitness of the Ameri-can attackers? Almost certainly not. What was needed to save the unfolding German catastrophe was fire-power: heavy fire-power from mobile artillery with the kind of speed and flexibility of manoeuvre that only well-trained, well-equipped and highly motivated panzer divisions could provide. Frightened young recruits, middle-aged men, Poles and Russians were not enough.

CHAPTER 14

D-Day: Foothold

Fritz Bayerlein, commander of the Panzer-Lehr-Division and only recently promoted to Generalleutnant, had been woken at 2 a.m. by a call from General Walter Warlimont of the OKW, who ordered him to put his division on alert and await instructions to move towards Caen. Having issued his own orders, Bayerlein took a car and hurried to see General Dollmann at 7. Armee Headquarters, who relayed to him new orders that the Panzer-Lehr should be ready to start moving at five that afternoon. Bayerlein protested – it was too early, too dangerous to move in daylight, he argued. If they were not to move right away, they should wait until dusk at the very least. Dollmann, however, was adamant. It was essential, he said, that the Panzer-Lehr be near Caen by the morning of 7 June. He also told Bayerlein to take completely different march routes to the ones his division had already carefully reconnoitered. At this, Bayerlein put his foot down.

Bayerlein was forty-five, thick-set and swarthy, and vastly experienced in fighting the western Allies. He was also a friend and trusted colleague of Rommel's, having served alongside him in North Africa. Bayerlein was not only experienced at commanding armoured units – he had commanded the Afrikakorps, for example – but also understood the devastating effects of Allied air power. 'In training,' he noted, 'I placed every emphasis on camouflage against air attack. We trained to move at night and dispersed in small detachments in woods and villages.' So good had been their camouflage discipline in the previous weeks, not once had any of his troops been attacked by Allied aircraft. He had made it absolutely *verboten* to move on any road during daylight. Now, however, he was being told to set off in broad daylight. It was madness. Bayerlein understood the need to move to the front swiftly, but he wanted his division to arrive full strength, not ravaged on the way there. The trouble was, getting to the front safely, in one night, simply wasn't possible.

'The nights were very short,' Bayerlein pointed out. 'We could move a maximum of only 10 or 12 kilometres during the hours of darkness.' This meant the most they could travel in darkness was 60–70km – about 40 miles – which was not enough. This was the fatal weakness of leaving the Lehr and other panzer divisions, such as the 12. Waffen-SS, so far behind the coast. 'I proposed that we rest during the day and resume the march the next evening,' said Bayerlein, 'but Generaloberst Dollmann, who underestimated the Allied air forces, said we had to keep moving.'

Confusion also reigned over the deployment of 21. Panzer. At Marcks's behest, General Feuchtinger had ordered his division to attack British airborne forces east of the River Orne. Major Hans von Luck, commander of the II. Bataillon, had become increasingly angry about the lack of orders. The hours of darkness were the ideal time to move – the whole division should have charged, hell for leather, towards the coast! But by the time Feuchtinger's orders arrived at around 8 a.m., half of von Luck's battalion was already engaged in defensive operations and he believed the critical moment to strike swiftly had all but passed. 'Too late, much too late!' he wrote. 'We were dismayed and angry.'

Then, at 10.35 a.m., new orders arrived from Marcks's corps headquarters. The division was now to attack to the north of Caen and to the west, not east, of the River Orne. This total change of plan threw the division into disarray. Already en route to the area east of the Orne, they had to stop and completely change their march routes. This was in no way a straightforward task. First, all units, which were inevitably spread out, had to be informed and then they had to manoeuvre heavy vehicles in the right order through narrow roads with enemy aircraft overhead. Those already east of the Orne could use only two bridges if they wanted to avoid a massive detour – one was in the suburbs and the other was a railway bridge near Colombelles. Already Caen was burning, with huge fires and thick smoke in the air. Rubble covered many of the streets in the Vaucelles suburb, while refugees were fleeing south and against the flow of traffic of 21. Panzer. A swift advance was impossible. Realizing this, Oberstleutnant Hermann von Oppeln-Bronikowski, commander of Panzer-Regiment 22, ordered his men to bypass Caen altogether; if that meant a longer journey, then so be it – better that than risk gridlock and possible annihilation in Caen.

The truth was, there were simply neither the troops nor the time to rectify a situation that was rapidly escalating out of control. Marcks was desperately firefighting and hoping to put right his earlier errors of judgement. His men were under pressure all along the front, but he had committed both 21. Panzer and the corps reserve far too prematurely and was now trying to plug the holes in the dam. Repeatedly changing his orders, however, was only making the situation worse, because by the time the units involved had changed direction, yet more precious time had been lost, and with every passing hour the Allies' foothold was getting stronger.

It didn't seem that way to the beleaguered British airborne troops guarding the bridges across the Caen Canal and River Orne. Earlier that morning, Denis Edwards and his seven-man section from D Company, the Ox and Bucks, had been ordered down to the village of Le Port to shore up the men from 7 Para. Colonel Pine-Coffin and Major Howard had tried to create a ring of defence around the two bridges so that every approach was covered. By defending Le Port, they were protecting the approaches on the western side of Pegasus Bridge from the north.

En route to the village, Edwards and his men had briefly paused under a tree. They had not eaten since leaving England and were both tired and hungry. Suddenly a long burst from a German machine gun rang out and bullets spattered the branches above them, showering them with twigs and leaves. A moment later, Colonel Pine-Coffin himself appeared with a young officer Edwards did not recognize. It was Lieutenant Richard Todd, sent earlier to defend Le Port.

'That is not too healthy, old boy,' said the colonel, turning to Todd. 'We had better deal with them, eh?'

Edwards watched them hurry off through a gap in the hedge, then heard several bursts from Sten guns. Silence ensued, until a few minutes later the two officers reappeared.

'Well, lads,' said Pine-Coffin. 'That's fixed him up.'

Edwards and his men followed them to the village, where they were told to defend a row of cottages to the south of the church. Only once they had scampered up to the second floor of one of the buildings did they realize the Germans were in the houses just on the other side of the street. They threw a couple of grenades across the road and through the windows opposite, then hurried out of the back of their cottage and into the next before realizing they would be better off getting clear altogether. As they jumped a brick wall at the end of the garden behind the houses, the garden behind was raked by machine-gun fire.

Lieutenant Richard Todd, meanwhile, had been moving about quite a bit, trying to help organize the depleted men from his company and ferret out snipers. At one point, two patrol boats had motored gently down the canal from the direction of the sea. As they drew near, Todd and his men had raked them with fire. After a brief return of shots, the German crews emerged from the wheelhouses with their hands in the air. 'So to add to our battle honours that day,' noted Todd, 'we were able to claim a naval victory.'

By about 10 a.m., Todd was starting to worry. Ammunition was low and he knew from conversations with Colonel Pine-Coffin that everyone was running short. Casualties were mounting too. German snipers had proved particularly deadly and effective.

Denis Edwards and his men were also wondering whether the Commandos would ever turn up. They were now in a field just to the south of the church at Le Port, where they were protected by the wall, but from where they could cover the gateway and wall around the churchyard. Soon a German appeared in the church gateway, then another and, after peering round, they stepped out into the field. At that moment, Edwards and his men opened fire, killing the men instantly. Soon after, they heard a German voice barking orders from the far side of the church, beyond the wall that separated it from the road. Hurrying into the churchyard and scampering from grave to grave, Edwards and one other reached the front wall, lobbed over several grenades, then ran back.

'You English in the church,' shouted a voice. 'You are surrounded and cannot escape. Leave your weapons behind and come out through the church gate and no harm will come to you.'

Two more of Edwards' men now ran into the churchyard and lobbed the last of their grenades. 'Have these then,' one of them shouted in riposte. 'That's all we're giving up.'

For the time being. None of them was sure how much longer they could hold out. All their grenades had gone and they had no idea what else was happening – either with the invasion or elsewhere around the bridges. Suddenly, the noise of battle quietened and a still descended over Le Port. It was strange, but then, faintly at first but becoming louder, Edwards heard a thin, reedy sound carrying across the air until it sounded like a mournful banshee wail.

'It's them!' shouted one of the men. 'It's them – it's the Commando!'

Relief swept over them, but they soon realized that in their excitement they had taken their eye off the ball: from the church tower, a German machine-gunner opened up, firing in the direction of the Commandos. They shot a few rounds up at the tower and were just considering rushing the church when they heard the low rumble and squeak of a Sherman tank. Moments later, two tanks were firing their 75mm guns directly at the tower. A large hole was knocked out, stone and rubble fell down, and it was the end for the machine-gunner. Hurrying through the church-yard, Edwards and his men emerged into the road to meet Lord Lovat's Commandos.

Soon after, they reached the two bridges, where both Commandos and armour poured across and joined the battle for Ranville and the Bréville Ridge beyond the DZs. It had seemed touch and go, but the men guarding the bridges had held on, justifying Montgomery's and Demp-sey's plan to bolster 3rd Division with Lovat's brigade. Although fighting was going on, so far there had been no sign of any concentrated counter-attack. It was, though, surely only a matter of time.

A concentrated counter-attack was exactly what General Marcks was trying to organize with General Kraiss, the commander of the 352. Divi-sion, but with very little success. Oberst Karl Meyer's men were still battling their way back across Normandy when they were given new orders to attack towards Caen and secure the lateral road that linked the city with Bayeux. Any troops from the 716. Division he came into con-tact with were to be absorbed into his *Kampfgruppe*. Also promised to him was a company of the 352. Division's Panzerjäger-Abteilung (tank destroyer battalion) with their StuG and Marder assault guns – tracked armoured vehicles with a fixed rather than a turreted gun. In response to these latest orders, Meyer quite reasonably argued that his men were strung out, battling against attack from the *Jabos* and until the assault guns arrived there was a limit to what could be achieved.

An hour later, at around 11 a.m., Meyer was called yet again. Kraiss had now decided there would be a massed and coordinated counter-attack at midday all along the invasion front. One of Meyer's battalions was to go towards Omaha to help with the attempt to throw the

Americans back into the sea. The rest were to strike towards Crépon as had been earlier ordered. This was hopelessly over-optimistic, however, because Meyer's troops were still spread out, dodging Allied aircraft, and there was still no sign of the assault guns, which were struggling to move even more than were the infantry. Midday came and went and the massed counter-attack was delayed by a further two hours. By that time the Germans at Omaha were struggling simply to plug the gaps in the line, let alone to mount a serious counter-thrust.

The problems were escalating rapidly. The divisional artillery were running short of shells – by midday they were down to their emergency reserve, which meant just three per hour. A number of officers and NCOs had been killed or captured, which meant there was a growing shortage of small-unit commanders. Leutnant Hans Heinze had been called back to take command of 5. Kompanie of Grenadier-Regiment 916, which was fortunate as, soon after, WN64 where he had been stationed had been overrun. He soon found his new company, which had also absorbed much of 8. Kompanie as well. They were in reasonable shape, but a lot of the men were Russians and morale was not good; they were particularly agitated by the number of *Jabo*s overhead. Of the Luftwaffe there was absolutely no sign. Nor were the American prisoners brought in doing anything to help. The bountiful equipment, rations and cigarettes only underlined just how short their own supplies were.

The Americans were, by this time, pushing quite a distance from Omaha. The village of Colleville, a mile inland, fell at around 12.30 p.m. Franz Gockel might have been just about still firing, but WN62 was now, in effect, isolated. Among those pushing inland were the Bowles twins, who had climbed the bluffs through a path that had been cleared. 'Achtung Minen' signs were all around and they passed a wounded man sitting up but with half a leg blown off. 'He was just sat there warning us about the mines,' said Tom Bowles. 'Guess he was still in shock or something.'

From the USS *Augusta*, however, it was very difficult to make much sense of what was going on. Everywhere he looked, Captain Chet Hansen could see an enormous concentration of craft, while the heavy warships, a little further back, continued to pound the coast. Hansen had already taken a ride on board a PT – patrol – boat close to the beach, but apart from seeing a mass of landing craft jammed up on the shore, it had been hard to tell what was happening. Heading back to *Augusta*, he had reported to General Bradley and then headed on a launch with General

Kean to USS *Achernar*, the command ship. After scanning the intelligence and initial radio reports, they were not much the wiser. 'Apparently,' noted Hansen, 'the situation is still very obscure.'

Back aboard, after eating a sandwich, Hansen and Kean were sent off on another PT boat to get on shore and report back. After switching mid-journey to a Higgins boat, they reached the shore and jumped down into 4 feet of water and on to Omaha Beach at around 1.30 p.m. Quite a sight greeted them: smashed landing craft with their backs broken, innumerable tetrahedrons and other obstacles, and debris everywhere – ammunition boxes, discarded assault vests, and lots of dead bodies, lying where they had fallen or washed up by the rising tide. One body floating in the water had a leg missing. Hansen could hear sporadic small-arms fire and watched a single file of soldiers heading up the bluffs along the cleared path in the minefields.

They met the beach master, a young naval captain who told them his CO had been wounded. As they were talking, an enemy artillery shell landed amid a concentration of more landing craft. Troops hurriedly scrambled ashore. Another shell came over and hit a truck that had just landed, throwing the driver some 30 feet into the air, where for a brief moment he seemed to hang before falling lifelessly back down on to the sand. The beach master told them a bulldozer driver had recently been similarly blown skywards, but had landed back all right, dusted himself down and then clambered on to another vehicle. This was the inexplicable lottery of war. 'There was continual though not severe artillery fire on the beach,' noted Hansen. 'While it was sporadic, it was not harassing the troops too badly.'

Kean reckoned they had seen enough, so they headed back out to sea and reported to Bradley, whom they found in the war room on board *Augusta*. A slightly clearer picture was emerging. The Utah landings had gone well. At Omaha, on the eastern, 1st Division side, the 18th Infantry was landing behind the 16th, but casualties had been high among both divisions. Too many officers and commanders had been killed or wounded, with a subsequent loss of control and, although they were now cleaning up the central part of the defences, the western end was still firing and causing further casualties and difficulties unloading.

'Bradley shows no sign of worry,' noted Hansen. Later, many years after the war, Bradley claimed he had been so worried he had privately considered evacuating the beach. This seems unlikely and probably has more to do with the post-war retelling of 'Bloody Omaha' than what he was feeling at the time. Of course he was worried. Lots of his men were being killed and wounded. Such things weigh on any commander, especially one as fundamentally decent as Bradley. But the truth is, up until around 2 p.m., Bradley had very little idea of just what was going on, and by the time he did, the outcome of the battle on Omaha was no longer in doubt, nor had it been for some time. As soon as strongpoints began to be knocked out, the defences at Omaha, only ever skin-deep, were going to unravel. Once again, it was a question of simple mathematics. The numbers of men and the amount of fire-power the Allies were hurling at the Germans were immense. The weight of fire the Germans were returning was not.

By this time, Karl Wegner was also struggling to keep going. Earlier, a frightened young conscript from a neighbouring strongpoint had arrived at their bunker, distraught. His officer had been shot in the back by some Russians who wanted to flee and, fearing for his own life, he had run to the next position, WN71, where Wegner was based, but had been wounded in the leg by shrapnel. Obergefreiter Lang had been incensed, and in a fit of mad anger had dashed back, lobbing several grenades into the bunker. Running back, he had been almost cut in two by machine-gun fire from the beach. Wegner and the two remaining comrades in the bunker had watched appalled.

That had left Wegner in charge – a responsibility he did not want. Soon after, they realized they had just one fifty-round belt of ammunition left – all that remained from 15,000 rounds. He decided he would use these to try to help them get away. They had two grenades, which they would throw out of either side. When they exploded, Wegner would use the smoke to cover him as he dashed for the nearest trench, then he would use his final rounds to cover the other two in turn. 'We all crouched in the entry way,' said Wegner. 'I took a deep breath and nodded to them. Both grenades flew out at the same time, explosions followed. I sprang through the doorway.'

Leutnant Hans Heinze had finally launched his counter-attack at around 1.30 p.m., but it was far from coordinated; instead it amounted to a more localized action to retake WN62b, the support bunker complex to WN62 further inland. He and his men managed to push back small groups of Americans who were pressing inland between WNs 62 and 64 and then recaptured WN62b, but were hammered by American naval gunfire. Heinze held on as long as he could, hoping the massed counter-attack would relieve them, but it never materialized. He was out of radio contact too, which didn't help. 'After a long time I knew we couldn't hold out any longer,' he said. 'I ordered the men to try and get out through the shelling by themselves, not in groups. This was the only possible way through that terrible fire.'

By 3.50 p.m., Oberst Karl Meyer was finally able to report that his infantry had linked up with the long-promised assault guns and that they were now on the attack in the direction of Asnelles and Crépon – the area inland from Gold Beach. To begin with, they pushed back the British troops, but the Tommies quickly dug in, reinforcements arrived, offshore shelling continued and *Jabos* played merry hell, so Meyer's men were soon falling back. At 5.30 p.m., a further signal reached 352. Division Headquarters. Kampfgruppe Meyer were now withdrawing or else would be overrun. Contact between the Fusilier-Bataillon and I. Grenadier-Regiment 915 had been lost. And there was worse news. 'The CO, Oberst Meyer,' the signal continued, 'is probably seriously wounded and in enemy hands.' In fact, he was dead, yet another German commander cut down that day.

Among those fighting Meyer's counter-attack had been the Sherwood Rangers, who had helped capture the village of Ryes and then had pushed on. The objective for Stanley Christopherson's A Squadron had been the higher ground overlooking the town of Bayeux, which they were to assault with infantry but also with the artillery of the Essex Yeomanry. Christopherson, however, could not find the Yeomanry's CO, who had failed to make the arranged rendezvous. The thought of a painfully slow and cumbersome journey in his tank didn't appeal, but then he came across a fully saddled horse tethered outside a house. Taking it, Christopherson galloped off. 'Never in my wildest dreams,' he noted, 'did I ever anticipate that D-Day would find me dashing along the lanes of Normandy endeavouring, not very successfully, to control a very frightened horse with one hand, gripping a map case in the other, and wearing a tin hat and black overalls!' But he did find the CO of the Essex Yeomanry, who was somewhat startled to see him on horseback. Christopherson suggested they attack right away and take Bayeux that evening, but the commander of the Essex preferred to wait until morning.

At Juno, the Canadians were making good progress, although Bob Roberts experienced an extraordinary event after they had cleared Saint-Aubin. Later in the afternoon, they were corralling some prisoners when suddenly they were surrounded by civilians offering them drink and thanking them for liberating them. A girl whom Roberts reckoned was perhaps eighteen or nineteen suddenly stepped forward and asked to have a look at one of the men's Sten guns. One of Roberts's mates handed it over and she brought it up to her face and was aiming it when an old Frenchman suddenly stepped forward and shot her. 'Shot her right between the eyes,' said Roberts. 'He said, "She was about to shoot you. She's a collaborator, she was about to shoot you."' It made a deep impression on Roberts. 'Suddenly we realized we were really at war.'

A little to the west, the Queen's Own Rifles had also pushed on, taking first Bernières and then pressing inland some 7 miles. 'We followed the fields,' noted Charlie Martin, 'picking out draws, sloughs and low ground when we could.' Later in the afternoon, the remnants of his A Company, alongside C and D Companies, captured the village of Anguerny and D Company that of Anisy. They had reached their D-Day objectives.

On the whole, the day was going pretty well for the Allies, with the ground troops all getting ashore and having spectacular support from the offshore naval guns and the air forces, which appeared to be marauding the skies at will, dropping bombs and strafing anything that moved. At Sword Beach, the Commandos had achieved their objectives, justifying their heavy front-loading on to 3rd Division, but the passage towards Caen, a major D-Day objective, was not going quite so well. Huge criticism has been poured on both Montgomery and Dempsey for giving 3rd Division an over-ambitious objective without the tools or plans in place with which to carry it out. The argument has been that far too much emphasis was placed on getting on to the beaches and not enough on then pushing inland.

This is possibly a little harsh, however. Not only was there some precedent for reaching such a goal, but quite a careful plan had been made for the capture of Caen. The infantry of 8th Brigade, who had landed first, were to take the long, low ridge about a mile inland, then two battalions of 185th Brigade, with the tanks of the Staffordshire Yeomanry, would pass through them. The planners believed, correctly, that once WNs 16 and 17 were captured, the path to Caen would be fairly straightforward. In this presumption they were quite correct, especially since the tanks of 21. Panzer had decided to skirt around the south of the city before turning north towards the coast. In Sicily the previous July, most of the troops had reached Syracuse on foot, but not all were expected to be so on D-Day. Ideally, the infantry would have been in half-tracks and trucks, of which the British Army had plentiful supplies. However, there had not been enough shipping for those, plus tanks, plus AVREs, so 8th Brigade were to advance to the ridge on foot, while one battalion of the infantry following behind would mount themselves on the tanks with mounted engineers and artillery in support. This would, in effect, be an armoured battle group.

So, there was a plan for taking Caen, and a not unreasonable one in the circumstances. The problem was the execution, because the tanks of the Staffordshire Yeomanry took longer to get off the beach than had been anticipated. This was largely because of a much higher tide than usual, which had not been expected. It meant there was only a narrow sliver of beach on which the tanks could manoeuvre and not enough paths cleared quickly enough through the minefields. Congestion and a slower than expected exit off the beach were the result, which meant that while the infantry was ready by 11 a.m., the accompanying armour was not.

The second problem was Oberst Ludwig Krug's defensive network at WNs 16 and 17, code-named Morris and Hillman by the British, who had accurately appraised these defences and bombed and shelled them heavily. Morris, at the foot of the slope, held four 105mm guns and was, on paper, a potentially tough nut to crack. In fact, the enemy troops there, mostly *Osttruppen*, had been more interested in brewing their own hooch than manning the guns and quickly surrendered. Morris was a walkover. Hillman, on the ridge behind, was a totally different kettle of fish. Here, Krug himself was still in command; he had trained his men well, and had also created a well-organized and coordinated defensive position; he had absolutely no intention of rolling over without a fight. It was not the fault of Montgomery or Dempsey, though, that Hillman hadn't been more effectively pummelled beforehand. No one could have predicted that, of all the strongpoints along the Normandy coastline, this was the best organized, best defended and best led. In fact, some 150 men were defending it – nearly five times as many as at WN62 at Omaha.

Covering an area of 600 yards by 400, it lay directly in the path of the British advance on Caen. It was also surrounded by dense and effectively laid minefields in plain view of nasty numbers of machine guns, mortars and Tobruks, each with effective interlocking fire. The Suffolks from 8th Brigade were given the job of taking Hillman, among them Arthur Blizzard and the Pioneer Platoon. He was only too happy to get rid of the Bangalore torpedo he had been carrying around since landing. At around 1 p.m., together with sappers from the Royal Engineers, they began clearing gaps in the wire. Blizzard managed to blow a good gap, but came under heavy fire as he did so. 'I nearly got kaput over it,' he said, 'but I got away with it.' Others were not so lucky. Casualties quickly mounted, including a number of officers and NCOs; Captain Geoff Ryley, A Company commander leading the assault, was one of the first.

The Suffolks were forced to pull back and wait for support, which came from the Staffordshire Yeomanry and 13th/18th Hussars, although they were supposed to be part of the armoured group pressing on towards Caen with the infantry of 185th Brigade. Meanwhile, the Norfolks tried to bypass the position well to the left, but were raked by machine-gun and mortar fire and in no time had 150 casualties. Oberst Krug's strongpoint, heroically and determinedly defended by men who, on paper, looked likely to throw in the towel quite early, were badly holding up the British advance on Caen because it took time to organize a more coordinated attack with tanks and artillery. Arthur Blizzard was eventually able to use his 'beehive', but although it blew a big hole in the concrete of one particular emplacement, it wasn't enough to get through the superior engineering work of Krug's strongpoint. 'What we really wanted was another one,' said Blizzard. 'We tried to get a tank up to put his gun through there but when there's action you can't get things done as you want.'

Armour and infantry from Utah Beach had hooked up with men from the 101st Airborne, and at Brécourt Manor the German defenders, who had fallen back around the manor house after Dick Winters's assault on the gun battery, had been cleared. Carl Rambo and his crew, however, remained stuck; having got through the minefields, his Sherman DD had ground to a halt and they had been unable to get it going again. It was in the way, so a bulldozer had pushed it clear and it had sunk down into the flooded area. They went back to the beach to try to get a replacement, but none was yet available, so the rest of the 70th Tank Battalion pressed on inland without them.

On the far side of the flooded area around the village of Chef-du-Pont and the hamlet of La Fière, Lieutenant-Colonel Mark Alexander was now temporarily commanding the 1st Battalion of the 505th PIR after what had been an eventful day. Soon after landing he had met up with Major Fred Kellam, commander of the 1st Battalion, and along with forty or so men they had begun heading south-west in the direction of the 505th's DZ. As they were crossing the main road linking Sainte-Mère-Église to

Cherbourg, they heard a small convoy approaching from the north heading towards the town. Quickly preparing an ambush, the paratroopers opened fire, killing more than twenty Germans and capturing a lot of communications equipment.

They had then continued on their way and Alexander successfully reached the 505th's command post, where the operations officer and a small staff had already set up a tent and were in radio contact with other units. Troops in Sainte-Mère-Église had seen off a German counter-attack, while Kellam and his men, their number increasing as the day progressed, were heading towards the Merderet, where heavy fighting was taking place.

Just before noon, word reached the command post that Kellam, along with the 1st Battalion's operations officer and a company commander, had all been killed. Alexander's job was to run the regiment from the CP, but leadership was needed urgently with so many already killed, so he headed to La Fière, hurrying there with his orderly, Corporal 'Chick' Eitelman. En route, they had a brief firefight with some Germans and Eitelman was hit in the leg. Despite Alexander's urging, Eitelman insisted on remaining with him. They reached the railway crossing above La Fière around 1.30 p.m. From there, a bridge crossed the river and a causeway led over the flooded area to the village of Cauquigny, some three-quarters of a mile away. The Germans counter-attacked across the causeway using old 1940-era French tanks, but the paratroopers held them off. Despite this, plenty of artillery and mortar shells were still being fired into the paratroopers' positions. Casualties were continuing to mount. And ammunition was getting low.

Later in the afternoon, Alexander took a medic and hurried from foxhole to foxhole in case there were wounded in need of attention. They found one man still alive but with a dollar-sized piece of his skull missing, exposing his brains. They picked him up and were about to take him to the aid station when the Germans sent over a concentrated barrage. 'They really schlacked that area,' said Alexander. 'Dirt and rocks were blowing in on us.' He and the medic sat in the foxhole trying to protect the wounded man, their ears ringing.

Meanwhile, not far away, at the La Fière railway crossing, the Dubosq family were continuing to give shelter and aid to the American paratroopers. Geneviève's father had brought back a wounded American in his boat from the flooded area and she had helped bring him into the house. 'I have never seen such a bad fracture,' she wrote. 'The bones have broken through the skin and the leather of the boot.' The man desperately needed a doctor, but they were cut off. Even worse, they had neither disinfectant nor dressings in the house. His name, he told them, was Lieutenant George Wingate. 'Mama uses boiled water and calva,' wrote Geneviève. 'We don't know if we are doing the right thing.' Monsieur Dubosq continued to take his boat out into the water to rescue more supplies, despite enemy fire from the far side, while his daughter kept watch on Lieutenant Wingate. For the Americans defending La Fière and for the Dubosq family suddenly and dramatically caught up in the middle of this battle, the situation was far from good.

Adolf Hitler had woken at around 10 a.m. on 6 June and had been told about the invasion, but then had prevaricated as he so often did. Neither he nor those at the OKW were sure that the Normandy assault was anything more than a diversion. Despite the Allies' enormous material strength, it was not clear how they were supposed to launch a second invasion. Frankly, it beggared belief, although 617 Squadron, the Dam Busters, had performed a clever and brilliantly flown operation in a looping box across the Channel, which, on radar, simulated an invasion fleet crossing towards Calais.

Not until 2.32 p.m. was 12. SS-Panzer given permission to move, and not until 4 p.m. were the rest of the panzer reserves released. Also at 4 p.m., some sixteen hours after the first report of enemy troops had reached them, SS-Panzergrenadier-Regiment 25, part of 12. SS-Panzer-Division 'Hitlerjugend', was finally given its employment orders, which were to attack the area around Carpiquet airfield to the west of Caen. 'The time had come!' wrote the regiment's commander, Standartenführer Kurt Meyer. 'The soldiers mounted their vehicles. Dispatch riders roared down the streets on their motorcycles; the combat vehicles' engines were bellowing.' Meyer was thirty-three and already a veteran of the Anschluss in Austria, the battles for Poland and France, and the Eastern Front. The son of a coalminer from Jerxheim, he was an early convert to Nazism, joining the Party at the age of nineteen and the SS in October 1931, when he was still only twenty. 'I have breathed in National Socialism as a religion,' he said at one point during the war, 'as my life, no matter whether it is called National Socialism or has some other designation. I have realized that that is the only right life for our people, that otherwise our culture would go to the devil.' Originally an SS policeman, Meyer was soon noticed and asked to join the Leibstandarte-SS

'Adolf Hitler', the Führer's own personal bodyguard. Originally known as SS-Verfügungstruppen, these combat SS units later became part of the Waffen-SS, while SS police and intelligence services, which included prison guards, were part of the Allgemeine-SS, or General SS.

Meyer was tough, unquestionably courageous and a natural leader of men. Time and again he proved himself, always leading from the front, and he also had a sharp tactical brain. Remaining with the Leibstandarte-SS throughout the early years of the war, he certainly had blood on his hands: he had ordered the burning of a village and the execution of all its inhabitants during the Battle of Kharkov in early 1943. He was far from alone and not just within the Waffen-SS; plenty of Wehrmacht commanders had committed similar atrocities in a war with the Soviet Union that was fought with particularly brutal violence. Underpinning Meyer's ideology was a rabid abhorrence of communism. His greatest fear in June 1944 remained the annihilation of the German people at the hands of communists.

He also suspected that one day, in the not too distant future, Germany would link arms with the western democracies against the threat of the Soviet Union. That, however, was for the future. For now, he faced the days and weeks to come with no small amount of anxiety. 'We knew what was in front of us,' he wrote. 'In comparison, the magnificent young soldiers looked at us with laughter in their eyes. They had no fear.' At least he knew he had trained his own regiment well. The division had been formed the previous summer and Meyer had ensured his fanatical young troops, nearly all of them teenagers, avoided drill and instead focused on physical toughening and the tactical and operational techniques outlined by General Geyr von Schweppenburg, commander of Panzergruppe West and responsible for the training of armoured troops. Meyer had also ensured his troops had extra rations to make them physically stronger after the stringent rationing back home. As they headed to battle, he was proud of them. 'They were imbued with a belief in the rightness and justice of the German cause,' he noted. 'The young soldiers went to war superbly trained. There were few divisions which had been trained as well.' That was perhaps overstating it, but both the 12. 'Hitlerjugend' and the Panzer-Lehr were fully motorized, fully trained and superbly well equipped. The men were motivated and highly disciplined. On the march, these troops looked impressive: fit, healthy, with the latest uniforms and riding an array of tanks, armoured cars, half-tracks and other vehicles. The contrast with the half-bitten, half-trained, half-equipped infantry divisions on the coast could not have been greater.

The bulk of Major Hans von Luck's II. Bataillon had finally got moving later in the afternoon. Their goal was to push north, clear the British Red Devils and Commandos from around Ranville and retake the two bridges. With the support of a panzer company, his reconnaissance battalion of half-tracks and armoured cars went straight into the attack and reached the village of Escoville, to the south of Ranville. 'Then all hell broke loose,' wrote von Luck. 'The heaviest naval guns, up to 38cm in calibre, artillery, and fighter-bombers plastered us without pause.'

The attack was stopped dead in its tracks as radio contact was lost, men desperately tried to take cover and the wounded streamed back. Hurriedly, von Luck managed to reach his forward commanders to tell them to break off the attack and start digging in. His were not the only ones in 21. Panzer to be stopped in their tracks, however. So too had been Oberst Oppeln-Bronikowski's panzers. After laboriously inching his way around the southern edge of Caen, he pushed north, in between the British and Canadians at Sword and Juno. Unfortunately for the panzers, the Staffordshire Yeomanry saw them coming and moved their Sherman Fireflies into an ambush position. These were equipped with a 17-pounder anti-tank gun, a weapon that could fire a shell at over 3,000 feet per second and at a velocity superior to that of the German 88mm. These Fireflies made short work of Oppeln-Bronikowski's panzers, knocking out thirteen in fewer minutes. Several panzers pressed on and reached the coast, but they achieved little and soon they were all pulling back. The intended massed counter-attack had had neither enough weight nor proper coordination and it had failed. With every passing hour, the Allies' foothold became stronger.

German troops were falling back from Omaha too. Franz Gockel, like Karl Wegner, had run out of ammunition, and American troops were all around them. Abandoning their bunker, crouching, Gockel and his surviving comrades hurried up the communication trench to try to make good their escape. Unfortunately for them, the trench zig-zagged up the hill in plain sight and one of the men was shot in the head and killed, while another was wounded. Then Gockel was hit in the hand. A comrade quickly bandaged it as best he could and they continued, crawling then running, inching their way along hedgerows and across fields in the direction of Colleville. Eventually, they reached a company command post on the edge of the village, only to learn that the Americans now held the village itself. Saint-Laurent, the next village to the east, was apparently also in American hands. The company commander had been killed. 'For us wounded there was no protection here,' wrote Gockel. 'Enemy planes flew over and attacked anything that looked like it was carrying troops.'

Gockel and other wounded men were bundled into a truck and taken towards their hospital in Bayeux at breakneck speed, away from the violence and terror of the day's fighting on the coast. From the lorry, he saw the invasion fleet out at sea, huge and menacing, barrage balloons floating above. In the fields lay dead cows, and rubble on the road, while a little further on a burial party was interring a number of the dead. Eventually, the truck could go no further and so the walking wounded were told to try to reach Bayeux by foot. As they trudged along the road, some farmers offered them a lift in their carts. 'Even in these,' added Gockel, 'we were not safe from the Jabos.'

Karl Wegner and his two comrades, meanwhile, had made it to the road into Vierville and, with a careful watch on the sky, headed in the direction of the village, only to come across a number of dead sprawled across the road. 'It looked as though a Jabo caught them in the open,' he said. Overcoming their queasiness, they rifled through the bodies for ammunition. Soon they met a number of other soldiers. A *Feldwebel* told them to fall in and they headed back away from the village soon after learning from another straggler that Vierville was in American hands. On they trudged, westwards, until they came across some other troops, including several officers, sheltering under a tree from the *Jabos*. One of the officers asked them what they were doing and where they had come from, but none of them answered in case they said the wrong thing and were shot for desertion. Instead, Wegner and his two friends were posted as replacements to 4. Kompanie of Grenadier-Regiment 914 and told to head towards Pointe du Hoc, where American troops were holding the battery. Their task was to wrest it back. Wegner was given some rounds of wooden bullets. These were normally training rounds only, but were good for keeping the heads of the enemy down – or so he was told.

The Allied tactical air forces were marauding almost entirely freely over Normandy. On this day only around 800 Luftwaffe aircraft were in the west and of those just 120 were fighters. One of them was flown by Leutnant Wolfgang Fischer, who along with eleven others had taken off at around 9.30 a.m. in his Focke-Wulf 190 with a *Nebelwerfer* rocket – a

'Moaning Minnie', or rapid-firing mortar – under each wing, with orders to fire the rockets at the invasion fleet. When they reached the Normandy coast, Fischer was over-awed by the scale of the invasion. They circled around, unmolested by Allied aircraft, then, after carefully aiming off at a large warship, Fischer fired his rockets. It was the first time he had ever done so and it gave him quite a shock. Whether they actually hit or not he couldn't tell but, now unencumbered, he turned towards the beach and flew over at 900 feet. 'I let fly at the mass of men and materiel packed below,' he wrote. 'After the spectacular and noisy fireworks that had accompanied the launch of the two rockets, the thumping of my cannon, drowned out by the roar of the engine, sounded like the harmless popping of a cap pistol.'

This was a very rare foray by the Luftwaffe, however, which flew only around eighty sorties – individual combat flights – all day. In contrast, the Allied air forces flew a staggering 14,674. Gabby Gabreski flew four times that day, while Archie Maltbie flew three. Over Omaha, Maltbie saw the fighting raging below. He even saw blood staining the sea close to the beach. Ken Adam and his flight of 609 Squadron Typhoons were roving further inland when, near Lisieux, they hit a column of Bayerlein's Panzer-Lehr, which was now on its way. Adam and his crew were not the only Allied fighters to hammer the Panzer-Lehr that day.

Feldmarschall Rommel finally reached La Roche-Guyon at around 9 p.m., by which time the various counter-attacks attempted had all been repulsed. Even Hillman had finally been overrun, although Oberst Krug would not personally surrender from his bunker until the following morning. All along the invasion front, as dusk fell, the Allies had the foothold they needed. The next few days would be crucial, however. The race to get men and supplies to the front was on, and in their efforts to win this particular race the Allied air forces had a vital role.

Casualties among those in the firing line had been considerable, although from the American perspective, perhaps not quite so high as has often been perceived. The 29th Infantry lost 321 dead; the 1st 107; V Corps, including tank crews and Rangers, 349; and the US Navy and Royal Navy 65, making a total of 842 Allied dead at Omaha, which amounted to around 2.8 per cent of all those landed there on D-Day. It was a lot, but nothing like as bad as it might have been or as the narrative has suggested. Total Allied casualties on Omaha – dead, wounded and missing – were higher at 4,725. On the other hand, much of the German crust defending the coastline had been swept away. Exact figures are impossible to determine, but the 716. Infanterie-Division, for example, no longer existed as a fighting unit. Men like Karl Wegner and Franz Gockel, who had somehow managed to survive the carnage, now found themselves among unfamiliar faces, hungry, exhausted and barely able to comprehend what had happened.

South of Juno Beach, Charlie Martin couldn't help shedding some tears. Half his company had gone – men with whom he had lived and trained for years had been cut down and were now dead or wounded. Towards midnight, a brief firefight broke out and several German prisoners were taken. Soon after, Martin spotted someone lighting a cigarette and bawled at him to put it out. It turned out to be the CO, Lieutenant-Colonel Jock Sprogge. 'Charlie,' he said to Martin, after taking his telling-off on the chin, 'it's such a sad day. We've lost so many good men.'

It had certainly been a sad day – a terrible day of scarcely imaginable violence. Yet converging on Normandy were not only many more Allied troops and supplies, but also among the very best troops in the entire German Armed Forces and many more besides. It was Germany's dilemma that their best-trained and best-equipped units were those that were mobile – the panzer divisions – and so had not been defending the crust of the Atlantic Wall. Had they been, it might have been a different story, but their very nature meant they were deployed inland, and even had Rommel had his way they still would not have been manning the coast itself. Instead, the Allies had come up against the very old and the very young, men recovered from debilitating wounds or dragged into the firing line against their wishes. Once, there had been infantry divisions brimming with young, lean, fit, motivated men, but by this fifth year of the war they had gone, consumed by long years of fighting in far-off lands – in the Soviet Union, in North Africa, in the Mediterranean.

Yet those men did still exist, in the panzer divisions – divisions bristling with fire-power and the best weapons in the German arsenal. Despite the innumerable problems facing the Germans, these troops still represented a potent threat to anyone taking them on – and especially in the difficult terrain of Normandy. In the weeks to follow, there would never be a greater concentration of panzer divisions anywhere in the war than here in this corner of north-west France. D-Day, for all its awfulness, was only the first of what would stretch out for another seventy-six long, difficult and brutal days until the battle for Normandy was finally done.

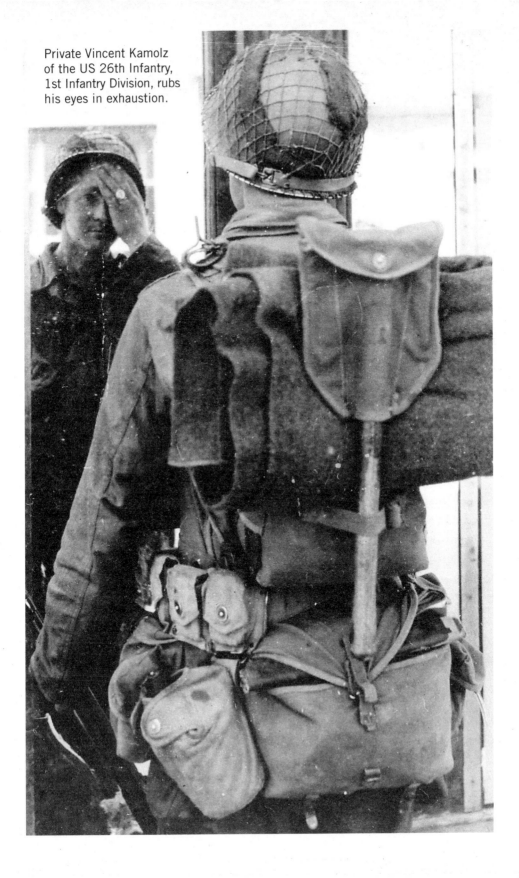

Private Vincent Kamolz of the US 26th Infantry, 1st Infantry Division, rubs his eyes in exhaustion.

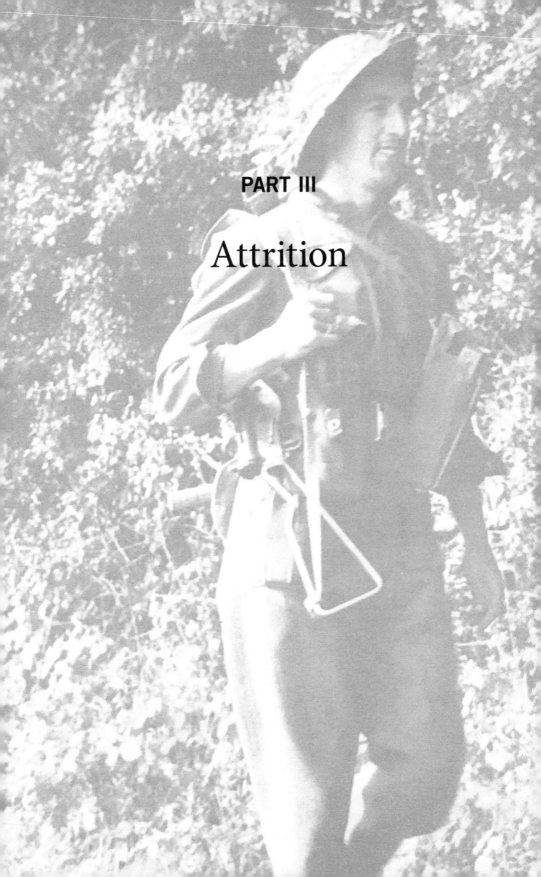

PART III

Attrition

CHAPTER 15

Bridgehead

CURRENT GERMAN STRENGTH IN Normandy amounted to around 78,000, so about half the number of the Allied troops that landed on D-Day itself. Admittedly, not all these troops were defending the crust, but a rule of thumb of any offensive operation is to have a 3:1 manpower advantage at the point of attack, and the Allies did not have that. It was another reason why there was an urgency to the Allied build-up over the following days. What's more, within OB West there were some 880,000 men, which was a lot. Most of these could, in theory, be sent to Normandy, although the Allied air forces were doing their very best to make sure that didn't happen any time soon.

Major Dick Turner had brought his 356th Fighter Squadron, one of three in the 354th Fighter Group, to Christchurch on the south coast of England on the evening of 6 June, but the next day was up again before dawn and soon after was briefing his pilots. The plan was to fly straight to the beachhead to provide air cover across the invasion front for one hour, and at first light they were in their Mustangs, heading across the Channel. Cloud cover had dropped a little and so they flew quite low, at around 4,000 feet, which meant they saw plenty of debris: bits of aircraft, oily patches and other flotsam.

As they neared the coast, Turner saw ships, boats and landing craft spread out for miles – an incredible visible show of strength. Making sure to waggle his wings as they passed over the warships – despite the new invasion stripes – he then led his squadron the length of the beaches. Materiel and vehicles covered the ground and he could even see columns of men and vehicles steadily moving inland; the Allies had a foothold, that was for sure. 'All looked orderly and peaceful from 4,000 feet,' he noted, 'but now and then a half-sunken ship, a burning vehicle or some unidentifiable wreckage would be visible.' He kept craning his neck for German fighters but saw only one, which tried to sneak in at low level and was promptly caught in devastating crossfire from two cruisers and fell into the sea trailing a long flame.

The Mustangs of the 354th Fighter Group were far from being the only fighters over the beachhead that morning. For the tactical air forces it was another maximum effort, with protective umbrellas flown over the beach as well as marauding inland: everything possible had to be done to slow and limit the ability of German units to reach the front. Ken Adam of 609 Squadron would fly twice that day, while some squadrons made as many as four or even five trips across the Channel. No wonder the Germans were feeling so utterly oppressed from the air.

Not only fighters were swarming over the Normandy front. Now that the cat was out of the bag, Allied bombers could concentrate on isolating Normandy more specifically. Lieutenant Smitty Smith of 550th Bomb Squadron and his crew had been on leave for a few days and so had missed D-Day, but were back in the air by 9 a.m. on Wednesday, 7 June. Their target was the railway marshalling yard at Niort in France, south-west of Poitiers, but when they got there they discovered others had already beaten them to it, so instead they headed for the secondary target, but that had also been destroyed. On they went to the next, a bridge, a long distance from the Normandy coast. The entire trip lasted the best part of the day. It had been their twentieth mission, which entitled them to add the Oak Leaf Cluster to the air medals they already had and a second Battle Star to their European Theater of Operations Medal. More importantly, it meant they only had five missions left until they finished their tour.

Smith was feeling reasonably upbeat about this when the captain, Moon Baumann, appeared looking morose.

'They've increased the tour to thirty missions,' he told them. 'Don't wait up for me. I'm going to the Club . . . Wanna go and have a drink?'

'No,' Smith replied. 'I think I'm gonna have a cigarette and puke.' He was utterly poleaxed by the news. 'I felt as if I were somehow dead,' he wrote. 'There was to be no future.'

Another bomber man not feeling particularly bright about the future was Lieutenant Joe Boylan of the 391st Bomb Group. They had been briefed late on D-Day to bomb a marshalling yard at Briouze, some miles south of Caen. Intelligence suggested the Germans would unload fifty tanks there the following morning; their job was to make sure they got no further. They would be flying their B-26 medium bombers at low altitude, a prospect that made Boylan feel heavy-hearted all night; he slept little, imagining the intense flak they would probably face at Briouze. Breakfast was a sombre affair, with no one talking much. At the briefing, nothing had changed from the previous evening. 'So all the negatives were in place,' wrote Boylan. 'This was going to be one hell of a mission.'

Soon after crossing the coast at just 1,500 feet, they approached the target. The town was small and the railway yard obvious, but of the unloading panzers there was no sign. Over the radio there was a brief discussion: should they look for another target or hit the station anyway? Someone pointed out that the train might be late and that by bombing the place they could still put it out of action, which might be just as effective. 'One could hardly argue with that,' noted Boylan. 'So we bombed the hell out of the rail yards and the train.' Much to his relief, he and his crew made it back safely, although one plane was shot down over Caen. 'Not too bad and this being the second day of the invasion!' he noted. 'We were scared to hell but we were coming out of this in pretty good shape.'

German reinforcements were reaching the front, however. Oberleutnant Cornelius Tauber had managed to escape the horror of being nearly grilled alive and had run into a group of Waffen-SS men. These had been from the reconnaissance battalion of the 12. SS 'Hitlerjugend' and Tauber had been immediately struck by the difference in mentality between these young, aggressive, confident men and those he had led in the bunkers. He had also watched agog as they calmly knocked out two Canadian Shermans with their *Panzerschreck* – hand-held rocket launchers – then shot all the crew. The SS men had been the advance guard, sent forward without permission, but the rest were on their way.

Standartenführer Kurt Meyer had reached the Caen–Villers-Bocage road at about eleven the previous evening, having witnessed a number of Typhoons attacking a column of SS-Panzergrenadier-Regiment 25. Vehicles were burning, while up ahead in the distance Caen could be seen on fire. 'A soldier was lying on the road,' wrote Meyer, 'a jet of blood shooting from his throat.' An ammunition lorry had then exploded. A refugee column had also been hit. Much to Meyer's delight, an old Frenchwoman was shouting, 'Murder! Murder!'

By midnight, he was standing before Generalmajor Wilhelm Richter, commander of 716. Division and one of the least talented of German generals, getting an apprisal of the situation. During the briefing, Oberst Krug rang and explained that British troops were standing on top of his bunker and he wondered what he should do. Richter was silent for a moment then told him to do whatever he thought best and put down the phone. Krug surrendered early that morning and was taken into British captivity. The 716. Division had ceased to exist. General Feuchtinger was also present and gave a picture almost as bleak: 21. Panzer wasn't in great shape either and it was rumoured the enemy were now at Carpiquet.

After the depressing reports from Richter and Feuchtinger, Meyer rejoined his men. Obergruppenführer Fritz Witt, the 12. Waffen-SS commander, ordered them to attack from the western side of Caen at noon, but already Meyer was discovering the difficulties of doing so. His driver had traded his normal armoured car for a smaller, less conspicuous *Kübelwagen*, but they had hardly started off before they were in a ditch after swerving to avoid bullets and cannons from fighters overhead. 'Where was our Luftwaffe for God's sake?' Meyer wondered.

He felt better once installed in the old abandoned Abbey d'Ardenne with its thick stone walls. There was also a church with two towers for observation. By the early hours most of his men were ready and in position to attack on the northern outskirts of Caen, but they were still missing their tanks. They did not start to appear until 10 a.m.; relentless fighter-bomber attacks had slowed them considerably, but by midday he had some fifty Panzer Mk IV tanks, although now they were being shelled by offshore naval guns. Climbing the church tower, Meyer looked out towards the coast and saw the sea thick with ships, and enemy tank formations near the town of Douvres. 'The whole expanse looked like an anthill,' he noted. 'And what was going on behind us – smoking rubble, empty roads and burning vehicles.' Then fighter-bombers came over and attacked the monastery, but although the men swore at this plague, little damage was caused on this occasion. Later that afternoon, they would counter-attack, and hard. Obergruppenführer Witt had told Meyer and all his units they must be ready to strike at 4 p.m. Meyer remembered General Guderian's great motto: '*Klotzen nicht kleckern!*' Strike hard, not softly.

General Dwight D. Eisenhower was a relieved man. He had prepared a note to announce the failure of OVERLORD in case of that eventuality, but in fact he had cause to be very pleased. Some 75,215 British and Canadian troops had been landed on D-Day alongside 57,500 Americans and more than 23,000 airborne troops. Rommel's Atlantic Wall had not prevented more Allied troops from penetrating into Normandy and, despite the violence and brutality of battle, they had done so with fewer casualties than had been expected or prepared for, even with the losses at Omaha. It was true they had not achieved all their objectives, but by 7 June Omaha was no longer threatened; at Utah, the 4th Division was well inland and hooking up with the airborne troops; while along the British and Canadian beaches, troops were now between 4 and 7 miles inland. Even with the unexpectedly stubborn resistance at Hillman, the British 3rd Division had managed to get more than halfway to Caen, while the Canadians were within spitting distance. Had Hillman succumbed as had Morris – and other strongpoints along the invasion front – then Caen would have been taken and seventy years of wise-after-the-event criticism would never have happened.

At any rate, soon Eisenhower would be on French soil himself. That morning, the 7th, he had been up early and, with Admiral Ramsay, set sail from Portsmouth in the fast minelayer HMS *Apollo*, which could speed across the Channel at 40 knots. Also now in Normandy was General Montgomery, who had boarded the destroyer HMS *Faulknor* the previous evening at ten, leaving Major-General Freddie de Guingand, his chief of staff, holding the fort in England, while he headed off with his Tactical HQ. Monty was a stickler for a good night's sleep – he argued, quite sensibly, that he needed proper rest so that his mind was always clear – and so had retired to his cabin with instructions not to be disturbed until 6 a.m.

On board *Augusta*, meanwhile, Captain Chet Hansen was woken at 4.40 a.m. with the warning that Monty would be alongside at around six. Having only got to bed at 1 a.m., he was exhausted. General Bradley, on the other hand, seemed as chirpy as ever. In fact, *Faulknor* got a little lost on the way over, but managed to get back on track and avoid any mines, and on cue joined them in the waters off Omaha, so Bradley, with Hansen in tow, crossed over to confer with Montgomery at around 6.30. 'Decision made in view of difficulty in establishing initial beachhead,' scribbled Hansen in his diary, 'that immediate effort be made to join Utah and Omaha at all possible costs as quickly as possible.' This was essential, and the build-up of forces also needed to continue without let-up and with the greatest of speed. Montgomery and Bradley were expecting a concentrated counter-attack on probably D plus 4 or D plus 5 – so around 10–11 June. Continued rough seas, however, were hampering the unloading process.

Right away, Montgomery wanted to see General Miles Dempsey, who was aboard HMS *Scylla*, but *Faulknor* couldn't immediately locate her. Furious signals were sent and soon after the British Second Army commander was tracked down and came aboard. It was now around 9 a.m. Dempsey had better news. Caen had not been taken, but his troops were progressing well. The opposition so far had been varied and had, in places, been stubborn, but there was no sign yet of a major coordinated counter-attack. On the other hand, it was evident that 21. Panzer-Division was organizing itself and that 12. SS-Panzer-Division was also moving up to the west of Caen – a prisoner from a reconnaissance unit of that division had been captured and interrogated. What was concerning Dempsey was the speed of unloading men and materiel. He had talked to Admiral Philip Vian, the commander of the Eastern Task Force, who had promised to do everything in his power to improve the situation, including bringing landing ships directly on to the beach – something that was already under way at Omaha. 'Unless the wind drops and the sea moderates,' noted Dempsey, 'the build-up is going to be very difficult.'

The rapid build-up of troops and the establishment of a watertight and connected bridgehead was the absolute priority for the Allied commanders. Achieving this trumped everything. While during the planning there had been lofty talk, from Montgomery especially, of driving beyond Caen on D-Day, deep concern had also been expressed that the entire enterprise might fail. On D plus 1, the mood in the Allied camp was this: huge relief that the invasion had so far gone considerably better than many had dared hope but not quite as well as the best-case scenario. There was, though, no complacency and the urgent need to join the bridgehead together and speed up unloading was, rightly, of paramount importance. The invasion could not, under any circumstances, be allowed to fail – a reality that trumped absolutely every other consideration.

Once they had ensured that threat had gone, the Allies could go all-out on the attack. It would be madness now, everyone agreed, for some units to press ahead too far without proper support, leaving themselves with vulnerable flanks and open to being cut off. What fighting the Germans so far had taught the Allies was that they always counter-attacked and their instinctive predilection was to be aggressive. Different units could, of course, push and probe forward but, broadly speaking, this needed to be done on a wide front at this early stage in the campaign. Montgomery's reputation had been founded on the build-up of overwhelming materiel and a steady and methodical drive forward using heavy fire-power to support the infantry and armour, and precisely this approach enabled the number of front-line troops to be kept comparatively small, which in turn saved lots of lives. It was a method that suited machine- and technology-heavy armies made up largely from conscripts from western democracies. Cut and dash might, conceivably, result in a decisive breakthrough, but far better, at this stage, to maintain pressure all along the front, which would, in turn, put pressure on the Germans in Normandy, whether it be the battle-scarred men pushed back from the coast, or those newly arriving.

Eisenhower reached Normandy before midday and during the next few hours the course of action for the days to follow was agreed without dissent or argument. Clearly, though, the focus of the fighting would be in two main areas. The first would be between Omaha and the Cotentin – it was essential that Isigny and then Carentan were taken swiftly – and then around Caen, where already, it seemed, German armour was beginning to concentrate, just as Montgomery had predicted.

'It is sometimes difficult in this life to admit that one was wrong,' Air Marshal Sir Trafford Leigh-Mallory wrote to Eisenhower on Wednesday, 7 June, 'but I have never had greater pleasure than in doing so on this occasion over the operations of the American Airborne Forces.' After all the fuss he had made and his unsettling hysteria, the least he could do was eat humble pie. For all the mayhem, there was no question the airborne operations had been considerably more successful than any the Allies had attempted before and that they had more than achieved their primary goal of securing the flanks and creating havoc for the defenders. More glider reinforcements had arrived at both the British and American areas during the evening and night of D-Day and again on the morning of 7 June; these had gone as well as most had hoped and far better than some, like Leigh-Mallory, had predicted. Out of the three battalions of the 325th Glider Infantry that had landed, for example, only fifty-seven men were missing, and around 90 per cent of the regiment was ready for action in support of the 82nd Airborne within a couple of hours.

The biggest problem was the time it was taking paratroopers to reach their designated areas. By midnight on D-Day, the 82nd still had only around 2,000 men and the 101st 2,500 – roughly a third to two-fifths of their strength. Had those still missing managed to move at a speed of just 1 mile per hour, then three-quarters of those dropped would have been able to go into action against their allotted objectives. All too many found themselves caught up in debilitating firefights or pinned down for hours on end, which absorbed huge amounts of time and also restricted their ability to move.

'On June 7,' wrote Lieutenant-Colonel Mark Alexander, 'we were under constant fire.' He was still commanding 1st Battalion, 505th PIR, while Brigadier-General Jim Gavin, the XO of the division, was commanding the men down the road at Chef-du-Pont. Most of the men had been digging in furiously and were now in foxholes along the hedgerows and around the buildings of La Fière. The task of the paratroopers was to make sure no German troops got across the causeway and threatened their positions and, with them, the Americans' western flank on the Cotentin. The issue was whether they could hold out, with dwindling ammunition, until reinforcements arrived. From his own foxhole, Alexander could see German infantry moving about in Cauquigny, the far side of the flood area, but he and his comrades had only .30-calibre machine guns, a handful of mortars and a single 57mm anti-tank gun which was down to just six rounds. This gun and the mortars had to be held back in case the Germans tried another assault across the causeway and the bridge.

At 8 a.m. a furious mortar barrage opened up, spraying jagged fragments, clods of dirt and grit along their positions. Then four tanks began trundling along the causeway, a Panzer Mk III in the lead, followed by ageing French models captured back in 1940. The 57mm gun was wheeled out and, when the tanks got close enough, paratroopers with bazookas jumped out of their foxholes and opened fire. The first two tanks were swiftly knocked out and the other two pulled back. More heavy artillery fire now rained down on them. Casualties began to mount rapidly.

Not far away, the Dubosq family were still doing their best to help the Americans. Geneviève was worried about her lieutenant with the shattered leg. Late the previous night she had gone to check on him and saw he was stricken with a fever, covered in sweat and barely able to talk. He was still alive the following morning, however, though how much longer he could survive without seeing a doctor, they weren't sure. Geneviève's mother had tried to find him some medical help. After milking the cows at the farm a short distance further back from the river, she handed out much of the milk to the Americans dug in there and asked them for a doctor. There wasn't one, but the paratroopers promised to send help to Lieutenant Wingate as soon as possible.

Later that morning, three Germans approached their house, unseen by the Americans. One had been hit in the leg and had lost a lot of blood, while a second had a bullet in his heel.

'Please, madam,' said the third, an unwounded officer, in good French, 'the boy has lost a lot of blood. He will die if you don't help him.'

Bringing them into the house, Madame Dubosq did what she could while the officer sat disconsolately and Geneviève gave him a bowl of coffee. Suddenly, one of the wounded Americans, Kerry Hogey, came into the room. He and the German officer stared at one another, then the German offered his hand. Cautiously, Hogey took it. 'I am astonished,' wrote Geneviève. 'Both men smile to each other and sit together by the fireplace.'

A Jeep arrived soon after and an American came in to see how Lieutenant Wingate was faring and to reassure him he would soon come back with medical help. On his way out, he turned to the German officer and said, 'Get ready to come with us when I'm back. You can show us where the Germans are.' After he'd gone, the German asked for a pen and some paper so he could write to his wife. 'I am going to die today,' he told them. 'I won't see my family again.' Madame Dubosq tried to reassure him, but he shook his head sadly. His comrades would shoot him if they saw him with the Americans. Sure enough, when the Jeep returned, the Americans gave Wingate some pills and left the rest with Madame Dubosq, then took the German officer away with them. They'd not gone a hundred yards when a German machine gun opened fire from the far side of the water. Those in the house could only watch helplessly.

Some hours later, however, they saw the German officer again, this time struggling in the water near the house. Madame Dubosq hurried out followed by her daughter. Geneviève's mother screamed at her to go back inside as rifle shots rang out, but it was clear Madame Dubosq could not manage alone and so, ignoring her mother, Geneviève ran to help. The German had been hit in the chest – blood was bubbling under the surface of the water. Weakened by his wound and from being in the water for some three hours, his strength was fading fast. Somehow, they managed to pull him half clear, Geneviève staying with him and keeping his head above the water while her mother ran for help.

Geneviève talked to him, desperately trying to reassure him. They talked of God, of his family, and she told him secrets she had never told anyone. Then he asked her to sing to him. 'Here I am,' she wrote, 'an eleven-year-old girl, singing a beautiful song in the middle of a swamp, with a dying man in my arms.' She was cold, exhausted and her body ached from holding his head up. The German appeared to be asleep but then awoke at the sound of Madame Dubosq returning. But after reminding them to post his letter to his wife, he closed his eyes once more and died.

Some miles to the west, the paratroopers of the 101st Airborne were feeling less imperilled and had successfully linked up with the 4th Infantry, while more men were continuing to flood in. Some kind of cohesion was gradually reasserting itself and a Division HQ was established with General Maxwell Taylor at the helm. The one major source of disappointment was that Carentan remained firmly in the hands of Fallschirmjäger-Regiment 6. The town and the canal and river locks and bridges had been the objective of the 501st PIR, with the 3rd Battalion of the 506th to help, but the latter had been cut to shreds by German *Fallschirmjäger* lying in wait as the Americans descended, and the rest of the 501st had simply been neither numerous nor strong enough to burst their way through. The dubious allocation of troops concocted by Taylor, Ridgway and the airborne planning teams, in which the most challenging – and important – objective had been left to a force not strong enough for the task, had come home to roost.

So it was that early on the morning of 7 June, the remaining two battalions of the 506th – some 225 men from the 1st Battalion and 300 from the 2nd – were ordered to head south through the Cotentin village of Vierville and on to Saint-Côme-du-Mont and then to Carentan. The fate of the 3rd Battalion, shot up the day before, was still not known to either regimental or divisional headquarters; on that second morning it was a lost battalion. Easy Company was put on alert at around 5 a.m. and, in the absence of Lieutenant Meehan, Lieutenant Dick Winters was still acting commander. 'Winters, I hate to do this to you after what you went through yesterday,' Captain Clarence Hester, the battalion ops officer, told him, 'but I want Easy Company to lead the column toward Vierville.' With the 1st Battalion ahead of them, Vierville was secured fairly swiftly and easily. Winters then led Easy in an attack on Angoville with the help of a couple of light Stuart tanks and they took the village even more easily. The company was then placed in reserve, while Dog

Company headed towards Côme-du-Mont. Here they had a tough fight and were unable to break through. They also took high casualties – the Dog Company commander, Captain Jerre Gross, was killed and so too was the 1st Battalion commander, Lieutenant-Colonel William Turner, shot in the head by a sniper in full view of many of his men. 'Combat in Normandy,' noted Winters, 'was proving an extremely dangerous business.' Now that Fallschirmjäger-Regiment 6 were primed and ready, it was clear they were not going to give up Carentan willingly.

Oberleutnant Martin Pöppel certainly had no intention of doing so. His 12. Kompanie in the III. Bataillon of Fallschirmjäger-Regiment 6 had been braced the previous evening for an attack, but reports from observation posts suggested the Americans had pulled back for the night. Pöppel had barely snatched any sleep at all but had been dozing early that morning when Allied bombers thundered over. Now, throughout this second day of battle, he and his men remained ready at their posts; most of the action, though, appeared to be coming from the far side of Carentan around Côme-du-Mont. News reached him that the I. Bataillon had already suffered heavily. Later, 9. Kompanie was ordered across the river and canal to help with the fighting raging there. Enormous explosions could also be heard to the north and to the north-east, which he reckoned must be coming from the enemy warships. 'We can also hear the noise of battle from that direction,' he noted.

Fierce fighting raged throughout much of the day to the west of Omaha Beach and around the batteries of Pointe du Hoc and Maisy. After their very easy destruction of the guns at Pointe du Hoc, the Rangers had found themselves isolated at the moonscape of the original gun position as the Germans had emerged from where they'd been sheltering underground and had then been reinforced. Rather like the 82nd Airborne on the banks of the Merderet, the Rangers had been valiantly holding out with rapidly depleting ammunition. Unbeknown to them, rescue was at hand from the rest of the Rangers who had landed at Omaha and from a company of the 116th Infantry, who were battling their way west through stiff resistance by the remains of the 352. Division and what reinforcements hurried forward.

Captain John Raaen had spent the night of D-Day out in the open to the west of Vierville. The day's fighting had ended when they met some stiff resistance as they pushed westwards along the coastal lateral road towards Pointe du Hoc. Quite a large Ranger force had been assembled – the 5th Rangers as well as three companies of the 2nd Rangers, Company

C of the 116th Infantry and even some Shermans of the 743rd Tank Battalion. 'The night of D-Day,' recalled Raaen, 'I learned the difference between a hay stack and a manure pile.' In the early hours of the 7th, he attended an O Group meeting with General Cota and senior officers in their group. He struggled to concentrate, though, as by this time he'd not slept in forty-eight hours.

Some Rangers had managed to break through to Pointe du Hoc the previous evening, only for the position to come under sustained attack twice during the night. By the morning, Colonel James E. Rudder had just under a hundred men, half of whom were wounded, including himself and the British Commando liaison officer, the 6-foot-6 Lieutenant-Colonel Tom Trevor. Now dug in nearby were Karl Wegner and his two comrades from their beach-top bunker, who with their new, hastily cobbled-together company had been moved westwards along the coast. Reinforced with extra ammunition, Wegner was conscious that a stand-off had occurred, even though they were more numerous than the Rangers they now surrounded. 'They were far better soldiers than us,' said Wegner. 'We couldn't make headway against them and they were too few in number to make a big attack against us.'

German troops had moved overnight so that, while the Americans now had a bridgehead around Omaha, there were plenty of men defending the coast between Vierville and Pointe du Hoc. The mission of the mixed Rangers and Company C, 116th Infantry group was to battle their way through and somehow link up with the beleaguered Rangers at Pointe du Hoc. First, though, they had to see off a counter-attack launched at seven that morning. It came a few hundred yards from where Captain Raaen was dug in, but seeing a number of Shermans standing by idly, he ran over to one, jumped on to it and knocked on the hatch. A bleary-eyed tank commander emerged and Raaen told him to unleash some fire-power against the German attack. Quickly getting into action, the Shermans helped force the enemy attack back. Soon after that, Raaen was ordered out on patrol with just three other men, treading very carefully for fear of enemy mines. Spotting two Germans up ahead, they opened fire and pursued them until they lost them. They then heard the revving of engines behind them and realized the column about to drive for Pointe du Hoc was getting going.

Rejoining the rest of the column, he was told to head to the 29th Division CP and report the Rangers' plans. This took him back to the beach, where, having made his report, he was able to take a Jeep, fill it with ammunition and drive it back up to Vierville and on to rejoin the relief column heading towards Saint-Pierre-du-Mont, the village before Pointe du Hoc. Several times, snipers took shots at Raaen's Jeep. One bullet skimmed his helmet and spun into his lap. Then a machine gun opened fire and, quickly using a hedge as cover, both he and Corporal Jack Sharp, who was with him, got out of the Jeep, took cover underneath and, having released the handbrake, crawled and pushed the vehicle past the next gap until they were clear. Soon after, they reached a fork in the road, which posed a dilemma – which direction should they take? After careful examination of spent cartridges and battle debris, they chose the right. This turned out to be the correct call, because soon after they finally rejoined the column and were able to distribute the ammunition.

The Ranger relief column reached Saint-Pierre-du-Mont at around 11 a.m., but although they were now only 1,000 yards from Pointe du Hoc, here German resistance stiffened. Artillery and mortars rained down, while snipers and machine-gun fire – from Karl Wegner among others – covered every approach and, although the Rangers and accompanying tanks returned fire, they were unable to force their way through. Now they were doubly surrounded – at Pointe du Hoc and at Saint-Pierre-du-Mont. Raaen was about to be sent off on a lone mission to find out what the situation was at Vierville and whether reinforcements were on their way, when an officer from the 29th Division arrived on a bicycle and assured them the 29th's 175th Infantry had just landed and that relief from the 116th was coming. It might have been, but not that day.

That evening, the Shermans pulled back along with some of the men. Raaen, although only a young captain, was left in command of the rest – three Ranger companies and Company C of the 116th. 'We had practically no anti-tank weapons,' he recalled, 'and so we just holed in expecting to be run over by German tanks.'

Across the invasion front to the north-west of Caen, the Canadians, and to a lesser extent the British troops from Sword, were coming to blows with the altogether more formidable armoured forces of the 12. SS 'Hitlerjugend' and the 21. Panzer-Division. By 1944, German infantry divisions had been reduced in size, so generally speaking had three regiments of two battalions each, rather than the older version of three regiments, each with three infantry battalions of around 900 men each. This meant their overall size dropped from around 15,000 to 12,000 men. Armoured divisions, on the other hand, and especially Waffen-SS panzer divisions, tended to be swollen and above their authorized establishment. The 'Hitlerjugend' Division was a case in point, with a total strength of 20,540 on 1 June, with substantially inflated battalions in its two panzer-grenadier regiments, all of which were motorized, as well as having just under a hundred Panzer Mk IV tanks and almost fifty Mk V Panthers. The division also had a self-propelled gun regiment (tracked guns that could move in their own right rather than having to be towed) and a lot of artillery support, with nearly 150 guns all told, including twelve 88mm high-velocity anti-tank guns attached to five of the six battalions, while the sixth still had six; there were seventy of these extremely potent guns in the division. This was a lot – a huge number compared with ordinary Wehrmacht infantry divisions and almost as many as an artillery-heavy British division.

Not all of the division had reached the front by the afternoon of Wednesday, 7 June, but Standartenführer Kurt Meyer's SS-Panzergrenadier-Regiment 25, which was in the van, could call on at least fifty artillery pieces and a similar number of tanks, as well as his highly mobile infantry, who were also bristling with mortars and machine guns: each of his three panzer-grenadier battalions had some 69 machine guns, except the III. Bataillon, which had a staggering 151. A gaping chasm existed between the best and least within the German armies; the British and Canadians who were about to come up against 12. SS were taking on troops of an entirely different calibre and level of equipment and firepower to the German infantry divisions they had encountered on the crust. It was like comparing the little leagues with the majors. What's more, quite regardless of the standard of training and leadership, the men of the 12. SS 'Hitlerjugend' were, almost without exception, highly motivated and, crucially, disciplined. They were men who were very unlikely to roll over easily and would do exactly as ordered.

Nor were they on their own that day, because on their right flank was half of 21. Panzer, reinforced by a hastily reconstituted battalion from the remnants of the 716. Division. Despite its losses the previous day, 21. Panzer still had plenty of Panzer Mk IVs and lots of powerful mobile artillery; Kampfgruppe Rauch, under Oberst Josef Rauch,* could, for example, call on twenty-four self-propelled 105mm guns as well as a further four 100mm guns.

Moving up from the north of Caen directly towards Kampfgruppe

---

* German *Kampfgruppen* were named after their commanding officer.

Rauch was an infantry brigade of the British 3rd Division, who had now passed through the men of the D-Day assault brigade. After their bloody battle at Hillman, the 1st Suffolks were dug in among woods near the tiny village of Le Bois du Mesnil. As far as Arthur Blizzard was concerned, it was still pretty hellish, even dug in there. 'That was a bad day,' he said. 'Jerry had us pin-pointed with mortars and 88s and stonked us day and night.' At one point during a pause in the firing, he and his mate, Alec Bailey, had been making a dash to the cookhouse (a couple of makeshift petrol-fuelled tins) when the shelling opened up again. When they eventually got back to their trench there was a large unexploded shell right in the middle of it.

To the west of them, the Canadians were pushing forward, with the North Nova Scotia Highlanders leading the advance – just one battalion – supported by some fifty Shermans of the Sherbrooke Fusiliers. Their advance was supposed to be supported by a Royal Canadian Artillery field regiment, as well as by offshore naval guns. Unfortunately, by late morning the artillery was still supporting the North Shore (New Brunswick) Regiment's attempts to capture the Distelfink radar station near Douvres; although its radar equipment had been destroyed, the strongpoint itself had not. Bob Roberts was among those making little progress there. Nor could the Nova Scotias call on naval fire support as planned, because the FOB – the naval forward observer, bombardment – could not make radio contact with the cruisers out at sea; there was just too much radio traffic and the interference across the airwaves was too great. To make matters worse, nor did the Canadian vanguard have their normal allotment of anti-tank guns – they had not yet been unloaded, for which the weather and choppy seas were largely to blame. This was why Dempsey was so worried about the slow rate of unloading; without the full complement of fire-power, his forward troops were vulnerable.

The countryside around Caen was very different from the western half of the invasion front, which was laced with small fields, bocage, and winding, softly undulating valleys. Here, the landscape was altogether more open, with wide fields no longer trimmed with a mass of dense hedgerows. From his viewpoint in the towers of the Abbey d'Ardenne, Kurt Meyer could see all the way to the beaches of Juno some 8 miles away. There were ridges and folds, but less pronounced, while the latticework of roads wove through a network of small and ancient villages, most no more than 1 or 2 miles apart. The landscape did, however, drop into dead ground just to the north of the airfield of Carpiquet, which could not be seen by any troops advancing from the coast – an ideal place in which to site waiting tanks and artillery, as Meyer was very well aware. The Nova Scotias, with the Sherbrooke Fusiliers in support, were advancing up the eastern side of the River Mue, with the airfield as their ultimate objective, although if they encountered heavy opposition they were to consolidate and secure the 'high ground' between the villages of Buron and Authie. Unfortunately, however, there was no high ground. Someone had misinterpreted their map.

By midday, the Canadians had managed to push back the blocking force of Kampfgruppe Rauch and get through the villages of both Villons-les-Buissons and then Buron by midday. Next on the road to Carpiquet was Authie; the airfield was now just 3 miles to the south-west.

From the Abbey d'Ardenne, Kurt Meyer was getting his men ready for the planned counter-attack, due to be launched at 4 p.m. This was to be a major drive forward, with both 12. SS and 21. Panzer operating side by side and with Panzer-Lehr joining in and securing their left flank as soon as they arrived and were in position to do so. Their orders from Marcks were to 'drive the enemy who had broken through into the sea and destroy him'. It was unequivocal. The arrival of the Canadians in front of him rather upset these plans, however, because they forced him to engage far earlier than intended and so without the kind of coordination that might have been achieved had they been able to stick to the 4 p.m. kick-off as ordered.

The Canadian advance reached Authie and then, as they probed forward once more, hit the 12. SS. Tank duels opened up in which both sides lost armour, while heavy shelling thundered into Authie, Buron and the ground in between. Meyer's men were now advancing all along the north-west of Caen. Smoke and the fog of war obscured Meyer's view, however, and, charged with adrenalin, he jumped on a motorcycle and sped towards his III. Bataillon as it advanced on Buron, speeding past some fifty Canadian prisoners who were being frog-marched towards the abbey. No sooner had he reached the open ground south-east of Buron than Canadian Shermans opened fire and shells began whistling around him. Diving for cover in a shell-hole, he was startled to find himself face to face with a Canadian soldier. They looked at each other warily, then the Canadian made a dash for it as more shells flew over.

Meyer eventually found Obersturmbannführer Karl-Heinz Milius, the commander of his III. Bataillon, between Authie and Buron. Heavy artillery fire was falling on Buron. 'One could no longer identify the village,' wrote Meyer. 'Smoke, explosions and flames marked its position.' By around 4 p.m. the Canadians were pulling back to Les Buissons as their artillery was finally arriving to give support. It was clear, however, that, although they were being pushed back and had taken heavy casualties, this was far from being a rout. The combined infantry and armour had taken a considerable toll on the Germans too – a toll that was worsening now the artillery was joining in. Obersturmführer Hans Siegel, whose II. Bataillon was also involved, discovered the effectiveness of Allied artillery fire at first hand. Although only a first lieutenant, he was a highly experienced 25-year-old who had fought in the Polish campaign as well as through much of the war on the Eastern Front. Commissioned back in 1940, he had won an Iron Cross First Class at Kharkov before being badly wounded and invalided out for more than six months. Now recovered, he was one of the tough, dedicated and battle-hardened officers who had been brought in to provide the backbone of the new 'Hitlerjugend' Division. This afternoon of 7 June, though, he was leading his 8. Kompanie of Mk IV panzers in an attack towards Cambes, a couple of miles north-east of Buron.

His was the lead tank when the shelling began, so he sped towards the edge of a wood for cover. Suddenly, a shell exploded above them, knocking a tree directly on to their tank, cutting off their visibility entirely and jamming the turret. 'We quickly turned back and forth,' said Siegel, 'but were unable to strip the monster from us.' Siegel then bailed out and was hurrying to get another vehicle when two more of his panzers were hit as they stopped to fire. His fourth tank had slid sideways into a shell crater, which meant all four were out of action before they had properly got involved in the battle.

These mounting losses were riling the men of Milius's III. Bataillon. Commanders always set the tone for the men serving under them and Milius was an old-school SS Nazi who had worked at Dachau concentration camp before the war. First in Authie and then in Buron, his men went on the rampage. Wounded Canadians were bayoneted and bludgeoned to death, and a number of those trying to surrender were shot. In Authie, eight prisoners under guard were executed, then two of the bodies were dragged on to the main road and a Mk IV brought up to run back and forth repeatedly over the corpses. When a French civilian was later authorized to remove the mess, he needed a shovel to do so. More prisoners were summarily shot in Buron.

As soon as the SS men tried to push north of Buron, however, they were cut to pieces in turn and, with the Canadian artillery now support-ing, Meyer had no choice but to recall his men. With the lead German units in retreat, the Canadians counter-attacked and managed to retake the shattered remains of Buron. Shermans of the Sherbrooke Fusiliers were now running down fleeing grenadiers. At long last, naval fire added support to the Canadians' efforts and that evening the entire area, includ-ing the villages of Cambes, Buron and Authie, over and through which the battle had raged all afternoon, were plastered by offshore naval guns, while once again fighter-bombers swooped in to strafe and bomb enemy positions. In a fit of murderous pique, a further eighteen Canadian POWs were shot in the grounds of the abbey that evening; of the 110 Canadians who died that day, at least 37 were executed while others were murdered by panzers deliberately guided to run over a number of wounded lying by the sides of the road. Witnesses recalled seeing the streets running with blood. However, the Germans were not the only ones murdering prisoners – the Allies were doing it too; Bob Slaughter, for example, had been expressly told not to take prisoners on D-Day. This had set an ugly tone for the rest of the campaign.

The battle demonstrated much else besides. The 12. SS, one of the best-equipped and most motivated divisions in the German Armed Forces, had been stopped by an initially under-gunned Canadian force only a sixth of its size. There had been no drive to the sea; the Allies had not been destroyed. This was in part because of the high level of training and excellent equipment of the Canadians, who yet again had punched above their weight – a feature of their performance throughout the war so far. It was also because fighting in this open ground around Caen was extremely difficult, especially when on the offensive, which necessarily meant moving up and out of concealed positions. In this regard, not very much had changed since going over the top from the trenches in the last war. The Canadians and British could take great cheer from having seen off this strong counter-attack, but the experience of the 12. SS and 21. Panzer that day also served as a warning. Being on the offensive in this eastern part of the battlefield was not going to be easy or straightforward in any way.

Normandy was going to be brutal.

CHAPTER 16

Fighter-Bomber Racecourse

With the Allied urgency to build up men and supplies rapidly, one of the most vital objectives was the capture of Port-en-Bessin. No. 47 Commando had spent the night of 6 June in the open on Mont Cavalier, marked up as Hill 72 on their maps. At its foot was a German bunker being used as a medical post, which the Commandos had quickly captured, taking the German medical officers prisoner. During the night, a group of Germans had arrived there thinking they would be attending morning sick parade, only to be met by Commandos with blackened faces. They were swiftly added to the growing prisoner count, although as the morning of 7 June broke the Germans still occupying the town were none the wiser that the Commandos were at their backs.

Up on the hill, as dawn arrived, Lance Corporal Frank Wright looked down the straight road that ran a mile or so into the town and small fishing port. Three strongpoints covered Port-en-Bessin, one on either side on the cliffs overlooking the town and sea beyond – labelled the Eastern and Western Features – and a third at the southern edge of the town, which appeared to consist of strengthened billets and ammunition store bunkers. The attack of 47 Commando was due to be coordinated with American artillery from Omaha and offshore naval gun support, but Colonel Charles Phillips and his HQ team could not make radio contact with the Americans. They did, however, manage to link with HMS *Emerald*, a light cruiser lying 5,000 yards off shore. It was agreed the navy would bombard both the Eastern and Western Features, then Second TAF would send in rocket-firing Typhoons. Immediately after that, at around 3 p.m., the Commandos would attack. A Troop was to assault the

Western Feature, B Troop the Eastern and X Troop the ammunition bunkers. The already depleted Q and Y Troops would remain in reserve at the hamlet of Escures, with Rear HQ remaining on Hill 72 to control the battle.

As planned, naval shells began screaming on to the cliffs either side a little after 2 p.m. Frank Wright and the rest of the assault troops could only watch as shell after shell screamed on to the German positions. The town was swathed in smoke as the Commandos set off and, since a grass fire had broken out on the Eastern Feature, there was no sign of it subsiding. Frank Wright and X Troop now passed through A and B Troops and at the crossroads before the town they turned left, westwards, towards the ammunition pits. Cornfields edged the sunken track and at the third field they came to they stopped and then, two at a time, passed through a gap in the hedge and into a ditch. This gave them cover as they looked out across another meadow, roughly the size of a football field, towards a man-made hill about 25 feet high. Trenches had been dug around it and they could see troops moving about. Lieutenant Armstrong, Wright's section officer, was now moving along, two or three men at a time, explaining in whispered tones the plan; in a nutshell, this was to fix bayonets and then charge the position.

'Any questions?' asked Armstrong.

Wright said nothing. No one did. They were all speechless, because advancing over an open field towards an enemy strongpoint seemed liked suicide.

'I hope they are going to notify our next of kin,' muttered Marine Brian Skinner.

At 3.50 p.m., right on cue, first one squadron of Typhoons roared in overhead, then a second five minutes later. Thundering in over the town, they shot off their rockets and cannons with impressive accuracy, then disappeared again. 'Our target,' noted Wright, 'had been transformed into a miniature volcano.' With smoke still in the air, Captain David Walton, the troop commander, raised himself up and gave the order to fix bayonets. Wright climbed out of the ditch, clicking his bayonet on to the end of his rifle. 'I must be dreaming,' he thought. 'This isn't really happening – I'll wake up in a minute.' Mortars and a few Bren guns gave them some covering fire, and then they were running and shouting and in moments had reached the foot of the mound, miraculously still alive. Pushing into a concrete entrance, Wright and his fellow Marines, black streaks on their faces and their blood up, emerged into a bunker to find about twenty Germans, all cowering. 'White faced, hands held high,' noted Wright, 'they were shaking uncontrollably.' Half an hour later, X Troop was marching back towards the town. As it turned out, their objective had been a walkover.

It was not so easy for A and B Troops, however. A Troop were climbing the Western Feature when they suddenly came under murderous fire from the harbour. Unbeknown to the Commandos, two small German flak ships had evidently entered the harbour since the last reconnaissance photos. The survivors kept going, only to be hit by machine-gun fire and grenades as they broke through the wire around the strongpoint. With more than half the force of fifty now dead or wounded, A Troop were forced to pull back. B Troop also came under heavy fire on the eastern side of the harbour, while the Germans then counter-attacked from the south towards Rear HQ, with Y Troop also coming under fierce attack. Suddenly, the entire operation appeared to be in jeopardy.

Help was at hand, however, when two destroyers, one of them the Polish *Krakowiak*, bombarded the flak ships. Some from X Troop, Frank Wright included, were also sent forward towards the Western Feature to shoot up the flak ships and keep the enemy gunners from firing at their own.

Wright was firing away when he heard the crack of a rifle from behind them and realized they were being sniped. Nearby, Taffy Evans was firing short bursts on the Bren. As Wright fed another clip of bullets into his Lee–Enfield, he glanced across at Evans, who he realized had stopped firing. To his horror, Evans was dead. Another crack rang out. 'I'm going to die here, now,' thought Wright, 'and won't know a thing about it, here on this fucking stupid hill – dear God, get me out of this.' Fortunately, Captain Walton then pulled them back into the town, where they waited, fearing a major counter-attack and worrying they were surely doomed. Unbeknown to them, however, the battle had already turned in their favour.

One of the flak ships had half-sunk and both had been abandoned. Meanwhile, Bren carriers with machine guns and mortars from the Heavy Weapons Troop had been able to get forward and, as darkness fell, a combined force from A and B Troops assaulted the Eastern Feature. Although the commander of the attack, Captain Terence Cousins, was killed, they successfully overran the strongpoint, taking nearly forty prisoners in the process. Early the following morning, it seems the enemy troops still in the Western Feature decided it was time to quit, because voluntarily they surrendered to a Commando they had taken prisoner the day before. At around 4 a.m., just as Wright and his fellows were advancing back up the Western Feature, Corporal Amos led a further twenty-three Germans down the hill and into the port. By the time the men of X Troop reached the strongpoint, the position was deserted. 'And we were over the crest,' noted Wright, 'and walking on to open fields and the rolling countryside beyond.' Port-en-Bessin had fallen. Now both artificial harbours, the Mulberries, could be swiftly brought over and put in place.

Captain Carol Mather, part of Montgomery's 21st Army Group Tactical HQ staff, did not come ashore until late in the evening on Wednesday, 7 June. He had not been on the same ship as his chief – Tac HQ had been spread out over a number of different vessels – and had lain off shore through much of the 7th, reading the wartime chapters of Vera Brittain's *Testament of Youth*. He couldn't help ruminating on the enormous casualties, less than thirty years earlier. 'What would be our fate?' he scribbled in his diary. 'Only time would tell.' It had been encouraging, though, to arrive at the Normandy coast and discover neither enemy aircraft overhead nor shelling. He landed on the beach, jumping ashore into a couple of feet of water, while Monty's staff car glided in and then emerged, dripping, on to the hard, damp sand. From the sea, the shore had seemed unnaturally tranquil, but once on the beach the urgency of battle was all around. 'There was the acrid, pungent smell of powder,' he recorded, 'of damp clinging dust thrown up from tracks and ruined buildings; then of evening earth and herbage, mingled with petrol fumes and tank exhausts.'

The journalist Ernie Pyle had also come ashore on D plus 1, reaching the battle-scarred beach at Omaha. 'Submerged tanks and overturned boats and burned trucks and shell-shattered Jeeps and sad little personal belongings were strewn all over those bitter sands,' he wrote. 'That plus the bodies of soldiers lying in rows covered with blankets, the toes of their shoes sticking up in a line as though on drill.' He then took a walk along the beach, marvelling at the enormous wastage, and not just the bodies still floating in the water. He was shocked to see entire landing craft knocked upside down, the remnants of Rommel's beach obstacles, and partly sunken barges. Piles of shells, rolls of wire, stacks of unused life jackets could be seen on the beach. It was, he thought, a 'shore-line museum of carnage'. He also found tins of shoe polish, toothbrushes, a pocket Bible with a soldier's name in it, and even a tennis racket. 'On the beach lay, expended, sufficient men and mechanism for a small war,' he wrote. 'They were gone forever now. And yet we could afford it.' Later, Pyle clambered up the bluffs and took his turn to look at the vast armada still out at sea and be awestruck by the spectacle. A group of prisoners were standing nearby, guarded by a couple of Americans. They too were gazing out to sea, as if in a trance. None of them spoke. 'They didn't need to,' wrote Pyle. 'The expression on their faces was something forever unforgettable. In it was the final, horrified acceptance of their doom.'

Overnight on 7/8 June, Karl Wegner and his comrades, who the day before had been defending Omaha, were ordered to fall back a short distance. They had also come under command of a new *Obergefreiter*, Paul Kalb, who arrived at their lines with an Iron Cross First Class on his chest, as well as the ribbon of the Iron Cross Second Class and an Eastern Front Medal. Their mission, he told them, was to hold the Americans where they were until reinforcements arrived. Every field, he said, was to be made into a fortress. Furiously, they began digging behind the dense hedgerows of the bocage. Wegner was scared and rather overawed by the Rangers he knew were opposing him. 'Willi and I were too jumpy to try and get sleep with these men against us,' he said. At one point they heard the familiar 'brrrrp' of their machine guns coming from the American lines and briefly hoped they had broken through there. Obergefreiter Kalb soon put them right, however. 'Wegner,' he said, 'the Amis are using MGs they captured from us so keep your foolish head down.'

Captain John Raaen had been expecting a German counter-attack all night, but because of the new dispositions it never came. In fact, Generalleutnant Kraiss had recognized that his beleaguered 352. Division was too stretched, too short of ammunition and too depleted to mount any more counter-attacks. For that to happen, they needed far greater reinforcements, which were not obviously forthcoming just yet. His division was collapsing and clearly he needed to fall back to the secondary defensive line his men had prepared. This would mean losing the stretch of coast between Omaha and Pointe du Hoc – a vital piece of land with commanding views across the invasion front – but as far as Kraiss was concerned that couldn't be helped. If he pulled his men back to the second defensive line, they would be behind the River Aure, which ran roughly west–east from Isigny, and a large part of the line would also be behind the flooded part of the Aure Valley that ran almost halfway to Bayeux.

At around 2 p.m. that day, Thursday, 8 June, General Marcks arrived at 352. Division HQ and there Kraiss told him he had already ordered some of his units to withdraw, fully aware that in doing so he had already disobeyed the Führer's orders not to give any ground at all. He told Marcks that if the no-retreat order were imposed, then his division would not be able to hold and the line would collapse. Marcks was silent for a moment, contemplating the potential enormity of this decision. At length he told Kraiss his men should continue to hold on to any coastal positions until the men there ran out of ammunition and that the division should be ready to help the arriving armour in a major counter-thrust towards Bayeux planned for the following day, 9 June. Kraiss agreed, although did not tell Marcks that he had already lost contact with all the remaining strongpoints.

So it was that, earlier that morning, Captain Raaen had sent out patrols and then had been preparing to push towards Pointe du Hoc when the American relief force, including armour, arrived. 'And we took Pointe du Hoc,' he said. 'What was there was the worst mess you have ever seen in your life. There was not a blade of grass, there was not a leaf, there was not a tree standing. Everything there was shattered.'

Carol Mather had woken to a gorgeous sunny morning and after a brief council of war had headed off on a recce of the Tac HQ. The first choice, Croix, had been rejected by Monty, so now Mather and Major Trumbull Warren, Monty's Canadian PA, headed to the Château de Creullet on the edge of the town of Creully, some 5 miles inland from Gold Beach. It seemed to fit the bill. It was secluded, had ample grounds behind a wall and iron gate, as well as plenty of outhouses. There was no question of occupying the house itself – that was far too First World War; rather, they would set up their caravans, trucks and tents under trees in the grounds and liberally drape them in camouflage nets. Tac HQ was designed to be highly mobile, spare but comfortable enough, efficient and highly pragmatic.

The chateau was only a few miles north of Bayeux, which had fallen that morning, Thursday, 8 June. Among the first to pass through the city had been the Sherwood Rangers, whose tanks were supporting the infantry of 56th Brigade. Stanley Christopherson's A Squadron had pushed into the town early on the 7th and, much to his relief, the Germans had already pulled back, part of Kraiss's withdrawal to the next line of defence. 'We were given a most enthusiastic and spontaneous reception by the inhabitants,' noted Christopherson, 'who appeared genuinely delighted to welcome us and demonstrated their joy by throwing flowers at the tanks and distributing cider and food among the men.' One enemy machine gun stubbornly held out in a house to the south of the town, however, but the building went up in flames after the Sherwood Rangers opened fire. Soon after, Christopherson was startled to hear a clanging bell followed by the Bayeux fire brigade hurtling past in their shiny helmets. Despite the machine-gun fire, they held up the battle, stormed into the house and put out the fire, then re-emerged with the machine-gun team as prisoners.

The following day, 8 June, they pushed on south, crossing the main N13 highway and, after a further 6 miles or so, were ordered to make a right hook towards the village of Audrieu and take up positions on a ridge, Point 103 on their maps, overlooking the villages of Saint-Pierre, Tilly-sur-Seulles and Fontenay-le-Pesnel down the other side of the hill. Along the top of the ridge a track ran roughly east–west, lined by beech trees, with woods beyond. Beyond Tilly lay the next ridge, which, although not especially high, offered a commanding position with clear views to the long ridge that barred the route south and which ran all the way past Saint-Lô, some 25 miles to the west. Moving his tanks forward of the track, Major Christopherson ordered them into fire positions in the trees beyond, directly overlooking Saint-Pierre. All seemed quiet down in the village but he sent Captain Keith Douglas, his second-in-command, and one of his troop commanders, Lieutenant John Bethell-Fox, down in their Shermans for a reconnoitre. There they discovered most of the civilians hiding in their cellars, but eventually they persuaded one old man to come out and he told them Germans were already in the village and tanks in Tilly. Agreeing discretion was the better part of valour, Douglas and Bethell-Fox beat a hasty retreat towards their waiting tanks only to walk straight into a German patrol. Both parties were so surprised they each turned and fled, Douglas firing his revolver wildly as he ran.

These were the vanguard of Generalleutnant Fritz Bayerlein's Panzer-Lehr-Division, which was finally reaching the front after a predictably torrid march from the Le Mans area, a distance of around 110 miles. The first air attacks had occurred soon after they had got moving on 6 June, leaving casualties of around twenty men and more than that number of vehicles. Bayerlein himself came under attack at around 7 p.m. They had pushed on overnight, but at dawn he had warned Dollmann again that to keep going during the day was courting trouble. Again, Dollmann insisted the Panzer-Lehr carry on. By 5 a.m. on the 7th, they were through Argentan, some 40 miles to the south-east of Caen, which they had found heavily bombed and burning. Just getting through the town had been difficult enough as a number of roads had become blocked. The next air attack arrived at around 5.30 a.m. as they were approaching Falaise. 'The main road Vire-le-Bény,' said Bayerlein, 'was so bad that it was called a *Jabo Rennstrecke*, or fighter-bomber racecourse.' 7. Armee had insisted they move in total radio silence, as though this would prevent the Allied air forces from spotting them. Instead, it just prevented the divisional command from having clear contact with the various units and state of advance. Bayerlein found himself repeatedly having to dispatch officers and even drive to the units himself to find out what was going on.

Late on the afternoon of the 7th, Bayerlein split off and drove to meet with Oberstgruppenführer Sepp Dietrich, the commander of I. SS-Panzerkorps, to whom Panzer-Lehr, 21. Panzer and 12. SS-Panzer were now subordinated. He caught up with the leading elements of the division near Thury-Harcourt, about 25 miles south-east of Bayeux. Along the way, Bayerlein passed dozens of wrecked vehicles, most of which were nothing more than smouldering steel skeletons. 'The section between Caumont and Villers-Bocage,' said Hauptmann Alexander Hartdegen, Bayerlein's aide, 'was the road of death. Sitting along the road were burnt-out trucks and bombed field kitchens and gun tractors, some still smouldering, the dead lying beside them. This horrible scene was the backdrop to our journey.' Soon after, they were attacked again, fighters hurtling down the road straight at them, cannons blazing. Not for the first time, they found themselves jumping out of a still-rolling car, headlong into a ditch. On this occasion, the fighters made several passes. The BMW staff car was destroyed and their driver killed. Bayerlein escaped with cuts and bruises and was able to get a lift in a *Kübelwagen* to his new HQ at Proussy. Panzer-Lehr had begun the journey even better equipped and supplied than 12. SS-Panzer, but losses on the way to the front were: 84 half-tracks, prime movers and self-propelled guns out of 700; 130 trucks, more than 10 per cent of their total; and five tanks. 'These,' Bayerlein pointed out, 'are serious losses for a division not yet come into action.' More importantly, of the trucks destroyed, forty had been carrying vitally precious fuel.

Also heading north-west with the Panzer-Lehr was Hauptmann

Helmut Ritgen, supply officer and deputy commander of the II. Bataillon, Panzer-Lehr-Regiment 130. Twenty-eight years old and married, with a young wife back home in Paderborn, Ritgen was, like all the officers in the Panzer-Lehr, a vastly experienced tank commander, having served with the 6. Panzer-Division in France in 1940 and later on the Eastern Front. Then in March 1943 he had been posted from a course at the Battalion Commander School in Paris, not to his old regiment but as a company commander to the newly formed Panzer-Lehr-Regiment at Wünsdorf near Berlin. His initial misgivings had been swiftly dispelled, as his fellow officers were all first-class, as was his panzer company. Furthermore, he immediately took to his new battalion commander, the urbane and aristocratic Major Prinz Wilhelm von Schönburg-Waldenburg.

They had now been together for over a year and Ritgen had every confidence in the Prinz, in his men, in the entire division, most of whom were *alte Hasen* – old hands. Not surprisingly, though, he was heading to the front with a heavy heart. 'We knew it would be difficult,' he wrote. And like everyone else in the Panzer-Lehr, his first taste of the front was from the air; even once darkness fell, their column still had to circle continually around bomb craters and wrecked vehicles, which slowed progress. By morning they were nearing the small town of Villers-Bocage when the *Jabos* came over again, hitting one of the precious fuel trucks and sending a column of thick black smoke high into the sky, which drew even more enemy aircraft to them. Ritgen found the noise and confusion hellish. His supply company eventually reached the village of Parfouru-sur-Odon, a mile or two east of Villers-Bocage, and, using the woods and well-rehearsed camouflage techniques, Ritgen's men managed to get everything hidden away and comparatively safe. Meanwhile, the battalion's Panzer Mk IVs all pushed on towards Tilly-sur-Seulles, from where they were expecting to drive towards Bayeux.

Bayerlein's orders on finally reaching the front were the same as those of 12. SS-Panzer and 21. Panzer: to drive the enemy into the sea and destroy them. Panzer-Lehr was due to join the left flank of 12. SS-Panzer at Bretteville-l'Orgueilleuse and attack towards the sea at Courseulles. They were just moving up, completely unaware even that Bayeux had already fallen, when his leading troops bumped into Keith Douglas and John Bethell-Fox of the Sherwood Rangers in Saint-Pierre.

From Omaha, the Americans continued to make steady progress. The Big Red One was moving south from Colleville, with the 18th Infantry pushing towards the town of Formigny. Tom and Dee Bowles were busy scuttling between units laying telephone wire. It was always a dangerous job, as they had to run, crouching, from one place to another and hope they weren't out in the open when the shelling began or if a sniper suddenly got a bead.

On the morning of 7 June, Dee Bowles and his buddy, Private Kirkman, had been laying wires and were heading back down a track towards one of the battalion's companies when a hidden German machine-gunner opened fire from 20 yards. Kirkman was shot through the ribs, while Bowles was hit twice in the arm, the back and his side. The force knocked them both backwards, off the road and into a ditch that ran alongside. Incredibly, both were still fully conscious; lying there, Bowles felt numb and was unsure where he had been hit or how badly. Together they managed to crawl about 50 yards until they reached some shrubs out of sight of the enemy gunman. Somehow they then both got to their feet, walked back up the road and managed to get some help.

Dee's twin, Tom, had been lying in a ditch trying to get some sleep when he was told the news. Hurrying up to the aid post, he found his brother still conscious but lying on the ground.

'Are you going to be all right?' he asked.

'Well, I think so,' Dee told him. Medics were giving him morphine and checking his condition.

'Can you lift yourself on to the stretcher?' one of the medics asked Dee.

'Yeah, sure,' he told them, but when he tried to lift himself up, he found he couldn't really move at all. Having been placed on the stretcher, Dee turned to Tom and asked him to take off his belt and canteens, which they had filled with whisky before heading across the Channel. 'I won't need that Scotch after all,' Dee told him. Tom was relieved that his brother could still joke. Perhaps Dee wasn't too badly hit. Perhaps he would be OK soon enough. Even so, they both realized Dee would be heading straight back to England.

'Well, so long,' said Tom. Then Dee was put on to a Jeep and taken away.

For all his cheeriness in front of his brother, Dee had been seriously wounded. Soon after, he passed out and when he woke up again he was already on a ship back across the Channel. There were stretchers of wounded men all around him and he was struggling with a desperate thirst. 'But they wouldn't give me no water,' he says. 'They didn't know how badly shot I was.' Eventually, after much pleading, they gave him a wet rag to put in his mouth. The next thing he knew, he was at the naval hospital in Southampton, where he underwent a number of operations. 'Only one of those bullets was real,' he says. 'And that went clean through my arm. The rest were all wooden. It's probably what saved me.'

Left in France, Tom worried about him. 'Of course, I thought about him all the time,' he says. 'If I'd have ever met a German at that time, I would have shot him – I wouldn't have taken no prisoners.'

There was little let-up for Tom Bowles and the rest of the 2nd Battalion. By the evening of 8 June, they had taken Formigny and Mandeville across the River Aure, where, fortunately for them, there was no flooding, and were pushing south again, the network of fields and the high bocage seeming denser with every passing yard.

CHAPTER 17

Linking Up

LIEUTENANT-GENERAL LEWIS BRERETON, COMMANDER of the US Ninth Air Force, had discovered during his time in Cairo and the Mediterranean that journalists would often ask him how the Brits and Americans got along, and he would always cite the answers given by his friends and colleagues, Air Marshal Mary Coningham and Brigadier-General Auby Strickland, who had commanded IX Tactical Command in the Mediterranean. In the morning, one would come over to the other's tent, they would ask how each other was, then they would suggest they shared a glass of gin. Coningham would produce the bottle of gin and Strickland a can of grapefruit juice. That, Brereton would tell people, was how the British and Americans get along.

It wasn't always plain sailing, yet, for the most part, the Allied air force leaders got on well. Spaatz and Tedder had a close, easy relationship, with one another and also with Eisenhower, while those running the tactical air forces also got on well. No one liked Leigh-Mallory much, but that didn't matter because he had been effectively sidelined by both Tedder and Mary Coningham, who had been given the title Commander, Advanced AEAF. This gave him, rather than Leigh-Mallory, operational control of the US Ninth Air Force as well as his own Second Tactical Air Force. It meant yet another Brit in charge of a key component of the Allied forces, which annoyed Brereton, who was getting increasingly frustrated about the dominance of the RAF, but on a personal level he had no issue with Coningham, a friend and fellow bon viveur. The two had worked closely for months. Among the air force commanders, the long periods of tent-sharing in North Africa were now paying dividends.

Coningham had ordered a maximum effort on D-Day and D plus 1, regardless of wear and tear on aircraft and the strain on crews, which was why fighter pilots like Gabby Gabreski were flying four times a day and bomber crews such as Ken Handley of 466 Squadron were flying two missions in a day. Much thought had been put into every aspect of the air operations. To ensure effective and accurate fighter cover over the beaches, Fighter Direction Tenders had been added to the invasion fleets, on which were radar, plotting rooms and ground controllers. These had worked very well, but perhaps the greatest triumph had been won earlier, leading to the almost complete no-show of the Luftwaffe on D-Day. In early 1943 the Americans had pushed hard for prioritizing the destruction of the Luftwaffe. The POINTBLANK directive, issued on 10 June 1943, had been driven by them and they had been absolutely right. D-Day had been possible because of it, and the firm footing the Allies now had was in large part due to the immense support the air forces had given those on the ground. Command of the Allied Air Forces might now be dominated by the RAF, but the USAAF had driven the strategy that was paying such dividends now.

An essential part of Allied strategy was to swiftly establish airfields in Normandy from which aircraft could operate as soon as was humanly possible. The level of planning to achieve this was immense, but the closer aircraft were to the front, the more they could fly. And the more they could fly, the easier the task would be for those Allied troops battling on the ground.

Brigadier-General Pete Quesada flew into Normandy on Thursday, 8 June, arriving on Emergency Landing Strip 1 at Pouppeville, just behind the southern part of Utah Beach, and nearly cutting down an engineer still trying to finish the airfield. He had come to confer with Bradley and the corps commanders, as well as to see how his airfields and advance parties were getting along. The challenges were many. In the pre-invasion plan, the Allies had hoped to be further south already, but first the delays in getting engineers, ground personnel and equipment ashore and then having to construct airfields while still being shelled and sniped had ensured that on D plus 2 only two airfields had been built in the American sector and just one in the British. That these three had been open for business in so short a time was, however, little short of a miracle. Many of the men involved had been drafted from AT&T, the company that was almost single-handedly responsible for implementing the telephone network across the USA. 'They were AT&T's best,' commented Quesada, 'and they could do anything.' At any rate, these engineers simply shifted west and created an airfield between Omaha and the village of Saint-Laurent-sur-Mer – behind Easy Red. Incredibly, airfield A-21 C was operational by evening that day.

Also ashore were the first radar sets, as well as offshore radar and ground control, the forward directing posts. It wasn't ideal – Quesada's new microwave early warning – MEW – radar ideally needed higher ground – but by the time he touched down at ELS-1, he did have some 1,600 engineers, ground crew and signals troops in Normandy. In all, Quesada alone had some 80,000 personnel ready to ship over to France, and every one of them knew exactly what they were supposed to do when they got there and where they were supposed to be. He was certainly anxious to be based in Normandy as soon as possible and, with scant regard for his own safety, he flew over again on 10 June. Just to the south of Pointe du Hoc, on the coastal road at the hamlet of Le Guay, IX Tactical Command HQ was set up alongside Bradley's embryonic First Army Headquarters. A mile to the south, at Cricqueville, A-2, a further US airfield, was being built. 'Headquarters IX Tactical Air Command,' signalled Quesada at 3.30 p.m. on the 10th, 'established on the continent.'

The troops on the ground also had reason to thank the contribution of the Allied naval forces, which had been phenomenal. The role of the navy in the success of D-Day has been all too often underplayed – and even rather taken for granted – yet in the most trying and difficult weather conditions imaginable they had cleared dense minefields and got the vast invasion forces successfully across the Channel, in order and on time, both men and truly huge amounts of materiel; on D-Day alone, 132,000 men and almost 20,000 vehicles were landed. In addition, there was the incredible amount of naval fire support, which not only destroyed vital enemy gun positions such as those at Longues-sur-Mer, but also helped turn the tide on the beaches, not least at Omaha. The destroyer USS *Carmick* alone fired 1,127 5-inch shells on D-Day; its effort was not exceptional. Offshore naval bombardment had continued to help the Allies push inland – performance on the ground improved considerably when communications with the naval forces were intact.

Admiral Ramsay had reason to be proud of his command and what they had achieved, although he was none the less furious that three S-Boats had managed to penetrate Allied naval defences and sink three LSTs on 8 June, which, added to the sixty-three landing craft destroyed on D-Day, amounted to serious losses. He was also equally frustrated that half a Kriegsmarine destroyer force moving up from Brest had got away. 'I wanted all to be sunk,' he noted in his diary, then added, 'The U-boats are approaching the Portsmouth area & will become active by Saturday. E-boats [S-boats] still a menace.' The following day he was flung into another rage when an LST carrying more than 250 wounded was kept at sea for several hours due to bad organization. 'Just a day of one d . . . d thing after another,' he noted, 'but the general trend of the operation is good & progressing.'

Nor were naval operations confined to warships and landing craft. Lieutenant Ambrose Lampen, aboard the ancient Channel paddle-steamer *Queen of Thanet*, had arrived at Arromanches, just to the west of Gold Beach, on the morning of 7 June, after his ship had weaved sedately along the Z-shaped channel cleared through the enemy minefields. Anchored a mile off shore, he could hear only the distant rumble of guns and see occasional flashes on the skyline. His task was to place the 'Corn-cobs' – old blockships that were to form the first breakwater. With the shelter they would provide in place, the Phoenixes and other elements of the Mulberry harbour could be brought in, swiftly assembled and put into operation.

The first blockship, *Alynbank*, arrived at 10.30 a.m. It had to be manoeuvred into position at 280 degrees, then sunk in such a way that it settled at the right angle. Working against this was the tide, which was now high but was about to start ebbing and might easily push the ship out to a different angle or off course entirely. 'The method of scuttling the ship was crude,' noted Lampen. There were charges either side below the waterline, each of which was supposed to blow a 4-foot hole. 'But no-one really knew what would be the effect of the blast, or how long the ship would take to sink.' The hope was that, while the ship sank, tugs would hold it in position. Unfortunately, the first attempt on *Alynbank* failed badly, as strong tidal currents took hold, the tugs lost control, and the ship swung round, settling at almost 90 degrees to where she should have been. This was the first Corncob to have been sunk and it could not have gone more disastrously wrong. Mortified, Lampen hurried back to shore in his small motor craft to see his boss, Captain Christopher Petrie.

'I saw the whole thing, Lampen,' Petrie said calmly. 'We should not have attempted it on the ebb tide. It was bad luck.' Nothing more was said, but Lampen felt certain his time as a 'planter' was over. None the less, he got the tug captains together and worked out how they might avoid this happening again, and the following morning, 8 June, they sank the next Corncob, the old tramp steamer *Saltersgate*, perfectly, her bows almost touching the misplaced *Alynbank*.

Rather than experiencing any sense of elation, however, Lampen felt shattered because a few minutes earlier he had seen Captain Petrie being escorted from Arromanches. 'I knew immediately what it meant,' he recorded. 'A fine gentleman had been caught between loyalty to this own subordinate and the inflexible ambition of his successor. For my mistake with the *Alynbank* he had been summarily removed from command and sent back into the oblivion of retirement.' There was little time for him to dwell on the unfairness of Petrie's dismissal, however, because there were more blockships to sink. He and his team were rapidly getting into the rhythm of the operation and by nightfall they had completed a third of the task.

By the evening of 10 June, Lampen and his men had completed the 'Gooseberry' harbour – the long breakwater of sunken blockships. Later, he climbed a track leading out of the town and walked up on to the cliff where the Germans had had a radar station; the broken Würzburg was still there. Looking out he could see the breakwater and the piers being put into place by the army engineers. Three 'spud' pierheads had already been situated, with 'whale' units – the individual parts of the pier – stretching back to the shore. On the beach, an LST was busy unloading, while further out, coastal steamers were unloading on to DUKWs, which beetled their way back to the shore. Both Arromanches and Gold Beach were hives of activity. Further along the coast, he could even see one of the other rows of blockships that were being established at each of the invasion beaches.

Lampen had also been elevated. Quite a team had been put in place to supervise the construction of the Mulberry B, but Lampen had now been given the additional post of 'planter' for the Phoenixes, the huge caissons that would make the main harbour wall. On Sunday, 11 June, they began positioning the Phoenixes, which had already been brought safely across the Channel and which would form the deepest part of the harbour. Having learned from *Alynbank*, he was determined not to put a foot wrong. His Phoenixes would be planted on a rising tide; Lampen realized that for the harbour to work successfully – and to last against whatever capricious weather might be thrown against it – each needed to be sited perfectly and, for that, timing was everything. And so this extraordinary offshore project progressed. Slowly but surely, almost a week after the invasion, the battle to win the build-up of supplies appeared to be in the hands of the Allies.

Meanwhile, the Americans were making progress to the west of Cricqueville. On 9 June the Rangers, along with the help of Company C, 116th Infantry, took both Grandcamp and the battery complex at Maisy. To help them they had the 58th Field Artillery, now attached, as well as the 743rd Tank Battalion, so were able to operate as an all-arms assault force. Captain John Raaen's first task was to clear the houses in Grandcamp of snipers. 'So I made up four teams of four,' he said, 'and put two on the right two on the left, and then leapfrogged the pairs from house to house. And we cleared about twenty or thirty houses that way.' The next day, after a night in ditches by the hedgerows, they joined the attack on the Maisy Battery itself, which they swiftly overran. This battery had been firing on them while they'd been holed up in Saint-Pierre near Pointe du Hoc, but, like all the German strongpoints along the Normandy coast, it had been worn down by air and naval fire and now by an overwhelmingly strong assault from inland. Concrete bunkers were all well and good, but they were immobile and dependent on the mutual fire support of others. When isolated, damaged and with ammunition supplies running short, such complexes often ended up becoming coffins instead, as had been painfully proved to the defenders since D-Day.

Sergeant Bob Slaughter and the 1st Battalion, 116th Infantry, swung inland a little way while the Rangers were attacking Grandcamp and cut across to the south of Maisy. Ahead were surviving elements of Grenadier-Regiment 914. Slaughter and his squad followed a squeaking Sherman tank as it trundled forward along a sunken road. High hedges lined the way, and Slaughter and his men took solace from the protection both these and the Sherman gave them, although because of the dust from the tank, he was happy to hang back a bit. Then sporadic mortar and the occasional larger shell began whistling over, until suddenly an almighty explosion up ahead pulsed through the ground. A fireball erupted and rolled in all directions as the Sherman hit a teller mine, blowing all the men inside to smithereens, as well as almost an entire squad of ten men who had been crouching behind the tank. Slaughter felt the blast and heat from some 40 yards back, and when the flame, dust and smoke began to settle, he saw that the 30-ton tank had been flung sideways into the ditch at the edge of the road. 'One minute they were healthy young men,' he wrote, 'and the next minute they were bloody arms and legs wrapped around bloody torsos.' They found body parts, including boots with the feet still in them, more than 25 yards away. Slaughter was far from being the only one to vomit. 'I thought I was getting used to seeing men killed in every gruesome way possible,' he added, 'but that teller mine explosion was one of the most horrific things I have ever witnessed.' After this, he vowed to keep his distance from tanks on roads.

The remnants of the shattered 352. Division were now pulling back to the *Hauptkampflinie* – the new main line of defence they'd prepared before the invasion. Leutnant Hans Heinze and his 5. Kompanie were among the first to reach it, having pulled back south of Colleville. After they had dug in, they watched as yet more Allied aircraft flew over; such overwhelming enemy air power and their huge materiel advantage was something Heinze had not experienced in Russia. After one pasting by Allied bombers, he found his friend Leutnant Heller, a veteran of France 1940 and the Eastern Front, quite unashamedly weeping over the loss of so many of his men since the invasion. 'If they would only fight us man to man,' Heller told him, 'we would have a chance. We can't fight their planes and bombs.'

Karl Wegner was among those exhausted German survivors continuing to trudge south and west. That day, Friday, 9 June, the division lost 2,000 men – a fifth of its fighting strength, and on top of the number that had been lost the two previous days. All day they were harried by *Jabos*, fighters and even bombers, while the roads were littered with dead horses and burning vehicles. 'Even though we fell back,' he said, 'other parts of our regiment were still fighting in the hedgerows.' Sometimes it was only a few men, but a machine gun or two and a couple of snipers could prove incredibly effective, holding up an entire American company and giving the rest precious time to make good their escape. As they trudged on, Wegner and his fellows kept a constant watch on the sky, but time and time again the *Jabos* dived down on them and they had to jump for cover and hope for the best. 'But always we asked the same question: where is the Luftwaffe?' he wrote. The most common answer was, 'They're all back home protecting Fat Hermann's medals.'

On the morning of 9 June, Generalleutnant Bayerlein was finally ready to enter the battle, with his artillery shelling the enemy positions on the ridge opposite where the British 8th Armoured and 53rd Infantry

Brigades were now dug in waiting to push forward. Above Saint-Pierre and Tilly-sur-Seulles, the Sherwood Rangers were feeling the heat. 'Point 103 became most uncomfortable,' noted Stanley Christopherson with typical understatement, 'and appeared to be the main target of German mortar and artillery fire.' His tanks were quite safe in the trees, but the moment they pushed forward they were exposed to enemy tanks down in the village. Eventually Sergeant Dring managed to push forward with his Firefly and, using the high-velocity 17-pounder gun, hit a Panther five times and knocked it out. Three Shermans were destroyed, although in each case the crews managed to get out. One of those hit was Lieutenant Mike Howden's tank. 'Mike's stammer prevented any kind of speech for half an hour,' noted Christopherson after Howden and his crew had escaped, 'and his complexion – which at the best of times is devoid of colour – was even whiter than snow.' But Christopherson did lose his second-in-command that day, Captain Keith Douglas, who was killed instantly by flying shrapnel. Douglas had been with A Squadron since Palestine and had fought with them all through North Africa. Arguably the greatest British war poet of the Second World War, he also wrote a superb book about his time with the Sherwood Rangers, *Alamein to Zem Zem*, which had been published before they left for Normandy.

Later that day, the Sherwood Rangers were withdrawn and their positions on Point 103 taken over by the 4th/7th Dragoon Guards. With the British in this sector coming up against the Panzer-Lehr, however, the Sherwood Rangers, along with all the infantry and armour of 50th Division plus the attached independent brigades, were needed once more, and the very next day were moved back up to Point 103. By then, Saint-Pierre had been taken in a combined infantry and armour assault backed by artillery, which, by this time, was in full support. Christopherson's A Squadron was on the left flank supporting the infantry. He and his men spent a sleepless night on the edge of Saint-Pierre expecting a counter-attack that never materialized.

On 8 June, the 1st Battalion, 505th PIR was finally relieved at La Fière, having spent two and a half torrid days holding the position and becoming increasingly chewed up by enemy artillery and mortar fire. By the time they moved out, Lieutenant-Colonel Mark Alexander had just 176 men left; he should have had over 500. More men were arriving, however. The 325th Glider Parachute Regiment took over and, with the help of some 100 men from the 507th PIR, charged across the causeway, finally taking the village of Cauquigny. It was costly, though, and not helped when the smoke laid down to mask their approach drifted away too soon, exposing them horribly. 'I was glad I didn't have that assignment,' said Alexander. 'I thought afterwards how lucky I was to no longer be there, and have to lead that daytime attack.'

To the south-east, meanwhile, the battle for Carentan was still going on. From the church tower in the town centre, Oberleutnant Martin Pöppel had one of the best views in the area. He could see either side of the Vire estuary to the north, back across to Saint-Côme-du-Mont to the north-west and even away to the east, while to the south, in the distance, the long, low ridge either side of Saint-Lô rose gradually, a patchwork sea of green spreading away from them. Out to sea was the overwhelming spectacle of the Allied fleet. 'Ship after ship, funnel after funnel,' he noted in his diary, 'a sight that absorbs everyone with its sheer military strength.'

As commander of the 12. Kompanie of the III. Bataillon, Fallschirm-jäger-Regiment 6, Pöppel was in charge of the battalion's heavy weapons – four 88s, four howitzers and a *Nebelwerfer* six-barrelled mortar. By this time, the I. Bataillon had been largely annihilated – just twenty-five men had escaped back across the flooded areas to Carentan – while II. Bataillon had been badly mauled at Saint-Côme and had been withdrawn across the Douve River. This left III. Bataillon bearing the brunt of any new American attack. Pöppel used his howitzers and 88s for harassing fire, safe in the knowledge that he now had all the regiment's artillery ammunition because all the other guns had been lost. Even so, Oberst von der Heydte, commander of Fallschirmjäger-Regiment 6, was not happy and early on 10 June rang Pöppel to ask him why he was using artillery rather than machine guns. Because, Pöppel told him, the MGs were completely ineffective at their current ranges. This prompted a major dressing down from the 'Old Man', but, even after Pöppel had ordered his guns to cease fire, another boom rang out and the colonel was back on the line complaining his mortars were now falling short.

A couple of hours later, three red Very lights rose into the sky, the signal that the enemy was attacking, so Pöppel ordered his guns to open up on pre-arranged targets with everything they had. Moments later, the phone was ringing again. A furious von der Heydte was demanding why he was firing his guns when he had given express orders not to? Pöppel explained why, but it cut no ice and he was relieved of his command with immediate effect. 'It's easy to imagine my bitterness,' noted Pöppel. 'My platoon leaders, who have gone through the whole business with me are furious as well, but there's nothing to be done. The scum up there always stick together.' He was now ordered to present himself at Regimental HQ, where he was made an aide-de-camp to the commander – in other words, an officer courier. It was quite a humiliation for someone of Pöppel's long experience and service.

If von der Heydte was becoming a little tetchy, it was understandable. He felt as though he was under attack from all sides, including his own. Ammunition was getting woefully short. Originally, he had been instructed to get extra supplies from an ammunition distribution point, but it turned out no ammunition had yet been stored there, so the regiment was assigned another and that turned out to have been destroyed already. Although he now asked for an air-drop resupply, by 10 p.m. on the 10th von der Heydte had already decided Carentan was untenable and that his men should fall back to a new line south of the town the following day, Sunday, 11 June.

However, earlier that evening Brigadeführer Werber Ostendorff, commander of the 17. SS-Panzergrenadier-Division 'Götz von Berlichingen', had reached the regimental CP, assuring them his panzers and artillery were making good progress and would soon be there to help split the Americans and drive them back. Perhaps von der Heydte did not believe him; perhaps he thought the situation too dire. At any rate, the evacuation order stayed. Only a single company of the III. Bataillon would remain in the town to hold up and frustrate the Americans.

Early on the 11th, Pöppel was told to report to LXXXIV. Korps HQ at Saint-Lô to ask for the regiment to be placed under command of 17. SS-Panzergrenadier-Division. This was granted and he was also able to grab a handful of much-needed maps before heading back on his motorbike along roads littered with burned-out trucks and other vehicles, shot up by the Allied air forces. He found von der Heydte at the new CP at the hamlet of Bléhou, some 7 miles south-west of Carentan. Making the most of the lull in the fighting, most of Fallschirmjäger 6 was withdrawn from the town that afternoon in full daylight, then at 10 p.m. orders were issued for a joint counter-attack with 17. SS for the following day, Monday, 12 June. They were signed not by von der Heydte, but by Brigadeführer Ostendorff.

Meanwhile, the 506th PIR had been moving up overnight to their jump-off positions for the assault on Carentan, unaware that only a skeleton force remained in the town. Already, US infantry and paratroopers had linked up a couple of miles to the north and bridges over the River Douve had been secured. General Maxwell Taylor had then ordered a three-pronged attack to take the town – from the north-east, from the east and with the 506th PIR attacking from the south-west – hence the night march to get them to their jumping-off position.

Easy Company had spent many months training at night, so many of the potential difficulties of crossing unfamiliar ground in darkness, of celestial navigation and of each man keeping in touch with the next had been rigorously overcome long before they ever left England. Dick Winters believed the only people who had concerns about night marches were the divisional and regimental staff who had never undertaken such training themselves. 'These shortcomings were evident on D-Day,' he noted. 'These staff officers encountered major problems getting orientated and finding their objectives.' From what Winters had witnessed so far, however, the junior officers had had no such difficulties. He predicted, though, that problems would arise when two battalions had to cross captured bridges over, first, the River Douve and then a spur, then turn west through swampy, flooded ground and get across two railway lines. The going was tough and, as Winters suspected, the regimental and battalion staff leading the march ran into problems, continually losing contact with the companies and changing battalion boundaries. 'All told,' he wrote, 'it was a rough night. We stopped, dug in, set up machine guns and bazookas, moved out, over and over.' None the less, by 5.30 a.m. they had reached their start point covering the main road south out of town towards Périers. If the 506th could successfully block this road, the Germans who were still in Carentan would be trapped and would only be able to escape by heading west through the flooded areas.

The only way to push into the town was to go straight up the road on which they now found themselves. Winters had deployed one platoon on the left and another on the right, with a third in reserve. The road was slightly raised, with slopes on either side down to shallow ditches. Minutes later, at the agreed H-Hour, Winters hollered at his men to move out and a lone machine gun opened fire from a building up ahead at the first of two intersections where two roads met on the edge of town. The men froze, so Winters pulled himself to his feet and, despite bullets pinging around him, began yelling, 'Move out! Move out!' as he ran to the head of his column; it was fortunate the MG42 was so inaccurate. His exemplary leadership got the men going, however, and, using grenades, they managed to kill the machine-gun team, while other enemy troops from the town fled south across the fields. Now having reached the second intersection, pre-arranged mortar and machine-gun fire zeroed in on the Easy Company men and casualties started mounting. Winters got a nick from a ricochet on his ankle, but they pressed on and were soon in the town, which they found deserted of enemy. Carentan had fallen.

'June 11 I shall long remember,' wrote Stanley Christopherson, 'and proved a very sad day for the Regiment and especially for myself.' Heavy fighting had been taking place ever since the Panzer-Lehr had first clashed with the British XXX Corps on 9 June. All around Saint-Pierre, Fontenay and Tilly the situation had been fluid, with both sides taking heavy casualties. The rolling countryside with its close fields and woods was 'unpleasant', as Christopherson described it, for tanks, with neither side managing to make much headway. Saint-Pierre had been captured, however, and while Christopherson and his A Squadron remained on Point 103, B and C Squadrons, along with Regimental HQ, pushed on down the hill and moved into the village.

At midday, in answer to a call over the net, Christopherson hurried down to the new regimental CP, which was in farm buildings at the northern edge of the village. There he learned that a direct hit had struck the CO's tank, known as *Robin Hood*, killing Major Mike Laycock, the CO, as well as Captain George Jones, the adjutant, and Lieutenant Laurence Head, the intelligence officer. Several others had been wounded. It was a shattering blow; Mike Laycock was a stalwart of the regiment – one of the pre-war Territorials who had set sail for Palestine, along with his horse, back in 1939. He had been CO for only a few days after the previous – and short-lived – commander had been wounded on D-Day. Christopherson and Laycock had been close friends; Christopherson considered him not only a fine person but an equally brilliant officer, someone who had been the backbone of the regiment.

Hauptmann Helmut Ritgen, whose men in the II. Bataillon of Panzer-Lehr-Regiment 130 were fighting against the Sherwood Rangers, suffered a similar tragedy that day. He had moved forward to Tilly with a supply column and to talk to Prinz von Schönburg-Waldenburg. On arrival at the battalion CP, he discovered a shell had just hit their field HQ, killing Obergefreiter Füssell, the Prinz's faithful old valet. The Prinz had been earlier called away to confer with the CO of Regiment 901, but on his return he was inconsolable; Füssell had been his greatest friend for twenty-five years, he told Ritgen. Furthermore, he was convinced the attack they had been ordered to carry out that afternoon was a mistake. 'He judged the terrain to be totally unsuitable for an armoured commitment,' noted Ritgen.

Ritgen tried to lift his spirits, but as he left him the Prinz said, 'Who knows if we all will die?' On this dramatic note, Ritgen headed back to Parfouru. At around 10 p.m., he was called upon by the battalion adjutant. While attacking Point 103, the Prinz's command tank had been hit in the turret. He and the communications officer were both killed instantly. A third officer also died in the action. Ritgen was stunned, but hurried forward with more supplies, finding the battalion moving into its positions for the night – known as 'leaguring' – and then headed on to speak to Oberst Gerhardt, the CO of Panzer-Lehr-Regiment 130. 'He temporarily entrusted me with the command of the battalion,' wrote Ritgen. 'How often in silence had I longed for this position, but not under these tragic and horrible circumstances. The death of the Prinz touched me deeply.'

CHAPTER 18

The Constraints of Wealth and the Freedom of Poverty

Now that the period of close cover above the invasion front was over, the tactical air forces were once again roaming more deeply. On Monday, 12 June, the Mustangs of the 354th Fighter Group were given targets to dive-bomb in northern France and all three squadrons set off together from Boxted in Suffolk. Leading the 356th FS to hit a railway bridge near Rouen was Major Dick Turner, and he was expecting it to be another fairly routine mission. They reached the target area without incident and, having successfully spotted the right bridge, Turner orbited it at around 5,000 feet, checking for any enemy flak emplacements, which would then help him decide how to attack the target. The most effective way was a 'concentrated' attack, in which each P-51 would follow the other along the same diving line. If the first one or two aircraft were either short or long in dropping their bomb, then those following would be able to adjust accordingly. The concentrated attack invariably led to the destruction of the target.

On the other hand, if there were enemy flak positions, then a concentrated attack was too dangerous because it would enable the gunners below to predict the line of the dive-bombers and hone their aim. The first few aircraft might get away with it, but those following almost certainly would not. A better option would be a 'coordinated' attack, in which some of the fighters targeted the flak emplacements and kept them busy, while the rest tried to hammer the target. A little bit of judicious reconnaissance, just as Turner was carrying out now above the bridge, usually paid dividends and ensured he kept his pilots in one piece. 'Besides,' he noted, 'my squadron-mates were all good friends.'

Peering down, he could see no sign at all of any flak, and so, licking his lips, he gave the order for a concentrated attack. Taking the lead, he led them down and dropped his two 500-pounder bombs with satisfying accuracy. In fact, it looked as though they had dropped all thirty-two of their bombs on the cherry; having climbed back up again, once the smoke and dust settled he could see the tracks at both ends all twisted and smashed, and the remains of the bridge now crumpled into the ravine below. With mission accomplished, they headed north-east, but Turner now decided to take his men on a little predatory hunt. They had received reports of more Luftwaffe units moving west, so he felt a quick look might not be a bad idea.

His hunch proved spot on. In under quarter of an hour, one of his pilots was excitedly pointing out a rough airfield below full of Focke-Wulf 190s tailed into the hedgerows. Turner looked left and, sure enough, there they were, half-hidden in the trees and foliage. Quickly looking around for flak once more and satisfied he could see none, he called the squadron to follow him and rolled over into a dive. As the nearest line of 190s came into view, he opened fire with his six .50-calibre machine guns, allowing the line of bullets to 'walk' on to the targets. In moments, two had caught fire and were billowing smoke. Pulling up from the deck in a shallow turning climb to port, he saw another, single, Focke-Wulf being refuelled near the edge of a second field. Rolling out level and pushing the stick forward to depress the nose of his Mustang, Turner opened fire again, hitting the fuel bowser and the 190 together in a brilliant flash of flame, before climbing out of the fray once more.

Glancing around, he saw his squadron were circling the airfield, while one or other dived down to attack a target. Mayhem reigned over the airfield, with burning fighters lining the edges, but Turner reckoned it was time to skedaddle; loitering at low level was not a good idea with the chance of other enemy fighters cruising about nearby. Calling his squadron to climb back up to 10,000 feet, he had just reached 1,500 when he saw a dust trail below and, looking down, saw it was a Ju88 about to take off. Seeing him coming, the Junkers pilot promptly aborted his take-off, but it was too late. 'I hit him just as he rolled to a stop,' noted Turner, 'and he exploded.'

With ammunition running low and the possibility of a hornet's nest having been stirred, Turner ordered them to head for home. All sixteen touched back down safely with no damage to a single plane. In addition to the bridge, they had accounted for twenty FW190s. 'And with my bonus Ju88,' added Turner, 'the total destroyed ran to twenty-one. It was a satisfactory day's work.'

The success of the Allied air forces was very welcome news, but the arrival of the first V-1 flying bombs over England earlier the next day most certainly was not. Most appeared to have fallen short over Kent, Suffolk and Essex, but a number also landed on London. 'Our attacks on CROSSBOW targets,' noted General Brereton, the Ninth Air Force commander, in his diary, 'must be resumed.' Time and again the CROSSBOW sites had been hammered, and even more so after Eisenhower had agreed to up the ante on 19 April; so now, just a week after the invasion, it had come as a great shock to discover that London was under attack.

One of those in the British capital that day was Lieutenant Mary Mulry, a nurse in the Queen Alexandra Imperial Military Nursing Service – the QAs – who had come to town on a rare day off to try to buy a trunk for their forthcoming deployment to Normandy. 'These buzz bombs are quite terrifying,' she wrote in her diary after a close call near Victoria Station. On her way to the Underground, she had heard the ominous buzz and had just managed to reach the station entrance when the engine cut and it dropped. 'I could hear the ambulance bells ringing as I descended the stairs,' she added. 'Londoners are remarkably phlegmatic and carry on with their normal lives in between dodging the doodlebugs.'

From neutral Ireland, Mary had left home in 1939, aged seventeen, and headed to London, since there were few jobs and even less money back home. Her older brother, Michael, had already emigrated to America, but Mary preferred England and had gained a position as a nursing probationer at Guy's Hospital in London. After war was declared she was evacuated to the Kent and Sussex Hospital in Tunbridge Wells.

Her first real taste of war had come during the retreat from Dunkirk in late May and early June 1940, when the hospital had been flooded with wounded servicemen. Then had come the Battle of Britain, much of which had played out in the skies above the hospital. Three years later, she had passed her State Registered Nurse exams and had moved back to London, to the Brook Hospital in Woolwich, where she had specialized in nursing fevers. Only in the spring of 1944 had she finally finished her training and applied to join the QAs. This army nursing service had been founded in 1902 at the end of the Anglo-Boer War to train up nurses to serve in the military and its ranks had grown from just over 600 in 1939 to some 12,000 by 1944. Mary had been desperate to join them, but her decision to leave Woolwich appalled both her hospital matron and her father, a fervent Republican who had fought the British during the struggle for Irish independence. Neither could deter her; and so, on 10 May, she had formally been called up to the QAs, one of some 165,000 Irish neutrals who chose to join the British Armed Services during the war. She had arrived at 101 General Hospital at Hatfield House in Hertfordshire, to the north of London, on 5 June. A large country house, it was the seat of the Earl of Shaftesbury, although was now being used as a military hospital – one that Mary found 'beautiful but rather frightening'.

On just her second day, she had woken to the news of the invasion. 'Tremendous buzz of excitement,' she wrote in her diary, 'clusters of people talking about the news.' Her brother, Michael, had joined the US Army and the two had met up in London a few weeks earlier – it was the first time she had seen him since he emigrated. Now, a week on from the invasion, she wondered whether she might see him over in Normandy. Their move across the Channel was now certain – they would be heading over there in a matter of days. First, though, she had to get back to Hatfield in one piece without being hit by a doodlebug.

Britain's war leaders were not quite so phlegmatic. The 1,000kg of Amatol the V-1 delivered was a destructive warhead and the British people, after long years of war, were understandably dismayed to find themselves facing a renewed Blitz. 'This new form of attack imposed upon the people of London was a burden perhaps even heavier than the air raids of 1940 and 1941,' noted Churchill. 'Suspense and strain were more prolonged. Dawn brought no relief, and cloud no comfort.' It was all the more reason to smash the enemy in Normandy quickly and charge across France to overrun the launch sites of these new terror weapons. Although the damage done was far less than anything wrought by the Blitz, the V-1 menace had now, at long last, arrived, and it hovered over the Allied – and especially British – war chiefs like a heavy shroud.

One even fell a little too close for comfort to General Eisenhower. Around 1 a.m. on the morning of 16 June, now back at Widewing, his SHAEF HQ at Bushy Park on the edge of London, he was reading in bed when the siren rang out. His friend and naval aide Harry Butcher hurried along to his room and suggested he head for the shelter. Eisenhower refused his entreaties, however, until they heard the clatter and bang of a V-1 exploding comparatively nearby. 'They say you have two seconds to find shelter when the hiss and put-put stop,' noted Butcher. 'So I decided that at least Butcher would retire to the shelter.' A few minutes later, Eisenhower joined him.

Certainly, the V-1 attacks almost immediately added a level of pressure and impatient expectation to the Normandy campaign that was out of all proportion to the actual damage they were causing – which was, in the big scheme of things, comparatively small. 'The Air Ministry estimates that the enemy is capable of launching 90 tons on the London area,' Brereton noted, 'which is cause for grave concern.' It was, however, very small beer indeed when compared with the gargantuan amounts of ordnance being dropped on Germany. The following day, for example, 617 Squadron alone dropped 1,230 tons of bombs on S-boat pens at Le Havre. The previous evening Bomber Command had hit a synthetic-fuel plant near Gelsenkirchen with 303 heavy bombers each carrying around 4 tons of bombs; this attack alone led to a loss of 1,000 tons of fuel per day for several weeks to come. Meanwhile a staggering 1,357 American heavies from the Eighth Air Force, each carrying around 2 tons of bombs, attacked a wide range of targets; Lieutenant Smitty Smith and his crew were among those hastily dispatched to hammer 'buzz-bomb' launching sites at Florennes in northern France. A sense of proportion was needed with regard to this new German pilotless blitz.

None the less, leaders in England were starting to get a little impatient. 'Last night,' noted Butcher on Thursday, 15 June, 'Ike was concerned that Monty couldn't attack until Saturday. Ike was anxious that the Germans be kept off balance and that our drive never stop.' In fact, the drive hadn't stopped. The Allies were indeed pushing forward; it was only a week and a half since D-Day, and the people back in London, looking at the two-dimensional maps with sea marked up as a flat, constant blue, were forgetting the many challenges the invasion had thrown up and continued to hurl at them. The build-up of supplies had been slower than anticipated; currently, the backlog was two days, which meant, for example, that the 150 British tanks of 33rd Armoured Brigade were reaching the front two days later than anticipated, which, in this early stage of the campaign, made quite a difference to the Allies' ability to punch through the gathering German defences with the kind of force that was needed. What's more, the enemy were showing no sign at all of retreating in stages as they had done in North Africa, Sicily and southern Italy, but rather seemed determined to hold on to every yard, even though this meant they remained in range of the Allies' enormous arsenal of offshore naval guns.

Even so, ten days after the landings, the Allies had reason to be fairly pleased. They had a continuous bridgehead, which was among the greatest short-term priorities, now some 50 miles long and between 8 and 20 miles deep. In the centre, on the boundary between the British and Americans, the US 18th Infantry were just over 20 miles inland, holding a salient around the town of Caumont. 'It was mainly little skirmishes,' recalled Tom Bowles. 'The Germans would try and push us back and we would fight them off.' Two, three, or more times a day, he would be sent up to the front to repair telephone lines. In fact, such had been the speed of advance of the 1st Division, who had fortunately pressed southwards into a gap between the Panzer-Lehr on the left and 17. SS-Panzergrenadier and the shattered remnants of the 352. Division on their right, that a chance for the Allies to unravel the entire German line was emerging. Yet the 1st Infantry Division, at this stage, did not have the armour, the artillery support or the reserves to be able to push beyond Caumont.

At the eastern flank, meanwhile, the mixed force of airborne and Commando troops were having a torrid time. They were rapidly becoming bogged down in the kind of attritional and largely static fighting for which such special *coup de main* troops were most definitely not designed. They were now holding a line that ran along the Bréville Ridge and roughly halfway between the Orne and Dives Valleys, and down through the village of Amfreville to the north and across to the Orne River; and which then cut across to Sainte-Honorine and on to the edge of Colombelles and the eastern outskirts of Caen. Both sides were furiously digging in, sniping and hurling shells and mortars at each other, with worrying echoes of the Western Front during the last war. 'At "stand to",' wrote Denis Edwards in his diary on Sunday, 11 June, 'Jerry gave us his customary dawn hammering and our lines took a thorough working-over, an exercise we called a "stonk".' He and the rest of the Ox and Bucks were now holding Hérouvillette. Edwards found that during the day he and his mates were smoking heavily – it was something to do and calmed the nerves, but they were now running low on cigarettes. That night, there were a lot of enemy patrols and they began to sense a counter-attack was on its way. The key bit of land, as Edwards was well aware, was the Bréville Ridge with its commanding position and views over the whole area and down to both valleys.

The paras still held the crest, but not strongly – just to the left of the Ox and Bucks were the men of 7 Para, including Lieutenant Richard

Todd, who, like Edwards, had not enjoyed being 'stonked' regularly for the past few days. Succour was at hand for him, however. Sunday, 11 June was his twenty-fifth birthday and orders arrived promoting him to captain and posting him to General Windy Gale's 6th Airborne HQ as GSO III (Operations). After a slap-up birthday lunch with fellow officers, he climbed into a Jeep with all his kit, bade his friends in the 7th Battalion farewell and sped off back to Ranville, stopping briefly en route at the field ambulance centre to get his still unhealed hand seen to.

The following day, the 12th, the weather was sunny and warm. Reinforcements had been arriving from a brigade of the 51st Highland Division, a veteran unit from North Africa and Sicily, which eased the pressure on the paras and Commandos, although not a moment too soon. Later in the day, 21. Panzer launched another counter-attack, with Major Hans von Luck's battalion now reinforced with *Nebelwerfers*, two motorcycle companies from the reconnaissance battalion and also some of Major Becker's assault guns. Kampfgruppe Luck opened the attack with the *Nebelwerfer* – 'Moaning Minnies', multiple rapid-firing mortars – and artillery, swiftly taking their objective, the village of Sainte-Honorine, from the Canadian paras. Von Luck went in close behind the motorcycles and saw the enemy lines for the first time. He was amazed by what appeared to be hundreds of broken gliders lying all around. As they quickly dug themselves in, he hoped they could use the slopes of Sainte-Honorine as a starting point for an attack on the ridge. 'Then began,' noted von Luck, 'the heaviest naval bombardment we had known so far.' He could actually see the warships out at sea firing, great stabs of flame erupting from their guns, followed by the scream of shells. The *Jabos* followed, swooping down apparently unhindered. 'A veritable inferno,' he added, 'broke over our heads.'

His *Kampfgruppe* had also attacked further to the north between Bréville and the hamlet of Oger, where the French of No. 4 Commando were dug in. Some German troops managed to get within a few hundred yards. Lieutenant Hubert Fauré lost five men in his troop that afternoon. Another man, Bégau, was hit by a piece of shrapnel that blew away half his face. 'There were only his eyes left,' said Fauré. 'It was horrible. The blood was bubbling.' Bégau was still alive, although caught out 50 yards ahead of their lines. No one moved, so Fauré jumped up and ran over to him, picked up the wounded man and carried him on his back. The Germans could have shot him easily, but he reckoned they respected him for picking up a wounded comrade and so left him alone.

Back at Divisional HQ, Captain Richard Todd found the atmosphere absolutely electric. There was great concern that the ridge might fall, but General Windy Gale now decided to counter-attack in turn, while the Germans were exposed and getting hammered by the naval guns and air forces. The attack would go in that night, at 10 p.m., with 12 Para leading, supported by the 13th/18th Hussars and preceded by a heavy artillery barrage. As darkness fell, the villages of Amfreville and Bréville were ablaze against the night sky. At Sainte-Honorine, the Canadians also counter-attacked and, after close, hand-to-hand fighting, von Luck was forced to recall his men and give up the village again. 'What more could we set,' he wrote, 'against this superiority in naval guns and fighter bombers?'

Bréville was taken and the ridge secured, but at a grievous cost to both sides, and especially 12 Para, who suffered 141 casualties out of the 160 with which they began the attack. The 5th Black Watch had also sustained around 200 casualties since their arrival the day before, massive losses that were already symptomatic of the brutal attrition of the fighting in Normandy. Von Luck was devastated by the day's fighting. 'We now finally gave up hope,' he wrote, 'of making any impression on the British bridgehead, let alone eliminating it.' Stalemate had arrived at the eastern flank, and the men began digging in along a line that would not budge for the next ten weeks.

Montgomery and Dempsey were, however, already launching Operation PERCH, their first attempt at a decisive breakthrough. This had been thought about before the invasion as a contingency in case Caen was not swiftly captured on D-Day or immediately after. Dempsey planned that 7th Armoured Division, the Desert Rats who had fought all the way through the North Africa campaign, would spearhead this drive towards Tilly. Another idea, code-named WILD OATS, involved a dash towards Caen by 7th Armoured and also the 1st Airborne Division, now waiting back in England to enter the fray. Leigh-Mallory had nipped that idea in the bud, however, and, because of delays and the weather, the Desert Rats hadn't been ready until 10 June in any case, by which time the Panzer-Lehr had arrived at Tilly. Dempsey's intelligence on that day reckoned there were about 500 enemy tanks now in Normandy and all the German divisions in the line had been correctly identified. 'A concerted blow by these formations is already overdue,' ran the Second Army intelligence summary for up to midnight on 9 June, 'and the enemy's choice of *schwerpunkt* is becoming increasingly difficult as the advance from Omaha continues.' The massed enemy counter-attack arriving before sufficient Allied forces had been built up had always been the biggest worry once they had achieved a toehold. Now that they had successfully established a firm bridgehead, the desire to push forward for a decisive breakthrough was balanced by concern that when the enemy counter-attack was finally launched, they had to be ready to meet and defeat it decisively.

However, the US 1st Infantry Division's taking of Caumont, 20 miles inland, the intense fighting around Tilly, and the 12. SS's defence of Carpiquet and the west of Caen meant a second gap had emerged. If the Americans could not realistically push further than Caumont, then perhaps the 7th Armoured Division could get their skates on and push through between Panzer-Lehr and 12. SS 'Hitlerjugend' instead. Their immediate target was the small market town of Villers-Bocage, some 15 miles south-west of Caen.

As hoped, at around eight o'clock on the morning of Tuesday, 13 June, an armoured column of the 4th County of London Yeomanry and 1st Battalion Rifle Brigade rolled into the town. This was the spearhead of the Desert Rats, which had hurried forward, throwing caution to the wind, without the usual probing reconnaissance units. With no sign of the enemy anywhere, this collection of Sherman and Cromwell tanks, half-tracks and trucks spread out in a long line along the main road through the town and paused, enjoying the enthusiastic reception of the townspeople, while the regiment's A Squadron pushed on to a notable knoll to the east of the town, labelled on their maps as Point 213. The gap, however, was only really a half-gap, because many of the Panzer-Lehr's support units – including those of Helmut Ritgen's II. Bataillon, Panzer-Lehr Regiment 130 – were still based a couple of miles to the east, not west, of Villers-Bocage.

Unbeknown to the British, watching this from just south of nearby Point 213 were Tiger tanks of the Schwere SS-Panzerabteilung 101 (101st Heavy Tank Battalion), rushed into the area ahead of other Waffen-SS panzer units and due to join the 'Hitlerjugend'. Commanding the Tigers was the panzer 'ace' Michael Wittmann, who decided to send three into action immediately, two against the British tanks on Point 213 and himself to the town. While the British column was standing motionless in the main street, Wittmann rumbled forward and attacked at almost point-blank range and with complete surprise. An entire troop of three

Cromwell tanks and one Sherman was knocked out in a matter of minutes, along with a number of half-tracks, trucks and carriers of the Rifle Brigade. As Wittmann pulled back and climbed out of the town, leaving a scene of carnage, his Tiger was disabled by a British gunner and he and his crew had to scramble away on foot. It had been an entirely opportunistic attack, without infantry support, and he had been very lucky that a British anti-tank gun, pointing directly at his Tiger in the opening moments of the attack, had not fired because the gunner was, at that very moment, relieving himself nearby; it could have all be so different.

Meanwhile, on Point 213, the now isolated British tanks were gradually picked off. The battle did not stop there, however, as more British and German troops arrived. In the afternoon, the roles were reversed as the Germans, carrying out their usual counter-attack, were ambushed in turn, losing six Tiger tanks and a similar number of Panzer Mk IVs. Since the Germans had only 36 Tigers in Normandy at that time, this was a substantial blow. Overall, the British lost 23–27 tanks, the Germans between 13 and 15.

Unfortunately for the Desert Rats and the British Army's reputation, the Germans had some press photographers hurry over to Villers-Bocage and take photographs of the devastation. Burned-out tanks, dead tank men and mangled vehicles made a sorry picture. The fact that just about any road behind the German lines, or in any place where they had been overrun, would have revealed an even grimmer picture of carnage on their own side was, understandably, kept quiet. So too were the facts that 21. Panzer had lost the best part of an entire battalion on D-Day and that, on 8 June, the Canadians had pushed back 12. SS 'Hitlerjugend' and had retaken Buron, Authie and then Kurt Meyer's HQ at the Abbey d'Ardenne, swiftly destroying thirteen of his tanks in the process.

At this difficult time, the people of the Reich needed some good news. Nazi propaganda had long had a penchant for elevating individuals as though they were movie stars, and Michael Wittmann was already a celebrated hero. The Nazi regime liked 'aces'. There were fighter aces, Stuka aces, U-boat aces, artillery aces and, of course, panzer aces. Pictures of these men looking square-jawed, wholesome and devilishly handsome – and it really was amazing how often they conformed to the Aryan ideal – were plastered on the front covers of magazines or featured in the *Deutsche Wochenschau* newsreels shown in the cinemas. They became household names, the pin-ups of the Reich. There were, of course, two major problems with this. The first was that, usually, these elevated individuals were actually part of a team. Wittmann never fired the gun on his Tiger, for example – his gunner did. Nor did the U-boat commander press the trigger mechanism on the torpedo. The second, perhaps bigger, issue was that all too often these aces then got themselves killed, which was very much bad, not good, PR.

At any rate, Wittmann's efforts at Villers-Bocage – good PR aside – achieved comparatively little. In truth, it has become one of the most over-blown episodes of the entire war, let alone the Normandy campaign, and really needs looking at not through the lens of dashing tactical chutzpah but through a wider prism. Was it really a massively wasted opportunity by 7th Armoured Division? Could the British have driven a terminal wedge into the gap between Panzer-Lehr and 12. SS? Probably not.

Successful exploitation tactics, going hell for leather with no regard to the flanks, usually says as much about those trying to defend against such an onslaught as it does about those attacking. It brought great successes for the Germans during the Blitzkrieg years at the start of the war, working brilliantly in France in 1940 because the French had a very top-heavy command structure that stifled initiative and its troops were not trained for either tactical flexibility of any kind or operational speed. Once the Germans burst through the crust, the French reserves, who had been trained for a far more ponderous and deliberate rate of manoeuvre, had neither the levels of command nor the communication to be able to respond and were defeated in detail. The Germans, on the other hand – or the mobile forces, at any rate – most certainly were trained for swift manoeuvre. *Bewegungskrieg* – the war of rapid manoeuvre – was their *modus operandi*; even in 1944 and handicapped by the lack of air power, tactical flexibility still lay at the root of the German way of war. They also had the added advantage of considerably better and more powerful anti-tank guns that could operate at great distances and with higher velocities than had been the case for either side back in 1940.

This all meant German troops were very unlikely to respond to a rapid thrust of the kind they had practised back in 1940 in the same way as, say, the French had done. Far more likely was a rapid organization of their strongest forces into a swift counter-attack. This would not be head-on, but at the base of the thrust – a decapitation, in effect. It would then leave the spearhead surrounded, cut off and very effectively removed from any further part in the battle, with all the ensuing disadvantages of having lost key manpower and equipment and all the effects on morale of having a spearhead annihilated. It might not have happened that way; the British *might* have achieved a decisive breakthrough, but, on balance, it was unlikely. And so was it worth the risk? Again, on balance, probably not.

There was, though, a reason why the Allies rarely operated with lightning speed or with the kind of tactical agility for which the Germans were renowned, and this was largely down to the constraints of their materiel wealth. The Allies had developed a method of beating the Germans that relied very heavily on fire-power and a huge number of support personnel, and which also ensured that the number of men at the coal-face of battle was, in the big scheme of things, comparatively small. Infantry, for example, made up just 14 per cent of the British and Canadian Army servicemen in Normandy, and armour even less. This was a good thing, because it unquestionably saved lives; the fewer men at the front line, the fewer became casualties. The Red Army and the Wehrmacht were proof of how inefficient and costly it was to have so many front-line divisions; it was why their wartime casualties were so much higher, even though the global effort of both Britain and the United States in the war so far had been far greater than that of the Soviet Union.

The flip-side of this fire-power, support-heavy way of war was that it took longer to organize. The rule of thumb was a simple one: the greater the fire support, the longer it took to both allocate and get into action. The artillery took time enough, but any kind of heavy air support took considerably longer. In Normandy, front-line troops had to coordinate efforts with the artillery, with the air forces and with the navy. As the Canadians demonstrated on 7 June, it was quite possible to hold up superior forces such as 12. SS, but it wasn't until the following couple of days, with all the artillery brought up and systems and communications properly in place, that they were able to drive the Waffen-SS men back. Perhaps this approach lacked a bit of tactical flair, but that is hardly a reason to criticize. What mattered was winning campaigns – which the Allies had been doing since the late summer of 1942 – and then ultimately the war. This required clear strategic thinking, superbly efficient supply lines and a mastery of the operational level of war – the level that has been so often relegated in the narrative of the Second World War. However, with good strategy, and superior control and understanding of the operational level, the tactical level of warfare would, to a very large extent, sort itself out as a matter of consequence. Shooting up a few British tanks single-handedly might seem very impressive, but that wasn't going to win the Germans the battle for Normandy, let alone the war as a whole, especially not if they were unable to manage the bigger picture very well, which they most certainly were not doing at present.

Nor were brilliant, highly experienced generals and commanders much of an advantage if they were hamstrung in their efforts to bring that flair and experience to bear. Allied generals have been repeatedly criticized over the years for being dull and methodical, and not as tactically ruthless as their German counterparts. At least, though, they were operating under very clear chains of command. The political leaders at the top, while sometimes meddlesome, were not totalitarian despots. Both Churchill and Roosevelt also had quite exceptional geo-political understanding and far-sighted strategic vision, and were supported by government ministers and by the Chiefs of Staff – the most senior commanders in their respective services – who were free to voice their opinions even if contradictory to those of their political chiefs. These also worked together as the Joint Chiefs of Staff (JCS), and operated as rational debating and balancing committees who were able to draw on and bring in others when necessary. Then there was Eisenhower, the Supreme Commander, a wonderful administrator and diplomat, who was also a superb facilitator and enabler, and collegiate in his approach. Under him were the component commanders, and while no one could deny that Montgomery was a difficult character, at least the channels of communication were clear and uncluttered. For the most part, an Allied divisional, corps, army or even army group commander knew where they stood, to whom they were subordinated, and they also knew they were being superbly supported by the long tail of supply and logistics behind them. This applied to the air forces and navy as much as it did to the army. Finally, while there were inter-service rivalries, for the most part the different services were all driven by a common goal. The quite exceptional coordination of effort between naval, air and ground forces in the first week of the invasion had enabled the Allies to overcome the many crises and challenges that had been thrown up so far. In fact, it was only by the harnessing of such a combined effort that an invasion of this scale had had even the slightest chance of succeeding.

The Germans enjoyed no such spirit of cooperation, as the men on the ground had not been supported by any naval forces worth talking about and almost no Luftwaffe. Throughout the war so far, the conflict had been fought in the air, on land and at sea. That Germany had never had the naval forces required to take on the West was because of faulty pre-war planning and strategy. Creating a large U-boat arm had been the only conceivable way of taking on Britain's – and America's – maritime power, yet they had chosen to build a surface fleet that could never hope to rival the Royal Navy, let alone that of the US Navy. Over the past six months, their Luftwaffe had also been ground down by British and especially American air forces that were better equipped, better trained, better supplied, and tactically and operationally superior. As German troops in Normandy were painfully discovering – and as they were in Italy too – an enemy with overwhelming air superiority has a huge advantage. The combatants able to fight in three different spheres were always likely to have the edge over a warring nation fighting in just one.

And then there was the chain of command. At the top was Hitler, master of all, whose word was final on absolutely everything. He was also by turns lazy, a control freak, overly obsessed with detail, and a hypochondriac who was taking a horrific cocktail of prescribed drugs on a daily basis, including a mixture of cocaine and methamphetamine given to him by his personal doctor. Hitler was also prone to irrational mood swings and changes of heart – perhaps unsurprising considering his daily intake – and used to his sycophants confirming his genius and to having his way on every single matter. The reverses in the war fed his paranoia and irrationality. He had a Combined Services General Staff in the OKW, but they didn't operate in the same way as the Allied Chiefs of Staff; rather, they were merely Hitler's mouthpiece. Nor did Hitler have geo-political understanding at all; he'd not travelled the world, he didn't speak other languages, his education was limited and he viewed everything – others, his enemies, the world – through the narrow prism of his own myopic vision. He commanded total subservience and discipline, and, as a result, his commanders were fighting a war with one hand tied behind their backs.

Another feature of his command style was his penchant for divide and rule, an old despot's trick to ensure he reigned supreme. In the military, this led to numerous factions and parallel command structures, so that unlike the Allies, where the chain of command flowed downwards in straight and clearly defined lines, German commanders were very often unsure of where exactly the buck stopped. This had been demonstrated glaringly in the disagreement between Rommel and Geyr von Schweppenburg, but now, a week into the invasion, it meant there was still a very muddled structure of command and control. On D-Day, it was General Marcks at LXXXIV. Korps who ordered 21. Panzer into action, but it was General Dollmann at 7. Armee telling Bayerlein when to march. On the other hand, by D plus 1, I. SS-Panzerkorps was telling 21. Panzer what to do. Geyr took overall command of Panzergruppe West on 10 June, but that did not include 21. Panzer – or did it? – while Panzer-Lehr, which was part of Panzergruppe West, had already been ordered into its position west of 12. SS at Rommel's behest. 'The chain of command from Panzer Gruppe West up was most unfortunate,' commented Geyr. 'At a moment everything depended on rapid action, orders were issued to just two and three-quarters panzer divisions by the following headquarters: I SS Panzer Corps, Panzer Gruppe West, Seventh Army at le Mans, Army Group B, OB West and OKW.' It was an absolute mess.

On top of that, Allied command of the sky and their very effective efforts at radio jamming and the pre-invasion destruction of radar and communications stations had also handicapped the Germans. The Allies could fly over at will and observe what was going on below, but with so little Luftwaffe, the Germans had nothing like these eyes over the battlefield. Bayerlein, for example, had insisted that not a single vehicle go within 500 yards of the Panzer-Lehr's divisional command post for fear of being targeted by Allied air forces.

Nor were others quite so successful at keeping their command posts secret. On the afternoon of 9 June, Geyr's Panzergruppe West HQ at the Château la Caine, 4 miles north-east of the town of Thury-Harcourt, was attacked by *Jabos*. General Sigismund Ritter und Edler von Dawans, the chief of staff, along with twelve other staff officers, were killed. Geyr, who was with General Max Pemsel at the time, escaped only by chance. Then, early on 12 June, when General Marcks heard that Carentan had fallen, he hurried off in his staff car – against the advice of his staff – to oversee personally a counter-attack against the town that had little chance of succeeding. Speeding along the main road north of Saint-Lô in broad daylight, his car was spotted by *Jabos* and shot up. With his wooden leg, he was not able to get out of the car quickly enough and was hit in the groin by a piece of cannon shell. Soon after he bled to death. So that was another general out of the picture.

On the other hand, the Germans in Normandy did still have a lot of very good, well-trained and, especially, highly disciplined troops, with more on their way, and despite the shortage of equipment among the infantry divisions, the German Army in the West did have a considerable amount of very good weaponry. Yet because of the comparative paucity of fire-power when compared with the Allies, they were often able to organize themselves more quickly. There were no air or naval forces to coordinate, nor, once at the front, huge columns of vehicles for which to find routes. There was, in fact, a freedom of manoeuvre in their comparative materiel poverty which gave them a flexibility the Allies could not share.

What's more, the terrain unquestionably favoured defence. In the west, the dense network of fields and hedgerows – the bocage – meant the Germans had a flexible defensive system that was, in many ways, more effective than any bunker. They provided cover and shelter and if a field or hedgerow was lost or about to be lost, they could simply fall back to the next one. One negative for the Germans operating in the bocage – and it was a major one – was their inability to see ahead very far. For much of the time they had little idea of what was coming towards them, or in what strength, although when it was dry the dust raked up by approaching Allied troops helped. Never had church towers been more used.

In the eastern part of the battlefield, however, around Caen, where the land was more open, there were plenty of places in which to dig in and take cover, whether it be dips in the ground, woods, villages or snaking valleys, but there were plenty of vantage points too. The Allied planners had identified this as the area the Germans would view as being of greatest strategic importance, and so it was proving. Geography from the invasion threat to Britain in 1940 meant that most British and Canadian troops had been on the eastern side of southern England, and so the Americans, when they began arriving in early 1942, moved into the western half. As they moved across the Channel, they kept the same orientation. It meant, though, that the British and Canadians were now facing the brunt of the panzer divisions being moved up to Normandy and could most likely expect even more.

Dempsey could see that the front was starting to congeal. The Allies also now knew that Hitler had declared his men must not give up an inch of ground and should fight to the last man, which meant they were less likely to retreat in stages as the Germans had practised elsewhere and were now doing in the battle north of Rome. If there was any lasting significance attached to Villers-Bocage, it was the realization that the Allies now faced a grinding and attritional slog against the growing German forces arrayed against them. The key would be to make sure the Germans could never mount a coordinated massed counter-attack. 'In the past twenty-four hours,' noted the Second Army Intelligence Summary

No. 10, the day after Villers-Bocage, 'the enemy has remained on the defensive and shown no inclination to use any of the reinforcements which have reached Second Army sector in an attempt to regain the initiative.' That assessment was entirely correct.

Montgomery also recognized that the chance for the swift capture of Caen had passed. Early on 13 June he had still thought it might be possible; the abrupt halt of the leading elements of the Desert Rats put paid to that and he revised his plans. The emphasis was now to be on drawing the enemy panzer forces on to Second Army and so keeping them away from the Cotentin. 'Caen is the key to Cherbourg,' he told Bradley, which had prompted much derision at First Army Headquarters. One of Montgomery's great failings was his inability to explain himself to his peers and subordinates either eloquently or with tact and charm, and yet, in essence, he was quite right. So far, the best enemy troops were homing in towards Caen rather than the western end of the bridgehead.

It was vital, though, that Dempsey's Second Army continue to chew up those German panzer divisions in the Caen sector and also the new units as they arrived, and to ensure the enemy could never mass their strength effectively, all the while building up his own forces to such a level that he could launch a major offensive of his own in the Caen area. Montgomery never launched any all-out offensive until he had such overwhelming materiel superiority that he knew his forces were going to win – or rather, until there came a point where they would not suffer a major reverse. Although this attitude has often brought criticism, actually it was simple good sense. Until that point arrived, however, all his troops could do was press forward, pushing and probing and grinding the enemy down with a never-ending assault of naval, air and artillery fire-power.

The pattern for the rest of the campaign had been set.

CHAPTER 19

Behind the Lines

FELDMARSCHALL ROMMEL WAS SPENDING his days hurtling from one headquarters to another. On 10 June he had visited Geyr von Schweppenburg and during the journey enemy air activity had been so bad he had had to take cover some thirty times. He had only just missed the air attack that hit Panzergruppe West's HQ that day and had not even been able to reach Oberstgruppenführer Sepp Dietrich at I. SS-Panzerkorps. The following day, Rommel had visited von Rundstedt to discuss the worsening supply situation, as the railway network, upon which the Germans were so heavily dependent, had all but collapsed due to the weight of Allied air attacks. He was also deeply frustrated that more men were not being sent to him. A number of units were on their way, including the II. Fallschirmkorps, and 77. Infanterie-Division from Brittany and 17. SS-Panzergrenadier had started to reach the front. Only on 7 June had Hitler agreed to release all mobile divisions in France, but none of them was progressing well. The OKW had not sent any of 15. Armee's units from the Pas de Calais, however, still for fear the Allies might launch a second landing. How on earth the Allies could possibly achieve such an operation was not explained. Von Rundstedt could do little to soothe Rommel's concerns.

Later that day, 11 June, and back once more at La Roche-Guyon, Rommel went for a walk with his friend and colleague Admiral Ruge. They ambled through the garden then up the hill behind the old castle in what became a two-hour chat in which Rommel gave full vent to his concerns. They had not prevented the landings, the initiative had been lost and, as far as he was concerned, the best solution would be to stop the war while

Germany still had some bargaining power. He believed the antagonism between the Americans and Soviets was where they had a chance to negotiate. He was aware Hitler wanted to fight to the end, but Rommel believed firmly that the nation came before the individual. They discussed what would happen when the war ended. The SS would have to be abolished and so would the Hitler Youth, which could be replaced by something else. The reconstruction of cities would need to be the first priority. Hitler also had blood on his hands. 'The butcheries were a heavy guilt,' Rommel told Ruge. 'The conduct of the war had been amateurish.' That was one way of putting it. It was, of course, just chat – and pie in the sky chat at that.

Just a few weeks earlier, Rommel had been back in thrall to Hitler, his faith restored, but it had been chipped away by the dispute over the command of the panzers and had completely dissolved since the invasion. Rommel was either full of vigour and energy, bristling with confidence, or consumed by a dark cloud of despair. He had shown this repeatedly in North Africa and again in Italy.

On 12 June, Rommel spoke to Feldmarschall Wilhelm Keitel, the head of the OKW, at Berchtesgaden and painted a bleak picture, as had von Rundstedt the day before. He implored Keitel to send someone senior from the OKW to the front to see for themselves. 'I've already briefed the Führer about it,' Keitel told him. 'You're going to get two panzer divisions from the Eastern Front.' These were to be the 9. and 10. SS, and would join 2. SS 'Das Reich', ordered up from the south of France, and 17. SS-Panzergrenadier, now mostly at the front. This was something, but these two divisions wouldn't reach the front for a couple of weeks. On the other hand, still within spitting distance in 15. Armee, were 1. SS and 116. Panzer-Divisions, ready for a second Allied invasion in the Pas de Calais that was never going to happen. Once again, the German command structure, the inadequate use of intelligence and the intractability of Hitler, still stuck away in Berchtesgaden, was proving a terrible handicap.

As if to drive home the point, the German counter-attack on Carentan failed. Launched early in the morning of 13 June, and using a combination of newly arrived assault guns, panzer-grenadiers and artillery of 17. SS, plus a handful of von der Heydte's *Fallschirmjäger*, they ran into American paratroopers of the 506th PIR, including Dick Winters' Easy Company. Winters himself was still commanding his men, despite the wound he had received in his leg the day before. 'June 13,' he noted, 'was about the tightest spot of the war for Easy Company.' Despite coming up against StuGs, Marders and other tracked assault guns, they managed to hold their positions. Their fellows in the 2nd Battalion had also been having a stiff fight. So too had Fox Company, who actually had been up ahead and had knocked out at least two enemy assault guns before falling back to be better in line with Easy and Dog Companies. The German attack, planned and executed under the orders of Brigadeführer Ostendorff, had not had the approval of von der Heydte, however. In order to maintain surprise, Ostendorff had insisted there should be no reconnaissance of enemy positions beforehand, nor any kind of artillery barrage before the attack in case this alerted the Americans. In fact, the American airborne troops had picked up on German planes, so were preparing to launch their own assault when the 17. SS attacked; Ostendorff had badly misread both his new enemy and the situation. Although the Americans initially struggled to contain the attack, the SS men very quickly became disorganized and commanders began losing control of their units. Von der Heydte reckoned it was clear the attack had failed by about midday. By 4.30 p.m. it most definitely had, as the recently arrived US 2nd Armored Division entered the fray alongside fresh infantry from the 29th Division.

The failed counter-attack by the 17. SS-Panzergrenadier-Division underlined another of the many problems facing the Germans. There has been a tendency to cast all these units as 'elite', when in fact all contained a fair number of troops new to combat and with varying degrees of training. The Panzer-Lehr could be considered 'elite' – or, at least, among the very best in the Wehrmacht, while 12. SS 'Hitlerjugend' were certainly well trained and disciplined. General Geyr von Schweppenburg reckoned the best included those two plus 2. Panzer and 9. SS-Panzer-Divisions. Of some of the others he was more critical. 'The division was bled white in Russia,' he said of 1. SS-Leibstandarte, the original Waffen-SS division, for example, 'and was unable to refill gaps resulting from casualties . . . Discipline was a sham; the NCOs were poor. The division did not have time for thorough training before the invasion.' By discipline, he meant training and combat discipline; 1. SS remained very well equipped and supplied, and every soldier would rigidly do as ordered. They remained a powerful force, but they were simply not as 'crack' or 'elite' as their reputation suggested.

Nor did 17. SS get a great write-up by Geyr, who thought it was poorly equipped and of questionable combat efficiency. In fact, it had only been formed the previous November and by 1 June, although 17,321 men strong, it lacked some 40 per cent of its allotted officers and NCOs. Most of the ordinary men were new to combat and had only had limited training. As a division it was woefully short of trucks, and had begun heading to the front from Thouars in central western France with just 245, a shortfall of a staggering 1,441 – around 80 per cent – which meant there was no way the division could move as one to the front. Only four of the six panzer-grenadier battalions could get moving on 7 June and not even all of those were fully motorized, while the remaining two had to move up to Normandy by bicycle – and it was over 200 miles from Thouars to Carentan. As a result, the division was arriving piecemeal, and had been thrown into battle before those leading elements had had a chance to get the lie of the land and operate as a whole. It meant their striking power was affected. Although not to the same degree, the same had been true of Panzer-Lehr and 12. SS.

The lack of mobility was why 18-year-old Willi Müller, of the 17. SS-Panzergrenadier-Division's Pioneer – combat engineer – Bataillon, had moved as far north as Saumur on the River Loire then remained where he was. Instead of heading on to Normandy, the engineer battalion had been ordered to build a temporary bridge across the river. Like many of the current crop of soldiers in the Waffen-SS, Müller had volunteered aged just sixteen. From the Bohemian town of Pikowitz, he had been packed off to basic training a few months later and then posted to the newly forming 17. SS, and specifically to the pioneers. Even now, in June 1944, his training remained fairly rudimentary.

A couple of days after those units now in Normandy had been thrown back from Carentan, Müller and his fellows were keeping watch on the Loire from their makeshift aerial observation stand when, at around 7.40 a.m., over a hundred enemy bombers appeared and bombed their newly built bridge. Looking through his binoculars, Müller thought the falling bombs looked like heavy rain. With the bombers gone, he and Oberscharführer Unger were sent forward to inspect the damage. As they neared, the smoke and dust began to settle and they were amazed to see the bridge still standing, although only just – large parts of it had collapsed, but they reckoned a motorcycle could just about still get across. Unger strode on to the bridge, but as Müller followed he noticed an unexploded bomb poking out a few inches above the main bridge deck. Bending down, he saw there were letters on it, but as he wiped clear the dust with his hand, another bomb detonated on the shore. Hastily he called Unger and, warning him about the UXB, they both hurried clear. 'As soon as we reached the shore another detonation took place,' he noted. 'It was the bomb I had dusted off.' Being on the banks of the Loire that morning had been almost as hazardous as being at the front.

While Rommel was desperate for someone from the OKW to visit the front, there was no shortage of Allied dignitaries arriving in Normandy, much to the chagrin of Montgomery, who, now firmly ensconced at his caravan camp at the Château de Creullet, was not at all interested in exchanging pleasantries and entertaining VIPs. Being charming and hospitable to his superiors was never something with which he felt particularly comfortable in any case. 'It is not a good time for important people to go sight-seeing,' he complained to James Grigg, the secretary of state for war. 'I do not want to take my eyes off the battle.' On 12 June, Churchill himself had descended, accompanied by General Alan Brooke, the chief of the Imperial General Staff, and the South African General Jan Smuts, former Boer War enemy but now ardent anglophile. It meant Monty cancelling a conference with Bradley, which annoyed him. It was a lovely June day, the sun shining down on them brightly. They lunched in the grounds of the chateau, Churchill enjoying himself enormously and relieved finally to have reached Normandy; it had been his intention to cross on D-Day itself until the king had personally intervened, pointing out the unnecessary risk of doing so. Churchill asked Monty how far they were from the front. About 3 miles, Montgomery replied. The PM wondered whether that was a continuous line, to which Monty replied, 'No.' 'What is there then to prevent an incursion of German armour breaking up our luncheon?' Churchill asked. Monty told him he thought that unlikely.

Three days later, however, Général de Gaulle arrived for a visit. British and American relations with de Gaulle were still not going well. Roosevelt continued to be mistrustful and de Gaulle remained resentful at the Allies' refusal to acknowledge his provisional government and at having been excluded from OVERLORD. Churchill and the British War Cabinet, however, had agreed to Eisenhower's proposal that de Gaulle be brought over from Algiers to be properly briefed. 'I am hopeful that your conversations with General de Gaulle will result in inducing him to actually assist in the liberation of France,' Roosevelt had written to the PM on 27 May, 'without being imposed by us on the French people as their Government. Self-determination really means absence of coercion.'

De Gaulle had only reluctantly flown to London on 4 June and when he met with Churchill had been furious to learn the Allies had been making preparations for administering civil affairs themselves and even introducing invasion currency printed in the US. The reasons were entirely pragmatic: there could be a lot of refugees, some form of law and order needed to be maintained, and, if the Germans decided to retreat using a scorched-earth policy and burned French money, it would not do to be caught short. De Gaulle had not seen it this way, however. Even Churchill lost patience with him when the Frenchman insisted on withdrawing all French liaison officers attached to Allied units in protest.

Now, finally, on Wednesday, 14 June, de Gaulle embarked for Normandy on the French destroyer *La Combattante*. They landed near Courseulles at around 2 p.m., de Gaulle silent and apprehensive, smoking incessantly. Since Montgomery was the Allied army C-in-C, it was only right that Creullet should be the first port of call, although it is hard to think of two other people in such positions both lacking the essential skills of tact and charm. At Tac HQ, they had been told to prepare a four-course meal, including sticky cakes. 'It was explained to the Chief,' noted Carol Mather, 'that this formed an indispensable part of a Frenchman's midday meal.' Monty was having none of it, however. Any meal would be given on his terms, not de Gaulle's. Three courses would be more than enough.

On arrival, de Gaulle spoke to Montgomery at length in French. It was a good job Monty couldn't understand, because de Gaulle was explaining how, now he was in France, he was in charge. Eventually, when he abruptly stopped talking, his ADC stepped forward and said, 'The General thanks you for your gallant liberation of France.' After their somewhat strained lunch, de Gaulle and his retinue sped to Bayeux, where the general stepped out of his Jeep and began walking the streets. 'At the sight of General de Gaulle,' he wrote, speaking of himself in the third person, 'a sort of amazement seized the inhabitants, who then burst into cheers, or into tears.' Men, women and children surrounded him until quite a crowd had grown, stopping all traffic. 'We thus walked on together,' he added, 'fraternally, overwhelmed, and feeling the joy, pride and faith in the nation surging again from the abyss.' He then gave a speech, declaring the CFLN were now liberating France with the help of the Allies.

The liaison officers from Tac HQ accompanying him painted a somewhat different picture, but it was unquestionably a big moment for de Gaulle, whose frustrations were entirely understandable, even though not helped by his ability to appear self-important, arrogant and ungrateful. It didn't occur to him, for example, that while walking through the streets and creating a throng he was holding up military traffic heading to the front around Fontenay and Tilly. Nor did he ask permission to make an unscheduled visit to Isigny and several other villages along the way. The Allies, and Monty especially, were all glad when he headed back across the Channel.

Despite de Gaulle's relegated status in the invasion, Frenchmen throughout the country were more than playing their part to help the Allied cause. As in Italy, Yugoslavia and elsewhere, something close to civil war had been erupting in France. There were still plenty of pro-Nazi and pro-Vichy men, and women, fighting on the side of the German occupiers, with battles raging between Maquis groups and other resisters – or 'terrorists', as the Germans called them – and the Milice, the French paramilitary anti-partisan force. Klaus Barbie, for example, the head of the SD – the *Sicherheitsdienst*, the SS secret intelligence service – in Lyons, had hundreds of volunteers still working for him, nearly all of whom were French. 'I was only a lieutenant,' he commented, 'but I had more power than a general.'

The balance was definitely shifting, however, as increasing numbers joined the Résistance movement. Motives varied: many were escaping obligatory service in Germany; others now simply sensed the time had come to choose what appeared to be the winning side. Others passionately believed in the cause. East of the invasion front, in the Surcouf area, Robert Leblanc was rapidly losing heart. On D-Day and the days immediately after it, he and his Maquis Surcouf experienced a frenetic time of high excitement, fear, adrenalin and then mounting disappointment: shoot-outs with Germans, the capture of collaborators, the exhilaration of taking precious German weaponry, the shock of losing close friends and colleagues, and the sense of guilt that came with it. The farmer who had hosted them on the eve of the invasion had been shot by the Germans. Leblanc had warned him not to return home for a few days and instead encouraged him to lie low and see how events worked out. But the farmer had cows to milk and the day-to-day chores of the farm, so he ignored the advice. The Germans were tipped off and the farmer killed. 'Poor people, but I can't be blamed for that,' Leblanc wrote in his diary. 'We've got so many dead to avenge. The bastards, they kill innocents!'

On the 7th, a German car was shot up and five Germans killed, but that same day Tintin and Bernard, two of his best young men, lost their lives in turn. That evening, in yet another barn, with the rain hammering down outside and having dodged a Milice patrol, Leblanc sat down to write his diary once more. He had been expecting Allied troops to land just to the south of the Seine, but so far there had been no sign and only rumours about what was going on further to the west. 'I must confess we are disappointed,' he wrote. 'I am disappointed. That's not how I had foreseen the big day. I expected a swarm of planes dropping arms and men. I am concerned about what comes next. But now we are almost 250 and we can only arm 100 men with minimal equipment!' He feared the worst.

The next day, Leblanc moved his headquarters again. More men were killed, then they moved yet again, walking 9 miles overnight and arriving at a farmhouse in the village of Thierville at 3.30 on the morning of the 10th. There was still no sign of any arms drops, nor any response to their frantic radio messages. Ammunition was now running low, as was food; it was hard to feed some 200 men when all were effectively on the run. By Sunday, 11 June, they were still holed up in Thierville, with the Milice patrolling the villages, arresting or shooting anyone suspected of resistance or 'terrorist' activities. Leblanc had a heavy heart. 'We used to say, "How smashed were we going to get when they are here!"' he noted in his diary sadly. 'Sure, they are in France, but not here. I feel down.' He also cursed the British and the Americans. He couldn't understand why they hadn't relied more on the Maquis. Didn't they realize the Résistance groups were primed to rise up and rid France of the Nazis? They were willing to lay down their lives for the cause, but they couldn't do it without weapons and bullets. 'Whatever happens next,' Leblanc scribbled, 'I will never change my mind: the Allies have underestimated us. They have screwed up the liberation of France!'

It was no wonder he felt so hung out to dry. A massive gulf existed between the resisters' expectations and reality. Leblanc and his men had simply assumed that the moment the Allies landed, planes would come over dropping gargantuan quantities of arms; the Maquis would take up those arms and a glorious battle of liberation would ensue, in which they would personally drive out the Nazis, string up the traitors and bring freedom and liberty once more. It had been intoxicating to think about and had been the focus of all their thoughts over the years, months, weeks and days leading up to the invasion. Leblanc had been swept away by the heroism of it, the romance even. In reality, they were on their own, with limited communications to the outside world and not really part of Allied plans at all. Few had military experience or very much weapons training; they were dependent on passion, patriotism, bare-faced courage and their own wits and intelligence. That was not enough for the Allied leadership, who wanted the local knowledge, courage and heart of the Résistance but only on their own terms. Those groups, like the Maquis Surcouf, without SAS or Jedburgh teams or SOE liaison officers, were seen as the ill-disciplined, politically febrile rabble they were. In the political vacuum of liberation, having lots of young politically active Frenchmen close to the front, armed to the teeth but without any training, held no appeal to the Allied leadership.

On Tuesday, 13 June, Leblanc accepted the inevitable. His Maquis was unsustainable until fresh arms drops reached them, and so, gathering all his men, he told them they faced three choices. They could stay with him and fight, they could go home, or they could go into hiding. Sixty-two decided to stay with him and sixty-two opted to go home; twelve went into hiding. 'Tears come to my eyes,' noted Leblanc, 'when a guy like Morpion says, "Robert, your old ones will never let you down. With or without weapons, we will follow you until the world's end."'

Meanwhile, the various Jedburgh and SAS teams were also working hard to train the Maquis and bring some kind of organization to their frequently ramshackle efforts. Major Bill Tonkin of 1 SAS, leading a mission code-named BULBASKET near Limoges, scored a spectacular success on 12 June. A local railway worker arrived in their camp near Pouillac and told them that a railway siding south-west of Châtellerault was jam-packed with eleven trains, all carrying fuel. This was destined for the Normandy front and specifically for 2. SS 'Das Reich', which had been ordered from Montauban, just to the north of Toulouse. A brutal culture of violence and intolerance existed within what was one of the original Waffen-SS divisions. Although containing a lot of new recruits, its beating heart – its officers and NCOs – were battle-hardened veterans of the Balkans and Eastern Front and it was these men, fanatical Nazis, who set the tone. They had also been brutalized by their experiences on the Eastern Front, where operations had been plagued by Russian partisans, who in turn dealt with any captured SS men with equally vicious violence. As far as the 'Das Reich' veterans were concerned, most resistant types were communists and therefore the scum of the earth and should be dealt with accordingly. This view filtered down to the new men who had joined the division since moving to France.

'Das Reich' were desperate to get to the front and into battle as quickly as possible and showed no mercy whatsoever to anyone who got in their way. When a company commander was shot and killed by a Résistance sniper, tempers flared badly. Believing the perpetrator was from a village called Oradour, they moved into Oradour-sur-Glane – an entirely different village – rounded up the women and children into the church and the men into barns, then shot the lot and set the buildings on fire. Some 642 were killed there on 10 June, more than 200 of them children.

On 12 June, their murderous mood worsened further. Tonkin had sent details of the petrol trains back to England and at 8 p.m. – just six hours after Tonkin's signal – two squadrons of Mosquitoes flew over, low and fast, dropping 10 tons of bombs and shooting up the trains with their cannons. The entire 100,000 gallons of fuel were destroyed, the fireball reportedly rising more than 8,000 feet into the air. This coordination of Allied effort, one that used special forces, intelligence, air power and improved technology to materially affect the ground war, really was incredibly impressive.

CHAPTER 20

The Grinding Battle

THE ALLIED TOEHOLD IN Normandy was getting stronger by the day. By Thursday, 15 June, five airfields had been built within the beachhead and in the next five days a further seven would follow. It was, by any reckoning, an astonishing achievement of organization and engineering, especially while under fire for much of the time. Airfield B-2 at Bazenville, near Crépon, was not due to become operational until the 16th, but at around 10.20 p.m. on the 15th, Spitfires of 602 Squadron came in to land there. Among them was a French pilot officer, Pierre Clostermann, who, along with his great friend and fellow Frenchman in the squadron Jacques Remlinger, was the first to be touching back down on French soil; Clostermann had not been in France since before the war. To celebrate, he and Remlinger had decided to forgo their normal RAF battledress and instead were wearing smart French dress uniforms and carrying a flask of French brandy.

Clostermann had missed the shock of defeat in France in 1940, although he was already a qualified pilot, trained as a teenager by a German, Karl Benitz. The son of a French diplomat, he had been a student at the California Institute of Technology in San Diego. While there, he managed to fly every day, practising aerobatics and building up the hours in his logbook.

When France fell, however, he decided he could wait no longer. His father had written to his son telling him he was going to Africa to join de Gaulle's Free French and suggested his only child should join the fight too. Pierre needed little persuading and so had begun his long journey to England and to becoming a fighter pilot in a front-line squadron in the

RAF. Four years on, he was highly experienced and flying with 602 Squadron alongside his long-standing friend Jacques. The squadron, once an auxiliary unit of pre-war 'gentleman fliers', now had Frenchmen, Canadians, New Zealanders and Australians among their number and had been honed into a very effective and combat-experienced front-line squadron.

Clostermann and Remlinger landed at Bazenville just behind Squadron Leader 'Max' Sutherland, who had immediately whipped up a thick cloud of dust. Clostermann had never seen anything like it, but it was an earthen airfield that had been dry for a couple of days and, stirred up by the slipstream of the propellers, it got everywhere. As Clostermann finally came to a halt and jumped down off the wing, he met two British soldiers whose eyes were only visible under a layer of dust and sweat. 'Well, Frenchie,' one of them said, 'you're welcome to your blasted country!' Remlinger came over, a handkerchief covering his mouth, and the two shook hands, back in their homeland at last, although rather than savouring this wonderful moment Clostermann was mostly consumed by feelings of regret that he had worn his finest uniform. He felt more like a circus clown than an officer of the French Armée de l'Air.

The pilots were quickly given some ground rules by a Canadian captain. They were not to stray from the airfield, nor cross from one side of the track to another. Nor were they to touch anything. 'The Huns have left mines everywhere,' he told them, 'and only half an hour ago a man was killed and two others wounded by a German sniper.' They were taken to a mobile canteen set up behind a hedge and given tea, biscuits and marmalade, liberally sprinkled with dust. At least there were plenty of anti-aircraft guns, each one surrounded by empty shell cases. The pilots were startled by this – they had barely seen any Luftwaffe at all since the invasion. A sergeant told them to wait until later that night, then they would understand.

It was around half past eleven and by now quite dark when Clostermann and Remlinger were sharing a smoke with a couple of Canadians. All seemed quiet, then suddenly they heard the faint whirr of aero-engines. They looked up, trying to locate the aircraft.

'Don't worry, Pierre,' said Remlinger, 'if it was a Hun the ack-ack would already have opened fire.'

Moments later they heard the whistle of bombs falling. The Canadians vanished and the two French pilots dived under a lorry, and then a bomb exploded, pulse-waves quivering across the ground, followed by a burning gust of air and splinters spattering the trees, lorry and tents around them. Then the ack-ack opened fire and the sky was suddenly full of moving tracer, making it appear as light as day. A Spitfire caught fire and more Junkers 88s thundered over, dropping a mixture of 1,000-pounders and smaller bombs while a Bofors gun continued firing. The ground shook, shrapnel, grit and dust spattered all around them, and the air seemed torn apart by the immense din. 'Deafened, battered,' wrote Clostermann, 'we crouched under our lorry, shivering with funk.'

The following morning, they finally emerged after their night under the lorry, grimy, cold and exhausted, with tongues as dry as sand, and were horrified to discover the truck was full of ammunition. Still reeling, they made their way to the field kitchen and queued for some tea, only to see their two Canadian friends. Clostermann had thought they had been killed by the bombs. 'Oh, you know,' said one of them, 'we are now pretty hot at sprinting. We've been here a week and we're unbeatable.' Moments later, three Focke-Wulf 190s screamed over at hedge height firing as they went, then were gone. By lunchtime, 602 Squadron was back at Ford, their base in southern England, where, despite not being France, things were considerably more comfortable and less dangerous.

The vast majority of people who fought in the Normandy campaign did not land on D-Day; most arrived days, if not weeks, later. Most Allied troops, however, reached those shores the same way as those who had splashed through the water on Tuesday, 6 June: by crossing the Channel by sea. On Thursday, 15 June, it was the turn of the 6th Battalion, the King's Own Scottish Borderers – or 6 KOSB for short – part of the 44th Lowland Infantry Brigade, which was in turn part of the 15th Scottish Division. Like so many units reaching Normandy – on both sides – they were new to combat and so untested in battle. They were, however, long in training, well equipped and, on paper at any rate, as ready as any to be flung into the fray.

Commander of 7 Platoon in A Company was Lieutenant Robert Woollcombe, just twenty-two years old and born and raised in London, rather than Scotland. Serving in the KOSB was, however, something of a family tradition. His grandfather had been colonel of the regiment in the last war and had even ended up commanding a corps at the Battle of Cambrai, while his uncle had also served with the regiment, although tragically had been killed in action in 1914 in the first months of the war. Robert had joined in 1941, although by 1944 few regiments remained true to their roots. Cornishmen served in Yorkshire regiments, Scots in London battalions, and men from Hampshire served with the Lancashires. Stanley Christopherson, for example, had never lived in Nottingham – he had spent much of his childhood in South Africa and had been living and working in the City of London when he joined the Sherwood Rangers. The war was mixing people up in a way that had been unthinkable beforehand.

The 6 KOSB had come ashore at Gold Beach and Woollcombe was amazed neither to hear nor see even the remotest sign of any fighting. 'At first sight,' he wrote, 'it looked like a methodical unflustered chaos that might have been some fantastic novelty at Blackpool.'

Also now landed and in Normandy were the 1st Battalion, the Northamptonshire Yeomanry, part of the 33rd Independent Armoured Brigade. Twenty-year-old Lance Corporal Ken Tout, a tank gunner in C Squadron, had felt quite intoxicated by the sight of the coastline. 'All through my young life,' he wrote, 'my hopes had simmered slowly up to this boiling, spilling delight of foreign adventure.' He had been brought up in the medieval market city of Hereford by parents who were devout members of the Salvation Army, so revival meetings and the strict, rather Jesuitical, code of living that went with them were part and parcel of his upbringing. 'You couldn't go to the cinema,' he said, 'you couldn't go to the dancehall, you didn't smoke, didn't drink, didn't do anything really, because it was a sin.'

As a result, the army was something of an escape, while the discipline seemed far from excessive. 'Comparative to my life at home,' said Tout, 'my life in the army was physically uncomfortable but psychologically good.' And he'd done well – so much so that he had been put forward for officer training just before D-Day, although after learning it would take nine months and that at the end of it he might not even return to the 1st Northants Yeomanry, he decided to stay put as an NCO; he neither wanted to leave his mates nor miss out on the chance to serve in the invasion.

Meanwhile, the battle continued. There was no major all-out offensive by the Allies nor counter-attack by the Germans, but bitter fighting none the less, marked by hard-fought-for local objectives, furious digging and cowering in foxholes as mortars and artillery banged and crashed back and forth. On 15 June Stanley Christopherson was promoted to lieutenant-colonel and given formal command of the Sherwood Rangers

Yeomanry. On the 16th, they were back in action supporting the infantry of 69th Brigade. As so often happened, however, keeping in communication with the infantry amid the smoke and heat of battle was difficult, yet tanks and infantry both added up to more than their individual parts when they managed to operate effectively side by side. Christopherson was frustrated by the problem, but was not sure where the solution lay. Then 69th Brigade was pulled back and a new division, the 49th, moved into the line and for the next three days they were supporting an entirely new infantry brigade as the Panzer-Lehr counter-attacked and pushed them back north of Fontenay. 'Some very unpleasant fighting took place around Cristot,' noted Christopherson, which from an understated fellow like him meant it was hellish. They had been holding the high ground when the infantry of the Duke of Wellington's Regiment cut and ran under the heavy weight of enemy fire. The Germans overran the positions, capturing abandoned guns and leaving the Sherwood Rangers to hold some wooded ground on their own. 'For a day,' noted Christopherson, 'the Regiment felt very naked.' The casualties continued to mount too.

It was hardly much of a picnic for the Germans either. After the sunshine, the rain returned and although that meant fewer *Jabos*, even when there was low cloud the Germans were not immune from enemy artillery. The slightest movement, it seemed, prompted a ferocious barrage within moments. Once, near Tilly, Hauptmann Helmut Ritgen and a number of his tanks were in a sunken lane when shells began falling all around. Although they weren't hit directly, shrapnel clattered about them, damaging periscopes and radio antennae, so essential for communication. Ritgen's driver completely lost his nerve and broke down, crying for his mother, and in his distraught state managed to get their Panzer IV stuck. When the firing briefly stopped, Ritgen and his gunner had to jump out, tie their tow cable to the tank behind and get pulled out. 'We were fortunate,' noted Ritgen, 'that Tommy waited until our hatches were sealed before starting the next barrage.' From the outside, their panzers looked a mess and with their antennas damaged they had no choice but to pull back.

Already, after ten days at the front, Ritgen recognized that the British had a completely different method of war. Germans always wanted to attack, but for the Tommies the priority was 'to do harm to their enemies and take care of themselves.' Despite the slight tone of condescension, destroying the enemy while saving the lives of one's own side was really quite a sensible approach to war, while Pavlovian counter-attacking and incurring large numbers of losses in the process perhaps was not always the right approach. Ritgen, however, believed – like almost every fighting German – that a swift counter-attack against the British enabled them to quickly regain ground lost. The catch, though, as he admitted, was that this always incurred losses, 'which we could not adequately replace, while the British received replacements during the night.' The military machine that could both look after its men and equipment better, and effectively make good its losses swiftly, however, was always going to be superior to the one that could not. Ritgen, like so many of his contemporaries, still believed in their aggressive tactical superiority, but this was largely because they had little else to offer and simply could not compete with the complete war effort of the Allies. It was, of course, why they were losing so badly and failing to gain any significant ground. The fighting against the Sherwood Rangers at Cristot was a case in point: they had made some progress, but not significant strides, and even though the British infantry had run, the attackers had still not been able to wrest the important high ground. In the process they had also lost yet more men. It was this aggressive tactical spirit, led first and foremost by the officers and senior NCOs, that was causing so many debilitating casualties – and not least among the Panzer-Lehr.

Further to the west, the Americans were pressing forward to the ridge line just to the north-east of Saint-Lô, which was being determinedly held by the Germans and which was the next main line of defence, as prepared before the invasion. Already the Americans had tried to hustle their way through the sparse German lines on 12 June, but through lack of heavy fire support had been unable to make any headway. It was along here that the shattered remnants of the 352. Infanterie-Division had retreated.

By Monday, 19 June, Leutnant Hans Heinze and the survivors of his 5. Kompanie, Grenadier-Regiment 916, had reached Le Mesnil-Rouxelin, just a few miles to the north of Saint-Lô. All his men were exhausted, filthy and hungry, having been in continual action since the invasion. They'd had almost no sleep, had been under fire almost constantly and many had bloody feet from all the marching they had done in worn-out boots. Soon after digging in, Heinze had been ordered to report to Oberst Ernst Goth, the regimental commander, at his command post in the nearby chateau. Heinze looked a sight as he presented himself and saluted: almost bearded, tattered uniform, mud, blood and grime on his face and hands. Goth berated him, yelling at him that a German officer should always look clean and presentable when reporting to a superior, regardless of the situation. He dismissed Heinze, telling him he had ten minutes to clean himself up. An orderly took his light summer jacket for a quick clean and also gave him a razor, mirror and basin of water. The razor, however, was blunt, the water cold and the soap non-existent. 'I put the razor against the skin of my cheek,' said Heinze, 'and began to scrape the blade down my face, taking hair and skin.' When he presented himself back in front of Oberst Goth, standing stiffly to attention, he could feel small drips of blood from where he'd cut himself running down his face and neck.

Karl Wegner and his comrades in Grenadier-Regiment 914, meanwhile, had reached the village of Saint-Clair-sur-l'Elle and had dug in around the road leading north, just south of the River Elle, which ran across their path. Because they were now so woefully understrength, they were widely spaced apart, but well positioned, with mortars and machine guns and well dug in along hedgerows. As previous fighting in Sicily and Italy had shown, well-placed machine guns and mortars, augmented by mines and snipers, could prove an effective barrier to Allied infantry. Even so, Wegner and his comrades were surprised the Americans didn't press them harder. 'One concentrated attack,' he said, 'would sweep us aside like toy soldiers.'

It was, however, more than the leading American troops could manage for very good reasons. Most had barely slept more than a few snatched hours, had been in heavy action, had had to cross flooded areas, dodge mines and snipers, and lacked artillery support. By the time they had attacked, the 352. Division had actually received some replacements and some support on their flanks. Among these was the 3. Fallschirmjäger-Division, now holding the line a little to the east around the key feature marked on Allied maps as Hill 192, between the villages of Couvains and Saint-Germain-d'Elle. Despite the reputation of all *Fallschirmjäger* units as superior troops, 3. Fallschirmjäger, like most other parts of the Luftwaffe, were severely under-trained and equipped.

Among those now dug in was Johannes Börner, still only eighteen years old and from Leipzig. Called up at seventeen in March the previous year, he had carried out his *Arbeitsdienst* – his labour service – then joined the Luftwaffe as ground crew before volunteering to join the *Fallschirmjäger* in January 1944. 'They asked us whether we would rather go to Russia as ground crew on Messerschmitt 109s or join the paratroopers,' said Börner, 'so I volunteered to become a *Fallschirmjäger*.' Posted to parachute school near Berlin, he underwent three weeks' intense training, which included the standard six practice jumps, and was then posted to Brittany to join the 15. Kompanie of the III. Bataillon, Regiment 5 of the 3. Fallschirmjäger-Division. 'We were really elite troops,' said Börner. Despite this claim, his paratrooper training had been a mere twenty-one days. In contrast, there was not an American paratrooper now in Normandy who had been training for less than two years.

At Finistère in Brittany, they carried out route marches, practised machine-gun and small-arms training, laid mines and prepared defences. They never once trained with tanks and only a limited amount with artillery. Then, early in the morning of 6 June, they began moving up towards Normandy. From Brest and the Finistère region to the front near Saint-Lô was more than 200 miles, and Börner and his comrades had to march the entire way, from dusk until dawn, reaching their new positions during Monday, 12 June. 'It was very hard,' admitted Börner. 'We were really tired and had blisters on our feet.' Despite this, they went into action immediately, because that same day the Americans tried to burst through.

Among those attacking was Sergeant Bob Slaughter in Company D of the 116th Infantry, who reached Couvains the same day. Digging in behind a hedgerow, he and his squadron had just finished camouflaging their position when Slaughter saw a new replacement officer wearing a fresh uniform move up and start scanning ahead with his binoculars. Moments later, a German high-velocity shell whooshed in, hitting the man squarely on the upper torso. 'The 2nd Squad and I were splattered with gore,' noted Slaughter, 'as the spotter was blown backwards, minus his head.'

On the afternoon of Thursday, 15 June, Montgomery visited Bradley. With V-1s now falling on Britain, the pressure to push the Germans harder and break out of Normandy was growing. All the senior commanders now in Normandy and those back in Britain had heard Monty's briefings on 7 April and 15 May, when he had spoken so confidently and shown the projected phase lines to which Bradley had so objected. It wasn't panning out quite as hoped, and those back in London and elsewhere looking at their maps had quickly forgotten just how well the Allies had done so far. Caen had been a D-Day objective, Cherbourg a priority. Both were still in enemy hands. So too was Saint-Lô, an objective that the Allies had hoped to capture in a matter of days.

At their meeting, Monty urged Bradley to take Saint-Lô swiftly, but Bradley told him the town was meaningless; what mattered was capturing the high ground on either side and that was what his forces would be assaulting the following day. They then set off by Jeep and car to see Major-General 'Lightning Joe' Collins, the US VII Corps commander, to discuss his plan of attack for Cherbourg. They passed through Grandcamp, Isigny and Carentan. Each was wrecked. Roads were pitted and littered with destroyed vehicles and rubble. Work parties were already trying to clear up, but it was a massive job. 'Carentan badly hit,' noted Chet Hansen, 'square was mass of rubble, still smell of burning wood. German barracks in center of town mass of discards as though they had picked up in a hurry and got out . . . churches were hit, demolished, windows broken. Shop fronts smashed, Civ. Affairs posters around warning of looting and pillage with death to offenders.'

They had their conference with Collins at his farmhouse CP near Sainte-Mère-Église. Collins, who had turned just forty-eight in May, had been the youngest divisional commander in the US Army when he was given the 25th Division back in 1942. He had led them during the final battles on Guadalcanal, which had so far proved the decisive campaign in the Pacific War against the Japanese. There, he had been faced by fanatical enemy troops and difficult terrain, yet had still earned the nickname 'Lightning Joe' for his speed of operations. Collins's philosophy was simple: always take the high ground wherever possible and get artillery forward. It was Bradley who had lined him up to take charge of VII Corps. The two had served together at West Point and then later as instructors at the Army Infantry School, where they became friends. Collins had also known Eisenhower briefly in the Philippines in the 1930s. Having returned to the US just before Christmas 1943, he was both available and keen to test himself in the cauldron of the campaign in Europe.

Collins had come ashore on Utah Beach on 7 June and hurried as many troops as the unloading would allow into the peninsula, ensuring the northern flank was secure and then pressing his forces to sever the Cotentin and trap the Germans to the north still defending Cherbourg. With 4th Division pressing northwards, he quickly brought in the 90th Division as well. The latter was new to combat in this war, but Collins hoped this would not hinder them. Their orders were to pass through the 82nd Airborne and push on towards Saint-Sauveur-le-Vicomte, a significant town and confluence of roads and railways heading north and likely to be stiffly defended. It was, however, held by the German 265. Division, newly arrived from Brittany and a low-grade unit with fragments of other units attached.

After two days of fighting through the hedgerows, the 90th had made little progress, however, so on 13 June Collins headed to the front to see them for himself. After calling in at the divisional CP, he and his party drove on, but could find neither any regimental or battalion headquarters nor any fighting. Eventually, he came upon a group of 90th men in a ditch alongside a road. Stopping, he asked the sergeant what they were doing and received an evasive reply. 'It was obvious,' wrote Collins, 'they were malingering.' Appealing to their sense of pride, he talked about the division's great record in France in 1918 and of the incredible fighting carried out by the 82nd, whom they had passed through on their way to the front, but the men were unmoved. Collins ordered them to get going and later reported his findings to their commander, Major-General Jay MacKelvie. 'He made no excuses,' commented Collins, 'but seemed at a loss as to what to do about the lack of fight in his division.'

Collins, however, knew exactly where the problem lay. Divisions were only ever as good as their commander. MacKelvie had had the division only a short while and Collins felt the lion's share of the blame lay with MacKelvie's predecessor, who clearly hadn't trained or toughened them up enough. On the other hand, MacKelvie wasn't the right man to shake them up either. This was war – men's lives were at stake, and there was simply no time to give commanders like MacKelvie the benefit of the doubt. Collins recommended to Bradley that MacKelvie be swiftly replaced by Major-General Eugene Landrum, another Pacific War veteran, and suggested bringing in the 9th Division, now landed, to drive west across the peninsula alongside the 82nd. Bradley accepted all Collins's recommendations. 'Still a good artillery man,' Chet Hansen noted of MacKelvie, 'everyone agrees on that. Probably not enough of a driver to be a good div commdr especially under hot mustard like Collins who demands ready action quickly.' Within 24 hours, this had all been put into action. Collins wasn't called 'Lightning Joe' for nothing.

It did mean, however, keeping the 82nd at the front longer than their fellows in the 101st, who had been withdrawn after Carentan and were due to ship back to England to rest and refit. The 82nd jumped off with their latest attack on 15 June, with Lieutenant-Colonel Mark Alexander's 505th PIR and the 325th Glider Infantry Regiment leading the charge to the upper River Douve and the town of Saint-Sauveur-le-Vicomte, which the 90th Division had so woefully failed to capture. To help him, Alexander had been given just two tanks, but they quickly proved their worth, as together with his men they took out one strongpoint after another. He found himself constantly in motion, flitting between company forward positions, his own battalion and regimental CPs.

By evening on the 16th, they had pushed the enemy back 15 miles and reached the eastern side of the River Douve, proving both the ineffectiveness of the German opposition and that Collins had been right to act swiftly over the 90th Division. He had also now brought the 9th Infantry Division into the line on the 82nd's right. Even so, how to get across was the next headache, because an opposed river crossing was not easy, even against third-rate opposition. Alexander now went ahead with his radio operator and orderly to survey the task, only to discover Bradley, Collins, General Matt Ridgway and Colonel Bill Ekman, the CO of the 505th PIR, already there. The Germans had failed to blow the bridge, so the plan was to hit hard and fast and get straight across, albeit behind a massive artillery barrage. 'Before you cross a river,' commented Alexander, 'you better know that you're going to have support, or they'll chew you up if you get out there by yourself. We were sticking our neck out, but the General sure provided an opening barrage.'

This was where fighting close to the sea played into the hands of the Allies. Naval warships as well as bombers and artillery flattened Saint-Sauveur in a brief but devastating barrage; as the Italians had discovered, when it came to saving towns and villages or the lives of Allied troops, it was the troops who always took priority. 'My 1st Battalion crossed the bridge immediately behind the 2nd Battalion without too much fighting,' recalled Alexander. 'The bombardment had pulverized St. Sauveur-le-Vicomte.'

Further to the south, meanwhile, on 16 June the Americans attacked the high ground to the north and east of Saint-Lô, again behind a heavy artillery barrage. Shells screamed in and exploded, smashing trees, buildings and churning up the ground. Karl Wegner had welcomed the pause of the past few days, but as the shelling began he hurriedly put on his helmet and crouched at the bottom of his foxhole. When eventually the barrage stopped, the Americans pressed forward with infantry and tanks. Still in his foxhole, Wegner could not see much, but not long after Obergefreiter Kalb yelled for them all to get up and pull back. 'One could feel the panic in the air,' said Wegner. 'I must admit that even I felt the to consider the same and visit Normandy. Much to everyone's surprise, Hitler agreed.

Rommel left later that afternoon, buoyed by the prospect and by Hitler's enthusiastic talk of the Me262 jet, of V-2s and rocket-fuelled aircraft projects. Von Rundstedt, on the other hand, thought the conference had been a complete waste of time. In this, he was right and Rommel wrong. There would be no handing over of complete tactical control to Rommel, no Me262s supporting the front, and no V-2s before the Normandy battle was done. Supplies would remain slow and insufficient. His men would continue to be stretched to breaking point.

Nor did Hitler ever make the trip to the front. Earlier that day, a rogue V-1 had veered off course, crashing and exploding only a few miles from Margival. Hitler was informed later in the day, with General Jodl, chief of staff of the OKW, urging the Führer to return to Bavaria. Just imagine, he pointed out, if another V-1 went astray and actually killed the leader of the Reich. Around the same time, reports of nearby Résistance activities reached Wolfsschlucht II. Suddenly the risks of touring Normandy seemed too great. In any case, with Rommel and von Rundstedt gone, the proposition of visiting a dangerous front over which marauding Allied fighters made any movement unsafe seemed dramatically less appealing. So, instead, the Führer decided to abandon such plans and return to the Berghof. He would never set foot in France again.

CHAPTER 21

The Great Storm

ON Sunday, 18 June, Montgomery issued new, revised, plans. Caen remained, like Cherbourg, a key objective, despite the realization five days earlier that it could no longer be taken swiftly or easily. He now ordered Dempsey to seize the city with a series of operations that would begin that day and reach their peak on 22 June with an attack to the east of the town and the River Orne. Bradley's First Army was to complete the isolation of the Cotentin Peninsula and then drive on Cherbourg, while continuing to try to get the high ground around Saint-Lô. By dusk on the 18th, men of the US 9th Division had reached the west coast of the Cotentin, just as Rommel had feared and forewarned, trapping the enemy forces to the north, including the 77. Division. It was now a matter of how long it would take and how many casualties the four German divisions in the north would inflict on the Americans, but the outcome was no longer in doubt. Before long, those German infantry divisions would be annihilated and Cherbourg would be in American hands. Montgomery, Bradley and Collins intended to begin the drive on Cherbourg the following day.

So far, Eisenhower had shown notable patience, understanding and support to his commanders and men fighting in Normandy. He had even now forbidden the visit of any further VIPs to Montgomery's headquarters. 'I won't have you bothered at this time,' he wrote to Monty on 18 June, 'by people who are not in position to help you directly in the battle.' The quid pro quo, however, was that Montgomery should now instruct his armies to press forward with no further delay. 'I can well understand that you have needed to accumulate reasonable amounts of artillery ammunition,' Eisenhower added, 'but I am in high hopes that once the attack starts it will have a momentum that will carry it a long ways.'

The war reporter Ernie Pyle was touring through the newly captured part of the central Cotentin and thought the countryside truly lovely. 'Everything was a vivid green,' he wrote, 'there were trees everywhere, and the view across the fields from a rise looked exactly like the rich, gentle land of eastern Pennsylvania. It was too wonderfully beautiful to be the scene of war.' None the less, he thought the ride was rather eerie because they drove for miles without seeing a soul. 'It was as though life had taken a holiday and death was in hiding,' he added. 'It gave me the willies.' They eventually stopped at a schoolhouse now being used as a POW collection point. More groups of German prisoners were arriving even while Pyle was there. He talked to one, a German doctor, who spoke English and appeared to be in good humour. 'I've been in the army four years,' he said, beaming, 'and today is the best day I have spent in the service.' Ahead, to the north, the Americans were continuing their drive on Cherbourg, but elsewhere French civilians were trying to carry on with their lives. Pyle's party drove on to Barneville, which had mercifully escaped the fighting. People quickly gathered around, asking questions and looking for instructions about what they should do and expect. One elderly man in blue denim overalls invited them to his café for a drink and gave them a concoction called 'eau de vie' – it was all he had left, as the Germans had drunk all his stocks of wine. They chinked their glasses, vived la France and knocked it back. Pyle and his companions found tears running down their cheeks – not from the emotion of it all but from their efforts not to choke and cry out in anguish as the searing hooch went down their throats. 'This good-will business,' noted Pyle, 'is a tough life and I think every American who connected with a glass of eau de vie should have got a Purple Heart.'

Along the invasion front, meanwhile, the flow of traffic continued across the Channel. The veteran US 9th Division, who, like the Big Red One, had seen combat in North Africa and also Sicily, had arrived in the Cotentin. Among the officers was 26-year-old Lieutenant Orion Shockley from Jefferson, Missouri, who had fought through much of the Tunisian and Sicily campaigns as an officer in Cannon Company, 47th Infantry Regiment, but then, after the battle for Sicily ended, had managed to get himself arrested and very nearly court-martialled. It was a ridiculous incident. General George S. Patton, commander of the Seventh Army in

Sicily, was a stickler for spit and polish, which meant wearing ties at all times and having all buttons fastened. One day in Palermo, Shockley saw a soldier being admonished for having a shirt pocket button undone after handing a base section captain a note. The soldier pointed out that he had just given the captain the missive, but was told he should have immediately buttoned it up again. Infuriated, Shockley walked over and said, 'Maybe you ought to take my name since my pocket is unbuttoned.' The officer did just that. Shockley immediately forgot all about it but was later hauled over the coals and was still officially under arrest when the 9th Division was posted to England. Once at sea and out of Patton's area, that was the end of the matter and Shockley was let off with a verbal reprimand, but it meant that once they were in England he was reassigned to the Service Company as special service officer. One of his tasks was to liaise with the USO – United Service Organizations – which provided entertainment for the troops. It gave him the chance to meet Hollywood stars like James Cagney and boxing champion Joe Louis – so the button incident turned out quite well for him in the end.

Now, however, he was in Normandy as XO in Company B, 2nd Battalion, 47th Infantry Regiment, and had been part of the fighting to cut the peninsula. After that, the battalion had been turned north and was now closing in on Cherbourg. A little under a year earlier, in Sicily, Shockley had been sweating buckets he'd been so hot. Here in Normandy it was often wet and cold. Once, he'd jumped a stream but the cliff on the other side had then collapsed and he slipped down into the water. Because the Germans were still shooting at them, he'd then spent over an hour crawling downstream until he could scramble out again. 'It was cold enough to make me very uncomfortable,' he wrote. 'It was night before I got into dry clothes.'

On 18 June, Lieutenant Mary Mulry was finally on her way to France. The previous day, she and her fellow QAs and medical staff of the 101st Military Hospital had been sent to an American transit camp in the New Forest, just outside Southampton. Much to their delight, the camp had a PX, an American services store, where they could stock up on chocolate, chewing gum and cans of fruit.

In the evening, they boarded their ship wearing tin helmets and battle-dress rather than starchy frocks and bonnets, and set sail at around 11.30 p.m. 'There was fear and anticipation,' she noted in her diary. 'What will it be like over there?' Out at sea there was even a mine alert and the engines were cut. Mary gripped her rosary beads and prayed, but eventually the all-clear was given and they continued on their way, by which time the weather was rapidly deteriorating. Everyone felt seasick, Mary included. As they neared the coast, a Luftwaffe air raid was in progress, the sky alight with flares and tracer and explosions. At around 4 a.m. a neighbouring vessel hit a mine and blew up, which shocked the nurses deeply. Landing craft were now trying to draw alongside, battling against the rising swell. Eventually Mary volunteered first to clamber down the net slung over the side of the ship, less from bravery than from a desire to get on to land as quickly as possible.

'Hold on until the exact moment I say,' said a voice behind her from the landing craft, 'and then jump backwards.' Already soaked, cold and frightened, she did as she was told and made the leap of faith. As promised, they caught her. 'Matron was the last to come down,' added Mary, 'which she did without too much loss of dignity.' Not too long after, they were coming ashore at Courseulles on Juno Beach. Temporarily given some stretchers to lie on in a barn, they grabbed some much-needed sleep, then later that morning clambered on to lorries and headed to Bayeux past broken tanks, black with burning, dozens of them with charred crew members hanging from them, half out of the turrets and escape hatches. 'There was mile after mile of destroyed armoured cars, trucks of all kinds,' Mary scribbled later, 'and stench of decaying maggot-ridden bodies.' After passing through Bayeux and heading down the road to Caen, they pulled into an orchard where in the days to come they would erect and begin operating their new field hospital. They would be much in demand.

Meanwhile, Lieutenant Yogi Jenson and the crew of HMCS *Algonquin* had been shuttling back and forth between Normandy and Portsmouth, carrying out fire-support, then anti-U-boat patrols as well. On the 19th they were off the mouth of the Orne providing fire-support for the beleaguered Commandos still dug in near the coast; they had barely moved since D-Day. That evening they came under fire from German 155mm guns, although their shells dropped short. The weather, however, was starting to whip up. 'The weather was too rough for efficient patrol,' noted Jenson, 'so we and three other destroyers anchored well to seaward.'

'Dark, cold and rainy day for our attack,' noted Chet Hansen in his diary that day, 'and air is hampered giving Germans additional days to stack up supplies to our V Corps front. Great break for him when air ceases to operate.' This was true enough, although it didn't stop the

British finally capturing Tilly-sur-Seulles from the Panzer-Lehr. The exhausted Sherwood Rangers might have been taken out of the line briefly, but not so the panzer crews of SS-Panzer-Regiment 12. For Kurt Meyer, it was a constant juggling act: on his right he needed to keep the Canadians at bay, while on the left he had to support the right flank of the Panzer-Lehr. The panzers counter-attacked again, but failed to make any headway and so, on the night of 18/19 June, pulled back on to the higher ground south of the town. By that time the rain was pelting down, the ground turning to mud. Tilly and the villages around were utterly wrecked; just one house was left standing in Tilly. It was a miserable part of the world to be that Monday.

This left Panzer-Regiment 12's left flank a little vulnerable, however, and among the troops sent forward to shore up the Panzergrenadiers still holding on to Fontenay was Obersturmführer Hans Siegel and his 8. Panzerkompanie. They moved their Panzer IVs into the northern section of the village, hiding them as well as they possibly could and then staying there in an anti-tank role for more than twenty-four hours without a break. 'This was a never-before experienced extremely difficult physical burden,' noted Siegel. 'Always on the look-out, not speaking to anyone. The crews isolated, not knowing what was happening elsewhere.' Tanks were not comfortable places; they were cramped and smelly and claustrophobic, yet Siegel allowed his men out only to answer the call of nature, fearing that the threat from shrapnel blast and small arms was too great. And so they stayed put, watching, straining their eyes, limbs turning stiff in the narrow confines of the turret and driving compartment. Siegel's draconian measures paid off, however. Their presence was not discovered. Nor did he lose a single man.

Both sides were exhausted and the British immediately went on to the defensive while they regrouped before the next planned attack. Hauptmann Helmut Ritgen pulled back his own tanks of II. Panzer-Lehr-Regiment 130 and for a change switched his CP from a hole in the ground under his panzer to a smashed farmhouse that had lost all its windows but which otherwise offered some shelter. Everyone was feeling the strain. 'The only consolation was that the Tommies had it no better,' he wrote. 'Unfortunately, they would be relieved after a short duration, and we would not.'

In fact, a major storm was now whipping up in the Channel, which would throw all the Allied plans into disarray. At Arromanches, the Mulberry B harbour was almost complete, as was the American one, Mulberry

A, at Port-en-Bessin. Lieutenant-Commander Ambrose Lampen and his team had managed to plant four more Phoenixes the previous day, the 18th, despite rising winds and despite them being 'A2s', which were some 50 feet high, the largest of the caissons, and also despite having to plant along the western breakwater and sideways to the tidal stream. They were getting good at it, though, the initial hiccup with the *Alynbank* now a distant memory, and they planted all four perfectly.

With gale-force winds howling across the coast, building waves up to 10 feet high on top of a heavy swell, the Mulberries were about to be tested to the full. Huge waves crashed against the blockships and over the Phoenixes, not just that day but all through the 20th and 21st as well. Amazingly, at Mulberry B the Phoenixes and the expensive Spud pier-heads also held, while the piers had been sited where protection was greatest and so also weathered the tempest. 'We were all proud to observe,' noted Lampen, 'that the unloading of stores continued uninterrupted throughout the storm.' That was true, but no new shipments could arrive during that time, while other vessels and craft hurriedly came inside to seek greater shelter so that the entire Mulberry was rammed with vessels. The misplaced *Alynbank* played a part in ensuring their safety as it lay across the direction of the wind. 'Under her lee,' noted Lampen, 'there was not a square yard of water unoccupied.'

There had been trouble enough, however: two Phoenixes at the western end had been badly damaged, while five others had developed gaps in their walls and a couple more had moved, but all in all Mulberry B had fared well, which was more than could be said for Mulberry A. Of the thirty-five Phoenixes that had been planted there, only ten remained intact, while two piers had also been wrecked. A week later, on 29 June, the decision would be made to abandon this entire harbour, built, transported and constructed at such enormous cost and effort, leaving just Mulberry B. The Gooseberry off Utah had largely been destroyed, while Rhinos and other landing craft the length of the invasion front had been smashed and broken against the shore.

Lieutenant Yogi Jenson had been aboard HMCS *Algonquin* throughout and had been shocked by the damage. It had reminded him of being in mid-Atlantic, and the scene of ships in great numbers rolling and tumbling on the surf brought to mind an eighteenth-century painting of a stormy seascape. 'Now was revealed flotsam of all kinds from that disastrous weather,' he wrote. 'Land craft had foundered and the occasional dead body floated by.'

The weather all across Europe during the war really had been terrible. The winter of 1942/3 had been pretty brutal, but that of 1943/4 had been even worse. It had set back Allied efforts in Italy, had massively hampered air operations and cast a terrible shroud of gloom over everyone unfortunate enough to experience it. Now, after a wonderful May, the month for which OVERLORD had originally been planned, France was experiencing the worst June in anyone's memory.

The effects of what quickly became known as the Great Storm were enormous. Some 800 vessels, most of them landing craft, were lost – a huge number, which could not be immediately replaced. The Allied build-up, already badly lagging primarily because of the poor weather earlier in the month, was put further awry. The number of troops landing was reduced by three-quarters and vehicles and other equipment by 50 per cent. By 22 June, British Second Army was three entire divisions short of the pre-invasion target. That was a lot. 'The strong north wind and low cloud continued all day,' General Dempsey recorded in his war diary. 'It prevented landing of stores and vehicles and the Air Force could not fly. It is proving a serious handicap to us as a large part of 8 Corps' vehicles have not been landed, and there is still insufficient ammunition for the operation.'

Montgomery and Dempsey now had to rethink their plans for their first major assault. At a commanders' conference on 22 June, Montgomery claimed that the build-up was now five to six days behind schedule. The trouble was, thanks to Ultra decrypts, Monty was very aware that the Germans were planning their own massed counter-attack at long last. To do this, they would need new infantry divisions to reach the front, take over the holding of the line from the panzer divisions now around Caen and to the west in order to allow them to pull back, reassemble and get themselves into some kind of order for a strike force that really might hurt the Allies, and specifically the British and Canadians in that sector of the front. From the secret intelligence he was receiving, it seemed likely the Germans would launch their attack at the end of the month, so there was now an urgent imperative for Montgomery to get his own assault in first and throw German plans off balance. Suffering a reverse in Normandy was simply unthinkable. A major operation, therefore, had to be launched in the Caen area and, of course, the hope was that it would break through and prove decisive; but in Montgomery's mind that was to be an added advantage rather than the primary objective.

Operation DREADNOUGHT, an attack to the east of Caen, had been ruled out as too difficult and risky, while a direct assault on Caen was also dismissed. This meant an operation driving southwards to the west of Caen was the only real option. Montgomery originally wanted to launch such an attack using three corps, which would make a potential decisive breakthrough far more likely. The shortfall in the build-up, however, had put paid to such lofty plans and so EPSOM, as the battle plan was code-named, had to be scaled back. Lieutenant-General Dick O'Connor's newly arrived VIII Corps would be the main strike force, while XXX Corps on the right – western – flank would strike first in an attempt to draw enemy troops away and also gain the important Rauray Ridge – a piece of higher ground that would be very useful to deny to the enemy when EPSOM was launched.

EPSOM would also be fought in two stages. To begin with, the attackers would drive south from around the village of Norrey through Saint-Manvieu and Cheux and then across the River Orne and up the other side to a dominating piece of high ground marked on their maps as Hill 112. Assuming all went to plan, VIII Corps' armour could then smash on through and break out into the ground beyond, circling back behind Caen and enveloping the city and all German troops caught behind. British armour was organized into two distinct roles. Independent armoured brigades – such as the 8th, to which the Sherwood Rangers were attached – were designed to give direct support to the infantry. Typically, one armoured regiment like the Sherwood Rangers would be temporarily attached to one infantry brigade, and one tank squadron to each infantry battalion. Armoured divisions consisted of tanks but also motorized infantry in half-tracks and Carriers, as well as numerous mobile anti-tank guns. They were trained to 'exploit', which meant to push through once an initial breakthrough had been achieved, with both speed and terrific force, and rapidly overwhelm any enemy forces beyond the original defensive line.

EPSOM was precisely the kind of set-piece battle on which Montgomery's reputation had been made. In support, the attackers would have some 700 field guns, which would lay down a heavy barrage before the attack was launched and then provide a rolling barrage as the infantry and armour pressed forward – in other words, they would be lobbing shells just ahead of the advance. The main width of advance would be just 2 miles in order to concentrate the *Schwerpunkt* – or main point of attack, to use a German term. Concentration of fire was a principle the British understood as well as the Germans. Naval warships would also offer support, as would, of course, the tactical air forces.

Several factors, however, suggested EPSOM might well fall short of its ultimate aim of achieving a decisive breakthrough. First was the shortfall of manpower. Second was the weather, which continued to be pretty dreadful. Tactical air forces really needed a high cloud base and, preferably, lots of sunshine, but in that last week of June northern Normandy was almost permanently covered in low ten-tenths cloud and drizzle, which helped the British not a jot. Third was the terrain. It was true it wasn't dense bocage, nor was it as bad as fighting through a city, but it still hardly favoured any kind of rapid operations. The Odon Valley, which ran roughly east–west, suddenly dipped quite steeply to the river, while the roads, the main arteries of any advance, were rough, narrow and winding. The ground rose steeply again on the southern side of the river before rising more gradually up to Hill 112. This was the kind of ground that most definitely defended the defender. EPSOM was not going to be easy.

On a two-dimensional map back at the Cabinet War Rooms or SHAEF HQ at Widewing, however, it all looked pretty straightforward and, with doodlebugs continuing to rain down on London and south-east England, a high level of expectation was placed on EPSOM to get the Allies back on track with the phase lines Montgomery had predicted on 7 April at St Paul's School. Monty tried to introduce a little note of caution, stressing how the weather was continuing to play merry hell with his plans, but this was not a time for pessimism. Confidence was what was needed and that had to come from the top. 'Of course,' noted Montgomery some time later, 'we did not keep to the times and phase lines we had envisaged for the benefit of administrative planning, and of course we didn't hesitate to adjust our plans and dispositions to the tactical situation as it developed – as in all battles. Of course we didn't. I never imagined we would.' This was an entirely reasonable comment. The trouble was, in the third week of June 1944 he did not explain this at all clearly to Eisenhower, or to Churchill or anyone else for that matter. They were still remembering that map of phase lines and his bravura pre-invasion performance that had spoken so confidently of being far to the south within a matter of days.

With the storm spent, the flow of Allied traffic to France continued. On Thursday, 22 June, the 356th Fighter Squadron flew to their new base in Normandy, airfield A-2 at Cricqueville, just south of Pointe du Hoc,

where Bradley and Pete Quesada had also set up their field headquarters. The 356th followed behind one of the other two squadrons of the 354th Fighter Group. The advance echelon had already gone ahead before the storm and, having received a report of a shortage of potable water, the pilots of Major Dick Turner's 356th FS had filled two 75-gallon drop tanks with fresh supplies. Then, shortly before they took off, the group finance officer rushed over to Turner and asked him to carry a sack of $75,000 in cash for the payroll in Normandy.

Despite a little anxiety at carrying such a precious cargo, they reached Cricqueville without incident, Turner heading in first to land. Flaps down, undercarriage down, approaching downwind, he was 50 feet short of the runway and 25 feet off the ground when he suddenly felt the aircraft stall. Turner realized his mistake immediately: normally, he was landing on almost empty, but with two drop tanks full of water, which was heavier than fuel in any case, plus a big bag of paper cash, his normal approach gliding speed had not been enough. He was now moments from a fatal crash as the Mustang lurched to the left and dropped a wing, and looked to be heading straight towards the runway Jeep control halfway down the strip. Hastily pushing forward the throttle and playing with the stick and rudder controls, he felt the P-51 reassert power in the nick of time, although he was struggling to pull up the port wing. Full right rudder and right aileron and full power, then suddenly he was climbing again and sped on above the airfield. Having recovered both control and his blood pressure, he rather sheepishly reminded those following him to increase approach speed by about 15 m.p.h. on account of the water load. 'It was a narrow escape,' noted Turner, 'and if I had applied power a fraction of a second later, I probably wouldn't have been able to recover.' Soon after, having made the necessary adjustments, he landed safely. There were now eleven operational airfields in Normandy and there would be even more in the days to come.

Out at sea, meanwhile, the Allied navies continued to provide enormous support. At dusk on 24 June, HMCS *Algonquin* began yet another coastal patrol alongside the British destroyer HMS *Swift*. Lieutenant Yogi Jenson came on watch at about 4 a.m. the following day, just as it was getting light, and soon after spotted a floating mine, which he shot and sank using a Sten gun.

'While you play around,' HMS *Swift* signalled moments after, 'may I anchor in your billet and you anchor in mine?'

Jenson replied yes, she could, and watched *Swift* steam ahead then lower her anchor. Immediately, there was a mighty explosion and an eruption of spray, followed by another; *Swift* had hit a couple of mines and had had her back broken. Already she was beginning to sink. Fortunately, all on board were rescued, but *Swift*'s misfortune had been *Algonquin*'s lucky escape. The following day, they returned to Portsmouth, their part in the great invasion over for the time being.

HMCS *Algonquin* might have returned to home waters, but with the abating of the storm the flow of men and materiel continued across the Channel to France, at a rate of around 14,500 men per day in both the American and the British and Canadian sectors – which amounted to the best part of two divisions in total every twenty-four hours. Now arriving in Normandy was 21-year-old William Biehler, from a German–American community in Summit, New Jersey; his grandparents had emigrated to the States in 1890. Not that the Biehler family were in any way for Germany. 'My folks were very definitely American-minded,' said Biehler, 'and they wanted to stay in America. They thought America was great.' Biehler was a highly intelligent and academic young man who had been at Rutgers University in his first year, majoring in chemistry, when the Japanese attacked Pearl Harbor. Drafted soon after, he was allowed to finish his sophomore year and even enrolled in the Army Specialized Training Program – a college officer-training scheme – with the hope of becoming an officer in the engineers. Soon after completing his basic training, however, he was told he was too short-sighted to be considered for officer material and was posted to the infantry rather than the engineers.

By mid-May, Biehler, all 6 foot 4 inches of him, had crossed the Atlantic, gone by train to Devon and immediately been put into a 'repple-depple' – a replacement depot. 'The repple-depples were terrible places,' he said, 'because nobody belongs to anything.' Unlike many of the troops that had already landed, or complete divisions that were crossing the Channel, those from the repple-depples had built up little sense of camaraderie or notion of regimental pride. They were simply spares to be slotted wherever needed. The storm delayed his shipload of replacement troops, so not until 22 June did Biehler wade ashore. Sporadic artillery firing was going on in the distance as they were marched off to another repple-depple, where he spent his first night. The following day he and the others were divided – some into one truck, others into another – and then rumbled off. When they eventually came to a halt it was at the Rear HQ command post of the beleaguered 90th Infantry Division, still at the base of the Cotentin. Biehler was put on to another truck and that was how he ended up in Company K of the 3rd Battalion, 357th Infantry Regiment. He was cold, hungry, his boots were still wet from wading ashore, and almost immediately he was led to a foxhole where he met his new buddy. He was now in A Squad of the 1st Platoon with three others – there should have been twelve in all, but, as he swiftly discovered, he was among the first of the replacement troops. The company had been decimated in their first, recent, fighting. 'I don't think,' said Biehler, 'they had more than thirty.' For the time being they were simply holding a line. Their turn, however, would come soon enough. The 90th Division would then have a lot to prove.

Another new division arriving in Normandy was the British 43rd Wessex, re-formed back in 1939 after being disbanded at the end of the last war and now about to enter combat for the first time since then. Among its infantry battalions were the 4th Dorsets, who came ashore at Arromanches on the 22nd. It was a further three days, however, before Sergeant Walter Caines and the rest of the battalion Signals Platoon finally finished unloading, by which time he had begun to feel really fed up, hungry and sick of being at sea. It was afternoon by the time the Signals Platoon reached the battalion concentration area near Bayeux. At last Caines had time for a quick hot meal – albeit of compo rations – plus a wash and a shave, and then attended an O Group with Lieutenant-Colonel Cowie, the battalion CO, and Lieutenant Hogan, the signals officer. They would be moving the following morning, and the day after would take over positions currently held by the Canadians. During the night it began raining again, but Caines managed to crawl under a truck and spent the night there. So far, he wasn't much impressed with Normandy.

Also now joining Second Army was the sister battalion of Ken Tout's 1st Northamptonshire Yeomanry, the 2nd Battalion, not part of an independent armoured brigade but of 11th Armoured Division. Having landed on Juno Beach just after midnight on 19 June – before the storm had really whipped up – they had moved inland to near Creully. One of the tank commanders of 2 Troop, A Squadron, was Corporal Reg Spittles. A pre-war member of the Territorial Army, he had been just a part-time soldier, but on 1 September 1939 had been ordered to report to the local drill hall in Northampton in the English Midlands and sworn in to serve for the duration. Since then, he had seen the battalion transform itself from its pre-war unit of just one obsolescent tank to a well-honed, fully equipped armoured battalion ready for modern combat. 'I suppose I could be looked upon as a war-time veteran,' he wrote, 'as I was twenty-five years old at that time and had been involved in many, many training exercises.'

The battalion had also been re-equipped with Cromwell tanks, the British Army's latest and new for the Normandy battle, while the battalion's ranks, since the previous autumn, had also swollen from the various training regiments in anticipation of the invasion and the campaign to follow, so there would be enough replacement crews available once the fighting began and inevitable losses began to mount.

Each tank commander had been instructed to organize his 'first crew', with whom they would initially go into combat. Most chose those who had been longest in the battalion, but Spittles was a man of independent thought who liked to buck the trend and so had chosen mostly 18- and 19-year-olds. From what he had seen of them, they seemed keener than a lot of the older lads. 'After all,' he scribbled, 'they were freshly trained compared to the casual way we older ones took our training.' There was Denny Wells, aged eighteen, from Hull, who was the gunner and a bit of a loner. Bill Bagguly, from Birmingham, was the loader and wireless operator, also eighteen but quick-thinking and naturally aggressive. Bill 'Benny' Benmore, from London, the third 18-year-old, was the driver, 'sharp as a tack' and totally reliable. Finally there was Bill Barnett, the co-driver and machine-gunner from Stafford, a very easygoing and mild-mannered 23-year-old. As it turned out, they had had the best part of nine months together before heading to Normandy and in that time Spittles had got to know them all well. So far, he had had no cause to regret his decision. The biggest test, however, would come the moment they went into combat – and that was going to be very soon in General Dempsey's Operation EPSOM.

The 101st British Field Hospital was now up and running in its fields near Bayeux, albeit in a number of canvas tents. Because they were so close to the front they had a number of Pioneer Corps to protect them. Mary Mulry thought they seemed wonderfully unmilitary – most were conscientious objectors or foreign nationals who had taken refuge in Britain. One officer she quickly befriended was a Polish Jew with a name she could not pronounce, so they all called him 'Chezzy'. He was cheerful, good humoured and could speak English, German and Russian as well as Polish; he was a professional pianist in civilian life. 'Chezzy has so much warmth and personality,' Mary wrote in her diary, 'that it knocks me over. Why are ugly people often more attractive than handsome ones?'

Conditions at the hospital were a little too primitive for Mary's liking. The nearest water supply was over a mile away, although the Pioneer Corps swiftly worked out a system for getting it directly to the hospital. Sterilizing equipment was also basic and relied on storing needles, scalpels and so on in spirit, while there were Primus stoves for boiling water. Their first patients were Germans. One, a young German sniper called Fritz, was caught by the Pioneer Corps after being shot in the leg. Mary thought he couldn't have been more than fifteen. He admitted he had been ordered to stay behind to fight for the Fatherland, and to begin with was 'very high and mighty', although the arrogant sheen soon disappeared when they offered him some food; he was ravenous.

Nor was his wound too serious. They gave him a stick and within a day he was hobbling about, the life and soul once he realized he was not going to be shot. Mary and the other nurses put him to work helping out on the ward, which he seemed quite happy to do. Three days later, two more Germans were brought in – another teenager like Fritz, also with a leg injury, and an older man in his thirties called Hans, who was married with children back home in Frankfurt. He was thrilled to have been caught and, apart from some superficial cuts and bruises and obvious malnutrition, was in reasonable shape. Like Fritz, they intended to keep him on to help out with odd jobs. 'Hans is quite unlike the jackbooted "Hun" whom we had anticipated,' noted Mary. 'He is polite and timid and makes me feel that he is one of the many pawns in this game of war.'

Further to the east, out of the Allied bridgehead, life was not getting any easier for Robert Leblanc and the Maquis Surcouf. By Wednesday, 21 June he'd been promoted to *capitaine* by the FFI, but he turned it down, feeling he did not deserve it and that it was merely a sop to keep him keen when all around him his Résistance movement was on the point of collapse; his instincts were almost certainly correct. The responsibilities that came with leading a Maquis and the almost daily dilemmas facing him were immense. The less successful they were, and the more they struggled for lack of arms, the greater the risk not just of being outgunned but of being betrayed. Times were desperate. People were hungry, fed up, scared, and if captured they could expect torture, harm to their families and execution. It was not surprising that some talked.

On Wednesday, 14 June, the GMRs – the *Groupes mobiles de réserve*, effectively the army of Vichy – who were operating in their area had sent word saying they wanted to join the Maquis Surcouf. But should Leblanc believe them, or was it a trap? Then a rumour reached him that his wife and four children, still at home in Pont-Audemer, had been arrested; this, however, later proved to be false. More of his men were killed the following day and then the group moved yet again. Some good news finally reached him on Saturday, 17 June, when they were told to get ready for an arms drop. That night they tramped 6 miles across fields and through woods with their lamps, but on reaching the rendezvous there was no sign of either the liaison team they had been expecting or of any Allied aircraft. Bitterly disappointed, they tramped back again, empty-handed.

On the 20th, the wives of three of his men, 'La Torpille', 'Ramoutcho' and 'Henry III' (they all had *noms de guerre*), were arrested and taken away; La Torpille's wife was mother to their seven children. They learned that the arrests were directly the result of betrayal by a local man who had been taken in by the Germans. 'He thought he would save his life,' scribbled Leblanc angrily. 'Instead of being killed for the sake of his country, he will be killed all the same, but covered with shame.' He and his section commanders were beginning to feel ever more cornered and it was putting them in a murderous mood; they now considered executing the several prisoners they were keeping – a German soldier and three female collaborators. They could ill-afford to carry such people, the local farmers in whose barns the Maquis were hiding didn't want these prisoners anywhere near, and the Germans had not shown any scruples about killing people, so why should they? Not only had plenty of his men – as well as innocent civilians – already been killed, but the swine had now locked up the mother of seven children! 'All that makes me sick,' he wrote. 'I order Bougnat to "lose" him somewhere' – such as one of the many chalk quarries round about into which the German soldier's body could be dumped.

Then there was the question of what to do with the three women prisoners. He decided one could be let go. Another, Marie-Thérèse, was, he thought dangerous, but he had no hard proof against her, so he asked 'Robert 1', one of his section commanders, to take her off his hands. Then there was 'XX001X', as he code-named her in his diary. They had captured her a couple of days before the invasion and found on her a picture of a

known Nazi Party official with a dedication to her. She had continued to deny she was a Nazi agent, but Leblanc was convinced the German lover was in the Gestapo. He had no hard proof, however, and no one wanted to take charge of her. Two days later, on 22 June, Leblanc made up his mind. 'I do not hesitate,' he jotted in his diary, 'between our security and the life of a woman who's always been working with and for the Boche.' Robert 1 agreed with this and offered to 'do the job'.

The travails, trials and tragedies of an ill-trained band of Résistance fighters was of little concern to Montgomery, Dempsey or Bradley, who were battling to get enough supplies unloaded as more German troops also reached the front. While it was true they already had superior numbers, it was not yet at an overwhelming level, and nothing like the 10:1 advantage enjoyed by the Red Army for their new offensive in the East; Operation BAGRATION had thundered into the German Heeresgruppe Mitte – Army Group Centre – on 22 June, three years to the day after the Germans had invaded the Soviet Union. For all the Allies' fire-power, however, they were still some way short of that kind of numerical superiority.

At 9.30 a.m. on Friday, 23 June, Dempsey issued new orders, bowing to the inevitable; he couldn't fight the weather. 'I postponed 8 Corps attack,' he wrote, 'until Monday 26 June.' This meant an eight-day delay, all told, since Montgomery had originally planned to launch the battle for Caen. It was necessary, though, despite the ticking clock, despite the arrival of more German panzer units around Caen, and despite ever more V-1s falling on London.

CHAPTER 22

EPSOM

STANDARTENFÜHRER KURT MEYER WAS a troubled man on the evening of Saturday, 24 June. Driving back to the 12. SS divisional command post, he looked down from the Rauray Ridge and saw trucks still burning on the Caen–Villers-Bocage road, lighting up the sky. They had been full of ammunition for his men but had been caught by the dreaded *Jabos*. Back at his CP, he listened to a situation update and saw only worried faces. 'Without talking about it openly,' he noted, 'we knew we were approaching a catastrophe.' His division was being chewed up. Panzer divisions were designed for movement, but instead they had been holding the line, largely static, as the Allies poured air, naval and artillery fire on to them. It had already cost the blood of some of Meyer's best men and had destroyed much of their precious equipment. 'We were already feeding on ourselves,' he added. 'Up to that point we had not received a single replacement for our wounded or killed soldiers or a single tank or artillery piece.'

In contrast, Stanley Christopherson, the still-new commander of the Sherwood Rangers, was now back up to scratch with replacement troopers and officers. He was happy enough to have these new boys, but worried that they lacked experience and knowledge of operating Sherwoods. They would have to sink or swim.

The regiment, rapidly becoming one of Second Army's main firefighting units, was back in action on Sunday, 25 June. At daybreak, with low cloud, mist and drizzle, Operation MARTLET began, with two brigades of British infantry from XXX Corps leading the attack, supported by 250 field guns. The brunt of the attack was directed at 12. SS. MART-LET and the main event, EPSOM, which would be launched at dawn the following day, might have been separate operations for Second Army, but as far as the Germans, and Standartenführer Meyer, were concerned, they were really one and the same. Meyer himself had managed to snatch just a few hours' sleep before being roused by this renewed British onslaught and immediately hurried forward to Fontenay where the remnants of his panzer-grenadiers were desperately trying to hold firm. The place was already pulverized; he could hardly recognize it, nor could he see much forward for all the smoke. Shells continued to crash into the village and around, and Meyer took cover in a crater as enemy tanks and artillery knocked out one after another of his anti-tank guns. He was still there when his I. Bataillon tank commander jumped in beside him to tell him he was preparing to counter-attack. Soon after, as the leading British tanks, the Sherwood Rangers included, began targeting the panzer-grenadiers, so the 12. SS panzers rumbled forward through the smoke. A comparatively rare tank-versus-tank duel erupted. Tanks on both sides were knocked out, filling the battlefield with thick, oily smoke. Then the leading company commander's tank was hit and turned a few metres to the left. The hatches opened and Obersturmführer Ludwig Ruckdeschel somehow clambered out, jumped down and staggered towards Meyer before collapsing. Some men rushed forward to pull him to safety; only then did Meyer realize Ruckdeschel had lost an arm.

Soon after, Meyer was told about a dangerous gap in the line to his left, between his troops and Panzer-Lehr. He hurriedly plugged it with his exhausted reconnaissance troops, the only men he could spare; he was being forced to commit his division piece by piece in precisely the way he knew to be fatal. Despite the best efforts of his worn-out men, Fontenay fell later that day. The key British objective, however, the Rauray Ridge, remained in German hands. Dempsey had hoped to possess this high ground, from which the entire battle front west of Caen could be surveyed, before EPSOM was launched, but it was not to be. Certainly, though, MARTLET had ground down 12. SS yet more, inflicting casualties they could simply no longer afford.

'All the luck in the world to you and Dempsey,' signalled Eisenhower that day to Montgomery. 'Please do not hesitate to make major demands for air support of any kind which could possibly be helpful to you. Whenever a justifiable opportunity offers itself, we must destroy the enemy with everything we have.' EPSOM would finally begin at dawn the following morning, Monday, 26 June.

For all the Allied fire-power and the long tail of support troops, it was still the infantry and armour, with a few engineers besides, who had to cover the hard yards. It was these men who had to emerge from their slit-trenches and their cover, get up and advance. The moment they did that, they exposed themselves to a mass of withering machine-gun fire, mortars and artillery. Machine guns and mortars especially were comparatively low cost for the enemy; they definitely punched above their weight in terms of the damage they caused per cost of weapon and of ease of getting them to and manoeuvring them around the battlefield. The most basic mortar was essentially a portable tube, a couple of legs and a plate on which the tube stood, and could be manhandled without further need for truck, horses or mules.

The Germans also had *Nebelwerfers*, which were much larger and came in different forms, but the most common by 1944 was the Nebelwerfer 42, which was a six-barrel rocket-launched mortar that looked rather like a giant rotating chamber on a revolver pistol but which required transport of some kind to move into position. They were fiendishly effective, and could fire a 21cm or 30cm mortar shell some 8,580 yards, which was about 5 miles. They had an added psychological effect, in that they screamed as they hurtled over, which was why the Allies called them 'Moaning Minnies' or 'meemies'. The combination of mortars of varying kinds, machine guns and even limited artillery – and the Germans still had quite a lot – could very easily make short work of any infantry and tank advance.

In many ways, it was not so very different from getting up out of the trenches along the Western Front in the First World War and walking across no-man's-land. Infantry had to hope their accompanying armour could knock out targets such as machine-gun nests and mortar positions before being hit by the variety of anti-tank guns the Germans had available, and both armour and infantry had to hope that the combination of artillery, naval guns and air power could fulfil a combination of roles: knock out enemy gun positions and suppress fire-power, and keep the heads down of those Germans not hit by the barrage – which was most of them, because foxholes were very effective against shelling; usually only a direct hit would wound or kill anyone. No matter how effective the fire support, infantry and armour still had to take that leap of faith, get up and walk or trundle across open and inevitably exposed land. There was simply no way around it.

Nor was the number of infantry available ever quite as large as it might seem on paper. For EPSOM, the newly arrived VIII Corps would be leading the assault. This contained three divisions, although only one of infantry, the 15th Scottish Division, which was to be leading the advance. This division, like all British infantry divisions, had three brigades of around 3,500 men each, which in turn had at their core three battalions each of around 845 men. Every battalion, such as Robert Woollcombe's 6th King's Own Scottish Borderers, had four rifle companies of 120 men each, plus a support company of mortars and anti-tank guns and engineers. Each rifle company was in turn divided into three platoons of thirty-seven men and a company headquarters. Woollcombe was commander of one of the three platoons in A Company, and this was divided again into the smallest infantry unit in the British Army, the section, ten men strong and commanded by an NCO, usually a corporal. The remaining seven men of the platoon made up platoon headquarters, which included the commander and the platoon sergeant, and a mortar team, plus runner.

The company commanders were briefed at O Groups by the battalion CO and his staff, and it was then their job to brief platoon commanders and so on down the chain. Battalions would be given an objective: a village, a stream, a wood, or ridge – generally something that was challenging but achievable. Companies would then also be given specific objectives – the church in the village, or the farmhouse on the right-hand side of the village, for example. Maps were standardized, 1:25,000 in scale and blocked into a grid, an inch to each block and with each block numbered laterally and longitudinally, so objectives would be marked up in pencil or crayon on the map with a six-figure reference. Platoon commanders and platoon sergeants would both have such maps. Company HQ – which would be on the move during an attack – would be equipped with a radio set with a frequency tuned in to battalion headquarters, which would in turn be linked to brigade headquarters. Making contact during the heat of battle could sometimes prove difficult as airwaves quickly became clogged.

The average rifleman would be told what his specific objective was, but how much of the bigger picture was explained would depend on what the platoon commander told him and how much the platoon commander himself had been briefed in the first place. Most soldiers had very little idea of the wider battle or of what was happening more than a few hundred yards – if that – either side of them. Once the platoons were out in the open, communication with the company headquarters was dependent on runners. The closer the attacking infantry drew to the enemy, the more smoke there would be. As the battle progressed, tanks, vehicles, guns and buildings would inevitably get hit and burn, which produced more smoke – often thick, choking smoke, which cloyed the throat, got into the lungs and made visibility hard, but which could also thin out and disappear incredibly quickly once troops were past it. Smoke hid targets, but the benefits of that could cut both ways. Battle could be incredibly confusing.

Generally, companies would move in platoons, which would in turn move in sections, the ten men usually spread 5–10 yards apart, one Bren-gun team per section. A report written after the Sicilian campaign noted that very rarely did British and German machine guns fire at the same time, which suggests machine-gunners would fire a burst, then get their heads down while the opposition fired back. Suppressing machine-gun and small-arms fire therefore helped, but if a mortar landed near where a section was advancing, it was quite possible for half or all of the section to be killed or wounded. Just like that. When attacking it was easy for both infantry and armour to take truly appalling numbers of casualties very quickly, and among those parts of the army casualties were proportionally every bit as high, and frequently higher, than they had been on the Western Front in 1914–18.

EPSOM was to be launched by two of the 15th Scottish Division's brigades moving forward supported by Churchill tanks of the 31st Armoured Brigade. Again, on paper, two brigades sounds quite a lot: six battalions, 5,400 men and three armoured regiments of fifty tanks each. However, a brigade would only ever attack with two of the three battalions – one would always be in reserve – so there were only four battalions attacking, not six. On top of that, 10 per cent would always be 'LOB' – left out of battle – in case the worst happened and the battalion was destroyed. This meant there would still be a cadre from the battalion around which it could be re-formed. Battalions adopted the same policy, with three companies forward and one in reserve, which meant that the lead elements of an attacking infantry division had, in fact, been whittled down to about 2,000 men, not 5,400, which wasn't very many from a division of 15,000. The same principle applied to the armoured regiment, so that instead of having 150 tanks in support there would be more like 80.

Reserve battalions and companies might still be introduced swiftly into the battle, but leading elements could easily be rapidly reduced by 50 per cent or more, with, as a very rough rule of thumb, a third of that number killed and the rest wounded or taken prisoner. The aim was to get to the German positions and grind them down in turn before the lead infantry and armoured units were too badly mauled themselves. Leading infantry battalions in a major set-piece battle would usually be relieved within twenty-four hours and replaced by follow-up brigades. Any major assault therefore needed strength in depth and preferably support on the flanks.

Nor should it be forgotten that, no matter how well trained or led the lead infantry units were, most were conscripts who had no desire whatsoever to be there and whose chances of living or being wounded or killed by a shard of flying shrapnel were, for the most part, entirely random. Whether soldiers were from a Western democracy or a totalitarian militaristic state, their commanders expected a lot of them. Any criticism directed at the fighting prowess of either side has to be tempered by acknowledging this, and also by understanding the terrain over which they were fighting, because advancing over the wide open fields to the west of Caen, with German eyes on literally every movement, was going to be no picnic whatsoever, no matter how many guns, warships and aircraft the Allies had in support. Marching towards the enemy as one of the lead infantry companies or in a leading Churchill tank was a very lonely place to be.

Monday, 26 June, around 3 a.m. Incessant, drizzling rain filled the pitch-black air as the 6th King's Own Scottish Borderers reached forward assembly area just beyond Secqueville and began digging shallow pits against the threat of enemy counter-battery fire. Lieutenant Robert Woollcombe huddled in his hastily dug scrape alongside his batman – his soldier-servant – covered in a gas cape against the rain. Two hours later, they were called to get up. A petrol cooker was blowing in a nearby barn and breakfast was being prepared for the men of A Company. Inside, the men huddled, not saying very much. This was the day. In a few hours' time they would finally be going into battle. Outside, it was getting light and the rain had finally stopped, although the landscape beyond, over which they would soon be advancing, was covered in mist. They cursed it; mist and low cloud were no good for the tactical air forces. Green camouflage paint was liberally handed out, weapons were checked and rechecked, magazines loaded and bayonets fixed to the end of rifles. Extra rations – tins of bully beef – were loaded into the smaller haversacks they carried, cigarettes put into top pockets. 'Everyone admirably controlled,' wrote Woollcombe, 'but an air of tension about them.' No one really knew what to expect.

Woollcombe watched the minute hand on his wrist watch reach 7.30. Right on cue, all 700 guns opened fire along with the naval guns off shore. They were guns of differing calibres, some concealed in fields just behind them, and the noise was immense, indescribable. The ground shook, as though shivering from the weight of the onslaught. 'Little rashes of goose flesh ran over the skin,' noted Woollcombe. 'One was hot and cold, and very moved. All this "stuff" in support of us! Every single gun at maximum effort to kill; to help us.' Everyone was smoking; it was steadying. Woollcombe wondered whether he ought to be giving his men some heroically inspirational pep-talk but realized words were totally superfluous.

Soon they were off, moving up behind the 8th Royal Scots and heading down a rough road as though on exercise. No counter-battery fire whistled over, but then their own guns stopped and Woollcombe felt a cold sensation in the pit of his stomach. Up ahead were the 12. SS. Just the name 'SS' was enough to inspire fear. The Canadians had already told them the SS men took no prisoners. It was as though they were going into battle against an entirely different breed of man, and a terrifying breed at that.

They now reached the shattered remains of Bretteville-l'Orgueilleuse, crossed the main Caen–Bayeux road and headed on towards Norrey-en-Bessin, past charred Shermans and blown-up Carriers and into a field that was to be their forming-up place. From behind, the guns thundered again and shells whistled over then exploded somewhere up ahead in a part of Normandy now riven by the chaos of war. Mist still shrouded the landscape. Not a single aircraft flew above them. Suddenly, swirling black puffs of smoke dotted the sky, followed by the rippling cracks of explosions as the sound caught up. German air-bursts – shells that exploded above the ground, showering jagged shrapnel. Major Gilbertson, the company commander, ordered them to lie down and then, when the shelling stopped, they moved on once more just as a bedraggled group of SS prisoners was marched past – helmetless, bewildered and sullen-looking youths in grimy camouflage smocks.

*

A couple of miles to the west, XXX Corps' MARTLET attack continued in a confusion of mist, rain and smoke. That same morning, A Squadron of the Sherwood Rangers moved through the shattered remnants of Fontenay. Leading them through the southern end was their new commander, Major John Semken, who turned a corner only to come face to face with one of the few Tigers now in Normandy. Fortunately, he had an armour-piercing round already in place and his gunner hit it at 30 yards, then followed up with six more in quick succession. All of them bounced off, but one hit the turret ring, disabling it in the process; quick firing and a gyro gun stabilizer were two great advantages of the Sherman's 75mm gun, even if it did lack the velocity of the best German tanks. At any rate, the Tiger crew quickly bailed out. 'I happened to be following,' noted Christopherson, 'talking to Brigade Headquarter on the wireless – in fact, John had just passed me, which was indeed most fortunate, otherwise the Tiger and I would have met and the result might have been very different.' The Sherwood Rangers pushed on, Sergeant Dring, their ace, knocking out four further tanks as they pressed on towards Rauray, 1½ miles from Fontenay.

Standartenführer Meyer, who had been planning a major counter-attack, was now facing the second thrust of EPSOM. Hastily issuing new orders, he cancelled this operation and told Obersturmbannführer Max Wünsche, the commander of SS-Panzergrenadier-Regiment 26, to hold Rauray, to which the Sherwood Rangers and infantry were advancing, at all costs. At his CP at Verson, he could hear his own artillery firing furiously. The situation was desperate. By field telephone one of Meyer's commanders was saying his anti-tank guns had been destroyed and that his men were being overrun by tanks and infantry at Cheux, when the line went dead as the wire was cut. His chief of staff pleaded with I. SS-Panzerkorps for help. The positions must be defended to the last round, came the reply; they were to fight for time, but II. SS-Panzerkorps was on its way and would be arriving soon. 'As so often in the past,' noted Meyer bitterly, 'command and control was being exercised from a tactical perspective and not strategic considerations.'

Meanwhile, the 6th KOSB were now advancing across fields towards Saint-Manvieu, C Company on the left, B behind a little on the right and A Company in the middle. Lieutenant Robert Woollcombe's 7 Platoon was in the lead and he was with the leading section, his runner beside him, on the right of the company, as they waded through high, thick corn. Sergeant Duke's section was about 100 yards to the left, with Corporal Macbeth's behind them and, behind them, Corporal Tam McEwan's section and the rest of Platoon Headquarters. A few hundred yards further back was Major Gilbertson with the company radio set and signallers and 9 Platoon. Nice and well spread out. The guns had briefly stopped firing and occasional stabs and burps of small arms could be heard somewhere up ahead. 8 Platoon overcame an isolated position of SS men, who, still stunned from the barrage, surrendered. Reaching a hedge, 7 Platoon stopped. In the field beyond were a number of pale objects – human faces? Germans? They fired a few bursts on the Bren then realized they were some of their own dead. Woollcombe felt sick. They advanced again and reached their first objective, the dried-up river bed of the Mue. Ahead, the Royal Scots were pushing into the hamlet of La Gaule with Churchill tanks, while the Royal Scots Fusiliers away to their left had reached the edge of Saint-Manvieu. In the next field, Woollcombe's men found a number of dead Germans, whom they all paused to look at with a mixture of curiosity and horror. One of them was blond and good-looking. Woollcombe had never seen a dead body up close before.

'Look,' one of his men said, having rifled through the dead man's possessions, 'he's only seventeen!'

They paused again and Gilbertson ordered Woollcombe to take eight men and patrol forward looking for snipers. Setting off through the corn, well spaced out, they worked their way along a hedgerow until they were several hundred yards from the rest of the company. Suddenly Private Black fired a short burst from his Bren. Woollcombe froze as an SS man rose from the corn, charged at him, then fell at his feet. He had been hit in the shoulder, which was bleeding profusely.

'Don't shoot – don't shoot!' he implored. 'Have pity! Don't shoot!' They swiftly disarmed him. Woollcombe found it a very strange experience to stare down at this man clutching his legs and pleading for his life. 'One did not blame him for his terror,' he wrote. 'Nevertheless . . . one felt no compassion.' He looked dishevelled and unshaven, with his grubby fair hair and pale blue eyes. He was twenty years old.

'Well done, my boy,' said Gilbertson in an avuncular manner to Woollcombe when they returned with their wounded prize. 'It was the acme of praise,' noted Woollcombe. 'The prisoner was taken away.'

Three new SS panzer divisions were now converging towards the Caen battle front: 2. SS, 9. SS and 1. SS, although General Geyr von

Schweppenburg had planned to use them in the massed panzer counter-attack that was the only conceivable means of knocking back the Allies. This, however, could only happen if the panzer divisions already in the line and in action were relieved by the infantry and pulled back in order to reorganize themselves for a coordinated assault alongside the new-comers. The knowledge of these intentions was what made Montgomery press ahead with EPSOM despite the shortfall of men and materiel compared to his original plan. Ideally, he would have postponed EPSOM further, but there could be no more delaying.

In fact, on 26 June the planned relief of the Panzer-Lehr by the newly arrived 276. Infanterie-Division got under way. Hauptmann Helmut Ritgen's panzer battalion, however, remained at the front for the time being, subordinated to an infantry regiment from the 276. Division that had no combat experience. Two of his companies were spread out across the entire divisional front in a largely static anti-tank role. Ritgen hated it as much as Kurt Meyer did; it went against all the principles of mobile panzer warfare that panzer men, especially, regarded as the way armour should be used. Yet such was Allied fire-power, responding to almost every single sound with an instant reply of screaming shells and mortars, there was little for it but to stay put, hardly daring to breathe, let alone fire up their engines. As Hans Siegel had discovered, sitting in the cramped and deeply uncomfortable belly of a tank for long hours was debilitating in the extreme. Now it was the turn of Ritgen and his men to suffer the same.

So far, the morning had gone reasonably well for the British, despite the lack of air support and the dismal weather. Inevitably, not all the advancing troops had managed to keep up with the rolling barrage and some of the supporting tanks had become caught up in the enemy minefields. There were also errors in map-reading and confusion caused by the smoke, rain and the enormously disconcerting effects of advancing into a wall of fire. Communications between infantry and tanks continued to cause problems too – it wasn't only Stanley Christopherson who was finding this frustrating. Flame-throwing Crocodiles, those particularly brutal new weapons of war, were used very effectively in Saint-Manvieu. Not only did they cause huge damage, they also had a powerfully debilitating effect on the morale of the enemy – and no wonder. Being enveloped by flames of oil and rubber shooting out like a jet from a lumbering tank was not a good way to go.

The action was by no means one-sided, however. Mortars, *Nebel-werfers* and artillery, together with well-concealed machine guns, continued to take their toll, although first Saint-Manvieu and then Cheux were cleared. However, the advance was not quick enough to keep to the planned schedule for getting on to the high ground south of the River Odon, and by mid-morning General Dick O'Connor was already wondering how to maintain momentum. Back in 1940, when he had commanded the Western Desert Force in Egypt, his small army of just 36,000 men had routed two Italian armies of 160,000 and he had done so by employing speed of manoeuvre and tactical flexibility and flair. O'Connor was not an unimaginative commander. Waiting in reserve was the 11th Armoured Division, who were designed, trained and ready for rapid breakout operations once the infantry and armour had smashed a hole in the German lines. However, O'Connor decided to throw them into the fray now – or one armoured battalion at any rate – to provide the impetus and drive to get EPSOM to its objective before the Germans could properly reorganize themselves.

Major-General 'Pip' Roberts, at thirty-seven the youngest general in the British Army and commander of 11th Armoured, was highly sceptical about this early use of his division; although the enemy had been driven out, Cheux had become a choke-point blocked with rubble and battle debris, while the roads leading down to the river were also narrow, winding and clogged with war wreckage. Moving rapidly with overwhelming force was going to be next to impossible. Still, O'Connor reckoned he needed more armour up front and so the 2nd Northamptonshire Yeomanry, 11th Armoured's reconnaissance battalion, was sent forward, starting its advance at 12.50 p.m.

Corporal Reg Spittles had been rudely awakened that morning by the opening of the barrage, which was firing all around him; their tanks were right next to a battery of 25-pounders. Hurriedly, he and his crew clambered into their Cromwell and hastily shut down the hatches to drown out the noise. His regiment's task that day was to hurry forward to the River Odon and occupy the three bridges, a troop on each, then report on the situation by radio. It all sounded so simple and was the kind of mission they had practised countless times. In England, though, villages and towns were always intact, but in Normandy they had already been reduced to rubble and passing through them, despite the enormous speed of the Cromwell, was no easy task. It took an hour and a half for them to get through Cheux and, while doing so, A Squadron's second-in-command, Captain Wyvell Raynsford, was shot and killed by a sniper, as was the FOO – the artillery forward observation officer – attached to them. At one point, as they became stationary, German troops rushed the tanks, hurling grenades. From the turret, Spittles lobbed out phosphorus grenades, then, once they had exploded, used the smoke as cover to step out of the turret and spray the surrounding area with his Sten gun. 'It was a case of survival,' he noted. 'I was too young to die just yet!'

They pushed through Cheux, then the hamlet of Le Bosq and, using the Cromwell's speed, hurried on, spreading out in battle formation. No. 4 troop pressed ahead and reached the Odon, while 1 Troop was held up by a ditch. Spittles' 2 Troop was in reserve, so held back while 3 Troop continued through a cornfield. One moment 3 Troop were speeding towards a ridge of trees and bushes, the next two of their tanks had stopped and were brewing up. Spittles was shocked; he had never seen a tank on fire before. 'I just thought, "Bloody hell!"' he noted. But then Major Bobby Peel, the squadron commander, came over the radio and said, 'You see what's happened – get up there!'

'Hello, Baker,' the troop's commander, Lieutenant Hobson, said to Spittles, 'you heard that. Take the lead. Away you go.'

With no small amount of trepidation, they moved forward, Spittles using the smoke from the burning Cromwells as cover, then pushing on at Lieutenant Hobson's urging up and over the ridge. Suddenly, there was the Odon Valley spread before him, with a number of Panzer IVs and even a couple of Panthers moving from one position to another. Reporting what he could see to Hobson, the message was relayed back to Major Peel, who promptly said, 'Then shoot the bloody things!'

Spittles did as he was ordered, directing fire towards the enemy, and was soon after joined by the rest of the troop, while 4 Troop attacked several gun and mortar positions down by the river. Spittles reported destroying a Mk IV and a half-track, machine-gunning the occupants in the process, then the enemy appeared to withdraw. At around 5 p.m. they were ordered to pull back to their start position, so turned and rumbled off down the ridge, their turret traversed backwards, and picking up several wounded crew from the burning tanks on the way. Rain was now sheeting down. 'The absence of rocket-firing Typhoons,' noted the battalion diarist, 'and the lack of artillery support, due to the death of one FOO and poor wireless comms between the other FOO and the Arty Regts had an adverse effect on the whole op.' That was as may be, but as

Spittles had discovered, there was a very great difference between exercises and real combat. It was inevitable that things would go wrong, that people would be killed or wounded. Front-line combat was brutal, disorientating and difficult.

Although the Cromwells had reached the Odon, the British advance as a whole was by this time, late on 26 June, 2 miles short of the river. The 6th KOSB moved up into the shattered wreck of Saint-Manvieu, where they found twenty-eight men from the Scots Fusiliers, all that remained from the company that had crossed the start line earlier that morning; casualties included the company commander, who had been killed. Rumours abounded of enemy resistance stiffening and of an enemy counter-attack. C Company hastily moved into the centre of the village, while A Company were pulled back into a copse to the west. Soon after, they moved again, this time to a farm near the corner of the churchyard at Saint-Manvieu. Both church and farm had been badly smashed. 'The yard was a slough of refuse and decay,' wrote Woollcombe, 'and by the gate was a large iron cage. Inside, two huge black hounds were spread-eagled in death, their mouths crawling with flies and maggots; the wretched beasts, locked in and forsaken, the once savage guardians of their world. They capped the desolation, invoking mingled revulsion and pity.'

They remained at stand-to, waiting nervously for an attack. Shells still hurtled overhead in both directions, then the enemy began stonking the road junction about 100 yards ahead. Woollcombe's 7 Platoon HQ was now on the northern side of the church wall, where once again they furiously dug slit-trenches. Woollcombe had absolutely no idea of what was going on. Rain continued to fall. A little distance away, three dead Fusiliers sat leaned up against the wall, their deathly skin pale in the dusk. Their presence, the thought of the sprawled, maggot-chewed dogs, the continual crash of shells and the rain all helped to cast a leaden pall of depression upon him the like of which he had never experienced before. 'It seemed there was no hope or sanity left, but only this appalling unknown and unseen,' he wrote, 'in which life was so precious where all rotted, and where all was loneliness and rain. This was the war. It was bloody.' To make matters worse, Lieutenant Seyton of C Company was killed soon after, shot through the brain by a sniper while on his rounds.

The promised counter-attack finally happened a little later, mostly against C Company. Meanwhile, A Company sat tight as British artillery responded furiously. Eventually, the fighting died away and the SS men

Amis were right upon our heels.' Hordes of men were hurrying towards the last bridge across the River Vire, a mile or so to their west; the road became clogged with troops and vehicles in full retreat, desperate to cross the bridge before it was blown by the engineers. Miraculously, they were not spotted by the *Jabos* and most managed to pull back safely. In fact, Wegner and his comrades in Grenadier-Regiment 914 were then ordered to halt and dig in around the village of La Meauffe, which was actually just before the bridge across the Vire. By dusk, the panic had subsided.

Their attackers had been 2nd Battalion of the 116th, with the 1st Battalion and Company D on their left, pushing through Couvains. Moving up along high hedgerows, Bob Slaughter and his men crossed hurriedly abandoned German trenches until up ahead they saw the steeple of Couvains' church. Suddenly, artillery shells and mortar fire started falling around them. Slaughter dived into a ditch for cover and when the shelling stopped he dusted himself down only to see a German arm, still in its sleeve, lying beside him. Trying not to think too hard about it, he got his men moving again and was approaching a gap in the hedgerow when he heard someone moaning. Stepping forward he came face to face with a German paratrooper – one of Johannes Börner's comrades from 3. Fallschirmjäger; Couvains was on the boundary between them and the 352. Division. The man had been badly hit by shrapnel in the upper thigh and, assuming he was staring down at a fanatical Nazi paratrooper, Slaughter's first thought was to end it there and then.

'*Kamerad, bitte*,' mumbled the man, who, Slaughter realized, was probably as young as he. Back on Omaha, Slaughter had told himself not to take any prisoners, but the wounded man looked filthy and desperate. 'That was then, this is now,' thought Slaughter. 'I couldn't just shoot a wounded human being at point-blank range.' Crouching down, he tied a tourniquet around the German's thigh, applied sulfa powder, gave him a drink of water and lit a Lucky Strike for him.

'*Danke*,' said the man, smiling weakly. 'God bless. *Guten* luck.'

They left him and pressed on through the village. The platoon sergeant was badly wounded, while Sergeant Romeo Bily had been killed instantly when a sniper's bullet hit him between the eyes. Shelling continued with unerring accuracy, which meant a spotter was watching their every move. Obviously, the man was up in the church steeple and only once the spire was destroyed were they able to clear the village and push on south.

Despite this, by dusk on the 18th the Americans had made only limited gains. They had successfully crossed the River Elle, but the high ground eluded them and, with heavy casualties, there was nothing for it but to pause, dig in and bring up reinforcements for another push.

While fighting raged near Saint-Lô and on the Cotentin, King George VI had been the next VIP to visit Normandy, reaching the beaches on Friday, 16 June. It was another disruption for Montgomery, but certainly a more welcome guest than de Gaulle had been and unquestionably a morale-booster for the British and Canadian troops. While the British monarch was touring the Normandy invasion front and being entertained by Montgomery at Château de Creullet, Feldmarschall Rommel was once again speeding from one headquarters to another, and in between desperately trying to secure more supplies and replacements.

His number-one concern that Friday, however, was the fate of the Cotentin Peninsula, which he accepted would now inevitably fall. On one level, it was possible to look at a map, as Hitler was doing back in Berchtesgaden, and think the situation did not seem too bad: after all, some seven divisions were arrayed against just four American. However, those German units were in a pitiful shape, with mounting losses and no replacements coming through. Facing the American drive north were the remnants of three divisions, with the 77. Infanterie furthest to the west and so, of the three, the only one that might reasonably be able to escape back to the south before the Americans cut the peninsula. Rommel now issued orders for 77. Division to fight and hold out as long as possible, but then to make sure they withdrew south to safety.

No sooner had Rommel made this decision than an order arrived from Hitler himself insisting the 77. Division must not retreat under any circumstances but must keep fighting for Cherbourg instead. Later, a further *Führerbefehl* – order from the Führer – reached Heeresgruppe B: the line to the south of Cherbourg was to be defended at all costs. No retreat to the fortress of Cherbourg was to be allowed.

On every level this was a ridiculous order. Hitler had always placed enormous faith in the concept of 'will'. Willpower alone, he believed, could achieve anything. All the German troops now defending the Cotentin needed to succeed was self-belief. It was, of course, fantastical nonsense; this was the same day the Americans broke through at the key town of Saint-Sauveur-le-Vicomte, two-thirds of the way across the pulled back. Around midnight, men of the 43rd Wessex Division, including the 4th Dorsets, arrived to relieve them. The 6th KOSB pulled back, marching through the rain to the comparative safety of a couple of miles back. Sergeant Walter Caines of the Dorsets had spent much of the afternoon getting ready to move into the line. 'Transport had to be marshalled,' he wrote, 'wireless gear had to be checked, batteries issued, and numerous arrangements had to be made as no-one knew quite what to expect.' And all this done while the rain continued to pour down.

It had also been a sobering day for Obersturmführer Hans Siegel and his 8. Panzerkompanie, who had been supporting the panzer-grenadiers in the battle raging around Fontenay and Rauray; he had lost several of his tanks in the process. Early that evening, Siegel was hastily refuelling and re-arming four Panzer IVs at a dump just to the north-east of Rauray when he was met by Obersturmbannführer Max Wünsche, the regimental commander, who told him to clear up a very recent breakthrough south-east of Cheux at Le Bosq. The 12. SS were straddling both MARTLET and EPSOM operations in a juggling act that saw their mobile forces speeding from one part of the battlefield to another, desperately trying to firefight and plug rapidly emerging gaps in the line. Siegel had only these four Panzer IVs available; they would have to do. A quick briefing of the crews followed, then it was back into their tanks, engines growling and hatches pulled down, Wünsche's good wishes swallowed up by the clanking and squeaking of the panzers as they got moving. They had all been in action virtually every day since 7 June and continually for over twenty-four hours. They were absolutely exhausted.

They set off across open fields with no cover at all, in a staggered formation with Siegel's tank leading. After just a couple of hundred yards, they spotted some British armoured vehicles and opened fire on the move, hitting and destroying three Carriers, each loaded with ammunition, which blew up angrily. Reaching a small copse in the lower ground that fell towards the River Odon, they rumbled forward and discovered an embankment the height of a man to the left of the road that ran south from Cheux to Grainville-sur-Odon. Up ahead, to the north, Siegel could see the smashed gables of Cheux, perhaps 1,500 yards away. This was perfect. Spacing the four Panzer IVs along this embankment so that just the turrets and the machine gun were above the mound and the rest of the body of the tank hidden below, he could not think of a better hull-down position.

Siegel jumped out of his tank and ordered a couple of his men to scout to the right, while he and his gunner carried out a quick recce to the left. They saw no one – just an abandoned *Kübelwagen* and, up ahead, to the right of the road, abandoned German guns with empty shell cases scattered around. It was eerily silent, but then Siegel spotted an earthen bunker and, with his gunner giving cover and his pistol at the ready, he approached the entrance. To his relief, he found a number of the gunners huddled there, out of ammunition and taking shelter.

Back at the tanks, the others had returned and reported grenadiers about 500 yards to the west, but not enough men to close the gap. This meant Siegel's four tanks would have to fill it. They were well placed: hull down, covering the road south and with excellent fields of fire. With dusk falling, they used one of the panzers to pull the abandoned guns back, along with the gunners, who now joined them by the hull-down panzers. 'This was done,' noted Siegel, 'as heavy rains sets in and under a pitch-black sky.' Siegel now took the *Kübelwagen* and sped to Grainville, where Wünsche had his CP in a farmhouse lit inside only with flickering candles. Cupboards had been pulled across the windows to protect them from shrapnel blast. Siegel was offered a mug of hot coffee. It tasted good. It was now nearly midnight.

Soon after, he was heading back to his four Mk IVs with fresh supplies of rations and ammunition for the guns. Making it safely back, he discovered the commander of the artillery, Sturmbannführer Schöps, was also there and Siegel was just talking to him when suddenly a British voice shouted out, 'Hands up!' and several figures jumped out of the trees and bushes. Clearly, a British fighting patrol had crept up on them and now had the startled group caught. But it was dark, and raining, and the German tank men and gunners dived for the cover of the commander's Mk IV as the Tommies opened fire. Only Siegel had the wherewithal to charge at the nearest, grabbing the British man's throat with his left hand and pushing away the gun barrel of his sub-machine gun with the other. As they both fell to the ground, the British man fired his entire magazine, but the bullets went harmlessly through Siegel's leather trousers without touching him at all.

With Siegel's hand still gripping the Tommy's throat, the man gasped, 'Help me! Help me!' Another figure – a second British soldier – now approached and fired, but hit his mate by mistake, not Siegel.

'Oh – I'm wounded!' the man on the ground groaned. Siegel pulled out his own pistol and fired it at the disappearing figure. He got himself back on to his feet, the Tommy now dead on the ground.

Suddenly there was silence but for the rain beating down on the leaves in the trees above. Siegel could feel the blood pulsing through his temples and staggered back to his panzer, only to discover Schöps crouching on his knees, gasping. Hurrying over to him, Siegel tried to lift him, but the Sturmbannführer merely slipped on his own blood. Dragging him to the cover of his panzer, Siegel looked around, wondering where the rest of his men in the other three panzers were – perhaps they had not heard the scuffle. Hurrying to the nearest, some 70 yards away, Siegel replaced the clip in his pistol as he ran. Nearing, he stopped again, momentarily paralysed as he saw two further Tommies silhouetted, standing on the panzer and pulling on the turret hatch, which was obviously being held down by the men on the inside. One of them said to the other, 'Hand grenade!'

Snapping himself out of his stupor, Siegel crept forward, the sound of his footsteps covered by the British soldiers on the tank and the sound of the rain. Slowly, he raised his arm, as he had practised on the firing range, and squeezed the trigger twice, one shot for each man. They fell just as the guard Siegel had set, finally woken by the pistol shots, fired his submachine gun at the turret. 'The crew inside the Panzer had been surprised by the scouting party creeping up,' wrote Siegel. 'No wonder: rain – exhaustion – midnight!' He was certainly not going to chastise them.

Siegel was just getting his breath back from the drama of the past few minutes when he heard the engine of his own panzer start up and, to his horror, saw and heard it pull out and retreat into the meadow behind, only for the engine to shut down again. Running after it, pistol at the ready, he wondered whether some other Tommies had captured it. As he neared, he crouched down, then crawled across the sodden ground to the rear exit hatch and tapped on it with his pistol grip. At first there was silence, then he called out the password and, to his great relief, heard the correct reply. It turned out the rest of crew, realizing there was trouble and with the whereabouts of their chief uncertain, thought they should get clear. There was also no sign of the gunner, but he eventually showed up half an hour later; he had been captured during the first scuffle, but in the dark and the rain had managed to make good his escape. Sturmbannführer Schöps, however, had bled to death, while several other of his men had been wounded.

What a night it had been for Siegel and his four panzers. It could have turned out so different. Siegel had been lucky – very lucky – to have escaped unscathed and with his tanks intact. Had the British patrol been successful, they would have cleared the gap in the line that had emerged earlier and which Siegel had managed to plug. As events turned out, however, the panzer commander was still alive and well, and his four tanks would be ready and waiting when dawn arrived the following morning, the second day of the EPSOM battle.

CHAPTER 23

Cherbourg and the Scottish Corridor

E VER SINCE D-DAY, THE 70th Tank Battalion had been attached to the US 4th Division, working their way northwards up the Cotentin Peninsula every step of the way with the infantry. In many ways, single tank battalions such as the 70th were operating much as the Sherwood Rangers and the British armoured regiments of the independent brigades. The problem was that the infantry regimental commander – or brigadier in the British instance – always outranked the half-colonel of the tank battalion or regiment. This meant tank units were always at the beck and call of the infantry. 'Send liaison officer to the 22nd Inf. at once to plan for the use of tanks during their attack today,' ran orders received by Lieutenant-Colonel John Welborn, the CO of the 70th, on 26 June. 'Report the number of tanks available for us w/the 22nd Inf. and # of tanks you recommend to be used.' There was no discussion, no debate. Welborn was being ordered to do so.

For the most part, the line of command was smooth enough and the tank men didn't mind playing second fiddle, but Sherman tanks were most effective when working hand in hand with the infantry, rather than as both scouts and fire-power. Sergeant Carl Rambo, for example, found that sometimes he simply had to refuse orders from infantry officers. On a number of occasions he had been ordered by the infantry to head down a road until they drew enemy fire. 'Now you didn't do that,' he said, 'unless you were in open country. Some did, but they aren't alive. You have to see what is ahead or have infantry spot a gun around the corner, or another tank.'

Usually, tank commander and infantry officer quickly learned how best to operate together, but the casualties among officers and senior NCOs were so high that no sooner was a relationship established than an officer would be killed or wounded and the process would have to start all over again, because one of the major weaknesses of Allied training was the lack of all-arms exercises. By and large, infantry, armour and artillery tended to train separately then learn on the job. It was a paradox that Allied troops should be so well and extensively trained in many areas – far more so than their German counterparts – and yet not at all in others.

During the battle for Cherbourg, Rambo's own Sherman and four others were fanned out as they supported an infantry attack against a machine-gun nest. All five tanks were hurling a lot of fire – high-explosive shells (HE) from the main 75mm gun as well as machine-gun fire – yet it didn't stop his own tank being hit by an enemy MG, the bullets pinging off his turret like hail off a tin roof. By now a veteran of two earlier campaigns in North Africa and Sicily, Rambo had experienced enough action to realize this didn't quite make sense. There was simply no way a lone German MG could be firing back after the saturation fire they been throwing their way. 'That machine-gun has got to be coming from a tank,' he radioed to the other four Sherman commanders. 'He's suckering us in. Be careful and don't move.'

Moments later, an infantryman ran over to warn him that a German panzer was approaching from behind, so his hunch had been right. Telling the others to hold firm, Rambo moved his own tank off, sheltering under some trees where he could see a little further and, sure enough, just around the corner was a panzer. Fortunately, a 57mm anti-tank gun was in position and able to knock it out, and the infantry and Shermans pressed on. Rambo and his fellow tankers in Company B were among the first into Cherbourg, although even as they reached the high ground overlooking the port and began picking their way into the outskirts, it was still a nerve-racking business being in a Sherman. In any building there could be a machine gun or enemy troops with *Panzerfausts*.

None the less, by Sunday, 25 June there were three US divisions surrounding Cherbourg, which was now being defended by remnants of the German 709. Division, a static infantry unit of low quality, as well as scratch groups from other divisions. It was Generalleutnant Karl-Wilhelm von Schlieben's misfortune to be commander of the 709. despite considerable experience as a panzer commander in France in 1940 and later on the Eastern Front; he had even commanded a panzer division at the Battle of Kursk, so the 709. Division had been something of a demotion. Then, on 23 June, he had been made Kommandant of Cherbourg, a poisoned chalice if ever there was one, and told to fight to the last man. 'Concentrated enemy fire and bombing attacks have split the front,' he signalled late on Saturday, 24 June. 'Numerous batteries have been put out of action or have worn out. Combat efficiency has fallen off considerably. The troops squeezed into a small area will hardly be able to withstand an attack on 25th.' The situation was hopeless.

On 25 June the US Navy brought up three battleships, four cruisers and screening destroyers to help bring the Cherbourg garrison to its knees while the three American divisions reached the edge of the town and began inching their way forward, clearing each street and strongpoint in turn. Later that day, General von Schlieben again appealed to Heeresgruppe B, pointing out that further fighting, and with it loss of life, would not change the outcome. Cherbourg was doomed. 'You will continue to fight until the last cartridge,' Rommel told him, 'in accordance with the order from the Führer.'

The following day, Monday, 26 June, the noose was tightened further around Cherbourg. Ernie Pyle had been attached to the 9th Division, one of the few veteran units in First Army. They had been in Tunisia, then Sicily, and, from what Pyle had seen of them over the past week, they had lost none of their fighting ability – as they had shown all too clearly in the swift severing of the Cotentin and since then in the drive north. Pyle thought they performed like a smooth machine, showing the tenacity to keep right at the neck of the enemy and never letting them regain balance after falling back. Now, on 26 June, he and two others, Charles Wertenbaker, a journalist for *Time*, and Robert Capa, the photographer for both *Time* and *Life* magazines, drove up to the CP of the 47th Infantry Regiment, now on the high ground overlooking the western side of the town and port. A number of prisoners were being brought in, many of them Russians fighting for the Wehrmacht. Below, there were some big fires in the town and rolling clouds of thick, black smoke rising upwards. Off shore, the big naval guns were hammering the enemy strongpoints, including the old forts and newer bunkers, all part of the Atlantic Wall. Guns fired, shells screamed, single rifle shots rang out and machine guns brrrped. 'The whole thing,' noted Pyle, 'made me tense and jump. The nearest fighting Germans were only 200 yards away.'

While they were still at the CP, Lieutenant Orion Shockley, the executive officer of Company B of the 47th Infantry, arrived. Despite the bruising sky, he was wearing a trench coat and, rather incongruously, dark glasses.

'Our company is starting in a few minutes to go up this road and clean out a strong point,' he said. 'There are probably snipers in some of the houses along the way. Do you want to go with us?'

Pyle most certainly didn't, but found himself saying, 'Sure.' Capa and Wertenbaker also agreed to come. So they set off, walking at the head of the company alongside Shockley. Pyle found himself ducking involuntarily when their own shells screamed over. Most of the men had two weeks' growth of beard and uniforms that were grubby and torn. They all looked exhausted and as though they had aged since landing in Normandy.

'Why don't you tell the folks back home what this is like?' said one of the men to Pyle. 'They don't know that for every hundred yards we advance somebody gets killed.' Pyle explained that he tried to do that all the time, but didn't push it; he understood – the fellow was exhausted, had seen too much action and too many of his pals fall. It was no wonder he was bitter. They paused by a small farm at the very edge of town and, with maps, Shockley explained how they were going to attack a series of concrete bunkers and machine-gun nests, which were at the end of a street on the edge of town. Behind was a hillside and farmland.

'A rifle platoon goes first,' he told them. 'Right behind them will go part of a heavy-weapons platoon, with machine guns to cover the first platoon. Then comes another rifle platoon. Then a small section with mortars, in case they run into something pretty heavy. Then another rifle platoon. And bringing up the rear, the rest of the heavy-weapons outfit to protect us from behind. We don't know what we'll run into, and I don't want to stick you right out in front, so why don't you come along with me?'

'Okay,' agreed Pyle, who by this time had stopped feeling scared.

They were about to start when suddenly cannon shells whipped and hissed over their heads. Everyone crouched beside a wall as more 20mm shells began hitting the farmhouse. The farmer, who moments earlier had been nonchalantly hitching up his horses, now fled. In his driveway were two dead Americans and a German. The shelling stopped and the order was given to get moving, out of the protection of the wall, across a small culvert and then right into the road. Shockley was yelling at the men. 'Spread it out now. Do you want to draw fire on yourselves?' he shouted. 'Don't bunch up like that. Keep five yards apart. Spread it out, dammit.'

Some men had Garand rifles, others had grenades at the ready, while several had the big Browning automatic rifles. One man carried a bazooka. Medics were interspersed among the men. They all seemed hesitant and cautious, more like the hunted than the hunters as far as Pyle could tell. 'They weren't warriors,' he wrote. 'They were American boys who by mere chance of fate had wound up with guns in their hands, sneaking up a death-laden street in a strange and shattered city in a far-away country in driving rain. They were afraid, but it was beyond their power to quit.' As usual, Pyle was unerringly observant and spot on.

Pyle made his own dash for it, safely reaching the street. The troops were hugging the walls on each side and he followed. Most of the house windows were shattered and there were bullets and cannon shell holes all over the place. Telephone wire lay everywhere, twisted and ugly. Some dogs suddenly tore down the street, barking and snarling. The street was winding, but soon they began to hear firing from up ahead – single shots, steady machine guns and the rapid brrupp of the German MGs. Word came back that the street had been cleared and a hospital liberated, which included a number of wounded Americans. Lieutenant Shockley, Pyle, Capa and Wertenbaker went on down the street and reached the hospital. Beyond, there appeared to be more fighting, although it was hard to tell what was happening; there would be some shooting, then an inexplicable lull, then some more.

In a street beyond the hospital, Pyle came across two Shermans, one 50 yards beyond the other. Pyle scurried towards the lead tank and was only some 50 feet from it when it fired its 75mm gun. 'The blast was terrific there in the narrow street,' he recorded. 'Glass came tinkling down from nearby windows, smoke puffed around the tank, and the empty street was shaking and trembling with the concussion.' Pyle ducked into a doorway, figuring the enemy would likely fire back. And so they did, just as the lead Sherman was backing down the road. A yellow flame pierced the belly of the tank with an immense crash. A second shot whammed into the pavement next to it. Smoke engulfed it, but it didn't burst into flames and a moment later the crew bailed out and sprinted manically for Pyle's doorway. The five men were all safe and began jabbering excitedly, relieved at their lucky escape. This was the third time they had had their tank knocked out and each time it had been swiftly repaired and put back into action. They had named it *Be Back Soon*. This time they had been hit on one of the tracks and now they began to worry because they had left the engine running. Eventually, when the firing seemed to have died down, they sneaked out, looked at the damage and one of them clambered back in to turn it off. Up ahead, a German truck stood in the middle of the road, blackened and burned. Not a soul could be seen. Everyone had vanished, but then an American infantryman came running up the street yelling for a medic and pretty soon one appeared from another building. Pyle followed and saw, on the corner, the remains of a smashed pillbox and another one beyond that – these were what the Shermans had been firing at and they had destroyed them both before being hit in turn by a third, beyond that.

There was now a lull in the fighting as infantrymen cleared each of the houses, working their way up from the ground floor first. Pyle followed. Puddles lay in the middle of the road, the few shops were boarded up and then, suddenly, walking towards them past the wrecked truck came a small column of Germans with an officer at the front waving a white flag – the men from the last strongpoint. Robert Capa sneaked out and took a photograph. American infantrymen, still on high alert, stood in doorways clutching their weapons and looking around them, but they let the Germans, some carrying two wounded on stretchers, walk on past them to the hospital. The objectives had been successfully taken and mercifully, on this occasion, without too many casualties.

Later that day, von Schlieben, Konteradmiral Walter Hennecke, the German Naval Commander, Normandy, and some 800 troops all surrendered; after that, most organized resistance ceased. Even so, in the western side of the city there was still the mighty thick-walled arsenal to overcome. The following morning, 27 June, the 47th Infantry were due to launch an assault with three battalions but, after an ultimatum was broadcast to the defenders, white flags appeared and a further 400 men surrendered. It was a significant victory for the Americans.

With the MARTLET and EPSOM battles raging, the 101st Hospital near Bayeux was filling up quickly. On her particular ward, Mary Mulry was now overseeing some thirty-five patients, including Germans, Welsh, Londoners, Poles, a couple of Free French, a civilian member of the Résistance, one Latvian and two Americans. Her friend Chezzy was proving a great help translating. 'Hans brings me a cup of tea as I sit at my desk to read the night report,' she wrote in her diary. 'This multi-national microcosm of a Europe at war is interesting and sad.' She had overheard a wounded Cockney say, 'Thanks, mate,' to Hans as he handed him a mug of tea and fixed his pillows. 'Why are they all so tolerant of each other inside this canvas tent, and killing each other outside?'

A couple of days later, a new consignment of battledress and also khaki knickers arrived; these were from the many thousands of different supplies that had to be delivered to waiting ships on the south coast of England, then taken across the Channel, unloaded and transported to the right location in a field in the middle of Normandy. Yet the system was working, despite the ever-urgent need for more tanks, shells, ammunition and gargantuan amounts of rations to feed hundreds of thousands of men each day. 'These pants are hilarious, huge and elasticated at the waist and legs,' noted Mary, 'but we could hardly have expected army supplies to have equipped us with glamour cami-knickers. It will be blissful to feel clean.'

On the 27th, a badly wounded young Englishman reached the 101st Hospital in a terrible state. Blind, stinking, covered in gunshot and shrapnel wounds, 'Len' none the less barely stopped talking, and quite cheerfully too, as Mary and her friend Taffy worked on cutting him out of his uniform. 'He completely ignores the appalling state he is in,' she noted. 'The British are renowned for the stiff upper lip but this is ridiculous.'

He told them what had happened to him. On D-Day, he had nearly drowned after being knocked into the sea. Someone had dragged him out of the water and he had collapsed on the sand next to a dead German. He had been fighting ever since. Then that day they had been attacking and he had dived into what he thought was a German slit-trench only to discover it was an enemy latrine. Moments later, a shell landed nearby, blinding him and spattering him with shrapnel. 'Although he is too shocked to realise it yet,' wrote Mary, 'most of his right leg has been blown off. His face is completely blackened from impacted shrapnel.' He had managed to crawl out of the latrine and take shelter by a British tank, shouting for help as he did so. Someone came to his rescue and together they tied a tourniquet around his thigh. He was then strapped to the bonnet of a Jeep, which was very bumpy, until another shell screamed over and blew the Jeep off the road, with Len still strapped to it. The Jeep was somehow righted and, incredibly, Len, still alive, was brought to the tented hospital. 'I fix him up with intravenous plasma and give him a shot of morphine,' wrote Mary. 'He will need sleep to prepare for major surgery in the morning.'

*

Only a dozen miles or so from the 101st Hospital, the fighting continued for that other Allied objective, Caen. By midnight on the 26th, Standartenführer Kurt Meyer had been feeling desperate. Earlier, when he had seen the slaughter of his young grenadiers, he had been unable to stop the tears streaming down his face. 'The heavy fighting,' he wrote, 'had caused high and irreplaceable losses. A breakthrough could not be prevented unless we had new units.' Those units were on their way: II. SS-Panzerkorps, with 2., 9. and 10. SS-Panzer-Divisions were all closing in, but, realistically, it would be the day after tomorrow before they could actively enter the fray. That meant 12. SS had to hold out along with support from 1. SS on their right and elements of Panzer-Lehr and 276. Infanterie for another day at least. That was a big ask, as Meyer was keenly aware.

His only cause for solace was the reappearance of his valet, Michel, a Cossack who had loyally stuck with him for several years. Michel arrived with a letter from Meyer's wife telling him she was pregnant with their fifth child. New life was developing among all this death, but by the following morning, 27 June, the desperation of the situation returned with vivid clarity with the onset of heavy British shelling.

Just a few miles to the north-west of Meyer's CP, Obersturmführer Hans Siegel's four panzers were still in position and had now, by first light, improved their situation further by spreading themselves out behind the embankment they had discovered the previous evening. In the grey light of dawn, Siegel could see it was actually a dried creek, known locally as the Ruisseau de Sabley, which straddled the Cheux–Grainville road and was, by chance, the most obvious axis of advance for the British as they resumed their efforts to cross the Odon and reach the high ground of Hill 112. It really was the ideal defensive position and, while four Panzer Mk IVs hardly constituted a major defence force, their hull-down position, machine guns and 75mm main guns presented a formidable obstacle to any British troops trying to get past them.

Siegel was already up and about, out of his panzer after only snatched moments of sleep, and checking what troops were on their flanks. He found the first some 300 yards to the left and tried to reassure them. Heading back, he was approaching the first panzer when enemy shells screamed over – a dawn chorus laid on just for him, it seemed. Fortunately, all fell wide and, although some hit the tree tops behind, most landed harmlessly in the wet soil. Then, to his horror, his men started up their tanks and began moving out. Only after he had run around waving his arms furiously did they stop. Rather apologetically, they explained that with him gone and under attack, they thought they ought to pull out. Siegel immediately ordered them back; they had a British advance to halt and they were most certainly not going to cut and run.

They were back in position in the nick of time, because up ahead a British attack was beginning. Now back in his panzer and connected to the other three by their radio sets, Siegel told his men to wait for the Tommy infantry to get close and then to use only the MGs – and on his command only; he didn't want to betray their presence by the use of their main guns. 'We let them come close and then hammer,' noted Siegel, 'at short distance, concentrated fire from four machine guns at the massed attackers.' In moments, the enemy infantry was pulling back, turning in panic. Soon after, tanks appeared and Siegel gave the order for them to open up with their main guns. Several British were hit and the rest pulled back, disappearing behind the crest of the rise.

As the sun came up, Siegel spotted movement away to his right. Fearing an outflanking manoeuvre, he decided to risk moving his panzer from its concealed position in order to get a better view. Having moved out, he peered through his field glasses and saw a group of Tommies dropping heavy packs on the ground; he couldn't understand what they were doing, but then one of his panzers fired, the shell tearing into them, a massive explosion and men cartwheeling into the air. So, thought Siegel, they were engineers handling explosive charges.

Meanwhile, Kurt Meyer had ordered some seventeen Panthers to counter-attack towards Cheux. Shorn of infantry, the Panthers were operating largely on their own and hit a wall of British anti-tank guns that were ready and waiting. For all the notoriety of the German 88mm gun, the British 17-pounder had an even higher velocity and at ranges of up to 1,400 yards could stop a Panther in its tracks – as they did this morning. The destruction of the Panthers and the failure of the 12. SS counter-attack illustrated yet again the huge difficulty of making any ground when on the offensive; in the Panther and Tiger the Germans might have had superior tanks in terms of fire-power and thickness of armour, but the British could bring to bear considerably more high-velocity guns of a similar potency.

The only slight solace for Meyer was the escape of some twenty men from his engineer battalion, which had been largely decimated the previous evening; the Panther attack had allowed the shattered survivors to avoid certain capture. Their commander, Sturmbannführer Müller, had reported to Meyer at the division CP soon after. 'His deep, sunken eyes told all,' noted Meyer. 'He no longer had an undamaged bit of uniform on him. His knees were bloody and lacerated; his face was hardly recognisable under the dust. One arm was in an improvised sling.'

Obersturmführer Hans Siegel and his four panzers were still successfully holding the line south of Cheux, however, when at 10.30 a.m. yet another assault wave of British infantry and armour pressed forward – the fourth of the day. Soon they were firing both their machine guns and main guns and, fully occupied with the attack up ahead, neither Siegel nor anyone in his crew spotted the outflanking manoeuvre away to the right. A lone British tank managed to get close enough to fire at the side of Siegel's panzer and an anti-tank shell suddenly ripped through the lower right-hand side. Frantically, Siegel ordered the turret to traverse to three o'clock, but while it was still moving a second shell slammed into them, hitting them front-right, and immediately the panzer was engulfed in flames. Hatch covers opened, the gunner bailing out to the left in flames, the loader to the right. Siegel tried to climb through the top of the turret but was caught by the throat by his microphone wire. Increasingly frantic, with flames licking the inside of the tank and choking smoke rapidly filling the belly of the beast, he tried to escape through the side hatch but bumped heads violently with the radio operator, who had had the same idea because his own hatch was blocked by the half-traversed gun. Pushing the radio operator through the hatch, Siegel was then engulfed in flames for a second or two before following, jumping to freedom only to nearly hang himself from the microphone wire. Dangling from the side skirt of the tank, thrashing for his life, he finally managed to snap the wire and collapse to the ground. Only the driver, Sturmmann Schleweis, was unable to escape, burning in the inferno, while the gunner, lying on the ground in flames, was leaped on by the others and the fire smothered. That Siegel was not more badly burned was entirely down to the leather clothing they were wearing, which had been purloined by Wünsche just for his own men. 'It was booty from Italian navy supplies,' noted Siegel, 'and saved the lives of quite a few men.' His own included. They now looked on as spectators while the remaining three panzers continued to hit British tanks and once again forced them back. For the fourth time that day, just four Panzer IVs had repulsed British efforts to reach the Odon.

With the battle dying down once more, Siegel handed command to his senior NCO and drove himself and his wounded crew in the

Kübelwagen back to the CP in Grainville. There he reported once more to Wünsche, who slapped him on the back as a medic gave him a pain-killing injection of morphine. Siegel would soon be back, but his burns were bad enough to keep him out of the battle for the time being. By then, however, seventeen Panthers had arrived and more panzer divisions were fast approaching the front.

A couple of miles to the north, the 6th KOSB were bivouacked in a field north of Cheux. Lieutenant Robert Woollcombe had been put in charge of a burial party; for sanitary reasons as much as anything, the dead were buried swiftly, in mass graves. Most were Highlanders. He found one officer, a young platoon commander like himself, looking slightly surprised and without a mark on him except for a dark stain near his kidneys. In his breast pocket was a slab of chocolate and a photo of his wedding, taken just before the invasion. Another man had a neat hole in his forehead, blue eyes still staring in amazement. Others were more badly smashed about. There were Germans too. It was a grim business.

That same day, the 43rd Wessex Division began moving in and taking over positions from the Canadians who had been holding the line a little to the east of the main EPSOM attack. The 4th Dorsets, though, were for the time being in reserve. Sergeant Walter Caines was among the lead units as they moved up a little after 9 a.m. Getting the battalion communications up and running was a priority. Caines drove up on his motorbike to the new battalion CP, which was in a farmhouse, and, with the signal truck arriving shortly after, began setting up the signals office in a barn so that field telephone lines and radios were in good working order within an hour. Everyone at Battalion HQ was wondering when the enemy would start shelling them as the Canadians had warned, but the Germans, it seemed, were holding on to their ammunition that morning. Instead, it was their own artillery that opened fire first. 'This was the first time we had heard such a thunderous barrage from our own guns,' wrote Caines. 'It kept up all day and at times one could hardly hear oneself speak.'

Later that day, Meyer's 12. SS lost Rauray, although not the Rauray Ridge, which still lay tantalizingly just out of reach for the attackers. A basic rule of thumb was that, the more dominant a piece of ground, the heavier it would be defended precisely because it was dominant. And because high ground meant the occupiers had eyes on anyone trying to approach, it was accordingly much harder to capture. The Sherwood

Rangers were once more in the thick of the action that day, although casualties were mounting again. With the infantry, they managed to battle their way into Rauray by around midday, discovering a number of abandoned and knocked-out enemy tanks, including Panthers, Mk IVs and even a Tiger, hidden among some scrub, and apparently completely undamaged. Christopherson found a crew who had earlier lost their own Sherman and, having painted out the German crosses and replaced them with their own fox's head, added it to the regiment's arsenal. Sadly for the Sherwood Rangers, however, XXX Corps HQ swiftly claimed it instead to send back to England. The Sherwood Rangers were most put out. Christopherson was even more distressed by the losses, including several officers and men who had been with him and the regiment since 1939. 'The capture of Fontenay and Rauray,' he wrote, 'had proved most costly. B Squadron could now only muster two officers and only seven out of their sixteen tanks.'

A couple of miles to the east, that same afternoon, leading infantry and armour of the 11th Armoured Division did succeed in reaching the River Odon, down a narrow, winding road. They found a bridge still intact and managed to emerge up the steep slopes beyond to establish a shallow bridgehead. Just a couple of miles to the south lay the dominant Hill 112, from where Caen could be clearly seen, as could the Bourguébus Ridge, Carpiquet airfield and even Mont Pinçon, 12 miles to the south-west. The plan was for 11th Armoured to push on the following day, secure this key piece of vital high ground and then possibly drive on, sweeping in a wide left hook, cross the River Orne a few miles further to the east and fold up the enemy around Caen.

This might have sounded simple enough, but it was a lot for one division to carry out, especially when it was known II. SS-Panzerkorps were about to join the battle. Overnight, they managed to get leading infantry and armour successfully across as planned, but by this time the 1. SS-Panzergrenadier-Regiment of the 1. SS-Leibstandarte 'Adolf Hitler' Division had arrived and, by morning, and now under temporary command of Kurt Meyer, they were ready to counter-attack. That day, Wednesday, 28 June, saw confused and scrappy fighting. Some twenty-five British tanks and accompanying infantry managed to reach the summit of Hill 112, but because of the narrow crossings over the Odon, the rubble, mines and the German counter-attack, not enough of 11th Armoured was able to get through and support an onward drive towards the River Orne, nor even sufficiently secure the hill.

That same day, Dempsey flew across the battlefield to confer with Bradley, who planned to renew his strike southwards on 1 July – although Cherbourg had fallen, there was still vicious fighting going on around Cap de la Hague in the north-west tip of the peninsula. In the evening, Dempsey issued orders to Pip Roberts's 11th Armoured to push on to the Orne, but he was well aware that in the 'Scottish Corridor', named after the 15th Scottish Division, that had been established from Saint-Manvieu south across the Odon, there was still plenty of fighting. '15 Div,' he recorded in his diary, 'is still involved in clearing up the situation at Grainville and 43 Div is in the area Cheux-St. Manvieu.' It was great that Hill 112 had been taken, but it was clear they would still need to watch their backs. The last thing Dempsey or anyone wanted was to find his spearhead pinched out on a limb, cut off and surrounded. As Monty had not tired of pointing out, there could be no reverses.

To the west on the Cotentin, on 29 June, with the capture of Cherbourg complete, the 9th Division turned west to clear the last pocket of resistance in the Cap de la Hague. Orion Shockley found it a tough fight. Enemy machine-gun fire made progress slow and by dusk he and his men discovered themselves caught in a minefield. One man trod on a Schu-mine. 'Others started to get him,' noted Shockley, 'but I ordered them to stop until we could probe a path to him which was clear of mines.' Fortunately, the man was still alive by the time they got to him, although he had a badly mangled foot and leg, and he was safely evacuated. They pressed on through the night and the next day, 1 July, captured a German weather station and strongpoint, finding it only recently deserted. With that, the fighting at Cap de la Hague was finally over.

Away to the south-east, the fighting around Caen had continued with heavily mounting casualties for both sides. Lance Corporal Ken Tout was still without a tank after his Honey had been taken, but the rest of 1st Northamptonshire Yeomanry had been in battle. Tout had talked to Michael Hunt, one of the drivers in 4 Troop. 'We got clobbered,' Hunt told him. 'It's the bocage, you see. The fields are so small. You go through one great hedge into a field and within fifty yards you have to cross through another hedge even thicker. And the orchards. And farm buildings. Ideal places for Jerry tanks to hide.' Hunt then reeled off a long list of those who had been killed or wounded. 'And three of Frank's crew,' he had continued. 'Brewed up. Didn't stand a chance. And Len Wright with a wound in his skull, and tanks going up on mines, and Jerry tanks with their great guns waiting behind the hedges . . .' So it went on. Tout was appalled, although the losses meant he was now attached as a gunner in a Sherman crew in 3 Troop, C Squadron.

By dusk on the 28th, both Dempsey and Dick O'Connor, the VIII Corps commander, were beginning to realize that EPSOM had almost run its course. They agreed that the following day they needed to both widen and deepen the Scottish Corridor across the Odon Valley. 'Until this is done,' noted Dempsey, 'the armd bde will not be pushed forward to R. Orne.' Then he added a little ominously, 'During the day two more Pz Divs came into action on the Army front – 2 SS Pz Div from St Lo and 1 SS Pz Div from the Paris area.'

Instead, though, they could use EPSOM to chew up these newly arriving panzer divisions and make sure there could be no coordinated panzer counter-thrust as General Geyr von Schweppenburg was planning. What's more, by morning on the 29th, the skies had cleared, which meant the Allied air forces could finally join the battle in strength. In fact, Standartenführer Kurt Meyer was awoken that Thursday by shells from offshore naval guns screaming over. As he tried to move up to the front from his CP, he soon found himself lying prostrate on a road in Verson, taking cover from the *Jabos*, which seemed to be swirling around the sky like hornets. Not far away, an artillery truck had been hit and was burning, its ammunition exploding and zapping about wildly. 'The street was too narrow to pass around it,' he wrote, 'and we had to wait for the vehicle to burn out.' An ambulance had also been hit and was on fire, the occupants all burned alive.

Dempsey, who was privy to Ultra decrypts of German radio traffic, knew the freshly arrived II. SS-Panzerkorps was planning to mount a series of counter-attacks all around the base of the bulge that day, which was why he ordered O'Connor to move troops up into the Scottish Corridor and hold firm. The original plan for a decisive breakthrough had developed into an opportunity to grind down the enemy. It was why Sergeant Walter Caines of the 4th Dorsets was briefed at an O Group that morning to take over from the 5th Duke of Cornwall's Light Infantry – or 5th DCLI – at what remained of shattered Cheux. The order was to have this completed by 3 p.m. Caines was later heading up with the first-line transport and troops, riding his trusty motorbike, when urgent orders were shouted for them to halt and quickly disperse. Doing as ordered, he was wondering what was happening when suddenly they were shaken by the thunderous roar of their guns. Word soon got around:

the enemy was attacking directly towards Cheux and the flanks of the Scottish Corridor. Their own anti-tank guns were hurriedly called forward to help the 5th DCLI, who were still holding out in the rubble of the village.

German troops were now less than a mile distant, their armour, artillery and mortars hammering away, but ferocious counter-fire again ensured they were unable to break through and, at Cheux, by late afternoon the battle had died down, allowing the 4th Dorsets to take over from the 5th DCLI, as had been originally planned. Sergeant Caines had begun setting up their telephone system and exchanges when the enemy launched another attack. Shells fell all around, although with nothing like the intensity of the response from their own artillery. Even so, Caines and his fellows were already wondering what would happen if the Germans broke through. Even with extra support, the 5th DCLI had yet to move out; in places the Germans were overrunning their positions. 'There was no time wasted,' noted Caines. 'Every precaution was taken and men were digging in like hell as shells were falling all around the battalion's positions.'

The Germans tried again on the 30th, but again made no headway. Kurt Meyer was desperate. 'It was impossible to gain ground against this superior firepower,' he noted, 'not to mention the absolute air supremacy.' His own division was in tatters after the past three weeks' fighting. Since then, he had not received one single replacement tank. Within twenty-four hours, meanwhile, the Sherwood Rangers, for example, would be back up to their full complement. 'The constant use of piecemeal tactics enraged me,' Meyer added. 'What had happened to the days of the big armoured offensives?' But what other choice had Geyr and Obergruppenführer Paul Hausser, the II. SS-Panzerkorps commander, had? The Führer had insisted they should not give up a yard, which meant they could not buy time by falling back and organizing themselves for a counter-thrust. The only way to prevent the British building up their bridgehead and then pushing on towards the Orne was to attack the moment leading units reached the front. As Dempsey and the British commanders were well aware, the moment the Germans counterattacked, as they always did, they could then hammer them with their superior fire-power. That was exactly what happened.

On the 30th, Dempsey and O'Connor took the decision to pull back from Hill 112 and so lose the vital high ground that had been so hard fought for, although a narrow bridgehead across the Odon was maintained. This has been repeatedly cited as a poor decision by weak-minded British commanders lacking the cut and thrust of their German opposite numbers. Neither O'Connor nor Pip Roberts, the 11th Armoured Division commander, could be described as lacking drive, however. It is possible they could have held on to Hill 112, but by the 30th there were no fewer than five panzer divisions surrounding the bridge-head and the danger of it being pinched out and severed was considerable. Had that been the case, the leading elements isolated there would have been surrounded and annihilated, and historians would undoubtedly have been even more unforgiving. On balance, the risks probably did outweigh the benefits of potentially being able to hold on.

By the end of 1 July, the EPSOM battle had effectively run its course for both sides. Kurt Meyer headed up to the top of Hill 112 that day and marvelled at the destruction he saw. Wrecked tanks from both sides littered the landscape, while of the trees that just a few days earlier had covered the hill there was now nothing left. Barely a square metre of earth lay untouched. The two-dimensional map gazed upon from afar and the violent reality on the ground were poles apart.

Both here and where the Americans were fighting in the bocage, it was becoming clear already that set-piece operations could rarely last more than four days; after that neither side had the strength or reserves to keep going. At that point, there had to be a pause while the remnants of the attack units took stock of their losses and retired to lick their wounds. The key factor then was which side could replenish their casualties – both men and equipment. In Normandy, the Allies were winning this hands down, and this is where their big war vision and operational brilliance really kicked in. Tactical elan definitely had a part to play, but it was as nothing compared with the ability to provide replacement tanks, guns, rifles and, of course, men. Already, in twenty-four days of fighting, the Germans had lost 62,603 men, which amounted to 2,608 per day.

EPSOM has often been seen as a failure. Surely, the critics have argued, with all that fire-power, the British should have been able to bludgeon their way through. And where was the imagination, where was the tactical flair? It is worth pointing out that 12. SS 'Hitlerjugend' Division, fresh to the front, despite having six times the strength of the Canadians, could make no headway over much the same ground back on 7 June, and also faced a counter-attack followed by stalemate. The critics of British fighting ability cannot have it both ways; they cannot claim the Germans were better trained, tactically more flexible and equipped with better weapons and then not chastise them for failing to break through the British and Canadian lines. At EPSOM, the British faced no fewer than seven panzer divisions in their sector. Against them, the British – the attackers, after all – had just one. And it is important to understand that the panzer divisions the British were taking on were among the very best military units left within the German Armed Forces. The British did not achieve the decisive breakthrough, but they pushed them back a good distance, resisted the counter-attacks of five panzer divisions and chewed up the enemy so badly that any further offensive action by the Germans in Normandy was unthinkable.

EPSOM, then, finished off for good any further chances of the Germans launching a decisive and coordinated counter-attack, formally acknowledged by Geyr von Schweppenburg on the 30th when he cancelled the attack he had been planning. If the outcome in Normandy had still been remotely in doubt before the battle, it most certainly no longer was now. The Allies would be victorious; it was a matter of when, not if. Tensions were understandably growing within the German command as it became increasingly clear they were losing the battle, but frustrations were mounting in the Allied command too. As June finally gave way to July, both sides were unquestionably feeling the strain.

CHAPTER 24

Trouble at the Top

Feldmarschall Erwin Rommel had been devastated by the Allied drives towards Cherbourg and around Caen. 'We are always told to save ammunition,' he complained bitterly over breakfast one morning at La Roche-Guyon, 'while the others save blood.' The 'others' were the Allies. It angered him that ongoing hopes rested on a handful of special weapons; V-1s and even V-2s, when they were finally brought into action, were not going to win them the war. Poor people, he added, should not be at war, and Germany was now most definitely poor, impoverished by long years of bitter conflict and, it seemed, facing an enemy of infinite materiel wealth. He had time and again relayed the critical situation to the OKW, but his warnings had fallen on deaf ears. No one in the OKW was going to tell Hitler what he did not want to hear.

On the evening of 25 June, Rommel had once more gone for a post-dinner walk in the grounds with his trusted naval commander, Admiral Ruge. The situation was now hopeless due to the enemy's overwhelming materiel superiority, Rommel told him. In terms of manpower, the Germans were scraping the barrel; the average age of the men in most of the infantry divisions was thirty-five and even thirty-seven, while the panzer divisions were mostly filled with boys. Panzer-Lehr had already lost 2,600 men from its fighting strength. Then there was the lack of fuel and other supplies, and those lackeys at the OKW were trying to blame him for this downturn of events! Nothing was to be gained at all from the Führer's order to hold out to the last man. Even fortresses like Cherbourg lost their strength when the Allies could bomb and pummel at will from the air and from the sea. But he had to be careful; he could disobey orders or cry dissent only so far. 'Caution had to be exercised,' noted Ruge, 'with regard to commissars and the Sicherheitsdienst.'

Whatever hope Rommel had had before the invasion of kicking the Allies back into the sea had now gone and he was once again consumed by deep despair. It was Alamein all over again, but worse. Resigned to the inevitable defeat that must surely come in Normandy, he hoped instead to play for time so there might be a political settlement. What he meant by that, exactly, is not quite clear. Probably, Rommel was unsure himself, but he was certainly feeling torn. German officers were brought up to believe in honour, and oaths of allegiance were taken incredibly seriously. All had sworn solemn allegiance to Hitler. Duty came first, above politics, and most believed it was their task to fulfil their orders, not question them. Yet the Wehrmacht, in allying themselves to Hitler and the Nazis, had sold themselves down the river; they had collaborated in a monstrous nationalist movement that had brought millions of deaths and led the country of which they were so proud to the very brink of the abyss. Rommel had been fortunate not to have commanded in the East, where violence and the slaughter of innocents had been raised to a terrible level, yet he had risen to field marshal; he was still a part of it, for all his insistence on fair play and behaving honourably. He had continued to hope Germany would win the war, and then what would have become of the world? Only now, with the spectre of defeat hanging over them, was he starting to think of a time when there would be no Hitler, no Nazis. Like his fellow Wehrmacht commanders, he had colluded with the regime and had been in thrall to the Führer. For all the soul-searching now over matters of honour, oaths and allegiance, there had been plenty of times when he and others could have done more to stop the madness. Instead, they had been willing and even enthusiastic participants.

Late on the evening of the 27th, Rommel and von Rundstedt were both summoned to see Hitler at Berchtesgaden, a ludicrous decision at such a crucial moment in the battle and one that was compounded by news the following morning that General Dollmann had suffered a fatal heart attack. At least, that was what his chief of staff, General Max Pemsel, reported; Pemsel later claimed Dollmann had taken cyanide. At any rate, his death coincided with the fall of Cherbourg and the rapidly deteriorating situation for his 7. Armee. During the British attack around Caen, Dollmann had repeatedly shown his ineptitude, constantly changing his mind, issuing wild orders and insisting that II. SS-Panzerkorps throw its newly arriving units into the fray piecemeal rather than allowing them to form up and counter-attack en masse as suggested by Obergruppenführer Paul Hausser, the II. SS commander. This meant now, as the Germans desperately tried to withstand the British assault, there was no army group commander, a hiatus over command of 7. Armee and another over command of II. SS-Panzerkorps. A lack of leadership – or, at least, a fractured and confused chain of command – at critical moments was not conducive to battlefield success.

Having met up with von Rundstedt en route to Berchtesgaden, Rommel told him he planned to speak frankly to the Führer and urge him to give up the war. When he was finally before Hitler, however, at around 6 p.m. on the 29th, the Führer refused to let him speak about the wider conflict; he was to stick to the military situation in Normandy only. When Rommel protested, he was asked to leave the room. He left Berchtesgaden soon after, having barely said anything at all; he had been pulled from the battlefront for a wasted purpose. In his absence, though, Hitler ordered the navy to send midget submarines, a thousand fighters and to line all the roads to Normandy with hidden anti-aircraft guns. This was to happen immediately, although how exactly was anyone's guess. The midget submarines were, to all intents and purposes, human torpedoes and the pilots could only function inside them by taking an appalling cocktail of methamphetamines and cocaine, drugs that had been trialled at the behest of the Kriegsmarine by inmates at Sachsenhausen concentration camp. That a handful of midget submarines would be able to turn the tide against the immense fleets lying off the Normandy coast showed just how disengaged the regime had become from reality. 'Then, if everything goes well,' Hitler added, 'perhaps we can launch a counter-attack on the Americans after all.'

Rommel was back at La Roche-Guyon on the evening of the 30th, but in his absence Geyr von Schweppenburg had, with Speidel's support, ordered the evacuation of the area around Caen and put in plans for the withdrawal of both SS panzer corps to a new line out of range of the Allies' offshore naval guns. His hope was that such a move would also buy them some time to reorganize the panzer divisions, rather than have them chewed up in static defence as was currently the case. Rommel, however, now countermanded this decision, but in the meantime von Rundstedt had forwarded Geyr's orders to abandon Caen to the OKW in Berchtesgaden. A furious Hitler immediately ordered Geyr's dismissal, although, paranoid that the panzer general might defect to the Allies, he quickly issued further instructions that he should not be told until his replacement had reached the front. This was to be the 48-year-old General Heinrich 'Hans' Eberbach, another Eastern Front man. He was, however, a hugely experienced soldier and commander. Having fought during the First World War, where, in 1915, he lost much of his nose, after the war he had joined the police before returning to the army in 1935. He fought in Poland and in France in 1940, before serving under Geyr during the invasion of the Soviet Union. He had remained on the Eastern Front ever since, repeatedly proving himself and rising up the ranks as he did so.

Nor was Geyr the only one to go. Von Rundstedt was also sacked and replaced by Feldmarschall Günther von Kluge, who had commanded an army in Poland and against France in 1940, but who since then had been commanding army groups on the Eastern Front. When he arrived at La Roche-Guyon on the afternoon of 3 July, he and Rommel argued, with von Kluge urging greater aggression and drive and Rommel pointing out that his new boss had never fought the Western Allies and had no idea of the degree to which enemy air power stifled their own offensive chances.

Although Allied air power was the matter about which the Germans seemed most obsessed, it was also an aspect that was causing tension in the Allied command. On 13 June, Lieutenant Joe Boylan had been one of the 391st Bomb Group pilots ordered to fly over to Normandy and hit Périers, a small, country market town some 10 miles south-west of Carentan. Home to around 2,600, it sat at a crossroads on the road heading north to Cherbourg and the Cotentin. If Périers was blocked, then a key supply route north would be denied to the enemy. With Collins's VII Corps still battling their way across the peninsula, this would definitely be a help. The first bombers had come over the day before, and now Boylan, his crew and a number of other B-26s flew to the town to finish the job. 'For us in the 391st,' wrote Boylan, 'it wasn't a significant target and one that didn't look like it would give us any problem in bombing.' He was proved right – they were untouched by either flak or enemy aircraft and all made it back safely. It had been a milk run. They had also done as ordered pretty efficiently; after they had gone, there wasn't much left. Some 127 locals were killed and almost all made homeless as Périers was reduced to rubble. The town had been sacrificed in the cause of liberation from the Nazi yoke.

Commanders justified such bombing in terms of saving lives in the long term, denying the enemy, and the price of war, and once one town had been flattened it was just a little bit easier on the conscience to flatten another. Even so, for the most part it was recognized that such action should be avoided if possible. On the other hand, the destruction of Périers showed that a comparatively small number of medium bombers, used to support ground operations, could bomb clinically and accurately, causing a considerable amount of destruction without the need to call on the strategic air forces, who were busy bombing factories and oil installations.

None the less, the following day, 14 June, Air Marshal Sir Trafford Leigh-Mallory had flown over alone to France to confer with Montgomery and had then annoyed his peers and subordinates by agreeing to use heavy bombers to directly assist the ground forces, something he announced as a fait accompli at the next commanders' conference. The Mediterranean veterans had begun muttering 'Cassino' – the town 60 miles south of Rome where, earlier in the year, strategic air forces had flattened the Benedictine monastery and then pulverized the town with no benefit at all to the troops they were supposed to be helping; the Germans had simply occupied the rubble, which had blocked the path of Allied armour. A cultural and architectural jewel had also been unnecessarily destroyed, and it had been widely considered a prime example of how not to use strategic air power. In fact, Cassino had taught Allied commanders that it was best to use strategic forces sparingly in direct support of ground operations. There were times when big four-engine heavies bombing from generally greater heights could help, but they were less accurate, not used to operating in tandem with ground troops, and experience showed it was all too easy for instructions to get lost in translation as they were passed down the line and for friendly troops to get hit in the process. Concern about hitting troops and ships on D-Day, for example, had caused the heavy bombers to over-fly and so their efforts had been largely wasted. Tedder, Spaatz and Harris were not keen on seeing heavies used in the way Leigh-Mallory proposed, while Coningham and Brereton were annoyed that such conversations had been going on without their consultation. Humiliatingly for Leigh-Mallory, the plan was firmly and swiftly cancelled by Eisenhower and Tedder.

For the most part, Anglo-American rivalries at command level have been over-egged by historians. On the whole, the senior commanders cooperated well with one another and in comparison with the German senior command, at any rate, the Allies were a marriage made in heaven. It has to be remembered, as well, that these men had gargantuan amounts of responsibility and it was only natural that, if they believed strongly about something, they should argue their corner. It was also the case that some people simply didn't get on, but usually this had little to do with national differences; rather it was a combination of personality clash and looking at a situation from different perspectives and requirements.

For all the immense dominance of Allied air power, tensions were rising with regard to its use and the different outlooks of those commanding the air forces and those in charge of the land battle below. One of the problems was Leigh-Mallory, who was not part of the Mediterranean gang of air commanders who had built up mutual respect, trust, friendships and had helped develop new tactics and operational systems together. Already something of an outsider, his lack of charm and prickliness only exacerbated the situation. No one, it seemed, wanted him as C-in-C of the AEAF; frankly, no one wanted the AEAF at all. Coningham, Brereton, Tedder and Spaatz would all far rather have established an overseeing air command within SHAEF, although in many ways Tedder had already created this in his role as Deputy Supreme Commander. Leigh-Mallory, however, simply dug in his heels. There was also a growing feeling that he was in far over his head. Nor had his hysteria over the use of airborne troops just prior to D-Day done much to help his standing.

Then there was Montgomery, whom none of the senior Allied commanders much liked either. He was a past master at rubbing people up the wrong way; the Americans resented being lectured by him while his fellow Brits had been brought up to show a little more modesty and self-effacement. Both parties disliked the air of superiority and condescension he tended to show towards them. Tedder and Coningham had spent long months with Montgomery in North Africa and after the victory at Alamein in early November 1942 had found him increasingly insufferable; nothing they had seen of him in the build-up to OVERLORD had made them change their minds. A big part of the pre-invasion plan had been to capture not only Caen swiftly but also the high, open ground to the south and south-east of the city, which would be ideal for massing airfields. Monty had been absolutely right to present such a confident and positive picture before the invasion, and his estimation that the Germans would withdraw in stages was entirely reasonable, based as it was on previous experience. After all, what else was there to go on? As everyone on both sides agreed, with the sole exception of Hitler, it made absolutely no military sense to fight on so close to the coast when they remained within range of the guns of the two most powerful navies in the world.

Montgomery, however, singularly refused to admit the pre-invasion plan was going off course and that his predictions had been incorrect. He was quite right in claiming that all plans change the moment battle is joined – it had been ever thus – and he was also right to point out that the British and Canadians were still drawing the mass of the enemy's mobile divisions. Nor was it his fault that the weather had been so atrocious. 'Should there be a serious and unexpected break in the weather before D + 14,' he had warned back in April, 'this will have a serious effect on the maintenance of both forces.' And so it had come to pass. The poor weather had not only set back the build-up but had restricted the amount of direct air support as well, and possibly decisively so during EPSOM; there was historic form of Allied air forces breaking up and destroying German ground attacks, and when the weather had been clear on 29 June, air power had greatly contributed to halting the enemy counter-attacks.

There was also, by 1 July, much for the Allies to celebrate. The invasion had been an enormous success, despite being launched in the most difficult of circumstances. Unquestionably, the Allies had also won the build-up race. Cherbourg and all the Cotentin Peninsula were now in Allied hands, and EPSOM and the fighting around Tilly had not only massively chewed up two of Germany's finest divisions, it had stopped dead in its tracks any possible coordinated German counter-attack. It might not have won the Allies the decisive breakthrough, but, despite its reduced scale, appalling weather and the very limited air support, it had achieved much. By the end of June, 452,460 Americans and 397,819 British and Canadians had been landed, along with a further 25,000 airborne troops who had jumped into Normandy; that was some 875,000 in all, numbers with which the Germans could not compete. The Allies were going to win; all the anxiety, apprehension and concerns about a failed invasion had been flung to one side.

Despite this, the failure to capture Caen swiftly was upsetting wider Allied plans, something Montgomery refused outwardly to acknowledge. In many ways, by fighting so close to the coast, the Germans were helping him. His lines of supply were shorter and, of course, there were those offshore naval guns, which were assisting him enormously to grind down the German forces. But it was also causing congestion and stifling movement. Before the invasion, he had stressed how important it was that build-up was rapid. 'It is essential,' he had said at St Paul's on 7 April, 'that the British forces should advance sufficiently far East and

South to allow room for the development of the RMA [rear military areas] and administrative installations at as early a date as possible.' He had also told his audience that Second Army's prime objective was that area to the south and south-east of Caen 'in order to secure airfield sites'; the tactical air forces had been planning on this ever since. Now, though, he was brushing off the failure to capture this ground swiftly as of little consequence. It was driving Coningham, especially, potty.

The trouble was that, despite the impressive number of airfields being hastily created in the bridgehead, there weren't enough. A large number of both American and British wings and groups were still operating from southern England, which meant they were less effective than they might be and less able to respond swiftly to the capricious changes in weather. All the air commanders were frustrated by the V-1 attacks as well. The launch ramps were narrow, very difficult to bomb accurately, and the control centres were deep underground and encased in spectacularly thick concrete. Neither the strategic nor tactical air forces liked hitting these CROSSBOW targets; they understood why they had to try, but it was frustrating sending bombers and fighter-bombers over when they were achieving very little and when it meant they couldn't be hitting oil installations, or railways or enemy columns. The sooner the ground forces got a move on so that they could have their airfields and the V-1 sites could be rapidly overrun, the better. And their impatience was being compounded by Montgomery's character.

Another reason for the growing tension was the dispersal of headquarters. In North Africa, Coningham had been instrumental in placing his air HQ right next to the Army Tactical Headquarters, something Montgomery had embraced and which had, for a time, worked very well. Now, however, not only was Coningham still in England, because that's where most of his air forces were, but Monty's main HQ was still near Portsmouth and that was where General Freddie de Guingand, his chief of staff, was based. De Guingand made up much of the charm shortfall and did much to smoothe ruffles and iron out misunderstandings caused by Monty's crass interpersonal skills. But he wasn't in Normandy and the air and ground HQs were no longer side by side. Issues could not be easily sorted out or explained, and so resentment grew.

On 27 June Churchill had written to Tedder asking to know what airfields were now up and running in Normandy. 'I had to report in reply,' noted Tedder, 'that our progress was well behind schedule.' On that morning, there were now thirty-five fighter and fighter-bomber squadrons in France. There were five airfields in the British sector and eight in the American, all of which had been created by Allied engineers. Not one German airfield had yet been captured, while two that had been created had been pulled out of service for being too close to enemy fire, while three of the American air strips were being used by C-47 Dakotas for flying in emergency supplies and so couldn't be used by fighters. By this time, the Allies had planned to have eighty-one squadrons operating from Normandy, so the shortfall was around 60 per cent. The Allies were now caught in a chicken-and-egg scenario: the lack of air power was hindering the chances of a swift decisive breakthrough, but without such a breakthrough there could be only limited numbers of airfields – and support – from the air forces. Montgomery felt the air forces could do more, but both Coningham and Tedder believed the ground forces were being too slow and ponderous. Neither party in this argument was right; weather and space were hindering air support, while the ground forces could not realistically move any faster than they were – not in this terrain and against the enemy forces arrayed opposite them.

On 25 June, all of 602 Squadron had moved across to France to their new base at Longues-sur-Mer, and while it was true that the Luftwaffe flew barely a hundred sorties on D-Day itself, that had changed as enemy units were brought closer to the front: over 200 fighters were flown in from Germany in the first thirty-six hours and a further 100 by D plus 4. By the end of June there were over 400 over the Western Front, and while that was a hugely inferior number compared with the Allies', it was enough to ensure that Allied fighters often found themselves tussling in the air with Me109s and Focke-Wulf 190s and facing increasing amounts of flak.

A few days later, on 29 June, the squadron had taken off on their third operation of the day at around 7 p.m., an armed reconnaissance over the battle front. They had swept south-east but, after the fine weather early in the day, suddenly the thick cloud was back and it began to rain. Pierre Clostermann found himself separated from the rest of the squadron, rivulets of rain running across his windshield and back through a tiny gap in the canopy until they began dripping, landing on his legs and creating a widening patch of damp. He dropped down lower, trying to pick out some features and feeling increasingly certain he would hit a high-tension electric cable at any moment. He was also lost. 'I began to feel the terror of being alone in a hostile world,' he noted. 'I began to expect a deadly stream of tracer bullets from every hedge, every cross-road, every wood.'

He decided to climb up above the cloud base, emerging at 10,000 feet and watching, slightly mesmerized, the shadow of his Spitfire dancing like a happy porpoise on the clouds, until suddenly he caught sight of ten black spots heading towards him. Moments later they were on top of him – Focke-Wulfs, massively outnumbering his lone Spitfire. His only hope was to dive into the clouds and then use his instruments to throw them off, but this was easier said than done. For one moment he found himself spiralling downwards with a pair of enemy fighters above, another turning in front and a fourth blocking his retreat. Where were the others? He could only see four; frantically, he craned his neck and glanced around, then pulled the stick hard towards him, climbing steeply and narrowly avoiding a stream of tracer, just as a nervous tremor in his left leg made it effectively useless. Crouching low to protect himself with the armour plate behind him, the G-forces made his oxygen mask slip off his nose and he couldn't get it up again. He was panicking, saliva running down his chin. More tracer and a glance in his mirror told him four 190s were on his tail, the closest just 50 yards behind.

Kicking hard on the rudder, he pulled the stick urgently into himself, then sideways and, although cannon shells hit his plane and a black veil from the G-forces crossed his eyes, the manoeuvre had shaken the enemy off; they passed beneath him as he hurled himself vertically towards the clouds. Somehow, self-preservation had kicked in. But he was still lost when, emerging briefly from the cloud, he spotted a 190 up ahead, probably separated from the others. Closing in behind him, Clostermann opened fire before he was spotted and hit the German with his first burst. 'He mowed down a row of trees along a road by a level-crossing,' wrote Clostermann, 'and crashed into the next field, where he exploded.' Staying low, he eventually recognized the Merville viaduct, which they had dive-bombed a few weeks earlier. He let fly at the reconstruction effort then set course for home, landing at B-9 with barely a gallon of fuel remaining.

The P-51 Mustangs of the US 354th Fighter Group were getting used to their new airfield at Cricqueville, although they were flying in a different manner now they were once again part of the Ninth Air Force and no longer escorting the heavies of the Eighth. That meant they rarely operated as a group; on most days the three squadrons would fly separately on a combination of fighter sweeps, beach patrols, dive-bombing and close support for the ground troops. 'The new set-up served to unify individual squadrons,' noted Dick Turner, 'as they ran missions as fighting units independent of other squadron action. But we all missed the big aerial battles with the Germans that old group missions yielded.'

They did, however, occasionally engage with enemy aircraft. On 28 June, Turner was leading his squadron on a patrol of the beachhead and was flying off the coast near Bayeux in the direction of Le Havre when up ahead he spotted a number of fighters diving from the cloud base a little way off to the east. Gunning the throttle, he manoeuvred his flight in an 'S' turn to the port so that he could approach the aircraft in a quartering head-on direction which would give him a better chance of quickly identifying them. They were still heading in his direction and he now realized it was a lone Me109 being pursued by Spitfires. For a moment, Turner wondered what the German pilot would decide to do, then watched as he turned southwards in the direction of Caen. 'I wasn't planning to waste time being polite to our allies,' wrote Turner. 'As it turned out, I was downright rude.' Whipping over his Mustang in a steep right turn, he sped towards the Messerschmitt, cutting behind him and ahead of the Spitfires. With the rest of his squadron following his lead, the Spitfires pulled up and abandoned the chase. Closing in, Turner let off a short burst, clipping the German's wing. The 109 now pulled into a shallow climbing turn to port, but Turner followed, closing tighter, and just as the enemy reached the edge of the cloud base, Turner pressed down on the gun button again, hitting him from the wing root up to the engine cowling. Trailing smoke and fire, the Messerschmitt disappeared into the cloud.

A moment later, the pilot tumbled downwards and his parachute opened. Turner circled and narrowly missed being hit by the burning wreck of the Messerschmitt, but continued to follow the pilot down. As the parachute neared the ground, Turner saw British troops running towards him and even raising their weapons. Only after he vigorously waggled his wings did they lower them again. Away towards Bayeux, in a wood near a chateau, he also saw the Me109 glide in and crash-land, and, making a mental note of the site, he opened the throttle once more and climbed back up to rejoin the rest of the squadron.

A little later, after safely landing back down at A-2, he grabbed his crew chief, Tommy, and a spare Jeep and drove over to the chateau near Bayeux. In the wood they found the Me109 more or less intact. The two men counted around 200 bullet holes in a gratifyingly concentrated area. They cut the swastika out from the vertical stabilizer and, with a few other souvenirs, headed back. 'There is nothing like a good air fight,' noted Turner, 'to keep fighter pilots on their toes and eager to go.'

While other squadrons could spend whole weeks never seeing another enemy aircraft, Turner and his 356th FS had to wait only another couple of days, because on 30 June, after heading out on a patrol southwards above the Vire–Caen area, they quickly spotted a number of aircraft high above them at some 30,000 feet. Climbing hard, they gave chase, being careful to keep behind them so as not to be spotted. After a quarter of an hour or so, Turner saw to his delight it was a flight of Me109s and, telling his squadron to keep as tight as possible, he closed in.

Turner picked out the 109 on the left but, misjudging the distance and impatience possibly getting the better of him, he opened fire too early. Immediately, the rest of the enemy flight broke to the right, with the Mustangs giving chase, but for some reason Turner's original target continued on his way and so, allowing for greater drop of his bullets, he opened fire again with a long burst that raked the Messerschmitt. Smoke streamed from the aircraft, but no visible flame, and Turner drew closer and gave him another burst of fire. The 109 wobbled and more smoke gushed from it, but there was no sign of the pilot bailing out or the plane spiralling out of control. Turner closed further to finish him off, hitting him across his wings and fuselage. Now the stricken plane yawed violently and flipped over into a dive. As it got lower, it burst into flames, enveloping the entire aircraft. Turner was watching this when tracers suddenly flashed past, followed by two 109s hurtling by at great speed. Unscathed, and following them down, he opened fire and hit one of them as he pulled out of his dive. Closing in, he fired again and watched the Messerschmitt blow apart mid-air. That was three in three days, and demonstrated the ever-widening gulf between the young, under-trained and inexperienced pilots of the Luftwaffe's fighter arm and the hardened, veteran Allied aces like Dick Turner. In an engagement there was simply no contest.

The bombers, meanwhile, continued to hammer enemy targets all across Europe. Lieutenant Smitty Smith and his crew in the 385th Bomb Group had flown sometimes two days in a row and at other times every other day, their completed missions mounting and the end of their tour drawing ever closer. On 20 June they had bombed a V-1 factory at Königsborn, their twenty-fourth mission, which should have meant they had just one to go. But then the rules were changed and they had to fly thirty-five before they could be sent home. Smith was disappointed to put it mildly – they all were – but was still grateful not to be a 'ground-pounder' down below in Normandy. Their bombardier, however, 'Eut' Eutrecht, had something of a breakdown on that flight. Having made the target, they all waited to hear him say 'Bombs away,' but there was nothing. Nor did the plane lurch upwards as normal with the release of the bombs. Instead, Eutrecht sat upright, mesmerized and frozen in place, unable to move. 'Ears' Moody, the navigator, eventually nudged him into action; their bombs dropped and they opened the throttles and did their best to catch up with the rest of the group. 'Eutrecht's subconscious had shut him down,' noted Smith. 'I knew from my own feelings that everyone of us on our crew, who had been exposed to this terrible virus, were all fighting our own demons and it was only time before it would take each of us, because there has to be a limit to the amount of abuse that can be taken.'

Despite this, they were packed off to Berlin the following day – Eutrecht included – and to bomb the Standard oil plant near Paris the day after that, so that was three trips in three days. On that trip, Ears Moody was hit by a shard of flak in the parachute, something he never normally wore. When Smith called over the intercom, all he could hear was a raging argument between Ears and Eut over a piece of chocolate – Eut said he had dropped it, Ears claimed he had found it and it was finders keepers. It was silly, unnecessary and another sign that nerves were getting stretched. Another couple of missions followed and then, having flown twenty-eight in less than eighty days, the entire crew was called in and told they were being sent to the 'flak farm' for two weeks' rest and recuperation. These were large English country estates where crew could rest, relax and get away from the war. Smith hated it, though. It was too grand, too formal. When another pilot there wet his bed and bunked off out of shame, Smith decided to join him. Signing himself out, he headed to London and together they took an expensive room at the Savoy, drank, dodged the V-1s and went to the Windmill Theatre, where he picked up two girls, then lost his nerve in the face of their self-confidence. 'The myth about "You Air Force guys with a gal on each arm and plenty of money" wasn't as great as it sounded,' he wrote. 'I was broke, if not broken, and it was time to go back to work.' He and his crew still had seven more missions to fly.

*

On 7 July, Eisenhower sent a letter to Montgomery, written in consultation with Tedder, urging him to expand the beachhead and get more room for manoeuvre as quickly as possible. 'I will back you up to the limit in any effort you may decide upon to prevent a deadlock,' Ike told him, 'and will do my best to phase forward any unit you might find necessary.' He even offered to send him an extra American armoured division. 'Please be assured,' he added, just to really underline the point, 'that I will produce everything that is humanly possible to assist you in any plan that promises to get us the elbow room we need. The Air and everything else will be available.'

By this time, Montgomery was actively moving to get Coningham replaced, while at the same time ignoring him as a channel for requesting air cooperation and instead turning directly to Leigh-Mallory. At the air commanders meeting on 7 July, Leigh-Mallory once again announced he had agreed to support Montgomery's latest attempt to capture Caen by sending over the heavies of Bomber Command. Operation CHARN-WOOD, the attack on Caen, was due to begin the following morning, which didn't allow very much time for planning. Neither Coningham nor Tedder was at the meeting, although Coningham's chief of staff reported that Second Army had requested the use of heavies to attack '4 aiming points consisting of concrete "hedge-hog" defences' and that on this occasion Mary had suggested heavies might be used. Air Chief Marshal Harris, who did attend, replied that he had 350 bombers standing by and that if the planned CROSSBOW target was abandoned he could up that to 450. Tedder later warned Leigh-Mallory against using Bomber Command; what's more, what had been an operation to destroy some quite specific German defences had now transformed into something much bigger. Tedder felt the plans had not been properly thought through, nor the limitations of such heavy bombing of the battlefield sufficiently understood. All the concerns about a repeat of Cassino that had been voiced three weeks earlier remained just as valid now.

By the time the 467 aircraft of Bomber Command set off, the original target agreed by Coningham had been changed from the fortified villages just to the north of the city behind the German main lines of defence. There was concern, as there had been on D-Day, that bombs might fall short, even from the comparatively low height of 8,000 feet, and hit their own troops, so the targets were adjusted so that they were closer to Caen itself. This compromise perfectly illustrated the shortcomings Tedder had warned about. Either the heavies were to be used to hit a specific target or they weren't. If the risks to their own troops of such an operation were too great, then Bomber Command should have been stood down rather than dropping lots of bombs where they weren't so needed.

The die, though, had been cast. Sergeant Ken Handley and his Australian crew in 466 Squadron were among those assigned to the raid. 'Another good daylight prang over target at 22.00 hrs,' noted Handley cheerily. 'Flak bursts against the clouds gave them a spotted appearance. Target was smothered in smoke where tank concentrations were.' Except there weren't any tank concentrations where the bombs struck, only the northern outskirts of the medieval city of Caen, which were ruined by 2,276 tons of bombs, dropped very accurately within 2½–3 square miles, but on a target that achieved little except create huge amounts of rubble, debris and craters across all the roads leading into the northern part of the city. The university was largely destroyed and some 350 civilians were killed. Very few German troops appear to have been hit.

Among the Allied high command there was mounting concern that the British and American armies were getting bogged down in a stalemate from which there was no obvious escape. The V-1s, those harbingers of death and destruction, were still droning over southern England, while in the East the Red Army was smashing huge swathes from German Heeresgruppe Mitte, contrasting starkly with the tiny movement forward in Normandy. The East, however, was not of such great strategic importance to Hitler; no vengeance weapons were being directed towards the Soviet Union, for example. Only in Normandy could Nazi Germany bring to bear its army, navy and Luftwaffe, even if these last two armed services were making little contribution. New generation U-boats were on their way, but once those Atlantic bases had gone, there could be no turning back to them, while once the Allies had established an even firmer foothold on the Continent, then stemming their flow would become almost impossible. Even Hitler understood this.

A sit-down of all the major Allied commanders might now have been time well spent, despite the distraction from the battlefield this would have caused Monty and Bradley. They could have taken solace from this appraisal of the differing strategic picture between the Eastern and Western Fronts, while a calm, measured assessment of the situation would have assured them that, while they appeared to be making little headway, the Germans were in a desperate situation which would, eventually, lead to their collapse. But Allied leaders were in a hurry, and allowing their increasing impatience to be fuelled by pre-invasion presumptions that had proved to be misconceived. So, instead, further assaults were ordered as the battering ram was pulled back for another shove. The ill-conceived bombing of Caen was part of this renewed bludgeoning.

CHAPTER 25

Bloody Bocage

T HERE WAS NOW ABSOLUTELY no let-up in the fighting as the Allies lined up along a broad front to try to hammer their way through the German lines. The casualties were enormous. All along the ridge line around Saint-Lô, new set-piece attacks were launched, while further west, now that the Cotentin Peninsula was finally, completely in American hands, Bradley could turn Collins's VII Corps south. His men were in for a torrid time, for while the focus had been on the battle northwards to clear the Cotentin and capture Cherbourg, the Germans holding the line to the south, on the other side of the flooded area stretching west from Carentan to Périers and beyond, had been digging in and strengthening their defences.

Among them had been Fallschirmjäger-Regiment 6, who in the second half of June had been making the most of the lull in their sector. They were now attached to the 5. Fallschirmjäger-Division, which had arrived from Auxerre in central France. Oberst von der Heydte was somewhat sniffy about his new division. Hardly any had received jump training and not more than 20 per cent of their officers had either proper infantry training or combat experience; most were drawn from disbanded Luftwaffe units elsewhere. 'Weapons and equipment were neither complete nor uniform,' he wrote, his despair all too obvious. 'Only 50 per cent of the units were equipped with machine guns; one regiment had no steel helmets; no heavy anti-tank weapons were available and there were no motor vehicles.' The *Fallschirmjäger* were proud to consider themselves elite troops, but this rabble were a sorry lot indeed. On the other hand, von der Heydte had received over 800 replacements by the end of June to help rebuild his battered companies, while into the line had also arrived several anti-tank battalions of assault guns and Panthers. 'Never before, either in Russia or in North Africa,' he added, 'had the troops of the 6. FS Regiment witnessed on the German side such an accumulation of materiel and troops for purely defensive purposes.' While the panzer divisions were massing around Caen, more units were arriving into the western half of the Normandy front; and while Cherbourg and the Cotentin might have fallen, the German 7. Armee meant to fulfil the Führer's orders to the letter. The Americans could expect a tough, bloody battle in the bocage, a landscape that unquestionably favoured the defender.

Fallschirmjäger 6 were now dug in just to the south of the small village of Méautis, only 4 miles south-west of Carentan; here the front line had not moved at all in nearly three weeks and the paratroopers meant to make the Americans pay for that still-painful loss. Oberleutnant Martin Pöppel, no longer in bad odour with Oberst von der Heydte, had been given back command of his old 12. Kompanie, the III. Bataillon's heavy weapons unit, and, although still under strength, had been given a new 150mm howitzer and a couple of 80mm mortars. 'Excellent progress is being made on the consolidation of our positions,' he noted on 22 June. 'The individual holes are now connected by trenches to create a unified line, and well-disguised observation holes have been driven through the earthen walls. The roads have already been mined, and each night our engineers are at work mining the land in front of our positions. Barbed wire, prepared by our supply men, is also being put into position.'

It was also their turn to try to knock down a troublesome church tower they were aware the Americans were using as an OP. On 1 July, one of their self-propelled guns, a 105, rumbled forward and fired no fewer than eight rounds but still failed to destroy the tower. The following day, Pöppel was told to try again with his 150mm. The first shot was too high, but the second tore a hole clean through from one side to the other. 'Eight shots,' noted Pöppel, 'each one better than the one before, but the monster just won't fall.' On the other hand, it seemed pretty unlikely the enemy could now make much use of it. Meanwhile, his best sniper had racked up a growing score of dead Americans. As if to show there were no hard feelings, they prepared a large white card with naked ladies drawn on it inviting the American commander and staff to a variety show called 'Parisian Women' on 6 July. During the night, a patrol planted it on a stake just before the American lines. 'The Americans,' noted Pöppel, 'will scarcely be able to believe their eyes when they see our little joke.'

The American infantry of the 83rd Division, now in Normandy and facing Fallschirmjäger 6, clearly had no intention of taking them up on the offer, instead opening their attack with a powerful artillery barrage in the early hours of Independence Day, 4 July. By 6 a.m. they had penetrated between II. and III. Bataillons and so Pöppel, instinctively inclined to an immediate counter-attack, suggested leading his reserve platoon to rectify the situation. Under the cover of their own mortars, they got up out of their trenches and hurried forwards, past bodies of dead Americans, until they reached a sunken road. Shells screamed overhead, bullets pinged and hissed. Then they heard English voices coming closer and, warning his men to get hand grenades ready, Pöppel raised his head and saw an American charging towards him with his Tommy gun at the ready. Snatching his MP40 sub-machine gun, Pöppel fired and cut him down, only to see another American emerging through a gap in the hedgerow. Raising his weapon, Pöppel fired again, but at the same moment so did the American and a bullet tore through his arm just above his right elbow. 'Damn it,' noted Pöppel, 'but at least the American has gone down as well.' Falling back into the cover of the sunken lane, he looked at his wound. It hurt like hell. His men had all moved on and he now lay there, listening to the sounds of battle, gripping his pistol in his left hand. Eventually the fighting quietened down and some of his men reappeared, including his batman, who helped him back to the field dressing station. He had been lucky – the wound was not fatal nor would he lose his arm. His time in Normandy, however, was over.

Now neighbouring the 83rd Division were the 4th Infantry, who had barely had time to draw breath before being sent south to attack through the flooded swampy area south-west of Carentan. Still attached to the 4th were the 70th Tank Battalion. On 6 July, before Collins's VII Corps had even really begun their attack, Sergeant Carl Rambo's Company A were flung against the bocage. They had a new platoon commander who, in Rambo's view, seemed keen to get himself wounded or killed in quick order. Attached to the platoon was a Sherman dozer tank. Only with this could the Shermans actually get through the high mounds and hedges of the bocage; ordinary Shermans simply rose up, exposing their weaker undersides, and were then unable to push on through. The dozer, on the other hand, could ram the hedgerow, punching first one and then a second gap through which the others could follow. The new platoon commander, ignoring Rambo's warning, went through first, telling the others to follow, and was promptly knocked out by an anti-tank gun hidden behind the hedge of the next field. Rambo's tank followed, his machine-gunner spraying the hedges up ahead and firing HE shells from the main gun, while from the turret he gave directions to the driver to keep moving. One crew stopped to try to rescue the first crew as they were bailing out, only to be knocked out as well.

Rambo kept calling his driver to move left, then right, but an 88mm shell still hit the corner next to the co-driver, knocking off a big chunk but fortunately otherwise not penetrating the main hull, stuffed as it was with ammunition. They now began backing off, firing all the time as one of the escaped crew clambered on to the back and was promptly shot in the leg. The dozer tank now turned to go back but was hit square in the side and caught fire. Although the commander began to clamber out, the flames got the better of him and he fell back inside, incinerated with the rest of the crew. Using the flaming tank as cover, Rambo backed out and took cover behind the comparative safety of another hedgerow. 'The maddest I ever got during the war was now,' recalled Rambo. The 2nd Platoon was waiting in reserve behind them and he called them to ask for help.

'What's the matter?' came the reply. 'Is the mud too deep up there?'

'No,' Rambo replied, 'it will dry real quick, we have four tanks on fire and I've been hit.'

They pulled back and later that afternoon dive-bombing P-47 Thunderbolts came over and plastered the enemy positions. Afterwards they discovered one of the newly arrived German Panthers had been dug in there. Four out of six American tanks had been knocked out in a matter of minutes. Fighting through the bocage was going to be tough. And slow.

A few miles to the north-west were the 82nd Airborne, still in the line despite being shock troops designed for *coup de main* operations, despite having suffered over 50 per cent casualties since D-Day, and despite their sister divisions having already been sent back to England. General Matt Ridgway had complained to Bradley about this, but the First Army commander had insisted his men fight this one further battle; then they could pull out and head back to England.

Lieutenant-Colonel Mark Alexander had been shifted across from the 505th PIR to the 508th, where he was once again performing the duties of XO. He wasn't happy about either; as far as he was concerned, he was a 505th man. What's more, he much preferred leading men from the front to playing an admin role, but his protestations fell on deaf ears. The decision to move him had been General Ridgway's and was done because he had concerns over the 508th commanding officer, Colonel Roy Lindquist. Ridgway worried he wasn't aggressive enough and more suited to a staff role. He wanted Alexander to come in and provide the aggression and front-line leadership while Lindquist managed the show. In effect, the roles of commander and XO were being reversed, albeit without the switch in status or rank.

The 82nd were given the capture of La Haye-du-Puits as their objective, another small Normandy country town that had the misfortune to sit on a confluence of roads heading north, south and east. The 505th were to take a ridge called Hill 131 and then the 508th were to follow through them and take the next feature, Hill 95, before pushing on to La Haye-du-Puits. As planned, Hill 131 was captured on 3 July, but the 2nd Battalion commander of the 508th was wounded by a mine and so for the attack on Hill 95 Alexander took over temporary command just as he had at La Fière.

His 2nd Battalion would lead the assault on Hill 95 at dawn the following morning, Tuesday, 4 July, so with half an hour of daylight left on the 3rd, Alexander crept forward to make his own reconnaissance. Crawling towards a wall, he managed to remove one of the stones and peer through with his field glasses. Directly ahead was a shallow valley of exposed open ground before the rise of the hill, but away to the left was a wood, which ran all the way up to the top of the hill. He also spotted two enemy guns on Hill 95 and was fairly certain one of them at least was an 88mm. Resolved to attack through the cover of the woods on the left-hand saddle of the hill, he returned to his battalion CP, phoned Colonel Lindquist and told him that to cross the open ground in a direct assault would be suicidal. 'They're shooting right down our throats from there,' he told him.

He had no sooner rung off than the Germans began mortaring their positions. Alexander heard the first mortar round coming but too late and was hit in the back by a couple of fragments. All he could do was lie there on the ground, cursing. The medics were not long in coming and, after bandaging him up, they put him into the front seat of a Jeep and drove him to the nearest field hospital. He had been severely hit and the blood quickly started to seep through the bandages and into the seat. By the time he finally reached the hospital, he was slipping in and out of consciousness, but American medical services were second to none and, after emergency surgery, the worst had passed. He would be in a bad way for a while, but Alexander would pull through.

This was a lot more than could be said for a number of his men. His own XO, Captain Chet Graham, took over command of the battalion and was ordered by Colonel Lindquist to attack directly, across the open land, rather than along the approach Alexander had suggested. As it was, there were only 225 men left in the battalion out of the 640 that had jumped on D-Day. Despite the odds, they crossed the open ground, stormed the hill and by around 4 a.m. on the 5th it was secured. But the cost had been horrific, with nearly 50 per cent casualties. It was, however, their last action for a while. Like the 101st Airborne, it was time for the 'All Americans' to be pulled out of the line and sent back to England.

The bocage was every bit as dense and difficult away to the north-east of Saint-Lô, where the Germans were now dug in along the low ridge that dominated the 15 miles or so of land to the coast. From the base of the Cotentin all the way to Caumont and beyond into the British and Canadian sector was a mass of small villages and hamlets, linked by narrow, winding roads and lanes, none of which was asphalted, but rather just grit and compacted earth. Every road, every sunken lane and every field was lined with those hedgerows on earthen mounds. Most fields were only a few acres in size. Colonel Tick Bonesteel, of the US 21st Army Group planning team, had warned the First Army planners about the potential dangers of this terrain and had even briefed the US 1st Division – the Big Red One – in some detail. Despite this, and despite much of First Army training in south-west England where, as in Normandy, the fields are small and the hedgerows every bit as high, the focus for training had been on fitness, on weapons, on beach assaults and on attacking fixed positions, but very little thought – if any – had been given to how they might attack an enemy dug in along hedgerows. 'So here was what I would call at least an imperfect terrain appreciation,' commented Bonesteel. 'We had not trained in the special fighting techniques needed to work our way through the bocage.'

The challenge was how to get through one hedgerow and across the field to the next without being cut to ribbons. The German defenders could position machine guns at each far corner behind the mound of a hedge. Riflemen would be dug in between the two corners. Further back, behind the next field or two, there would be mortar teams. No matter how the Americans tried to break through the hedge, they would be exposed and mowed down by twin machine guns that had every part of the field covered. In many ways, the hedgerows offered the Germans a far better defence than concrete bunkers. Concrete was fixed and rooted to the spot, whereas hedgerows offered much more flexible defence because troops could move about behind them and could also always pull back to the next field. The problem for the Germans, as their extensive training instruction pamphlets were quick to point out, was that in hedgerow country the forward view was often not particularly good. Certainly during the first fighting inland after the invasion they had been trying to second guess where the enemy might attack and in what strength because they had no aerial reconnaissance to act as their eyes on the ground.

From the ridge around Saint-Lô, however, the Germans were, for the most part, able to look down on the Americans from what they called the *Hauptkampflinie* – HKL – the main line of defence, which had been earmarked by the 352. Division before the invasion and prepared with a web of foxholes and firing positions. Key roads and crossroads, meanwhile, were zeroed with well-placed anti-tank guns, such as the much-feared 88mm and the Pak 40 75mm, which was a similarly high-velocity and lethal weapon. To defend the ridge effectively they didn't need a huge number of troops. Some well-placed artillery, as many mortars as possible, a decent number of machine guns and trained snipers could hold up the advance of a much bigger attacking force very effectively. The Germans were materially poor, but they had enough of those weapons to stop the Americans in their tracks.

An important and particularly troublesome feature for the Americans was Hill 192, near the village of Saint-Georges-d'Elle, which had commanding views all the way back to the coast and which was covered by a patchwork of dense hedgerows, sunken lanes and copses. The 2nd 'Warrior' Division, on the right flank of the Big Red One, had been given the job of clearing this feature. They had first attacked on 11 June, but had made no headway at all, then launched a second assault on the 16th. Although they had managed to reach the summit, they had been pushed off again and four days later had to pull back; there had not been enough artillery support or nighttime patrol work to pin down enemy positions, but the real problem was how to penetrate the hedgerows without the infantry getting massacred. Although air power and artillery could unquestionably help, what was really needed were Shermans working alongside the infantry. Ideally, a Sherman would burst through the middle of the hedge, fire its 75mm at each corner and knock out machine-gun nests, then spray the entire hedgerow with MG fire while the infantry fanned out from behind. The trouble was, the mound underneath the hedge, and then the hedge itself, were too much for the tank, which merely rose up and was unable to push through. Dozer tanks could work, as they had for the 70th Tank Battalion, but generally only those units that had landed on D-Day had them. This inability to get through the hedgerows was making the tanks almost redundant; 'Kraut Corner' and 'Purple Heart Draw' had become death zones for the 2nd Division boys the moment they got up from their foxholes as the machine-gun heavy 3. Fallschirmjäger-Division defending the ridge exacted a terrible toll.

The men of the US 29th Division weren't making much headway either and by 1 July were spending their days crouching in ever more sophisticated foxholes as both sides snipered, mortared and shelled one another. That day, Sergeant Bob Slaughter was making further improvements to his foxhole when the chaplain arrived with news from home. His father had died in May from an aneurism, aged only forty-nine; he could barely take in the news. 'There was,' he wrote, 'no time to grieve.' In any case, he was daily staring death in the face himself, particularly since they were dug in on a forward slope with the enemy just beyond on the other side of a shallow ravine. One platoon was particularly in the firing line and when the section commander, Staff Sergeant Mackay, was killed by a sniper, Slaughter was ordered to go and take over.

He hurried along a sunken lane, crouching as he made his way towards his new platoon's positions. All the men were taking refuge in their foxholes and it bothered Slaughter that no one seemed to be keeping a watch out. Realizing he needed to show some leadership, he slowly raised his head over the hedgerow, looking out either side of him. A matter of seconds later, his helmet flew off and he fell forward on his hands and knees, blood gushing down his face. For a moment, he felt sure he would die, but he had been lucky; a sniper's bullet had hit the small peak of his helmet and exited through the liner, grazing his head as it went. It was no wonder, though, that the Americans could barely move.

Snipers, however, could not work very well at night and this enabled the Americans to carry out extensive patrols to capture enemy troops and pinpoint positions which could then be relayed back to the mortar teams and artillery. Karl Wegner, now dug in on the ridge opposite Bob Slaughter and the rest of the 29th Infantry Division, hated the nights.

'The hedgerows were our allies during the day,' he said, 'but at night they were no one's friends.' It was during a night patrol, for example, that Kraut Corner – which overlooked any advance along the road up the ridge towards Point 192 – was finally subdued. On the night of 6 July, Lieutenant Ralph Winstead of the 38th Infantry, 2nd Infantry Division, led a small patrol and inched forward across the field, under cover of both darkness and pre-arranged mortar and artillery fire, until they were mere yards from the German machine-gun position on the other side of the hedgerow in the corner of the neighbouring field. Gently extending a Bangalore torpedo, they fired the charge then stood up and charged the position, shooting eleven men, capturing key documents and returning safely to their own lines.

Meanwhile, around Caen, the fighting continued. The Canadians of 8th Brigade were given the task of capturing Carpiquet airfield before the main attack on Caen was launched. For much of the past three weeks, the Queen's Own Rifles had been dug in between Bretteville-l'Orgueilleuse and Le Mesnil-Patry; it was through these lines that British VIII Corps had moved up for the EPSOM battle. On 3 July, they had reached the village of Marcelet, barely a mile west of Carpiquet airfield, which was still in the hands of Kurt Meyer's 12. SS 'Hitlerjugend'. German signal intelligence had picked up on increased Canadian radio traffic and correctly guessed an attack was imminent, so were ready, although Meyer felt certain the attack would signal his division's entry into Valhalla.

His 12. SS had long since reached a point where it could no longer properly function. His Panzergrenadier-Regiment 26 had been reduced to the strength of a weak single battalion; it had arrived in Normandy with three full-strength battalions. His panzer strength had been reduced by around three-quarters. His reconnaissance battalion had just one mixed company left – perhaps a hundred men – while his combat engineer battalion had been effectively annihilated. One entire battalion of artillery had also been obliterated. Ammunition was low and his entire division had been reduced to that of a *Kampfgruppe*; only Panzergrenadier-Regiment 25, still defending the western half of Caen, remained in reasonable order. Despite this, Oberstgruppenführer Sepp Dietrich, his superior at I. SS-Panzerkorps, continued to give 12. SS the lion's share of defending Caen; on their right was a weak Luftwaffe field division, while 21. Panzer remained to the east of the River Orne. Dietrich was a good Nazi and brave soldier, but not the sharpest tool in the shed. Like many senior Waffen-SS officers, his origins were as a street fighter; he had had little education, no military staff training and had most definitely been promoted above his capabilities, but increasingly men like Dietrich were given the task of keeping the German effort going. What they lacked in training and military sense, they made up for in loyalty. Dietrich was nothing if not loyal to the Führer.

Meyer was resigned. He knew the Führer's order to fight to the last round meant the end of the division. 'We wanted to fight,' he wrote. 'We were prepared to give our lives, but the fighting had to have a purpose. I bristled at the thought of allowing my young soldiers to bleed to death in the city's rubble. The division had to be preserved for a more flexible form of combat.' He was quite right; German successes in the first years of the war had been based around flexibility, rapid manoeuvre and the ability of the commanders in the firing line to use their training, experience and judgement to make tactical decisions. That flexibility had gone the moment Hitler himself had taken over as C-in-C of the army back in December 1941 following the failure to capture Moscow.

At Carpiquet village and the airfield Meyer had only around 200 men, although he also had several tanks hidden among the wrecked hangars in an anti-tank role, as well as a battery of 88s and some *Nebelwerfer*s, all of which were zeroed in on key roads and positions. Weakened they might be, but in defence these men still posed a considerable threat, as the Canadian 8th Brigade discovered when they attacked on 4 July, with the usual immense artillery and naval barrage marking the start of their assault. Meyer was up with his panzer-grenadiers in the hangars on the southern side of the airfield when the barrage began, watching from the entrance to a bunker as the village on the far side disappeared in smoke and dust, while hangars and airfield buildings were obliterated. Above, Typhoons swirled, among them Ken Adam and the men of 609 Squadron. As the Canadian infantry and armour emerged from the smoke, however, Meyer's defenders came out from their dugouts and foxholes and opened fire. The Winnipeg Rifles were particularly hard hit, cut to pieces by the German 88s and machine guns.

Sergeant Charlie Martin's A Company were on the right of the Winnipeg Rifles and were ordered to take ground and some of the buildings and shattered hangars on the north-eastern edge of the airfield. Despite heavy artillery support, it was a challenge, because here the ground was flat and open, and once again there was nothing for it but to keep going and hope that smoke and the fog of war would give them enough cover.

A Company moved onwards, platoons spaced apart and with one ten-man section leading while the other two gave covering fire then leap-frogged forward. Having taken over several buildings, the Queen's Own Rifles were told to dig in and hold. 'It was terrible,' noted Martin. 'We had to dig in along the runway and in part of the old hangar building. The enemy were watching every move.'

Although the defenders tenaciously held on to the southern side of the airfield, Meyer's men were unable to hold Carpiquet. Bad as it had been for the attackers, it had once again been worse for the SS men, whose inevitable counter-attack equally inevitably failed. Of the panzer-grenadiers defending the village, not one officer or NCO had survived. Meyer pleaded with Dietrich to be allowed to withdraw, but once again his request fell on deaf ears. The Führer's order stood.

By 7 July the 1st Northamptonshire Yeomanry had moved eastwards a little way to the village of Fontaine-Henry and strung out along a hedge on a rising slope. Ahead lay Lébisey Wood and, beyond that, the medieval city of Caen. Lance Corporal Ken Tout had yet to go into action, although he had already seen more than enough of death to take the edge off his earlier excitement at the adventure of it all. First, there had been the burned-out German tank near Creully. Curiosity got the better of them, so he and his new crew mates clambered on to it and made the terrible mistake of taking a peek inside, where the blackened, wizened crew still sat. 'The roasting of human flesh and the combustion of ammunition and the defecation of a million voracious flies,' wrote Tout, 'created an aura of such sense-assaulting horror that we recoiled.' Then there had been the growing stench of a dead German not far away, so they had been ordered to bury him. Digging the grave, the soil still soft from the rain, had been no great hardship and they had made sure it was nice and deep in the hope that it would eradicate the terrible, pervasive, sickly sweet smell. Once dug, they hurriedly picked him up to swing him into the hole, but the arm Tout held disintegrated. After vomiting, they shovelled the decomposing remains into the pit and hurriedly piled on the earth. It had not been a dignified burial ceremony for the poor fellow.

The rumour was they would be heading into Caen, but before they were ordered to move out they watched RAF Bomber Command fly over and lay waste to the northern half of the city. Tout and his mates could hear the heavies coming long before they saw them: a deep drone that grew louder and louder until the thunder seemed to resonate inside their skulls. Even when they first spied them, they appeared like specks, far too small for the enormous noise, which then, incredibly, grew even louder, so that every part of the air seemed to be utterly consumed by this immense thunder. They tried to count, but soon gave up as dozens became hundreds – an enormous, barely comprehensible vision of titanic power. Stabs of tracer began arcing up from the ground, an extraordinary light show in its own right, but the enormous fleet roared on, apparently untroubled. Then the bombs began to fall and from where they waited by their tanks they felt the concussion and shock waves that followed. 'Give 'em hell, boys!' they cheered. Once this wave of gargantuan destruction had passed, they learned they would be attacking the city the following morning alongside the British 3rd Division and the Canadians, part of Operation CHARNWOOD.

'That's it then,' said Tommy Tucker, the crew's loader. 'All the other buggers in the British and Canadian armies have had a go. Now it's the NY that has to liberate Caen.'

'Hope the Jerries have gone home before we get there,' added Stan 'Hickie' Hicken, the driver.

Operation CHARNWOOD, the attack on Caen, was yet again preceded by an immense battering ram of fire-power from naval guns, artillery and the tactical air forces. 'Our cellar shook at all its corners,' noted Kurt Meyer, who was sheltering in his CP near the south-west edge of the city. 'Plaster and dust settled on the candlelit map.' Attacking from the north-west, the Canadians overran Authie and began hammering the Abbey d'Ardenne, Meyer's first CP and now held by Obersturmbannführer Karl-Heinz Milius and his Panzergrenadier-Regiment 25. By afternoon, all his II. Bataillon company commanders had been killed. On their right, the 16. Luftwaffen-Felddivision was breaking. Meyer gave Milius permission to evacuate the abbey that night, including all the wounded sheltering in a makeshift field hospital in the cellars.

Earlier that morning, the men of 1st Northants Yeomanry had moved up towards Lébisey Wood. Ken Tout marvelled at the sight of several thousand infantry and tanks spread out in attack formation ready to move off, although, disconcertingly, spreadeagled sideways in a hedge near to where they had paused, a British dispatch rider lay dead, as though crucified, flung by a bomb blast, his motorbike hurled even higher.

It was afternoon by the time they rumbled forward, through Lébisey Wood and into open ground with views across the wide valley of the

River Orne to the chimneys of Colombelles, the industrial edge of Caen. Infantry parted either side of them.

'Operator, load 75 with AP,' the commander, Corporal 'Snowie' Snowdon, called out over the intercom. The gunner's seat was on the right of the turret and the main 75mm gun, with the loader on the far side, and the commander sitting behind, with his head sticking out above the turret. All wore headphones. The Sherman was unique among tanks in Normandy in having a gyro-stabilizer on the gun, which meant it could fire with greater accuracy while on the move than other tanks. Tout, as gunner, and the commander and loader sat in a wire-mesh conical basket that rotated with the turret, while the driver and co-driver sat beyond, to the left and right respectively, their access point a hatch each forward of the turret. They could drive with their heads above these hatches, or could close them, lower their seats and use periscopes instead. From his position next to the gun, Tout used a periscope and had control of the turret and gunsight, which had cross-hairs for aiming. The commander, however, had an override switch with which to traverse the turret rapidly should he need to. At his feet, Tout had two buttons – the right for firing the 75mm gun, the left for triggering the .30-calibre machine gun. Ammunition was stored everywhere, both armour-piercing – AP – which was solid steel, and HE, which had a charge in the tip and exploded either on a delay or on impact. It was stacked upright around the turret and down in the hull beside the driver and co-driver. The proximity of all this explosive charge so close to the heads of the crew and in such a confined space wasn't something the men wanted to think about too much.

'Hullo, all stations, Yoke,' could now be heard over the 'A' set frequency but still audible on the intercom. This was the C Squadron commander. 'There are undesirable elements somewhere among those chimneys. See if you can knock them down.'

They loaded the gun with HE and Tout peered through the telescope, his forehead resting against the rubber cushion, and fired a ranging shot, the whole tank shuddering from the recoil. He could follow his own stab of tracer as the shot sped towards the target but fell short.

'Short! Up two hundred,' called out Snowdon.

Tout fired again as an enemy shell hit the ground uncomfortably close by, then fired some more, as did the others in the battalion, but the concrete chimneys remained intact, apparently immune at that range. Soon they disappeared entirely, screened by smoke.

Around the same time, Standartenführer Kurt Meyer was nearly buried alive when his command post building was hit by bombers of Second TAF. Fortunately for him, he had already taken to the cellar, although the blast had blown out the candles and the air had been so thick with dust that he and his staff had barely been able to breathe. One young soldier, knocked down the cellar entrance by the concussion wave, had become hysterical. All their radio vehicles up above had been destroyed.

It was dark by the time C Squadron, 1st Northants Yeomanry, moved off towards the city ruins. Ken Tout's tank was leading. One moment they were trundling through grassy fields and the next they were grinding over rubble, the Sherman lurching up, then down, as they manoeuvred over craters and mounds of brick and stone. 'For what's it worth,' said Corporal Snowdon, 'we are now in Caen.' They were all shocked. Caen – or at least its northern part – had gone. A wilderness of ruin remained, made worse by the appalling, cloying stench of death. They climbed up a steep mound of rubble, then slid and rocked down the other side. Tout couldn't see anything through his scope and told the commander.

'That's OK,' Snowdon replied. 'It's just as bad up here. If we need to, just blast away regardless with the seventy-five and hope it scares them more than they scare us.'

They climbed another mountain, tipped over the top, then Hicken, the driver, lost control and the tank stalled. Tucker began singing the old nursery rhyme 'The Grand Old Duke of York'.

Snowdon jumped down and told Tout to keep watch while he went to confer with the Ulster Fusiliers and the squadron commander, Lieutenant Bobby McColl. Eventually he returned and clambered back up to the turret.

'No way forward,' he said. 'Bobby agrees. Ulsters say no use staying here. We came. We saw. We conquered. And a fat lot of use it was.' Certainly, no enemy was firing. Not a soul appeared to be living in the wreck of Caen apart from them.

They still had to get out of the crater in which they now found themselves but, having started the tank, Hicken managed to reverse them back. 'We scrunch around in the ruins of people's lives and homes,' wrote Tout, 'and follow back the way we came.'

Late that night, Kurt Meyer had once again appealed to Dietrich to allow him to evacuate the city and once again his request had been turned down. This time, however, Meyer decided to disobey and issued orders for his men to start pulling out – that is, what men he had left. Milius's regiment had been all but destroyed. Not only had the II. Bataillon lost its officers, so now had the III. Bataillon, which had been reduced to little more than a hundred men, 15 per cent of its fighting strength. 'The soldiers of 12. SS Panzer Division were at the end of their physical endurance,' wrote Meyer. 'They had gone to war weeks before with fresh, blooming faces. At this point, camouflaged, muddy steel helmets cast shade on emaciated faces whose eyes had, all too often, looked into another world. The men presented a picture of deep human misery.' As it happened, General Hans Eberbach, Geyr von Schweppenburg's replacement, also ordered the withdrawal from Caen that night, to the eastern side of the Orne.

After five days of sitting precariously in a foxhole at one end of the airfield, Sergeant Charlie Martin, for one, was mightily relieved when the SS men at last pulled back. It had not been good for the nerves. They had finally emerged and crossed the open ground to the south; the battle for the airfield had cost the battalion another seventy men, including Martin's mate Frank Mumberson, who lost an arm. He headed off to the field hospital on the back of a Carrier, his stump heavily bandaged, smoking a cigar. 'See you in Blighty!' he called out as he left. Martin watched him, exhausted, filthy and shattered by his first month of battle.

CHAPTER 26

Living Like Foxes

'FELT TOO ILL AND tired to write this for a few days,' Mary Mulry wrote in her diary on 9 July. 'Len had his bandages removed this morning. He can identify objects with his left eye although there is a great deal of blurring. It is good news. Everybody is happy for him.' Considering the appalling state Len had been in when he arrived, it was little short of miraculous that he was still alive let alone could see. It was a credit to Mary and all the doctors and nurses at the hospital, but also down to rapidly improving surgical techniques and the introduction of penicillin, the wonder drug that was so effectively combating bacterial infections. This was new medical science and something the Germans did not have. American hospitals were even better; one in four cases reaching US field hospitals in Normandy would be made fit again to head back into the line. By the standards of the war, this was a remarkable achievement, especially since these tented hospitals were operating in alternating conditions of mud and terrible dust.

The variety of wounds was extraordinary and Mary found herself having to deal with non-physical injuries too, another area where huge strides had been made. One officer, Lieutenant Martin, was just twenty years old, newly passed out of the military college at Sandhurst, but, although unscathed, was completely withdrawn and could no longer speak. 'This young man needs far more time than we can give him,' noted Mary. 'He needs sedation, reassurance and speech therapy.' On the other hand, she was touched to see how others on the ward were reacting to him with compassion and warmth. Lieutenant Martin could not stop shaking, so some of the 'up' patients were helping him to eat.

Plenty of cases, however, were beyond anything modern medicine could do to help. One day, a convoy of young Canadians from the Carpiquet battle reached the hospital, all charred from a terrible friendly-fire incident when they had been mistaken for Germans and torched by flame-throwers. Stretchers of charred bodies filled the tent, some men quietly dying, others screaming. 'Their bodies were black, their appearance horrific,' wrote Mary. 'We gave them morphia and more morphia and watched helplessly as they died. We moved the dead out of the ward and got on with trying to save the living. They were all so young and frightened.'

A generation earlier, millions of young men had been slaughtered along the Western Front, but even those men had been regularly rotated in and out of the front line, while between the big offensives – and any individual would be unfortunate to take part in more than one a year – not a huge amount happened. There was relentless shelling, and night patrol work, and there were snipers too, but these hazards were familiar to anyone fighting in Normandy. Now, though, men could be in the line for weeks at a time. Those like Bob Slaughter and the boys in the 116th Infantry, or the 4th Infantry, or the Canadians of 8th Brigade or the tank men of the Sherwood Rangers had been in the thick of it almost without let-up. And what was true of the Allies was doubly so for the Germans; Karl Wegner had been on the hoof since D-Day. So too had Hans Heinze and Kurt Meyer. Heinze's 5. Kompanie was suffering from desertions, especially from the *Volksdeutsche* – ethnic German troops from outside Germany. Deserting was a risky thing to do – if caught they would be summarily executed. None the less, Heinze could understand why they might hand themselves in. 'Our star was setting,' he said, 'so who could really blame them?'

Sergeant Charlie Martin and those of his mates in A Company who had survived intact were finally moved into a rest area on 12 July, although they were still in range of enemy shellfire. Here a mobile bath unit was set up where the men could get a shower for the first time since boarding their ships in England before the invasion. Martin had not changed his underwear since then either and, having stripped off, threw it away. The men were supposed to swap their dirty underwear for a new set, but the quartermaster running the bath unit told Martin that since he didn't have any to hand in he couldn't claim a new set. At this, Martin saw red and, picking up a Bren gun and still naked, chased him through the camp yelling at him. 'When I went back to the mobile bath,' he noted, 'there was no trouble about getting my new underwear. It had suddenly become quiet, in fact, so I helped myself to a spare set.'

The Germans suffered great shortages of water. For much of the time around Tilly, Hauptmann Helmut Ritgen and his men simply couldn't get near the River Seulles. 'Undressing and bathing were excessive luxuries,' he noted, 'but one took every opportunity to shave.' The long summer days, often quite warm even when overcast, combined with the strain on the nerves meant he and his men were always thirsty. Because of the lack of water, they took to drinking local cider, calvados, wine and even cognac, although for some reason this rarely made any of them drunk. They also smoked as many cigarettes as they could get their hands on. One of the great perks of overrunning British troops was the resultant bounty of food and especially cigarettes. Their own rations only ever came up at night and were generally pretty unpalatable.

Walter Caines and the men of the 4th Dorsets managed to do some washing in the line on 4 July. The sun came out, strong and warm, so they washed their clothes in a stream and were even issued some clean underwear there and then. This had also been Caines's first set since leaving England. Digging in, though, was a large part of daily life. Caines found himself in the front line, digging in, then pulled back a short distance, then back up at the front again. It was relentless and, as a senior NCO in the Signals Platoon, he also had to set up the signals equipment and break it down again every time. They got good at it, though. Wherever possible they would use old smashed doors, bits of wood or branches as extra cover. Charlie Martin reckoned the best kind of foxhole was L-shaped, with one man on watch in the shorter part and the other trying to get some sleep in the longer length.

Bob Slaughter was back in the line four days after being shot in the head – his only days out of the line since D-Day – and joined a slit-trench with a young prep-school boy from Maryland, called Private Lewis Cass. Slaughter, despite being only nineteen, called him 'Junior'. Their foxhole was covered with wood and topped with piled earth. Here they lived, like rats in the ground. 'Junior and I were a pitiful sight,' wrote Slaughter. 'Fine yellow dust sifted through the cracks of the roof and stuck to our sweaty skin and eyes.' Their eyes were bloodshot and swollen and, when nature called, they simply lay down and did their business into a receptacle of some kind in their trench. Although replacements were coming in all the time, Slaughter reckoned anyone who survived a week could consider themselves an old-timer. Mostly they were living off K-rations, boxes of cold food – processed meat, chocolate, hard biscuits, candy – which came in slightly different versions for breakfast, lunch and supper. They were designed to give troops enough daily energy, but men soon lost weight. Slaughter noticed their ribs, shoulder blades and Adam's apples all starting to stick out. Their uniforms were filthy, as were their hands, ingrained as they were with oil and mud. Nor was young Lieutenant Martin the only one to be tipped over the edge. Stanley Koryciak was a teenage soldier in Slaughter's Company D. Having landed on D-Day and fought well through the hedgerows, he had none the less lost several close friends. He suddenly started acting strangely and crying a lot; during heavy shelling he even became hysterical. It was clear he was suffering from combat stress and so was sent back to the kitchen area for a break; it was hoped that a couple of days out of the line, a few hot meals and some rest would see him right as rain. Instead, he blew his brains out.

'In general,' noted Helmut Ritgen, 'we lived in the ground like foxes.' They were under fire much of the time – by day from *Jabos* and also artillery, mortars and offshore naval guns, while by night artillery and mortars continued to rain down. Ritgen reckoned he could sleep through a barrage so long as it was not directly heading towards him, although sleep was never very deep. Major John Semken, commander of A Squadron, the Sherwood Rangers Yeomanry, was so exhausted during the battle for Tilly that he slept right through an artillery barrage even though the guns were firing from only a couple of hundred yards away. For the most part, Ritgen spent the night sleeping in a slit-trench underneath his panzer. He even set up the II. Bataillon command post under a panzer. In spite of the close, stale air, fumes and oil stains, it was felt this was a better option than risking living above ground.

So too did Ken Tout and Reg Spittles, who would often dig a hole in the ground and then drive their tanks over it for extra protection. Once during EPSOM, Reg Spittles and his squadron were pulled back for the night and ordered to leaguer up in an area already occupied by the infantry. Spittles was out of his tank and just about to tell his driver to switch off when a voice said, 'Do you think you could put your tank just a bit forward?' It was raining and the two men occupying the slit-trench wanted the Cromwell over them to keep them dry. Spittles was happy to oblige, because he and his crew intended to try to snatch a few hours' dozing inside the tank.

Being in a tank crew was exhausting, because manning such beasts was physically demanding and then, at the end of each day, there were maintenance checks to carry out, as well as refuelling and restocking of ammunition. This all took time and no one could get any rest until it was finished. Eating tended to be done on the fly. 'You were totally independent for eating and sleeping purposes,' said Ken Tout. 'You just ate as and when.' When on the move or out of the line, it was possible to barter for food from local farmers. Lots of tank crews kept chickens in a box either on the back or even in the hull as a supply of eggs. The whole of Normandy was strewn with dead animals, and as long as the beast hadn't already begun to rot, soldiers would readily cut them up. 'We were able to add to our rations,' said Tout, 'not an immense amount but enough to tip the scale.'

Operating a tank was not a natural occupation, however. It could get very, very hot inside and, although there were hatches, it didn't take long to fill with fumes, especially when moving a lot and firing. A stench of oil, sweat, urine, cordite and rubber pervaded the tank. Throats would quickly become dry and eyes would sting. Panthers were incredibly cramped inside despite their size. There was no way of linking the driving compartment with the turret. Inside the turret, the space was barely big enough for three men – the commander, gunner and loader. In a Sherman there was a recoil guard but, for all its complexity, there were no such precautions in the Panther; loaders, especially, must frequently have had an arm, shoulder or even head crushed.

Casualties in tanks were every bit as bad as, if not worse than, those of the infantry. The German Panthers and Tigers and the British Churchill tanks had the thickest armour, but every tank was susceptible to being hit and 'brewing up'. Shermans, Cromwells and Panzer Mk IVs were more vulnerable because they had less armour and not such a big gun as the Panthers and Tigers, so they needed to be closer to be effective. Shermans became known as 'Ronsons' after the American cigarette lighter or 'Tommy cookers' because if hit by a high-velocity shell they would often burn. Different parts of the tank had greater thickness of armour – the turret and front glacis, for example, were generally the strongest. A high-velocity 88mm shell, however, did not have to penetrate completely to kill the crew. A shell might only penetrate the size of a penny, for example, but that might be enough to punch out a ring the size of the shell's diameter on the other side. A large part of this would hit the nearest hard object but the rest – the spawling – would amount to thousands of molten bits of steel that would be flung around the inside of the tank and then cool into jagged shards. If these hit the explosive charge in the ammunition stacked within the tank, then the consequences could be catastrophic. The kinetic pressure inside the tank caused by the shell could also be fatal. If a tank started to burn then the crew had only moments to get out; on other occasions the combination of blast and pressure meant the entire inside blew up with everything in it. Not uncommon was the sight of a turret, several tons in weight, bursting into the air like a champagne cork. Very, very few tank crews survived more than a week or two in the front line without their tank being knocked out in some shape or form; it might be a broken track, or something quite minor, but the moment the tank stopped in the middle of an action, it became a sitting rather than a moving target, which in turn made it considerably more vulnerable.

On 7 July, twelve days after originally planned, the Panzer-Lehr finally began moving westwards to help support the defence of Saint-Lô, although it was planned that it should, for the time being, avoid contact with the enemy. It was to be the reserve mobile force. One of Hauptmann Helmut Ritgen's panzer companies was to stay behind for a couple of days longer, while the rest set off that night. Even though the distance was only a matter of 25 miles or so, it still took them the best part of three nights to shift to their new positions as they wound their way through rough, narrow roads, pitted with bomb craters and wreckage.

They finally reached their assembly area near Pont-Hébert at around midnight on the 9th and were immediately flung into an attack, something they had been assured would not happen. Such, though, was the desperate nature of the situation and the threat from the latest American push. It meant they had had no time for any kind of reconnaissance, nor any appreciation of the kind of dense bocage in that part of Normandy. 'The bocage,' noted Ritgen, 'allowed for neither wide fields of fire, nor movement on either side of the few narrow roads, tank commitment was difficult.' Every single American and British tank crew would have agreed with his assessment.

Inevitably, the counter-attack failed completely. As in the open ground further to the east, so it was in the bocage: attacking successfully – and decisively – was extremely difficult. Ritgen lost two more of his officers that night and even more in the days that followed. Because of the short-age of fire-power and dwindling numbers of infantry, his panzers were being forced to act as anti-tank gunners, blocking roads and potential choke-points. What's more, because of the infantry shortage, they were being committed for longer than was bearable and were suffering the same if not worse artillery and mortar response to movement in the American sector as they had in the British and Canadian. 'My crews suffered greatly from the inability to move,' Ritgen noted, 'with swollen limbs and shattered nerves.' By 15 July, he had lost fifteen officers from the battalion since their deployment to Normandy; of the lieutenants with whom the battalion had left Germany, not a single one now remained. Nor was the situation much better with the NCOs. It was bad for morale as well as combat effectiveness. Ritgen was suffering from the burden of responsibility, from witnessing the loss of so many of his men, from the relentlessness of the action. Even when away from the front line there was no escape. What had happened to his II. Bataillon was representative of the division as a whole. It had arrived in France supremely well equipped, but from the moment it began its move to Normandy it began to be chewed up, bit by bit, day by day. Soon there would barely be a division left at all. And the Americans had not even launched their main offensive yet.

While the Allies had unquestionably won the battle of the build-up, more and more German troops were reaching the front. As with the first reinforcements posted to Normandy, they were arriving piecemeal, one unit at a time, torturously heading along roads and rail lines broken by incessant Allied air attacks or by Résistance networks, SAS teams and Jedburghs. Strict new instructions were issued to all who were attempting to travel these routes. 'March on several roads. Avoid main roads!' ran the new instructions. 'Every man of the unit must know the destination (write it down!) Reason: if a marching platoon is blown apart by an air raid, each vehicle and each soldier must nevertheless reach the marching destination. Do not use closed passenger cars during aviation weather! If necessary, place observers on foot boards or fenders!' It went on with details about guards, camouflage, the right process for awaiting road repair units, the distance vehicles should keep from each other. It was accepted there would be losses. The key, these new instructions made clear, was to try to keep these to a minimum.

It made the journey to Normandy an agonizingly slow one, as Artillerie-Regiment 277 discovered. Attached to the 277. Infanterie-Division, they had been based near Béziers in the south of France and were given their marching orders on 23 June. Kanonier Eberhard Beck was an 18-year-old gunner in 10. Batterie of heavy 150mm sfH18 howitzers. Born in Tirana, Albania, he had been drafted very reluctantly and would never have dreamed of wearing a uniform had it not been for the war. In the south of France conditions had been spartan and tough, but at least it had been quiet and he had dutifully attended his training, albeit without much enthusiasm. Now he was heading to the front and to battle. It did not appeal at all; he just wished the war would be over.

The journey began on trains, which were slow and often interrupted, but after reaching the River Loire they marched the rest of the way, the barrels and gun carriages towed separately by horses, just as they had been in the days of Frederick the Great. 'It was incredibly cumbersome when a horse lost a shoe and then came the command, "Shoeing master forward!"' wrote Beck. 'Such actions paralyzed everything. It disordered the whole unit, disrupted and delayed the advance.' As they finally neared the front, so they were joined by infantry units trudging alongside them, despite the instructions for them to march separately and spaced apart. Repeatedly as they passed this procession of horse-drawn artillery, they asked Beck and his comrades when the new miracle weapons would be arriving.

On the last night of marching, as Beck and his comrades neared the front, they saw the sky lit up with shellfire and flares: the ongoing battle for Caen. And then they were in the ruins of Évrecy, just a couple of miles south-east of Hill 112. 'Fields and streets were brightly lit by the fire of the front,' he wrote. 'It twitched and flashed along the entire length . . . One was tired from the march and very upset. The gunfire became louder, brighter and brighter.' They moved up to straddle the road between Évrecy and Esquay-Notre-Dame, which led up past the northern side of Hill 112 and on towards Éterville and Caen. It was around 2 a.m. on Sunday, 9 July. Beck was assigned to the second gun, which the horses pulled into a narrow, uneven lane lined by high trees. After a few hundred yards they pulled off the track and into a clearing surrounded by more trees, which would give them some much-needed cover. Beck clambered up one tree to cut way some of the branches and as he did so enemy shells screamed over. Soon after, they suffered their first casualty. One of the horse drivers was killed as he took the horses away from the guns. 'It was said his head,' noted Beck, 'had been ripped off by a shell.' The next task was to start digging a foxhole. Beck was exhausted; they all were. And hungry. At first light, a kitchen wagon arrived with some hot food at their firing position. All was well until more shells whistled over, the horses reared and the food canister was knocked over.

Later that day, he and his comrades went to explore their new surroundings and met some SS men from the 9. 'Hohenstaufen' Division. Beck and his mates could only marvel at the SS men's camouflage smocks, shiny new weapons and latest equipment. Beck had respect for these men but did not envy them. 'For us,' wrote Beck, 'the war was long lost, we had to survive. We knew that these units were ruthlessly led into the fire.'

Unbeknown to Eberhard Beck, he had arrived just a day before Second Army launched its latest attack, Operation JUPITER. Although much of Caen had now fallen, the Germans were still stubbornly holding the ground to the south-east on the far side of the River Orne and they still held Hill 112, which both General Miles Dempsey and General Hans Eberbach, Geyr's replacement, were well aware was a vital piece of high ground. And while General O'Connor's decision to pull back from the hill ten days earlier might well have been the right one, there was no denying it was going to be a tougher nut to crack for a second time. Holding the line were the 9. SS- and 10. SS-Panzer-Divisions, both in far better condition than 12. SS and now with all their units arrived at the front. Additionally, they had the Schwere SS-Panzerabteilung – Heavy Tank Battalion – 102 of Tigers attached, as well as an array of 88mm and anti-tank guns and the 277. Infanterie-Division also joining II. SS-Panzerkorps. It was the 43rd Wessex Division who were to assault the hill, supported by Churchills and flame-throwing Crocodiles.

Supporting the Wessexmen was the usual heavy artillery. Sergeant Walter Caines had never experienced anything like it. He could hardly hear himself think. The barrage was followed by the arrival of Typhoons overhead, strafing enemy positions with rockets, bombs and cannons. The first objectives were taken easily, largely because Eberbach had already ordered his men back to a line straddling Hill 112. Caines had set up the signals equipment near the battalion's start line. Enemy 'Moaning Minnies' and shells screamed over, but the first prisoners were also being brought in; Caines thought they looked exhausted and terrified. A few hours later, word reached the battalion CP that Éterville, right on the Évrecy–Caen road, had been successfully captured, so Caines and the rest of the Signals Platoon moved up with Battalion Headquarters to the shattered remains of the village church. 'Shells rained down upon us as we entered,' noted Caines, 'and it was truly terrifying and most nerve-racking. It appeared to us that we would not have an easy stay in this village and to be quite honest, I thought that if every attack was to be like this, I could not guarantee my own life longer than a few days.'

Vicious fighting continued all day. With their thick 150mm frontal armour, 30mm greater than any other tank on the battlefield, the Churchills were, on paper, a good option for supporting the advancing infantry, and to begin with progress was good. Not only was Éterville taken, so too was Maltot beyond, while both tanks and infantry managed to rumble up the shallow, steady and wide incline to the ridge of Hill 112. As they neared the summit, however, the waiting array of Tigers and 88s on the far side was able to blast them at short range. Not even the Churchills' frontal armour was enough. The 31st Armoured Brigade lost 39 tanks that day, most left strewn and burning amid the crater-pitted open ground of the hill.

Later, 43rd Division commander Major-General Ivor 'Butcher' Thomas ordered another brigade of tanks, this time thinner-skinned Shermans, to push on through the Churchills, but the new and young Brigadier Michael Carver point-blank refused, leading to an angry exchange between the two. Carver, though, was in situ and could see that his Shermans would be entering an attack more suicidal than that of the Light Brigade at Balaclava. He unquestionably made the right decision.

In the meantime, Walter Caines had watched large numbers of casualties stream back into the village; the medical officer and his team were struggling to cope. Caines and his men were feverishly digging in – he reckoned he was digging for two hours solidly, while smoking endless cigarettes and taking swigs from his water bottle. The company runner commented on how calm he seemed. 'Little did he know,' noted Caines, 'how scared I was.' Moments later, two Bren Carriers just 60 yards away were hit and burst into flames. Caines realized the armoured car with the radio link to the gunners was in danger of being hit by the exploding ammunition on the burning Carriers. It was parked in a lane blocked by several abandoned motorbikes but, with a couple of men, he dashed across and pulled the bikes out of the way just as a shell screamed over his head and hit a wall behind them. But they were still in one piece and the armoured car was now able to move to a safer position.

At 3 p.m. their positions were taken over by the Cameronians and they were able to pull back to the edge of a wood, where they discovered a number of dead Germans. They had barely had a chance to replenish batteries and catch their breath when word arrived that the Hampshires were all but surrounded in Maltot and needed help. Accompanied by tanks, they set off, only to be hammered as they reached the edge of the village. Caines was following with the signals team and Battalion Head-quarters but, as they crossed the open wheatfield before the village, machine guns raked them. 'It was hell,' wrote Caines. 'No-one dared put his head above the corn. As soon as Jerry observed the slightest move-ment, a long burst of fire would be the reply.' They remained there, pinned down, until about 7 p.m., when they were finally ordered to pull back.

It was too late for A Company, however, which had led the attack on Maltot; the entire company had been killed, wounded or captured. The survivors now frantically dug in along a line they were told to hold at all costs. Caines discovered most of his signals equipment had been destroyed during the attack, while the signallers moving up with the companies had either lost or abandoned their wireless sets; two signallers had been badly wounded, two captured and at least one killed. It had been a terrible day for the 4th Dorsets; a terrible day for the entire division.

At dawn the next day, Tuesday, 11 July, Caines and his fellows stood to, dog tired and fit to drop. It had been the worst twenty-four hours of his life. 'Something I will never forget as long as I live,' he wrote, 'seeing men fall, and hearing the wounded cry and moan with pain.' They were also raven-ously hungry. One of the cooks and some of the men managed to salvage a few compo ration packs from some knocked-out Carriers and so everyone got something. More worrying to Caines was the loss of his cigarettes – he had become something of a chain-smoker since arriving in Normandy – but he managed to scrounge enough to keep himself going.

The German mortars opened just after first light and soon they could see the enemy forming up for a counter-attack. Caines watched one of the forward observation officers directing the artillery behind them from a scout car. 'We thanked God for this,' noted Caines, 'as within a few moments down came our murderous artillery barrage, crash, crash. They could be seen bursting on the edge of the corn field amongst the Jerries.' Two tanks were on fire in moments.

The battle petered out by evening. Yet again, the British had probed forward with their infantry and armour, and once more they had stalled against the well-dug-in Germans with their machine guns, mortars and high-velocity anti-tank guns. But equally as predictably, the Germans had then launched a series of furious counter-attacks, at which point Allied fire-power kicked in and stopped them dead in their tracks. The following day, the 12th, the 4th Dorsets were out of the line and the sur-vivors were able to wash, shave and clean themselves up. There was little chance to rest, however, for all the kit of those killed had to be unloaded from the rear echelon vehicles, then sifted and sent to the next of kin. Caines sorted out the kit of those in the Signals Platoon with Corporal Penny. Tears came to his eyes as he looked through the photographs of the wives, sweethearts and families of the boys he had lost.

Yet more men were reaching the front, and the first experience of combat was for many a terrible shock – a hellish experience for which no amount of training could prepare them. On 12 July, 17-year-old Willi Müller and the rest of the 17. SS-Panzergrenadier-Division's Pioneer-Bataillon finally arrived a month after the division's first units. The journey up had been predictably awful – agonizingly slow and harried by *Jabos* all the way – and much to the annoyance of Müller and his comrades they were taking over positions that had been held by the I. Bataillon of SS-Panzergrenadier-Regiment 38 on either side of the village of Tribehou. As soon as they arrived, reconnaissance parties were sent out. One group almost immediately ran into some Americans and were promptly captured, while Müller, packed off in a *Schwimmwagen* – an amphibious vehicle – with his comrades Lange and Speidel, was lucky not to get killed. Setting off towards the village of Les Champs-de-Losque, just a few miles to the south-east, they were soon attacked by a *Jabo*. Hurriedly stopping the car, they jumped out and straight into another unit, whose adjutant explained that his commander had been killed and American tanks were breaking through. Suddenly, the next *Jabo* dived down on them and Müller flung himself against the hedgerow as bullets hissed and zipped around him. When the planes had gone, he returned to the road only to discover the *Schwimmwagen* and his two comrades had disappeared. Müller couldn't believe they had abandoned him, then realized that the adjutant must have commandeered them both to take him straight away to the battalion command post to report the American breakthrough.

Stranded and alone, he tried to get back to base, but it was several miles away. He began running, but suddenly the road was under fire from American artillery, the shells screaming over. Every time he heard the tell-tale whistle, he dived into the hedgerow, tried to make himself as small as possible, then got up again and carried on running. At one point he found an old bicycle. One of the tyres was flat, but he wasn't going to worry about that; anything to get him back. Eventually he saw a car coming towards him and, hailing it, was relieved to see it was their own adjutant. Brought back, he was once again sent off to fulfil the original recce mission with Lange and Speidel. It seemed crazy, but on the other hand the battalion had only just moved in, the ground was unfamiliar and, if the Americans really were breaking through, they obviously needed to know about it and to find out where exactly the penetration was taking place.

They set off again, stopping only when they spotted a frightened and helmetless German, who told them the Americans were all around them. As if on cue, they heard the chatter of an American machine gun behind them. Müller and his mates decided they couldn't possibly be taken prisoner; if it came to it, they would take their egg grenades and blow themselves up. 'How did we come to such a terrible idea?' wrote Müller. 'In our subconscious, we knew it was unworthy for a Waffen SS soldier to be captured. Thank God it didn't come to that!' In fact, once darkness came the sound of battle stopped, so they began walking, eventually reaching the piquets, who were *Fallschirmjäger*. It was now past midnight and they didn't know the password, but managed to convince the guards of who they were. Allowed to pass, they pressed on and soon found the remains of their two companies. Müller's first day at the front had certainly been memorable: he had been repeatedly strafed from the air, shelled, had twice got lost, then found himself surrounded by the enemy and contemplating suicide. 'Can a seventeen-year-old forget a day like that?' he wondered.

On the other side of the hedgerow, William Biehler had reached the front and joined his rifle platoon in the 90th Division, now back in the line with something to prove. His 1st Platoon of Company K, 357th Infantry Regiment were in action on 6 July, part of VII Corps' broad push southwards, and were attacking through the bocage along an old Roman axis road that ran from the village of Saint-Jores to Le Plessis-Lastelle. By the time Company K attacked, at around 3 p.m. that afternoon, they were approaching some high ground immediately to the south of the hamlet of Beau-Coudray.

Here, the aces were all with the defenders. Just to the north of Beau-Coudray was a particularly dense network of fields, and that had been hard enough to capture. Just to the south, the ground was on a rise and laced with a series of parallel hedgerows that ran roughly west–east, so at 90 degrees to the axis of the American advance. It is hard to find a more dense patchwork of hedgerows anywhere in Normandy, with some of the fields only 20–30 yards wide. There were gaps in the corners of the field that Biehler and the 1st Platoon were attacking, so the first two men went through and were immediately blasted backwards by artillery fire.

'Medic!' someone shouted.

'I don't think a medic's going to help them,' said Biehler as he looked down at their lifeless bodies, blood pouring from their mouths. But they had been taught never to pause and to always keep going, so Biehler and his new fellows in his squad ran past and into the field. 'The machine guns were firing,' he recalled, 'and the first two were killed and there's three left out there. All of a sudden I look around and there's nobody else there but me. So I got up and ran back.' They were up against the machine-gun rich Fallschirmjäger-Regiment 15, the latest German paratrooper unit to reach Normandy. Safely back behind the hedgerows, Biehler and his comrades radioed for artillery and air support. Soon American shells were screaming over, then P-47 Thunderbolts turned up and plastered the German positions. It didn't stop them from getting bogged down at Beau-Coudray, however, and Biehler and his mates in the 3rd Battalion were dug into foxholes and had to see off some fourteen counter-attacks by the enemy between then and 11 July. During one attack, Biehler was aston-ished to see the *Fallschirmjäger* charge across the field, gleaming bayonets fixed to their rifles and martial music playing from their lines. 'We just fired until we almost ran out of ammunition,' he said. It was enough to stall the attack, however. Yet again, the same pattern was being replayed: attack with the infantry, take the hits, fall back, wait for the counter-attacks, hammer the enemy. It was slow, attritional and costly, but there was no real alternative.

Second Lieutenant Richard Blackburn first went into action just a few miles to the west of the 90th Division, at the town of La Haye-du-Puits. Blackburn, who had turned twenty-five on 3 July, was from Bedford County, Pennsylvania, and, although he had been eligible for the draft from 1940, had not been called up until February 1942. As a college graduate, he had initially been singled out for staff work, but he had done well in his training, was physically strong and bright enough to apply for Officer Candidate School, even though that meant applying for the infantry, something he had vowed never to do. He had accepted, though, that he could do more to help win the war by carrying a rifle than by sit-ting behind a desk filling out endless forms. A devout Christian, he believed it was his moral duty. 'After much thought and prayer,' he wrote, 'it just seemed the right way to go.'

On 4 July, he had reached Normandy as a replacement officer, one

Left: Canadian troops of Charlie Martin's battalion, the Queen's Own Rifles, pose by the city sign for Caen on 9 July 1944. By the time they finally took the town, there wasn't much of it left. The level of destruction in Normandy and the number of towns and villages pulverized was horrific.

Above left: British troops awaiting a counter-attack in hastily dug trenches and foxholes between Hills 112 and 113 on 16 July 1944. One exhausted Tommy has a kip while his mates keep watch.

Above right: A Stuart light tank equipped with a hedge-cutter, conceived, developed and built with immense speed by the Americans in July 1944.

Left: US troops street-fighting, July 1944.

THE ALLIES' MATERIEL STRENGTH

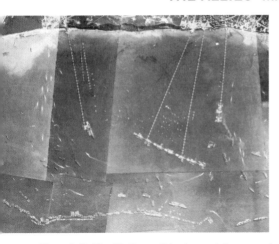

Above left: The Mulberry B harbour at Arromanches, a phenomenal achievement and a huge contribution to continuing the flow of supplies.

Above right: Incredibly, railway tracks and carriages were run straight off landing ships. Allied logisticians were not afraid to think big.

Above: Vast numbers of trucks were brought over, then safely parked in huge fields like this one. Unlike the Germans, the Allies had little to fear from the skies above.

Left: Bulldozers were much needed in Normandy and were also shipped in huge numbers.

A convoy of supply lorries (**below left**) and fuel pipelines (**below right**), swiftly laid to keep the enormous number of vehicles in the Allied armies running.

Never had armies in the field been so well serviced. Allied armoured units were supported by large numbers of low-loaders (**below**), tank-wreckers (**below middle**), mobile workshops and (**right**) field maintenance units.

Below left: Hedge-cutters being mass-produced in the field, using blow torches to cut up and weld Rommel's beach obstacles into teeth to put on the front of the tanks.

Below right: While hedge-cutters could cut through hedgerows like butter, dozers were equally effective.

ALLIED FIRE-POWER

The Allied way of war was to use infantry and armour to goad the Germans into counter-attacking and then hammer them with their immense weight of fire-power. **Above left**: A British 155mm gun blasts enemy targets. **Above right**: A US Sherman of the 3rd Armored Division with an up-gunned 76mm high-velocity gun and a hedge-cutter. In terms of the gun, this was on a par with the Panther and Tiger.

Above left: The same was true of the British Sherman Firefly, equipped with a 17-pounder anti-tank gun, which had a greater velocity than the fabled German 88mm. **Above right**: An American M10 tank destroyer. Tank destroyers were developed by the Americans and were equipped with an anti-tank gun, were fast and manoeuvrable but lightly armoured.

A US M4 high-speed tractor tows a heavy 8-inch howitzer of the 153rd Field Artillery Battalion.

GERMAN FIRE-POWER

A camouflaged StuG, an effective low-profile assault gun on a Panzer Mk III chassis.

Panthers. Mechanically complicated but well armoured and powerfully gunned, they were understandably feared by Allied troops.

A group of *Fallschirmjäger*. Under-mechanized they may have been, but they were bristling with machine guns – more so than ordinary infantry units.

The panzer 'ace' Michael Wittmann in the turret of his Tiger.

Above left: A Panzer Mk IV – comparable with the Sherman and Cromwell, and the most common of German tanks by a considerable margin. **Above right**: Not all 'eighty-eights' really were 88mms, but this is the classic dual-purpose anti-tank/anti-aircraft high-velocity gun in action.

Below left: An Sd.Kfz 'Wespe' assault gun, developed by adding a 105mm howitzer on to the chassis of an obsolescent Panzer Mk II. **Below right**: A Pak 40 75mm anti-tank gun. The Germans were skilled at positioning and camouflaging such weapons.

THE BRUTALITY OF NORMANDY

The fighting in Normandy was absolutely brutal, with average daily casualty rates that exceeded the worst battles of the First World War. **Left**: A British ammunition truck is hit and explodes during the EPSOM battle, 26 June 1944. **Below**: Lines of dead await burial.

Left: German dead of 1. SS-Panzer-Division lie beside another column caught out in the open.

Below left: A dead soldier floats in the flooding around the base of the Cotentin.

Below: Hungry French civilians carve up a horse that has been killed in the fighting.

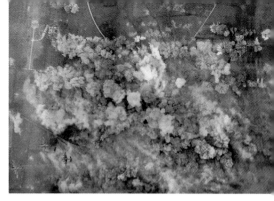

Above left: Generals Bradley (**left**), Eisenhower (**centre**) and Ira T. Wyche of the 79th Infantry Division confer at Bradley's tented HQ.

Above right: Villers-Bocage, briefly liberated by the Allies on 13 June, disappears under smoke as Allied strategic heavy bombers pulverize it on 4 August. Ninety per cent of the town was completely destroyed.

Left: American troops of the US 4th Armored Division pass through Folligny on 31 July 1944 during the breakout after COBRA.

Below left: Saint-Lô. Two French children look down on the ruins of their shattered city.

Below right: By the time the ancient city of Falaise was finally captured by the Allies, the German armies in Normandy were imploding and desperately fleeing through the narrow gap still left open.

Above left: Operation TOTALIZE. Allied heavy bombers hammer German positions as planned on 9 August.

Above right: Long columns of Shermans of the Polish Armoured Division ready to move forward during TOTALIZE.

It is hard to overstate how important Allied air power was during the battle for Normandy, and no aircraft better symbolizes that dominance than the extraordinary rocket-firing Hawker Typhoon, here taking off from an airfield in Normandy (**left**) and (**above right**) firing a salvo of four of its eight rockets.

Below: The Corridor of Death. One of the most beautiful areas of northern France was devastated by the terrible carnage of two annihilated armies trying to flee. The roads and lanes were clogged with dead men, horses and wrecked vehicles.

of the toughest cards to have been given, and was assigned to Company A, 121st Infantry Regiment in the 8th Infantry Division, joining the company on 13 July under Captain Arthur Kaiser, a kindly fellow, who immediately welcomed him in but warned him sombrely to remove his lieutenant's tabs from his collar as the Germans would purposely target officers. Blackburn was shocked by the scene of death and destruction around him. Just a few feet away from where he and Kaiser were talking lay two dead Germans, their bodies bloated with gases, their skin distorted.

The following day, Friday, 14 July, the battalion attacked south towards the Ay River. The ground was a continuous stretch of swampland, ankle-deep to begin with but then knee-deep. They immediately came under small-arms, mortar and artillery fire. Bullets began to ping and hiss past Blackburn as they approached the jump-off point for the attack, and he could feel his heart pounding, although curiously he didn't feel scared exactly. He thought about what might happen to him but was glad he could still think. Dead men lay in the swamp, on the roads and in the ditches. Collapsed buildings, once homes, were in ruins. Smashed vehicles were burning, their occupants with them.

Now came the order to move forward into attack and Blackburn was moving forward, urging his men. There was nothing glorious about it, he realized. It was brutal, violent, and death hovered above each man. Somehow, though, he got through, the objective taken, and so began the process of digging in, his first experience of every infantryman's task. Within a few days, his newcomer's sheen had gone. Several days' growth of beard covered his filthy face; he was dirty, smelly and living in a hole in the ground. 'It was very difficult,' he wrote, 'getting accustomed to the fact that a German soldier was always in the next hedgerow, in a window in the next house, in the ditch just ahead, or behind the next tree, waiting to kill me.'

By mid-July there was still no sign of a decisive breakthrough for the Allies, but they were making ground, chipping away at the enemy, grinding them down and whittling away at their strength. They were learning too. The US 2nd 'Warrior' Division had been stuck below the ridge around Hill 192 since 11 June, but when they launched their third major attack on 12 July they did so with the support of one armoured field artillery regiment, two extra battalions of the neighbouring Big Red One, and an armoured regiment as well. What's more, despite the enormous losses over the past month, replacements had arrived and ensured the assaulting battalions were doing so at pretty much full strength, which was more than could be said for the 3. Fallschirmjäger-Division defending the position. That day, the Americans finally took Hill 192, advancing 1,500 yards and getting very close to the vital Bayeux–Saint-Lô highway.

The following day, Thursday, 13 July, the *New York Times* reporter Hanson Baldwin arrived at Bradley's headquarters and proceeded to lecture Chet Hansen and other staff, making little effort to conceal his contempt for the Allies' limited progress inland. 'Disregarding the bocage country we fight in,' noted Hansen, 'and the terrain which hinders our movements, the swamps which canalize our advance, the lack of space in which to maneuver and the necessity for build-up before we break out, he asks why we haven't gone more quickly.' Hansen was quite right to feel indignant. Baldwin was doing what others back in England were doing: looking at a two-dimensional map and comparing the Normandy battle with that raging on the Eastern Front, where the rapid Soviet advances had already cost the Red Army hundreds of thousands of casualties – the kind of losses that could only be absorbed by a totalitarian regime like that of Stalin's, where the lives of his men counted for nothing. The democratic Allies, with their conscript armies, were simply not going to squander the lives of their young boys so recklessly, and their commanders and war leaders were better people for taking this approach. Huge materiel support was the way to go, with ever-improving technology and tactics. For all Baldwin's contemptible and arrogant lecturing, the Allied way was working. If Eisenhower, Montgomery, Bradley and others could have been flies on the walls within the HQs and command posts of their adversaries, they would have taken great heart. The dam had not broken yet, and there were still disappointments to come over the course of the next week, but they were close. The breakout for which they had been striving since D-Day was now within reach.

A Canadian Sherman crew from the South Alberta Regiment rest to the south of Caen, 28 July 1944.

PART IV

Breakout

CHAPTER 27

A Brief Discourse on Weapons and the Operational Level of War

THERE IS A PERSISTENT myth that despite materiel wealth, the Allies were facing a German Army equipped with far better weaponry. It is a myth that needs to be knocked on the head. In terms of small arms – pistols, rifles, sub-machine guns and machine guns – there really wasn't much of a difference.

American troops tended to fetishize the German Luger, a pistol that was designed in 1898, although the wartime version dated to the P08 version first produced ten years later. It was a perfectly adequate semi-automatic pistol that fired a 9mm slug, although far more common was the Walther P38. A number of other pistols, such as smaller Sauers and other Walthers, were issued to Luftwaffe and tank crews. Pistols were used for very close-quarter combat and at ranges of up to 10–20 yards they were, frankly, much of a muchness. If a person found himself in a situation where he needed to use his pistol, the most important thing was to make sure he killed the person trying to kill him, so the bigger the bullet (calibre) and lower the velocity, the better. Smaller bullets from higher-velocity pistols might easily pass through a victim quite neatly, but a lower-velocity and bigger slug would hit its target and the kinetic energy spread out on impact, causing much greater damage. At close quarters, it was generally best to try to kill one's enemy with a single shot.

This was why the American Colt .45 semi-automatic, first in service in

1911, was the one to have if there was a choice in the matter. It was solid as a rock, packed a punch and did what it promised on the packaging. The British and Canadians had a lot of these – they were issued to airborne forces, Commandos and tank crew, as well as to some infantry officers. The British also had revolvers, which were powerful, but it was not ideal to have to fiddle around reloading individual bullets with shaking fingers in the heat of battle. American Lieutenant Orion Shockley experienced this difference in calibres first-hand in Cherbourg. On the outskirts, he was on the right flank of a platoon as they approached a barracks-style building. As he started around one corner of the building, he heard a noise and, pulling out his British Webley .38-calibre pistol, saw a lone German emerge. 'Achtung!' Shockley yelled at him, but the soldier swung his MP40 at him. Shockley fired, hitting his adversary in the shoulder, but, rather than being knocked down, the man just staggered and tried to fire his sub-machine gun again. Shockley fired a second time and on this occasion hit him in the head and killed him. 'Examining his wounds, we learned a lesson,' he noted. 'A .38 calibre gun did not carry the shocking or knockdown power of a .45 calibre bullet.'

In terms of rifles, the German Mauser-breech K.98 was the least effective. It could take only five bullets at a time and the bolt came back so far that anyone aiming it had to move their face away and re-aim each time he fired. The British Short Magazine Lee–Enfield Mk IV had a shorter bolt and a magazine that could take ten rounds and could be topped up at any point, and because the short bolt didn't require any movement of aim, its user could fire double the rounds per minute of his German adversary. The Americans had bolt-action Springfields and, more commonly, the M1 Garand, which was the first semi-automatic rifle to enter service and therefore had no bolt. It held eight rounds, but could not be replenished until all eight had been fired. All were well built and reliable, and a good marksman could fell a man at 400 yards using any one of these weapons.

Sub-machine guns were also close-quarters weapons, ideal for laying down considerable numbers of bullets in quite a wide area. These would be best used to clear buildings and trenches, and in close hedgerow fighting. The Americans had the Thompson, which was heavy at 10 lb, but which also fired the bigger, more lethal .45-calibre slug and which in the US, British and Canadian armies generally had a 30-round stick magazine. The Americans also had the M3 'grease gun', which was only 8 lb and smaller, but which also fired a 30-round magazine of .45-calibre bullets. It was cheap, simple, but a little unreliable and generally not popular.

Its unreliability issues would be ironed out, but they hadn't been by the summer of 1944.

Another sub-machine gun with a mixed reputation was the British Sten gun, which was of even simpler construction, could easily be reduced into different parts so packed down very well, was light and was incredibly cheap to make. It was known to fire a bit too easily and the magazine, which fed two bullets alternately into a single chamber, could jam, but its early shortcomings had been largely resolved by D-Day. Because it was so simple, there was less to go wrong and it was pretty indestructible. It fired a 9mm bullet, so could use captured German ammunition should the opportunity arise, and it also had a magazine that extended sideways from the left, so could be fired lying down, something no other sub-machine gun could do unless angled sideways.

The Germans had MP38s and more commonly MP40s, essentially the same weapon, and known to Allied troops as Schmeissers. These were fine bits of kit, beautifully made and balanced. Over ranges of 75 yards, the Thompson and MP40 were fractionally more accurate, but weapons such as these were generally used at ranges of 30 yards or less, in which case there was nothing to choose between them. The MP40 was incredibly expensive and over-engineered – especially so at this stage of the war, when the Germans were short of just about everything.

The same could be said for their light machine guns. The very expensive MG34 had been largely replaced by the MG42, but this still took 75 man-hours to make compared with 45–50 man-hours for British and American machine guns. It had a rapid rate of fire of some 1,400 rounds per minute, which was incredibly useful in an ambush or when initially attacking men landing on a beach, but there was a pay-off: it was something of a scatter gun, so not very accurate, and because of the very rapid rate of fire, with some fifteen bullets each detonating a small charge in the breech every second, quickly overheated. Very strict firing discipline was needed, as well as multiple barrel changes, which meant German squads – or *Gruppen* – had to carry at least six spares, all of which had multiple inspection stamps on them. Such attention to detail was partly because of excellent engineering standards that the Germans were simply unable to get out of their system, and partly because they used so much slave labour and were understandably concerned about sabotage. It still added time and money, however. Every MG42 cost some 250 Reichsmarks, around $10,500 in today's money.

The Americans had the Browning Automatic Rifle, or BAR, which was a halfway house between rifle and light machine gun, and fired a 20-round magazine. It cost half the price of an MG42 to produce. The BAR was good as far as it went, while the Americans also used the heavier, belt-fed .30-calibre Browning M1919, which was superb: solid, reliable, and fired at a sensible and effective rate with unerring accuracy. The British had the Bren, which was also very reliable and extremely accurate, hardly ever needed a barrel change – each was engineered to fire at least 250,000 rounds – and had a helpful wooden grip on the barrel, which made it easier to carry and also to change its barrel when this finally needed to be done. It was magazine- rather than belt-fed.

Despite the different approaches and rates of fire, all these weapons operated at an effective rate of fire – rather than an actual rate – of around 120 rounds per minute. In other words, they all had their strengths and weaknesses. In an ideal world, both sides would have probably liked to have had a combination of all varieties. It is certainly not true, however, to say that the MG42 was the best machine gun of the war, as has been repeatedly claimed over the years. Fastest rate of fire, yes, and a fine weapon in many ways, but with disadvantages too. Overall, there wasn't a huge amount to choose between the various small arms of the differing combatant nations.

While the merits or otherwise of German small arms has been the subject of feverish debate, this pales into insignificance compared with opinions about tanks and anti-tank guns. In this, the Germans have long since been held to have had the upper hand, while British tanks, especially, have been the object of exasperated contempt. This was true even during the war. In the summer of 1942, for example, the British minister of supply, Oliver Lyttelton, was forced to defend British tank and anti-tank production in Parliament, patiently pointing out that British anti-tank guns were as good as those of the Germans and ditto their tanks. At the time, he was quite right.

Allied combatants themselves really fed the debate, as they saw Tiger and Panther tanks and 88mms at every turn. Letters, diaries, memoirs and interviews all talk about being fired at by 'eighty-eights'. Sometimes they really were 88mms – or Flak 36s as they were officially known – but the Germans had a lot of other artillery, such as heavy howitzers like the 150mm that Eberhard Beck was operating, as well as many others besides, and not just German ones, but also guns pilfered from all corners by their earlier conquering armies. It could make the quartermaster's task tricky, because the German armies in Normandy were using a staggering number of different calibres, not to mention different firing tables. General Hans Eberbach, now commanding Panzergruppe West, reckoned he had 133 batteries, or some 400 guns, not including flak. 'But since ammunition was so scarce that firing had to be kept at a ratio of 10:1 to the British expenditure,' he noted, 'the many guns and rocket launchers were of little use to me.' This was perhaps overstating matters, but certainly among Panzergruppe West's arsenal were twenty-four Italian heavy guns that fired so badly that, once they had used all the available ammunition, Eberbach ordered their demolition; they were more hassle than they were worth.

Most German anti-tank guns, however, were not the 88mm dual-purpose anti-aircraft/anti-tank gun, although there were, admittedly, a good number of those. This was a heavy weapon of some 5 tons and, because it was designed primarily to shoot down aircraft, it had a high profile that made it vulnerable. It could, however, fire an 88mm-diameter shell at around 2,690 feet per second, which meant very often those coming under fire only realized what was happening once it had already reached the target – which could sometimes be too late.

All anti-tank guns, though, were high-velocity. That was the entire point: to hurtle a shell on a flat trajectory with an enormous amount of power and energy. Howitzers – field artillery – by contrast, were designed to lob shells great distances, and not in a direct-fire scenario but blindly, behind a hill, for example, with the aid of spotters and observers to direct their fire who would be further forward. For both types of gun, there were high-explosive and armour-piercing shells, depending on the target. As a rule of thumb, the bigger the shell, the bigger the explosion, damage and crater. Despite the term '88' being used by Allied troops as a catch-all for all German anti-tank weapons, the mainstays were actually the Pak 38, which fired a 50mm shell, and the Pak 40, which fired a 75mm round. Both were lower-profile weapons, lighter, much more versatile and more easily towed by horses as well as by vehicles. Although these were the most common, there were also numerous others, mostly converted captured guns and also a specialist 88mm anti-tank gun, the Pak 43, which could fire at 3,280 feet per second and had a much lower profile.

By the middle of July, the number of German tanks and assault guns that had reached Normandy was around 2,500. Of those that would take part in the campaign, only two were King Tigers and a mere 126 were

Tigers, despite the propensity for Allied troops to spot them lurking around every corner. There were many more Panthers, some 655 in all, but most common was the Panzer Mk IV, which looked a bit like a smaller Tiger and was therefore, unsurprisingly, the cause of a lot of mis-identification. This was a medium tank comparable with the basic 75mm-gun Sherman; in fact, their guns were very similar. There were also a lot of StuGs, some 453 in all, which were assault guns with fixed turrets welded on to Panzer Mk III chassis. Although the turret couldn't rotate, they were low-profile, reasonably reliable and easier to drive and maintain than most other German tanks. On top of these were some 114 Jagdpanthers, high-velocity assault guns, and also a miscellany of converted French tanks captured in 1940 and others such as those in 21. Panzer adapted specially by Major Becker. This meant that the number of high-velocity gunned tanks and assault guns amounted to less than 1,000 all told.

For the most part, Allied tanks were medium tanks of around 30 tons and equipped with medium-velocity 75mm guns and machine guns. Towards the end of the Normandy campaign, after much concern about the quality of British armour had been voiced at home, a number of crews were surveyed about what they thought of their tanks. Cromwell crews were generally pleased with their mount, including Reg Spittles and his fellows. They were fast, mechanically reliable and easy to maintain. 'They have, of course,' wrote the report, 'the same complaint as Sherman equipped brigades, ie, that their armour and armament are both lighter than those of Panthers and Tigers.'

This was true of the majority of Allied tanks, but they did also have up-gunned versions of the Sherman tank – the Firefly, in the case of the British and Canadians, which had the 17-pounder high-velocity gun, and the 76mm high-velocity-gun Sherman for the Americans. It is true they lacked the armour of the Panthers and Tigers, but they certainly had the killing power and, as the campaign continued, so their numbers grew. Most British Sherman-equipped regiments, for example, had one Firefly per troop, but increasingly this number was doubling. The Allies also had other fearsome weapons in their arsenals, such as the British and Canadian flame-throwing Crocodile. Incidents were recorded of enemy troops fleeing the moment they saw these monstrous tanks. Although Tigers were feared for both their gun and apparent immunity, Crocodile tanks seem to have prompted an equivalent level of terror among the Germans. 'The two attacks were completely successful,' ran a report on a

Crocodile action near Secqueville on the Orne, 'and the enemy decided to leave these villages as soon as he saw the Crocodile in action.' Who could blame them? Few weapons on display in Normandy were more horrifically brutal than a tank spouting a mixture of burning petrol, oil and rubber in a 120-yard-long jet. 'The enemy are frightened of it,' ran another testimony in the report, 'and our own troops are encouraged by it.'

None the less, most criticism of Allied tanks was directed at the comparative lack of armour and the weakness of the 75mm gun on the Sherman, Cromwell and Churchill, especially when compared to the Tiger and Panther. Even Tigers, however, were vulnerable to high-velocity anti-tank guns, and the Allies had considerably more of those and even more times the amount of ammunition. The British 17-pounder, American 3-inch and 76mm anti-tank guns all had high-barrel velocity and, with it, killing power. During extensive analysis of battle damage on their own tanks and on those of the enemy carried out by 21st Army Group, one Panther was shown to have been hit and knocked out by a 17-pounder shell that had first hit a soft-skin vehicle, gone straight through it, then through a barn wall of brick and stone 18 inches thick and only then hit the tank. 'Actually,' ran the report, '6 shots in all were fired, all of which passed through the barn. The strike on the Panther is on the lower nose plate and the tank was burned out as a result.' What's more, just arriving in Normandy were the new armour-piercing discarding sabot rounds – or APDS. The armour-piercing shell was covered in a casing which discarded during its trajectory and which enabled an even greater velocity – some 4,000 feet per second – which made it comfortably the highest-velocity and most powerful anti-tank weapon/shell combination on the battlefield. It lost accuracy beyond 2,000 yards, but such distances were rarely exceeded and so this was not much of an issue. APDS-firing 17-pounders, soon to be arriving in some numbers, were very effective tank killers.

Both the British and Americans had really enormous numbers of anti-tank guns, way more than the Germans. Each British infantry division, for example, was supported by three field artillery regiments, each of twenty-four 25-pounders, so seventy-two in all, as well as an astonishing seventy-eight 6-pounder anti-tank guns and thirty-two of the phenomenal 17-pounders, which had a velocity that was slightly greater than the 88mm flak gun and the equal of the Pak 43. These guns had a low profile and were incredibly easy to move into position using a combination of trucks – 'gun tractors' – and half-tracks. A 17-pounder could be reversed into a hedgerow or similar cover, spread its forks, have a shell in the breech then fire in less than half a minute. On top of that, a light anti-aircraft regiment was attached to each division, including seventy-one 20mm cannons – the same calibre as used in Spitfires and Typhoons, for example – as well as thirty-six 40mm cannons and eighteen self-propelled 40mm cannons mounted on tank chassis. Since there was very little Luft-waffe to shoot at, especially during daylight hours, it was not at all uncommon for these anti-aircraft weapons to be used in a ground-attack role instead. Cannons such as the Bofors 40mm fired at around 2,890 feet per second, so certainly had the velocity to be effective direct-fire ground-attack weapons. They were quick-firing too, at around 120 rounds per minute.

The Americans had a similar level of support in terms of artillery and anti-tank guns, although the set-up was not quite as regimented as for the British and Canadians. Each infantry battalion had a heavy-weapons company, equipped with either six of the smaller 37mm or, increasingly, 57mm anti-tank guns, which were US versions of the British 6-pounder – so fifty-four in all per division. Each regiment also had attached six 105mm howitzers. In addition, the division would have four artillery battalions, three of twelve 105s each and one of twelve 155mm howitzers – so a lot of fire-power all told.

The 6-pounder was ideal in the close hedgerow fighting, as it was a lot lighter than the British 17-pounder. There was also the 3-inch anti-tank gun, pushed through by General Leslie McNair, the head of the army ground forces. The 3-inch, a towed gun, was too heavy and difficult to manoeuvre to make it effective in the bocage, but, although it was some-thing of a pet project of McNair's, the US was also unique in developing specific tank destroyer (TD) battalions and, of the thirty based in the UK on the eve of D-Day, nineteen were entirely self-propelled and included a number of exciting new high-velocity tracked armoured vehicles. The Tank Destroyer Center had been established in the US in 1942 to help develop and train what was, in effect, a new and separate branch of the army to sit alongside the infantry, armoured, airborne and other strands of the US army ground forces, although it never received official equal bill-ing. McNair was one of the pioneers of the TD battalions and fervently believed that tanks should be kept free to operate with infantry and des-troy unarmoured enemy troops, and that enemy armour should be taken on primarily by specialist mobile anti-tank weapons. Part of the new TD doctrine was a sense of fearlessness among its men; anti-tank operations were not to be essentially defensive but, rather, would be aggressive, with mounted anti-tank guns operating in tank-hunting parties.

McNair wanted these units to be powerfully armed, fast and agile. This way, they would be able to manoeuvre themselves better than the slower, more ponderous tanks, and so get themselves more easily into a favourable position from which to fire. In North Africa, however, they had proved rather unsuccessful, partly because commanders like General Patton had failed to understand how they should be used and partly because the TD battalions were aggressive in the face of enemy tanks, where their minimal armour worked against them, rather than being aggressive in their reconnaissance and ambushing. Nor was concealment particularly easy in the desert of southern Tunisia. Those, however, had been the early days; by D-Day the tank destroyer doctrine was more developed and its men better trained. They were now hard-hitting fighting units, of around 800 men each, and equipped with superb radios and communications – each TD battalion had no fewer than ninety SCR619 sets – as well as anti-aircraft protection and thirty-six towed or self-propelled 3-inch or 76mm high-velocity anti-tank guns. They were capable of destroying enemy anti-tank guns as well as panzers, and of acting as an advance guard and also covering withdrawals. The M10 tank destroyer was equipped with the 3-inch gun, while the M18 Hellcat had the 76mm, and both could zoom along at 50 m.p.h.

Although the TD battalions were not included in the initial waves on D-Day, they soon caught up and were deployed wherever needed; as a rule of thumb one TD battalion tended to be attached to each infantry division along with one tank battalion. In addition to the thirty-six anti-tank guns each battalion possessed, they also came with more than forty .50-calibre heavy machine guns and sixty-two bazookas. A TD battalion lacked armour, for sure, but certainly brought speed, agility and lot of fire-power into the equation.

Nor were the plain old Shermans quite so out of their depth against German tanks as is often depicted. A study of the actions of the Sherwood Rangers Yeomanry was made during the 'most unpleasant' fighting Stanley Christopherson admitted experiencing in and around Rauray on 27 June. One Sherman struck a Panther on its side while it was travelling at around 12 m.p.h. at 80 yards' range, 'and he brewed it up with one hit through the vertical plate above the back bogie.' Then there was the Tiger attacked by John Semken and his crew, which was hit head-on at 120 yards. Three shots were fired in rapid succession before the Tiger could fire one in return. The Tiger crew bailed and Semken's gunner then put in a further three rounds and the tank brewed up – four shots had scooped on and gone into the tank through the roof, with one ricocheting off the track and up into the sponson. Sergeant Dring, the SRY's leading panzer ace, shot up a Panzer Mk IV at 200 yards and watched it burn. He then engaged a Tiger at 1,000 yards. The Tiger fired once at him but missed; Dring's crew then pumped five rounds into the enemy beast without any further retaliation and the German crew bailed out. This tank was later recovered and sent to England. Next, the imperturbable Dring met a Panther at a crossroads and hit it at 500 yards with one shot of armour-piercing in front of the sprocket; again, the crew bailed and 'It brewed up.' As if this wasn't enough, Dring then took on another Tiger at 1,400 yards, just outside Rauray, firing six shots in rapid succession, of which four hit and the last set it on fire. Initially, Dring thought he had missed and hit the wall behind, but one of his crew pointed out, 'you don't see a brick wall spark like that.' 'This tank has been seen,' added the report, 'and is much shot up.' Nor was that the end of Sergeant Dring's heroics. He then engaged a further Mk IV at 1,200 yards, fired two ranging shots of HE and then a further AP round, which went through the tracks, into the lower chassis and began burning.

What this and numerous other such incidents showed was that it was entirely possible for an ordinary 75mm-gun Sherman to destroy the best enemy tanks in Normandy. Admittedly, these all happened at comparatively short range, but the only time Allied tanks were engaging at long range was during the battles in the open country around Caen and, even then, as a proportion of the fighting as a whole, tank-on-tank engagements were actually pretty rare. At close quarters, as experienced in town or village fighting, the Sherman actually had some important advantages. First, it could fire more quickly. Second, its turret could traverse faster than those of German tanks. Third, because of its unique stabilizing gyro, its gun was more accurate while operating on the hoof. Fourth, it was generally more manoeuvrable, largely because it was less complex. The transmission on a Tiger, for example, was a six-speed, semi-hydraulic pre-selector gearbox designed by Ferdinand Porsche. It sounded complex and it was. The Panther's gearbox was also a work of engineering brilliance, but altogether too complicated for the average teenage driver straight out of basic training. To change gear required pulling on two levers simultaneously, while the driveshaft ran through the belly of the tank and was almost entirely inaccessible to the crew. To

get to the engine required moving the turret into the right position, lifting one hatch, then unbolting a further, larger hatch and employing a heavy lifting crane. On the Sherman, by contrast, engine access was from the rear and sat on simple mountings. An engine could be taken out and replaced with only modest lifting gear in about a couple of hours. The gearbox, meanwhile, was a simple four forward and one reverse manual construction that operated in exactly the same way as that of a car – which, of course, Americans, and even Brits, had lots of back home, but which Germans did not.

Every tank was an incredibly complex piece of equipment, so the fewer parts the better and the less complex the better. But more than that, when the Americans, particularly, built tens of thousands of Shermans, they also built thousands of mobile workshops, tank transporters and tank wreckers. Knocked-out tanks were very swiftly pulled from the battlefield and either put back into action right away, taken to workshops further back, or broken up and butchered for parts. The entire system was incredibly well thought through and effective, and it helped enormously to ensure as many tanks as possible were available on any given day.

If Allied crews had their tank knocked out and they were still in one piece, they would try to lie low and keep out of the way, then, when the fighting died down or the immediate danger passed, they would hurry back to regimental headquarters either on foot or by catching a lift. In the case of the British and Canadians, within a matter of just hours a new Sherman would arrive, driven up by the men from the delivery regiments in the Royal Armoured Corps (RAC). These replacement tanks were brought in from England, shipped to Arromanches, driven straight off on to the jetties, then taken to the various rear military areas. Transports of various kinds would be shuffling back and forth continuously. In the meantime, the damaged tank would be rescued by the Light Aid Detachment (LAD). Sometimes a tank might be repaired on the spot by a mobile workshop – a truck with every conceivable tool in the back, as well as winches and lifting gear – but otherwise it would be either towed out or lifted on to a tank transporter. Only if it was completely burned-out would it be left on the battlefield, although eventually it would be cleared away and broken down for scrap.

Each regiment also had its own support troops, known as B Echelon. Once it became dark, tanks would pull back and 'leaguer up' – usually each troop in a circle with the guns pointing outwards or backed into a hedgerow or somewhere with natural camouflage. Depending on how close they were to the front, they might dig a hole in the ground, sleep underneath the tank or pull a tarpaulin out from the side. B Echelon would arrive in 'soft-skins' – trucks, Jeeps, weapons carriers – with more ammunition, basic spare parts, jerry cans of fuel, and rations. Unlike the Germans, no British tank crew, or tank battalion, was ever short of support. The system was much the same for the Americans, whose supplies, if anything, were even more efficient and plentiful.

The Germans had a similar system. The equivalent of the British LAD was the Panzer Maintenance Detachment of nineteen men and two shop trucks. Each panzer regiment then had a panzer maintenance company of between 120 and 200 men and did have lathes, electricians and some lifting gear. The prime mover was an 18-ton half-track Maybach capable of pulling 20 tons. Heavier tanks were shifted by coupling several of these Maybachs together. The Germans did not have the kind of low-loaders, tank wreckers or tractors available to the Americans and British; no country was as capable of building big, powerful prime movers as the Americans. The Germans also had panzer maintenance platoons, usu-ally attached to each tank battalion; Hauptmann Helmut Ritgen, for example, had a maintenance platoon serving his battalion, and they could, on paper at any rate, replace engines and transmissions and carry out welding. Ritgen's battalion was equipped with Mk IVs, however, which were far easier to maintain than Panthers or Tigers.

On paper, then, the German system seemed efficient enough. Prob-lems arose, however, on a number of different levels. First, from 1942 onwards the urgent and pressing need for new tanks like the Panther and Tiger had taken precedence over other aspects of armour production, such as the manufacture of spare parts. By 1944, tank battalions were always short of parts and far too many tanks had to be abandoned for want of a new gasket, cog or pinion. Second, the reduction of training across the board coincided with the increase in both numbers and var-ieties of German tanks – there were thirteen different variants of the Mk III, for example – as well as the massively increased size and sophistication – and complication – of certain models such as the Pan-ther and Tiger. All too often, repairing stricken panzers was simply beyond the abilities of the maintenance teams.

The contrast with the Americans simply could not have been starker. At the start of the war, there had been two Americans for every motor-ized vehicle in the USA, but that figure had been forty-seven in Germany. The United States had tens of thousands of mechanics and they had the

capacity, time and materials to ensure those with mechanical skills were superbly trained for the task they were assigned, whether it be tank, truck, gun or aircraft maintenance. Third, in Normandy the Germans no longer had enough fuel or prime movers, and even though divisions such as the Panzer-Lehr and 12. SS set off to the front at full strength, the traumatic journey to Normandy soon put paid to that. It was one of the reasons why Bayerlein was so angry and distraught at the losses to his soft-skins en route. Without them, his tanks could not be supported, and tanks that could not be properly supported in the field were no good to anyone. 'Any nation that anticipates conducting large-scale military operations in a distant theater of war,' wrote a US study on German tank maintenance, 'can conserve the combat efficiency of its armour only if proper tank maintenance is performed in the field.' It was hard to argue with that, but the German armies in Normandy were unable to abide by this simple but essential tenet. By mid-July, both the Americans and the British (and Canadians) had around 3,500 tanks each in theatre, a huge number. The Germans had brought up, in total, a thousand fewer. The difference between the two sides was that the Allies were able to maintain and even grow those figures, but the Germans were not. For them, the line on the graph was going ever downwards.

Yet while the operational level was executed so much better by the Allies, it would be wrong to suggest their armour was necessarily inferior. It really wasn't just about the guns and armour, despite what was often believed at the time and has been perpetuated in many quarters ever since. There were other factors about the Sherman, the most numerous of all tanks in Normandy, that often get ignored, but which made it an immensely practical tank to have among the Allied armies. Ever since the Battle of Alamein in October and November 1942, the Allies had been on the advance. As the Axis forces retreated, so they blew up bridges in their wake, which meant Allied engineers then had to bring forward bridging equipment. The best and most effective way to do this was by laying a Class 40 Bailey bridge, which could take 40 tons at any one time. A Sherman was 30 tons; even with crew, fuel, ammunition, kit and wood on the side for extra protection, it still weighed less than 40 tons. If it were heavier, like the 56-ton Tiger, it would not be able to get across. The Cromwell was a similar weight but could also travel at 50 m.p.h., faster than any other comparable tank, and would be a huge advantage as and when British armour managed to get into open countryside. Its time would come.

Shermans also fitted neatly into liberty ships and landing craft, as well as being very easy to maintain compared with most German models. When considering the advantages and disadvantages of any particular armoured fighting vehicle – AFV – it is essential to look at it in the round, not just from the perspective of its armour and gun, and these practical advantages of the Sherman were very important indeed.

By contrast, the Tiger was not only incredibly complex, it was also very thirsty, yet fuel, along with food, was one of Nazi Germany's biggest shortcomings. Tigers had to be transported as close to the front as possible by rail, but because they were so big they were too wide to fit on to the continental railway loading gauge. The solution was to give the tank narrower tracks for travel, which would then have to be taken off and switched for much wider combat tracks once it reached the front. Under the watch of enemy *Jabos*, this was a complicated and time-consuming exercise. The tank then had to be driven the rest of the way, the crew hoping they didn't break it en route before it actually got into action. Only 1,347 Tigers were ever built – compared with 49,000 Shermans and 74,000 Sherman chassis, which, because of their uniformity, were converted into assault guns, troop carriers and other AFVs – and of those Tigers it is estimated half were lost to lack of fuel or mechanical failure.

One of the problems facing the Germans was that, because they were not a particularly automotive country even before the war, they had a much smaller pool of drivers, mechanics and large vehicle factories in the first place. As the war progressed and training was cut and cut again, and fuel became ever scarcer, so their tanks demanded a larger share of available fuel. This meant huge corners had to be cut. From prisoners captured in Normandy, it became clear to the Allies that a lot of Panther and even Tiger drivers had gone into action with as little as ten hours' training, a woefully insufficient preparation for operating beasts so mechanically complex. It was no wonder Sergeant Dring's crew were able to best several Panthers and a Tiger in one action. Most prisoners grilled about their German armour reckoned that, on average, at least five Panthers out of a company of twenty-two would be permanently in workshops undergoing maintenance. A Tiger company was fourteen tanks and it was estimated that at least two would always be out of action and in the workshops, which usually amounted to 5–10 days. Engines overheating, blown gaskets, broken final drives, a lack of maintenance and bad driving were the most common cause of mechanical problems.

Then there were other small but not insignificant differences. The

suspension, track and wheel systems on the Tiger and Panther were complicated and not easy to repair. The Panther, for example, had eighteen wheels, all interlinked, including the drive wheels, on each side, so thirty-six in all, with the suspension system on the far side. Shermans, on the other hand, had eight each side, including the drives, and the three twin-suspension bogeys on each side were on the outside of the tracks so they could be easily accessed and replaced if damaged. All were simply bolted on. This kind of practicality and ease of repair was really important in the fury and heat of battle when maintenance of the front – and effort – was of paramount importance. Broken tracks were very easy to repair, but the suspension and wheels on a Sherman could be replaced, if necessary, without removing the tracks at all. On a Tiger or Panther – or a Mk IV for that matter – the entire track and wheel system usually had to be removed to repair one part.

Nor was the bocage any better for panzer divisions than it was for the attacking American troops. 'We could only knock out enemy tanks at a maximum range of 200 yards,' said Fritz Bayerlein, 'as the hedges concealed everything further away. The German tanks are built for long range firing.' This was true enough; the Panthers and Tigers, especially, as well as upgunned StuGs, had been designed with the open steppe of Russia and the equally wide-open North African desert in mind. Big, heavy tanks were a nightmare to operate in such close country. 'We could not use the Mark V cross-country in Normandy,' he added – nor the Tiger, had he been given any. As far as he was concerned, the Cromwell was the best suited to the bocage with its 'sharper angle of approach. We believed it had been specially built for use in Normandy.'

However, there was no doubting that in open country, such as that around Caen, British tanks were vulnerable, less to Panthers and Tigers but more to anti-tank guns. Allied tank crews understandably viewed combat from their own experiences and it often seemed as though these incredible German weapons were making mincemeat of them and displaying overwhelming superiority. German tank crews, however, had to contend with many more enemy anti-tank guns, vastly overwhelming artillery, naval guns and, of course, the *Jabos*, about which they were even more obsessed and fearful than Allied troops were about Tigers and 88s. Most Allied troops never got to see this German perspective, however.

The vulnerability of tanks to anti-tank guns also applied to the bocage country, where pretty much all fighting was short-range and where they were vulnerable to hidden 88s, Pak 40s and even Pak 38s and other German anti-tank weapons, such as the hand-held *Panzerschrek* rocket-launcher and the *Panzerfaust*. Colonel Tick Bonesteel had suggested to the First Army planners that they urgently request the bigger Pershing M26 tank, which was now rolling off the assembly lines but had yet to be shipped to the ETO. General George S. Patton, generally considered the leading armour expert and soon to be commanding US Third Army in Brittany, had advised against this 46-ton heavy because of the support it would require in terms of parts, fuel and shipping. It was certainly too big for a Class 40 Bailey bridge, but did have a 90mm high-velocity gun. On the other hand, its armour was less than that of a Tiger and similar to that of a Panther, with 102 mm of frontal armour and 55 mm on the sides; the Churchill had 150 mm of frontal armour, while the Tiger had 100 mm and a 120mm-thick gun mantlet. This meant that even in close hedgerow country the Pershing would have been vulnerable to anti-tank weapons, while not as easy to maintain or manoeuvre. For clearing enemy troops, mortars and lesser guns from bocage country, the Sherman's machine guns and 75mm main gun were very effective. The secret to winning in the hedgerows was rapidly to develop new tactics and techniques, and, despite the horror and shocking devastation men like Lieutenant Richard Blackburn saw on arriving at the front, by the middle of July this was starting to happen.

It has to be remembered that, in terms of their armies, Britain, America and even Canada had been at ground zero in June 1940, a mere four years earlier. The United States had had a tiny army in September 1939, almost no tanks, just seventy-odd fighter planes and not one single producer of high explosive. Britain had lost the fighting power of her very small army in France following the retreat from Dunkirk and had never intended to have a large army in the first place; that had been France's role in the pre-war alliance. Suddenly, they had found themselves facing a terrible danger that threatened the free Western world. Four years on, they had not only expanded already large navies but had built the world's two largest air forces and armies of millions, superbly well equipped and supported. Any criticism of tanks has to be tempered by the truly astonishing achievement of building such armies so exponentially quickly and with the operational infrastructure to sustain them. Furthermore, Allied war leaders had worked out a method of defeating the enemy that was, by the standards of the day, comparatively cost-effective in terms of the lives of their young men. The Allied war effort should be not only applauded but marvelled at. It was a truly incredible achievement that had happened only because every fibre of their respective nations had been ploughed into their war effort with a focus and cool-headed pragmatism that has never been rivalled or equalled at any point in world history.

The trouble was that it was the poor infantry and the tank crews who had to put their necks on the line and head into the hedgerows and across the open ground to face the full fury of the enemy. When tanks started brewing up left, right and centre, and the terrible losses began to mount, it was no wonder morale took a hammering. It was also no wonder that those getting hammered began to have weapons-envy, especially when they saw a much bigger Tiger or Panther loom over the horizon or lurch around a corner. Resentment and a feeling of the inadequacy of their own equipment was entirely understandable, not least because they were, in effect, the sacrificial lambs of the Allied armies. The British and American way of war was far more efficient, better supported and supplied than any other of the combatant nations, but despite the 'steel not flesh' wider strategy, and despite the fire-power-heavy approach to war, there was simply no avoiding the work of the infantry and armour. To destroy the Germans and bring their immense fire-power to bear, there had to be a bait. And that bait was the poor bastards in the infantry and armour.

CHAPTER 28

Crisis of Command

O N D-DAY, LEUTNANT RICHARD Freiherr von Rosen had just rejoined Schwere Panzerabteilung (Heavy Panzer Battalion) 503 at Ohrdruf troop-training depot. From an aristocratic Prussian family, he had been brought up on an estate in Altenburg, in the hills south of Dresden, and in 1940, when he was just eighteen, he had been thrilled to join the army's exciting new panzer arm. He started in the ranks, as was the case for every soldier, and then became a *Fahnenjunker*, an officer candidate. He had earned his right to attend *Kriegsschule* – military school – and had duly become an officer in the army's spearhead, the elite. By 1944 he had seen much action: he had been there at the start of Operation BARBAROSSA, had survived Russian winters and the previous July had been wounded in the Battle of Kursk. Patched up and rested, he was now glad to be back with his old unit. His commander, Hauptmann Rolf Fromme, had appointed von Rosen as special duties officer at Battalion HQ and one of his first tasks had been to prepare for the visit of Feldmarschall Heinz Guderian, then still the inspector-general of panzer troops, who was due to visit on 15 June. Guderian remained, in many ways, the father of the panzer arm, so a visit from this great warrior was an honour indeed.

Guderian had been guest at the officers' party and during the dinner he made a point of coming over and sitting with the lieutenants at their table, speaking gravely about the situation on both the Western and Eastern Fronts. 'If we do not succeed in destroying the enemy bridgehead in the next fourteen days,' he said of Normandy, 'the war is lost for us.' Coming from a man such as he, this made an especially deep

never a FM – only a Colonel-General

impression on von Rosen and his fellow officers, although over the next couple of weeks he tried to put it out of his mind and focus on the exacting demands of preparing for front-line action once more. Their movement order finally arrived on 27 June; they were to pull out of Ohrdruf at six the following morning, von Rosen's twenty-second birthday as it happened, and head to the Normandy front.

As was standard for any new units heading to Normandy, Schwere Panzerabteilung 503's journey was one of constant interruptions by Allied air attacks and long detours to avoid smashed bridges, so they did not reach their railhead until 2 and 3 July, then laboriously moved up to the front over the ensuing nights, arriving in darkness on the 7th. The following day they were attached to 21. Panzer-Division, and von Rosen was now given command of the fighting *Staffel* (squadron) of 3. Kompanie. Leaguered up in fields and woods to the south-east of the battered city of Caen, the battalion's tank companies took it in turns to be on alarm duty, although for a few days they were not called upon. Instead, they used the time to acclimatize to their new surroundings. The fighting here, von Rosen realized, was very different to that along the Eastern Front; here the enemy's mastery of the air was undisputed.

On Thursday, 11 July, von Rosen was woken by a dispatch rider at around 5 a.m. and warned to get his company at immediate alarm readiness and to hurry to the battalion command post. There he was briefed: the Canadians had broken through between Cuverville and Colombelles and now occupied the high ground just to the north of the chimneys and factory complex there. The roads east of the city lay dangerously open to the enemy and a large number of British tanks had been reported moving forward. His 3. Kompanie was to destroy them, push back the enemy and restore the front line, then hold and await further orders.

Von Rosen saluted and hurried back to his company. Their Tigers had already been run up and were ready and waiting. His instructions were swiftly passed on: they were to mount up, get to battle-readiness, then pull out. Thirty minutes after the alarm, the company rolled at top speed and within fifteen minutes they had reached Giberville, a mile east of the Orne and south-east of Colombelles. There they were held up when the immense vibrations of the passing Tigers caused a damaged house to collapse on top of one of them. 'Nobody was hurt but it had to be dug out first because the company could not pass, the road being too narrow for more than one panzer at that point,' noted von Rosen. 'It always happens when one is in a rush!' Leutnant von Rosen, meanwhile, clambered down from his own Tiger and hurried forward on a motorbike; he found the artillery OP of the StuG Battalion 200 in a room above a bakery. Peering through binoculars, he soon spotted a number of British Shermans below in the battle-scarred village of Sainte-Honorine. These were clearly their targets.

Hastening back, he was relieved to see his Tigers were now clear and they moved off again, although as they reached the northern end of the village they came under fire. Von Rosen now ordered two platoons to fan out, with a third in reserve, while he took up position in his tank in the centre. Immediately, they began receiving hits, although the shells mostly bounced off harmlessly, but once they were all in position von Rosen gave the order for them to advance at full speed. Much to his annoyance, there was no reaction at all from his men, so he repeated it, this time in a sharper tone of voice. Again, nothing happened. His Tigers continued to fire from where they were, although already they were hitting their marks as Shermans started to brew up, thick black smoke rising from the burning wrecks.

'If you don't attack at once,' von Rosen now yelled into his microphone, 'I shall turn my turret to six o'clock and fire behind me!' But there was still no reaction. Enemy shells were hitting his Tiger, clanging and pinging off the armour or hurtling just past. Only then did he realize his radio aerial had been shot away – that was why no one had responded to his orders! For a moment he wondered what to do, but swiftly decided there was nothing else for it but to attack alone.

Off his Tiger went, speeding forward for several hundred yards. Much to his relief, the others had clearly realized what was happening and were now following, his men trusting to their good training rather than depending on verbal orders. The technique was like an infantry advance: one platoon advancing while the other gave covering fire. For a while the enemy tanks disappeared behind the smoke, but soon it cleared. 'Every round we fired hit a Sherman,' he wrote, 'which then burst into flames.' The British tanks began falling back. Von Rosen's Tigers were now in open country with little cover, and a spotter plane soon began circling overhead. Moments later, enemy shells were screaming in, the ground shaking and convulsing as if in the middle of an earthquake. Dust, grit and smoke swirled around them, blinding and choking them; von Rosen had never experienced anything like it, not at any point on the Eastern Front. Quickly signalling them to pull back 500 yards, he thought they were safe – only for them to come under attack again. His Tiger received a direct hit, the sound deafening and reverberating, stunning them all. The lights went out inside, but much to their surprise they were all alive and uninjured apart from the ringing in their ears.

For eight hours they were pounded. Von Rosen was shocked by the level of accuracy achieved by the Allied naval gunners and, despite repeatedly changing their position, with every move another salvo would straddle them. None the less, although there were a number of hits and welded seams were ripped and torn apart, the Tigers were still functioning and his crews in one piece. Finally, once the spotter plane disappeared, some semblance of peace returned and von Rosen took the opportunity to jump out and walk forward to have a look at the wreckage. In all, he counted eleven enemy tanks, including a couple of Fireflies, plus five anti-tank guns. He also discovered two abandoned Shermans, which had collided and obviously become stuck; in the heat of battle, the crews had scarpered. These he managed to get towed back in triumph.

Von Rosen's Tigers had halted British plans to clear the south-eastern outskirts of Caen in preparation for Second Army's next big offensive, Operation GOODWOOD. Infantry from the 51st Highland Division and armour from 148th Royal Armoured Corps had swiftly laid down a smokescreen and pulled back into Sainte-Honorine. 'Our first engagement in Normandy was successful,' commented von Rosen, 'but was only of local significance and could not influence the overall situation.'

He was quite right, but once again this small firefight had illustrated the difficulty of making ground in this unhelpful terrain. Before the invasion, Montgomery had recognized that the countryside around Caen did not favour sweeping armoured exploitation, but he had also presumed Rommel would not choose to fight so close to the coast. He had expected him to pull back to a series of flexible defence lines from where the German mobile divisions could better manoeuvre for a counter-attack far out of range of Allied naval guns. And that was exactly what Rommel would have done had he been unable to push them back into the sea immediately; it was what he had suggested to Hitler at Margival on 17 June. Now, though, the bridgehead was becoming immensely crowded; almost every field was covered in airfields, rear military area camps, depots and field hospitals. Southern England of May 1944 had been transported to Normandy and packed into an even smaller area. What options there were for bursting through the mass of divisions arrayed around Second Army were limited by the sprawl of Caen, now mostly lying in ruins, and large numbers of rivers that all worked against the Allied axis of advance. Ideally, they might mount one massive, broad-front attack either side of Caen, but there was not the space or even quite enough artillery or ammunition to pull off such a massive assault. It is hard to overstate the difficulties confronting the Allies. Montgomery now faced four enemy corps, including seven panzer divisions and six of infantry. It was true that all those panzer divisions had, by now, become badly mauled – 12. SS especially so – but a few fresh units, such as Schwere Panzerabteilung 503, were still arriving and a handful of Tigers could play merry hell with an attacking force, as von Rosen's company had shown. There was simply no avoiding pushing infantry and armour forward into the open, but then the casualties began to mount – and to what was fast becoming an unacceptable level. It was a conundrum, but one that was being further exacerbated by political considerations.

During his time as Eighth Army commander, Montgomery had been largely protected from the kind of political and high command issues that plagued his superiors. He had been far away in North Africa when his immediate CO, General Sir Harold Alexander, a supreme diplomat and man-manager as well as a fine battlefield commander, had expertly shielded him from Churchill's impatience for swift action. Eisenhower and Alexander had then together taken on this mantle of buffer between the front line and London and Washington, first in Tunisia, then in Sicily and finally in southern Italy. Now, though, Montgomery was operating far closer to home, Alexander was commanding Allied forces in Italy, Freddie de Guingand, Monty's chief of staff, was still holding the fort in Portsmouth, and Eisenhower's and just about everybody else's patience with him was beginning to wear a little thin. In part, this was because of the evolving situation and in part it was because of Monty himself, who was becoming increasingly insufferable the more the pressure for swift and decisive action mounted.

Eisenhower, Bradley and Montgomery had all been seeing a lot of each other recently as they tried to rethink their plans to break out of the current impasse and as Ike sought to help his beleaguered battlefield commanders. On Friday, 30 June, for example, Bradley visited Monty's Tac HQ, newly moved to a hillside near the village of Blay, a few miles west of Bayeux and closer to First Army. They found him in a particu-larly spikey mood.

'I say,' he said to Bradley, looking at Chet Hansen, who had been recently promoted, 'now do you have a major for an ADC? Simply a dog's body, you know, a whipping boy. I would not have an ADC who is more than a captain.'

What on earth compelled him to say such a thing? It was insulting to Bradley, insulting to Hansen, whom Monty had seen so many times before, and just so spectacularly rude, offensive and unnecessary. Bradley, not rising to the bait, patiently explained that he promoted his aides to the rank he believed they were capable of attaining elsewhere were they not working for him.

'Messenger boys, simply messenger boys,' muttered Montgomery, determined to have the last word. He then launched into an insulting critique of the superbly designed American M1 steel helmet. It is hard not to cringe recounting this conversation. Montgomery and Bradley needed to work side by side, hand in hand, with unity of purpose and with mutual respect and fellowship. How much harder it was when a small Englishman in corduroys and a sweater was sitting there being so appallingly discourteous, provocative and rude. It is hard to fathom why he behaved so.

Two days later, they were back at Monty's Tac HQ, this time with Eisenhower. Monty was still wearing the same corduroys and sweater; Hansen wondered when he ever washed them. His two puppies were there, Hitler and Rommel, a fox terrier and a spaniel; Hitler had been given to him by some BBC journalists. 'Hitler and Rommel both get beaten when necessary,' he told the journalist Phyllis Reynolds, 'but both are coming to heel well.' It was a shame his wit didn't come to the fore more often. After conferring, they all went out to look at a Panther and at John Semken's Tiger, which had been brought in; it was hard not to be impressed by their size, although they were aware of the mechanical limitations. 'We'll give him a battle when our stuff comes in,' Montgomery told them and reported that some forty-two enemy tanks had been knocked out the day before.

A week later, Caen had finally fallen, but there was still no breakthrough. Back in England, the V-1s continued to buzz over. The horizontal blast effect of each was enormous, shattering windows and causing casualties in a wider area than more conventional bombs; Londoners had once again gone back to sleeping in shelters and in Underground stations. Everyone was getting fed up, while on the map it looked as though the huge amount of fighting in Normandy was getting the Allies nowhere. In fact, on the map board, the Allies looked horribly penned in and even vulnerable.

On 10 July, Montgomery met again with Bradley and this time Dempsey. Montgomery's chief planning officer, Brigadier Charles Richardson, had already told Monty and Dempsey that he was worried about the state of the infantry and urged them to make more liberal use of the plentiful amounts of armour now available. Bradley was also gearing up for a major offensive, but told Montgomery his forces needed more time to manoeuvre southwards before he launched his attack north-west of Saint-Lô. This operation had already been given the code name COBRA and Bradley, taking Eisenhower's promise of air support at his word, intended to have heavy bombers drop some 4,000 tons on a tightly designated area. 'I've been wanting to do this now since we landed,' he told Chet Hansen two days later. 'When we pull it, I want it to be the biggest thing in the world. We want to smash right on through.' He imagined attacking with three divisions and a mass of armour, with tank destroyers in support, driving straight through this big gap created by the bombers. But he wasn't ready yet. Montgomery was persuaded by this plan, but also accepted it was paramount to keep as many of the panzer divisions around Caen as possible so that First Army was mostly confronting the less-trained and -equipped German infantry. Already they had intelligence that the Panzer-Lehr had switched west; they did not want any more to do so.

On the other hand, mounting casualties was one of the prime political considerations troubling Montgomery and one that had been brought into sharper focus earlier that day when he met with General Ronald 'Bill' Adam, the adjutant-general. The British Army, Adam told him plainly, was suffering a manpower shortage that was about to become severe if they weren't careful.

By the end of June, there were some ninety-five infantry battalions in England, which, on the face of it, seemed like quite a lot. Only five, however, were regular rifle battalions, while the remaining ninety were a mixture of territorial, reserve or holding battalions; of these, only twenty-six were up to strength, while the rest were far from being the full complement and were either unfit for operations on the Continent, still undergoing transiting, already earmarked elsewhere – such as Burma and Italy – or were 'Lower Establishment' and suitable only for home defence. So as far as deployment to Normandy was concerned, there wasn't a lot in the pot. There were also some 172,815 men in Anti-Aircraft Command, and 50,000 had been earmarked to be transferred to 21st Army Group. The V-1 attacks had put a halt to this, however; British people needed their protection once more and, politically, withdrawing home-based anti-aircraft gunners and sending them to the front line in France was, for the time being at any rate, no longer on the cards.

Britain's global reach was enormous, with its contributions to the Italian campaign, naval forces all around the world – the Pacific Fleet was due to be formed in August – the campaigns in Burma and Normandy, as well as its vast air force. Of course Britain did have more manpower, but it had sensibly continued to put a lot of it into factories. Germany, on the other hand, had pulled its industrial labour force out of the factories and given them rifles, replacing them with inefficient slave labour, and was now losing the war. Britain was not prepared to make the same mistake, but nearly five years at the heart of a global conflict was taking its toll; only Germany had been in it longer, and that by only two days.

What was equally obvious, however, was the growing military strength of the United States and the USSR. Very soon there would be more American troops and materiel in France than British. Patton's Third Army was already being shipped over to Normandy and was preparing to be activated and thrown into the battle in a matter of weeks, while on 14 July the decision was finally made to go ahead with Operation ANVIL, the US-led invasion of southern France. Britain's war leaders were now looking ahead to the peace that would follow, whether that came before the year's end or into 1945. The Americans would eventually go home, but the Soviet Union threatened to bring communism to Europe, something Britain feared almost as much as National Socialism. Britain was a part of Europe and a neighbour – and had already made a huge contribution to liberating it from the Nazi yoke; it was vital it continued to do so. From Churchill downwards to Montgomery, it was understood that Britain needed to be sitting at the table with the USA and Soviet Union when the war was won. It was no wonder Montgomery was concerned about casualties.

More than that, however, Britain's and America's entire war strategy had been built around keeping those at the coal-face to a bare minimum, and they should be applauded for that rather than castigated in any way. For both personal and humane reasons, Montgomery, no matter his shortcomings of character, was never reckless with the lives of his largely conscript army; nor was Bradley. They wanted to win as quickly as possible, but with as few lives lost as possible. It was a very difficult and narrow line to tread, but it was also why they were so ready to use air power and fire-power to help them. Within British Second Army, for example, a mere 7 per cent of manpower was in tanks; 16 per cent only were infantry, 17 per cent artillery, 13 per cent engineers, 5 per cent signals and a whopping 42 per cent service corps. First Army was much the same. It was brilliant that the Allies could fight – and win, as they were doing – with so few men in the immediate firing line. This really was a far, far more efficient way of fighting than the path taken by Germany or Japan or the USSR, but it did mean there would be times when progress seemed slow and the map was hardly shifting. Montgomery *could* have ruthlessly burst through the German lines now, and had he been a Soviet leader – or a German commander – he would have done so. The cost, however, would have been heavy, too heavy, and it was not one he was prepared to bear. Nor were any of the other British and American war leaders, for that matter. What they couldn't understand, however, was why, with the Allies' overwhelming fire-power, they couldn't break through without losing vast numbers of casualties. It was Montgomery's singular inability to convey why this was the case that was at the root of the rising tension now. He was not a bad general; he was a very good one. So too was Bradley. But while Bradley had the innate personal skills to reach out to the lowliest GI as well as to generals and politicians, Montgomery's insufferable arrogance and gaucheness drove people against him. It has unquestionably tarnished his reputation ever since.

That same day, Monday, 10 July, following his meetings with Bradley and Dempsey, Montgomery issued a new directive in which he made it clear he intended to expand the bridgehead across the Orne, south-east of Caen, but not push much further. He wanted to use the British and Canadians to anchor the Germans in their sector and not much more; even this was to be undertaken only if it could be done without too much cost. 'I am not prepared to have *heavy* casualties to obtain this bridgehead over the Orne,' he announced in his directive that day, 'as we shall have plenty elsewhere.' On seeing this, Tedder in particular felt Monty was being far too cautious, despite the concerns over the approaching manpower shortage, and he said as much to Eisenhower.

In the days that followed, however, the next planned British assault began to take shape, although the idea for GOODWOOD was not really Monty's but rather that of the Second Army commander and was rather more ambitious than Montgomery had originally intended. Miles 'Bimbo' Dempsey has been rather overshadowed by the dominating personality of Montgomery, yet he was no shrinking violet and a far more forceful commander than has often been supposed. Intelligent, incisive and a clear thinker, he was good at listening but was also willing to impose himself. With Bradley needing more time, Dempsey saw an opportunity to help keep the bulk of the panzer divisions in the British and Canadian sector while at the same time further chewing up their strength and possibly even breaking through at last. Such a breakthrough, he reckoned, might well be possible; he knew all too well that Coningham and Tedder were itching to get to the high ground beyond the Bourguébus Ridge, while a drive to Falaise, some 20 miles south-east of Caen, would not only tie up the German forces still facing Second Army but might well draw those from further west too; it would be impossible for the Germans not to respond, which would clearly help Bradley and COBRA.

Montgomery, however, warned against such lofty ambitions and so GOODWOOD was somewhat scaled back on 15 July. However, it was still to be a major effort using all three armoured divisions brought together into Dick O'Connor's VIII Corps in an effort to minimize the number of infantry directly involved. The Canadians were to play a part, clearing Colombelles and the rest of the eastern outskirts of Caen. Dempsey was also taken with Bradley's ideas for carpet-bombing ahead of COBRA, something Eisenhower and Tedder were both prepared to support. Once again, however, there was a breakdown in translation. Despite Monty dampening down his plans, Dempsey still made it clear to O'Connor that he thought a breakthrough to Falaise was possible. It was, however, very much in keeping with Dempsey's command style and belief that it was better to give his men an ambitious objective and not achieve it than not to be ambitious enough and then find themselves unable to exploit success for lack of a plan.

Trouble, however, was brewing. Montgomery had first signalled Eisenhower about GOODWOOD on 12 July, before the plan had been scaled back. This more positive and aggressive original plan had evoked an enthusiastic response from Eisenhower and Tedder, who reacted by offering him their full support. 'Eisenhower and I,' noted Tedder, 'decided that the reply should be worded in such a way as to make it clear that we expected Montgomery to go ahead, even if the weather ruled out full support.' Eisenhower then sent a very positive reply the following day: 'We are enthusiastic on your plan. We are so pepped up concerning the promise of this plan that either Tedder or myself or both will be glad to visit you if we can help in any way.'

They should have known Montgomery better after all this time.

Monty always did what *he* thought was best, and anything less than a direct order – and Eisenhower's response was not that – wasn't going to sway him from his amended, scaled-back course of action. In his mind, Montgomery was very clear about what he expected for GOODWOOD. Dempsey and O'Connor and the Second Army staff still had greater ambitions, however, and Tedder and Eisenhower most certainly expected Second Army to go all out and achieve that decisive breakthrough. In other words, at this vital moment, the Supreme Command, army group and army were all singing from a slightly different hymn sheet.

Meanwhile, Allied air power continued to be the dominating factor as far as the Germans were concerned. Bad weather had continued to hamper Allied ambitions enormously, yet more airfields were springing up within the bridgehead and so more aircraft were arriving. On 1 July, the advance elements of 609 Squadron had reached Normandy and moved into B-10 at Plumetôt, 4 miles north of Caen. They had landed in Dakotas and had also brought Group Captain Billy, their goat and squadron mascot, to whom they were all very attached. 'The question of leaving him behind seems never to have risen,' noted the adjutant, 'even though his most fervid sponsor, Johnny Wells – who considered that to embark on an operational mission without first saluting Group Captain Billy was sheer stupid bravado – had a week earlier handed over 609 to its first Belgian CO, Manu Geerts, DFC.'

Flight Sergeant Ken Adam had not been too concerned about giving up the comfortable existence they had had back in England. After all, it was exciting to be part of this great invasion force and to feel they were finally getting the enemy on the run. Flying in amid vast amounts of dust on 2 July, they were operating from B-10 but camping out at B-5, which was further from Caen and enemy shelling. Adam didn't mind. His tent was comfortable enough: he and his good friend Norman Merrett had a campbed and sleeping bag each and a canvas washstand to share. They felt a bit vulnerable at night with the odd Luftwaffe bomber coming over, although Adam had slept easier again since going to bed with his tin helmet covering his most vital parts.

Losses were mounting. Five pilots had been killed in May and four in June, which was around 40 per cent of the squadron's pilots. 'Squadron detailed to attack tank concentrations S.E. of HOETOT,' recorded the squadron diary on 11 July. 'Target located by Red smoke.' Twelve tanks were spotted and rockets fired. 'F/Sgt Bliss appears to have been hit by flak after attack and is reported missing.' Despite there being little action from the Luftwaffe, the dangers to these pilots were still immense. Typhoons were ground-attack aircraft, used to operating at very low altitudes; when they attacked, they might well be doing so at only a few hundred feet off the deck. This meant there was very little room for manoeuvre should anything go wrong, and there was often little chance to bail out. If a plane went in, the pilot invariably went in with it.

New tactics were being adopted. As well as marauding far and wide, they would also be called in to support specific operations on the ground. In France, where precision was so important, a new system was adopted, copied from the First Tactical Air Force in Italy and introduced by Air Vice-Marshal Harry Broadhurst, commander of 83 Group, and Pete Quesada's opposite number in Second TAF. This was known as 'VCP' – visual control point – whereby an experienced RAF ground controller would travel about the front line in an army tank and, equipped with a radio set tuned to the correct squadron frequency, would direct the Typhoons on to very precise targets, often beside an artillery observer. These were called 'Rovers'. The pilots, working in flights of four, would operate a 'cab-rank' system: with the same maps as the controller on their knees, they would take it in turns to take off, climb to 8,000 feet above their air strip and circle around waiting to be directed on to a target. 'The controller would say, "Right, here's the grid reference, and in fifteen seconds you'll see red smoke. Go down and attack,"' recalled Adam, 'and then we'd find a Tiger tank or an 88mm gun and fire our rockets.' Flying so often and at such low altitudes, it was not surprising the squadron began to suffer.

'It was hard,' admitted Adam of the number of losses. To avoid dwelling on such matters, there was a lot of drinking in the evenings and much time spent gambling. If he woke up the following morning with a hangover, he usually found that flying at 10,000 feet with the oxygen on full would soon clear his head. What was absolutely certain, though, was that now the weather appeared to be improving they could expect ever more flying. The Allied commanders on the ground were depending on the tactical air forces more, not less, and this applied to the USAAF every bit as much as to the RAF.

Lieutenant Archie Maltbie and the rest of the 365th Fighter Group had moved to France at the end of June and were flying almost non-stop. So too were the 354th. On 3 July, Major Dick Turner was asked to provide fighter escort for Pete Quesada and the Supreme Allied Commander himself, General Eisenhower. Ike had asked for a tour of the Saint-Lô battlefield from the air and Quesada had suggested they take a Mustang that the 354th had modified by removing the fuselage fuel tank and replacing it with a second seat, which they used occasionally to demonstrate tactics to new pilots. Turner had taken off to escort the two generals in a brand-new P-51 only to suffer a drop of oil pressure. Much to his acute embarrassment, he had been forced to land hastily back down again. Fortunately, his two other pilots had stuck to the Supreme Commander like glue. Safely on the ground, Bradley thought both Ike and Quesada looked as sheepish as schoolboys. Eisenhower had urged him to fly faster, but Quesada had kept them at around 250 m.p.h. 'Gosh,' Quesada told Chet Hansen, 'I wish I had opened her all the way.'

Harry Broadhurst had set up his Tac HQ right next to that of Miles Dempsey, just as Pete Quesada had his next to Bradley. In both cases, ground and air commanders got on very well and would often dine with one another. Chet Hansen and Bradley had certainly become very fond of Quesada and there is no question that, by living in each other's pockets, the two commanders were better able to understand the problems and limitations each faced and to deal with them better. After the fall of Cherbourg, Quesada had told his men to understand that their work was really only just starting. On 6 July, for example, General Joe Collins asked Quesada for help when his troops below were struggling to get going; this was the same day Carl Rambo and the Shermans of 70th Tank Battalion had been stalled. Two fighter groups, ninety-six fighters in all, flew up and down the battle front. At around 3.30 p.m. they caught some Germans in the open, ravaging them with 1,000 bombs and strafing. They also answered calls to attack specific targets, using 250lb fragmentation bombs that caused minimum craters but sprayed a wide area with shrapnel and blast. This was not pinpoint targeting, but such was the ever-growing paranoia and obsession of German troops with Allied air supremacy that the arrival of *Jabos* was often enough to stall an attack or ensure they immediately went to ground. It was noticeable that, on days of good weather, the Allied ground troops tended to make more progress than when it was wet and overcast. The trouble was, the weather continued to prove capricious – a day of sun and warmth, maybe two, then the rain clouds would reappear.

Whatever concerns and troubles Montgomery and the Allies were facing, they were as nothing compared with those confronting the Germans.

On the Eastern Front, Marshal Konstantin Rokossovsky's forces had smashed through the German Heeresgruppe Mitte and now Heeresgruppe Nord was being hammered too. A 50-mile gash had been cut through their lines in just two days of bloody fighting. Unlike at Caen, there was no concentration of panzer forces on the Eastern Front to stop the enemy, while the Luftwaffe was even more absent than it was over Normandy.

The latest German intelligence picture suggested General Patton was about to launch a cross-Channel invasion at any moment; that wasn't so far off the mark, although Patton and his Third Army were headed for Brittany, not the Pas de Calais as the Germans expected. On 15 July, Rommel wrote to Feldmarschall von Kluge, his new superior at OB West, that he had now lost 97,000 men since 6 June but had received just 6,000 replacements, while seventeen tanks had been sent to replace the 225 that had been lost. Air power, especially, but also naval and artillery fire, was smashing Heeresgruppe B to pieces. In fact, the real figure was worse than that: over 100,000 men lost by 7 July. Johannes Börner was still dug in near Saint-Lô, but he was one of only 35 per cent of the 3. Fallschirmjäger-Division still fighting, for example. The 353. Infanterie-Division was down to a fighting strength of around 180 men. Rommel asked von Kluge to pass this directly on to Hitler. The two had had something of a rapprochement after their first, explosive meeting. On 11 July, following the fall of Caen, von Kluge had arrived at La Roche-Guyon looking visibly shaken and dog tired, his earlier confidence gone. He now accepted that Rommel's assessment had been right. Rommel was also bitter that he had been ordered to hold fast at Caen. The 16. Luftwaffen-Felddivision had been smashed and 12. SS gutted. The losses, he felt, had been much higher than they needed to be. There were also incidents of basic ineptitude.

'What do the people think who view the situation so completely differently?' Rommel asked over breakfast on the morning of 12 July. 'One should not act according to wishful dreams, but soberly according to reality.'

On Monday, 17 July, Standartenführer Kurt Meyer was summoned to I. SS-Panzerkorps headquarters, now in a densely wooded area near Bretteville-sur-Laize, some 10 miles south of Caen. His shattered division was completely out of the line, resting and hoping to refit around Potigny, to the north of Falaise. Travelling to Bretteville should have been straightforward but, once again, his journey was interrupted by the near constant presence of *Jabos* patrolling the dead-straight Roman road, so he was an hour late arriving. When he did so, he found Dietrich, Eberbach and von Kluge sitting in the shade of a tree, all bitterly complaining about the continued and strait-jacketing interference from the OKW. Invited to join them for lunch, Meyer was astonished to hear Sepp Dietrich, that most loyal of SS men, openly condemning the conduct of the war in Normandy. 'During the course of the conversation,' noted Meyer, 'it became apparent that there was agreement between the commander-in-chief, the commanding general and myself on the impossibility of the present situation.'

The reason for his summons was twofold. First, the continuing British operations around Hill 112 had seen the 272. Infanterie-Division pushed back; Maltot, where the 4th Dorsets had been so badly hammered, had fallen; 12. SS was now on alert to return to the front. Second, Rommel was due to arrive and when he did so he made a point of recognizing the efforts of 12. SS since the invasion. He also asked for a frank assessment of the situation. Meyer told him they could expect the British to strike again around Caen any day. The troops defending there would continue to fight, he told Rommel, and continue to die, but they would not be able to prevent the enemy from rolling over them and advancing on Paris. The Allies' overwhelming air supremacy made any kind of tactical manoeuvring impossible. Even moving the smallest units swiftly could not be carried out because of the control Allied air forces had over anything that moved. He urged Rommel somehow to find them some air support of their own. 'We are not afraid of the enemy ground forces,' he told him, 'we are powerless against the massed employment of the air force, however.'

Rommel responded furiously. Did Meyer think he was travelling around Normandy with his eyes closed? Did he really believe he hadn't been screaming for air support? He had warned the OKW over and over about Allied air power – he had seen it first-hand in North Africa. 'But the higher-ups know better, of course!' he snarled. 'They don't believe my reports any more! Something has to happen! The war in the west has to end! But what will happen in the east?'

Soon after, Rommel left them. Dietrich warned him to be careful and not to drive along any main road. He also suggested taking a *Kübelwagen* rather than his big Horch staff car. Rommel brushed away his concerns with a smile and drove off.

Rommel was sitting in the front seat, next to Gefreiter Daniel, his regular driver. In the back seat were his two aides, Hauptmann Hellmuth Lang and Major Neuhaus, along with Feldwebel Hoike, there specifically to be Rommel's aircraft lookout. It was around 6 p.m. and they had just left the town of Livarot, heading north back towards La Roche-Guyon, when two Canadian Spitfires from 412 Squadron dived down towards them, sweeping in from the left and behind. From 300 yards, the lead Spitfire, flown by Flight Lieutenant Charley Fox, opened fire with his 20mm cannons, which spattered against the road then hit the side of the Horch, sending splinters into Rommel's face, while another shell hit Daniel in the shoulder. Badly wounded, the driver lost control of the speeding car, which careered off the road several hundred yards further on and crashed into a ditch. Lang was unscathed, Neuhaus slightly injured and Daniel fatally wounded, while Rommel was thrown forward and smashed his skull.

The field marshal, unconscious, was taken to a Luftwaffe hospital at Bernay. For a while it seemed touch and go as to whether he would live, but the following day he regained consciousness and the worst appeared to have passed. It did, however, mark the end of his remarkable career as a soldier. Yet another German general had gone, and this was the biggest scalp of them all.

CHAPTER 29

GOODWOOD

BOTH SIDES SPENT CONSIDERABLE energy on developing new tactics, introducing new weaponry and ensuring their men were adequately trained, although the training graph unquestionably showed a downwards trajectory for the Germans, while for the Allies battlefield skills were, for the most part, heading upwards, as well-trained but green troops gradually absorbed the best lessons of all – those learned in combat. Allied memoirs of the fighting and after-action reports often talk about the superb fighting skills of the enemy, while post-war analysis suggested that German fighting soldiers were, man for man, better than any others. These claims have been forensically disproved since, but analysts were also guilty of conflating battlefield skill with a willingness – or, rather, determination – to keep fighting in the face of unspeakable danger and losses. Fighting skill is one thing, discipline is another. If Hitler told his men not to give any ground, generally speaking that's what happened, from the OKW lackeys that were his mouthpiece, to Rommel, to corps, divisional, regimental, company, platoon and *Gruppen* commanders. If it didn't, they would be shot. In the First World War, the Germans executed fewer than fifty men for desertion. In the Second World War, they would execute 30,000 – or two entire divisions' worth. And that figure errs on the conservative side.

On the other hand, if German troops weren't especially well trained, why was it taking the Allies so long to battle through the hedgerows? Well, largely because it didn't require a huge amount of training to sit in a foxhole behind a hedge and fire a machine gun, rifle, mortar or *Panzerfaust*. What was needed was discipline and courage. The Germans, a

few Ost-Bataillone excepted, always had discipline; they were from a totalitarian, militaristic state, after all. Then there were the panzer divisions, which varied wildly in training standards and fighting ability, but which were, as Eberhard Beck discovered when talking to men from the 9. SS-Panzer-Division, more willing to fight fanatically than reluctant conscripts like him and his fellows in the 277. Artillerie-Regiment. That meant they were more aggressive, more willing to fling themselves into the firing line. Combine this with decent weaponry, and they were transformed into the so-called fanatical Nazi elite panzer divisions that litter so many eyewitness accounts by Allied troops. Certainly this made them a pretty fearsome enemy, but it didn't mean they were especially well trained. There is a difference, and it's one that has often been lost in the narrative.

Both the British and Americans were learning all the time, but there is no question that the Americans, especially, had a willingness to soak up new tactics and absorb lessons. For all the concerns about how long it was taking the Americans to grapple their way through the bocage, actually it was only around six weeks from D-Day until the middle of July and in that time they had significantly increased the bridgehead and captured the Cotentin and Cherbourg – all of which had been done in dense hedgerow country and with only gradually increased armour, artillery and tank destroyer support. Rather than getting chewed over for their tardiness, Bradley and his First Army should have been given a massive pat on the back. It had taken six months to take Tunisia, thirty-six days to take Sicily and long months in the wet, cold and miserable winter of 1943/44 to get from Naples to Rome, so there was past experience to draw upon. And what was six weeks in the big scheme of things? Before the invasion, Montgomery had reckoned it would take them ninety days to get to Paris. They were currently about halfway through that.

In any case, the Americans were getting better with each passing week, if not day. There was a willingness to learn that was endemic and equally a willingness to innovate. An example is the way in which troops learned to blast holes in the bocage big enough to allow a tank to pass. Once this big conundrum had been solved, a major stumbling block was removed, because it meant armour could push through with infantry following, sheltering behind their protective armour. The Sherman could then spray the opposite hedgerow with machine-gun fire and blast out the machine-gun posts with its main gun. Then the infantry could fan out, clear up and move on. Dozers were one method; assaulting with combat engineers to blast a path for the armour was another; while a third method was the development of steel forks on the front of a Sherman tank.

During an inspection tour at the very end of June on a quiet sector of the line near Saint-Germain-d'Elle, US V Corps commander Major-General Leonard Gerow turned to the commander of F Troop, 102nd Cavalry Squadron, Captain James Depew, and asked if he had done anything to deal with the hedgerow problem. Depew admitted they had not yet come up with anything. Gerow told him to find a solution and fast. That same night, Depew called a meeting of his officers and senior NCOs. Staff Sergeant Curtis Culin said he had an idea. The problem, Culin pointed out, was that the Sherman and the hedge acted like two cars coming together bumper to bumper. What was needed, he reckoned, was something like a snowplough, which could use the momentum of the tank to get through the hedge rather than banging into it head-on.

Depew liked the sound of this and presented the issue to his squadron maintenance officer, Lieutenant Steve Litton. Litton suggested something like a fork – strong and long enough to dig in and pull up the roots of the bushes and trees in the hedge, and easy to bolt on to the front of the Shermans – and, in fact, these remarkable tanks came with a set of loops at the front on the lower hull. Litton thought maybe the beach obstacles that had littered Omaha and Utah could be used – they were made of strong steel and had good cutting edges to rip the bottom out of landing craft. Perhaps, he suggested, they could be cut and welded to the front of a tank.

Two days later, Depew reported that a prototype had been developed and was ready for testing. At first, the tank drew up and then pushed against the hedge so that the tracks began rising up the mound, just as it did without the fork on front. But then they had another go, charging straight at the hedge, and this time the Sherman sliced straight through as effortlessly as if it had been butter.

Word quickly spread up the chain of command until it reached Bradley, who in turn mentioned to Eisenhower that he was about to see a new device that could cut through hedgerows. Bradley was given his demonstration on 14 July, standing alongside General Gerow. Both were hugely impressed. 'So absurdly simple that it had baffled an army for more than five weeks,' noted Bradley, 'the tusk-like device had been fashioned by Curtis G Culin, Jr, a 29 year-old sergeant from New York City.' In fairness, it had been a joint effort, with Lieutenant Litton responsible for the design of the hedge-cutter.

These hedge-cutters became known as 'Rhinos'. Bradley immediately ordered the chief of First Army's Ordnance Section to supervise the construction and installation of as many of them as possible. First Army Ordnance then assembled welders and welding equipment within the beachhead and from rear areas in England. These teams used scrap metal from the German beach obstacles to construct most of the devices. Between 14 and 25 July, more than 500 hedgerow cutters were made, while by the end of the month 60 per cent of all First Army's Shermans were equipped with the device.

While these admittedly arrived mostly too late for the hedgerow battles north of Saint-Lô, they were now available for the COBRA assault and what might follow. In no other army in the world would the initial idea of a mere NCO be listened to, then proved and embraced so emphatically. The US Army was truly a people's army of civilian conscripts, not constrained by regimental tradition, and that gave it a freedom to innovate in a rapidly evolving world not shared by either the British or Germans.

Other innovations were adopted by both the Americans and British, including improved means of communication between infantry and armour. Telephones had been placed on the back of tanks, for example; these were trial-and-error developments and were certainly something Stanley Christopherson, for one, believed needed further honing. For the most part, however, the British and Canadians followed one approach, the Americans another; because they were coalition partners and fighting together but independently of one another, there was little common doctrine, although tactical developments were shared. The same was true for the air forces. Pete Quesada, for example, got on very well with both Coningham and Broadhurst, but was developing different tactics for his air forces, not least because the fighting in the bocage was different to that experienced by the British and Canadians in the area around Caen. The RAF was using the cab-rank system and VCP – visual control point – but Quesada, in the build-up to COBRA, was now hatching an even more refined system for directly supporting the ground troops. It was yet another example of innovation and rapid implementation being developed in Normandy.

'Bradley liked me, and I liked him a hell of a lot,' recalled General Quesada. While the planning for COBRA was taking place they were talking daily, with Quesada urging the First Army commander to assemble his armour on a very narrow front so that they could smash their way through and then keep going. Quesada was belying his lack of ground operations experience, but he said, 'Look, Brad, if you will concentrate your armor, I will tell you what I will do. I will keep over every column that you establish a flight of bombers from daylight until dark.'

'You will?' Bradley replied.

'Yes, I will,' answered Quesada.

'For every column I establish?'

'Yes, and further than that, Brad, we'll do something else that I think will be a tremendous help. We will put in the lead tank of every column an aircraft radio, so they can talk to the flight that's above them.'

That wasn't all. In the same conversation, Quesada also offered to put a pilot in the leading tank. Suddenly, in the space of one simple conversation, an exciting new tactical development had been born, one they then began to thrash out verbally. Quesada's fighters were now using high-frequency radios and were also being controlled from the ground by their MEW radars as well as by radio and high-frequency direction finding. What Quesada was proposing was a development of the cab-rank and Rover system used by the RAF, but with important differences. By flying directly above an armoured column, the pilots could see ahead. If they spotted an 88, or enemy troops, they could warn the column below and could either deal with it themselves or help the armour to defeat it. Because there was to be a direct verbal link between the lead tank and the pilots above, friendly-fire incidents, which had been not uncommon so far in the campaign, would be reduced. In fact, because of the direct radio link, the gap between the armour below and the actions of the fighter-bombers above could be narrower, which would also help the armour get on to their targets more quickly.

That very afternoon, they trialled putting an aircraft radio in a tank with a pilot alongside and found the system worked very well. Within a matter of days, they had practised it on a larger scale. Flights of four P-47 Thunderbolts flew in turns, thirty minutes at a time, over an armoured column, which meant they could maintain a permanent air umbrella over any armoured advance, striking targets and providing advance searches. It also meant an armoured column could dash forward with less concern about its flanks, because any movement on that score was likely to be spotted from the air. Keeping up such an umbrella would absorb a lot of Quesada's fighters, which would then not be available for interdiction tasks, but it did not have to be kept up all the time; rather, it could be implemented as and when required – such as for Operation

COBRA. The Armored Column Cover had been born. It was a potentially devastating development of air–land integration forged from the bloody bocage battles of Normandy.

While preparations for COBRA got under way, Dempsey's Second Army launched Operation GOODWOOD. The planning of this battle underlined precisely why, so far, British and Canadian efforts had been concentrated on the western, not eastern, side of Caen. Only six bridges crossed the Orne and Caen Canal, over which three armoured divisions, with their thousands of vehicles and men, had to pass. This meant leaving the artillery on the western side, where they would be less effective. Because this was an armour-led operation, the attack was going to be very light on infantry. In other words, largely unsupported British armour would be advancing under the noses of German high-velocity anti-tank guns well dug in above them. Most of the time, the inferior range of British tank guns didn't particularly come into play. As they advanced towards the Bourguébus Ridge, however, it almost certainly would.

It didn't take a brilliant military tactician to work out that this was asking for a bloody nose. But what to do? Eisenhower and Tedder were pushing for a breakthrough; Montgomery now had 3,500 tanks and yet was also being warned to conserve his infantry stocks, and attacking to the west had twice failed to produce a decisive breakthrough. It was most likely for this reason that Monty had insisted on a more limited operation, recognizing that his armour would probably take some hits but that, overall, they could continue the chewing up of German forces, especially if supported by heavy carpet-bombing by the RAF and USAAF. After all, Eisenhower and Tedder had offered to support any offensive operation. On the other hand, if Montgomery told them he was substantially scaling back Dempsey's original plan, would they support GOODWOOD quite so fully? Then what would become of his armour?

The instructions issued for GOODWOOD, however, reflected the mixed messages for the battle's aims. In his 'Notes on Second Army Operations 16 July–18 July', Montgomery hand-wrote his instructions to Dempsey. Under the title, 'Object of this Operation' he wrote:

> To engage the German armour in battle and 'write it down' to such an extent that it is of no further value to the Germans as a basis of the battle.

To gain a good bridge-head over the River Orne through Caen, and thus to improve our positions on the eastern flank.

Generally to destroy German equipment and personnel.

Only Dempsey and O'Connor were given these notes – they were not distributed to any of the divisional commanders, nor to Eisenhower or Tedder for that matter. In fact, to Tedder's follow-up signal of enthusiastic encouragement, Monty replied:

Three things important.

First: To hold the ring between now and 18 July and delay enemy moves towards lodgement area to greatest extent possible.

Second: To examine every means so that the Air can play its part on 18th and 19th July even if weather is not 100 per cent.

Third: Plan is successful promises to be decisive and therefore necessary that the Air Forces bring full weight to bear.

This was deliberately disingenuous and non-specific, because Montgomery knew perfectly well that both Eisenhower and Tedder had greater expectations for GOODWOOD than he thought possible. Perhaps they would get lucky and a decisive breakthrough would happen, but Monty certainly wasn't going to bet on it. But he did want that full air support all the same.

O'Connor's orders to his commanders, on the other hand, gave a more specific objective: the area 'Bourguébus–Vimont–Bretteville-sur-Laize'; this latter village was the site of Sepp Dietrich's I. Panzerkorps CP, some 10 miles south of Caen and well beyond the Bourguébus Ridge. 'If conditions are favourable,' O'Connor had added, 'subsequently exploiting to the south.' These reflected Dempsey's own ambitions for GOODWOOD, but they were certainly more far reaching than Montgomery's.

Because of the lack of space and the limiting constraints of trying to pass 44,892 men, 1,098 tanks and 11,772 vehicles of three British armoured divisions across six bridges in one short period of darkness, it was General Pip Roberts' 11th Armoured Division that would lead off and head over first. His instructions were to make for the Bourguébus Ridge and, ideally, beyond it, but his motorized infantry were first to clear up two villages near the start line of the attack. Roberts, understandably, was worried that his armour would then get too far from his infantry – and that was not good practice, as the infantry were the eyes of the tanks and needed to prevent lurking Germans with *Panzerfausts* attacking and to stop enemy infantry from clambering aboard and killing the crew. Armour could not really work entirely on its own in an attacking role. When Roberts questioned this, however, O'Connor insisted he do as ordered, although he allowed him to cover Cagny then pause while the Armoured Guards Division caught up; he also turned over some of the artillery's half-tracks and self-propelled guns to act as armoured personnel carriers. Dempsey's vision for GOODWOOD dictated the battle plan, not Montgomery's. The concern, though, as Montgomery had correctly gauged, was that it was demanding too much in circumstances that were not suited for a breakthrough. Not the terrain, the constraints of time, the Germans' high-ground advantage or the sudden lack of infantry made this look like an odds-on success. The die, however, had been cast.

Under instructions from Tedder, Air Chief Marshal Sir Arthur Harris ordered a maximum effort from RAF Bomber Command, with 1,056 heavies attacking at first light. These would be followed by nearly 500 medium bombers of Ninth Air Force and a further 539 heavies from Eighth Air Force. More than 2,000 bombers would be hitting the German positions. That was a huge number; Hamburg, for example, had been destroyed by 3,500 bombers over three nights back in July 1943. Bomber Command's targets were Colombelles, Cagny, and the villages of Touffréville, Sannerville and Banneville, a roughly diagonal area of some 4 miles by 4 that extended south-east from Caen and covered the gently rising slopes and ridge line; Cagny village straddled the Bourguébus Ridge and was a key German position and OP.

Among those attacking were Ken Handley and his Australian crew in 466 Squadron. Handley was finally coming towards the end of his tour, but he approached this mission with the same phlegmatic attitude that had seen him through so far. Like most of the heavies, they carried 8,000 lb of bombs – 4 tons. 'A good early morning prang on tanks and enemy gun installations in the battle area prior to a breakthrough,' he noted; even Bomber Command aircrew had been promised GOODWOOD would prove decisive. '1,000 aircraft took part at heights of 6-8,000 ft.' It was also their 'christening with flak', as Handley termed it; they had been very lucky to come through entirely unscathed so far. A jagged piece cut through the Perspex nose, missing the bomb-aimer by a matter of inches. 'Otherwise pleasant,' noted Handley.

It certainly wasn't pleasant for those on the ground. Leutnant Freiherr

Richard von Rosen had been at a party the previous evening organized by the battalion ordnance officer, but it had broken up quickly once they began to be shelled, and more heavily than usual. Von Rosen wasn't sure how to interpret this, but he inspected the sentries of 3. Kompanie, warned them to wake him if anything happened, then crawled under his panzer, Tiger 311, and slipped into his slit-trench alongside his gunner, Unteroffizier Werkmeister.

He was awoken early the following morning, at around five, by the thunder of aero-engines and, creeping out of his slit-trench, moved through the foliage that was camouflaging them and watched 'Christmas tree' marker flares dropping slowly to the ground all around them. Bombs began whistling down and just 200 yards away enormous geysers of earth erupted into the sky, followed by a violent pressure wave that almost knocked him off his feet. As he dashed for his Tiger, more bombs fell, nearer this time, the tank shaking and the pressure painfully stabbing his ears. 'From now on, I could not think,' he wrote, 'I was as helpless as a drowning man tossed into raging seas.' The air was filled with the whistling of bombs and von Rosen curled up tightly, pressing himself into the ground. Wave after wave of bombers flew over, the ground trembling, the air sucked from them, the whistling, the explosions, the churning up of soil, rock and grit. Von Rosen felt profoundly and completely helpless. There was simply no escape. All he could do was cover his ears, crouch as small as possible and hope.

Suddenly, a very close eruption flung him and Werkmeister across their slit-trench and covered them in earth. Momentarily, both were knocked unconscious, but when they came to they saw that the side of their slit-trench had caved in and that Tiger 312 was ablaze; their own panzer had been lifted and shifted to one side too, all 56 tons of it. Then it began again, another wave thundering over and more bombs falling. Von Rosen lay under his Tiger with his fingers in his ears and his blanket stuffed into his mouth to stop him from screaming.

The attack lasted about an hour and a half. Four of the Allies' targets were accurately marked using Oboe, a blind-bombing navigation system, while the fifth was also well marked by the pathfinders. The American bombers then followed and in all some 6,800 tons of bombs were dropped in a series of attacks. Von Rosen couldn't believe how the landscape had been transformed. 'Of the once so beautiful parkland nothing remained but shredded trees,' he wrote, 'churned meadows and giant bomb craters so numerous they overlapped – a grey, repulsive moonscape and a mist of dust which made breathing difficult. Through the thick fog it was possible to see the red glow of trees and cornfields burning.'

Dazed men, struggling to regain their senses, began emerging. Von Rosen had lost two Tigers from his company; one had been flipped upside down and was sitting on its turret. Both crews were dead, most of them eviscerated. His maintenance detachment had also been killed and their equipment destroyed. Platoon leaders congregated around him; von Rosen knew he had to act swiftly. Some Tigers were still in working order, but others had tracks broken or trees across them. Behind his own tank, just a few yards away, was a huge crater that would have swallowed him whole had the bomb been released a nano-second earlier.

Once the tanks and infantry of 11th Armoured Division got going they initially made good headway, following behind a rolling artillery barrage. However, the closer they got to the bombed areas the harder progress became, as they had to pick their way through the large number of craters. From the start position just to the west of Escoville, it was between 6 and 8 miles to their first objectives, which might not have looked so very far on the map but was quite a lot of ground to cover, especially now that much of it had been churned up by the bombing. The 3rd Royal Tank Regiment and other leading tanks had reached villages around Bourguébus by around 10.30 a.m., but as they neared Hubert-Folie they were suddenly on their own, beyond the range of the artillery and terribly exposed. Enough Germans had emerged from their slit-trenches and enough artillery, self-propelled guns and panzers had survived to give the leading British armour a hammering.

It wasn't long before Leutnant von Rosen and his men heard the sound of enemy tanks getting near. Radio contact with the battalion command post was down and his men and tanks too shattered by the experience to be able to think clearly, let alone fight. Scrambling over craters and debris, von Rosen hurried on foot and eventually found Hauptmann Fromme, who ordered him to get what tanks and men he could ready as soon as possible and create a blocking force between Manneville and Cagny. Enemy naval shells were now screaming over and repeatedly von Rosen had to take cover as he scampered back towards the remnants of his company. His III. Platoon still had all its tanks; three Tigers of I. Platoon were write-offs; and II. Platoon hoped to get two up and running soon. Whether this would be soon enough was anyone's guess. All the

Tigers had suffered damage of varying degrees and needed to go to the workshop, but that would have to wait, and by 10 a.m. they had six roadworthy.

An hour later, several Shermans appeared in front of them. Opening fire, the Tigers' shots were horribly wide; the bomb blast had recalibrated their guns. Von Rosen now planned to hit the enemy in the flanks, so ordered his Tigers to head south-west towards Cagny, then turn west to the farmstead of Le Prieuré, but en route two more of his Tigers were hit and brewed up, so he ordered his remaining four to pull back by 200 yards. When the fighting seemed to die down for a while, he hurried on foot to the battalion CP at Manneville. By this time, he had sixteen dead.

Major Hans von Luck only reached the battle at around 9 a.m., so missed the bombing. Having been awarded the Knight's Cross, he had been given a few days' leave in Paris, where he had been reunited with his beloved fiancée, Dagmar. By the time he finally arrived at his regimental CP and met his I. Bataillon commander, the news was grim. The officer seemed all at sea; all contact with the rest of both I. and II. Bataillons had been lost. Fuming, von Luck abandoned any thoughts of breakfast and instead ran to a panzer Mk IV that was at his disposal, yelling at his adjutant to contact Division HQ and ask for reserves to be sent forward urgently. Then, having offered his driver a cigarette, he told him to take the main road to Caen. At Cagny he was appalled to see British tanks fast approaching and with no sign of anyone firing back. Finding some abandoned 88mm flak guns, he ordered them to be moved into the northern end of the village and, telling the gunners to keep firing, he headed back to his CP.* Having feared that half his regiment had been destroyed, he was relieved to find Major Becker with news of his assault-gun batteries.

'One battery has been completely knocked out by bombs,' Becker told him. But, he explained, two batteries on the left flank were intact and were currently supporting the grenadiers of I. Bataillon. The other two batteries were about to go into action any moment on the right flank, where Major Kurz, using his initiative, had set up a defensive blocking

---

* Hans von Luck's account has often been called into question, but there were certainly tanks being knocked out later from Cagny and there were also Luftwaffe flak guns around Caen. Although not picked up by Allied aerial reconnaissance, the evidence of events suggests these were exactly as von Luck always claimed. I see no reason to doubt his version of events.

position with his II. Bataillon men. Soon after, the adjutant returned. Feuchtinger had no reserves but was sending the reconnaissance battalion. Von Luck's orders were to prevent any breakthrough to the east along the ridge.

Meanwhile, the Canadians had been brought in to clear the southeastern outskirts of Caen, and particularly the industrial area of Colombelles and the village of Giberville, both on the eastern side of the Orne. The Queen's Own were given Giberville as their objective on what was to prove a difficult day for the regiment. A Company attacked from left of the village, C and D from the right, and, making the most of the bombing to mask their advance, were approaching the village by around 7 a.m. They came under heavy machine-gun and small-arms fire and all three platoon commanders were killed, while one of Sergeant Charlie Martin's great mates, George Bennett, took five bullets in the stomach and two of his other pals were wounded.

The village was taken later that morning along with the capture of a large number of 16. Luftwaffen-Felddivision troops. One wounded prisoner had had his leg patched up but, as the stretcher-bearers took him away, he pulled out a pistol and shot several of them, killing one and wounding two more. Charlie Martin and several others jumped on him, grabbed the pistol, broke his arm and roughed him up before a group of prisoners took him away with a note attached explaining what he had done. 'A cruel and inexplicable act,' was Martin's verdict. 'But we never heard anything further.'

Later in the day, some of the A Company men pushed forward south from the village and took up positions along the railway line. They were soon counter-attacked, however, as at least two companies of Germans burst through from behind a thick hedge that had screened them. Seeing what was happening, Charlie Martin sent one man off to Company HQ to call in artillery and mortar support, then, his men giving him covering fire, he hurried forward to warn those still holding out by the railway embankment to fall back out of the way quickly. Most were able to pull back successfully, although largely because Buck Hawkins remained behind on the Bren to cover their retreat. Hawkins, though, was hit in the chest and killed just as he was finally about to withdraw himself. Martin was distraught – the whole company was. Hawkins had been quite a figure; at thirty-nine, he had been a lot older than most, married with children back home. But he was also a stalwart with a quick sense of humour and utterly fearless, a man who seemed to embody the spirit of the company. 'No words could express our feelings for Buck,' admitted Martin. 'The pain that day cannot be described.' The company was now down to about 50 per cent strength. They had taken their objective but at a terrible price.

Also suffering had been the lead units of 11th Armoured Division. The 2nd Northants Yeomanry had been waiting to follow up behind the 3rd RTR and were moving forward by around 11 a.m., although as they passed near Démouville they engaged and destroyed two German self-propelled guns. Not until 4.30 p.m. were they ordered to go to the rescue of 3rd RTR. In A Squadron, Corporal Reg Spittles and his crew had already pushed up the railway embankment that ran south-east out of the city, his 2 Troop taking the lead. Moving on through the arches, they rumbled past the Cormelles factory complex, stopping around 500 yards further on, along some rough ground behind bushes, to look at their objectives. Almost immediately they came under fire and the troop sergeant's tank was hit and brewed up. Spittles moved his tank forward and, jumping down, helped the troop sergeant to get the gunner and loader clear. He then drove back to their start point with the crew on the back, deposited them and headed back once more. It had not been a good start.

While fighting continued around Bra and Hubert-Folie, further east the British attack had run out of steam. Hans von Luck reckoned the worst had been halted by around midday and reported as much via a restored radio link to Feuchtinger. The divisional commander, in turn, told him 1. SS-Panzer-Division was being urgently brought back into the line, while Kurt Meyer's 12. SS was also being brought back up. 'The 1. SS will arrive today in the late afternoon,' Feuchtinger told him, 'the 12. SS not before midday tomorrow. We *must* hold until then.' In fact, von Luck was not far wrong, although by this time the British and Canadians were on to the ridge and over the other side. The infantry of 3rd Division, operating on the left flank of the attack, had pushed into Troarn, where the Paras had blown the bridges on D-Day, while the Guards and 7th Armoured Divisions had overrun Cagny despite von Luck's best efforts. They then pushed on, over the ridge to the village of Bourguébus itself, quickly renamed 'Bugger's Bus' by the Tommies. 11th Armoured Division were still holding Bra and Hubert-Folie, while the 2nd Canadian Infantry Division had pushed south from the city.

None the less, by 4 p.m. the fighting seemed to have quietened down in the Manneville area and, with 1. SS-Panzer-Division on its way, Hauptmann Fromme told Richard von Rosen to take his surviving

Tigers back to the maintenance teams, using the roadworthy ones to tow those that were knocked out. Before his Tiger 311 set off, von Rosen had another look at the upturned Tiger 313 and it now occurred to him to check the escape hatch on the turret. Seeing it was slightly ajar, he leaned over and called out, and was amazed to get a reply. The hatch was wedged, though, and no matter how hard he tried to move it, he could not make it budge. Nor could the trapped men inside. Eventually, with the help of three others, they managed to ease it open enough for those inside to inch their way out. 'We brought them out more dead than alive,' noted von Rosen. 'Now it was time for us all to get the hell out of there.'

Fighting continued all the way along the ridge and beyond. General Eberbach was furiously trying to make sense of what was going on, but not until mid-afternoon were the dazed and confused Germans able to mount any serious counter-attack, and even then they were hammered in turn by *Jabos*, naval shelling and anti-tank guns. Flight Sergeant Ken Adam, for example, flew twice that day, attacking enemy gun positions in the morning and then carrying out an armed reconnaissance and shooting up 1. SS-Panzer-Division as they moved up to the front. At around 6.30 p.m. Corporal Reg Spittles finally rejoined his squadron at Bra, where they engaged the 1. SS now entering the fray. They were finally pulled back for the night at around 11 p.m., although were back in action the next day.

By this time, however, General Dempsey had accepted there would be no dramatic breakthrough. Eberbach was amazed the British didn't push on through overnight, but it was impossible to coordinate fighting of this scale in the dark, even with flares, and the casualties were considerable. The following day he kept pushing the gains made on the 18th, but the front was stiffening again as more German reinforcements arrived, including those two SS panzer divisions. Reg Spittles was back in action in Bra on the morning of the 19th, when his tank was hit on the back by an enemy shell. Because it was in the first salvo, they were not closed down, so he, his gunner and loader were all hit by shrapnel, albeit not badly. Everything on the outside of the tank was stripped off, however, including the radio aerial, and Spittles no longer had any comms at all, either internal or external. He set off to find the 7th Armoured Division and a unit of Cromwells to see if they could help. 'This they did,' he noted, 'fitters sorted the tank, the Medical Officer patched our wounds up.' They rejoined the regiment the next day, by which time it had begun to rain and GOODWOOD had been brought to a halt, to the relief of the soldiers on both sides.

Later that Thursday, 20 July, Spittles was wounded again. The Germans began to shell their leaguer. Because of the heavy rain, he and his crew decided against sleeping in a sodden slit-trench under their tank and so were trying to get some rest in a lorry instead. As soon as the shelling began, they quickly got out of the vehicle, but not before another nearby, on which boxes of ammunition were stored, was hit and exploded, shrapnel flying everywhere. 'Unfortunately,' scrawled Spittles, 'one rather large part found me, almost breaking my back and one arm.' With severe bruising and a bad gash, he was evacuated to a field hospital.

Of all the British battles in Normandy, GOODWOOD is the one for which Montgomery has suffered the most criticism. It has been pointed out that some 400 British tanks were lost that day, and for a mere 7 miles' gain. Four hundred tanks! In one day! Eisenhower, for one, was furious. As he pointed out to Harry Butcher, 1,000 tons per mile seemed excessive even for the resource-rich Allies. Tedder was also seething and, had he had his own way, would have sacked both Montgomery and Leigh-Mallory, who he felt was increasingly plotting behind Coningham's back. 'On 20 July,' wrote Tedder, 'I spoke to Portal about the Army's failure. We were agreed in regarding Montgomery as the cause.'

Some qualification here is needed. First, from Montgomery's point of view GOODWOOD achieved exactly what he had expected and was not a failure. Second Army enlarged the bridgehead east and south-east of Caen, and the battle got his troops on to the Bourguébus Ridge. It also chewed up large numbers of German troops and brought 12. SS and 1. SS rushing to the rescue, which meant there would be no more panzer divisions heading into the American sector. It wasn't a great battle plan, but it was Dempsey's, not Montgomery's, and that was why they were unable to push on; without proper infantry support, the armour was too much out on a limb. The British armoured divisions were designed for exploitation, for advancing fast and wide once the breakthrough had been achieved. It was the independent armoured brigades that were supposed to achieve that breakthrough, operating hand in hand with the infantry. Unfortunately for Second Army, however, because of the terrain and because the Germans had fought, on Hitler's orders, so close to the coast, the armoured divisions had been used in a way for which they had not been designed or created.

Then there was the matter of tank losses. Reg Spittles pointed out that the 2nd Northants Yeomanry lost thirty-seven tanks at GOODWOOD out of fifty-two in the battalion. Of the 185 men manning those tanks, however, only 25 were casualties, which suggests most of the tanks that were knocked out of action did not brew up. In fact, the figure of 400 tanks for the day also needs re-addressing. Detailed reports by the Military Operational Research Unit (MORU) examined all tank casualties and categorized them into those destroyed and burned; those badly damaged but repairable in rear-area workshops; and those repairable near the front but taking longer than 24 hours. Their findings confirmed that, although 493 tanks suffered some kind of damage, only 156 were written off. In all, only 136 tank crew were killed, although the infantry, which was supposed to be preserved, lost 3,432 killed, wounded or missing between 18 and 22 July in the GOODWOOD battle; 300 of those, however, were Canadians who found themselves entirely encircled and forced to surrender to the 1. SS-Panzer-Division on 21 July.

That final figure of tank losses, however, rather illustrates why the Allies were winning the war, because a phenomenal 218 of those tanks were back in action within just twenty-four hours of being reported knocked out, and a further 62 within a matter of days. As darkness fell, swarms of British tank wreckers and gun tractors had poured on to the battlefield and retrieved all but the blackened, burned-out hulls. LADs and workshops toiled furiously with an abundance of tools, winching gear and spare parts and got them ready again. Montgomery had 3,500 tanks on the eve of GOODWOOD. Some 156 permanent losses were something they could easily absorb. And 156 was a long way short of the 400 usually bandied about when GOODWOOD is discussed.

German losses amounted to eighty-three tanks and assault guns, the strength of one entire panzer division, and included twenty-six Panthers, seven Tigers and three 72-ton King Tigers, the only ones in Normandy. General Eberbach had to accept that the remaining, battered, half of 16. Luftwaffen-Felddivision had been 'swept away', as had elements of 21. Panzer. 'The local reserves had been annihilated or shattered,' he added, 'their guns smashed before they ever fired a shot.'

Montgomery might have been quick to take the plaudits and bask in the glory when it came his way, but he also took the flak on the chin. He had been in a tricky position before GOODWOOD and, when it fell some way short of Eisenhower's expectations, he made no effort to point the finger of blame at anyone else; the more ambitious plan, and the use of the armoured divisions in a striking role, was Dempsey's, after all. GOODWOOD had, in fact, more than achieved all Monty's expectations for it, and, all things considered, at quite a small cost. He would ride out the storm, however, as he had known he would; back home in England, he had a powerful supporter in General Sir Alan Brooke, the British chief of the Imperial General Staff, who knew there was no one else ready to take Montgomery's place, nor, frankly, anyone better to handle the largely civilian armies of which he had charge. What's more, Montgomery had the people's vote. No one was going to sack Monty.

Yet once again, whatever crisis seemed to be facing the Allies, it was as nothing compared with that confronting the Germans, for on Thursday, 20 July, as the GOODWOOD battle petered out, an assassination attempt was made on Hitler's life, and it very nearly worked. This stunning event would fling the German defence of Normandy into even further disarray.

CHAPTER 30

Saint-Lô

No matter that GOODWOOD achieved Montgomery's ambitions for the battle, there is no doubt that by the third week of July morale was taking a dip across all the Allied forces, and that was a potentially dangerous state of affairs. Most troops at the front had no idea just how parlous the condition of the German forces really was; as far as most were concerned, they were hitting a brick wall of fanatical, highly trained Nazis. In fact, the opposite was closer to the truth: the Germans were hitting a brick wall of immense Allied fire-power and slowly but surely bleeding themselves to death, and now that Hitler had survived an assassination attempt, the German commanders in charge could expect even tighter – and more disruptive – interfering from the top.

On Thursday, 20 July, Oberst Claus Graf von Stauffenberg had managed to bring a briefcase packed with explosives into a meeting with the Führer at Hitler's Wolf's Lair headquarters in East Prussia and the bomb had exploded. Miraculously, Hitler had survived with only superficial wounds; really, he had the luck of the devil. The coup had failed, the immediate ring-leaders had been shot and the witch-hunt had begun. Ever since, much speculation has raged over Rommel's precise involvement, but it seems certain he was not involved at all; perhaps he had heard about a plot to overthrow the Führer, but the approaches made to him were always so heavily laced with non-specific and multiple interpretations that he may very well not even have fully realized what was being proposed. He certainly did not take any bait to join the conspirators. His chief of staff, Speidel, was more involved, although probably less so than his post-war memoirs made out. There was little doubt, though, that Rommel had been suggesting to his senior commanders that it was time to make peace with the Western Allies. Conversations such as the one Kurt Meyer overheard on his arrival at I. SS-Panzerkorps CP on 17 July had been taking place. Had Rommel not been wounded, it is possible he might have surrendered to the Allies, although this would have been considerably less likely after the failed bomb plot just because, to do so, he would really have needed the support of Hausser, Dietrich and Eberbach, and probably of von Kluge. Grumbling and complaining about the conduct of the war and the hopelessness of the OKW – whom everyone hated – was one thing; surrendering, unthinkable in the ideology of the SS, was quite another. But Rommel *was* wounded and no longer part of the equation in Normandy, and speculation on this score, though interesting, is ultimately pointless.

Hitler, increasingly paranoid even before the attack and his mind already addled by the daily cocktail of drugs, now saw treachery at every turn. Incredibly, the day after the assassination attempt, von Kluge wrote to the Führer, forwarding Rommel's missive of 16 July. After fourteen days at the front, von Kluge wrote, he had come to the same conclusion as Rommel about their prospects in Normandy. 'The moment is fast approaching when this overtaxed front line is bound to break up,' he added. 'And when the enemy once reaches the open country a properly co-ordinated command will be almost impossible.'

Not surprisingly, these reports from the front went down spectacularly badly at Hitler's headquarters. Von Kluge's days were now numbered, and there would be no retreat – that was unthinkable. They were to keep fighting and destroy the Allies. Reaction among the troops to the news was broadly one of shock. 'The terrorist act was rejected equally by all units,' noted Kurt Meyer. 'The soldiers had no sympathy for the 20 July conspirators.' Hauptmann Helmut Ritgen, who had known von Stauffenberg when they had both been in 6. Panzer-Division, was also shocked. 'Although I loathed Hitler,' he wrote, 'his death would have been for us, at least temporarily, a disaster and caused such confusion that the enemy would have been confirmed in his goal of the destruction of Germany.' Eberhard Beck and his colleagues in 277. Artillerie-Regiment took a somewhat different view, however. 'His death could bring us a turnaround,' Beck noted, 'and we hoped very much that this senseless war would end.' His commander, Leutnant Freiherr von Stenglin, visited all his gun crews and told them that not only had the assassination failed, but orders had arrived that from now on they were to use only the Nazi salute, not the more traditional military one. It was clear von Stenglin was appalled. 'We were all disappointed by the failed assassination attempt,' added Beck. Soon after, von Stenglin disappeared and no sign of him was ever found again. Leutnant Richard von Rosen found the news deeply unsettling, especially since the perpetrators all seemed to be aristocrats. 'Young man, don't let it get to you,' Hauptmann Fromme told him, 'we shall protect you.' 'It was a pity that Rommel was out of action,' added von Rosen. 'We had great faith in him. A word from him now would have helped us greatly.' Willi Müller was also 'unsettled' by the news, and this seems to have been the overwhelming reaction. It was disconcerting at a time of already considerable uncertainty.

The Panzer-Lehr had by now long completed their move and were in the line to the west of Saint-Lô, with 17. SS on their left and 2. SS-Panzer next to them, which meant for the first time the Americans were confronted by two panzer and one SS panzer-grenadier divisions. That they had got there pretty much unscathed was largely because of the poor weather, which had prevented the usual amount of air cover. Helmut Ritgen's II. Panzer-Regiment 130 had arrived on the night of 10 July and were immediately thrown into a counter-attack early the following morning. Fighting on unfamiliar ground with no time for reconnaissance was a recipe for disaster, and so it proved. 'As feared,' noted Ritgen, 'the division attack failed completely, with frightful losses.' By 15 July, Ritgen had lost fifteen officers.

Opposing them were the veteran US 9th Division and, as the 47th Infantry counter-attacked in turn, Lieutenant Orion Shockley and his men bypassed an orchard although mortars and small arms were coming from its direction. No sooner had they gone past than Thunderbolts swooped over, turned and headed back towards them. Shockley and his men thought they were going to be attacked, but instead the P-47s fired and dropped bombs on the orchard, driving a number of tanks out from their cover. Shockley watched all this in amazement, then suddenly several tanks rumbled past. As the last ones went by, one of Shockley's men jumped out and fired a bazooka, which hit the tank but didn't stop it. A German soldier, badly wounded, fell off on to the road. Shockley walked up to him and the man raised an arm as if asking for help. 'I saw that there was no hope for him,' noted Shockley, 'and felt a pang of regret for the whole war and what it did to people. I had seen many of my buddies wounded and killed, but somehow this incident got to me.'

Shockley and his men managed to advance three-quarters of a mile that Wednesday, 12 July, and over the days that followed it was the same, with more of his men getting wounded and killed along the way. One man was hit in the stomach by shrapnel. 'Lieutenant, I'm going to die, ain't I?' he said, a statement of fact, rather than a question. His stomach had been sliced open and he was holding his intestines with both hands. Shockley called for a medic and tried to help; the man was taken to hospital but died a few days later. The following day, 16 July, Shockley's good friend Captain James Cameron was killed when his Jeep went over a mine. They had been together since fighting through North Africa. The day after that, another friend, Lieutenant Paul Buffalo, was also gone, killed by shell fragments. By the 20th, Shockley was given command of the company.

Shockley had already seen enough violence to last a lifetime, but now at Esglandis, while they waited for the launch of COBRA, a company commanders' meeting was called. No sooner had they arrived at the battalion CP than the enemy began sending over shells. The first landed nearby, so they all ran for cover. First out of the tent were Captain Minton and Lieutenant Roger Murray, to whom Shockley had just been talking. A second shell whistled in and a fragment sliced off Minton's head while a second hit Murray.

'Ow, I'm hit,' he said as he was neatly cut in half just a few feet in front of Shockley. He was dead by the time he hit the ground. Knowing shells dispersed more in distance than to the side, Shockley dived into a foxhole away from the incoming blasts as a further one hit a tree, showering the two men in the trench below and killing them too. It had not been a good few days.

'The hedgerows were terrible,' said Lieutenant John Rogers, a platoon commander in Company E of the 67th Armored Regiment, part of the US 2nd Armored Division. The division was known as 'Hell on Wheels' and it was a kind of hell in that country. 'We were there for eighteen days and eighteen nights,' he said, 'just slugging it out.' They all found it deeply frustrating, but they just could not penetrate – not in any depth. The dozer he had fixed on to the front of his Sherman helped, but it seemed to him like a particularly brutal slugging match in which neither side was gaining much.

Both sides confronted that third week of July with morale at a low ebb. Desertions were on the rise. The grinding violence of the campaign was so debilitating. Death lay everywhere, covering the once beautiful countryside with a pall of putrefaction. Every field, it seemed, held the carcasses of cattle and horses blasted by the war. Most would fill up with gases, which made a carcass roll over with its legs sticking in the air. One day, Reg Spittles was peering through his binoculars and spotted a German machine-gunner sitting in his slit-trench enjoying the sunshine. Ahead of him, though, was a dead cow, already swollen in death. Spittles and his crew were several hundred yards away and safe in their tank, so Spittles asked his machine-gunner to fire a burst at the cow, which he did. The reaction from the German was everything Spittles had hoped for. Swiftly gathering his weapon and ammunition belts together, he looked around, then hopped out of his foxhole. 'Finally taking a cigarette from his mouth,' noted Spittles, 'he looked to the direction of where the firing had come from and with a big smile shook his fist in our direction.'

Just as often, the stench was from those killed in action and left on the battlefield. It seemed to infuse everything. Equally bad were the appalling sights of what could happen to the body of a once strapping young man. Near Tilly, along a lane that was continually used by the Sherwood Rangers, Stanley Christopherson noticed a dead German soldier protruding on to the track. Every time a tank passed, his arm was crushed, over and over until there was nothing left but mashed bone and flesh, like constantly run-over road-kill. Reg Spittles also repeatedly passed a knocked-out Panzer IV. One of the crew was hanging out of the turret, dead, and with every day his rotting corpse changed – the skin swelled, then darkened, until eventually the head and arm fell off completely.

The constant shelling, the violence, the stench, the discomfort – it was relentless. Even while GOODWOOD was going on, the British were still attacking around Hill 112 and the neighbouring Hill 113 to the south of the Odon. Lieutenant Robert Woollcombe had been there with the 6th KOSB and the 15th Scottish Division on and off since the end of EPSOM. He had been certain he would be killed there, although so far that frequently self-fulfilling prophecy had not come to bear; he had been lucky, though. Some seventy-five men in his A Company had gone up Hill 113, but only thirty-two had come back down again. He had learned that only by huddling in his foxhole did he have much chance of survival, but as an officer he would often be summoned to Battalion HQ. 'The journey back to this vicinity was a rather cat-like procedure,' he wrote. 'It entailed the usual walk-run, the periodic halts in order to listen, the agonising pause before the swift shrill hiss of another "stonk" coming over; hollow-eyed, stubbly-chinned men bolting for cover, the clatter of rifles, spades and trench headboards being knocked over – and your landing with a bump on top of somebody in a strange trench for momentary refuge. The hard, heavy explosions and the trench shaking tiny rivulets of dislodged earth over you, the whirr of spinning metal, dust flying, and silence.' The battalion lost nine officers on Hill 113. Just a month earlier, Woollcombe had been one of the junior subalterns. Now he was the senior one.

Just across the valley, partly responsible for the shelling Woollcombe was trying to dodge, was Kanonier Eberhard Beck. Ammunition restrictions meant their firing was limited, while they were still in range of British counter-battery fire and were losing friends and comrades as a result. His friend Paumann was killed instantly by a shrapnel fragment; Fritz Arnold, due to be heading to *Kriegsschule*, was wounded; Kanonier Ludwig Gröger, with whom Beck had trained, suffered a breakdown and was taken to hospital. Beck never saw him again. Then Leutnant von Senglin disappeared. Beck missed his mother and even contemplated giving himself a 'home shot' – a wound that would get him out of there. 'I just wanted to get out of this misery,' he wrote. It also bothered him that he had never been with a woman.

The British weren't the only ones getting over a troublesome ridge line. Following the fall of Hill 192 on the high ground to the north-east of Saint-Lô, the whole of the American line was pushing further south, inexorably, while by 17 July the 29th Division was finally closing on the town itself. Sergeant Bob Slaughter had rejoined his platoon in time for the assault and, by the time the 29th finally entered the shattered remains of the town, they had been in the line for forty-two days straight. Slaughter could scarcely get his head round the number of friends he had lost; just in the past couple of days on the Martinville 'Ridge of Death', less than 2 miles to the north-east of Saint-Lô, his good buddy Sergeant 'Ajax' Browning had been killed, as had his trusted machine-gunner, PFC 'Fats' Williams. Slaughter reckoned a part of him had died with those two on that ridge. 'Hearing the news of who had gotten hit was always hard,' he noted, 'and every day, new faces replaced seasoned infantry men.'

Obergrenadier Karl Wegner and his *Gruppe* in Grenadier-Regiment 914 were among those defending the ruins of Saint-Lô and had been holding out on Hill 122, just to the north of the city. For the past six weeks, since the trauma of D-Day, he had stuck close to Obergefreiter Kalb and his friend Willi. A bond of deep comradeship had been forged. Overnight, in the darkness of 17/18 July, they had tramped back along with the remnants of their company, now just a few dozen men, past discarded equipment and wreckage in the ditches by the track. 'Karl, any fool can see that we're beaten,' Kalb told him. 'There is no hope of holding this lousy French ruin.' But those were General Kraiss's orders: the town, although completely wrecked, was to be defended. Wearily, they had begun digging in yet again.

The following day, though, the defence of Saint-Lô quickly unravelled. By late afternoon word reached them that the Americans were actually behind them, and then shells started coming in – shells fired by their own artillery. If they were surrounded, which it seemed they were, then it was clearly time to scarper. Kalb and his small *Gruppe* now got up out of their foxholes and began skirting through the city, peering round corners, then making a dash for it. Then, while taking a quick peek, Kalb was shot in the hand. Wegner fired a burst from the machine gun, then they bolted down another alley, but around the next corner they ran straight into some American armoured vehicles. As they tried to turn back, Willi slipped, knocked into Kalb, but was then hit by a volley of bullets. Kalb pulled him back out of the firing line, but Willi was badly shot up, and screaming in pain and panic. Cradling his head and holding his hand, Wegner looked down at his dying friend while Kalb desperately tried to dress the wounds. Willi's screams faded away and the colour drained from his face. He began to cry softly. 'Karl,' he mumbled, looking up at Wegner, 'through all this just to die in the rubble, it makes no sense.' Then he was gone.

Kalb took Willi's things – his photos of his wife, his wedding ring and identity disc – wrapped them in a handkerchief, then replaced his own helmet with his cap and told the others that he would go first and, if everything was all right, they should follow. Holding his arms up above his head, he stepped out. Glancing one more time at his dead friend, Wegner followed. 'Thank God,' he said, 'it was all over.'

It was almost over for Leutnant Hans Heinze too. Also trapped in Saint-Lô, he and his last few men had suddenly seen American tanks bearing down upon them. Caught in the open, Heinze now tried to buy his men some time by taking a *Panzerfaust*, running into the centre of the road and firing it at the lead tank. The blast of a shell knocked him to the ground and when he came to he realized he was lying on the ground with his right arm and side badly wounded. Curiously, his first thought was that he'd never be able to play tennis again. His second was that he needed to move quickly or be crushed by the Sherman bearing down on him. Pulling out a handkerchief, he frantically waved it and, to his amazement, the American tank commander stopped and allowed Heinze's men to grab him and pull him clear. Even in the midst of this hell there were still, it seemed, moments of humanity.

Not only was Heinze's life saved, he was taken to an aid post and then put on an ambulance and taken south, out of the ruins of the city. Lying in the van, he looked up to see a mass of bullet holes in the roof. Groggily, he asked the driver how many times he'd been shot at. 'Almost every time we drive we are strafed,' the driver told him. He explained the Allies believed they were using ambulances to deliver ammunition and supplies to the front. For the Germans there really was no escaping the ever-present dominance of Allied air power. Heinze, though, did make it in one piece to the field hospital. His Normandy campaign was over.

Wednesday, 19 July was a busy day for General Omar Bradley. In the morning at his HQ encampment he conferred with his corps commanders for COBRA, having already briefed his generals on 12 July. Key to the plan was to attack on a narrow front, rather as Pete Quesada had been urging him to do, though it went against the instincts of most American commanders, who tended to prefer a broad-front approach so that they could exert pressure all along the line and make the most of materiel advantage. With the air assault key to the whole operation, however, greater focus was needed for COBRA. Joe Collins's VII Corps would take the lead, his armour surging forward the moment the bombers had cleared a path.

Then it was a short flight to England to discuss the air plan. At 1.30 p.m. Bradley and Quesada, with Chet Hansen in tow, took off in thick fog, but touched down at Northolt near London in better conditions. Brereton and Coningham were there to meet them, Brereton looking small and trim behind his wire spectacles, Coningham big and red-faced. They headed off to Bentley Priory in a convertible Buick, where Leigh-Mallory, lean, curt and with few smiles, was waiting. Spaatz too – calm, confident and bristling with shrewd intelligence – and also Tedder, wiry and small, chewing on his pipe and 'quivering with alertness'.

Bradley had expected a hard sell of his air plan for COBRA, especially after GOODWOOD, but it was received enthusiastically and carefully thrashed out. Fighter-bombers of the Ninth would strike first, hitting German defences immediately south of the Saint-Lô–Périers road at H minus 30. Then Spaatz's heavies would bomb the 7,000-yard width and to a depth of 2,500 yards behind the German main line of resistance, which was the road, with each bomber carrying forty 100lb bombs. This meant the entire 7,000 by 2,500 yard area would be saturated with some 72,000 bombs. Nor was that all. The heavies were to be followed by medium bombers, then yet more fighters. 'General was pleased with what he had gotten,' noted Hansen. In all, the Panzer-Lehr, the division holding that sector of the line, would be pasted by 1,800 heavies, 300 medium bombers and 350 fighters. If the Germans had had any remaining doubt about the overwhelming fire-power of the Allies, they would no longer have any after this attack.

Also discussed was exactly where the troops should be behind this awesome bombing effort. Bradley wanted them as close as possible, so that they could sweep in before the Germans had had a chance to recover, but the air men suggested they should be at least 3,000 yards away. Bradley countered with 800 yards; they eventually settled on 1,200. Then came discussion over the angle of attack. Bradley and Quesada argued that it should be west–east, parallel to the start line; the bomber men had other ideas, however, pointing out that trying to get the planned force of bombers into an area just 1½ miles wide would be impossible. Other considerations of navigation, radar and enemy flak all came into play, but the most pressing was the narrowness of the width. Heavy bombers took up a lot of air space. Leigh-Mallory, who had no real experience of bombers, disagreed and sided with Bradley and Quesada, but the conference ended without the matter being properly resolved.

By 5 p.m. they were done and flew back to Normandy, from where they took another quick flight from airfields A-1 to A-3, and then on to see Collins at VII Corps HQ. Bradley had already grown to trust Collins and gave him considerable leeway to plan for COBRA. Collins and his staff had been working hard over the previous week, but had divided the operation into three phases. First would be the breakthrough, and he wanted 9th and 30th Divisions on the left and right, with 4th Division in the middle. The 9th and 4th would head southwards to Marigny, then the 9th would swing to the west and strike towards Coutances near the coast; this way they might envelop 2. SS, 17. SS and various infantry units, cutting off their retreat. It was a daring and exciting proposition. Meanwhile, the 4th would fall into reserve, protecting against any counter-attack from the south. The 30th Division would drive south and then east, protecting the left-hand flanks. Then could come the armour – 2nd and 3rd Armored Divisions with the Big Red One loaded up into vehicles. This would be the exploitation phase and dramatic speed of action was key. The third phase could be consolidation as his forces struck for, took and held key towns and nodal points.

'Everything is now committed,' noted Hansen on the evening of 19 July. 'Tight squeeze to get it into line in time but it can be done.' Six divisions would be used, supported by over 1,000 artillery pieces and 140,000 shells stockpiled and ready for VII Corps' drive, plus a further 27,000 put aside for VIII Corps, which would follow with its own thrust south a little to the west. In all, some 1,269 Shermans, 694 Stuart light tanks and 288 tracked tank destroyers were available. It was an immense amount of force, greater than anything yet concentrated for one operation in Normandy. As they were about to leave, Bradley told Collins he was planning to have fighters drop belly tanks of napalm on to the assault area too. 'That's giving them the works all the way around,' added Hansen in his diary. It certainly was. The following day, Collins issued VII Corps Field Orders 6.

CHAPTER 31

COBRA

'THIS WAS MEANT TO be the day of the attack,' jotted Chet Hansen on 21 July, 'but we are weathered out.' The rain was sheeting down, turning everything quickly to mud. The previous evening Eisenhower had been over. 'When I die,' he had said, peering out from Bradley's tent at the rain, 'they can hold my body for a rainy day and bury me during a thunderstorm, for this weather will be the death of me yet.' Airfields were inoperable and much of the front seemed to have ground to a halt. The fighting never completely stopped, though, with plenty of shelling still going on and, east of Caen, clashes between the Canadians and 1. SS-Panzer-Division. Troops were being shifted around after GOODWOOD, with most of Second Army moving back west of Caen and the bulk slotting in next to the Americans in the middle of the line. The area around Caen was now the domain of First Canadian Army, operational under Lieutenant-General Harry Crerar, who had been brought over to Normandy by Lieutenant Yogi Jenson and the crew of HMCS *Algonquin*.

In all, there were some 640,000 British and Canadian troops in Normandy and 812,000 US troops. The Germans, by comparison, had sent 490,000 troops to Normandy, but had already lost nearly 117,000 and had received a measly 10,078 replacement troops. This meant the Allies had a 3.8:1 manpower advantage, which was much healthier than it had been on D-Day and the days that had followed.

Despite this, Montgomery was hopeful but not confident of an American breakthrough with COBRA, so was keen to keep up the pressure. Fighting continued around Hill 112 and, on 22 July, the 43rd Wessex Division attacked again in what was called Operation EXERCISE. It was an example of how the Allied armies were learning in this difficult campaign. Time was given to planning, forward reconnaissance was carried out, and infantry, armour and artillery agreed a plan beforehand that they were then able to execute. 'It has been said of this battle,' noted the division war diary, 'that it was a set piece in which all the precepts of the training manuals were fulfilled.' Two Wiltshire infantry battalions, working in tandem with Churchill tanks, overwhelmed the enemy, captured and then secured the village of Maltot, a wreck of a place that had changed hands several times over the past fortnight; this was where Walter Caines and the 4th Dorsets and 1st Hampshires had suffered so badly. On the 22nd, however, the inevitable counter-attacks were dealt with and seen off, and some 400 prisoners taken, which somewhat offset the loss of 300 Canadians the day before. Casualties among the attackers were, all things considered, slight. The dead of the earlier fighting were still strewn in the village, which was little more than piles of rubble. The stench was appalling, but at least the clear-up could now begin. The Wessexmen's battle here, small in scale, was none the less important. It showed they were both adapting and learning.

The following day, Sunday, 23 July, was also misty and grey, with yet again no possibility of launching COBRA. Three days of clear weather, Bradley reckoned he needed. Quite rightly, he wasn't prepared to jeopardize this battle through impatience; it wasn't D-Day, after all, with its constraints of tide and moon. It was still frustrating, though, with everyone keyed and raring to go.

'Dammit,' Bradley muttered as he looked up at the sky. 'I'm going to have to court-martial the chaplain if we have very much more weather like this.'

Instead, Bradley had a meeting with General George S. Patton, who was now in Normandy and itching to get into the battle. A God-fearing, swearing, no-nonsense shooter from the hip, Patton remained America's best-known general in theatre. Always immaculately dressed, he was definitely a firebrand and a career cavalryman who had served in the Mexican War as well as in France in 1918. In Tunisia, he had been commander of II Corps before handing it over to Bradley so that he could prepare for the invasion of Sicily, where he had commanded US Seventh Army and commanded it well. Patton believed in aggressive action and, tactically, was pretty astute, although he also had the shortest of fuses and a tendency to blow up before pausing to see the other person's point of view. This had got him into trouble, not least after the Sicilian campaign when he had slapped a man suffering from combat fatigue, a condition with which Patton had no truck whatsoever.

Eisenhower, having sacked Patton after this incident despite being a long-standing friend, had brought him back to lead Third Army, which was always going to be brought into the battle at a later stage. 'It is Hell to be on the side lines,' Patton had written to his wife on D-Day, 'and see all the glory eluding me.' Nor had he been particularly impressed with Bradley's handling of the campaign, which he had been following in forensic detail; but although Patton got results, he was certainly more willing than most Allied commanders for his troops to die in the process. So desperate was he to get into the fight that he offered to pay Eisenhower $1,000 for each week earlier than planned that Ike brought him over. Third Army had not been given the operational go-ahead yet, but Patton had come over on 4 July, landing in a C-47 at A-21, Saint-Laurent-sur-Mer, and immediately heading down to Omaha Beach in a Jeep. Word soon spread and, because of all the unloading still going on, quite a crowd quickly gathered. 'I'm proud to be here to fight beside you,' he said, standing up and speaking in his curiously high-pitched voice. 'Now let's cut the guts out of those Krauts and get the hell on to Berlin. And when we get to Berlin, I am going to personally shoot that paper-hanging son of a bitch, just like I would a snake.' Those listening lapped it up. Patton was nothing if not a showman.

He had been back and forth a few more times since then. He had as many high hopes for COBRA as Bradley, because as soon as First Army reached Avranches, his Third Army would start moving down south from its build-up and staging areas in western Normandy. South of Avranches, Patton's forces would sweep into Brittany, where they would clear the Brest Peninsula and then turn eastwards. They were, Hansen admitted in his diary that day, far behind schedule, which was one of the reasons for Patton's impatience – before the invasion he had expected to be over in the fight long before now – but there was real hope for COBRA. Palpable hope.

This sense of hope was conveyed to Ernie Pyle and other war correspondents when Bradley called by to give them an informal briefing. He didn't hold back, explaining in graphic detail what he was going to do with the help of the air force. Pyle was thrilled, and although the army commander didn't actually mention the word 'breakout', those accompanying him did. 'This is no limited objective drive,' Pyle was told. 'This is it. This is the big breakthrough.'

By Friday, 21 July, in anticipation of the action, Pyle had joined the 4th Infantry Division, who were to be in the middle of the attack. He spent that first night comfortably enough in a tent at the division's command post, the second in a rickety old farmhouse a little closer, then on Sunday, 23 July, he kipped down in an orchard even closer; but then when the attack still didn't happen, for the next night he moved even further up to the start line and dug himself a hole behind a hedgerow so an 88 wouldn't get him.

COBRA was due to be launched that day – 24 July – with H-Hour at 1 p.m. Leigh-Mallory had flown over but, having arrived, felt the sky was too overcast and visibility not good enough, so promptly ordered a postponement. The air armadas, however, were already on their way and although most got the message and turned back, not all did. Three groups of fighter-bombers still roared over, parallel to the start line, and so attacking lengthways, west–east. Although the first formation of heavies then arrived, they turned back because of bad visibility, while of the second formation only thirty-five dropped their loads, not from a parallel course but at right angles, north–south. So too did the 300 bombers of the third formation, who dropped some 550 tons of bombs. Tragically, twenty-five men from 30th Division were killed and 131 wounded, although less because the men were too far forward and more because the bombardier of one box of bombers had had trouble moving his bomb-release mechanism and had inadvertently released some of his load by mistake; the fifteen aircraft behind him had then followed suit.

Bradley, Collins and Quesada had watched this half-attack with mounting horror. 'How the hell did it happen?' Bradley asked Quesada. But Quesada had no idea, nor did he find out until he finally got through to Leigh-Mallory, now back at Bentley Priory. As far as Bradley and Quesada were concerned, Leigh-Mallory had agreed on a west–east parallel attack, which, they had assumed, would bring less risk to the men below. This was not quite correct, nor had it ever been resolved after the 19 July conference; heavies were just as liable to bomb wide as they were short. Leigh-Mallory now told Quesada that Spaatz and General Jimmy Doolittle, the commander of the Eighth Air Force, had insisted on a perpendicular attack, north–south. The west–east approach was impossible – there wasn't enough space, nor could that many bombers attack in a narrow corridor in just an hour as Bradley had insisted. So a choice had had to be made: the heavies would attack north–south or cancel. Bradley had to acquiesce. Now that a half-hearted attack had alerted the Germans, it was, he believed, essential that COBRA be launched as soon as possible. That meant 1 p.m. the following day, Tuesday, 25 July. 'The human truth,' commented Quesada, 'is that people heard what they wanted to hear.'

Even before the Panzer-Lehr had left Tilly for the westward move, General Fritz Bayerlein had lost over 5,000 men from the 17,000 he had had before the invasion, and a large proportion of those were fighting men. Then there was the disastrous counter-attack that had been imposed upon him, in which he had lost a further twenty tanks and more than 500 men. With almost no replacements coming through, this meant that by 24 July, the Lehr, just seven weeks ago one of the best-equipped and -manned divisions in the entire Wehrmacht, had already been reduced, before COBRA's launch, to a skeleton force. Repeatedly, he proposed withdrawing. 'It was hopeless,' he said. 'We were ordered not to yield a foot of ground.'

By 24 July, Bayerlein had one regiment in reserve and the rest forward. His aide, Hauptmann Alexander Hartdegen, sensed something was up and suggested to Bayerlein that they might well come under a major attack, but the general wasn't so sure. When the bombers approached at 1 p.m. that day, Bayerlein thought they would be heading further south, but then the bombs began to fall. His command post was an old chateau at Le Mesnil-Amey, which was only about 3 miles south of the bombing zone and due west of Saint-Lô. Fortunately, it had very thick, medieval stone walls and Bayerlein was able to climb the tower and watch through the arrow slits and castellations with comparative impunity. He saw artillery positions blasted and the front line appeared to have been wiped out. All communications with the forward troops was gone, so once the bombing was over he sent out dispatch riders to investigate the situation, while he drove as far forward as he could then walked the last part to the CP of Panzergrenadier-Regiment 902 in La Besnardière, a mile or so west of his castle. The commander had virtually nothing left. He then walked to Hébécrevon and learned that 275. Infanterie-Division had also been effectively destroyed. Eventually, he managed to get a line through to Generalleutnant Dietrich von Choltitz, who had taken over from Marcks as LXXXIV. Korps commander, and told him he could not possibly hold the front without reinforcements from at least one other regiment. Choltitz told him he had nothing to spare, but reiterated the Führer Order: there was to be no withdrawal.

Among those who had flown on 24 July was Lieutenant Truman 'Smitty' Smith, on his first flight as 1st pilot. After their mission on 14 July, a long trip to the Alps, Moon Baumann, the man who had piloted them on their first thirty-two missions, had got drunk and later woken up Smith and other crew mates screaming, 'Bail out!! Bail out!! We're on fire!! Bail out!!' He had then jumped off his bed, sheet clasped to his chest like a parachute, and hit his head on the concrete floor, which knocked him out and gave him a big gash. He had been grounded for his trouble and Smith given the 1st pilot job on their crew.

Ten days on from this dramatic incident, they were heading to Saint-Lô, with a new co-pilot whom Smith neither liked nor trusted and a different bombardier, as Eut Eutrecht was also still *hors de combat*. 'Based on what I had seen of my co-pilot's abilities,' noted Smith, 'I was reluctant, make that "scared", to let him fly.' But hand over controls he did, only for the new boy to nearly ram the bomber in front. Smith was about to grab the controls when his co-pilot grinned and pulled back; he had done it on purpose to scare him. It was hardly the time or place for such a joke. Half an hour later, Smith took over again and vowed to keep it that way. Then, over Saint-Lô, there was too much cloud and they turned round and went back. Now they were heading over again, although this time Smith had told the co-pilot that he would do all the flying and that all he required was for him to watch the oil-pressure gauges.

Down below to the north of the kick-off line, Ernie Pyle was watching from a farmyard about 800 yards back. 'And before the next two hours,' he wrote, 'I would have given every penny, every desire, every hope I ever had, to have been just another 800 yards further back.' Also watching were Bradley, Quesada, Collins and other assembled generals and senior staff officers. 'We sat in a little café partly destroyed in earlier fighting,' wrote Collins, 'adjacent to the command post. Starched lace curtains hung in the open windows.' First over again were the fighters, 350 in all, who roared in, parallel, dropping bombs on quite specific targets with what appeared to be unerring accuracy. Pyle watched them peel down in groups, bombs cracking, machine guns chattering, engines whistling and screaming. 'It was all fast and furious,' noted Pyle, 'yet distinct.' Then they became gradually aware of a rising drone, deep and filling the air.

It was the heavy bombers. Huge strips of coloured cloth had been laid on the ground below to denote the boundary.

'My God, look at those Germans run!' called out Smitty Smith's co-pilot.

Smith smacked him with a backhand. 'Watch the Goddam gauges!' he ordered.

They were the bottom aircraft of a three-plane element, of the bottom flight, of the bottom squadron, of the bottom group – without doubt, the most lonely and vulnerable position to be in any bomber formation when the bombs started falling, which they now were, tumbling in clusters; and when the lead ship in their squadron made an adjustment to avoid the bombs coming down towards him, so too did his wingman, which meant Smith also now needed to bank sharply to avoid being hit. 'And while we didn't get hit by a single bomb,' he wrote, 'we ended up less than a thousand feet above the ground and naturally, as far away from the group as I could get.' Dropping their own bombs, Smith banked again and turned for home, his part in the great bombing over.

Pyle watched them. They seemed slow, steady. 'I've never known a storm, or a machine,' he wrote, 'or any resolve of man that had about it the aura of such a ghastly relentlessness.' Around him, others had gathered to watch, having climbed out of their foxholes despite orders to the contrary, including Lieutenant Richard Blackburn and some of his men in the 121st Infantry, who were due to attack that day with the rest of the 8th Division. To begin with, the bombs were dropped very accurately, but the wind began to drift the smoke north towards the American lines. With so many explosions, grit and dust, the lines marked on the ground soon disappeared. Pyle had been quite transfixed by this incredible spectacle, but then realized, as they all did with sudden, mounting horror, that the bombs were starting to fall wide. Men were diving for foxholes as the bombs began exploding around them. 'I had heard my share of exploding artillery shells and bombs,' noted Blackburn, 'but none could compare to this barrage of bombs.' He dived into a narrow trench, frantically reciting the 23rd Psalm. Not far away, Ernie Pyle found a wagon shed, dived for the ground, then wriggled like an eel to get under a cart. 'The feeling of the blast was sensational,' he wrote. 'The air struck us in hundreds of continuing flutters. Our ears drummed and rang. We could feel quick little waves of concussion on the chest and in the eyes.'

Also watching, although safely further back, was Tom Bowles, who, along with the rest of the Big Red One, had moved from Caumont after six largely uneventful weeks there and was now in reserve and primed for the drive towards Coutances. 'You never saw so much dust,' said Bowles. 'It was so bad you couldn't see nothing.' Lieutenant Orion Shockley had realized what was happening a little earlier than some and had ordered his men to fall further back once the bombing began, although it didn't stop some of them from getting wounded. Then, after the heavies had gone, it was time for the medium bombers. From where he was sheltering, Shockley had seen General Leslie McNair, the commander of Army Ground Forces who was over in Normandy on an inspection tour, standing about 150 yards away when the B-26s came over. Bombs started to fall, eruptions ripped the ground apart, and smoke and dust covered the scene of where McNair had been standing. He was the most senior American general to have been killed in the war so far. A further 110 others were also dead, while 490 more had been wounded.

When the bombing began again, General Fritz Bayerlein honestly thought his time had come. He had fought in North Africa, on the Eastern Front, in France, but nothing had prepared him for this. 'The three days by St.-Lô,' he said, 'were the worst I have ever experienced.' Everything before seemed to have been erased. All communications with the outside world had been destroyed. In the front line, the casualties were considerable: some 1,000 men, 25 tanks and 10 assault guns, which amounted to two-thirds of his entire fighting force, as well as a *Fallschirmjäger* regiment, which was effectively annihilated. 'The whole place looked like a moon landscape,' he said, 'everything was burned and blasted. It was impossible to bring up a vehicle or recover the ones that were damaged. The survivors were like madmen and could not be used for anything.' This was true. Men were wandering around, deranged. They had literally lost their minds from the experience.

Hauptmann Helmut Ritgen had been due to move his panzer battalion into reserve on the 24th, but this had been postponed by twenty-four hours, which meant he and his surviving Mk IVs were still based at Saint-Gilles, a mile south beyond the bomb zone, and when the bombing began he and his men all took shelter in the farmhouse being used as their CP. Although a number of cows were killed and shrapnel seemed to rain down on them incessantly, once the bombers had gone they dusted themselves off and were relieved to find their panzers, although a little battered, were all in one piece.

With the bombers gone, the American infantry began moving

forward, picking their way across the scarred landscape. Lieutenant Orion Shockley's 47th Regiment was among the hardest hit by the American bombing, although none of his men in Company B was killed. The 3rd Battalion was so badly cut up, however, that 1st Battalion had to take over the lead in cutting the road, and that meant Company B was now in the van of the COBRA attack. They crossed the road, moving cautiously. The German dead were everywhere, as were the wounded, most of whom swiftly surrendered. Shockley noticed a number of them were bleeding from the nose, ears and mouth. Then the attackers came under heavy fire from Ritgen's tanks and from the surviving German artillery. There was a fury and intensity to the firing unlike anything Shockley had ever experienced. 'Shock, if we survive this barrage,' Lieutenant Klauz, his XO, said to him as they huddled in a bomb crater, 'I think we will make it through the war.'

In the middle, 8th Division also got going, Lieutenant Richard Blackburn and his men crossing the road and cautiously pushing forward across the battle-scarred landscape. He had not lost any men either, but the death of General McNair and the tentative push of the infantry meant that, by evening, there was an air of profound disappointment among the senior American commanders. Eisenhower, for one, was done with using strategic air forces in this way. 'I don't believe they can be used in support of ground troops,' he groused to one of Bradley's aides. 'That's a job for artillery. I gave them a green light on this show but this is the last one.'

The following morning, Wednesday, 26 July, it looked even more as though COBRA was failing. The Germans appeared to have recovered. Artillery fire and mortars were stalling the advance of the three infantry divisions, which were continuing to make only very slow progress. The worry was that they would soon become completely bogged down in yet more inching-forward, attritional fighting and that the Germans would regain some kind of balance. None the less, Collins, as corps commander, reckoned the Germans must still be reeling from the previous day. 'I sensed that their communications and command structure,' he wrote, 'had been damaged more than our troops realized.' He was quite right; chaos reigned. Bayerlein was unable to communicate with anyone except by foot; he had no link at all to von Choltitz or Hausser and no real idea of the enemy's precise aims or intentions. The breakthrough was now within the Americans' grasp after all.

With this in mind, late on Tuesday, 25 July, Collins had ordered up his armour. The mounted infantry of the Big Red One was to strike hard for Coutances that morning, Wednesday, 26 July, alongside Combat Command B of the 3rd Armored, while 22nd Infantry of the 4th Division was to mount up and join the 2nd Armored Division in a strike south. What he wanted was mounted infantry and armour to strike hard and swiftly. Among those now rumbling southwards were Carl Rambo and the tanks of 70th Tank Battalion, using dozers and Rhinos to smash through the hedgerows beyond, and also Lieutenant John Rogers and the 67th Tank Regiment, who were advancing with the men of the 22nd Infantry sitting on the back of their Shermans.

That Wednesday was also the first day of Quesada's Armored Column Cover and Rogers had a pilot with him in his tank. Later that day, as the advancing VII Corps came up against the hastily cobbled together armour of Panzer-Lehr, the P-47s were quickly called down and soon stopped the panzers in their tracks. 'It really worked wonderfully,' said Rogers. 'It was constant, constant, constant, just one flight after another.' Saint-Gilles, where Helmut Ritgen had had his CP, was cleared, then so was Canisy. Fighters flew cover constantly. 'We'd have call letters and call signs for them on their radio,' remembered Lieutenant Archie Maltbie, still flying with the 388th Hell Hawks, 'and our pilot on the ground would call us in. He'd say, "Hey, we got some tanks in this forest over here, we're gonna put a pink shell in there and you guys go in and take them out."' At other times it would be a roadblock or some other specific target.

'Everyone is overjoyed with the rapidity of their movements,' noted Chet Hansen on Thursday, 27 July. 'The 2nd Armored spearheaded towards the south in great sweeping advances, while the 3rd Armored broke down the road towards Coutances, rocking the German back on his heels, confounding him with their movement.' That day, Bradley issued new orders. There was to be a full-on advance towards Avranches, the hinge into Brittany. After the disappointments of COBRA's launch, it seemed the dam had finally burst. This was the breakthrough the Allies had all been hoping for.

The endgame in Normandy had begun.

CHAPTER 32

BLUECOAT

T HE SAME DAY AS COBRA, Tuesday, 25 July, the newly operational Canadian First Army launched Operation SPRING, using the infantry of II Corps and with armour support from the British 7th Armoured and Guards Divisions to drive south from Caen. On the map, they were up against seven enemy divisions arrayed to the south of Caen, of which five were panzer: the 116. Panzer-Division, almost full strength, had now reached Normandy, although was not yet in the line. However, directly confronting the Canadians were just two divisions, one a low-quality infantry unit and the other the 1. SS-Panzer, less depleted than some others. In defence, and well dug in, this still made them quite an obstacle and the Canadians' initial attack made little headway. Lieutenant-General Guy Simonds, the II Corps commander, was in tears at SPRING's failure, but Montgomery had never viewed it as much more than a holding operation and that was what it proved to be. Instead, he now turned to how he could best support the American breakthrough. SPRING had shown the bulk of the surviving German armour was still rooted in the area to the south and south-east of the city, whereas the enemy line seemed weaker further west around Caumont, now held by the 15th Scottish Division.

It was Dempsey who came up with the plan for a thrust from the Caumont area towards Mont Pinçon, the highest point in Normandy. This objective was to be given to XXX Corps under Lieutenant-General Gerard Bucknall, while on his left flank would be General Dick O'Connor's VIII Corps, recovered from GOODWOOD. Having spent much of the campaign fighting through open terrain around Caen, they would be heading for the rolling hills and dense bocage of what was known as 'la Suisse

Normande'. British armour had not cottoned on to the idea of hedge-cutters and dozers – there had been no need – but now would be driving south into the kind of countryside that had so beleaguered the Americans in the Cotentin and before Saint-Lô. But there could be no shirking such challenges. The line here was held by infantry divisions and elements of 10. SS-Panzer; it was unquestionably currently a weaker part of the line and, with the Germans reeling further to the west, this plan, Operation BLUECOAT, seemed like the best chance of capitalizing on US First Army's success and possibly driving in at the sides of the ring of panzer divisions south of Caen. BLUECOAT would jump off on 30 July.

In the western half of the line, the Germans were now flooding back as the Americans poured through the breach in the dam. By 26 July, it was clear to Hausser that his front was collapsing. Marigny, 12 miles south of the COBRA start line, fell to the Big Red One and the 3rd Armored, while 2nd Armored advanced 7 miles. On the German left flank, the American VIII Corps also began their drive south, taking the ruins of Périers. 'The centre and the left wings,' recorded Hausser, 'had to be withdrawn. The only remaining difficulty was that of obtaining Army Group's permission.' Even von Kluge, however, realized that unless these forces, which included not only 17. SS but also the comparatively intact 2. SS 'Das Reich', were urgently pulled back, then they would all be encircled and annihilated.

Word of the collapse on their right reached the Pionier-Bataillon of 17. SS shortly after 9 a.m. that morning and by 4.45 p.m. they had received the order to withdraw due south as quickly as possible and to head for Roncey, about 18 miles away and south-east of Coutances. 'Impossible due to enemy action,' noted Willi Müller in his diary, but by 9.20 p.m. they had managed to fall back. 'Dissolving out without enemy action,' he wrote at 3 a.m. the following morning, 27 July. Also falling back was Hauptmann Helmut Ritgen, whose panzer battalion had now been attached to the Panzergrenadier-Lehr-Regiment 901. Every road of retreat seemed to be patrolled by Thunderbolts. 'One had to play Russian roulette,' noted Ritgen, 'by trying to outwit the pilots while they rose back into the air after descending to attack.' It didn't work for long, however. First all radio communications were lost, then his panzer was hit and he had to abandon it, although all his crew were safe. Heading south on foot, they spotted American tanks up ahead but managed to dodge them and make good their escape.

Willi Müller and his fellow pioneers were also marching on foot, and no longer only by night; if planes came over, they jumped into the ditches beside the roads or fled to the nearest cover, whether it be a hedge or a wood. By 8 p.m. they had reached the village of Belval, a few miles east of Coutances. At 8.22 p.m., they received orders to make contact with 3. SS-Panzer-Regiment, from 'Das Reich'. Two of their Panthers were just a kilometre away and a further four were a little beyond that, but they couldn't locate them so kept going. At 5 a.m. the following day, Friday, 28 July, they were told to head to Cerisy-la-Salle to try to link up with the 'Das Reich' men. By 9 a.m. they finally reached the Panzer-Regiment 3 command post, where they found the Panthers. At least they now had something to ride on and could stop marching.

Pursuing them was the American 9th Division, although they were following behind the main armour spearheads; Lieutenant Shockley and his men still found themselves mopping up rearguards and having to stop to take cover from enemy shelling. Further to the west, Lieutenant Richard Blackburn and the men of the 8th Infantry Division reached Coutances on 28 July, although too late to encircle the SS divisions and remnants of German infantry. Because of the swiftness of the advance, some of the towns through which they passed remained largely untouched, but others were completely and utterly wrecked. In some areas he found it difficult to walk properly for all the dead and rotting corpses of soldiers and their horses. 'There were scores and scores of dead Wehrmacht soldiers everywhere,' he wrote, 'with their skin turned a sickly green in death.' And not only were the dead left in Coutances – the Americans also discovered 66 tanks, 204 other vehicles and 11 guns completely wrecked and burned out, and a further 56 tanks and 55 vehicles abandoned. It was a considerable haul.

Avranches fell on 27 July. The following day, the commander of 2. SS 'Das Reich', Obersturmbannführer Christian Tychsen, was killed in a firefight with American troops, while Obergruppenführer Hausser, the corps commander, was fired at and had to throw himself into a ditch to escape. Von Kluge blamed Hausser for the collapse but couldn't – or wouldn't dare – sack an SS general, so fired Max Pemsel, Hausser's chief of staff, instead and relieved von Choltitz, commander of LXXXIV. Korps, replacing him with Generalleutnant Otto Elfeldt. None of these command changes was the remotest bit helpful, because suddenly new men, unfamiliar with the terrain, situation or units involved, were being flung into situations of utter mayhem and expected to get an immediate grip on the reins – an impossible task. But it was increasingly the German way; the number of command changes in Normandy was astonishing. By contrast, the Allies were unquestionably benefiting from the continuity of command being exercised in their campaign. Allied sackings were not unknown, but they were rare.

By that day, Friday, 28 July, Helmut Ritgen had safely made it to Saint-Denis-le-Gast. All his panzers had been lost, as had most of those in the entire Panzer-Lehr. He did, however, now have a motorbike and sidecar, which he shared with his dispatch rider, and was heading to see Bayerlein at a commanders' conference when they were pounced on by Thunderbolts. It was too late to dismount, but they swerved left, the bullets of the Thunderbolts missing them by inches.

By Saturday the 29th, Willi Müller and his Pionier-Bataillon were travelling as passengers on Panther tanks, heading south towards Saint-Denis-le-Gast from Roncey. Word then reached them that they and the remainder of LXXXIV. Korps had been encircled. Desperately, Müller's column tried to find a route out; it seemed there was a road that had not yet been cut that led to Saint-Denis-le-Gast. Soon after, however, up ahead Müller could see the *Jabo*s descending on a crossroads at the edge of a village, their engines screaming as they dived. 'It horrified us,' he wrote. 'We also had to cross this intersection.' They were saved by the weather. Before long, the cloud thickened and it began to rain; suddenly the *Jabo*s had gone and Müller and his companions moved on, over the crossroads and beyond, clear of the encirclement. Others, however, were not so lucky. In their desperation to flee the entrapment, horse-drawn and motorized vehicles were stacked up nose to tail for some 3 miles. To begin with, just one fighter group had attacked this mass of vehicles, but as soon as General Quesada heard what was happening he diverted others. In all, a further 100 tanks, 250 vehicles and other horse-drawn wagons were left in flames. It was mayhem for Germany's 7. Armee, which was very rapidly disintegrating. Not one division could now muster more than a *Kampfgruppe* in strength.

That same day, Hauptmann Alexander Hartdegen, General Bayerlein's aide, was captured and brought to see General Bradley. He spoke quite openly about Rommel's battles over the use of the panzers and where they should be positioned before the invasion. He also told them about the Führer's order to defend every inch. 'General Bayerlein and Rommel felt this was useless murder,' Hansen noted, hastily writing down Hartdegen's testimony. 'Bitter about Stalingrad and Caucasus, bitter about SS with pick of replacements and officers.' Hartdegen also told them he hated Hitler and would do anything to end the war quickly. 'Felt Hitler was committing suicide with the German people,' recorded Hansen. They took him outside and showed him a park stuffed full of trucks, tanks and mountains of equipment. Hartdegen broke down and wept. 'If only we Germans had this,' he said.

Later, Eisenhower showed up at Bradley's HQ. He was elated – elated and relieved, and joked that if they were in Paris for Chet Hansen's birthday in October, they would take over the biggest hotel and have the biggest party in the world until everyone got tight. It was that kind of day, when even a Supreme Commander was so giddy with excitement he could make rash promises. After dropping Ike at the airfield, Hansen returned to join Bradley and his deputy, General Courtney Hodges, for a steak supper while they marked up their maps with the latest advances, which now amounted to some 30 miles. 'We eagered,' added Hansen, 'for good news from the front.'

On Sunday, 30 July, Lieutenant Richard Blackburn was glad to go to a short church service led by the chaplain in an orchard. Most of the company attended without much coaxing. It was raining, as it had been on and off for the past few days, but then, suddenly, halfway through their prayers, the clouds parted and great shafts of sunlight shone down. That day, Blackburn's 121st Infantry enjoyed a pause, but the armour continued to surge ahead. By now, 2. Panzer-Division had been brought over from the Caen area, while 116. Panzer-Division was also on its way as von Kluge desperately tried to stem the collapse. On the 30th, the 4th Armored Division managed to seize a key bridge over the River Selun at Pontaubault. This bridge was the gateway to Brittany. As July drew to a close, the Germans were completely reeling, with most of 7. Armee's armour gone, some 20,000 troops taken prisoner and countless dead and wounded.

It was now time for Patton's Third Army to enter the battle and, with it, US 12th Army Group was activated with Bradley as its commander. This meant that from Tuesday, 1 August, Montgomery was no longer C-in-C of all Allied ground forces, but instead, as had always been planned, he took sole charge of 21st Army Group, which made him equal to, rather than above, Bradley. D-Day might have been a predominantly British operation, but a shift was about to take place. Not only had the US Army's first army group become operational, but the number of US troops in France had exceeded those of the British and Canadians. The United States had just become the dominant partner.

Further to the east, the British had been planning and getting ready for BLUECOAT. It had actually been an extraordinary feat of logistics to get VIII Corps switched all the way to the Caumont area without being detected. Armoured units had moved at night and the corps' white knight symbol had been painted out. Dummy radio traffic was transmitted to fool the enemy, although rather than these deception measures, it was Eberbach's hunch that the British wouldn't be capable of mounting an armoured thrust through such terrain that ensured they were caught off guard when BLUECOAT was finally launched.

Weakened though the panzer divisions might have become, more and more infantry units had also been brought up from Brittany and now, finally, from 15. Armee too – units that had been held back in case of a subsequent Allied amphibious invasion. By the last week of July, there were four German corps facing the British and Canadians. The ground around Caumont, however, fell into the area of General Erich Straube's LXXIV. Korps. The key piece of terrain, Straube declared to his men, was Point 309, to the south of Caumont, not Mont Pinçon as Dempsey had concluded. This hill, Straube ordered, was not to be given up under any circumstances.

Among the British now gearing up for the battle was newly promoted Captain Robert Woollcombe, now second-in-command of A Company, the 6th King's Own Scottish Borderers. After Hill 113, the chance to rest and refit in Caumont had been gratefully taken, and they had been especially pleased to occupy the old positions of the Big Red One, who were only too glad to hand over large numbers of surplus supplies. 'This windfall,' noted Woollcombe, 'covered the entire floor of a farmhouse attic knee-deep.' It included cigarettes, chocolate, tinned fruit and enough lavatory paper for an entire brigade. There were even boxes of cigars.

The Sherwood Rangers Yeomanry were moving up too, having also taken over from the Americans, in this case from Lieutenant John Rogers and the 67th Tank Battalion. The Sherwood Rangers had just taken on a lot more replacements, both officers and ORs; since the invasion, they had already lost forty tank commanders, killed or wounded. That was around 80 per cent. The 24th Lancers, also of 8th Armoured Brigade, had been so badly mauled they had been broken up – the SRY received some of them – and their place taken by the 13th/18th Hussars. The King's Own Scottish Borderers, meanwhile, had been sent a number of Northern Irishmen. At the start of the war, local regiments had been filled with local people. Five years on, they were filled with all sorts.

Behind the usual bombing and artillery barrage, on 30 July both corps started on BLUECOAT, jumping off either side of Caumont. Dick O'Connor's VIII Corps on the left saw the 15th Scottish Division lead off. Supporting them were the 6th Guards Brigade. O'Connor had made it clear he wanted the very closest of infantry and tank cooperation; they would be heading through dense country and it was essential, he told his commanders, that they worked together. Fortunately, they had trained together back in England before the invasion, so their staffs and senior officers were quick to cooperate. It made such a difference, and what's more, their advance benefited from the number of Crocodiles and mine-clearing flail tanks that were now part of their arsenal. Particularly impressive was the attack on Hill 309, the main objective for the first day. It was defended by the 326. Infanterie-Division, originally formed from Eastern Front veterans, but another static division with little or no transports.

Although the British infantry became held up with hedgerow fighting, the Churchills pressed on alone and took the summit by 7 p.m.; these tanks could climb peaks and mounds that others could not and, perhaps more than any other tank, were suited to operating in the bocage. The infantry then followed and secured the feature overnight. This was no small achievement. That day, yet another German general was killed, this time Leutnantgeneral Victor von Drabich-Wächter, commander of the 326. Infanterie. Next day, 31 July, VIII Corps pushed on and took the next hill. Three monstrous Jagdpanther high-velocity assault guns knocked out eleven Churchills in no time, but British versions of the M10 tank destroyer, equipped with 17-pounders, soon joined the battle and their superior guns helped force the Jagdpanthers to withdraw.

Leading the XXX Corps attack, meanwhile, was 50th Northumbrian Division on the left, heading towards Villers-Bocage, and the 43rd Wessex Division on the right, with 8th Armoured Brigade directly supporting them. Stanley Christopherson, who had a wonderful sense of humour and was rarely without a smile, rather struggled with the po-faced martinet Major-General Ivor Thomas, the Wessex Division commander. He was known as 'Butcher', but 'Von Thoma' to the Sherwood Rangers, after the German general in Tunisia. 'He was a wiry little man,' noted Christopherson, 'with piercing little eyes, a long nose, which protected a bristling moustache, devoid of any sense of humour and a hard relenting driver, but a good soldier whom I am convinced enjoyed his fighting and discomfort.' It was hardly a ringing character assessment, but they didn't need to be bosom buddies, and while there might not have been a lot of jokes in Thomas's CP, he had already proved an effective divisional commander. The Wessexmen made good progress that Sunday as the sun beat down hot and strong for a change. It also helped that they'd trained in the tight fields and sunken lanes of rural Kent before the invasion; the ground they crossed was not at all dissimilar.

Cahagnes fell on 31 July, with almost 200 prisoners taken and a further 100 Germans killed. The 4th Dorsets had been in reserve, but on that day were given a ridge beyond the village to capture. They were ready at 4 a.m., had breakfast at 8.30 and then attacked, although not as a whole battalion. Instead, they pressed forward with fighting patrols alongside the 7th Hampshires and this proved very effective. Sergeant Walter Caines managed to keep communications open with radio sets only. In the evening, once the intelligence from the various patrols was brought back, an attack on the ridge was made at around seven. 'This ridge was captured,' noted Caines, 'without a single casualty.' More patrols were sent forward to try to find out exactly where the enemy was. They returned with a number of prisoners. 'Everyone dug in as usual,' added Caines. The following morning, Tuesday, 1 August, it remained blisteringly hot and there was still not much sign of the enemy. The Germans had, Caines noted, been a tough nut to crack so far, and he, for one, felt uneasy. It was quiet. Too quiet.

That day, though, the 7th Armoured Division, the Desert Rats, were to pass through between the two infantry divisions and seize the town of Aunay-sur-Odon, a few miles to the south of Villers-Bocage. Their orders were that speed was very much of the essence, yet they managed to get themselves held up by pockets of resistance, minefields and too many vehicles trying to pass through too few, too narrow roads. Their problems were compounded by lack of visibility caused by early-morning mist and, when it lifted, they found themselves on forward slopes where they soon began to be picked off by Panzer IVs of Oberst Oppeln-Bronikowski's 21. Panzer *Kampfgruppe*, who had been hurriedly sent to the rescue and were now dug in, hull down, and keen to stop the British advance dead in its tracks.

It did seem, however, as though the Desert Rats had lost some of the chutzpah and elan that had so marked their earlier career in the war. Bucknall, the XXX Corps commander, now urged Major-General George Erskine, CO of 7th Armoured Division, to get a move on and throw all caution to the wind. The corps artillery, he added, was very much available to help. Dempsey in turn was losing his patience. 'You may lose every tank you've got,' he told Bucknall, 'but you must capture Aunay by midnight tonight.'

It didn't happen, however. Erskine wasn't prepared to push his men that hard; neither were his junior officers willing to make the potential levels of sacrifice needed to push on to Aunay. The Desert Rats had first gone into action against the Italians under General Dick O'Connor in the Western Desert in 1940. They had fought all through the North African campaign, then in Sicily and again in southern Italy. Of course, much of their personnel had changed, but not all, and if this was a cadre of men who felt they had more than done their bit in this war, it was, in fairness, entirely understandable. Both Bradley and Montgomery had wanted the invasion forces to have a mixture of experience and men new to combat, but it was perhaps no coincidence that Collins was also currently worrying that the Big Red One, veteran division of Tunisia and Sicily, was now under-performing and lacking drive.

Meanwhile, the Wessexmen and 8th Armoured Brigade were carrying out a daring night move south on the right flank of 7th Armoured to take the village of Jurques, some miles south of Cahagnes. 'It was a terrible night,' noted Walter Caines, 'troops were lifted on tanks, and were continuously dropping off to sleep.' Caines was following, as usual, by motorbike, his third of the campaign after the previous two had been destroyed, and feeling on edge about potential enemy resistance opening fire at any moment, but also absolutely exhausted and struggling to keep awake, as they ground their way forward at little more than 5 m.p.h.

At 5.30 a.m. on the 2nd, the column halted on the edge of Jurques. Firing could be heard up ahead and word got back that the leading company had met resistance. 'A few fanatics were holding out in the village itself,' wrote Caines. 'These fools were quickly dealt with and were no more.' They pushed on through the village, but then Caines was told that the signals scout car, which had been travelling behind the lead company, had hit a mine and been destroyed; the adjutant had been killed and so too had the control operator, Corporal Penny. The signal officer had survived, but had suffered burns to his face and arms. To make matters worse, just beyond the village they ran into far more serious resistance as artillery, self-propelled guns and machine guns opened up; like 7th Armoured, they had now hit Oberst Oppeln-Bronikowski's *Kampfgruppe* from 21. Panzer.

Responsibility for the battalion's signals now rested with Caines, but then word arrived that the two signallers with B Company had also been killed. Several tanks were knocked out and D Company's commander, Major Letson, was also badly wounded. Caines now had just one wireless set but couldn't reach brigade, so dispatch riders were sent instead, while in the meantime the 4th Dorsets and their accompanying armour managed to push through and take the next village of La Bigne. Incredibly, however, within an hour and a half of the signals scout car being hit, a brand-new one arrived, complete with fresh equipment. It is hard to think of a better indication than this of the superb British logistics now operating in Normandy. It was no wonder the Allies were winning. The Dorsets now dug in and further supplies came forward. Shelling continued through the afternoon and into the night as Caines and his depleted team worked to lay telephone lines and repair those broken by shelling. At first light the following morning, 3 August, every man was given a hot meal and issued with chocolate and cigarettes, another vital filip in the British quest to keep up morale. 'I was so tired and literally worn out,' noted Caines, 'that I gave up all efforts to dig in properly.' No one in the signals ever had much time to themselves, as they were always busy with the upkeep and maintenance of the lines.

VIII Corps, meanwhile, had been in danger of getting too far ahead of XXX Corps on its left, so 15th Scottish and their accompanying armour had paused to allow the Wessex Division to catch up, but had used the time to see off repeated counter-attacks in which, as usual, the Germans had exposed themselves and got progressively chewed up. Meanwhile, 11th Armoured Division, on the right, which had been supposed to offer flank support only, drew alongside 15th Scottish only to be urged on by O'Connor, and by 11 a.m. the following day, 31 July, having unusually moved through the night, they attacked the village of Saint-Martin-des-Besaces. While this was happening, a remarkable incident took place. Reconnaissance scouts from the 2nd Household Cavalry had been probing forward, looking for gaps in the German defences. With their eyes focused on the fighting at Saint-Martin-des-Besaces, the German defenders failed to notice a Dingo scout car and an armoured car speed past. Led by Captain Dickie Powle, the reconnaissance party motored on a further 6 miles, reaching a bridge across the River Souleuvre, which gave them a potential route to Le Bény-Bocage 2 miles further on, a village that stood on a ridge of high ground bestriding a road that led south-east towards Falaise. If they could take that village quickly, it would unquestionably be a great triumph. With the armoured car acting as cover, the Dingo sped forward and crossed the bridge. The cavalrymen then dispatched the sentry and, despite the difficulties of sending radio signals across rolling and wooded countryside such as this, eventually relayed a message back. Within a matter of hours, the advance of 11th Armoured was thundering down the same road and on up the ridge beyond to take Le Bény-Bocage and, from there, the town of Vire, which lay on the main west–east road to Falaise and to which the Americans were also now advancing.

In some ways, it had been a lucky strike as the road taken lay on the border not just between two German divisions, but also between Panzer-gruppe West and 7. Armee, but in the confusion and hiatus it was not clear who was going to reach Vire first, the British or the Americans. Meanwhile, 15th Scottish had also continued to drive south. The 6th KOSB went into action on 1 August wearing roses in their helmets to commemorate the Battle of Minden in 1759 during the Seven Years' War. Supported by eight artillery regiments and swarms of rocket-firing Typhoons, they attacked across the main road from Avranches to Villers-Bocage, gained the woods on the far side and found a number of knocked-out Panthers and large numbers of enemy dead. It had been an exemplary assault of combined arms reminiscent of the kind of confident coordination and cooperation the Germans under General Guderian had employed in 1940 to such devastating effect. Most of the dead, Woollcombe noted, were shockingly young, boy conscripts of the 276. Infanterie-Division. 'But it seemed we were hardened by this time to any sight,' he wrote. 'We trod among the bodies of the blonde boys with hardly a thought.' He was then sent on a patrol down into the woods on the far side of a narrow valley to see if there were any enemy left alive. He found only the dead.

Progress that day, 1 August, was not as dramatic as it had been the previous two days, but by this time the entire German front was in danger of complete collapse. With the greatest threat still a British and Canadian breakthrough in the eastern half of the front, von Kluge now ordered II. SS-Panzerkorps from the Caen sector to try to stem the flow of the British drive from Caumont. On 2 August, 11th Armoured managed to take and hold the next ridge line, the Perriers Ridge, which overlooked the main Vire–Falaise road. For the next few days, 10. and 9. SS-Panzer-Divisions desperately tried to push the British back off the ridge, but to no avail. General Pip Roberts was following one of Joe Collins's mantras: always head for the high ground and then don't let go.

A little further east, 15th Scottish continued to sweep south, and were now coming up against 2. SS-Panzer. The rest of 21. Panzer, meanwhile, had also been pulled across from the Caen sector and pushed in beside them on their right. This meant there were now four panzer divisions facing VIII Corps' thrust. On the extreme right, the 2nd Northants Yeomanry had been given the unenviable task of bridging the gap between VIII Corps and the Americans on their right. None of the Yeomen was very happy about operating on their own without infantry, although to begin with it had been all right, as the gap had been a narrow one and they had been close to the rest of the drive south. By 2 August, however, they were holding an area about 7 miles wide, each squadron spread out worryingly far apart. They were in bocage country too. 'Even a troop of three tanks,' noted Reg Spittles, who had only just returned from hospital, 'were out of sight of each other and had to rely on radio contact.' This was asking for trouble and, sure enough, they got it. By the following day the reinforced Germans had realized the Northants Yeomen were on their doorstep and so counter-attacked with panzers and grenadiers. B Squadron lost six tanks that first day, but by the evening of the 4th the 2nd Battalion had been reduced to just fourteen tanks.

On 4 August, 50th Division took Villers-Bocage, completely flattened since the leading tanks of the Desert Rats had pushed into the town on that early morning in June. The same day, the 6th KOSB were back in action. It was blisteringly hot as they attacked the leeward side of a ridge near Montchauvet into stiffening resistance. *Nebelwerfers* screamed over, mortars exploded and the tanks of the Welsh Guards were engaged with Tigers. As dusk fell, Captain Robert Woollcombe watched the entire crest burning, as hayricks, farmsteads and undergrowth all flamed furiously. 'A profusion of Nebelwerfers wailed over the scene,' he wrote, 'and A Company were unable to capture their objective for the simple reason that it was on fire.' By the morning, however, with the rest of the division moved up and more Crocodiles come to lend a hand, they were over and beyond.

Further east, Dempsey had finally lost patience with Bucknall and Erskine and both were sacked. It was Dempsey's call, not Montgomery's as is usually claimed, but it had Monty's backing. It was the right decision too, for while it was much better not to sack commanders in the field, occasionally it was needed. Collins and Bradley had made changes at 90th Division, for example – twice now, because Major-General Eugene Landrum, Mackelvie's replacement, had also been removed – but those had been the only ones. Both Dempsey and Montgomery were deeply mindful of not pushing their troops too hard, but it was a narrow line to walk: go too soft and the battle would drag on, resulting in even greater casualties; push too hard, however, and there could be slaughter, setbacks, a major dip in morale, or worse. Yet at Aunay, XXX Corps had not been facing 21. Panzer for long; the latter had been replaced in the line by another poorly equipped infantry division. What's more, the cross-over should have given 7th Armoured an opening to strike hard. It was essential Dempsey had confidence in his commanders; he had lost that with Bucknall and Erskine. Bucknall was outraged, which rather underlined the rightness of the decision, and was replaced by Lieutenant-General Brian Horrocks, who had commanded a corps under Monty in North Africa before getting wounded.

Aunay did finally fall to the Desert Rats, however, by which time only the church and one other building were still standing; engineers had to be brought in to clear the rubble and debris. Dead Germans littered the streets but, as they had retreated, the enemy had laced the place with booby traps and mines, something they had become fiendishly good at in Italy; it was a very effective way of slowing an Allied advance. A little to the west, meanwhile, the 4th Dorsets were called forward on the morning of the 4th to attack and take the village of Ondefontaine. Resistance was stiff. The advancing infantry of D Company were cut down by machine guns and mortars, and artillery shelling continued all day. Walter Caines was struggling with a severe shortage of manpower and, for once, a lack of equipment; they had used so much wire since 30 July that he had almost none left. It was up to Lance Corporal Harris and himself to keep the entire battalion in contact and they had to do so while dodging the shells. Harris had his helmet badly dented by a piece of shrapnel at one point; only a mug of tea given to them by a cheerful company runner did anything to restore their composure. Later, and in quick succession, Caines was shot at by a sniper then forced to leap for his life as a volley of shells came over. 'I really did feel scared,' he confessed, 'probably because I had been without sleep for so long. Somehow, I felt I should say a prayer, so laying on the ground, clasping my hands tightly together, I quietly prayed.'

The following day, with contact to brigade broken, he was sent back on his motorbike for instructions. They were to attack Ondefontaine again, this time with the full weight of artillery behind them, as well as the support of the Sherwood Rangers Yeomanry. It was a sombre O Group that Caines attended later that morning: hardly any officers were left and no replacements had reached them over the past few days; casualties across the entire battalion had been heinous. 'The unit had certainly taken a knocking,' noted Caines, 'a blow on the jaw I will never forget, but we were not downhearted, every man was prepared to rise and box on.'

Major John Semken's A Squadron of the Sherwood Rangers led the attack that evening, but had to advance down the one and only approach road – always a deeply nerve-racking experience for the lead tank – and in view of the high ground on their flank on which the Germans had their OP and tanks. Unable to take the village that night, they tried again the following morning, the 4th Dorsets and Sherwood Rangers going in together after another heavy artillery barrage. Stanley Christopherson's friend, Peter Seleri, the commander of C Squadron, was wounded in the process by a mortar fragment; it was not life-threatening, but it meant another officer had been lost for the time being. Seleri was ever cheerful and Christopherson knew he would miss him greatly, although perhaps not his radio style when in action. 'He was prone to using long and ponderous words,' wrote Christopherson. 'Instead of saying, "In wood to my left front, three enemy tanks moving left to right, am engaging," he would monopolise the air by reporting, "I can without question discern three moving objects in yonder wood, which give me an unquestionable impression of resembling three Tigers which appear to portray hostile inclinations. It is my intention to offer immediate engagement," much to the frantic impatience of the other tank stations.'

The attack, however, was successful and that morning they moved in among the ruins of the village, over yet more dead Germans. 'Ondefontaine,' wrote Caines, 'was now in the Fighting Fourth's hands.' So too was Mont Pinçon, finally captured the same day, 6 August, by the Wessexmen after a brutal fight against 21. Panzer. The 5th Wiltshires, down to just two companies, had only sixty-three men standing by late afternoon; it was their sister battalion, the 4th Wiltshires, who eventually claimed the crest with the help of bold action from the 13th/18th Hussars.

BLUECOAT had run its course, but it had been a huge success for Second Army, who had demonstrated a new level of tactical verve and flexibility, harnessed to operational skill of the highest calibre; it proved hard lessons had been learned during the past two months of vicious fighting. For all the frustrations of the Allied high command, eight weeks was really not very long, especially not in the context of the entire war, and what had been achieved deserves greater accolades than have often been awarded. By the beginning of the second week of August, the Allied forces in Normandy were on the cusp of a stunning victory. There was, though, one more twist to be played out in this bitter battle.

CHAPTER 33

LÜTTICH

LEUTNANT RICHARD VON ROSEN had missed the British attack south to Aunay and Mont Pinçon because immediately after the GOODWOOD battle he had been given three days' leave in Paris. German troops were rarely given time off and especially not during a big battle, but with most of his tanks in the workshop and nothing much for him to command, he and the adjutant, Oberleutnant Barkhausen, could be briefly spared. They were still in Paris when Hauptmann Scherf arrived at their hotel to tell von Rosen that his surviving panzers had been handed over to 2. Kompanie and that he was to report to the troop training depot at Mailly-le-Camp near Châlons along with the rest of his 3. Kompanie to pick up some new Tigers. Having reached Mailly-le-Camp, however, it turned out his precious new Tigers had yet to leave Germany – it was ever thus at this stage of the war – and not until 3 August did they finally arrive.

Nor were they Tigers but Tiger IIs, or *Königstiger* as they were better known – more than 70 tons of the heaviest and thirstiest combat tank in the world. It was an awesome, huge beast, earmarked for a battle that was already lost and where there was precious little fuel or the infrastructure needed to keep this monster in the fight. Really, at this stage of the campaign, it is hard to think of a more pointless weapon of war to send to Normandy; if anything mechanical went wrong with these tanks, they would be going absolutely nowhere. As it was, they had arrived at Mailly with a large amount of their equipment missing.

Von Rosen thought he ought to present himself at the battalion CP to report on the situation. 'On this journey,' he noted, in which he passed through the area of the Maquis Surcouf, 'I came into contact for the first time with the French Résistance movement, the Maquis. There was some danger, but I came out of it unscathed.'

All over France, the Résistance was performing heroically and proving of great help to the Allied cause, but it was notable that these sabotage efforts were far more successful where there was some kind of higher Allied control. Decisions over where support was given varied, but for the most part it was focused on areas where sabotage could be most effectively applied to stop or hinder the movement of enemy troops. On the other hand, it was also important there were not hordes of over-armed Résistance fighters getting in the way of the Allied breakout when it finally happened, one of the main reasons why the Maquis Surcouf had been rather abandoned.

Still no arms had arrived since D-Day, and they were struggling. Robert Leblanc, their beleaguered leader, continued to spend much time moving from one hiding place to the next, all the while contending with increasingly fractious members of his group. Resisters were being denounced and arrested, while Leblanc was dealing with those known to have betrayed them with equal brutality. One lady, 'Madamoiselle XX014X', had been suspected of being a spy and had then backed up a German who had been accused of rape. 'I decide that this old shrew will be hanged,' scribbled Leblanc in his diary. 'First, because she deserves it. Secondly, because everybody in Campigny will be relieved. And it will make an example for those who consider denouncing us. We are at war, I make war!' He sounded like the Germans or the Milice. The mademoiselle was killed on 4 July by seven of Leblanc's men, who hit her on the head with a rifle butt, though initially not hard enough. Fighting back, she bit the hand of the man, who grabbed her and screamed for help, but they hit her again – and again – and then hanged her from a tree. Father Deuve, the sacristan at Saint-Étienne-l'Allier, who was accused of denouncing some of the Maquis Surcouf, was also hanged, but from the church tower. Another man accused of denunciation in Fourmetot was snatched, brought before the town mayor, publicly beaten, then hanged from a street lamp in front of the town hall. It was barbaric.

Meanwhile, more of Leblanc's men were getting arrested, while another splinter group of resisters were robbing others in the name of the Maquis. 'It's anarchy,' wrote Leblanc on 6 July. It certainly was, and it was not clear how they were achieving anything very useful in their quest to help the Allies and liberate France from the Nazi oppressors.

The BBC had been urging the people to demonstrate against the

Germans on Bastille Day, 14 July, and Leblanc dutifully obeyed by organizing a large service at the graves of some of his fallen comrades. The night attack they had planned, however, had to be cancelled because there were too many Germans about – alerted, no doubt, by the demonstrations of defiance earlier in the day. By 3 August, Leblanc was still on the move, this time to his thirty-fifth hideout. The news from the front sounded better, but life was still as tough, dangerous, and his Maquis Surcouf, short of arms and ammunition, was achieving little apart from fuelling the local mood of mistrust and violence. As if to prove the point, three more of his best maquis were caught and killed, with others arrested the following morning. 'Pelican, Jean l'Abbé, Raspail dead!' he wrote. 'All the liaisons cut! Mireille and Raymond arrested! What a disaster!'

One area where resistance was proving very effective was in Brittany, where the Allies had focused a lot of effort. Here, they had pumped the Maquis and FFI full of arms. The French SAS team had also been parachuted in there on D-Day, while Général Pierre Koenig, head of the FFI from Britain, was based at SHAEF and had been in regular contact with Bradley. The new 12th Army Group commander now announced that all the resistance in Brittany would come under the direct orders of General Patton and his Third Army, but should carry out sabotage and guerrilla activities through the region. On 3 August, the BBC made repeated radio announcements urging the FFI and Breton Maquis to rise up and begin such action. By the following day, however, Patton's other armoured spearhead, 6th Armored Division, had already sped off down the peninsula in a cloud of swirling dust, so Koenig asked permission to parachute in his designated commander, Colonel Albert Eon, and deputy, Colonel Passy, from England, right away so that they could take control of Résistance operations. This was agreed, albeit on the understanding that Eon and Passy did so at their own risk, as neither had yet carried out a single practice jump. Both men landed successfully the following night, 4 August, as did a further 150 French from 3 SAS, who parachuted in to protect the railway bridges at Morlaix, east of Brest. On the night of the 5th, ten US gliders then landed between Vannes and Lorient, packed with Jeeps, weapons and ammunition for the FFI, while the next day, 6 August, contact was made with an American armoured patrol.

By that time, however, most of the peninsula of Brittany had been cleared, much to the befuddlement of General Middleton, the VIII Corps commander, which was now part of Third Army. Ever since his armour had gadded off into the distance, Middleton had had little idea of where they were. On 2 August, he had learned they had sped on past Saint-Malo, which Middleton had ordered to be taken first, as he worried the hinge there, between Normandy and Brittany, looked weak. Patton, on the other hand, had ordered him to go hell for leather for Brest, which was exactly what 6th Armored had done. Middleton now couldn't locate Patton to argue for a greater concentration on the Dinard–Saint-Malo area and so felt he had to appeal to Bradley.

'Some people are more concerned with the headlines and the news they'll make than the soundness of their tactics,' huffed Bradley. 'I don't care if we get Brest tomorrow or ten days later. If we cut the peninsula, we'll get it anyhow. But we can't risk a loose hinge.' If the Germans now decided to counter-attack with three divisions, he added, they would make them look very foolish. It would be embarrassing for Patton too. Middleton suggested they turn 79th Infantry down towards the hinge. Bradley was not happy about having to overrule Patton, but Middleton was right – the 79th was closest and there was no time to lose. Bradley later chastized his Third Army commander, but Patton shrugged it off. 'Brad went over the situation,' noted Hansen, 'and George laughed, put his arm round the old man, told him he did the right thing.' So that was all right. In the meantime, his 4th Armored had surged towards Rennes, which they encircled the following day.

This lightning fast cavalry charge across Brittany was very much the Patton way. His arrival into the fray could not have been more perfectly timed, as the situation was ideal for the kind of warfare he preferred. 'Self-confidence, speed and audacity,' were his watch-words. With Bradley now 12th Army Group commander and his former deputy, General Courtney Hodges, having taken over First Army, there had been a sudden and dramatic surge in the number of US forces in France. Among the newcomers were two more entire corps, XV and XX, which had been held back since mid-July, and also XII Corps, which was currently staging into Normandy as the surge south took place. For the first time, French units were arriving too; now landing with XII Corps was Général Philippe Leclerc's US-equipped 2nd Armoured Division.

Nor was that all. XIX Tactical Air Command, which had been operating under IX TAC, now became operational too. Mary Coningham's Second TAF Headquarters moved across the Channel and set up shop in Normandy, while Ninth Air Force Headquarters was due to follow. More men, more tanks, more guns, more fighter planes, more bombers. The full might of American industry, begun a mere four years earlier after a series of meetings between President Roosevelt and certain leading captains of industry, had in barely comprehensible rapid time transformed itself into a Titan of mighty war-materiel manufacturing. It was unprecedented in world history and utterly remarkable. For the Germans, it must have seemed as though the American forces were like some horrific Hydra's head; no matter how many *Nebelwerfer* rounds they fired, or how many 88s or Panthers or machine guns they dragged into the battle, there were yet more Americans coming towards them.

The biggest challenge, it seemed, was getting these immense numbers of American troops and quantities of materiel south and into the open where they could manoeuvre and begin the giant wheel towards the east. Most troops were still landing on Omaha and Utah, then heading down through the wreckage of Saint-Lô, Coutances and Avranches. Only two routes were realistically usable; they converged both at Coutances and at Avranches before splitting again, and both were lined with dead Germans, dead horses, upturned carts, burned-out tanks and vehicles, and the rubble of destroyed buildings. However, bulldozers were hurriedly sent south to clear paths through this wreckage and, once again, the incredible Allied logistical system ensured those vital bits of equipment, as well as the engineers and service corps to man and oversee such work, were readily and swiftly available.

By 1 August, it was blindingly obvious to all the senior German commanders in Normandy that the battle was lost, and when Eberbach suggested to von Kluge that they rapidly pull out and retreat behind the River Seine, he was echoing the thoughts of Hausser, Dietrich et al. There was some good sense to such a move. Normandy was clearly lost, yet much of Germany's 15. Armee was still behind the Seine, because only now that Patton had arrived with the US Third Army did the Germans finally accept there would be no Allied invasion in the Pas de Calais. They could salvage whatever they could of their 7. Armee, with Panzergruppe West holding the eastern flank as they did so, then the remaining armour of I. and II. Panzerkorps could also pull back. With much of 15. Armee already behind the Seine, there was less travelling for those divisions to do, which was a good thing given the Allies' total domination of the skies – a domination that was becoming more evident with every passing day. As nearly two months' fighting had proved with crystal clarity, the more German troop movements, the more they would be chewed up just in the process of getting from A to B.

The OKW rejected this plan out of hand, and in so doing they were, as ever, reflecting their Führer's take on the matter. Hitler wanted to play for time; he planned to prepare the next line of defence protecting Germany's western borders. The old Siegfried Line, or West Wall, had been neglected, but work on it was now furiously under way. Hitler reckoned he needed between six and ten weeks, however, to get it ready. The Allies, he surmised, would need ports, so these were to be defended to the last round and the last man, and for as long as possible, tying down Allied forces and denying them the port facilities in the process. In fact, the Allies had already thought of that in Brittany. SHAEF had expected the retreating Germans to wreck harbour installations and so planned to create a new harbour themselves on the Quiberon Peninsula in southern Brittany. Meanwhile, huge amounts of materiel were coming ashore at Mulberry B, and continuing to arrive in landing craft and landing ships on the beaches of Normandy. The Allies had so far conducted the entire campaign without a previously established port.

To von Kluge, this insistence on holding the 'fortresses' meant only one thing: the inevitable loss of between 180,000 and 280,000 men, as well as equipment. Since there was to be no withdrawal behind the Seine, the only alternative was some frantic attempts to plug the gaps in the dam. II. SS-Panzerkorps was pulled out of the Odon Valley and was due to be handed over to 7. Armee, but then the British attacked southwards with their BLUECOAT offensive and so they were turned instead to stem the flow of that. Now the south of Caen was vulnerable, with 12. SS the only panzer division in the area and the gap in the line filled with infantry units from 15. Armee. And, of course, all these movements of divisions had to be done at night and in the most difficult possible circumstances.

And then came the bombshell. On 2 August, a directive from Hitler reached von Kluge ordering him to counter-attack towards Avranches, for although all his forces in Normandy were already committed, six infantry and one further panzer division were now all heading to Normandy from both the Pas de Calais and southern France. Whether they would get there in time was a moot point, but it seemed likely that three infantry divisions would be reaching the front within the next few days.

On 3 August, General Walter Warlimont, the head of planning at the OKW, arrived at the front. Again, Eberbach suggested a retreat to the Seine was the only possible course of action, but Warlimont told him that was 'politically unbearable and tactically impractical.' Von Kluge, like Eberbach, told Warlimont there was absolutely no chance of this counter-thrust being successful, especially not with the Allied control of the air. But this fell on deaf ears. Hitler's perspective was not entirely without logic; after all, the Normandy front was shorter than the Seine, and the river was hardly an ideal defensive line. On the other hand, events were moving very fast, the situation was changing almost by the hour not just the day, and already, by 4 August, that front line in Normandy was rapidly extending southwards and in danger of spreading east like a pool of blood under a man who has been fatally shot. On 4 August, it was still possible to retreat to the Seine using the Caen area as a pivot. Within another day, maybe two, or three at most, it might not be.

If ever there was an example of bad decisions being made far from the front on the evidence of a two-dimensional map rather than taking on board what was happening on the ground – and, more importantly, in the air – then this was it. With von Kluge doubling up as commander of both Heeresgruppe B and OB West, Hitler had now effectively assumed the latter role. Post-bomb-plot, he mistrusted his Wehrmacht generals even more and his insistence on micro-managing had worsened. His mind was made up: von Kluge was to assemble an armoured force using eight of the nine panzer divisions now in Normandy and strike west towards Avranches, supported by a thousand fighters, the Luftwaffe's entire reserve. It was to be called Operation LÜTTICH.

Meanwhile, Patton's forces were sweeping through Brittany. Rennes was encircled by 4th Armored Division on 3 August, but it was recognized that some infantry was needed to help them actually get into the town and that was to come from the 8th Division. That same day, Lieutenant Richard Blackburn and his company paused for a rest in the pouring rain, but he managed to find a shed with some straw and get his head down in the dry for a change. He was exhausted; they all were. Over the past few days they had passed through Coutances, Granville and Avranches, following a trail of destruction that he found profoundly depressing. Once he saw a dead cow hanging in the fork of a tree about a hundred feet up. Another time he passed a knocked-out German tank with a crewman hanging half out but burned to a crisp. They also travelled through the wreckage of the Roncey encirclement, past scores of dead and smashed vehicles. One wounded horse was still alive, kicking and struggling, so he took out his pistol and put it out of its misery. Then there was the German soldier he saw running for dear life, but who then suddenly lost his footing and tripped. A moment later he was crushed by a tank. Subsequent tanks went over him too until there was nothing left but flattened pulp. 'Events like these left me feeling like a limp, wet rag,' noted Blackburn. 'Seeing human bodies mutilated beyond belief left a huge scar on my memory.'

The following day, Friday, 4 August, half of the 8th were sent to clear Rennes, while the rest, including the 121st Infantry, paused before turning towards Saint-Malo, the weak hinge that so troubled Bradley and Middleton. To the relief of all the men, however, and not least Lieutenant Blackburn, a mobile shower unit had been brought up, along with fresh, clean uniforms. Blackburn threw away his old set – he had been wearing them solidly for a month.

By the beginning of August, First Army had also driven deep to the south, with General Joe Collins's VII Corps striking towards the small town of Brécy. Orders that day from General Hodges, the new First Army commander, directed his men to wheel towards the south-east. The Big Red One, and specifically Tom Bowles and the 18th Infantry Combat Team, had just taken Villedieu, and Collins now urged the men of the 1st Division to push on towards the town of Mortain, some 14 miles south of Vire. On 3 August Collins met Major-General Clarence Huebner, the 1st Division commander, at a crossroads south of Brécy and pointed to a feature on his map, Hill 317, which dominated the surrounding countryside.

'Ralph,' Collins told him, 'be sure to take Hill 317.'

'Joe, I've already got it,' Huebner replied, grinning.

The following day a gap was developing between VII Corps and XV Corps on their right, so Collins ordered the Big Red One to push south and fill the hole, while 30th Division was brought in to take over the Mortain area. This left 9th Division now on their left near the village of Saint-Pois and the 29th Division immediately on their left to the north at Vire, converging on the town with the British striking from the north as part of BLUECOAT. The 116th Infantry were clearing the hills around the town, having taken the village of Moyen on 1 August.

A few days later, on 6 August, it was the 1st Battalion's task to take Hill 203, and Sergeant Bob Slaughter had a feeling it was going to prove a tough one to crack. As they jumped off that morning, they immediately came under mortar and shell fire and then, to make matters worse, Company D realized they had to get over a crossroads where German artillery had clearly already zeroed their guns. The men had to calculate how long it took between salvoes then make a dash for it, but the trouble was, they were carrying heavy equipment such as machine guns and mortars; running with this was no easy matter. Sergeant Crawley timed his sprint well and made it across, only to get hit in the thigh by shrapnel some 50 yards further on. Bob Slaughter then got across but paused to help his buddy, who was already losing considerable amounts of blood. Having tied a tourniquet and given him a shot of morphine, Slaughter then hurried to join the rest of the platoon as they picked their way down beside a rocky stream. Hill 203 lay just up ahead. When he finally caught up with the rest of the men, he was out of breath and didn't hear the *swish-sh-sh* of the mortar bomb coming in until it was too late. Landing some 8 feet behind them, it killed one man and wounded two others, including Slaughter, who felt a red-hot fragment hit him just above his right kidney. To begin with it didn't hurt too badly, but he was struggling to stand. A lieutenant helped patch him up, but by then Slaughter was in difficulties. Crawling to the safety of some rocks near the bed of the little stream, he remained there until eventually, at dusk, a corpsman arrived in a Jeep, patched him up, put him on a stretcher on the bonnet and took him back to the 45th Evacuation Hospital. Bob Slaughter's time in the Normandy firing line was over.

For Operation LÜTTICH, von Kluge had managed to assemble only four panzer divisions, not eight, along with the remnants of 17. SS. This force was to be commanded by General Hans Freiherr von Funck, who had recently arrived in Normandy to lead one of the new formations coming into the battle, XLVII. Panzerkorps. He was a competent, highly experienced panzer commander, although not much liked by his peers, and it would have made more sense for Eberbach to command the attack as he had been in Normandy for over a month and knew the ground; also, the men involved had all been in Panzergruppe West, now renamed 5. Panzerarmee. In fact, four hours before LÜTTICH was due to begin, Hitler ordered Eberbach to take over from Funck, although it was far too late to insist upon such changes of command. Perhaps, though, since it was doomed to failure, who was in charge was, frankly, neither here nor there.

Throughout the Normandy campaign, the moment German troops assaulted they tended to be absolutely hammered as the full weight of Allied fire-power rained down upon them. The danger to the Allies had always been a coordinated full-strength counter-thrust by multiple panzer divisions bristling with weaponry and fresh, gung-ho troops, but that danger had long ago passed as these elite Wehrmacht and SS divisions had been ground down. The only one of Funck's divisions that was in good shape was the newly arrived 116. Panzer, but its commander had been so pessimistic about the operation he had not even got his regiments ready in time. In all, Funck had around 300 tanks for this attack, although because of the usual difficulties of moving troops and the excessively complicated switch around of various units on narrow roads, watched constantly through daylight hours by the *Jabos*, the support tail for LÜTTICH was nothing like sufficient.

While it was true that they were at long last out of range of Allied naval guns, there were now many more Allied air forces operating over Normandy and, with improved weather, the movement of the LÜTTICH force, kicking up dust, made them an obvious target, even though the operation was launched amid heavy ground mists in the early hours of Monday, 7 August. Even worse for the Germans was the fact that Bradley knew the assault was coming. Given Ultra clearance, he was able to see decrypts of German Enigma-coded radio traffic decoded at Bletchley Park throughout 5 August, revealing troop movements that seemed to indicate the Germans were planning some kind of counter-attack. By 2 p.m. on the 6th, it was revealed they would be attacking westwards, with further details of the attacking force just before 8 p.m. Another decrypt at eleven minutes past midnight on 7 August was passed on to Bradley, reporting a German attack towards Mortain. As a consequence of this invaluable information, Bradley had brought up several divisions in case a crisis developed, including Third Army's XX Corps. None the less, Mortain was swiftly overrun by 2. SS, although the key piece of high ground, Hill 317, was not. Here, the men of 2nd Battalion of the 120th Infantry Regiment, part of the American 30th Division, had dug in and could not be budged despite a hellish rain of fire.

In the afternoon, as the mists began to clear, 2. Panzer joined in, striking further to the north. The Luftwaffe had been ordered to support LÜTTICH with a maximum effort. The thousand fighters Hitler had earmarked did not materialize, although several hundred took off from forward airfields around Paris. Some did get through to harass American lines of supply, but these were few and far between. Most were pounced upon before they had even taken off, while many of the rest were forced away by marauding Allied fighters some way short of the Mortain area. 'In fact,' said Generalmajor Rudolf-Christoph Freiherr von Gersdorff, Pemsel's replacement as chief of staff at 7. Armee, 'not a single German airplane reached the ordered operational area.'

Major Dick Turner and his fighter squadron of Mustangs had had a fruitless mission in the morning, but in the afternoon were sent up a second time to scout for German airfields and any sign of the Luftwaffe around their known landing grounds in the Paris area. 'We had hit the regular airfields used by the Germans so much,' noted Turner, 'they were abandoning them for open fields, highways or almost any level area close to forests which would provide camouflage.' After circling over Chartres, he led them east and, after a short while, spotted something down below in a large field bordered on two sides by woods. Diving down to 3,000 feet, he saw wheat sheaves in the fields but could also make out the familiar shape of Me109s underneath. Telling the rest of the squadron of his discovery, he made a pass on one of the 109s, opening fire as he did so, and was pleased to see strikes and then the aircraft explode and burn. 'For the next five minutes,' wrote Turner, 'we gave the concealed airdrome a good working over.'

Turner didn't spot any ground fire, but one of his men was hit all the same, although he managed to nurse his P-51 most of the way back and then bailed out over an American tank formation, who gave him a ride; he was back at their airfield later that day. On that sweep alone, Turner reckoned he and his squadron destroyed at least nineteen Messerschmitts on the ground. It had been a good haul, and while they had been shooting up Luftwaffe airfields, Thunderbolts and Typhoons, including the P-47s of the 388th Hell Hawks, had been attacking the leading panzer units as they tried to advance, unhindered by the threat of the Luftwaffe, peeling off and diving repeatedly on to the armoured columns, dropping bombs, firing rockets and hammering them with cannons and machine guns. 'The absolute air supremacy of the Allies,' noted Gersdorff, 'made any further movement by the attack units impossible.' Already by noon, 1. SS-Panzer had stopped short of Juvigny-le-Tertre, some 16 miles east of Avranches, because of the loss of tanks and the impossibility of advancing under the weight of *Jabos* hammering them. Around 1 p.m., they were forced to pull off the roads and take cover.

Everywhere, the German advance was faltering under the weight of aggressive counter-attacks by the Americans and continued attacks from the air. By evening 7. Armee was repeatedly asking von Kluge for a decision about what they should do: continue attacking until they were annihilated, or withdraw and pull back? The answer eventually arrived at around 10 p.m., and came via Hitler and the OKW. They were to keep attacking and 12. and 10. SS were to be moved in support of them.

By then, however, 12. SS was already embroiled in another battle to the south of Caen. The endgame was beginning to be played out in Normandy. Almost surrounded, the German forces in Normandy now faced not only defeat but annihilation.

CHAPTER 34

Tank Battle at Saint-Aignan

O N 7 AUGUST, THE British prime minister visited the front and made a point of seeing General Bradley. 'I came to tell you,' Churchill said as he greeted him, 'how magnificently we believe you are doing.' It was gracious of him and his praise entirely justified; it was precisely the kind of gesture that did much to further Allied relations. The PM charmed them all with his enthusiastic interest and grasp of the situation. 'Good God,' he said, looking at the mass of divisions now plotted on his map, 'how do you feed them?' Bradley laughed and explained they had cleared two roads south and that these were used twenty-four hours of every day in supplying the front.

Operation ANVIL, now renamed DRAGOON, was about to be launched in the south of France; Eisenhower had insisted on it and had got his way, although such was the emerging success in northern France that Churchill still wondered whether it was worth the effort. 'Why break down the back door,' he said to Bradley, 'when the front is already opened by the American Army?' There was also a brief discussion about the German counter-attack, but Hansen, observing these conversations, noted that no one was very worried about it. Nor did they need to be. LÜTTICH was merely serving to hasten the end in Normandy, not extend the campaign as Hitler hoped.

There was a noted feeling in Normandy that the British and Canadians weren't doing as well as the Americans – something that reflected the attitude to Montgomery rather than to the British and Canadian troops under his charge. Yet whatever antipathy there might have been towards this unquestionably difficult fellow, actually the British and

Canadians had done considerably better than the advances on the map suggested. In two months they had ground down seven of Germany's very finest divisions to the point of collapse, pushing them back bit by bit and learning important lessons as they went along. No other force in the entire war to date had achieved that against such a concentration of armour and with only three armoured divisions of their own. Their efforts should in no way be belittled.

The plan now, however, was to finish the job by finally striking south to Falaise, a task given to Canadian First Army, and more specifically II Corps, under General Guy Simonds, who after the setback of Operation SPRING was keen to prove his mettle and that of his men. Simonds was just forty-one and, although he had been born in England, his parents had moved to Canada when he was still a young boy. From a long line of generals and East India Company men, the military was very much in his blood. A gunner, he had attended staff colleges in England and Canada and, despite SPRING, was highly rated by Montgomery. Bright, imaginative and an innovator, he was certainly not a man to rest on any laurels but instead was constantly striving for tactical improvements, which was very much to his credit. Lean, with dark eyes and a trim moustache, Simonds cut rather a dashing figure. For Operation TOTAL-IZE, as the push for Falaise was named, Simonds wanted to try something different.

The men of the 1st Northants Yeomanry learned what this was going to be on the afternoon of 7 August, as the sun beat down, strong and warm. Lance Corporal Ken Tout had been stripped to his waist as he zeroed the gun sights on their Sherman. They had known all day they were going into battle that evening – a night attack was part of Simonds' innovative approach; certainly a combined-arms nighttime attack was something new in Normandy.

'Do you think the Germans will really stay asleep with all this lot chugging around the countryside in the dark?' one of the lads had asked. The answer was no, but Simonds hoped the German infantry, very new to the line, would be thrown by a surprise assault in the dark. Lieutenant Bobby McColl, the troop commander, joined them by their tanks at around 5.30 p.m. Everyone stood up.

'Business this time, lads,' he said. 'For real. Orders are simple. Keep rolling. Keep moving. Keep in sight of the tail light of the tank in front.' All the villages had been fortified by the Hun, he told them. If anyone got lost, they should follow the green tracer from the Bofors guns firing over them. The colonel, David Forster, and squadron officers then arrived for a briefing and pep-talk. Colonel Forster seemed to struggle to find the right words; he quite openly hated sending his young charges into battle. 'The Germans are now almost surrounded,' he told them. 'We are being asked to slam the door on their retreat.' He reiterated that they were to keep moving. The objective was the village of Saint-Aignan-de-Cramesnil, code-named 'Fly By Night', and they were expected there by 3 a.m. Forster tapped the silver regimental badge on his black beret. 'Our little silver horse does not look very savage,' he said. 'But he can gallop across country. Good luck!'

The plan was to try to smash through the first line of German defence this coming night, then at first light consolidate and wait for the heavy bombers to blast a way through the rest of the German lines. Two columns of all arms – armour, mobile infantry and anti-tank artillery – would make the night assault, the infantry in half-tracks and new armoured personnel carriers, developed by the Canadians from Sherman chassis, called 'Kangaroos'. Then the armour, including the newly arrived Polish Armoured Division, would strike on towards Falaise. Night advances were fraught with difficulties, but searchlights, flares and radio beams would help Forster's columns navigate their way through. A second wave of infantry would then follow up and finish off the enemy forward lines, while the two columns of armour surged ahead after the bombing.

9.15 p.m. 'Driver, start up!' said Snowie Snowdon, Ken Tout's tank commander. The Northants Yeomanry and the rest of the 33rd Armoured Brigade were partnering with infantry from the 51st Highland Division, while on the other side of the road the Canadian column would be led by the 2nd Infantry and 2nd Armoured Brigade; this time, Charlie Martin, Bob Roberts and the men of the 8th Infantry Brigade were not in the spearhead.

Tout and his fellow crew all wore their tanker overalls, black berets and a variety of non-regulation shoes: hobnailed boots were no good in or on a tank. Some wore rubber-soled plimsolls; Ken Tout had a pair of brown shoes from Stead & Simpson. Headset on – simple headphones over the top of his beret were the only way they could communicate over the din of the engine, the gun and the barrage already booming behind them. They trundled up the slope from Cormelles. Much of the ground round about was churned up, cratered and blasted, but they advanced through cornfields, following the green Bofors tracer – then suddenly someone appeared to have turned on a light switch. Looking through his periscope from inside the Sherman turret, Ken Tout thought it seemed eerie, almost inexplicable.

'That is artificial moonlight,' said Snowdon. 'Searchlights shining on the clouds. It should help a little.'

It was at around midnight that the first wave of bombers came over, some 660 Lancasters and Halifaxes dropping about 4 tons each, pounding the ground and villages on the flanks of their advance. Huge concussive waves pulsed through the ground and into their tank as each cluster of bombs detonated. The light was strange – dim and grainy close by, but up ahead brilliantly clear as spouts of flame rose above the trees. Tout sat in the turret next to Snowdon, watching, and saw a tank thrown lazily into the air then plunge back down again into the trees. 'The physical sensation here on the turret,' wrote Tout, 'is that of standing on a beach during a cyclonic storm.' Warm, foul-smelling air rushed over them and dust blew in their eyes. And this a thousand yards from the bombs.

They pressed on, past burning trees and fires, across the pitted, desolate, devastated lunar landscape of GOODWOOD, up and down craters, the tank swaying and lurching, until eventually they emerged into still largely untouched countryside of hedges, sunken lanes and fields. By 1 a.m. the fighting had begun and by 1.20 a.m. Tout was answering Snowdon's instructions, spinning the turret, his eye to the telescope, pressing his foot on to the firing button, then on the co-axial machine-gun firing button. HE rounds, and the gun crashed, the breech hurtled back, jamming against the springs, then slid forward again into position for another round, the automatically opening breech spewing out choking cordite fumes. Another shot, then another and another, dust, smoke and grit swirling up, creating a second darkness and obscurity around the darkness of the night. For all involved it was deeply confusing, chaotic and cacophonous.

By 3.15 a.m. they had reached Fly By Night – Saint-Aignan-de-Cramesnil – and the regiment paused. Tout was able to clamber out of the turret and stretch his legs. Earlier he had struggled to keep images of murderous SS hordes and Tiger tanks out of his mind, but now it was a bit calmer and there were some Black Watch infantrymen about to talk to. 'Behind us and to our right rear the moonlit night is ruddy with flashes,' noted Tout. 'But here all is doom quiet, silver frosted. Is it possible that the Germans have not realised that we are here?'

They had, but had been simply blown away; the 89. Infanterie-Division, low-grade, poorly trained and equipped, had arrived only three days earlier, hastily shipped in from Norway, and had now largely ceased to exist, its men fled, killed, wounded or captured by the combination of air power, artillery and monstrous mechanized all-arms columns. All the first objectives had been taken, and the British column had suffered just forty casualties, the Canadians a number more – some 340 – but a penetration of 4 miles wide and 5 deep had been achieved. The next phase was to consolidate these gains by mopping up any enemy pockets, wait for the bombers to come over at 1 p.m. and blast a hole in the next line of German defences, then to push through two more armoured divisions, the 4th Canadian and the 1st Polish.

In fact, the first part of TOTALIZE had been so completely successful that, had the two columns pressed on, they might well have bludgeoned their way through the 12. SS, still woefully understrength and completely thrown by the sudden rupture of the front. This, however, was where the constraints of wealth played a part. General Simonds and his commanders were not aware of just how successful his plan had been and did not have a clear enough picture to change tack and go hell for leather right away without the help of the bombers due an hour after midday. In any case, the bombers could not be so easily cancelled at short notice, and they did represent a lot of explosive power. So, instead, the attack force sat around on their objectives twiddling their thumbs.

Kurt Meyer had hurried forward towards Bretteville-sur-Laize soon after he heard the first bombs falling, only to find the village impassable. He was also shocked to see terrified German soldiers pouring back down the road. Speeding off in his *Kübelwagen*, he recognized that if anyone was going to halt this attack it was going to be his 12. SS 'Hitlerjugend' Division; he certainly couldn't rely on the rabble streaming back from the front, nor on the 85. Infanterie-Division, also newly arrived and of equally poor quality as the 89. Meyer reached Standartenführer Mohnke's SS-Panzergrenadier-Regiment 25 CP a short while after and a little later was joined by General Eberbach, who had also come up to the front to see the situation for himself. Together they agreed a plan of action. Meyer had just forty-eight panzers in all, since some of his arsenal had already been sent to Mortain – the rest of the division had been due to follow – so had to make do with *Kampfgruppen* of grenadiers, panzers, anti-tank guns and mortars. Two were sent to take back the high ground around Saint-Aignan and west of Saint-Sylvain, and a third was told to occupy and defend the high ground to the west of the road.

*

The Northants Yeomanry had moved forward out of Saint-Aignan on 8 August, with C Squadron in fields due south of the village. No. 3 Troop, including Snowie Snowdon's tank, were sitting on the edge of some trees. Directly in front of them, a track led down into a narrow, curving gully, perhaps 15 feet deep and a football pitch wide, before climbing again to a mass of hedgerows and, beyond that, a farmstead, marked Robert-mesnil on the map. Stretching away from their position were cornfields running all the way across to the main Caen–Falaise road, and beyond that the wall of a small country chateau. No. 2 Troop had pushed down into the gully, planning to climb out again into the hedgerows to watch on Robertmesnil. No. 4 Troop were on the left, spread through the edge of the wood, while No. 1 Troop were beyond them. An orchard stood to the immediate left of Snowdon's tank, where the Black Watch were digging in. A Squadron were spaced out on their right and B Squadron behind. They were, they knew, in the vanguard of the TOTALIZE advance and were waiting for the SS men to counter-attack, part of the consolidation before the heavy bombers of the Eighth Air Force came over. But right now, mid-morning, absolutely nothing was happening.

'Sitting here like this,' said Stan Hicken, their driver, 'we might just as well be watching a cricket match. Nothing happening, nobody moving, bloody monotonous soul-destroying waste of time.'

Hicken had clearly been tempting fate, because soon after, at around 10.30 a.m., there came a loud slam and crash, and from the chatter on the battalion net it seemed the CO's tank had been hit. In Snowdon's tank they could only speculate on whether the colonel and his crew were badly hurt or worse, but then B Squadron's commander was hit too. All remained quiet in their little sector, though, until around 11.15 a.m. Corporal Stanley in 2 Troop suddenly came on the net. 'Hallo, Roger 2 Baker. Alert! I seem to see movement half-left, a hundred yards left of roof but cannot yet identify. 2 Baker, over.' Everyone liked Stanley. He had grown a small Hitler moustache for a laugh and was very much the squadron joker. He kept everyone cheery. From the gunner's position in the turret of Snowdon's tank, Ken Tout peered through both his periscope and the more magnified telescope, traversing the gun as he did so.

A sudden shuddering wham, loud and close across the background noise of artillery fire.

'Two Baker, I'm bloody hit!' shouted Stanley. 'Bail out! Hornet at . . . Gawd!'

'Hornet' meant an enemy tank or assault gun. But where did he mean?

Tout traversed again, frantically searching, then saw something, solid-topped, between the hedges. He stamped on the firing button, the breech whammed backwards, the muzzle spouted fire and the Sherman rocked in recoil. Multiple flashes now hammered into the far hedge beyond the gully. Eventually Snowdon ordered ceasefire. They were worried about Stanley, but there was no sign of a fire or of a Sherman brewing up. Maybe he had got out. Perhaps they all had. Beyond in the hedgerows, though, smoke was rising – thick smoke with no flames. The German gun. Then more waiting.

Heading towards Saint-Aignan that same day, Tuesday, 8 August, were the Tigers of Schwere Panzerabteilung 101 commanded by Sturmbann-führer Michael Wittmann, the celebrated panzer ace, feted throughout the Reich and only just back with 12. SS after being called to the Wolf's Lair to be awarded the Swords of the Knight's Cross by Hitler himself. Wittmann's fame and celebrity had grown since his one-man shooting spree in Villers-Bocage a week after the invasion, but either over-confidence and recklessness or the pressing orders of Kurt Meyer to grab and hold the high ground had led him to advance towards Saint-Aignan directly across the open fields in front of the 1st Northants Yeomanry a little after 12.30 p.m.

They were first called out by 3 Charlie, A Squadron's Firefly with its big 17-pounder, and the words sent tremors of fear through Ken Tout.

'Hullo, Oboe Able to 3 Charlie,' Tout heard the A Squadron troop leader say. 'I see them now. Keep under cover and hold fire until about 800 yards. Then fire at the last one while I pepper the others. Over.' The idea was to hammer the enemy with HE, not with much hope of destroying any of them, but to confuse them and cover them in smoke, making them continue hatch-down. Hopefully, their visibility would then be so poor they wouldn't be able to fire back very effectively.

'Oboe Able to 3 Charlie. Near enough. Fire! Over.' The commander of 3 Charlie acknowledged and ordered his gunner to fire. The big gun blam-crashed and hit the last Tiger, which now erupted into flames, much to the delight of the Yeomen, then 3 Charlie reversed into cover while the 75s of A Squadron fired their HE rounds and the Tigers began firing back blind. Blam-crash again, the Firefly's shell hissing towards its target in less than a second.

'Oboe Able to Oboe. Second Tiger brewing. Am keeping third busy while Charlie brings to bear. Over.'

'Oboe, bloody good show. Over.'

The third Tiger's 88 and 3 Charlie's 17-pounder now fired almost simultaneously, but the panzers, including a fourth, were also being attacked by the Sherbrooke Fusiliers from behind the wall by the chateau and, although all Shermans rather than Fireflies, they were firing from only around 150 yards. A moment later a third Tiger was hit. Tout saw flames erupt beyond the trees in front of him.

Who exactly hit Wittmann's tank has been the subject of feverish debate ever since, but what is clear is that a shell penetrated the main part of the tank, which was almost fully loaded with ammunition, igniting the shells inside, which, combined with the immense kinetic energy, generated a massive explosion that blew the entire turret, weighing some 15 tons, high into the air and, with it, Wittmann and his crew. Lower-velocity 75mm guns could destroy a Tiger, but generally only at weak spots like its backside or by knocking out tracks. Everything about the violence of the Tiger's end points to it being that of a high-velocity gun. And the only one of those firing at that moment was 3 Charlie, whose gunner was Trooper Joe Ekins.

That was not the end of the firefight, however. Not long after, some twenty Panzer IVs began engaging them, the squadron net alive with frantic chatter as enemy tanks were hit and they then began being knocked out in turn.

'Two Charlie! Behind you! Behind you, I say! 2 Able, traverse right! Charlie! Charlie!' came the frantic voice of one of 2 Troop's commanders. 'Oh my God, 2 Charlie is brewing. 2 Able, can't you traverse right? Right! Traverse . . . Oh my God . . . bail out . . . bail!' Suddenly, Snowdon's tank seemed horribly exposed, with Tout desperately traversing the turret and peering for all his life's worth through the telescope. 'The day degenerates into chaos, noise, flame, smoke, grilling sunshine, stinking sweat, searing fear, billowing blast,' wrote Tout, 'and our tank shuddering and juddering even as it stands still on the exposed, oh so exposed ridge crest.' They now moved forward, slowly, Tout and Snowdon craning their eyes to see a sign of the enemy panzer that had knocked out all of 2 Troop. Then Tout saw it, in among the trees and hedge at the edge of the gully – a box-like shape that didn't fit.

'Hornet! Hornet! Hornet!' shouted Snowdon. Tout elevated the gun, crosswires on to the shape, then stamped down his foot and boom! The gun fired, crashing back and forward again. While the tracer of his round shot through the air, another flash came back and a further tracer sped towards the panzer. The German shell was wide, but Tout's and the second shell seemed to have hit – a puff of smoke, a shape jerking backwards and then thick, black smoke tinged with flame. Tout fired again, then one further time. The panzer was dead.

The firing died down, but soon after the bombers arrived – 681 heavies, Fortresses and Liberators, the first bombs landing worryingly close to Tout and his comrades. The tank men fired off yellow smoke and then the bombs began falling further on, where they were supposed to – another giant hammer blow of carnage, obliterating yet more French villages in the process, and while this latest rain of bombs was whistling down, two more Mk IVs were engaged and brewed up near the Falaise road. Then the bombers were gone and suddenly the battlefield – their battlefield around Saint-Aignan – fell silent again. Tout was able to pause and think about what had happened and what might happen to him, to his crew, if they were hit. Fear gripped him once more. 'The clutching feeling at the heart,' he wrote, 'piercing sensation in the throat, ice-cold prickles up the nape of the neck and under the ears, burning fire behind the eyes, within the cheeks and across the eyebrows.'

Meanwhile, away to the west, despite demands from Hitler to renew the attempt to strike for Avranches, LÜTTICH was getting nowhere. The panzer divisions had been savaged the previous day, 7 August, from the air. Eighty-one panzers were destroyed, fifty-four damaged and a further twenty-six simply abandoned for lack of fuel, mechanical failure or because the crews bailed out rather than face the relentless attacks from the air. Hundreds of trucks, armoured cars, half-tracks and other vehicles were destroyed.

Willi Müller was now in the ruins of Mortain, his pioneer battalion just a few hundred strong and attached still to the 2. SS 'Das Reich' Division – or what was left of it. They were not able to achieve very much – mere bit-players while the armour was slaughtered, holding Mortain while the Americans stubbornly clung to Hill 317. Elsewhere, American divisions continued to chip away, although not without suffering casualties of their own. On 8 August, the 47th Infantry of the 9th Division was in action near Saint-Pois, between Vire and Mortain, fighting back against LÜTTICH. Lieutenant Orion Shockley was hit twice – first when an American tank opened fire and its shell killed his runner and sent a piece of fizzing shrapnel into his back. Fortunately for Shockley, it wasn't too bad; the shard was removed, his back patched up and he continued leading his men. Next, his company was ordered to take a hill position. Crossing a road, his canteen, hooked on to his waist, was hit, soaking his leg. Later, the Germans called a truce in order to get their wounded clear. Shockley went forward to meet the delegation and discovered that the German medic holding the makeshift flag of truce had emigrated to the States before the war, but had gone back to Germany to visit family in 1939 and been conscripted. He had no wish to fight at all, least of all against Americans, which was why he had become a medic.

South of Caen, meanwhile, TOTALIZE was moving into its final phase. Quite inadvertently, Meyer's ordering of his men to counter-attack meant they had not been where the bombers struck; instead of being bombed to death, they were being shot to pieces by the British, Canadians and Poles on the ground, albeit not without taking some of their enemy with them, as had been proved at Saint-Aignan. In all, five of Wittmann's seven Tigers had been destroyed, however, including the three in the action by the Northants Yeomanry and Sherbrooke Fusiliers. On the opposite side of the road, Meyer's other counter-attack fared equally badly as his grenadiers were cut down and panzers knocked out, the remnants pulling back before the next armoured advance got under way. TOTALIZE had slowed down, not because of 12. SS's counter-attacks, but because this multifaceted force of armour, infantry, artillery and heavy strategic bombers, drawn from the United States, Canada, Britain and Poland, had stuck rigidly to a battle plan that had looked perfectly reasonable the day before, but which had initially developed better than expected. Because there were so many different parts – and nationalities – to bring into the equation, it had been impossible to tinker with the timings. The third phase of TOTALIZE, the armoured thrust, had begun bang on time at 1.55 p.m., regardless of Meyer's counter-attack; what the SS men saved by avoiding the bombers, they had lost in action during their counter-attacks. And Wittmann, the hero panzer ace of the Reich, was dead.

To the south of Saint-Aignan, the Northants Yeomanry were still in position, consolidating, and seeing off several waves of grenadiers attempting to attack. They had mowed them down with their machine guns and with HE rounds, then the artillery started hurling over shells as well, at first a bit too short for comfort, but then with unerring accuracy. Calm returned, and at around 2.30 p.m. Snowdon's crew were ordered into the gully. Some of the survivors had already been picked up, but they were missing others, including Corporal Stanley. They found the three Shermans at the edge of the trees, one to the left, another to the right and the third a little further ahead on the left. Two were still smoking. Snowdon clambered down and told Tout to jump down too.

'Ken, have a look at those two Shermans out front,' he said, 'and I'll go check the farthest one. Fast's you can.'

Tout could see Stanley sprawled in his turret on the nearest Sherman. The corporal was staring at him, watching him all the way. Climbing up on to the back, Tout leaned down and touched Stanley's hand. It was already cold. There was no sign of any wound, but he couldn't have been more dead. Tout jumped down and hurried on to the next tank – wandering around, exposed like this, was nerve-racking to put it mildly. He reached it, but the tank had not brewed up. Through the turret he could see someone in the driver's compartment, so he moved around to the front of the turret and lifted the hatch. He wished he hadn't. Trooper '173 Judge', as he was always known, was sitting there, his hands on the levers, feet on the pedals, perfectly upright but minus his head. 'The mess on the floor is black,' noted Tout. 'Flies have already found it.' He then found Ernie Wellbelove, the third missing tank man, lying in the grass not far away, also dead. These were three men they had been talking to, laughing with, just hours earlier. Friends. Comrades-in-arms.

Tout pushed on through the bushes, unable to resist his curiosity, and found the Mk IV he had hit and the machine responsible for knocking out 2 Troop. The tank commander was still in the turret – or his top half, at any rate. A shell – possibly Tout's shell – had done for his lower half, removing it as neatly and brutally as the one that had removed 173 Judge's head. Snowdon now waved to Tout and he ran back, sickened by what he had seen.

Several hours later, the grenadiers attacked again and, this time, no sooner had the Shermans opened fire than rocket-firing Typhoons swooped in and finished the enemy off. Ken Tout watched them scatter and flee, and soon after they saw some prisoners coming towards them, keen to stress they were not SS. Tout and Rex Jackson, the co-driver, clambered out to wave them on their way to the rear. Gesturing with his pistol, Tout accidentally fired a shot, sending one of the men to the ground, pleading for mercy. Jackson pulled him up, stuffed a cigarette into his top pocket and told him to 'skip it' with a light push. 'Your war's over. Thank God for that,' Jackson said. 'Our ruddy picnic goes on.'

TOTALIZE was running out of steam, however. The Poles, in their first action, had struggled to manoeuvre and had also suffered from the friendly fire of the bombers – as had the Canadian 4th Armoured; in all, there had been some 315 casualties from the bombing, which underlined just how difficult it was, in 1944, to use strategic heavy bombers in support of ground operations. Such tragedies exemplified the limitations of dropping a vast number of bombs from hundreds upon hundreds of large four-engine bombers over a short period and on a confined space. There were also communications issues between the Poles and the artillery, which contributed to the slow advance, as did the stoic efforts of the German artillery, *Nebelwerfers* and mortars. Forty Polish tanks were knocked out in short order; once again, well-positioned anti-tank guns, in open country, could wreak havoc. As both sides had repeatedly proved since D-Day, it was much easier defending than it was attacking. By dusk, the Poles had advanced only 2½ miles.

The Northants Yeomanry were finally pulled back into leaguer at 11 p.m., and Ken Tout and his crew did not get a chance to sleep until after 1 a.m., by which time they had been on the go, non-stop, for over twenty-seven hours. They were exhausted, utterly spent. Twenty of the battalion's tanks had been lost that day. Even at this stage of the war, when the Germans were emphatically losing, the fighting was still relentlessly brutal. And it would continue that way until the campaign was finally over.

CHAPTER 35

The Corridor of Death

A T THE 101ST BRITISH General Hospital, Lieutenant Mary Mulry had been as busy as ever. Facilities were improving with every passing week and social life was equally on the up as the front moved further south and the threat from enemy shelling and even the Luftwaffe melted away. There were RAF dances, naval officers' dances, trips to Bayeux and lots of attention from dashing young officers. One day, Mary was taken on a drive around the battle-torn countryside by a Canadian friend and was shocked by the levels of devastation. 'What an awful waste of life and property all this is and so much destruction,' she noted, 'and yet there is a feeling of constant chance and excitement. I should, I know, hate it all – and the human suffering is appalling – but I must admit to enjoying the excitement.'

Meanwhile, the fighter planes of the enlarged Ninth Air Force and Second Tactical Air Force continued to wreak devastation. They had never been busier. Many of the squadrons were mounting as many as five missions a day, a heavy workload by any standards. Wednesday, 9 August, dawned with mist hanging over the airfield, but it promised to be a warm, clear day, and at B-7, now home to 609 Squadron, even before the liaison officers had stepped into the large, dark-green intelligence tent for the morning briefing, it was obvious to the assembled pilots that there would be plenty of flying that day.

At least none of the pilots could ever complain about being kept in the dark. Daily briefings were held in the 'inter ops' tent for the two squadrons that shared the airfield and made up 123 Wing – 609 and 198 – providing each and every pilot with impressive amounts of information about the progress of the Allies. In attendance were liaison officers from the army and navy, as well as their own intelligence officers and the met officer. Such detail was essential: often very little ground separated their own side from the enemy and the role of the Second TAF was to help the army, not hit them by mistake. Flight Sergeant Ken Adam listened carefully to the briefing by the army liaison officer, then the met officer, until finally it was the wing commander's turn. Around 10 a.m., once the mist had burned off, 609 would send up a flight on an armed reconnaissance mission over the Falaise area. If they saw any clear targets they were to hit the enemy hard.

Adam's friend Norman Merrett took part in that first flight of the day. They spotted enemy tanks moving north-west 6 miles south-east of Falaise and attacked, knocking out two. Another armed recce took off at 1.45 p.m. and once again they found targets, opening fire on an enemy column on the Falaise–Argentan road and leaving a truck and a further tank in flames. Adam was then one of eight men in A Flight chosen to fly a third armed recce later that afternoon. Shortly after 4.30, he was walking briskly towards his Hawker Typhoon, large and imposing as it stood motionless alongside a number of others under the cover of some trees at the airfield perimeter. His ground crew were already there. Ammunition boxes were stacked nearby, as were piles of rockets. Adam took the parachute off his wing, put each fur-booted leg in turn through the straps, then brought the other two straps over his shoulders and clipped them all together into the buckle. A quick glance at the four rockets loaded under each wing, then he put his boot into the retracting footrest, heaved himself up on to the scuffed, paint-chipped wing-root and clambered into the cockpit.

With its thick wings and huge, protruding radiator jutting from underneath the nose, the Typhoon certainly had none of the finesse and elegance of the Spitfire, but it was an extremely effective gun-platform as well as exceptionally quick. It could also carry a 1,000lb bomb, while Adam had discovered he was pretty good at firing its rockets: during training that spring he had regularly fired with an average error of 50–60 yards; with eight 60lb warheads exploding, that still created an enormous amount of damage.

In the cockpit, Adam immediately put on his helmet and, as he always did before a mission, turned the ring on his finger three times. Having given the signal to his ground crew, he strapped the oxygen mask to his face and fired the starter cartridge, the huge 24-cylinder Napier Sabre engine bursting into life amid clouds of thick, acrid smoke. The noise was enormous and the airframe shook violently. Adam switched on the oxygen immediately to avoid breathing in the lethal carbon-monoxide fumes that swept into the cockpit. Closing the bubble-perspex canopy, he watched his ground crew take away the chocks, their faces covered with scarves, and wave him round towards the wire-mesh – PSP – runway amid clouds of dust whipped up by the propeller.

The Typhoons took off in pairs and by the time it was Adam's turn the dust was so thick he could barely see a thing. Such was the power of the Sabre engine that the torque from the propeller caused the aircraft to veer violently to the right unless the pilot heavily corrected the yaw by pressing down hard on the port rudder. He was well used to this foible by now, but even so, taking off, especially with such poor visibility, was a hazardous occupation and had to be done blind, using the gyro – the aircraft compass – to keep him straight.

They immediately climbed steeply and turned northwards, out to sea. Normally Adam could see the silver barrage balloons shielding the Mulberry harbour glinting in the sun, but not that morning: Normandy was draped in soft, grey cloud. Merrett took them to 8,000 feet, then they turned and flew inland once more. Circling over their patrol area, they soon spotted a cluster of scattered enemy transport – trucks, lorries and smaller vehicles – so Merrett led them down, their engines screaming, plunging at nearly 600 m.p.h.

As they hurtled over the enemy vehicles, Adam released half his rockets, two at time, and pressed his thumb down on the gun button. Their efforts were clearly striking home. Balls of flame and columns of thick, black smoke erupted into the sky. All eight Typhoons managed to escape the fray and climbed once more before attacking a wood they thought might be hiding more enemy equipment. Firing their remaining rockets, they left it in flames. Looking back, Adam saw smoke rising high into the sky. A little over ten minutes later, all eight aircraft were touching back down again at B-7.

This pace would be kept up over the days that followed as a ridge of sustained high pressure settled over Normandy, bringing with it hot, dry weather. Three missions by the squadron on the 10th were followed by two on the 11th, one on the 12th and a further two on the 13th. The Hell Hawks and 354th Fighter Group were just as busy. This almost continual bombardment was hammering yet another nail into the coffin of the German campaign as it continued to unravel. Late on the 8th, Le Mans had fallen as Patton's troops continued their rapid sweep eastwards. This was a huge blow to the Germans, because it was the main supply base for 7. Armee and well to the south-east of the Normandy battlefield. Hausser, now promoted to Oberstgruppenführer, had been one of the last to leave, sneaking out in an armoured car with only an orderly and his driver. By now, Patton had a dozen divisions south of Avranches and Bradley ordered him to swing one of his corps north towards Alençon as part of a massive encirclement to close in on the Germans in Normandy. 'Our lead elements on the flankward sweep,' noted Chet Hansen, 'are now well beyond Le Mans, approximately 80 miles from Paris. General [Bradley] is amazed at failure of Germans to grasp seriousness of the situation and feels they are either dumb or thoroughly oblivious to our intentions.'

The German command changes continued. Von Kluge now ordered Eberbach to hand over command of 5. Panzerarmee to Sepp Dietrich. Instead, Eberbach was to command Panzergruppe 'Eberbach', subordinated to 7. Armee, and launch a renewed attack towards Avranches. It was madness. With what? They wouldn't have the giant Tiger IIs Leutnant Richard von Rosen was finally bringing from Mailly-le-Camp – they had been shot up by *Jabos* and badly damaged while on their railway wagons. Von Rosen, who had been in the turret of one at the time of the attack, had also been wounded by shrapnel. It was symptomatic, however, of the dire situation in which the Germans now found themselves. They could barely move at all, let alone attack. Eberbach was incensed by this shift of command none the less. 'Dietrich's totally unqualified for the job!' he complained despairingly, although a lack of command qualifications was the least of their problems. By now, the remains of those divisions that had begun LÜTTICH were almost back at their jump-off points, yet they were being expected to break through with even fewer troops and less equipment. 'It was unaccountable that OKW could not see this,' noted Eberbach, 'after Stalingrad, Tunisia, Crimea, and Krementschug.'

Carl Rambo and the 70th Tank Battalion reached Mortain on 9 August and there they remained for three days. They pulled into a field just short of the town, put their tanks in a ring and got them camouflaged. Their task was to hold their position, because for the time being they did not have the strength to attack. 'All we could do was sit there and let them shell for several days,' said Rambo. 'They blew that earth all to pieces, but never did scratch one of us.' When they finally moved, it was only a few fields further on. Rambo saw a panzer and, as it was sideways to him, he told his gunner to hit it low. Three shells in quick succession whammed into the tank and it began to smoke. 'We got him,'

Rambo told his crew, then ordered them to turn away, firing as they went. Soon after, his gun became so hot that a round got jammed. When they were clear, the gunner jumped out and, using the ramrod that was always left on the main side of the tank beneath the turret, he eventually managed to loosen it and get it clear.

The Germans eventually, and finally, pulled back on the 11th – with the beleaguered 2nd Battalion of the US 120th Infantry still holding out on Hill 314; they were relieved the following morning, having lost 277 killed, wounded and missing. It had been a heroic stand that had done much to limit the German advance. 'Enemy takes Alençon and Argentan,' noted the war diary of the 17. SS-Pionier-Bataillon. 'Fifth and Seventh Armee threatened to be encircled.' Willi Müller and his comrades retreated 15 miles that night, then had to abandon their *Schwimmwagen* when the engine seized for lack of oil. They managed to get a ride in a different vehicle and were told to keep going. They passed through one town, then another, then a third, where all the Germans were clearing out. Then they reached Bellême, east of Alençon and well clear of Normandy, where Müller and his comrades were astonished to find the town already decked with British, French and American flags – he even saw one woman getting flags ready from her upstairs window. 'She abandoned her plan,' noted Müller, 'when she noticed us.'

Eberhard Beck and the gunners of the 277. Infanterie-Division were also pulling back, although not yet out of Normandy. They had remained near Évrecy, but the British were pushing southwards in their part of the line too, between the BLUECOAT area around Aunay and Mont Pinçon and the Canadians south of Caen. On the morning of 9 August, the gunners had reached a former flak position. Although Beck wasn't quite sure where they were, it was near a village and he managed to find a mattress from an old house, which he and one of his comrades put at the bottom of their foxhole as soon as they had dug it. Then enemy shells started screaming over again and by evening they were packing up once more. 'We had to hurry,' wrote Beck. 'The enemy was on our tail.' They had just 300 rounds left, which were placed behind the guns, but the horses were already saddled up and waiting, and they now realized they simply didn't have time to load the ammunition up. Instead, they would fire the lot now in hopes of stalling the Tommies. Beck was on No. 2 gun. 'Whole battery, fire!' came the orders.

The barrels were soon glowing red with the heat. Dusk was falling; it was time to move off again. By first light they had reached their next firing position, beside another former anti-aircraft battery that had been unable to protect itself; it had been destroyed from the air. 'We were not supposed to stay in this position for twenty-four hours,' he noted, 'and it didn't take long before we were spotted by the enemy.' Beck dug in again as shells whooshed over, exploding too close for comfort. Their commander, Leutnant Niesmayr, then called them all together. The enemy had broken through, he told them, and some of them would have to act as infantry from now on. Müller was reassigned as a runner and told to report to the regimental CP. Air bursts were now being fired – shells that exploded at waist height, showering the area with shrapnel. Müller saw one man running for cover only for another shell to burst above him. 'His head was torn off by a shell,' he recorded, 'and he ran a few more steps until he collapsed covered in blood.' No one at the CP could tell him anything, so he hurried back to their battery firing position where once again they were packing up to move out.

TOTALIZE, meanwhile, continued on 9 and 10 August. Sergeant Charlie Martin from the Canadian Queen's Own Rifles was back in the thick of it, attacking Quesnay Wood, which ran either side of the Roman road and where the 12. SS anti-tank guns were dug in; Meyer's men had been helped by the arrival of a self-propelled anti-tank company. The Queen's Own had been supposed to attack alongside Polish tanks, but these had not shown up because they had been accidentally hit by Allied bombers. The Canadian infantry attacked anyway, with artillery support, but were unable to clear it; the Queen's Own lost a further eighty-five men, including another of Martin's great mates, Jimmy Browne. 'When he was killed by a sniper's bullet,' noted Martin, 'sadness filled the air like lead.'

TOTALIZE had burned itself out by 10 August, but while the breakthrough had again not occurred, they had at last pushed on south well beyond Caen and stretched 12. SS and the remaining infantry to breaking point. It had certainly been a bleak couple of days for Kurt Meyer and his men. 'The enlisted soldiers and the officers presented a pitiful picture,' he noted. They were, he knew, at the end of their tether. 'Why didn't we call it quits? Why did we continue this senseless struggle?' His division pulled back and handed over to the 85. Infanterie on 12 August. By this time, Meyer had just twenty armoured fighting vehicles left, 300 grenadiers, four 88mm flak guns and a handful of other guns. His division, which had arrived in Normandy with 20,504 men, was now less than 1,000 strong.

Everywhere, the Allies were pressing forward, with one exception: the original eastern flank on the far side of the River Orne north-east of Caen. Here, Denis Edwards, Richard Todd, Hubert Fauré and Frank Wright were all still in much the same place as they had been immediately after the invasion. It had been like the Western Front of 1914–18, with the men dug in, rotating in and out of position but essentially moving very little as both sides held their ground. 'We have been in Normandy for seventy days or so,' Denis Edwards scribbled in his diary on 15 August, 'and during that time we had never moved more than a few miles from our bridges.' German counter-attacks along that part of the line had been repulsed, while the British and Canadian effort had been southwards; after all, there was little point trying to attack eastwards over the flooded Dives Valley.

British Second Army, meanwhile, continued on from the gains made by BLUECOAT, while the Canadians now launched Operation TRACTABLE, the latest drive on Falaise. A tantalizing opportunity was rapidly opening up to trap the remains of the bulk of the German armies in Normandy in a devastating encirclement. Because of LÜTTICH, a large part of the German forces had concentrated to the west of Falaise. Now that the counter-attack had failed, however, they were being pressed from all sides. If the Allies were quick, there was a chance for the American troops now to the south of the ancient Normandy city and the British, Canadians and Poles to the north to seal off the Germans' escape route. Already, this narrowing corridor was being referred to as the 'Falaise Gap' or 'Pocket'.

On 13 August, Sergeant Walter Caines attended an O Group of the 4th Dorsets where they were given an intelligence briefing on the current situation. 'We were informed that troops well to our left had gone well past the town of Caen and that the Americans had driven well south,' he noted, 'and were now tightening the neck of the Falaise Gap.' The following day, the brigade attacked the village of Proussy, some 14 miles south-west of Ondefontaine, which they had captured during BLUE-COAT. The 4th Dorsets' objective was a hill at the edge of the village. They attacked through enemy shelling, but Caines reckoned the enemy had been pretty well plastered by their own artillery and the companies were able to advance swiftly with only a few casualties. 'Many prisoners were captured during this push,' wrote Caines, 'all seemed fully prepared to give themselves up to us. Some of them were a pitiful sight to see, they looked unshaven, hungry and very badly clothed.'

Yet although most of Brittany had been swiftly overrun, because of

Hitler's fortress order the defenders of Brest, Lorient and Saint-Malo had all done as ordered and so far had refused to throw in the towel, which meant some unpleasant and difficult fighting continued long after Patton's armour had swept up most of the peninsula. And it was the infantry who had been left to fight it out, while Patton's mobile forces turned east.

The American 121st Infantry, for example, had been given Dinard as an objective, a small and comparatively insignificant town on the opposite side of the narrow estuary from Saint-Malo. In four days of bitter fighting between 8 and 12 August, Lieutenant Richard Blackburn's 1st Battalion had got nowhere against a mass of enemy strongpoints, while the 3rd Battalion, moving on their flank, had managed to become encircled, something that would have been ridiculous in the circumstances of the rest of the campaign had it not been so tragic. Because, strategically, Dinard was of little importance, and because most of Third Army was now driving east, there had been precious few troops with which to relieve the beleaguered 121st. The encircled 3rd Battalion had held out for four days without any resupply at all before finally being relieved with the help of the 331st Infantry. Blackburn's Company A had begun the push to Dinard with 180 men and six officers, but by the time they resumed their drive on 13 August they had only three officers and around a hundred men. On Sunday, 13 August they were finally approaching the town. Although the campaign was nearly over, they were still expecting a tough fight and Captain Arthur Kaiser, the Company A commander, sought out Blackburn. The two had been become close friends, a deep camaraderie forged over the past five weeks of intense combat. Kaiser was on edge, however, and wanted to make a pact that, should one or other of them not make it through the day, the survivor would write to the other's parents, explaining exactly how he had been killed and then visit them when he eventually got home. Blackburn agreed and they shook hands on it. It left Blackburn feeling deeply unsettled, however.

Their attack was supported by artillery and Kaiser planned to assault with three platoons up and Blackburn following with 4 Platoon plus the mortars and machine guns. Bang on schedule, at 9.30 a.m., the guns stopped firing and Kaiser came over to Blackburn to talk through some last-minute instructions. They were on their knees looking at a map when enemy fire began whooshing in and exploding around them. Just as Kaiser stood up to move, a shell hit the tree above them – neither had heard it coming in, so it must have been an anti-tank round – and shrapnel burst all around.

'Oh, Blackie, no . . .' said Kaiser and collapsed. Horrified, Blackburn laid him down as blood sprayed from his friend's chest. 'As I took my hands away from the Captain's lifeless body,' he wrote, 'they were completely covered in blood; and I realized his chest had been ripped open by several large pieces of shrapnel.' Blackburn reeled in shock and despair. Tears were streaming down Kaiser's grimy face, even though he had died in moments. Blackburn struggled to absorb the enormity of what had happened; he had seen countless dead, but it was the shock of his friend being alive and talking to him one moment and then gone the next that he found impossible to fathom.

He was wounded himself, with small shrapnel fragments in his arm and hip, but, with Kaiser dead, he was now company commander. Pausing a moment, he briefly closed his eyes and prayed for guidance. Then he was up and ordering his men forward – they needed to get moving – although with each pace he felt a shot of pain in his hip. Realizing his backside was also covered in blood, he quickly dropped his trousers and had a medic pour sulfa powder on to his wounds and patch him up. Another soldier had been killed nearby, while a further man had lost a leg. Blackburn knew he had been lucky and, although it was painful to walk, he decided he had to stay with the company.

The attack was successful and they captured the German gun crew that same afternoon. Blackburn realized it was more than likely that these were the men that had killed Kaiser and the others. As the Germans walked towards them with their hands aloft, he heard several of his men flick their safety catches. 'But I was always taught to do what was just and to love mercy,' he wrote, 'even in a world that seemed to have gone mad.' He ordered his men to hold their fire.

The final assault on Dinard jumped off at 9 a.m. the following day, 14 August. Initially they secured their objectives rapidly, until by the afternoon they had to cross open ground and once again came under withering fire. They pressed on, however, and by around 4 p.m. had reached the water's edge and finally the guns fell silent. Some 13,000 prisoners were taken in the Saint-Malo–Dinard operation, but at a terrible cost. In Company A, there were just eighty-four men left from the 180 that had begun the advance on 8 August. The number was about to be reduced to eighty-three, as Blackburn now finally went to the first aid collection unit, standing in the queue of walking wounded. Buildings were still burning and smoke rising into the sky, while the streets were littered with battle debris and the dead, both Germans and civilians. The smell was overpowering. Once Blackburn was seen he was swiftly told he would not be returning to his unit any time soon. Rather, he was being evacuated back to England. Richard Blackburn's Normandy campaign was over.

Back in action in VIII Corps' sector were the men of the 2nd Northants Yeomanry. Just ten days earlier, after BLUECOAT, Reg Spittles and his fellows had had just fourteen tanks, but now, once again, they were back at full strength of sixty-five, including a new Challenger – a Cromwell equipped with a new turret and armed with a 17-pounder. On the night of the 14th they reached the edge of Vassy, a small town some 25 miles due west of Falaise. By morning, however, the infantry found the town had been evacuated and so they pressed on, the speed of the Cromwells taking them all the way to Flers, some 12 miles to the south, that same day.

The German evacuation from Flers was the attempt to withdraw the westernmost parts of 7. Armee. Hitler was still insisting on counter-attacking with Eberbach's phantom panzer force, but this was clearly now impossible. On the evening of 14 August, von Kluge left La Roche-Guyon and drove to the front to confer with Sepp Dietrich at 5. Panzerarmee headquarters. It was agreed the situation was utterly hopeless, but early the following day von Kluge headed to meet with Eberbach and Hausser at Nécy, about 6 miles south of Falaise. En route, he was attacked by *Jabos* and his radio car destroyed. The field marshal was now completely uncontactable and no one knew where he was, which meant he was unable to exercise any kind of command. Late that evening, Hitler agreed that Hausser should be in temporary charge, but before that order reached 5. Armee von Kluge reappeared. It was patently clear to all that the withdrawal order was already too late, but still needed none the less. None of them dared defy the Führer, however, despite the carnage on the roads and despite the near complete encirclement.

Meanwhile, Operation TRACTABLE had jumped off on the 14th as the Canadians began their renewed drive to Falaise in an effort to close the gap. The Germans were now completely encircled, so the hope was to drive swiftly south and cut off those still in the pocket. Once again, this was General Simonds' plan and he decided to follow a similar format to TOTALIZE. There would be combined-arms columns, heavy bombing and lots of armour to push through, although this time they would attack in daytime, but with smokescreens to cover their advance.

Coningham's Second TAF attacked first with medium bombers at

11.37 a.m., then 805 aircraft of Bomber Command began arriving at 2 p.m. For the most part, the bombing was incredibly accurate until, half-way through the raids, some aircraft began dropping their bombs on a quarry where a Canadian artillery regiment was located. The Canadians set off yellow warning flares; unfortunately, through one of those terrible, inadvertent but tragic mistakes that happen in war, the marker flares were also yellow that day. Down below, Sergeant Charlie Martin could see what was happening. 'Talk about fear! We were helpless,' he wrote. 'Other British planes, who seemed to know better, were swarming their own bombers, shooting and stunting, trying to warn them away.' All they could do was pump out more yellow smoke, but this was literally adding fuel to the fire. Most managed to take cover in their slit-trenches, but thirteen men were killed, fifty-three injured and a number of vehicles and guns destroyed. Charlie Martin was nearly one of the casualties, but had taken cover in a nearby house rather than his slit-trench. When it was over, he discovered his trench had taken a direct hit.

The smokescreens also caused confusion, and then the Canadians, British and Poles of II Canadian Corps had to cross the River Laize. Heavy fighting took place all afternoon as 12. SS and the last remnants of the German infantry divisions fought against overwhelming enemy fire-power. Kurt Meyer lost another old and trusted friend that afternoon, Sturmbannführer Karl-Heinz Prinz, commander of II. SS-Panzer-Regiment 12. 'Once again I was witness to the last battle of a warrior friend,' Meyer wrote. 'Prinz had been with me on all fronts since 1940.' It was an artillery shell that did for him, thousands of them screaming over and hammering the German positions. Typhoons also swooped in with their rockets while Meyer was with one of his regiment commanders, Max Wünsche, on Hill 159, a commanding position already being attacked by tanks and infantry. Rockets exploded around them and Meyer felt a burning pain on his head; blood ran down his face. Feeling giddy, he glanced back at the road – his *Kübelwagen* had vanished, but then it reappeared with one of his men at the wheel. Urging Meyer to jump in, together they sped off; later, as dusk fell and with the Allies through Potigny and nearing Falaise, Meyer pulled his men back.

The following day, the 15th, Simonds was able to send his armoured divisions around the ever-weakening blocking force and Falaise finally fell the next day, Wednesday, 16 August. The remnants of 21. Panzer were split in two: one *Kampfgruppe*, with all the tanks, fell into the Falaise Pocket, but Major Hans von Luck's battle group remained just outside. He was now given orders to set up a blocking position near Vimoutiers, close to where Rommel had been wounded. At La Roche-Guyon, von Kluge had been waiting all morning for an answer to his request to withdraw. At 12.45 p.m., he finally rang General Alfred Jodl at the OKW. 'No matter how many orders are issued,' von Kluge told him, 'the troops cannot, are not able to, are not strong enough to defeat the enemy. It would be a fateful error to succumb to a hope that cannot be fulfilled and no power in this world can accomplish his will through an order it may give. That is the situation.' Calling off, he then ordered Speidel to prepare the withdrawal orders. When there was still no response at 2.30 p.m., von Kluge finally issued the withdrawal nine minutes later. The field marshal was promptly sacked for this – after all, Hitler needed someone to blame – and replaced with Feldmarschall Walter Model, who would not be able to reach the front for at least two days.

Fighting continued. Ken Tout spent a few days as a gunner in a Firefly, as they headed to Saint-Pierre-sur-Dives to try to close the gap. By 17 August, because of a shortage of tank commanders, he was given command of a Sherman instead. Stanley Christopherson and the Sherwood Rangers had been in action pretty much continually since BLUECOAT. On 17 August, they helped capture Berjou, halfway between Vire and Falaise and at the western end of the Falaise Pocket. They took the hill in a classic example of all-arms cooperation, but not without suffering more losses as shells and mortars rained down on their assault. C Squadron had, by then, lost all its officers except the commander. That evening, after Berjou had fallen, Christopherson walked to the end of the village and looked down on the Noireau River. 'From there,' he noted, 'I had a wonderful view of the surrounding country and could fully appreciate why the mortar and shellfire had been so accurate. The Germans could see every movement that we made.'

'Between August 7 and August 17,' noted Lieutenant Orion Shockley, 'we lost fifty-three men to mortar, artillery, machine-gun and rifle fire.' Of these, eleven had been killed. By 17 August, he and his company were near Saint-Hilaire-de-Briouze, 12 miles south of Falaise and part of First Army's sweep around the south of the pocket. It was getting dark as they approached the village and, as they reached the road through, a German half-track came slowly round the bend. Shockley stepped out and shot at it with his pistol, hitting a door but nothing more and the half-track rumbled on – one that had got away.

Most did not, however. The countryside around Falaise was – and is – stunningly beautiful, normally an Eden of green fecundity and tranquil rural charm. Villages linked by weaving, narrow country lanes dotted this pastureland of woods, fields and streams. Yet in this third week of August, it had become a scene from hell as desperate German troops tried to escape through the last remaining routes available. Saint-Lambert-sur-Dive and Chambois, once two of the most lovely villages in all Normandy, had become a death trap as men, tanks, half-tracks, horses and wagons funnelled into the fords and narrow bridges across the river. No longer waiting only for nighttime, in this August heatwave they were easy prey for the *Jabos*. Major Dick Turner and the fighter boys of the 354th, now operating from a new base not far from Rennes, were in action every day. Between 14 and 18 August, Turner flew five patrols, strafing German columns and shooting up anything that moved.

From his blocking position, Hans von Luck could see the endgame of the Normandy battle being played; he had a grand view and watched the *Jabos* swooping down and the mushroom clouds of exploding bombs. He recalled an old Crusader knight's poem: ' "Man, horse, and truck by the Lord were struck." ' It had come to his mind twice before – near Moscow in December 1941, in North Africa in 1943. And now.

Charlie Martin, meanwhile, was in Maizières, a few miles to the north-east of Falaise. He had already seen his fill of carnage and destruction, but what he now witnessed was on an entirely different scale. The sunken roads were littered with the dead, with burned-out equipment and vehicles. 'This was an awful price of war,' he noted, 'the bodies of enemy soldiers, dead horses and cows, broken wagons, disabled anti-tank guns and burned trucks.' The stench was overwhelming. Much to his distress, he saw too many civilians among the dead. Liberty was coming at a very heavy price in Normandy as one town or village after another was flattened and lives were destroyed. The levels of destruction were truly titanic: Caen largely obliterated, along with Saint-Lô, Coutances, Vire, Aunay, Villers-Bocage and Falaise, birthplace of William the Conqueror. In between, far too many villages had been completely erased. The typhoon of war had, indeed, been terrible.

The gap was finally closed on the afternoon of Saturday, 19 August after the Poles, who had learned valuable lessons of combat in quick time, had taken the key Hill 262, Mont Ormel, up which one of the prime German escape routes wound its way. From here, all the way down to the Dives Valley, the road was thick with carnage. Truly, this was a scarring picture of defeat and the very terrible cost of war. But the battle for Normandy was over.

Postscript

ON 22 AUGUST, FLIGHT Sergeant Ken Adam saw the battlefield himself, three days after the gap had been closed and the last German troops had managed to get away. The squadron had been given a rare day off, so he and a number of other pilots took a truck and drove over to the Falaise area. He soon wished he hadn't. Their truck became stuck among a long British armoured column moving at a snail's pace through the devastation. The road – or what was left of it – was choked with wreckage, swollen corpses and dead cattle and horses. 'The smell was terrible,' he recalled, and although they all put handkerchiefs over their faces, it did little to help; the sickly sweet smell of death stuck to their clothes for days to come. 'This was my first contact on the ground with the dead and what had been the enemy,' he said. In the air, most pilots were somewhat removed from the realities on the ground. Being so close to the horror came as a profound shock. Strangely, however, Adam felt more affected by the sight of bloated, rotting horses and cows than he did the many enemy dead. As a German Jew, he and his family had been cast out; they were no longer his countrymen lying there, but the enemy, just as they were to everyone else in the squadron. It really was, though, a pitiful and appalling sight. Just beyond Saint-Lambert-sur-Dives, for example, was a lane that ran down to a ford in the river, from which another winding, narrow road, lined by hedgerows, ran up to the village. The lane on either side of the ford and the crossing point itself were absolutely filled with the carnage. It was impossible to walk a clear path through the density of corpses, broken wagons, abandoned Panthers, assault guns, field guns and other detritus. Black-and-white photographs survive of this destruction and, even though there is no colour and no smell, it is hard not to bring a hand to the mouth at the horror of it all.

Some did get away. Willi Müller was one and so was Hauptmann Helmut Ritgen, who had been pulled out of Normandy along with the rest of the Panzer-Lehr survivors before LÜTTICH. The newly promoted Oberführer Kurt Meyer also got away, although only just and with only a handful of men; he had been fortunate that the division had been stationed in that area before the invasion and he knew the lay of the land well. Eberhard Beck was captured on 21 August, his ordeal finally over.

For the victors, there was little rest, particularly not for the armoured units, who now sped forward in the most rapid extended advance in history. At no other time in Europe have attacking armies covered quite so much territory – it eclipsed even the astonishing German advance across France back in 1940. The River Seine was crossed by 25 August; that same day Paris fell, and without being destroyed by the retreating Germans first, as Hitler had ordered. Among the first troops into the city were those of Général Leclerc's French armoured division. By 10 September, the Allied armies had liberated Belgium and stood at the borders of Germany and Holland, helped by the speed of the American tank destroyers and British-built Cromwell tanks. These lighter tanks and TDs often get hauled over the coals for not being Panthers or Tigers, but those mechanically unreliable monsters could not have achieved what the Allies did in the days that followed the end of the battle for Normandy.

Much criticism has been poured on to the Allied efforts in Normandy, but this has often been made by armchair historians too quick to be dazzled by rapid-firing machine guns, big tanks, fiendish anti-tank guns and the supposed tactical acuity of the Germans. The British and Canadians have been blamed for being too stodgy, too ponderous and too scared to take risks. Even the Americans have come under the cosh for unimaginative tactics and for being too slow in the hedgerows. This criticism is, however, both misplaced and unfair. For all the Allies' firepower and incredible logistics arm, it was the infantry and the armour who had to take most of the ground and no one can justifiably criticize these men – mostly conscripts from democratic countries rather than from totalitarian militaristic states – for being slow. The risks were simply enormous, the sacrifice immense. The Sherwood Rangers Yeomanry, for example, lost 44 officers even though the full establishment was only 36. A further 175 men of other ranks were lost from 200 in tanks in the regiment during the Normandy campaign. The 116th Infantry lost 100 per cent of its fighting strength. The incredible conveyor belt of replacements kept them going, but these units in the front line in Normandy suffered appallingly. Of course mistakes were made, and different decisions might have made a difference, but, on the whole, these citizen armies performed incredibly well.

By any reckoning, it was certainly a great Allied victory. Just 50,000 Germans and two dozen panzers escaped the Falaise Pocket. Johannes Börner, of the 3. Fallschirmjäger-Division, was one of only twelve men from his company that made it. Two entire armies – 7. Armee and 5. Panzerarmee – had been effectively annihilated, including almost all their guns and 2,500 tanks, and it had been achieved in 74 days, or 77 if one includes the final bit of fighting in Normandy, which ended on 22 August – that was, in fact, nearly two weeks better than Montgomery had surmised before the invasion. It is true the campaign did not pan out exactly as he had predicted, but Monty and all the senior commanders who signed up to the OVERLORD plan could be forgiven for assuming that the Germans would retreat in stages as they had in the past. As Rommel pointed out to Hitler at Margival on 17 June, it made no military sense to fight so close to the coast while in range of Allied naval guns. Rather, the criticism of the day from Tedder et al. was a result of frustration with the V-1 campaign, Montgomery's unfailing ability to get up the nose of his peers and his inability to admit the campaign was going anything other than entirely to plan. It wasn't, but it didn't really matter because, in the end, they did better than anticipated. That should not be forgotten.

Time, however, allows a more nuanced and balanced picture, and one in which the operational level of war, so often ignored, is reinserted. The management of these armies, air forces and navies was truly astonishing. As the Germans discovered, it was very difficult indeed to fight offensively in Normandy, especially when their enemy was so much better at fighting wars than they were. As Michael Wittmann's blaze of glory showed at Villers-Bocage, it was not much use pulling off a small tactical engagement if every other part of the war effort was found wanting. At almost every level, the Germans were failed by their high command. They simply never had enough of anything and were forced to dance to the Allies' tune, not the other way around. The grinding down of their celebrated panzer divisions, drawing them into battle in detail and before they were ready, ensured they could never manoeuvre and operate in the way they were designed to do. For far too long, the picture has been painted of the British, especially, banging their heads against a brick wall of panzer divisions, when in fact it was the other way round.

The German command structures were ridiculous – unwieldy, divisive and deeply unhelpful to the men and generals forced to work around these parallel commands, vacillations and hash of orders. Not only was Hitler too far away, but for much of the time so was Rommel, then von Kluge and the army commanders. While Monty and Bradley camped out near the front, Rommel remained at the luxurious chateau of La Roche-Guyon. Even once it was plain where the main invasion was, he still stayed put. Had he not been endlessly driving back and forth to the front, but actually closer to where he should have been, he might have avoided the near-fatal shooting he suffered on 17 July.

Churchill was incredulous over how so many Allied mouths could be kept regularly fed. The logistics were mind-bogglingly complicated and quite superbly executed. By 4 September, for example, the Mulberry B had delivered 39,743 vehicles, 220,231 personnel and, in total, 517,844 tons of supplies. Then there were the beaches, which on average, collectively, continued to deliver some 16,000 tons of supplies per day. Enough fuel was provided to keep over 100,000 Allied vehicles on the road. On average a tank used 8,000 gallons of fuel a week and an entire armoured division some 60,000 per day. It was an incredible amount and yet it was provided, mostly by four ship-to-shore pipelines that were built in each beach area and which allowed a tanker to discharge 600 tons of fuel per hour. Code-named 'Tombola', it was another ingenious innovation. In mid-August, the PLUTO pipeline was laid under the sea from England and also became operational. That was a further technological breakthrough, as it needed to be strong enough to withstand the pressure of lying on the sea bed while also large and sturdy enough to cope with a constant flow of fuel. The Germans, meanwhile, had focused much of their innovative energy on weapons such as the V-1s, which killed a fair number of civilians but not one combat serviceman at the front.

In all, thirty-seven German divisions fought in Normandy, amounting to some half a million men, and by the end of it well over 300,000 had been killed, wounded, lost or captured. Exact figures are impossible to confirm; one army record claims the 12. SS lost just 8,000 from their original strength of 20,500, but this is a low figure for a division that escaped from the Falaise Gap before it was closed by the Allies with no more than a few hundred men at the absolute most. The 12. SS had effectively ceased to exist by the end of Normandy, while 21. Panzer lost its entire arsenal of 167 tanks and assault guns along with some 350 officers and 12,000 other ranks. In fact, of the seven panzer divisions trapped in the Falaise Pocket, only around 1,300 men and just two dozen tanks escaped – from 140,000 of the best-equipped and best-trained divisions the Germans had and a total of around 2,500 panzers that had been sent to Normandy. Those are staggering statistics and a demonstration of just how crushing the defeat of the cream of German units really was.

The Allies lost some 209,000 casualties out of over 2 million brought across the Channel, 83,045 for 21st Army Group and an even higher 125,847 from the US ground forces, of whom around 37,000 were killed. In addition, the Allied air forces suffered some 16,714 dead, a huge number, while the suffering of the French amounted to 15–20,000 dead, mostly as a result of Allied bombs. Excluding German POWs, that amounts to a daily casualty rate of around 6,870, worse than the Somme, Passchendaele and Verdun in the First World War, three battles usually viewed as a benchmark for wanton slaughter.

Of the men and women featured in this narrative, most survived, although many only just. Henry Bowles recovered from his six bullets and rejoined his brother in the Big Red One in time for the Battle of the Bulge in December 1944–January 1945. Bob Slaughter made it back too, as did Richard Blackburn. Others were wounded later on, such as Bob Roberts and John Raaen, although the latter remained in the US Army and rose to become a general. Hans von Luck survived the war and then ten years in a Gulag in the Soviet Union, and later became a highly successful businessman, importing coffee from South America. He also became a favourite contributor to British Army battlefield studies and staff rides. 'He was absolutely charming,' recalls Dr Peter Caddick-Adams, who knew him well from those tours, 'and could drink absolutely anything without any apparent effect.' A regular of Canadian battlefield studies post-war was Hans Siegel, who also recovered from both wounds and the war. Richard von Rosen also survived and later married the daughter of Caesar von Hofacker, who had been executed for his part in the July plot against Hitler. He died in 2015, aged ninety-three. Helmut Ritgen was another guest of the Soviet Union but survived, as did Cornelius Tauber, Willi Müller, Eberhard Beck, Karl Wegner and Franz

Gockel. Wegner and Gockel regularly returned to Normandy in later life and struck up friendships with former adversaries.

Kurt Meyer was captured in September 1944 and taken to Britain, where in bugged conversations with other prisoners he revealed the depths of his devotion to National Socialism. After the war, he was tried for war crimes, and specifically for the murder of Canadian prisoners at the Abbey d'Ardenne on 8 June. Although he was cleared of issuing direct orders for their execution, Meyer was none the less found guilty of their deaths as the commanding officer of the men who carried out the execution. Sentenced to death, he was reprieved and given a life sentence, which was then commuted. By 1951 he was back in Germany and was released from prison in 1955. Two years later, he published his memoirs, *Grenadiere*, which painted a picture of heroic duty and airbrushed any notion of criminality. They remain, though, a vivid account of frontline action with the Waffen-SS.

Of the pilots and aircrew, Bert Stiles finished his bomber tour, transferred to fighters and was killed in action in November 1944. Gabby Gabreski clipped a wing during a ground attack in Germany in July 1944, crashed his plane and was captured. It had been his last flight before flying home. After the war, he stayed in the United States Air Forces and flew in Korea. So too did Dick Turner, who was posted home soon after the Normandy campaign was over. Ken Adam remained with 609 Squadron until the end of the war and went on to become a celebrated filmset designer. He was responsible for most of the early Bond production design, as well as that of *Chitty Chitty Bang Bang*, and later won an Oscar for *The Madness of King George*. His Oscar stood in a corner of his study next to a scale model of his Typhoon. Both Truman Smith and Ken Handley finally completed their tours just before the end of the Normandy campaign and survived to live long and fruitful lives. Stanley Christopherson also made it to the end of the war. By this time, the Sherwood Rangers had collected sixteen battle honours since the invasion and over the course of the war became the single unit in the British Army with more battle honours than any other. Later in life, this unfailingly charming and cheerful fellow suffered terrible bouts of depression brought on by his wartime experiences. So too did John Semken; his war came to an end after five long years in March 1945 when he suffered a complete breakdown.

Charlie Martin returned to Canada with his English wife; so too did Bob Roberts, although he later moved back to Britain and spent much of his married and professional life on the south coast of England. Yogi Jenson remained in the Royal Canadian Navy before retiring to Nova Scotia and becoming a much-loved artist and writer. Robert Woollcombe survived the war and wrote several books, including a timeless classic about his time in the war, *Lion Rampant*. Reg Spittles also survived and lived a long life, handwriting his memoirs and donating them to the Bovington Tank Museum. Ken Tout got through the war, married, had children, and had a long and successful career working for various charities, before retiring to the Sussex coast. Ambrose Lampen, whose efforts creating the Mulberry at Arromanches can still be seen today, emigrated to California. Denis Edwards, Hubert Fauré and Frank Wright all made it through, as did Richard Todd, who became one of Britain's best-known film stars. He portrayed Guy Gibson in *The Dam Busters* and even took the role of John Howard in the movie *The Longest Day* about D-Day. Mary Mulry continued nursing until the end of the war, then married and settled in England.

Orion Shockley also made it through the war, as did Carl Rambo. So too did Mark Alexander and Dick Winters. The latter became world-famous after the release first of Stephen Ambrose's book *Band of Brothers* and then the internationally acclaimed and successful HBO TV series of the same name. Walter Halloran went through the rest of the war and later served in Vietnam too. They all lived to old age. The legendary war correspondent Ernie Pyle, however, did not. Offered the chance to go to the Pacific, he was covering the Battle of Okinawa in April 1945 when he was shot and killed by a Japanese machine-gunner. He was deeply mourned in America, where he had become one of the best-loved writers in the country.

Of the commanders, Günther von Kluge committed suicide on 20 August 1944, while Rommel recovered from his accident only to be implicated in the Hitler plot. Visited by two SS men at his home in October 1944, he was given a choice: to swallow cyanide right away and have a state funeral, or to allow himself to be arrested, put on trial, found guilty and executed for treason. After bidding his beloved wife and son farewell, he took the cyanide. After the war, Speidel tried to make Rommel out as a great hero and committed to ousting Hitler, but there is, in reality, no proof at all that he was involved. Speidel himself somehow survived the post-July-plot witch hunt and later served in the West German army. Fritz Bayerlein commanded a corps and later an army, and was, like Heinrich Eberbach and Geyr von Schweppenburg, captured at

No: two generals   — becoming its head!

the end of the war. All three later helped the Americans with interviews and written studies of German perspectives in the war.

Montgomery and Bradley both remained in post and wrote post-war memoirs – in Bradley's case twice over, with Chet Hansen ghosting one of the versions for him. Eisenhower served two terms as president of the United States. Pete Quesada remained in the air force and lived to old age, but Mary Coningham was killed in a plane crash over the Bermuda Triangle in January 1948, while both Trafford Leigh-Mallory and Admiral Bertram Ramsay were similarly killed in flying accidents, both before 1944 was out. General Patton also died prematurely, this time in a car accident in Germany after the end of the war, by which time he had become one of the most celebrated and well-known Allied generals of the war. Like Monty, however, he has remained something of a controversial figure ever since.

Robert Leblanc managed to survive the internecine spats and threats of betrayal, later commanding a semi-formal battalion of French troops. After the war he was feted as a hero of the Résistance. Geneviève Dubosq also survived the war, as did all her family. Général Charles de Gaulle did indeed become the democratically elected president and so the leader of free France after all.

Normandy, and indeed all of France, took some time to recover from the ordeal of the war. Normandy, especially, took long years to rebuild its shattered cities, towns and villages. For a while after, wrecked tanks and other detritus littered the countryside, and farmers were able to make a tidy sum from the large amounts of scrap metal they accumulated; the remains of Michael Wittmann's Tiger ended up in a farmer's barn for decades. Gradually, though, and especially once the combatant nations had created large cemeteries for the thousands slain in the battle, Normandy became an important place of pilgrimage. Its church towers were rebuilt, the tank tracks disappeared and normal life returned. Today it is a stunningly beautiful part of the world. On Utah, Omaha, Gold, Juno and Sword, there are now holidaymakers, kite-surfers and children enjoying the lush sands and sea. Old bunkers remain, however, while museums have sprung up all along the coast. The war is big business – Normandy thrives on the battle of 1944, not that anyone could possibly resent this burgeoning economy after all the suffering they endured.

The story of the battle itself has evolved, the narrative changing as the world changes, and much of it is mired in myth. It is important, though, to remember what happened there, back in 1944, and to recognize the

enormous sacrifice and carnage. It was a terrible battle, and what followed, until the final surrender in May 1945, was every bit as horrific.
Yet out of this tragedy a better world did emerge – and certainly a better
Europe. For the main combatant nations, long years of peace ensued – a
peace still enjoyed to this day.

Not so long ago, I climbed up to Mont Ormel, the site of the end of the
Normandy battle. It is a gorgeous spot. From this wonderful vantage
point it was possible to see the entire Falaise Gap laid out before me. It
twinkled in the summery sun, a picture of tranquil beauty, of myriad
fields, small villages, church spires and lush farmland. It was almost
impossible to believe that down below and on the road just to the left of
where I stood there had once been such terrible scenes of suffering and
desolation. It was a reminder of the extraordinary regenerative power of
the world in which we live, but also that we must look after it and remember how easily we can throw this haven back into turmoil.

Glossary

ADC	aide-de-camp
C-in-C	commander-in-chief
CO	commanding officer
Corncob	individual blockship sunk to make an offshore breakwater
Corps	army unit consisting of two or more divisions
CP	command post
Division	army unit of all arms, usually with a focus in either infantry or armour – the basic military unit by which size and scale of a force was judged in the Second World War
Fallschirmjäger	German paratroopers
FOB	forward observer, bombardment (naval)
Gefreiter	corporal
Gooseberry	row of Corncobs forming a breakwater
HE	high explosive
Heeresgruppe	Army Group
Leaguer	night-time position of tanks out of the front line, usually in a circle with the guns pointing outwards
Maquis	group of French resistance fighters
OB West	*Oberbefehl West*: German Army Command in the West
Oberst	colonel
Obersturmbannführer	lieutenant-colonel
OKW	*Oberkommando der Wehrmacht*: German Combined Operations Staff
OP	observation post
Phoenix	largest part of the Mulberry; a caisson, a block of the harbour wall
PIR	Parachute Infantry Regiment

PSP	pierced steel plating (for creating all-weather airfield runways)
RAMC	Royal Army Medical Corps
RCN	Royal Canadian Navy
RTR	Royal Tank Regiment
Schwere Panzerabteilung	Heavy Tank Battalion
Spud	floating pier end that could rise and fall with the tide
Standartenführer	Waffen-SS equivalent of *Oberst*
Sturmbannführer	Waffen-SS equivalent of major
TI	target indicator
TURCO	Turn Around Control
VCP	vehicle collecting point
Whale	section of floating pier
WN	*Widerstandsnest* – strongpoint

Constructing the caissons, or 'Phoenixes', that will make up the walls of the Mulberry harbours.

The Mulberry B Artificial Harbour at Arromanches

A sketch from the papers of Lieutenant Ambrose Lampen.

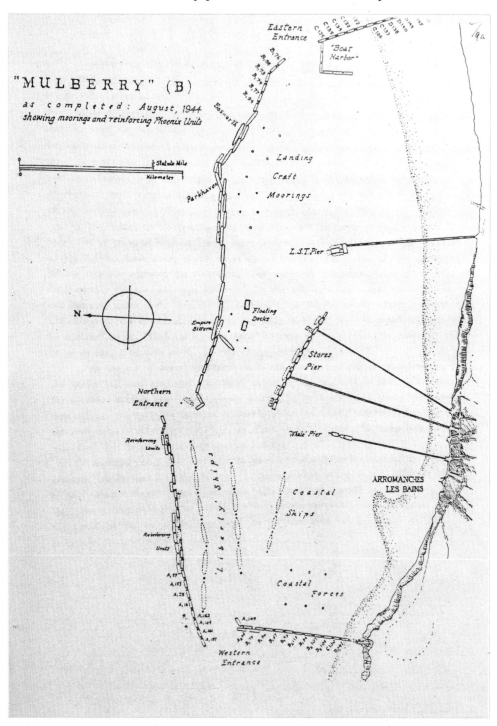

British Infantry Battalion

War strength: 36 officers, 809 men. Total 845.

	Battalion Headquarters	Headquarter company			Support company					4 rifle companies (A, B, C, D)	
		Headquarters	Signal Platoon	Administrative Platoon	Headquarters	3in mortar Platoon	Carrier Platoon	Anti-tank Platoon	Pioneer Platoon	Headquarters	Platoon x 3
Battalion Commander *Lieutenant-colonel*	1										
Second in Command – *Major*	1										
Major/Captain		1			1					1	
Adjutants (Captain)	1										
Captains								1	1	1	
Subalterns	1		1	1		1	1	1	1		1
Quartermaster				1							
TOTAL OFFICERS	4	1	1	2	1	1	1	2	1	2	1
Warrant officers and other ranks	45	5	35	51	8	41	60	51	21	14	36
TOTAL	49	6	36	53	9	42	62	53	22	16	37

Personnel attached 1 Chaplain (*Royal Army Chaplain Department*)

	Battalion Headquarters	Headquarters	Signal Platoon	Administrative Platoon	Headquarters	3in mortar Platoon	Carrier Platoon	Anti-tank Platoon	Pioneer Platoon	Headquarters	Platoon x 3
Medical Officer (*Royal Army Medical Corps*)	1										
Armourers and car mechanics (*REME*)				3		1	1	2			
Cobbler (*Royal Army Ordnance Corps*)				1							
Cooks (*Army Catering Corps*)				15							

Breakdown of 21st Army Group Personnel

August 1944[1]

ARMS

Royal Artillery	18%
Infantry (inc. airborne troops)	14%
Royal Engineers	13%
Royal Armoured Corps	6%
Royal Corps of Signals	5%
TOTAL	**56%**

SERVICES

Royal Army Service Corps	15%
Pioneer Corps	10%
Royal Electrical and Mechanical Engineers	5%

Royal Army Medical Corps	4%
Royal Army Chaplain's Department	
Royal Army Ordnance Corps	
Royal Army Pay Corps	
Royal Army Veterinary Corps	
Royal Army Educational Corps	
Intelligence Corps	10%
Army Physical Training Corps	
Army Catering Corps	
Corps of Military Police	
Military Provost Staff Corps	
TOTAL (for services)	**44%**

[1] *Percentages based on 660,000 men.*

[2] *The relative strength of the artillery resulted from doctrines evolved from First World War experience.*

Royal Regiment of Artillery

A single corps that recruited, trained and instructed in the use of the various means of this arm. All the units were numbered and kept the traditional name of the regiment.

Composition

1. Regiments from the Regular Army or Territorial Army.

2. Regiments from the former mounted cavalry of the Territorial Army (Yeomanry), transferred to the Royal Artillery. Traditionally they kept their original name at the same time as having a number – e.g. 153rd (Leicestershire Yeomanry) Field Regiment, Royal Artillery, TA.

3. Regiments of the Royal Horse Artillery transferred to the armoured divisions, of which certain batteries preserved the traditions of the Honourable Artillery Company.

4. Regiments coming from converted infantry battalions.

5. Counter-mortar batteries. Groups for detecting mortars by radar or sonar. They were incorporated into the divisions from July 1944.

6. Searchlight batteries. Searchlight units attached to general reserve anti-aircraft regiments.

7. Air observation post squadrons. Light aircraft squadrons used for observation and artillery spotting, attached to the army or army corps. The pilots and the observers belonged to the Royal Artillery, whereas the aircraft and the ground staff were the responsibility of the RAF.

The Artillery Regiments (anti-tank, anti-aircraft, light and heavy)

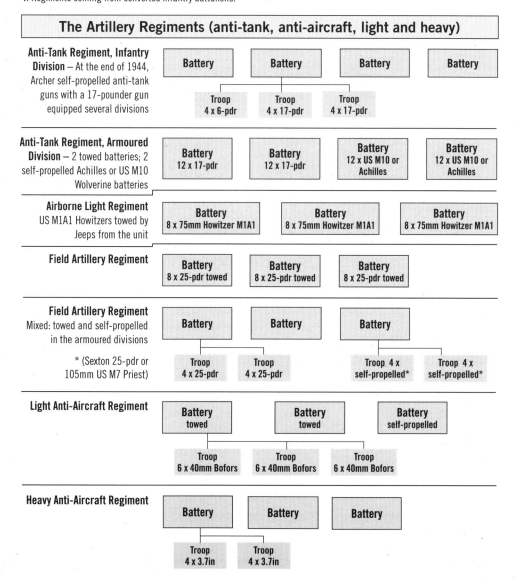

Anti-Tank Regiment, Infantry Division – At the end of 1944, Archer self-propelled anti-tank guns with a 17-pounder gun equipped several divisions

- Battery
- Battery
- Battery
- Battery
  - Troop 4 x 6-pdr
  - Troop 4 x 17-pdr
  - Troop 4 x 17-pdr

Anti-Tank Regiment, Armoured Division – 2 towed batteries; 2 self-propelled Achilles or US M10 Wolverine batteries

- Battery 12 x 17-pdr
- Battery 12 x 17-pdr
- Battery 12 x US M10 or Achilles
- Battery 12 x US M10 or Achilles

Airborne Light Regiment US M1A1 Howitzers towed by Jeeps from the unit

- Battery 8 x 75mm Howitzer M1A1
- Battery 8 x 75mm Howitzer M1A1
- Battery 8 x 75mm Howitzer M1A1

Field Artillery Regiment

- Battery 8 x 25-pdr towed
- Battery 8 x 25-pdr towed
- Battery 8 x 25-pdr towed

Field Artillery Regiment Mixed: towed and self-propelled in the armoured divisions

* (Sexton 25-pdr or 105mm US M7 Priest)

- Battery
- Battery
- Battery
  - Troop 4 x 25-pdr
  - Troop 4 x 25-pdr
  - Troop 4 x self-propelled*
  - Troop 4 x self-propelled*

Light Anti-Aircraft Regiment

- Battery towed
- Battery towed
- Battery self-propelled
  - Troop 6 x 40mm Bofors
  - Troop 6 x 40mm Bofors
  - Troop 6 x 40mm Bofors

Heavy Anti-Aircraft Regiment

- Battery
- Battery
- Battery
  - Troop 4 x 3.7in
  - Troop 4 x 3.7in

43rd (Wessex) Infantry Division (Commander: Major-General G. I. Thomas)

Created: September 1939 (*First-line Territorial division*) **NW Europe Campaign:** 24 June 1944–31 August 1945 **BATTLES: 1944** – 25 June–2 July: *River Odon* / 4–18 July: *Caen* / 18–23 July: *Bourguébus Ridge* / 30 July–9 August: *Mont Pinçon* / 17–27 September: *Nederrijn* **1945** – 8 February–10 March: *Rhineland* / 23 March–1 April: *Rhine*

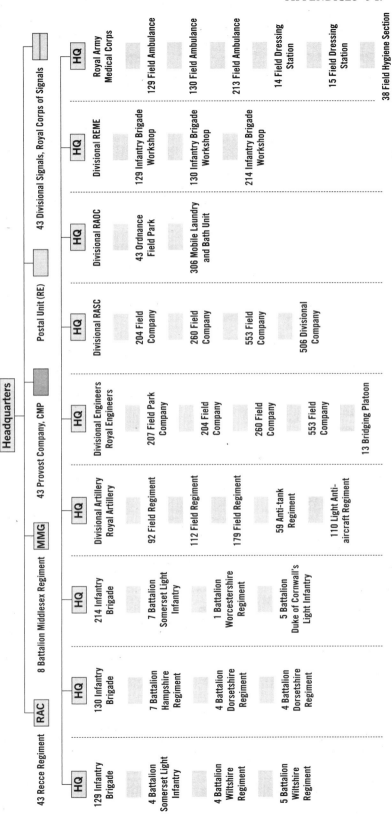

Commanders of the 129th Brigade: Brigadier G. H. L. Luce (wounded; died 14 Nov. 1944); Brigadier J. O. E. Vandeleur (15 Nov. 1944)

Commanders of the 130th Brigade: Brigadier N. D. Leslie; Brigadier B. B. Walton (17 Aug. 1944); Brigadier B. A. Coad (7 Oct. 1944) **Commander of the 214th Brigade:** Brigadier H. Essame

British Armoured Regiment

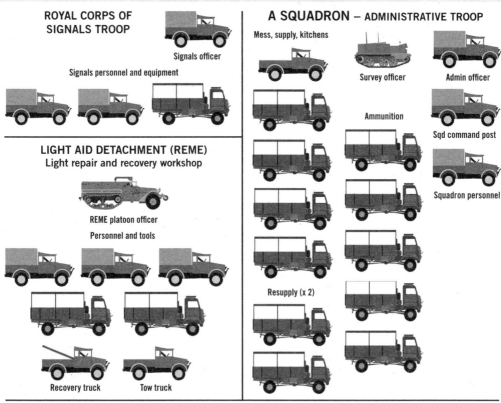

ROYAL CORPS OF SIGNALS TROOP

Signals officer

Signals personnel and equipment

A SQUADRON – ADMINISTRATIVE TROOP

Mess, supply, kitchens

Survey officer

Admin officer

Ammunition

Sqd command post

Squadron personnel

Resupply (x 2)

LIGHT AID DETACHMENT (REME)

Light repair and recovery workshop

REME platoon officer

Personnel and tools

Recovery truck

Tow truck

COMMAND POST SQUADRON 3 squadrons (A, B, C)

Workshop lorry

Liaison Jeep

OP tank

OP tank

Squadron commander's tank

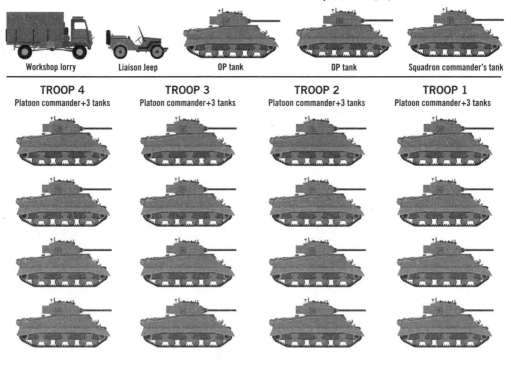

TROOP 4	TROOP 3	TROOP 2	TROOP 1
Platoon commander+3 tanks	Platoon commander+3 tanks	Platoon commander+3 tanks	Platoon commander+3 tanks

Command Post personnel

Regimental HQ light vehicle

REGIMENTAL HQ
CORPS COMMANDER'S COMMAND POST

4th tank

OP tank (Forward observation)

OP tank (Forward observation)

Regimental commander's tank

AA PLATOON
Platoon commander +7 tanks

LIASON PLATOON
Platoon commander
+ 8 Scout cars

RECON. PLATOON
Platoon commander
+10 tanks

ADMINISTRATION PLATOON (Includes 8 motorbikes)

Liaison

Second in command

Liaison

Workshop

Survey officer

Medical evacuation

Signals officer

Quartermaster

Officers' mess

Ammunition trucks

Mess water tankers

Mess trucks

Transport trucks

Workshop

German Order of Battle, 1–6 August

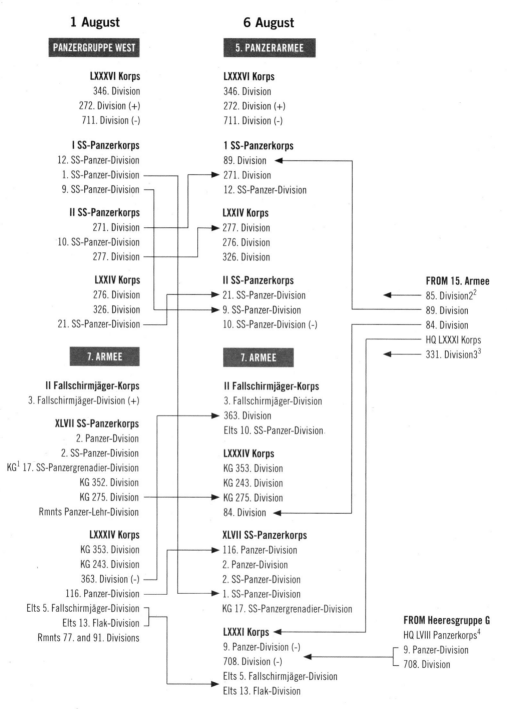

1 August

PANZERGRUPPE WEST

LXXXVI Korps
346. Division
272. Division (+)
711. Division (-)

I SS-Panzerkorps
12. SS-Panzer-Division
1. SS-Panzer-Division
9. SS-Panzer-Division

II SS-Panzerkorps
271. Division
10. SS-Panzer-Division
277. Division

LXXIV Korps
276. Division
326. Division
21. SS-Panzer-Division

7. ARMEE

II Fallschirmjäger-Korps
3. Fallschirmjäger-Division (+)

XLVII SS-Panzerkorps
2. Panzer-Dvision
2. SS-Panzer-Division
KG[1] 17. SS-Panzergrenadier-Division
KG 352. Division
KG 275. Division
Rmnts Panzer-Lehr-Division

LXXXIV Korps
KG 353. Division
KG 243. Division
363. Division (-)
116. Panzer-Division
Elts 5. Fallschirmjäger-Division
Elts 13. Flak-Division
Rmnts 77. and 91. Divisions

6 August

5. PANZERARMEE

LXXXVI Korps
346. Division
272. Division (+)
711. Division (-)

1 SS-Panzerkorps
89. Division
271. Division
12. SS-Panzer-Division

LXXIV Korps
277. Division
276. Division
326. Division

II SS-Panzerkorps
21. SS-Panzer-Division
9. SS-Panzer-Division
10. SS-Panzer-Division (-)

7. ARMEE

II Fallschirmjäger-Korps
3. Fallschirmjäger-Division
363. Division
Elts 10. SS-Panzer-Division

LXXXIV Korps
KG 353. Division
KG 243. Division
KG 275. Division
84. Division

XLVII SS-Panzerkorps
116. Panzer-Division
2. Panzer-Division
2. SS-Panzer-Division
1. SS-Panzer-Division
KG 17. SS-Panzergrenadier-Division

LXXXI Korps
9. Panzer-Division (-)
708. Division (-)
Elts 5. Fallschirmjäger-Division
Elts 13. Flak-Division

FROM 15. Armee
85. Division[2]
89. Division
84. Division
HQ LXXXI Korps
331. Division[3]

FROM Heeresgruppe G
HQ LVIII Panzerkorps[4]
9. Panzer-Division
708. Division

---

[1] *Kampfgruppe*
[2] *En route to 5. Panzerarmee. Leading elements south of Rouen, 6 August.*
[3] *En route to 7. Armee. Leading elements near Briouze, 6 August.*
[4] *HQ LVIII Panzerkorps assumed command of 271. and 277. Divisions on Panzergruppe West front, 2 August. It was reassigned to 7. Armee, 6 August.*

German Infantry Division
2-regiment type: total strength 9,859

DIV HQ
- MAP REPRO SEC
- MIL POLICE

FUS CO (CYCLE)
- CO HQ
- RIFLE PLAT
- RIFLE PLAT
- RIFLE PLAT
- 81mm MORT SEC
- FLAME-THROWER SEC

SIG BN
- BN HQ
- TEL CO
- RADIO CO
- LIGHT SIG CLM

INF REGT
- REGT HQ
- REGT HQ CO
- INF BN
- INF BN
- INF BN
- INF HOW CO
- AT CO
- LIGHT INF CLM

INF REGT
- REGT HQ
- REGT HQ CO
- INF BN
- INF BN
- INF BN
- INF HOW CO
- AT CO
- LIGHT INF CLM

ARTY REGT
- REGT HQ
- REGT HQ BTRY
- LIGHT ARTY BN
- LIGHT ARTY BN
- 88mm AT GUN BN

AA AT BN
- BN HQ
- AT CO (MTR-DR)
- AA CO (SP)

ENGR BN
- BN HQ
- ENGR CO
- ENGR CO (CYCLE)

DIV SERV
- DIV SUP
- WORKSHOP CO
- ADM
- MED UNITS
- VET CO
- FLD POST OFFICE

KEY
AA = anti-aircraft
AT = anti-tank
HOW = Howitzer
MTR-DR = motor-driven
SP = self-propelled

UNIT	Personnel	Light MGs	Heavy MGs	81mm mortars	120mm mortars	Flame-throwers	20mm anti-aircraft guns	75mm anti-tank guns	88mm anti-tank guns	75mm infantry howitzers	150mm infantry howitzers	105mm gun/howitzers	Motor vehicles	Motorcycles	Horse-drawn vehicles	Horses
Division HQ	150	2											48	15		
Foot Co.	120	16		2		2							5	3	5	20
Signal Bn	402	11											86	20	6	25
Infantry Reg.	2,645	178	24	18	12			3		6	2		51	44	244	631
Infantry Reg.	2,645	178	24	18	12			3		6	2		51	44	244	631
Artillery Reg.	1,755	43							12			24	52	28	106	968
Anti-aircraft/ Anti-tank Bn	350	17					12	14					88	24		
Engineer Bn	397	22	4	4		14							3	7	35	68
Division Services	1,395	30											159	33	86	391
TOTAL	9,859	497	52	42	24	16	12	20	12	12	4	24	543	218	726	2,734

Waffen-SS Panzer Division — Total strength 17,262

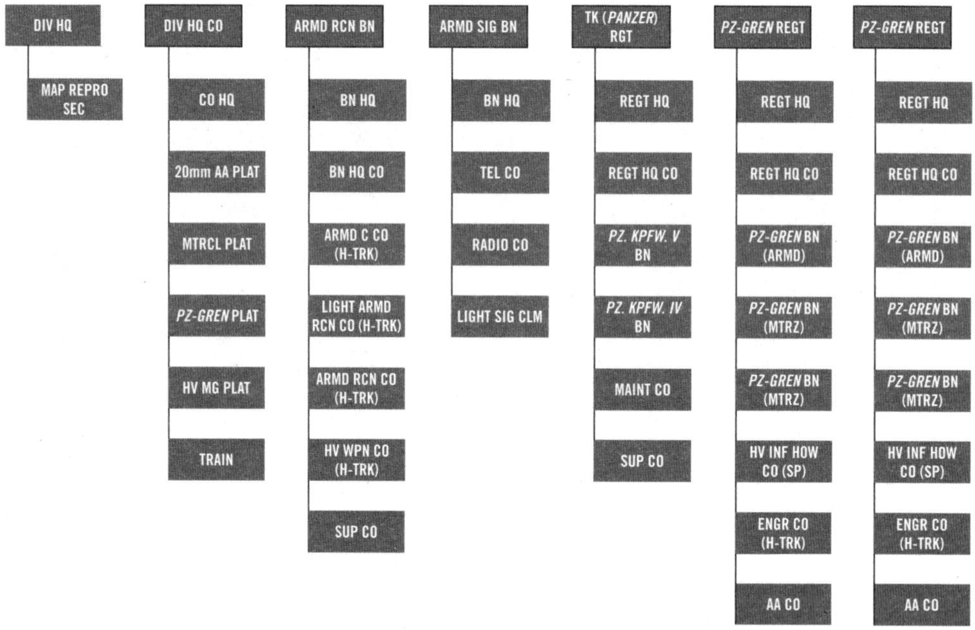

Organizational chart (columns):

- **DIV HQ** → MAP REPRO SEC
- **DIV HQ CO** → CO HQ · 20mm AA PLAT · MTRCL PLAT · PZ-GREN PLAT · HV MG PLAT · TRAIN
- **ARMD RCN BN** → BN HQ · BN HQ CO · ARMD C CO (H-TRK) · LIGHT ARMD RCN CO (H-TRK) · ARMD RCN CO (H-TRK) · HV WPN CO (H-TRK) · SUP CO
- **ARMD SIG BN** → BN HQ · TEL CO · RADIO CO · LIGHT SIG CLM
- **TK (PANZER) RGT** → REGT HQ · REGT HQ CO · PZ. KPFW. V BN · PZ. KPFW. IV BN · MAINT CO · SUP CO
- **PZ-GREN REGT** → REGT HQ · REGT HQ CO · PZ-GREN BN (ARMD) · PZ-GREN BN (MTRZ) · PZ-GREN BN (MTRZ) · HV INF HOW CO (SP) · ENGR CO (H-TRK) · AA CO
- **PZ-GREN REGT** → REGT HQ · REGT HQ CO · PZ-GREN BN (ARMD) · PZ-GREN BN (MTRZ) · PZ-GREN BN (MTRZ) · HV INF HOW CO (SP) · ENGR CO (H-TRK) · AA CO

UNIT	Officers	NCOs	Privates	Rifles/carbines	Pistols	Sub-MGs	Light MGs	Heavy MGs	81mm mortars	120mm mortars	Flame-throwers	150 or 210mm rocket projectors	20mm anti-aircraft guns
Division HQ	32	31	78	95	44	3							
Division HQ Co.	3	37	179	138	65	19	16	2	2				4
Armoured Reconnaissance Bn	27	223	692	434	300	206	147	4	10		6		
Armoured Signal Bn	16	103	396	444	69	51	35						
Tank (Panzer) Reg.	70	614	1,087	816	719	245	296						6
Panzer-Grenadier Reg.	89	598	2,555	1,957	852	443	284	38	20	12	24		43
Panzer-Grenadier Reg.	89	598	2,555	1,957	852	443	284	38	20	12	24		43
Armoured Artillery Reg.	89	473	1,605	1,636	409	255	109	12					
Anti-aircraft Bn	22	148	654	729	73	47	22						18
Bn Rocket Projector	14	101	358	380	40	53	18					18	
Assault Gun Bn	15	111	218	294	80	70	22						
Anti-tank Bn	20	166	327	271	142	100	47						
Armed Engineer Bn	26	132	826	654	254	102	99	6	6		20		
Division Services	64	292	1,529	1,708	165	13	86						
TOTAL	576[1]	3,627	13,059	11,513	4,064	2,050	1,465	100	58	24	74	18	114

[1] Including 62 officials
[2] Including 359 armoured vehicles

ARMD ARTY REGT
- REGT HQ
- REGT HQ BTRY
- OBSN BTRY
- LIGHT ARTY BN
- LIGHT ARTY BN
- MED ARTY BN
- HV ARTY BN

AA BN
- BN HQ
- BN HQ BTRY
- HV AA BTRY
- HV AA BTRY
- LIGHT ARTY BTRY
- LIGHT AA CLM

ROCKET PROJECTOR BN
- BN HQ
- BN HQ BTRY
- ROCKET PROJECTOR BN
- ROCKET PROJCTR BTRY
- ROCKET PROJCTR BTRY

ASSAULT GUN BN
- BN HQ
- BN HQ BTRY
- ASSAULT GUN BTRY
- ASSAULT GUN BTRY
- ASSAULT GUN BTRY

AT BN
- BN HQ
- BN HQ CO
- AT CO
- AT CO
- AT CO
- SUP CO

ARMD ENGR BN
- BN HQ
- BN HQ CO
- ENGR CO (MTZ)
- ENGR CO (MTZ)
- ENGR CO (MTZ)
- BR CLM K
- BR CLM J

DIV SERV
- SUP
- ADM
- MED
- MAIN UNITS
- MP DET
- FLD POST OFFICE

KEY
AA = anti-aircraft H-TRK = half-track
AT = anti-tank MTZ = motorized
BR = bridging SP = self-propelled

20mm anti-tank guns	28/20mm anti-tank guns	37mm anti-aircraft guns (SP)	75mm anti-tank guns (mtr-dr)	75mm anti-tank guns (SP)	75mm tank guns (long)	75mm tank guns (super-long)	88mm anti-aircraft guns	75mm infantry howitzers (SP)	150mm infantry howitzers (SP)	105mm gun howitzers (mtr-dr)	105mm gun howitzers (SP)	150mm howitzers (mtr-dr)	150mm howitzers (SP)	170mm guns	Panzerkampfwagen IVs	Panzerkampfwagen Vs	Motor vehicles	Motorcycles
																	32	8
				3													31	28
35				13													193	22
																	114	14
		8			64	62									64	62	313	53
								12	6								527	88
								12	6								527	88
										12	12	12	6	12			534	40
							12										181	16
																	107	8
				22													100	11
			12	31													135	17
3	3																212	52
																	323	85
38	3	8	12	69	64	62	12	24	12	12	12	12	6	12	64	62	3,329[2]	530

General Montgomery (*left*) with the Supreme Allied Commander, General Dwight D. Eisenhower (*right*).

Timeline: Normandy 1944

January

WEDNESDAY, 12

Meeting at Gen. Sir Bernard Montgomery's new HQ at St Paul's School, London, of senior commanders, including Gen. Omar Bradley and Gen. Sir Kenneth Anderson (then slated to command Second Army).

SATURDAY, 15

Montgomery demands 5 x division landing. Adm. Sir Bertram Ramsay agrees subject to necessary lift and naval forces being available.

FM Erwin Rommel appointed commander of Heeresgruppe B.

MONDAY, 17

Eisenhower discusses with Ramsay need to move out of London. Ramsay suggests Portsmouth.

WEDNESDAY, 19

Eisenhower speaks to senior members of combined staffs about importance of unity and close cooperation.

FRIDAY, 21

Big meeting to finalize outline of OVERLORD plan. 5 x division assault agreed. Ramsay explains naval implications and requirements.

THURSDAY, 27

Gen. Miles Dempsey takes over command of British Second Army.

February

TUESDAY, 1

Photo session of senior commanders for OVERLORD.

SATURDAY, 19–THURSDAY, 24

Luftwaffe raids on London by day and night.

TUESDAY, 29

Ramsay holds meetings of senior generals and admirals.

March

WEDNESDAY, 15

Large naval meeting at Admiralty to discuss anti-U-boat measures for OVERLORD.

SUNDAY, 19

Rommel summoned to see Hitler at Berghof.

SATURDAY, 25

Allied bombing policy conference.

April

FRIDAY, 7

1st day of Ex. THUNDERCLAP at St Paul's, including Chiefs of Staff, Sec. for War (Sir James Grigg) and all main generals, admirals and air marshals of higher command of forces for OVERLORD. Monty gives 1½ hour talk on army plan. Ramsay gives 1 hour talk on naval problems that would affect army and air plans.

SATURDAY, 8

2nd day Ex. THUNDERCLAP. Finishes 1.45 p.m.

WEDNESDAY, 19

Eisenhower agrees to give greater bombing priority to German V-1 and V-2 weapons sites.

SATURDAY, 29

Ramsay meeting with Eastern Task Force commanders. Discussions of H-Hour.

May

MONDAY, 1

Senior commanders meeting. Discussions about beach obstacles and H-Hour.

WEDNESDAY, 3

Op. FABIUS begins – D-Day dress rehearsal.

SUNDAY, 7

'Appreciation on Possible Development of Operations to Secure a Lodgement Area' distributed.

MONDAY, 8

Hitler divides up command of panzer divisions in the West.

MONDAY, 15

Big Presentation of Plans Day.

FRIDAY, 19

RAF Bomber Command hits Orléans.

SUNDAY, 21

CHATTANOOGA mission – Eighth Air Force fighters attack railway targets and destroy 91 locomotives.

MONDAY, 22

CHATTANOOGA mission Day 2.

Night: RAF Bomber Command hits marshalling yards at Orléans and Le Mans.

WEDNESDAY, 24

RAF Bomber Command hits marshalling yards at Aachen.

THURSDAY, 25

Eighth Air Force hits bridges along the Seine.

SATURDAY, 27

RAF Bomber Command hits marshalling yards at Aachen.

SUNDAY, 28

Gen. Galland learns Me262 will be used as a bomber not a fighter.

Huge aerial battles over Germany. 78 German fighter planes lost.

TUESDAY, 30

Rommel on inspection tour along Normandy coast.

June

FRIDAY, 2

10 a.m.: Commanders' meeting. Weather is main point of discussion. Agree to stick to current plan and loading to proceed.

Montgomery gives final pep-talk to staff at 21st Army Group HQ.

SATURDAY, 3

Invasion troops embark.

Rommel visits FM Gerd von Rundstedt in Paris.

9.30 p.m.: Commanders' meeting: agreed to stick to 5 June.

SUNDAY, 4

4.15 a.m.: Eisenhower decides provisional postponement discussed the previous evening should stand.

Gen. Charles de Gaulle arrives in London from Algiers.

9.30 p.m.: Group Capt. James Stagg announces a gap in weather is coming. Ike decides to go on Tuesday, 6 June.

Rommel leaves France to visit his wife in Germany, then goes on to visit Hitler.

MONDAY, 5

4.15 a.m.: Commanders' meeting at Southwick House. Eisenhower confirms D-Day will go ahead on 6 June with airborne operations starting that night.

Intelligence summary from OB West HQ reports no imminent threat of Allied invasion.

TUESDAY, 6 – D-DAY

See separate timeline, p. 567.

WEDNESDAY, 7

12. Waffen-SS Panzer-Division counter-attack to west of Caen held up by Canadians. Vicious fighting along River Merderet west of Ste-Mère-Église.

101st Airborne capture St-Côme-du-Mont.

Rangers battling to hold Pointe du Hoc.

Fighting all along front.

Bayeux liberated.

THURSDAY, 8

4 a.m.: 45 Royal Marine Commando capture Port-en-Bessin.

82nd Airborne take Cauquigny.

352. Division falls back to second line of defence.

Sherwood Rangers reach Point 103 north of Tilly-sur-Seulles.

Maj.-Gen. Pete Quesada, commander IX Tactical Command, lands at ELS-1 near Utah Beach.

Construction of Mulberry harbours begins at Port-en-Bessin and Arromanches.

FRIDAY, 9

Poet Keith Douglas killed.

Americans capture Grandcamp and Maisy Battery.

Lead elements of Panzer-Lehr enter battle at Tilly-sur-Seulles.

SATURDAY, 10

British Second Army launches Op. PERCH.

Battle for Carentan reaches climax.

2. Waffen-SS 'Das Reich' murder 642 French civilians at Oradour-sur-Glâne near Limoges.

SUNDAY, 11

Last German troops pull out of Carentan.

US troops link up between Utah and Omaha Beaches.

MONDAY, 12

US troops from Utah and Omaha meet near Carentan.

Joint 6. Fallschirmjäger/17. Waffen-SS counter-attack on Carentan.

Carentan battle ends.

Gen. Marcks killed by RAF.

Troops from 51st Highland Division reinforce British Commandos and Paras on British eastern flank.

21. Panzer counter-attack east of River Orne.

Winston Churchill visits Normandy.

1 SAS blow up German fuel trains near Châtellerault.

TUESDAY, 13

First V-1s fall on England.

German counter-attack towards Carentan fails.

Lead elements of British 7th Armoured Division halted at Villers-Bocage.

WEDNESDAY, 14

Op. PERCH halted.

Ongoing fighting at Villers-Bocage.

More than 300 heavy bombers of Bomber Command hit Le Havre.

De Gaulle visits Normandy and makes speech in Bayeux.

THURSDAY, 15

In Pacific, Americans launch assault on Mariana Islands.

Five Allied airfields built within the bridgehead by this time.

Americans renew effort to sever Cotentin Peninsula.

FRIDAY, 16

King George VI visits assault beaches via HMS *Amethyst* accompanied by Ramsay. Visits Monty at Creully.

Americans attack high ground to north of St-Lô.

SATURDAY, 17

Rommel meets von Rundstedt and Hitler at Margival.

SUNDAY, 18

Montgomery issues new plans: priority is capture of Cherbourg and Caen.

Evening: Americans reach west coast of Cotentin, cutting off all German forces to the north in process.

Panzer-Lehr counter-attack around Tilly and Fontenay.

Night: Panzer-Lehr pull back to high ground around Rauray and south of Tilly.

MONDAY, 19

Great storm begins in Channel.

American drive on Cherbourg begins.

TUESDAY, 20

Great storm continues.

WEDNESDAY, 21

Great storm ends – Mulberry A has been largely destroyed.

THURSDAY, 22

Op. BAGRATION launched on Eastern Front.

Montgomery and Dempsey agree plans for MARTLET and EPSOM.

FRIDAY, 23

Ramsay crosses to Normandy to inspect Great Storm damage.

Due to weather and troop build-up, Dempsey delays EPSOM until 26 June.

SATURDAY, 24

More troops on both sides reaching front.

Battle for Cherbourg continuing.

SUNDAY, 25

British XXX Corps launches Op. MARTLET towards Rauray Ridge. Rauray village captured.

MONDAY, 26

British Second Army launches Op. EPSOM.

TUESDAY, 27

Cherbourg garrison surrenders to Americans.

12. SS counter-attack west of Caen halted.

British VIII Corps gets across River Odon at Buron – 'Scottish Corridor' created up towards Hill 112.

Evening: Rommel and von Rundstedt summoned to see Hitler at Berghof.

WEDNESDAY, 28

By morning British 11th Armoured Division bridgehead over River Odon.

Hill 112 captured by British.

Two more SS panzer divisions enter EPSOM battle.

Rommel and von Rundstedt at Berghof.

THURSDAY, 29

Gen. Dollmann dies and replaced by SS-Gen. Paul Hausser.

German panzer counter-attacks in EPSOM battle repulsed.

FRIDAY, 30

Last German forces in Cotentin Peninsula surrender.

Further German counter-attacks in EPSOM battle.

Gen. Dempsey and Gen. O'Connor agree to pull British troops back from Hill 112.

Rommel back at La Roche-Guyon.

July

SATURDAY, 1

End of EPSOM battle.

Geyr von Schweppenburg sacked as commander Panzergruppe West and replaced by Gen. Hans Eberbach.

Von Rundstedt also sacked as commander OB West and replaced by FM Günther von Kluge.

MONDAY, 3

Von Kluge reaches La Roche-Guyon and immediately argues with Rommel.

Americans launch attack towards La-Haye-du-Puits.

TUESDAY, 4

Op. WINDSOR launched: Canadian assault plus 79th Armoured Brigade on village of Carpiquet.

Americans attacking southwards.

WEDNESDAY, 5

Fighting around Carpiquet and St-Lô.

THURSDAY, 6

Fighting around Carpiquet and north of St-Lô.

FRIDAY, 7

Eisenhower writes to Montgomery urging him to speed up operations.

Panzer-Lehr move to St-Lô sector.

Bomber Command attacks northern edge of Caen with 467 heavy bombers.

SATURDAY, 8

Op. CHARNWOOD launched.

SUNDAY, 9

British and Canadian troops enter Caen.

Panzer-Lehr counter-attack north-west of St-Lô.

MONDAY, 10

British and Canadian troops occupy Caen.

Op. JUPITER launched by British to retake Hill 112.

Montgomery issues new directive.

TUESDAY, 11

Op. CHARNWOOD halted.

Op. JUPITER halted.

Vicious fighting at base of the Cotentin Peninsula.

Panzer-Lehr counter-attacks near St-Jean-de-Daye.

WEDNESDAY, 12

Montgomery signals Eisenhower about plans for Op. GOODWOOD.

Bradley briefs his generals about Op. COBRA.

Heavy fighting in western sector.

US 2nd Division launch attack north-east of St-Lô – Hill 192 captured.

THURSDAY, 13

Heavy fighting in western sector.

FRIDAY, 14

Americans still pressing southwards around St-Lô.

Op. ANVIL authorized.

SATURDAY, 15

Montgomery authorizes scaled-back version of Op. GOODWOOD due to launch 18 August.

SUNDAY, 16

German counter-attack around St-Lô ends.

MONDAY, 17

Rommel wounded by air attack. Von Kluge takes over.

Americans closing in on St-Lô.

TUESDAY, 18

Op. GOODWOOD launched.

US forces capture St-Lô.

WEDNESDAY, 19

Continued fighting in GOODWOOD battle.

Gen. Bradley to England to brief air commanders on COBRA.

THURSDAY, 20

Failed assassination attempt on Hitler at the Wolf's Lair.

FRIDAY, 21

Op. GOODWOOD runs out of steam.

Op. COBRA postponed due to poor weather.

SATURDAY, 22

Op. EXPRESS – 43rd Wessex Division
and 7th Royal Tank Regiment attack
Hill 112 sector and capture Maltot.

SUNDAY, 23

First Canadian Army becomes
operational under Gen. Harry
Crerar.

COBRA postponed again due to poor
weather.

MONDAY, 24

Op. COBRA postponed by 24 hours,
although some Eighth Air Force
heavies still bomb targets. 25 US
troops killed.

TUESDAY, 25

Op. COBRA launched, preceded by
carpet-bombing by 1,500 heavy
bombers.

Op. SPRING: Canadian II Corps aim
to push on to Verrières Ridge
supported by Guards Armoured and
7th Armoured Division.

WEDNESDAY, 26

Americans pushing southwards.

IX Tactical Air Command introduces
Armored Column Cover for first
time.

THURSDAY, 27

Marigny in US hands. Clear that
German front opposite US First Army
is crumbling.

British and Canadians facing 645
tanks, 92 infantry battalions.
Americans facing 200 tanks, 85
infantry battalions.

Avranches falls to US First Army.

Montgomery issues directive for
Op. BLUECOAT around Caumont.
XXX and VIII Corps moved west
for this.

FRIDAY, 28

British Second Army moving troops
in preparation for BLUECOAT.

Americans continue to push south
from St-Lô.

SATURDAY, 29

The Roncey Pocket – over 100 panzers
and 250 German vehicles lost to air
attacks.

SUNDAY, 30

Americans seize key bridge at
Pontaubault.

British Second Army launches Op.
BLUECOAT.

August

TUESDAY, 1

Op. ANVIL – planned Allied invasion
of southern France, renamed
DRAGOON – scheduled for 15
August.

Von Kluge at 7. Armee Tac HQ:
'Gentlemen, this breakthrough means

for us and the German people the
beginning of a decisive and bitter end.
I see no remaining possibility of
halting this ongoing attack.'

21st Panzer-Division counter-attack
against British fails.

Hitler tells von Kluge to prepare a counter-attack. Von Kluge's hopes of falling back behind Seine are dashed.

II. SS-Panzerkorps committed to defend against BLUECOAT.

US First Army has captured 20,000 German troops in six days.

Gen. George S. Patton takes operational command of US Third Army.

Wednesday, 2

Americans clear most of Villedieu.

Dempsey sacks Lt-Gen. Gerard Bucknall as commander of XXX Corps. Replaced by Lt-Gen. Brian Horrocks.

Hitler orders von Kluge to prepare for major counter-attack west towards Avranches.

Thursday, 3

US 4th Armored Division approaching Rennes. Gen. Bayerlein says this 'had a shattering effect, like a bomb-burst upon us'.

Maj.-Gen. Erskine sacked as 7th Armoured Division commander. Replaced by Maj.-Gen. Gerald Verney.

Friday, 4

Villers-Bocage, now flattened, captured by British 50th Division.

Rennes captured by US Third Army.

Saturday, 5

British Second Army pressing on towards River Orne.

Sunday, 6

British capture Mont Pinçon.

British cryptanalysts learn of German plans for Op. LÜTTICH.

Monday, 7

Germans launch Op. LÜTTICH counter-attack towards Mortain.

Op. TOTALIZE launched.

Panzer ace Michael Wittmann killed.

Tuesday, 8

Op. TOTALIZE continues.

Le Mans captured by US Third Army.

Wednesday, 9

Germans back at Op. LÜTTICH start point.

Thursday, 10

Op. TOTALIZE halted.

Friday, 11

US troops retake Mortain.

Saturday, 12

US Third Army takes Alençon.

Sunday, 13

Germans becoming trapped in Falaise Pocket.

Monday, 14

Op. TRACTABLE launched by Canadian First Army.

Tuesday, 15

Allied landings in southern France – Op. DRAGOON.

Wednesday, 16

Falaise captured.

Thursday, 17

FM Walter Model takes over command of German armies in West and orders retreat.

FRIDAY, 18

Germans desperately trying to retreat through 'Corridor of Death'.

SATURDAY, 19

US, Polish and Canadian troops meet across neck of Falaise Pocket.

Normandy battle ends

FRIDAY, 25

Paris liberated.

Timeline: D-Day

00:07   German sentries spot low-flying aircraft north of Carentan in Cotentin Peninsula.

00:10   First US pathfinders jump on Cotentin to mark parachute zones for C-47 pilots who will arrive in the next few minutes.

00:16   First of 3 British gliders lands less than 50 metres from the bridge of Bénouville – the Pegasus Bridge. Men of D Company, Ox & Bucks, led by Maj. John Howard, hurry out and attack bridge.

Merville's German battery attacked by 5 Avro Lancaster bombers of RAF's 7th Squadron.

00:17   Second of 3 British gliders lands near Pegasus Bridge.

00:18   Last of 3 Horsa gliders lands near Pegasus Bridge.

00:20   6 Albemarle aircraft drop 60 pathfinders from 22nd Independent Parachute Company on DZs N, V and K east of Orne.

00:35   2 Horsa gliders land near the Ranville bridge (Horsa Bridge). The 3rd glider planned for the operation is missing.

00:50   5th Brigade, 6th British Airborne Division, commanded by Brig. Nigel Poett, dropped near Ranville.

01:10   36 French paratroopers, gathered in 4 teams, jump over Brittany, in forest of Duault and near Plumelec.

All German troops under orders of LXXXIV. Korps, from River Orne to St-Malo, on alert.

01:21   Pathfinders of 82nd Airborne Division jump over Normandy above Cotentin to attempt to mark 3 landing zones for rest of division (DZs N, O and T).

01:30   Gen. Dollman, German 7. Armee commander, orders general alert. Sirens of Pointe du Hoc Battery activated to signal appearance of Allied bombers.

01:50   In Paris, near Bois de Boulogne, Marinegruppe West chief of operations Adm. Karl Hoffman summons the various staffs following accumulation of alarming reports and sends message to Germany: 'Report to the headquarters of the Führer that it is the invasion.'

01:55   Take-off in England of bombers of US Eighth Air Force. 1,198 aircraft deployed in total.

02:00   FM von Rundstedt made aware of alerts following discovery of paratroopers, notably reported by 352. Infanterie-Division.

02:05   1. Panzerjäger Kompanie of Infanterie-Regiment 716 leaves Biéville to patrol along Orne Canal in direction of Bénouville and Ranville bridges.

02:29   Force U ships arrive off Utah Beach and drop anchor 24 km from shore.

02:40   Von Rundstedt reports by radio to German 7. Armee that he does not believe this a large-scale landing.

02:51   Force O ships arrive off Omaha Beach and drop anchor 23 km from shore.

03:00   US soldiers from Force O off Omaha begin to embark in landing craft.

US soldiers from Force U off Utah Beach begin to embark in landing craft.

RAF bombards targets in Caen.

03:20   Gen. Gale, commander of 6th Airborne Division, is parachuted with his staff above 'N' drop zone near Ranville.

03:30   Troops and vehicles of 21. Panzer-Division ready to be deployed.

03:35   55 Horsa gliders containing forces destined for British 6th Airborne Division land as part of Operation TONGA in Ranville area.

03:54   52 American Waco gliders containing forces destined for US 101st Airborne Division land as part of Operation DETROIT north of Hiesville.

04:00   Liberation of Ste-Mère-Église by US soldiers of 3rd Battalion, 505th PIR, 82nd Airborne Division. The American flag is hoisted at the town hall.

52 American Waco gliders land as part of Operation DETROIT north-west of Ste-Mère-Église.

Von Rundstedt asks Supreme Command at Berlin for permission to deploy 2 divisions to coast.

Violent aerial attack by Allies on German strongpoints WNs 44, 47 and 48.

04:10   Panzergruppe West alerted to Level 2 (intervention time of 1½ hours max.).

04:13   Staff of 352. Infanterie-Division give order of movement to Oberst Karl Meyer of Grenadier-Regiment 915, to be deployed in the direction of Montmartin–Déville, by bridge to west of Neuilly.

04:25   Staff of 352. Infanterie-Division give order of attack to Regiment 914 against paratroopers south of Carentan.

04:30	Lt-Col Terence Otway launches survivors of 9th Battalion, 3rd Brigade, 6th Airborne Division in the assault on the Merville Battery.
04:45	Pocket submarines *X20* and *X23*, in charge of marking the route of the Allied armada, arrive nearly 1 km from Normandy shore.
	Lt-Col Otway shoots a yellow rocket towards the sky, spotted off shore by the cruiser *Arethusa* – a sign that he is now in control of the Merville Battery. 70 British officers, NCOs and soldiers killed during the assault.
05:10	First shots of naval artillery on German coastal positions by HMS *Orion* cruiser off Gold Beach, then by cruisers *Ajax*, *Argonaut*, *Emerald*, by Dutch gunboat *Flores* and 13 destroyers.
	Attack on Mont-Canisy German battery by 18 Marauder bombers of USAAF.
	Free French warships *Georges Leygues* and *Montcalm* bombard German naval battery at Longues-sur-Mer, which opened fire on warship USS *Arkansas*.
05:20	Gen. Edgar Feuchtinger, commander of 21. Panzer-Division, arrives at his CP in St-Pierre-sur-Dives.
05:25	3 German gunboats fleeing from Ouistreham on Caen Canal intercepted by Maj. Howard's men at Pegasus Bridge: one destroyed, another stranded nearby, while third takes refuge further north in area of Le Maresquier.
05:30	Soldiers of first wave of Force S (Sword Beach) embark in landing craft.
	First Allied dive-bombing of day, near Falaise.
05:31	Eastern Task Force warships led by Rear-Adm. Philip Vian open fire on British and Canadian beaches of Gold, Juno and Sword.
05:35	29 US amphibious tanks from 741st Tank Battalion launched 6 km off Omaha Beach. 27 sink en route to beach.
05:37	German guns of Longues-sur-Mer Battery open fire on destroyer USS *Emmons* and cruiser USS *Arkansas*.
05:45	Bombardment by naval artillery of Houlgate, Mont Canisy and Villerville batteries.
05:50	Battleship USS *Texas* fires for the first time on the US sector of Omaha.
05:52	USS *Arkansas* opens fire again.
05:55	329 British Liberator bombers attack German coastal installations.
	A ship in charge of guiding landing craft to Utah Beach, PC*1261*, enters an area polluted by mines and strikes one. Other ships sink a few minutes later for same reason.
05:58	Sunrise. Weather is grey, the swell very important, low clouds let out short rains. Wind force 3 to 4.
06:00	270 American Marauder bombers drop 4,404 bombs of 110kg each on targets along Normandy coast.

Engineers from 3rd Parachute Squadron RE and paratroopers of 1st Canadian Parachute Battalion blow up bridge of Robehomme on River Dives.

06:06 Severe aerial bombardments reported on strongpoints located at Arromanches, Ste-Honorine and Colleville.

06:27 Omaha Beach: end of barrage bombardment on coast.

06:29 Omaha Beach, Dog Green and Dog White sectors: landing of 32 amphibious tanks (Companies C and B of 743rd Tank Battalion).

06:30 Omaha Beach: air attack by 18 x Marauder bombers on Pointe du Hoc, then USS *Texas* fires on German battery.

Gen. Feuchtinger, 21. Panzer-Division commander, gives order to attack bridgehead of British 6th Airborne Division beyond River Orne.

06:31 Utah Beach, Uncle Red area: landing of 2nd Battalion, 8th Regiment, US 4th Infantry Division.

06:35 Omaha Beach: landing of first assault wave of 116th Regiment, US 29th Infantry Division.

Utah Beach: landing of second assault wave of elements of 8th Regiment, US 4th Infantry Division.

06:36 Omaha Beach: landing of second assault wave of 116th Regiment, US 29th Infantry Division.

06:40 Gen. Dwight D. Eisenhower wakes up after short nap and is reassured by optimistic call from Adm. Ramsay.

06:42 US Rear-Adm. Kirk, commander of West Naval Training, reports 'everything is going according to plan'.

06:45 Utah Beach: landing of 32 amphibious tanks of 70th Armored Battalion. 28 reach the shore.

Omaha Beach: landing of second wave of assault.

B-25 medium bombers of 8 and 342 Squadrons, RAF (including French group 'Lorraine') complete creation of smokescreen to protect Allied armada.

General Speidel places 21. Panzer under orders of German 7. Armee.

07:00 Omaha Beach: landing of second wave of assault continues.

07:10 Omaha Beach: 88mm gun at WN61 put out of action after direct hit from either naval artillery or Sergeant Turner Sheppard's Sherman tank.

07:11 Omaha Beach: Col Rudder's 225 Rangers, delayed by erroneous navigations and a strong sea current, land 41 minutes late at Pointe du Hoc.

07:15 Pointe du Hoc: Rangers from Task Force C on their way to Dog Green (Omaha Beach) because they have not received the signal to request reinforcements from Pointe du Hoc.

Omaha Beach: German Grenadier-Regiment 726 reports that WN60 is severely bombed and that 20 landing craft, spotted by WN37, are approaching.

Gold Beach: landing craft equipped with 127mm rocket launchers open fire on coastal defences.

07:20   Omaha Beach: Grenadier-Regiment 916 reports amphibious tanks identified in area of Vierville-sur-Mer.

End of naval bombardment on Gold, Juno and Sword.

Sword Beach: landing of tanks of 22nd Dragoons transported aboard 10 LCTs.

07:25   Gold, Juno and Sword Beaches: de-mining and obstacle-clearing special tanks land.

Gold Beach: landing of British 50th Infantry Division, led by Maj.-Gen. Graham.

Sword Beach: landing of AVRE tanks of 5th Assault Regiment RE, 79th Armoured Division.

07:30   Paratroopers of 3rd Battalion, 502nd PIR, 101st Airborne Division, seize beach exit No. 3 to west of Utah Beach, near Audouville-la-Hubert.

Omaha Beach: surviving Rangers from Company C reach plateau east of exit D-1, Vierville-sur-Mer.

07:32   Sword Beach: landing of Kieffer (Free France) Commando in front of Colleville-sur-Orne.

07:40   Omaha Beach: LCI *91* hit by a mine and by German artillery, causing death of 73 soldiers.

07:45   Pointe du Hoc: Rangers set up temporary HQ in crater in front of L409A anti-aircraft bunker (37mm gun), east of German battery.

Omaha Beach: German soldiers at WN70 announce breakthrough of 6 US tanks, 3 of them at strongpoint WN66.

Omaha Beach: C (Task Force C) consisting of Companies A and B of 2nd Rangers Battalion about to land on edge of Dog Green and Dog White areas. All 5th Rangers Battalion heading for Dog Green.

Juno Beach: landing of 3rd Canadian Infantry Division led by Gen. Keller.

08:00   Utah Beach: 4 battalions have landed.

One of the 2 x 210mm Skoda K52 guns of Crisbecq Battery put out of action by Allied warships.

Omaha Beach: US soldiers reach top of dune WN60.

Omaha Beach: landing of men of 5th Battalion of Rangers, who were originally to land at Pointe du Hoc.

Sword Beach: landing of an anti-tank section which gradually reduces to silence the different German defensive positions.

08:05   Juno Beach: 3rd Canadian Infantry Division reports explosion of about 16 shells per minute on Mike Green beach area.

08:09   Omaha Beach: all amphibious tanks destined to land on Fox Green have sunk between their starting point and the beach.

08:20   Omaha Beach: Grenadier-Regiment 726 reports that 88mm at WN61 is out of use and that landing craft spotted in front of WNs 37 and 37a.

Gold Beach: landing of 7th Battalion, Green Howards, 69th Infantry Brigade, 50th (Northumbrian) Infantry Division.

Sword Beach: landing of whole of 4 Commando, 1st Special Service Brigade.

08:24   Omaha Beach: landed troops report they are under the fire of Maisy's batteries.

08:25   Omaha Beach: WN62 infiltrated by US soldiers while WN61 is attacked from front and back. German radio communication to Port-en-Bessin is interrupted.

Gold Beach: landing of Royal Marines 47 Commando.

08:30   Omaha Beach: counter-attack of Grenadier-Regiment 915 to regain control of WN60.

Omaha Beach: Gen. Cota establishes his CP on the beach.

C Company of 1st Canadian Parachute Battalion blow up bridge at Varaville on River Dives with help of sappers of 3rd Parachute Squadron RE.

08:45   Omaha Beach: Grenadier-Regiment 916 reports WN70 is in US hands. 3 tanks pass through WN66 and upper casemate of WN62 is destroyed.

Sword Beach: landing of Royal Marines 41 Commando.

08:55   Omaha Beach: Artillerie-Regiment 352 struggles to maintain radio contact with WN60.

08:57   Omaha Beach: Grenadier-Regiment 726 reports 30 enemy tanks landed between WNs 35 and 36.

09:00   Second 210mm gun of Crisbecq Battery put out of action by Allied ships.

Pointe du Hoc: Rangers repulse a counter-attack led by 1. Kompanie, Infanterie-Regiment 916.

Omaha Beach: WN60 strongpoint (Fox Red area) protecting F1 exit silenced by men of US 1st Infantry Division.

Sword Beach: survivors of the Kieffer Commando storm the casino bunker in Ouistreham.

09:05   Canadian soldiers land on Mike Red (Juno Beach) and report that situation is excellent.

09:15   352. Infanterie-Division reports loss of strongpoints WNs 65, 68 and 70.

Men of Lieutenant Shave of 3rd Parachute Squadron RE blow up railway bridge of Bures on River Dives.

09:17   Landings announced by Allies: 'Under the command of General Eisenhower, Allied naval forces, supported by strong air forces, began landing Allied armies this morning on the northern coast of France.'

09:20   Maj.-Gen. Clarence Huebner orders ships off Omaha Beach to fire new naval artillery barrage on German defences, despite risk of killing US soldiers. It lasts 28 minutes.

German battery of Longues-sur-Mer ceases firing.

09:25   Sword Beach: in Ouistreham, the amphibious support tank requested by Kieffer arrives in front of the casino bunker and opens fire, allowing the French Commandos of 1er Bataillon de Fusiliers Marins Commandos to storm the position.

Omaha Beach: Artillerie-Regiment 352 reports WNs 35 and 36 are destroyed, while guns of WN40 destroy 4 tanks and 3 landing craft.

Gold Beach: 12 Focke-Wulf 190 fighters attack beach.

Juno Beach: locality of Bernières liberated by men of North Shore Regiment and Queen's Own Rifle Regiment.

Sword Beach: Hermanville liberated by South Lancashire Regiment while the 1st Suffolks land.

09:48   End of second artillery barrage on Omaha Beach.

RAF reconnaissance patrol reports presence of armoured vehicles north of Caen.

09:55   352. Infanterie-Division reports all radio contacts with Grenadier-Regiment 916 are broken down.

10:00   Omaha Beach: 2 US destroyers approaching within half mile of shore to support isolated groups trying to get out of beach.

Omaha Beach: about 200 soldiers of 1st Battalion, 116th Regiment, US 29th Infantry Division climb cliff and reach Vierville-sur-Mer.

Omaha Beach: W64 silenced by US troops.

Sword Beach: British soldiers of 4 Commando reach port of Ouistreham where German defence is concentrated.

General Marcks decides to counter-attack with 21. Panzer-Division.

General Feuchtinger ordered to counter-attack with his tanks along River Orne against British paratroopers of 6th Airborne Division.

Hitler wakes up at Berghof after having been up late the night before, listening to Wagner's music.

10:15   Omaha Beach: at WN62 by Colleville Draw, 2 x 76.5mm guns are destroyed at the same time by naval artillery.

10:30   Omaha Beach: 2 x 75mm guns of Pointe de la Percée put out of action by destroyer USS *McCook*.

Omaha Beach: WN65 at junction between Easy Green and Easy Red beach sectors and protecting E1 exit is stormed by US soldiers.

Feuchtinger ordered to move 21. Panzer-Division to west of Orne Canal and to engage it north of Bayeux–Caen line.

11:00	German radar station at Pointe de la Percée attacked off Omaha by destroyer USS *Thompson*, which fires 127mm shells.
	Gold Beach: 7 beach exits cleared.
11:27	Omaha Beach: Grenadier-Regiment 916 reports that attackers hold the heights of St-Laurent-sur-Mer beach. Commander of Infanterie-Division 352 again orders counter-attack.
11:45	Omaha Beach: 1st Battalion, 18th Infantry Regiment, US 1st Infantry Division lands.
12:00	Utah Beach: 4 beach exit routes (causeways) are controlled by paratroopers of US 101st Airborne Division.
	Utah Beach: 2nd Battalion, 8th RCT enters Pouppeville.
	Utah Beach: Dog Company, 501st PIR reaches village of Angoville.
	Pointe du Hoc: last 6 defenders of observation post surrender to Rangers.
	Pointe du Hoc: Col Rudder sends message 'Arrived at Pointe du Hoc. Mission completed, urgent need of ammunition and reinforcements. Many losses.'
	Omaha Beach: due to lack of ammunition, the Houtteville Battery (4,500 metres from beach near Colleville-sur-Mer) refuses an order to fire salvoes against landing craft on approach. The battery only fires with one 105mm gun after the other.
	London: Churchill delivers speech in House of Commons, informing MPs of the liberation of Rome and the beginning of the Normandy landings.
12:14	Omaha Beach: Americans reach church of Colleville-sur-Mer.
12:23	Omaha Beach: men of 18th Regiment, US 1st Infantry Division climb bluffs and head towards Colleville-sur-Mer.
13:00	Omaha Beach: WN72 strongpoint (Vierville-sur-Mer, Dog Green area) under US control.
	Sword Beach: men of 1st Suffolk Regiment storm the Morris strongpoint south of Colleville-sur-Orne.
	Sword Beach: Germans counter-attack to seize WN21 (British code name 'Trout') defended by 41 Commando led by Lt-Col Gray.
13:30	Aerial bombardment of Caen.
13:41	Omaha Beach: German resistance in front of Dog Green, Easy Green, Easy Red and White Red sectors has stopped.
14:00	Pointe du Hoc: German defenders of Werfer-Regiment 84 abandon the battery on its western flank.
14:13	Omaha Beach: destruction by destroyer USS *Harding* of the bell tower of church of Vierville-sur-Mer supposed to house German artillery observers.
14:58	Omaha Beach: Artillerie-Regiment 352 reports that village of Colleville-sur-Mer has fallen once again into enemy hands.

15:00   Omaha Beach: 2 US destroyers approach shore to support the landed troops.

Omaha Beach: Grenadier-Regiment 916 counter-attacks US troops between WNs 62a, 62b and 64.

About 80 French resistance fighters shot dead at Caen prison by Gestapo because they could not be moved (the first are shot from 10:00 a.m., the rest in the afternoon).

Gen. Marcks asks Col von Oppeln-Bronikowski to counter-attack with 21. Panzer-Division: 'The fate of Germany and this conflict depends on the success of your counterattack.'

15:26   Omaha Beach: failure of German counter-attack led by Grenadier-Regiment 916 in Colleville-sur-Mer.

15:30   Sword Beach: British control port of Ouistreham.

15:45   Sword Beach: men and tanks of 2nd Battalion, East Yorkshire Regiment and 13th/18th Royal Hussars storm WN14.

16:00   German counter-attack towards bridge of La Fière, 2 miles from Ste-Mère-Église, defended by US paratroopers of Able Company, 505th PIR, 82nd Airborne Division.

Gold Beach: WN35 at Le Hamel under control of 1st Royal Hampshire Battalion.

Aerial bombardment of city of Caen. Bombing of German battery at Mont-Canisy by 37 Marauder aircraft, which drop 61 tons of bombs on the site.

Von Rundstedt authorized to engage his two armoured divisions.

16:20   25 German tanks belonging to 21. Panzer-Division counter-attack near Périers-sur-le-Dan.

17:00   Omaha Beach: Maj.-Gen. Huebner lands on Easy Red beach area.

Omaha Beach: bell tower of church of St-Laurent-sur-Mer, which houses German snipers, is destroyed by American naval artillery.

Omaha Beach: Omaha's westernmost strongpoint, WN73, stormed by men from 5th Rangers Battalion and 116th Regiment, US 29th Infantry Division.

17:10   Grenadier-Regiment 916 informs HQ of Infanterie-Division 352 that St-Laurent-sur-Mer has fallen into hands of enemy.

18:00   Juno Beach: in St-Aubin-sur-Mer, last German defenders of coastal installations in Nan Red sector surrender.

Sword Beach: men of 2nd Battalion, East Yorkshire Regiment storm Daimler fortified point (WN12) to Ouistreham.

18:10   Omaha Beach: Grenadier-Regiment 915 reports that it has bypassed the Americans from the rear at Colleville-sur-Mer castle and that its wounded can no longer be evacuated.

18:25   Pointe du Hoc: Gen. Dietrich Kraiss, commander of Infanterie-Division 352, orders Grenadier-Regiment 916 to counter-attack.

18:30   Omaha Beach: 26th Infantry Regiment, US 1st Infantry Division, begins landing.

18:54   Destroyer USS *Harding* once again bombards the steeple of church of Vierville-sur-Mer. Shooting ends at 18:57.

19:00   Omaha Beach: in locality of Colleville-sur-Mer, violent fighting between US troops and German defenders.

19:25   Pointe du Hoc: Germans launch counter-offensive in east towards Rangers positions with elements of Le Guay's strongpoint.

19:35   Destroyer USS *Harding* pours fire on to bell tower of church of Vierville-sur-Mer.

19:40   Pointe du Hoc: Kraiss informed of German advance and told 9. Kompanie, Grenadier-Regiment 726 is surrounded by enemy in east and south.

Omaha Beach: German artillery barrage on beach in Colleville-sur-Mer area, where landing operations are continuing. Some losses within US troops.

20:00   6 German tanks make breakthrough to Lion-sur-Mer then fall back.

1st Suffolks still fighting Hillman strongpoint, defended by men of Grenadier-Regiment 736, south of Sword Beach.

French Commandos of 1er Bataillon de Fusiliers Marins reach locality of Le Hauger.

20:15   Hillman strongpoint stormed by men of Suffolk Regiment and tanks of 13th/18th Hussars after hard fighting.

20:51   Last elements of 6th Airborne Division land with 256 gliders on landing zones of Ranville – LZ N – and north-west of Bénouville – LZ W – Operation MALLARD.

20:55   Beginning of airlanding operations, involving 36 Waco and 140 Horsa gliders towed by 176 Douglas C-47s.

21:00   Attack led by 3 companies of 21. Panzer-Division south of Juno Beach fails.

Pointe du Hoc: 24 Rangers of Company A, 5th Battalion reach Pointe du Hoc Battery from Omaha Beach.

21:30   Rommel arrives back at La Roche-Guyon from Germany.

22:30   Aerial bombardment of city of Caen.

After heavy fighting, liberation of town of Tailleville, defended by Grenadier-Regiment 736.

Men of 1st Royal Hampshires liberate locality of Arromanches.

23:00   Pointe du Hoc: counter-attack by 40 German soldiers belonging to the 1. Kompanie, Regiment 914, Infanterie-Division 352, launched against Rangers at Pointe du Hoc Battery.

Notes

Abbreviations used in notes

AFHRA	United States Air Force Historical Research Agency, Maxwell AF Base, AL
BA-MA	Bundesarchiv-Militärarchiv, Freiburg
BTM	Bovington Tank Museum, Dorset
CCL	Churchill College Library, Cambridge
DDE	Papers of Dwight D. Eisenhower
IWM	Imperial War Museum, London
LHCMA	Liddell Hart Centre for Military Archives, King's College, London
MdC	Mémorial de Caen
NWWIIM	National World War II Museum, New Orleans
TNA	The National Archives, Kew, London
USAHC	United States Army Heritage Center, Carlisle Barracks, PA
WSC	Winston Churchill, *The Second World War*

Prologue

4   'Here we are on the eve . . .': cited in Sir Trafford Leigh-Mallory's notes, TNA AIR 37/784. Although Eisenhower's words are given in speech marks, it is pointed out that these are the gist of what he said not 100 per cent verbatim

5   'Gentlemen I am *hardening* . . .': cited in Omar N. Bradley, *A General's Life*, p. 241

1 The Atlantic Wall

11   'We found no cheer . . .': cited in Vince Milano and Bruce Conner, *Normandiefront*, p. 37

12   'How is this possible?': ibid, p. 35

16   'In our circle . . .': Friedrich Ruge, *Rommel in Normandy*, p. 50

16   'He had a good sense of humour . . .': ibid, p. 49

17   'Our friends from the East . . .': cited in B. H. Liddell Hart (ed.), *The Rommel Papers*, p. 467

17   'I have to be satisfied . . .': cited in David Irving, *The Trail of the Fox*, p. 315
19   'Provided we succeed . . .': ibid, p. 313
19   'Subject: fundamental questions . . .': Ruge, p. 144
19   'It was to be hoped . . .': ibid
21   'On this beach . . .': ibid, p. 155
22   'Irrefutable documentary proof . . .': cited in ibid, p. 157

2 Command of the Skies

34   'Mary Coningham was . . .': General Elwood Richard 'Pete' Quesada, interview 3, AFHRA
35   'The strategic British . . .': cited in Richard G. Davis, *Carl A. Spaatz and the Air War in Europe*, p. 352
35   'Considering that they are all . . .': Churchill in WSC, Vol. V, p. 466
35   'I and my military advisors . . .': DDE, Vol. III, doc. 1,630, p. 1,809
37   'The ratio in which . . .': Adolf Galland, *The First and the Last*, p. 201
38   'It had been a long . . .': Wolfgang Fischer, *Luftwaffe Fighter Pilot*, p. 98
39   'Its pilot immediately . . .': ibid, p. 124
39   'Start travelling!': ibid, p. 125
40   'There is no torture . . .': Richard E. Turner, *Mustang Pilot*, p. 78
41   'The fighter arm . . .': Galland, p. 269

3 Understanding Montgomery and the Master Plan

43   'This is going to be quite a party!': cited in Carol Mather, *When the Grass Stops Growing*, p. 244
43   'Perhaps you will have him to dine . . .': ibid, p. 245
50   'This exercise is being held . . .': TNA CAB 106/1031
50   'Some of us here know . . .': ibid
52   'If projected phase lines . . .': Omar N. Bradley, *A General's Life*, p. 233

4 Countdown

55   'And, you know, when I joined . . .': cited in Holger Eckhertz, *D-Day Through German Eyes*, p. 94
55   'Every morning I thought of my brother . . .': ibid
55   'The Atlantic Wall . . .': ibid
56   'Feuchtinger had to delegate . . .': Hans von Luck, *Panzer Commander*, p. 167
56   'Gentlemen, I know the English . . .': cited in Werner Kortenhaus, *The Combat History of the 21. Panzer Division*, p. 68
56   'From my knowledge . . .': ibid
58   'In view of the thin . . .': Friedrich Freiherr von der Heydte, *A German Parachute Regiment in Normandy*, p. 6, B-839, USAHC
58   'Weapons from all over . . .': ibid, p. 8
58   'Emplacements without guns . . .': ibid
59   'A large percentage . . .': cited in Vince Milano and Bruce Conner, *Normandiefront*, p. 50

59   'Herr Major, we have . . .': ibid
59   'The weakest point . . .': Friedrich Ruge, *Rommel in Normandy*, p. 169
59   'The corporal was lying . . .': Arthur Blizzard, IWM 17979
61   'The success of any tank . . .': Stanley Christopherson Diary, February–6 June 1944
61   'I lay you 10–1 . . .': cited in ibid
62   'So, yeah . . .': Tom Bowles, author interview
62   'I know we had some guys . . .': Henry D. Bowles, author interview
62   'The men were honed . . .': John Robert Slaughter, *Omaha Beach and Beyond*, p. 89
63   'Sergeant, are you and your men . . .': ibid, p. 84
64   'The essence of his technique . . .': Carol Mather, *When the Grass Stops Growing*, p. 246
65   'He either fears his fate . . .': Montgomery of Alamein, Field Marshal the Viscount, *Memoirs*, p. 244, and Mather, p. 247
65   'Then everyone burst out . . .': Mather, p. 247

5 The Winds of War

69   'If our planning . . .': DDE, Vol. III, no. 1,682
74   'I hesitate to increase . . .': TNA AIR 37/772
74   'However, a strong airborne . . .': ibid
74   'Brad, the best of luck . . .': Chester B. Hansen Diary, 2/6/1944
75   'We are done with the heavy . . .': ibid
77   'Gentlemen, the fears . . .': LHCMA LH 15/15/29
77   'Are we prepared to take a gamble . . .': ibid
77   'Pleasant dreams . . .': ibid
78   'Are there any dissenting . . .': ibid
78   'The fair interval . . .': ibid
78   'It's a helluva gamble . . .': cited in Stephen E. Ambrose, *The Supreme Commander*, p. 416
79   'The question is . . .': ibid
79   'Stagg, we've put it on . . .': LHCMA LH 15/15/29
79   'Lay and thought . . .': ibid
79   'OK. Let's go.': Ambrose, p. 417

6 Big War

82   5,552,000 tons . . . : cited in Duncan S. Ballantine, *U.S. Naval Logistics in the Second World War*, p. 170
82   'Damn, he did unbelievable things . . .': Charles 'Tick' Bonesteel, USAHC
83   'It is a most complicated . . .': Robert W. Love, Jr., and John Major (eds), *The Year of D-Day: The 1944 Diary of Admiral Sir Bertram Ramsay RN*, 24/3/1944
85   'They *must* float up and down . . .': WSC, Vol. V, p. 66
86   'Every detail was there . . .':, A. M. D. Lampen, *Naval Reminiscences*, LHCMA V/7
86   'It's been decided . . .': ibid, V/9

87   'However, there's no point . . .': ibid
87   'I became familiar . . .': ibid, VI/4
88   'No single question . . .': cited in *Battle Summary No. 39: Operation "Neptune", Landings in Normandy, June 1944*, TNA, p. 24
89   'Made 16 . . .': Ramsay Diary, 29/5/1944
90   'Everybody who was supposed . . .': General Elwood Richard 'Pete' Quesada, interview 3, AFHRA
90   'Goddam it, Pete . . .': ibid
91   'You have to have . . .': ibid
91   'The air forces were fighting . . .': ibid
92   'I stayed up . . .': Ernie Pyle, *Brave Men*, p. 351
92   'The Germans will have to . . .': ibid, p. 354
92   'From a vague . . .': ibid, p. 356
93   'I tried to visualise . . .': Stanley Christopherson Diary, 5/6/44
93   'I immediately set about . . .': ibid
94   'This was the invasion . . .': Chester B. Hansen Diary, 3/6/1944

7 Air Power

95   'Constant enemy air attacks . . .': cited in James A. Wood (ed.), *Army of the West*, p. 35
95   'Paris has been systematically . . .': cited in Major L. F. Ellis, *Victory in the West*, p. 111
95   'Large-scale strategic . . .': ibid
96   'In fact, the whole crew . . .': Truman Smith, *The Wrong Stuff*, p. 37
96   'There was an overpowering . . .': ibid, p. 136
97   'I'm not going.': ibid, p. 137
97   'This was the fourth . . .': ibid
98   'Once the pilots and crew . . .': Joseph J. Boylan, *Goon's Up*, p. 228
98   'One of our planes got it!': ibid, p. 227
100   'Living outside Germany . . .': Ken Adam, author interview
101   'We were the last in . . .': ibid
101   'Junior Soesman hit . . .': Ken Adam, logbook
101   'Target well pranged': TNA AIR 27/2103
103   '*Where* within this entire . . .': F. H. Hinsley et al., *British Intelligence in the Second World War*, Vol. III, Part 2, p. 64
104   'the arsehole from the Berghof': cited in Ralf Georg Reuth, *Rommel: The End of a Legend*, p. 170
104   'highly animated': Friedrich Ruge, *Rommel in Normandy*, p. 172

8 D-Day Minus One

109   'Well, here it is . . .': Mark J. Alexander and John Sparry, *Jump Commander*, p. 173
110   'I want to be there . . .': cited in ibid, p. 174
111   'There has been no . . .': F. H. Hinsley et al., *British Intelligence in the Second World War*, Vol. III, Part 2, p. 63

114 'Airborne troops . . .': Ridgway Papers, Box 2a, USAHC
117 'In D Company . . .': Denis Edwards, *The Devil's Own Luck*, p. 19
117 'Apart from flying training . . .': ibid
117 'I smoked a great many . . .': ibid, p. 33
118 'My muscles tightened . . .': ibid, p. 35
118 'You've had it chum . . .': ibid
119 'In my opinion . . .': Latham B. Jenson, *Tin Hats, Oilskins & Seaboots*, p. 215
119 'I have just been informed . . .': ibid, p. 222

9 D-Day: The First Hours

120 'This time, no more . . .': Robert Leblanc, *Journal du Maquis*, ed. Alain Corblin, 5/6/1944
121 'I make the most of the minutes . . .': ibid, 5/6/1944
121 'Two minutes from cast-off . . .': cited in John Howard and Penny Bates, *The Pegasus Diaries*, p. 117
122 'Probably the only thing . . .': Denis Edwards, IWM 23207
122 'Relief, exhilaration . . .': Denis Edwards, *The Devil's Own Luck*, p. 43
124 'Are you scared?': Bert Stiles, *Serenade to the Big Bird*, p. 5
124 'Maybe this is D-Day . . .': ibid, p. 79
124 'D-Day. Honest to God.': ibid, p. 80
125 'Hello Four Dog . . .': Howard and Bates, p. 123
126 'Fate had led me . . .': Richard Todd, *Caught in the Act*, p. 143
127 'Gentlemen, in spite of your excellent . . .': cited in Winston G. Ramsay (ed.), *D-Day Then and Now*, Vol. I, p. 238
128 'All units are . . .': Hans von Luck, *Panzer Commander*, p. 172
132 'Though I had been . . .': Dick Winters, *Beyond Band of Brothers*, p. 81
133 'The regiment is . . .': Friedrich Freiherr von der Heydte *A German Parachute Regiment in Normandy*, p. 4, B-839, USAHC
136 'It burned very nicely . . .': Edwards, *The Devil's Own Luck*, p. 45
137 'No mistake . . .': Leblanc Diary, 5/6/1944
137 'Nobody is killed . . .': ibid
137 'Highest Alarm Status . . .': Franz Gockel, *La Porte de l'Enfer*, p. 79; cited in Vince Milano and Bruce Conner, *Normandiefront*, p. 71
137 'In our lightweight uniforms . . .': Gockel, p. 80
138 'Thousands of ships . . .': cited in Milano and Conner, p. 72

10 D-Day: Dawn

140 'They immediately made me . . .': John Raaen, NWWIIM
140 'We trained hard . . .': ibid
143 'The Allies are landing!': Geneviève Dubosq, *Dans la nuit du débarquement*, p. 73
143 '*Venez ici* . . .': ibid, p. 79
144 'Suddenly, I am . . .': ibid, p. 88
144 'We are extremely . . .': ibid, p. 99
144 'Here comes a car . . .': Malcolm Brannen, CRAOU

144   'Don't kill . . .': ibid
144   'So I shot . . .': ibid
147   'We saw the red . . .': Ken Handley Diary, 6/6/1944, IWM 3198
147   'successful': TNA AIR 27/1926
147   'Coming in over base . . .': Ken Handley Diary, 6/6/1944
148   'It was one of the most . . .': Francis Gabreski, *Gabby: A Fighter Pilot's Life*, p. 159
149   'We got flak . . .': Archie Maltbie, NWWIIM
149   'I'm not ashamed to say . . .': cited in Vince Milano and Bruce Conner, *Normandiefront*, p. 74
150   'It was only the beginning . . .': Franz Gockel, *La Porte de l'Enfer*, p. 82
150   'The earth trembled . . .': ibid, p. 83

11 D-Day: The American Landings

153   'What a stupendous sight . . .': Latham B. Jenson, *Tin Hats, Oilskins & Seaboots*, p. 224
154   'The invasion has now . . .': Chester B. Hansen Diary, 6/6/1944
154   'Attention on deck!': John Raaen, *Intact*, p. 5
156   'So we agreed . . .': Walter Halloran, author interview
157   'On the ship going to North Africa . . .': cited in Marvin Jensen, *Strike Swiftly!*, p. 22
157   'They really saturated . . .': ibid, p. 135
158   'nice and easy': ibid
158   'A rolling pin . . .': Franz Gockel, *La Porte de l'Enfer*, p. 83
160   'We'll start the war . . .': cited in Antony Beevor, *D-Day*, p. 118
160   'He was nearly dead . . .': cited in Jenson, p. 140
161   'Fire, Wegner, fire!': cited in Vince Milano and Bruce Conner, *Normandiefront*, p. 78
162   'Now was not the time . . .': cited in ibid, p. 79
162   'Here, we were facing . . .': Gockel, p. 87
162   'If you stopped . . .': Walter Halloran, author interview
162   'There's five soldiers . . .': ibid
163   'I don't understand . . .': Hansen Diary, 6/6/1944
163   'After H-Hour . . .': John Raaen, NWWIIM
164   'They crossed the beach . . .': Maryland Military History Society Archives, Company B, 1st Battalion, 116th Infantry, mdmhs.org/29div/interviews
164   'The enlisted men . . .': ibid
165   'When I pulled back the bolt . . .' Karl Wegner, cited in Milano and Conner, p. 84
165   'We expected A and B . . .': John Robert Slaughter, *Omaha Beach and Beyond*, p. 108
166   'It was demoralizing . . .': ibid, p. 109
166   'Slaughter, are we going . . .': ibid, p. 110
167   'The scene was one from hell . . .': Raaen, *Intact*, p. 39
167   'Headquarters! Over here!': ibid, p. 40

12 D-Day: The British and Canadian Landings
168 'Any minute now . . .': Latham B. Jenson, *Tin Hats, Oilskins & Seaboots*, p. 225
169 'Ten boats stretched . . .': Charles Cromwell Martin, *Battle Diary*, p. 5
170 'I was struck speechless . . .': cited in Holger Eckhertz, *D-Day Through German Eyes*, p. 70
170 'Are we sorry . . .': ibid, p. 71
171 'Our MG was running very hot . . .': ibid, p. 76
172 'Come on, be quick . . .': ibid, p. 78
172 'I began to understand . . .': ibid
173 'I looked into the MG room . . .': ibid, p. 80
174 'He certainly appeared . . .': Stanley Christopherson Diary, 6/6/1944
175 'Move! Fast! . . .': Martin, p. 6
176 'It was a great gun . . .': Bob Roberts, author interview
176 'Right out in the country . . .': ibid
176 'Because you didn't know what . . .': ibid
176 'When the explosions began . . .': cited in Eckhertz, p. 100
176 'However great the pressure . . .': ibid
177 'There was nothing . . .': Bob Roberts, author interview
178 'All I could see . . .': ibid
178 'They thought it was . . .': ibid
178 'Come on, let's . . .': ibid
179 'They screamed as they . . .': Eckhertz, p. 105
180 'I saw that his legs . . .': ibid, p. 108
180 'Up at 5.00 hours . . .': Revd. Leslie Skinner, *The Man Who Worked on Sundays*, 6/6/1944
181 'Chaos ashore . . .': ibid
181 'sneaking desire': Stanley Christopherson Diary, 6/6/1944
183 'It was terrific . . .': Arthur Blizzard, IWM 17979
183 'Jerry was machine-gunning . . .': ibid
184 'The most difficult challenge . . .': Hubert Fauré Oral History, MdC
185 'The shock was so strong . . .': ibid

13 D-Day: The Turning of the Battle
187 'I'm sorry, Lieutenant . . .': Dick Winters, *Beyond Band of Brothers*, p. 85
187 'Move, for Christ's sake . . .': ibid, p. 86
187 'This entire engagement . . .': ibid
188 'No make me dead!': ibid, p. 88
188 'Perhaps the Germans were short . . .': ibid
189 'I took a final look . . .': ibid, p. 89
189 'I was thirsty as hell . . .': ibid, p. 91
189 'Everything is in his favour . . .': General Miles Dempsey, Ronald Lewin Papers, CCL
190 'So the enemy invasion . . .': cited in David Irving, *The Trail of the Fox*, p. 335

190   'Normandy! Normandy! . . .': cited in Daniel Allen Butler, *Field Marshal*,
      p. 480
192   'With every casualty . . .': Franz Gockel, *La Porte de l'Enfer*, p. 90
193   'Hey, Captain, look . . .': John Raaen, NWWIIM
193   'What's the situation . . .': ibid
194   'Our attitude was . . .': ibid
195   'Absolutely none . . .': ibid
195   'You could see bullets . . .': Tom Bowles, author interview
196   'You could see the shells . . .': Henry D. Bowles, author interview
197   'I am not ready . . .': Frank Wright, IWM 23819
197   'It was not altogether pleasant . . .': Stanley Christopherson Diary, 6/6/1944
198   'I had a feeling . . .': cited in Holger Eckhertz, *D-Day Through German
      Eyes*, p. 110
198   'Our gunners in their enthusiasm . . .': ibid, p. 111
199   'I looked back . . .': ibid, p. 114
199   'He missed the gunner . . .': Hubert Fauré Oral History, MdC
200   'Kieffer was not . . .': ibid
200   'Some of our battle positions . . .': Fritz Ziegelmann, B-432, USAHC

14 D-Day: Foothold

202   'In training I placed . . .': cited in P. A. Spayd, *Bayerlein*, p. 156
203   'The nights were very short . . .': Fritz Bayerlein, ETHINT 66-ML-1079,
      USAHC
203   'Too late, much too late!': Hans von Luck, *Panzer Commander*, p. 178
204   'That is not too healthy . . .': Denis Edwards, *The Devil's Own Luck*, p. 51
205   'So to add to our . . .': Richard Todd, *Caught in the Act*, p. 177
205   'You English in the church . . .': Edwards, p. 53
206   'It's them! . . .': ibid, p. 54
207   'He was just sat . . .': Tom Bowles, author interview
208   'Apparently, the situation . . .': Chester B. Hansen Diary, 6/6/1944
208   'There was continual . . .': ibid
208   'Bradley shows no sign . . .': ibid
209   'We all crouched . . .': cited in Vince Milano and Bruce Conner,
      Normandiefront, p. 99
210   'After a long time . . .': ibid, p. 114
210   'The CO, Oberst Meyer . . .': Telephone Diary of the 352nd Infantry
      Division (Coastal Defense Section Bayeux), USAHC (provided by Fritz
      Ziegelmann)
210   'Never in my wildest . . .': Stanley Christopherson Diary, 6/6/1944
211   'Shot her right between the eyes . . .': Bob Roberts, author interview
211   'We followed the fields . . .': Charles Cromwell Martin, *Battle Diary*, p. 14
213   'I nearly got kaput over it . . .': Arthur Blizzard, IWM 17979
213   'What we really wanted . . .': ibid
214   'They really schlacked . . .': Mark J. Alexander and John Sparry, *Jump
      Commander*, p. 192

214   'I have never seen . . .': Geneviève Dubosq, *Dans la nuit du débarquement*, p. 116

215   'Mama uses boiled water . . .': ibid, p. 120

215   'The time had come! . . .': Kurt Meyer, *Grenadiers*, p. 216

215   'I have breathed . . .': Kurt Meyer, TNA WO 208/4177

216   'We knew what was in front . . .': Meyer, *Grenadiers*, p. 216

216   'They were imbued . . .': ibid, p. 214

217   'Then all hell broke loose . . .': von Luck, p. 179

218   'For us wounded . . .': Franz Gockel, *La Porte de l'Enfer*, p. 97

218   'Even in these . . .': ibid, p. 104

218   'It looked as though . . .': Karl Wegner, cited in Milano and Conner, p. 107

219   'I let fly . . .': Wolfgang Fischer, *Luftwaffe Fighter Pilot*, p. 137

220   'Charlie, it's such a sad day . . .': Martin, p. 16

15 Bridgehead

226   'All looked orderly . . .': Richard E. Turner, *Mustang Pilot*, p. 85

226   'They've increased . . .': Truman Smith, *The Wrong Stuff*, p. 166

227   'So all the negatives . . .': Joseph J. Boylan, *Goon's Up*, p. 231

227   'One could hardly . . .': ibid, p. 232

227   'Not too bad . . .': ibid

227   'A soldier was lying . . .': Kurt Meyer, *Grenadiers*, p. 216

228   'Where was our Luftwaffe . . .': ibid, p. 220

228   'The whole expanse . . .': ibid, p. 222

229   'Decision made in view of . . .': Chester B. Hansen Diary, 7/6/1944

230   'Unless the wind drops . . .': TNA WO 285/9

231   'It is sometimes difficult . . .': TNA AIR 37/772

232   'On June 7 . . .': Mark J. Alexander and John Sparry, *Jump Commander*, p. 193

233   'I am astonished . . .': Geneviève Dubosq, *Dans la nuit du débarquement*, p. 147

234   'Here I am . . .': ibid, p. 176

234   'Winters, I hate . . .': Dick Winters, *Beyond Band of Brothers*, p. 97

235   'Combat in Normandy . . .': ibid, p. 98

235   'We can also hear . . .': Martin Pöppel, *Heaven and Hell*, p. 179

236   'The night of D-Day . . .': John Raaen, NWWIIM

236   'They were far better . . .': cited in Vince Milano and Bruce Conner, *Normandiefront*, p. 135

237   'We had practically . . .': Raaen, NWWIIM

239   'That was a bad day . . .': Arthur Blizzard, IWM 17979

240   'drive the enemy who had . . .': Hubert Meyer, *The 12th SS: The History of the Hitler Youth Panzer Division*, Vol. I, p. 134

240   'One could no longer . . .': Kurt Meyer, p. 224

241   'We quickly turned back . . .': cited in Hubert Meyer, Vol. I, p. 147

16 Fighter-Bomber Racecourse

244   'Any questions?': Frank Wright, IWM 23819

244   'Our target . . .': ibid

244 'I must be dreaming . . .': ibid
245 'White faced, hands held high . . .': ibid
245 'I'm going to die here . . .': ibid
246 'And we were over . . .': ibid
246 'What would be . . .': Carol Mather, *When the Grass Stops Growing*, p. 255
246 'There was the acrid . . .': ibid, p. 257
246 'Submerged tanks and . . .': Ernie Pyle, *Brave Men*, p. 360
246 'a shore-line museum . . .': ibid, p. 366
246 'On the beach lay . . .': ibid, p. 367
247 'They didn't need to . . .': ibid, p. 369
247 'Willi and I . . .': cited in Vince Milano and Bruce Conner, *Normandiefront*, p. 145
247 'Wegner, the Amis . . .': ibid
248 'And we took Pointe du Hoc . . .': John Raaen, NWWIIM
248 'We were given . . .': Stanley Christopherson Diary, 7/6/1944
250 'The main road . . .': cited in P. A. Spayd, *Bayerlein*, p. 157
250 'The section between . . .': cited in Paul Carrell, *Invasion! They're Coming!*, p. 113
250 'These are serious losses . . .': cited in Spayd, p. 159
251 'We knew it would be difficult . . .': Helmut Ritgen, *The Western Front, 1944*, p. 57
252 'Are you going to be . . .': Tom and Henry Bowles, author interview

17 Linking Up

255 'They were AT&T's best . . .': General Elwood Richard 'Pete' Quesada, interview 3, AFHRA
256 'Headquarters IX Tactical . . .': cited in Thomas Hughes, *Over Lord*, p. 144
257 'I wanted all to be sunk . . .': Robert W. Love, Jr. and John Major (eds), *The Year of D-Day: The 1944 Diary of Admiral Sir Bertram Ramsay RN*, 8/6/1944
257 'Just a day . . .': ibid, 9/6/1944
257 'The method of scuttling . . .': Ambrose Lampen, *Naval Reminiscences*, LHCMA VII/7
257 'I saw the whole thing . . .': ibid, VII/9
258 'I knew immediately . . .': ibid
259 'So I made up . . .': John Raaen, NWWIIM
259 'One minute they were . . .': John Robert Slaughter, *Omaha Beach and Beyond*, p. 127
260 'If they would only fight . . .': cited in Vince Milano and Bruce Conner, *Normandiefront*, p. 155
260 'Even though we fell back . . .': ibid, p. 147
260 'But always we asked . . .': ibid, p. 148
261 'Point 103 became . . .': Stanley Christopherson Diary, 9/6/1944
261 'Mike's stammer . . .': ibid

262 'I was glad I didn't have . . .': Mark J. Alexander and John Sparry, *Jump Commander*, p. 197
262 'Ship after ship . . .': Martin Pöppel, *Heaven and Hell*, p. 184
262 'It's easy to imagine . . .': ibid, p. 202
264 'These shortcomings . . .': Dick Winters, *Beyond Band of Brothers*, p. 102
264 'All told, it was a rough . . .': ibid, p. 102
264 'Move out! . . .': ibid, p. 104
265 'June 11 I shall long . . .': Stanley Christopherson Diary, 11/6/1944
266 'He judged the terrain . . .': Helmut Ritgen, *The Western Front, 1944*, p. 60
266 'He temporarily . . .': ibid, p. 60

18 The Constraints of Wealth and the Freedom of Poverty

268 'Besides, my squadron-mates . . .': Richard E. Turner, *Mustang Pilot*, p. 86
268 'I hit him just . . .': ibid, p. 87
269 'And with my bonus . . .': ibid, p. 88
269 'Our attacks on . . .': Lewis H. Brereton, *The Brereton Diaries*, 13/6/1944
269 'These buzz bombs . . .': Mary Morris, 13/6/1944, IWM 4850
270 'beautiful but rather frightening': ibid, 5/6/1944
270 'Tremendous buzz of excitement . . .': ibid, 6/6/1944
270 'This new form of attack . . .': WSC, Vol. VI, p. 35
270 'They say you have . . .': Harry C. Butcher, *Three Years with Eisenhower*, 16/6/1944
271 'The Air Ministry estimates . . .': Brereton, 14/6/1944
271 'Last night Ike was concerned . . .': Butcher, 15/6/1944
272 'It was mainly little . . .': Tom Bowles, author interview
272 'At "stand to" . . .': Denis Edwards, *The Devil's Own Luck*, p. 77
273 'Then began . . .': Hans von Luck, *Panzer Commander*, p. 187
273 'A veritable inferno . . .': ibid
273 'There were only his eyes . . .': Hubert Fauré Oral History, MdC
274 'What more could we set . . .': von Luck, p. 187
274 'We now finally . . .': ibid
274 'A concerted blow . . .': TNA WO 285/9
281 'The chain of command . . .': Leo Geyr von Schweppenburg, B-466, USAHC
282 'In the past twenty-four hours . . .': TNA WO 285/8
283 'Caen is the key to Cherbourg': cited in Chester B. Hansen Diary, 17/6/1944

19 Behind the Lines

285 'The butcheries were . . .': Friedrich Ruge, *Rommel in Normandy*, p. 183
285 'I've already briefed . . .': cited in David Irving, *The Trail of the Fox*, p. 350
285 'June 13 was about . . .': Dick Winters, *Beyond Band of Brothers*, p. 108
286 'The division was bled white . . .': Leo Geyr von Schweppenburg, B-466, USAHC

287   'As soon as we reached . . .': Willi Müller, *Vom Pionier-Bataillon in der Normandie zum Panzerjagdkommando in Sachsen*, p. 74

288   'It is not a good time . . .': cited in Alistair Horne, *The Lonely Leader*, p. 154

288   'What is there then . . . ?': WSC, Vol. VI, p. 11

288   'I am hopeful . . .': Francis L. Loewenheim et al. (eds), *Roosevelt and Churchill: Their Secret Wartime Correspondence*, No. 544, p. 501

289   'It was explained . . .': Carol Mather, *When the Grass Stops Growing*, p. 263

289   'The General thanks you . . .': ibid, p. 264

289   'At the sight of General de Gaulle . . .': cited in Charles Williams, *The Last Great Frenchman*, p. 258

290   'I was only a lieutenant . . .': Peter McFarren and Fadrique Iglesias, *The Devil's Agent*, p. 49

290   'Poor people, but I can't . . .': Robert Leblanc, *Journal du Maquis*, ed. Alain Corblin, 6/6/1944

291   'I must confess . . .': ibid, 7/6/1944

291   'We used to say . . .': ibid, 11/6/1944

291   'Whatever happens next . . .': ibid

292   'Tears come to my eyes . . .': ibid, 13/6/1944

20 The Grinding Battle

295   'Well, Frenchie . . .': Pierre Clostermann, *The Big Show*, p. 171

295   'The Huns have left . . .': ibid, p. 172

295   'Don't worry, Pierre . . .': ibid

296   'Deafened, battered . . .': ibid, p. 173

296   'Oh, you know . . .': ibid

297   'At first sight . . .': Robert Woollcombe, *Lion Rampant*, p. 37

297   'All through my young life . . .': Ken Tout, *By Tank*, p. 10

297   'You couldn't go . . .': Ken Tout, author interview

298   'Some very unpleasant fighting . . .': Stanley Christopherson Diary, 20/6/1944

298   'For a day . . .': ibid

298   'We were fortunate . . .': Helmut Ritgen, *The Western Front, 1944*, p. 61

298   'to do harm to their enemies . . .': ibid, p. 63

299   'which we could not . . .': ibid

300   'I put the razor . . .': cited in Vince Milano and Bruce Conner, *Normandiefront*, p. 208

300   'One concentrated attack . . .': ibid, p. 192

300   'They asked us . . .': Johannes Börner, author interview

301   'It was very hard . . .': ibid

301   'The 2nd Squad . . .': John Robert Slaughter, *Omaha Beach and Beyond*, p. 128

302   'Carentan badly hit . . .': Chester B. Hansen Diary, 15/6/1944

303   'It was obvious . . .': J. Lawton Collins, *Lightning Joe*, p. 208

303   'He made no excuses . . .': ibid
303   'Still a good artillery man . . .': Chester B. Hansen Diary, 14/6/1944
304   'Before you cross . . .': Mark J. Alexander and John Sparry, *Jump Commander*, p. 215
304   'My 1st Battalion . . .' : ibid, p. 217
304   'One could feel . . .': cited in Milano and Conner, p. 204
305   'That was then . . .': Slaughter, p. 130
307   'The fortress of Cherbourg . . .': Hans Speidel, *Invasion 1944*, p. 90
308   'Cherbourg will fall in a week.': ibid, p. 91
308   'There's no front line . . .': ibid, p. 93

21 The Great Storm

310   'I won't have you bothered . . .': DDE, Vol. III, Doc. 1759
311   'Everything was a vivid green . . .': Ernie Pyle, *Brave Men*, p. 374
311   'It was as though life . . .': ibid
311   'I've been in the army . . .': ibid, p. 375
311   'This good-will business . . .': ibid, p. 378
312   'Maybe you ought . . .': Orion C. Shockley, *Random Chance*, p. 83
312   'It was cold . . .': ibid, p. 125
312   'There was fear . . .': Mary Morris, 18/6/1944, IWM 4850
313   'Hold on until . . .': ibid
313   'Matron was the last . . .': ibid
313   'There was mile after mile . . .': ibid, 19/6/1944
313   'The weather was . . .': Latham B. Jenson, *Tin Hats, Oilskins & Seaboots*, p. 231
313   'Dark, cold and rainy . . .': Chester B. Hansen Diary, 19/6/1944
314   'This was a never-before . . .': cited in Hubert Meyer, *The 12th SS: The History of the Hitler Youth Panzer Division*, Vol. I, p. 251
314   'The only consolation . . .': Helmut Ritgen, *The Western Front, 1944*, p. 65
315   'We were all proud . . .': Ambrose Lampen, *Naval Reminiscences*, LMHCA VIII/5
315   'Under her lee . . .': ibid
315   'Now was revealed . . .': Jenson, p. 232
316   'The strong north wind . . .': General Miles Dempsey Papers, TNA WO 285/9
318   'Of course we did not . . .': Montgomery of Alamein, Field Marshal the Viscount, *Memoirs*, p. 254
319   'It was a narrow escape . . .': Richard E. Turner, *Mustang Pilot*, p. 92
319   'While you play around . . .': Jenson, p. 233
320   'My folks were . . .': William A. Biehler, Rutgers Oral History Archives
320   'The repple-depples were terrible . . .': ibid
321   'I don't think . . .': ibid
322   'I suppose I could . . .': Reg Spittles, 'Story No. 24', BTM Archives
322   'After all, they were . . .': ibid
323   'Chezzy has so much warmth . . .': Mary Morris, 20/6/1944, IWM 4850

323   'very high and mighty': ibid
323   'Hans is quite unlike . . .': ibid, 23/6/1944
324   'He thought he would . . .': Robert Leblanc, *Journal du Maquis*, ed. Alain Corblin, 20/6/1944
325   'I do not hesitate . . .': ibid, 22/6/1944
325   'I postponed 8 Corps . . .': Dempsey, TNA WO 285/9

22 EPSOM
326   'Without talking . . .': Kurt Meyer, *Grenadiers*, p. 242
326   'We were already . . .': ibid
327   'All the luck in the world . . .': cited in Hubert Meyer, *The 12th SS: The History of the Hitler Youth Panzer Division*, Vol. I, p. 335
332   'Everyone admirably controlled . . .': Robert Woollcombe, *Lion Rampant*, p. 53
332   'Little rashes of goose flesh . . .': ibid, p. 54
333   'I happened to be following . . .': Stanley Christopherson Diary, 26/6/1944
333   'As so often in the past . . .': Kurt Meyer, p. 242
334   'Look, he's only seventeen!': Woollcombe, p. 60
334   'Don't shoot – don't shoot! . . .': ibid, p. 61
334   'Well done, my boy . . .': ibid, p. 62
337   'It was a case of survival . . .': Reg Spittles, 'Story No. 41', BTM Archives
337   'I just thought . . .': ibid
337   'The absence of rocket-firing . . .': TNA WO 171/860
338   'The yard was a slough . . .': Woollcombe, p. 65
338   'It seemed there was no hope . . .': ibid, p. 67
349   'Transport had to be marshalled . . .': Walter Caines Journal, p. 6, IWM 306
340   'This was done . . .': cited in Hubert Meyer, p. 378
340   'Help me! . . .': ibid, p. 379
341   'The crew inside the Panzer . . .': ibid, p. 380

23 Cherbourg and the Scottish Corridor
343   'Send liaison officer . . .': cited in Marvin Jensen, *Strike Swiftly!*, p. 157
343   'Now you didn't do that . . .': ibid, p. 158
344   'That machine-gun . . .': ibid, p. 172
345   'Concentrated enemy fire . . .': cited in G. A. Harrison, *United States Army in World War II: Cross-Channel Attack*, p. 432
345   'You will continue . . .': ibid, p. 434
345   'The whole thing . . .': Ernie Pyle, *Brave Men*, p. 399
346   'Our company is starting . . .': ibid
346   'Why don't you tell . . .': ibid, pp. 399–400
346   'A rifle platoon goes first . . .': ibid, p. 400
346   'Spread it out . . .': ibid, p. 401
347   'They weren't warriors . . .': ibid

347 'The blast was terrific . . .': ibid, p. 404

348 'Hans brings me a cup . . .': Mary Morris, 24/6/1944, IWM 4850

349 'These pants are hilarious . . .': ibid, 26/6/1944

349 'He completely ignores . . .': ibid, 27/6/1944

349 'Although he is too shocked . . .': ibid

349 'I fix him up . . .': ibid

350 'The heavy fighting . . .': Kurt Meyer, *Grenadiers*, p. 248

351 'We let them come close . . .': cited in Hubert Meyer, *12th SS: The History of the Hitler Youth Panzer Division*, Vol. I, p. 394

352 'His deep, sunken eyes . . .': Kurt Meyer, p. 249

352 'It was booty . . .': cited in Hubert Meyer, p. 396

353 'This was the first time . . .': Walter Caines Journal, p. 6, IWM 306

354 'The capture of Fontenay . . .': Stanley Christopherson Diary, 27/6/1944

355 '15 Div is still involved . . .': General Miles Dempsey Papers, TNA WO 285/9

355 'Others started to get him . . .': Orion C. Shockley, *Random Chance*, p. 148

355 'We got clobbered . . .': Ken Tout, *By Tank*, p. 15

356 'Until this is done . . .': Dempsey, TNA WO 285/9

356 'The street was too narrow . . .': Kurt Meyer, p. 251

357 'There was no time . . .': Walter Caines Journal, p. 8, IWM 306

357 'It was impossible . . .': Kurt Meyer, p. 252

357 'The constant use . . .': ibid

24 Trouble at the Top

360 'We are always . . .': Friedrich Ruge, *Rommel in Normandy*, p. 194

361 'Caution had to be exercised . . .': ibid, p. 196

362 'Then, if everything goes well . . .': cited in David Irving, *The Trail of the Fox*, p. 478

363 'For us in the 391st . . .': Joseph J. Boylan, *Goon's Up*, p. 232

366 'Should there be . . .': TNA CAB 106/1031

366 'It is essential . . .': ibid

367 'I had to report . . .': Arthur Tedder, *With Prejudice*, p. 555

368 'I began to feel . . .': Pierre Clostermann, *The Big Show*, p. 181

369 'He mowed down . . .': ibid, p. 184

370 'The new set-up . . .': Richard E. Turner, *Mustang Pilot*, p. 93

370 'I wasn't planning . . .': ibid, p. 97

371 'There is nothing like . . .': ibid, p. 99

372 'Eutrecht's subconscious . . .': Truman Smith, *The Wrong Stuff*, p. 179

372 'The myth about . . .': ibid, p. 243

373 'I will back you up . . .': DDE, Vol. III, 7/7/1944

373 'Please be assured . . .': ibid

373 '4 aiming points . . .': TNA AIR 37/1057

374 'Another good daylight prang . . .': Ken Handley Diary, 7/7/1944, IWM 3198

25 Bloody Bocage
376 'Weapons and equipment . . .': Friedrich Freiherr von der Heydte, *A German Parachute Regiment in Normandy*, p. 26, B-839, USAHC
377 'Never before . . .': ibid, p. 25
377 'Excellent progress . . .': Martin Pöppel, *Heaven and Hell*, p. 210
377 'Eight shots . . .': ibid, p. 217
377 'The Americans will scarcely . . .': ibid
378 'Damn it . . .': ibid, p. 220
379 'The maddest I ever got . . .': cited in Marvin Jensen, *Strike Swiftly!*, p. 183
380 'They're shooting right down . . .': Mark J. Alexander and John Sparry, *Jump Commander*, p. 227
381 'So here was what I would call . . .': Charles 'Tick' Bonesteel, USAHC
383 'There was no time . . .': John Robert Slaughter, *Omaha Beach and Beyond*, p. 132
384 'The hedgerows were our allies . . .': cited in Vince Milano and Bruce Conner, *Normandiefront*, p. 217
385 'We wanted to fight . . .': Kurt Meyer, *Grenadiers*, p. 254
386 'It was terrible . . .': Charles Cromwell Martin, *Battle Diary*, p. 37
386 'The roasting of human . . .': Ken Tout, *By Tank*, p. 19
387 'Give 'em hell, boys!': ibid, p. 20
387 'That's it then . . .': ibid, p. 21
387 'Our cellar shook . . .': Meyer, p. 259
388 'Hullo, all stations, Yoke . . .': Tout, p. 22
389 'For what it's worth . . .': ibid, p. 24
389 'That's OK . . .': ibid, p. 25
389 'No way forward . . .': ibid, p. 26
389 'We scrunch around . . .': ibid
390 'The soldiers of 12. SS . . .': Meyer, p. 266

26 Living Like Foxes
391 'Felt too ill . . .': Mary Morris, 9/7/1944, IWM 4850
391 'This young man . . .': ibid, 4/7/1944
392 'Their bodies were black . . .': ibid, 5/7/1944
392 'Our star was setting . . .': cited in Vince Milano and Bruce Conner, *Normandiefront*, p. 235
392 'When I went back . . .': Charles Cromwell Martin, *Battle Diary*, p. 45
393 'Undressing and bathing . . .': Helmut Ritgen, *The Western Front, 1944*, p. 63
393 'Junior and I . . .': John Robert Slaughter, *Omaha Beach and Beyond*, p. 137
394 'In general, we lived in the ground . . .': Ritgen, p. 63
395 'You were totally independent . . .': author interview
395 'We were able to add . . .': ibid
396 'The bocage allowed . . .': Ritgen, p. 96
397 'My crews suffered . . .': ibid
397 'March on several roads . . .': *Ausbildungshinweis* Nr. 33, BA-MA

398   'It was incredibly cumbersome . . .': Eberhard Günther Beck, *Tagebuch*, p. 7, BA-MA
398   'Fields and streets . . .': ibid, p. 12
398   'It was said his head . . .': ibid
399   'For us, the war was long lost . . .': ibid, p. 13
399   'Shells rained down . . .': Walter Caines Journal, p. 16, IWM 306
400   'Little did he know . . .': ibid, p. 17
401   'It was hell . . .': ibid, p. 19
401   'Something I will never forget . . .': ibid
401   'We thanked God . . .': ibid, p. 21
403   'How did we come . . .': Willi Müller, *Vom Pionier-Bataillon in der Normandie zum Panzerjagdkommando in Sachsen*, p. 88
403   'Can a seventeen year-old . . .': ibid, p. 89
404   'Medic! . . .': William A. Biehler, Rutgers Oral History Archives
404   'The machine guns . . .': ibid
404   'We just fired . . .': ibid
404   'After much thought . . .': Richard Blackburn, *In the Company of Heroes*, p. 93
405   'It was very difficult . . .': ibid, p. 155
406   'Disregarding the bocage . . .': Chester B. Hansen Diary, 13/7/1944

27 A Brief Discourse on Weapons and the Operational Level of War

412   'Examining his wounds . . .': Orion C. Shockley, *Random Chance*, p. 127
415   'But since ammunition . . .': cited in Samuel W. Mitcham, *Panzers in Normandy*, p. 56
416   'They have, of course . . .': 21st Army Group AFV Technical Report, 355.486.1 BTM
416   'The two attacks . . .': ibid
417   'The enemy are frightened . . .': ibid
417   'Actually, 6 shots . . .': ibid
419   'and he brewed it up . . .': ibid
420   'It brewed up.': ibid
420   'you don't see a brick wall . . .': ibid
423   'Any nation that anticipates . . .': 'German Tank Maintenance in World War II', Department of the US Army, No. 20-202, June 1954, p. 44
425   'We could only knock . . .': Fritz Bayerlein, ETHINT 66-ML-1079, USAHC, p. 35
425   'We could not use . . .': ibid

28 Crisis of Command

428   'If we do not succeed . . .': Richard Freiherr von Rosen, *Panzer Ace*, p. 226
429   'Nobody was hurt . . .': ibid, p. 232
430   'If you don't attack . . .': ibid, p. 233
430   'Every round we fired . . .': ibid
431   'Our first engagement . . .': ibid, p. 235

432 'I say, now do you have . . . ?': Chester B. Hansen Diary, 30/6/1944

433 'Hitler and Rommel . . .': cited in Alastair Horne, *The Lonely Leader*, p. 183

433 'We'll give him a battle . . .': Chester B. Hansen Diary, 2/7/1944

434 'I've been wanting . . .': ibid, 12/7/1944

434 By the end of June . . . : These statistics are cited in John Peaty, 'Myth, Reality and Carlo D'Este', *War Studies Journal*, Vol. 1, No. 2. D'Este made a big point about the number of rifle battalions in England and argued that Britain was shirking in Normandy and overly relying on America's young men to carry out much of the fighting. John Peaty has dissected D'Este's accusations in considerable detail and emphatically disproved the suggestion.

436 'I am not prepared . . .': cited in Arthur Tedder, *With Prejudice*, p. 560

437 'Eisenhower and I . . .': ibid, p. 561

437 'We are enthusiastic . . .': DDE Vol. III, 12/7/1944

438 'The question of leaving . . .': Frank Ziegler, *The Story of 609 Squadron*, p. 290

438 'Squadron detailed . . .': TNA AIR 27/2103

439 'The controller would say . . .': Ken Adam, author interview

439 'It was hard.': ibid

440 'Gosh, I wish I had opened . . .': Chester B. Hansen Diary, 5/7/1944

441 'What do the people think . . .': cited in Friedrich Ruge, *Rommel in Normandy*, p. 217

442 'During the course . . .': Kurt Meyer, *Grenadiers*, p. 270

442 'We are not afraid . . .': ibid, p. 271

442 'But the higher-ups . . .': cited in ibid

29 GOODWOOD

446 'So absurdly simple . . .': Omar N. Bradley, *A Soldier's Story*, p. 342

447 'Bradley liked me . . .': General Elwood Richard 'Pete' Quesada, interview 3, AFHRA

449 'Notes on Second Army . . .': cited in John Baynes, *The Forgotten Victor*, p. 199

450 'Three things important . . .': cited in Arthur Tedder, *With Prejudice*, p. 562

450 'If conditions . . .': Baynes, p. 200

451 'A good early morning . . .': Ken Handley Diary, 18/6/1944

452 'From now on, I could not . . .': Richard Freiherr von Rosen, *Panzer Ace*, p. 247

452 'Of the once so beautiful . . .': ibid

454 'One battery has been . . .': Hans von Luck, *Panzer Commander*, p. 194

455 'A cruel and . . .': Charles Cromwell Martin, *Battle Diary*, p. 46

456 'No words could express . . .': ibid, p. 50

456 'The 1. SS will arrive . . .': von Luck, p. 200

457 'We brought them out . . .': von Rosen, p. 251

457 'This they did . . .': Reg Spittles, 'Story No. 14', BTM Archives

458 'Unfortunately, one rather large . . .': ibid

458 'On 20 July . . .': Tedder, p. 562

459 'swept away': cited in Samuel W. Mitcham, *Panzers in Normandy*, p. 77

30 Saint-Lô

462 'The moment is fast approaching . . .': cited in James A. Wood (ed.), *Army of the West*, p. 145

462 'The terrorist act . . .': Kurt Meyer, *Grenadiers*, p. 273

462 'Although I loathed . . .': Helmut Ritgen, *The Western Front, 1944*, p. 97

462 'His death could bring us . . .': Eberhard Günther Beck, *Tagebuch*, p. 19, BA-MA

463 'Young man . . .': Richard Freiherr von Rosen, *Panzer Ace*, p. 257

463 'unsettled': Willi Müller, *Vom Pionier-Bataillon in der Normandie zum Panzerjagdkommando in Sachsen*, p. 106

463 'As feared . . .': Ritgen, p. 96

463 'I saw that there was no hope . . .': Orion C. Shockley, *Random Chance*, p. 152

464 'Lieutenant, I'm going . . .': ibid, p. 153

464 'Ow, I'm hit.': ibid, p. 161

464 'The hedgerows were terrible': John Rogers, NWWIIM

464 'We were there . . .': ibid

465 'Finally taking a cigarette . . .': Reg Spittles, 'Story No. 3', BTM Archives

465 'The journey back . . .': Robert Woollcombe, *Lion Rampant*, pp. 90–91

466 'I just wanted . . .': Beck, p. 16

466 'Hearing the news . . .': John Robert Slaughter, *Omaha Beach and Beyond*, p. 137

467 'Karl, any fool . . .': cited in Vince Milano and Bruce Conner, *Normandiefront*, p. 239

467 'Karl, through all this . . .': ibid, p. 245

467 'Thank God . . .': ibid, p. 246

468 'Almost every time . . .': ibid, p. 250

468 'quivering with alertness': Chester B. Hansen Diary, 19/7/1944

469 'General was pleased . . .': ibid

470 'Everything is now . . .': ibid

470 'That's giving them . . .': ibid

31 COBRA

471 'This was meant . . .': Chester B. Hansen Diary, 21/7/1944

471 'When I die . . .': ibid, 20/7/1944

472 'It has been said of this battle . . .': cited in John Buckley, *Monty's Men*, p. 147

472 'Dammit. I'm going to . . .': Chester B. Hansen Diary, 23/7/1944

473 'It is Hell . . .': Martin Blumenson (ed.), *The Patton Papers*, p. 464

473 'I'm proud to be here . . .': ibid, p. 477

474 'This is no limited . . .': Ernie Pyle, *Brave Men*, p. 456

474 'How the hell . . .': General Elwood Richard 'Pete' Quesada, interview 8, AFHRA

475 'The human truth . . .': ibid

475 'It was hopeless . . .': Fritz Bayerlein, ETHINT 66-ML-1079, USAHC, p. 43

476 'Bail out!! . . .': Truman Smith, *The Wrong Stuff*, p. 266

476 'Based on what . . .': ibid, p. 273

476   'And before the next . . .': Pyle, p. 434
476   'We sat in a little café . . .': J. Lawton Collins, *Lightning Joe*, p. 240
476   'It was all fast and furious . . .': Pyle, p. 459
477   'My God, look . . .': Smith, p. 276
477   'And while we didn't . . .': ibid, p. 277
477   'I've never known . . .': Pyle, p. 460
477   'I had heard my share . . .': Richard Blackburn, *In the Company of Heroes*, p. 160
477   'The feeling of the blast . . .': Pyle, p. 461
478   'You never saw so much . . .': Tom Bowles, author interview
478   'The three days . . .': Bayerlein, ETHINT 66-ML-1079, USAHC, p. 47
479   'Shock, if we survive . . .': Orion C. Shockley, *Random Chance*, p. 164
479   'I don't believe . . .': Chester B. Hansen Diary, 24/7/1944
479   'I sensed that their . . .': Collins, p. 242
480   'It really worked wonderfully . . . .' John Rogers, NWWIIM
480   'We'd have call . . .': Archie Maltbie, NWWIIM
480   'Everyone is overjoyed . . .': Chester B. Hansen Diary, 27/7/1944

32 BLUECOAT

482   ' The centre and the left . . .': Paul Hausser, B-179, USAHC
482   'Impossible due to . . .': Willi Müller, *Vom Pionier-Bataillon in der Normandie zum Panzerjagdkommando in Sachsen*, p. 111
482   'One had to play . . .': Helmut Ritgen, *The Western Front, 1944*, p. 114
483   'There were scores and scores . . .': Richard Blackburn, *In the Company of Heroes*, p. 163
484   'It horrified us . . .': Müller, p. 115
484   'General Bayerlein and Rommel . . .': Chester B. Hansen Diary, 29/7/1944
485   'Felt Hitler . . .': ibid
485   'If only we Germans had this.': ibid
485   'We eagered for good news . . .': ibid
486   'This windfall covered . . .': Robert Woollcombe, *Lion Rampant*, p. 112
488   'He was a wiry . . .': Stanley Christopherson Diary, 29/7/1944
488   'This ridge was captured . . .': Walter Caines Journal, p. 27, IWM 306
489   'You may lose every tank . . .': cited in John Buckley, *Monty's Men*, p. 158
489   'It was a terrible . . .': Walter Caines Journal, p. 28, IWM 306
489   'A few fanatics . . .': ibid, p. 28
490   'I was so tired . . .': ibid, p. 29
491   'But it seemed . . .': Woollcombe, p. 113
492   'Even a troop . . .': Reg Spittles, 'Story No. 32', BTM Archives
492   'A profusion of Nebelwerfers . . .': Woollcombe, p. 114
493   'I really did feel scared . . .': Walter Caines Journal, p. 31, IWM 306
494   'The unit had certainly . . .': ibid, p. 32
494   'He was prone . . .': Stanley Christopherson Diary, 6/8/1944
494   'Ondefontaine was now . . .': Walter Caines Journal, p. 33, IWM 306

33 LÜTTICH

496   'On this journey . . .': Richard Freiherr von Rosen, *Panzer Ace*, p. 257
497   'I decide that this old . . .': Robert Leblanc, *Journal du Maquis*, ed. Alain Corblin, 30/6/1944
497   'It's anarchy.': ibid, 6/7/1944
498   'Pelican, Jean l'Abbé . . .': ibid, 4/8/1944
499   'Some people are . . .': Chester B. Hansen Diary, 2/8/1944
499   'Brad went over . . .': ibid, 2/8/44
499   'Self-confidence, speed . . .': George S. Patton, *War As I Knew It*, p. 354
501   'politically unbearable . . .': Heinrich Eberbach, A-922, USAHC
503   'Events like these . . .': Richard Blackburn, *In the Company of Heroes*, p. 166
503   'Ralph, be sure . . .': J. Lawton Collins, *Lightning Joe*, p. 250
505   'In fact, not a single . . .': Rudolf-Christoph Freiherr von Gersdorff, B-725, USAHC
506   'We had hit . . .': Richard E. Turner, *Mustang Pilot*, p. 110
506   'For the next five . . .': ibid
506   'The absolute air . . .': Gersdorff, B-725, USAHC

34 Tank Battle at Saint-Aignan

507   'I came to tell you . . .': Chester B. Hansen Diary, 7/8/1944
507   'Why break down the back door . . .': ibid
508   'Do you think . . .': Ken Tout, *By Tank*, p. 40
508   'Business this time . . .': ibid, p. 41
509   'The Germans are now . . .': ibid, p. 42
509   'Our little silver . . .': ibid
509   'Driver, start up!': ibid, p. 43
510   'That is artificial . . .': ibid, p. 46
510   'The physical sensation . . .': ibid, p. 49
510   'Behind us and to our right . . .': ibid, p. 70
512   'Sitting here like this . . .': ibid, p. 86
512   'Hallo, Roger 2 Baker . . .': ibid, p. 89
513   'Hullo, Oboe Able . . .': this incident in ibid, p. 92
514   'Two Charlie! . . .': ibid, p. 94
514   'The day degenerates . . .': ibid
515   'The clutching feeling . . .': ibid, p. 99
517   'Ken, have a look . . .': ibid, p. 110
517   'The mess on the floor . . .': ibid, p. 111
517   'Your war's over . . .': ibid, p. 119

35 The Corridor of Death

519   'What an awful waste . . .': Mary Morris, 16/8/1944, IWM 4850
522   'Our lead elements . . .': Chester B. Hansen Diary, 10/8/1944
522   'Dietrich's totally unqualified . . .': cited in Samuel W. Mitcham, *Panzers in Normandy*, p. 143

522 'It was unaccountable . . .': ibid, p. 144

522 'All we could do . . .': cited in Marvin Jensen, *Strike Swiftly!*, p. 194

522 'We got him.': ibid, p. 195

523 'She abandoned her plan . . .': Willi Müller, *Vom Pionier-Bataillon in der Normandie zum Panzerjagdkommando in Sachsen*, p. 133

523 'We had to hurry . . .': Eberhard Günther Beck, *Tagebuch*, p. 26, BA-MA

523 'Whole battery . . .': ibid, p. 24

524 'We were not supposed . . .': ibid, p. 27

524 'His head was torn . . .': Müller, p. 27

524 'When he was killed . . .': Charles Cromwell Martin, *Battle Diary*, p. 60

524 'The enlisted soldiers . . .': Kurt Meyer, *Grenadiers*, p. 283

525 'We have been in Normandy . . .': Denis Edwards, *The Devil's Own Luck*, p. 138

525 'We were informed . . .': Walter Caines Journal, p. 35, IWM 306

525 'Many prisoners were . . .': ibid

527 'Oh, Blackie, no . . .': Richard Blackburn, *In the Company of Heroes*, p. 173

527 'But I was always taught . . .': ibid, p. 181

529 'Talk about fear! . . .': Martin, p. 61

529 'Once again I was witness . . .': Meyer, p. 294

530 'No matter how many . . .': cited in Jean-Paul Pallud, *Rückmarsch!*, p. 67

530 'From there I had . . .': Stanley Christopherson Diary, 17/6/1944

530 'Between August 7 . . .': Orion C. Shockley, *Random Chance*, p. 179

531 '"Man, horse, and truck . . ."': Hans von Luck, *Panzer Commander*, p. 205

531 'This was an awful price . . .': Martin, p. 67

Postscript

532 'The smell was terrible . . .': Ken Adam, author interview

536 'He was absolutely . . .': Peter Caddick-Adams, author interview

Selected Sources

PERSONAL TESTIMONIES

Author Interviews

Adam, Ken
Beamont, Roland 'Bee'
Börner, Johannes
Bowles, Henry D.
Bowles, Tom
Byers, Bill
Halloran, Walter
Mann, Douglas

Mather, Carol
Munro, Les
Neil, Tom
Roberts, Eldon 'Bob'
Semken, John
Tout, Ken
Watson, Stuart
Waughman, Rusty

Cornelius Ryan Archive, Ohio University, Athens, Ohio

Brannen, Malcolm D.
Cass, E. E. E.
Cota, Norman
Damski, Aloysius
Feuchtinger, Edgar
Freyberg, Leodegard
Gunning, Hugh
Hayn, Friedrich
Hermes, Walter

Keller, Robert
Morrissey, James
Oppeln-Bronikowski, Hermann, von
Pemsel, Max
Tempelhof, Hans
Thornhill, Avery
Voight, Bill
Wünsch, Anton

Imperial War Museum, London

Blizzard, Arthur
Todd, Richard

John Kane Interviews

Seekings, Reg

Legasee: The Veterans' Video Archive, London

Corbett, Frank
Downing, Eric
Eagles, Charles

Renouf, Tom
Sullivan, Bob

Mémoriale de Caen, Normandy

Fauré, Hubert
Zivolhave, Otto

National World War II Museum, New Orleans, Louisiana

Bailey, Richard
Baumgarten, Harold
Bell, Bryan
Brueland, Lowell K.
Denius, Frank
Farley, Dan
Ford, Richard
Gross, Clayton Kelly
Hawk, John 'Bud'
Lomell, Leonard

Maltbie, Archie
McCarthy, George
Raaen, John
Rice, Darold
Rogers, John
Utero, Cosmo
Venverloh, Joseph
Wichterich, George
Witmeyer, John James 'JJ'

Robin Schäfer Interviews

Leuffert, Karl
Seiler, Hermann

Rutgers, The State University of New Jersey

Biehler, William H.
Farrell, Francis
Johnson, Franklyn
Kingston, Clifford
Logerfo, Peter J.

Parisi, Joseph
Waters, John

US Air Force Historical Research Agency, Maxwell, Alabama

Gabreski, Francis 'Gabby'
Quesada, Elwood R. 'Pete'

US Army Heritage Centre, Carlisle, Pennsylvania

Bonesteel, Charles H.
Haley, Joseph M.
Ziegelmann, Fritz

Forrest Pogue Interviews

Alanbrooke, Viscount Sir Alan
Bonesteel, Charles H.
Bradley, Omar N.
Corbett, Paddy
De Gaulle, Charles
Dempsey, Miles
Gleave, Tom

Hughes-Hallett, John
Ismay, Hastings
Morgan, Frederick
Mountbatten, Admiral Lord Louis
Paget, Sir Bernard
Robb, James M.
Williams, E. T. 'Bill'

US Army Historical Division, Foreign Military Studies Series: Interviews

Bayerlein, Fritz
Rommel, Lucie
Schweppenburg, General Leo Geyr von, *Interview: Panzer Tactics in Normandy*

UNPUBLISHED REPORTS, MEMOIRS, PAPERS, ETC.

Bovington Tank Museum, Dorset

21st Army Group Administrative Statistics
21st Army Group AFV Technical Issues, 355.48.5
21st Army Group AFV Technical Reports, 355.486.1
Baulf, H. E. A., *Nine Elms: A Tank to Remember*, unpublished memoir
Casualties and Effects of Fire Support on the British Beaches in Normandy, 355.48.5(4)
Current Reports from Overseas, Nos 46–57
Overlord Outline Mounting Plan
Spittles, Reg, 'Stories' No. 3, 14, 24, 32 and 41

Bundesarchiv-Militärarchiv, Freiburg

Beck, Eberhard Günther, *Tagebuch*
German Tank Production
Training Instructions, Nos 29–39

Churchill College Archives, Cambridge

Lewin, Ronald, Papers

Eton College Library, Eton

Henderson, John, Papers, Diary, Photographs

Gettysburg Museum, Pennsylvania

Winters, Richard 'Dick', Papers

Ike Skelton Combined Arms Research Library, Fort Leavenworth, Kansas

70th Tank Battalion, 3663
737th Tank Battalion, 3608
741st Tank Battalion, 3522
893rd Tank Destroyer Battalion, 3518

Imperial War Museum, London

Caines, Walter, Papers
Green, T. W., *Reminiscences*
Guillotin, Claude, *Memoir*
Handley, Ken, Papers
Harris, J. R., Diary
Mulry, Mary, Diary
Wright, Frank, Papers

Liddell Hart Centre for Military Archives, King's College, London

Churcher, J. B., *A Soldier's Story*
Hutton, Michael, *Just a Bit of Time*, unpublished memoir
Jowett, George, *One Man's Long Journey*, unpublished memoir
Lampen, Ambrose, *Naval Reminiscences 1941–1944*, unpublished memoir

O'Connor, Richard, Papers
Wilmot, Chester, Papers
US Armed Forces Oral Histories

National Archives, Kew, London

1st Northants Yeomanry War Diary, WO 171/859
2nd Northants Yeomanry War Diary, WO 171/860
4th Somerset Light Infantry War Diary, WO 171/1372
4th Wiltshire Regiment War Diary, WO 171/1394
5th Wiltshire Regiment War Diary, WO 171/1395
6 KOSB War Diary, WO 171/1322
21st Army Group Combat Reports, WO 205/422
602 Squadron, Operations Record Book, AIR 27/2078
609 Squadron, Operations Record Book, AIR 27/2103
AEAF Historical Record, AIR 37/1057
Airborne Air Planning Committee, AIR 37/773
Appreciation of Possible Developments, WO 205/118
Daily Reflections by Sir Trafford Leigh-Mallory, AIR 37/784
Dempsey Papers, WO 285
Employment of Air Forces in Operation Overlord, AIR 37/772
General Montgomery Planning Notes, CAB 106/1031
German POW Prisoner Statements, WO 232/10A
Montgomery Notes for Address to Senior Officers Before Overlord, PREM 3/339/1
Observations on RAF Bomber Command's Attack on Caen, AIR 37/1255
Overlord: An Assault by an Infantry Battalion, WO 205/422
Personnel & Morale, WO 163/53
Probability of Hitting Targets, WO291/1330
Report by Air Marshal Sir Arthur Coningham, AIR 37/867
Survey of Casualties, WO 205/116

National Archives and Records Administration, College Park, Maryland

4th Infantry Division after-action reports
29th Infantry Division after-action reports
82nd Airborne Division, reports, papers, etc.
101st Air Division, reports, papers, etc.
United States Army, *Notes From Normandy*, Vol. II, No. 27

Naval Historical Branch, Historic Dockyards, Portsmouth

Curtis, Rupert (ed.), *Chronicles of D-Day and the Battle of the Build-Up*

US Air Force Historical Research Agency, Maxwell, Alabama

91st Bomb Group War Diary
354th Fighter Group War Diary
388th Fighter Group War Diary
391st Bomb Group War Diary

US Army Heritage Center, Carlisle, Pennsylvania

Memoirs

Bayerlein, Fritz, *Panzer Lehr Division*, A-902
—, *Panzer Lehr Division*, A-903
Eberbach, Hans, *Panzer Group Eberbach and the Falaise Encirclement*, A-922
Elfeldt, Otto, *LXXXIV Corps*, A-968
Gersdorff, R. von, *The Argentan–Falaise Pocket*, A-919
—, *Normandy, COBRA and Mortain*, A-894
Groppe, Theodor, *SS versus Wehrmacht*, B-397
Hansen, Chester B., *Diary*
US Army Historical Division, Foreign Military Studies Series: Written Studies
Hausser, Paul, *Seventh Army*, A-907
—, *Seventh Army*, A-974
Heydte, Friedrich Freiherr von der, *A German Parachute Regiment in Normandy*, B-839
Holtzendorff, Hans-Henning von, *Reasons for Rommel's Success in the Desert*
Krämer, Fritz, *I SS Corps in the West in 1944*
Kraas, Hugo, *12th SS Panzer Division*
Pemsel, Max, *Battle of Normandy – Comments*, C-057
Ruge, Friedrich, *Rommel and the Atlantic Wall*, A-982
Schramm, Percy E., *OKW War Diary 1 April–18 December 1944*, B-034
Zerbel, Alfred, *Combat Operations of 6th Parachute Division in Northern France in 1944*, A-956

Other Unpublished Memoirs, Doctorates, etc.

Boylan, Joseph J., *Goon's Up*
Christopherson, Stanley, Papers, Diary, Photographs
Colvin, H. E., Diary
Neave, Julius, *The War Diary of Julius Neave*
Thomas Alexander, Hugh, *The Other Air War: Elwood 'Pete' Quesada and American Tactical Air Power in World War II Europe*, University of Houston, 1994
Wharton, Bill, Letters

CONTEMPORARY PAMPHLETS,
BOOKLETS AND TRAINING MEMORANDA

Army Life, War Department Pamphlet 21-13, US Government Printing Office, 1944

Basic Field Manual: First Aid for Soldiers, FM 21-11, US War Department, 1943

The Battle of the Atlantic: The Official Account of the Fight Against the U-Boats, 1939–1945, HMSO, 1946

Combat Instruction for the Panzer Grenadier by Helmut von Wehren, 1944; English translation by John Baum

Company Officer's Handbook of the German Army, Military Intelligence Division, US War Department, 1944

The Development of Artillery Tactics and Equipment, War Office, 1951

Der Dienst-Unterricht im Heer by Dr. Jur. W. Reibert, E. S. Mittler & Sohn, Berlin, 1941

Field Service Pocket Book, various pamphlets, War Office, 1939–1945

France, Vol. II, Naval Intelligence Division, 1942

France, Vol. III, Naval Intelligence Division, 1942

Germany, Vol. III, Naval Intelligence Division, 1944

German Infantry Weapons, Military Intelligence Service, US War Department, 1943

The German Squad in Combat, Military Intelligence Service, US War Department, 1944

German Tactical Doctrine, Military Intelligence Service, US War Department, 1942

German Tank Maintenance in World War II, Department of the US Army, No. 20-202, June 1954

Gunnery Pocket Book, 1945, The Admiralty, 1945

Handbook of German Military Forces, TM-E 30-451, US War Department, 1945

Handbook on the British Army with Supplements on the Royal Air Force and Civilian Defense Organizations, TM 30-410, US War Department, September 1942

Handbook on the Italian Military Forces, Military Intelligence Service, US Army, August 1943

Infantry Training, Part VIII – Fieldcraft, Battle Drill, Section and Platoon Tactics, War Office, 1944

Infantry Training: Training and War, HMSO, 1937

Instruction Manual for the Infantry: Field Fortifications of the Infantry, 1940, H.Dv. 130/11; English translation by John Baum

Instruction Manual for the Infantry: The Rifle Company, 1942, H.Dv. 103/2a; English translation by John Baum

Instruction Manual for the Infantry: The Machinegun Company, 1942, H.Dv. 130/3a; English translation by John Baum

Instructions for British Servicemen in France 1944, HMSO, 1944

Merchantmen at War, Prepared by the Ministry of Information, HMSO, 1944
Pilot's Notes General, Air Ministry, 1943
The Rise and Fall of the German Air Force (1933–1945), Air Ministry, 1948
R.O.F.: The Story of the Royal Ordnance Factories, 1939–48, HMSO, 1949
Der Schütze Hilfsbuch, 1943, by Oberst Hasso von Wedel and Oberleutnant
    Pfasserott, Richard Schröder Verlag, Berlin, 1943
Shooting to Live by Capt. W. E. Fairbairn and Capt. E. A. Sykes, 1942
Statistics Relating to the War Effort of the United Kingdom, HMSO, November 1944
Tactics in the Context of the Reinforced Infantry Battalions by Generalmajor
    Greiner and Generalmajor Degener, 1941; English translation by John Baum
TEE EMM: Air Ministry Monthly Training Memoranda, Vols I, II, III, Air
    Ministry, 1939–1945
Truppenführung: On the German Art of War, edited by Bruce Condell and David
    T. Zabecki, Stackpole, 2009
We Speak From the Air: Broadcasts by the RAF, HMSO, 1942
What Britain Has Done 1939–1945, Issued by the Ministry of Information, 1945
Whitaker's Almanac, 1940
Whitaker's Almanac, 1942
Whitaker's Almanac, 1944

OFFICIAL HISTORIES

American Battle Monuments Commission, *American Armies and Battlefields in
    Europe*, US Government Printing Office, 1938
Aris, George, *The Fifth British Division 1939 to 1945*, Fifth Division Benevolent
    Fund, 1959
Behrens, C. B. A., *Merchant Shipping and the Demands of War*, HMSO, 1955
Blumenson, Martin, *United States Army in World War II: Breakout & Pursuit*,
    Historical Division Department of the Army, 1970
Cosmas, Graham A., and Cowdrey, Albert E., *United States Army in World War
    II: Medical Service in the European Theater of Operations*, Historical Division
    Department of the Army, 1992
Craven, Wesley Frank, and Cate, James Lea, *The Army Air Forces in World War
    II*, Vol. II: *Europe: Torch to Pointblank*, University of Chicago Press, 1947
—, *The Army Air Forces in World War II*, Vol. III: *Europe: Argument to VE Day,
    January 1944 to May 1945*, University of Chicago Press, 1951
Duncan Hall, H., and Wrigley, C. C., *Studies of Overseas Supply*, HMSO, 1956
Echternkamp, Jörg (ed.), *Germany and the Second World War*, Vol. IX/I:
    *German Wartime Society 1939–1945: Politicization, Disintegration, and the
    Struggle for Survival*, Clarendon Press, 2008
Eisenhower, Dwight D., *Report by the Supreme Commander to the Combined
    Chiefs of Staff on the Operations in Europe of the Allied Expeditionary Force*, 6
    June 1944–8 May 1945, HMSO, 1946
Ellis, L. F., *Victory in the West*, HMSO, 1962

Fairchild, Byron, and Grossman, Jonathan, *United States Army in World War II: The Army and Industrial Manpower*, Office of the Chief of Military History, 1959

Foot, M. R. D., *SOE in France*, HMSO, 1966 (Original First Edition)

Hancock, W. K., and Gowing, M. M., *British War Economy*, HMSO, 1949

Harrison, G. A., *United States Army in World War II: Cross Channel Attack*, Historical Division Department of the Army, 1951

Hinsley, F. H., *British Intelligence in the Second World War*, HMSO, 1993

Hinsley, F. H., et al., *British Intelligence in the Second World War*, Vol. I: *Its Influence on Strategy and Operations*, HMSO, 1979

—, *British Intelligence in the Second World War*, Vol. III, Part 1, HMSO, 1984

—, *British Intelligence in the Second World War*, Vol. III: Part 2, HMSO, 1988

Howard, Michael, *Grand Strategy*, Vol. IV: *August 1942–September 1943*, HMSO, 1972

Hurstfield, J., *The Control of Raw Materials*, HMSO, 1953

Institution of the Royal Army Service Corps, *The Story of the Royal Army Service Corps 1939–1945*, G. Bell and Sons, 1955

Knickerbocker, H. R., et al., *United States Army in World War II: Danger Forward: The Story of the First Division in World War II*, Society of the First Division, 1947

Lindsay, T. M., *Sherwood Rangers*, Burrup, Mathieson & Co., 1952

Militärgeschichtliches Forschungsampt, *Germany and the Second World War*, Vol. V: *Organization and Mobilization of the German Sphere of Power*, Part 1: *Wartime administration, economy and manpower resources, 1939–1941*, Clarendon Press, 2000

—, *Germany and the Second World War*, Vol. VI: *The Global War*, Clarendon Press, 2001

—, *Germany and the Second World War*, Vol. V: *Organization and Mobilization of the German Sphere of Power*, Part 2B: *Wartime administration, economy and manpower resources, 1942–1944/5*, Clarendon Press, 2003

—, *Germany and the Second World War*, Vol. VII: *The Strategic Air War in Europe and the War in the West and East Asia, 1943–1944/5*, Clarendon Press, 2015

Naval Historical Branch, *Invasion Europe*, HMSO, 1994

Palmer, Robert R., Wiley, Bell I., and Keast, William R., *United States Army in World War II: The Procurement and Training of Ground Combat Troops*, Historical Division Department of the Army, 1948

Parker, H. M. D., *Manpower: A Study of War-Time Policy and Administration*, HMSO, 1957

Pogue, Forrest, *United States Army in World War II: The Supreme Command*, Historical Division Department of the Army, 1954

Postan, M. M., *British War Production*, HMSO, 1952

—, Hay, D., and Scott, J. D., *Design and Development of Weapons*, HMSO, 1964

Rapport, Leonard, and Northwood, Arthur, *Rendezvous with Destiny: A History of the 101st Airborne Division*, 101st Airborne Association, 1948

Richards, Denis, *Royal Air Force 1939–1945*, Vol. III: *The Fight is Won*, HMSO, 1954

Risch, Erna, *The Technical Services, United States Army in World War II: The Quartermaster Corps: Organization, Supply, and Services*, Vol. I, Historical Division Department of the Army, 1953

Rissik, David, *The D.L.I. at War: The History of the Durham Light Infantry 1939–1945*, The Depot: Durham Light Infantry, no date

Roberts Greenfield, Kent, et al., *United States Army in World War II: The Organization of Ground Combat Troops*, Historical Division Department of the Army, 1947

Scott, J. D., and Hughes, Richard, *The Administration of War Production*, HMSO, 1955

Wardlow, Chester, *United States Army in World War II: The Transportation Corps: Movements, Training, and Supply*, Office of the Chief of Military History, 1956

Warren, John C., *Airborne Operations in World War II, European Theater*, USAF Historical Division, 1956

Webster, Sir Charles, and Frankland, Noble, *The Strategic Air Offensive Against Germany, 1939–1945*, Vol. III: *Victory*, HMSO, 1961

—, *The Strategic Air Offensive Against Germany, 1939–1945*, Vol. IV: *Annexes & Appendices*, Naval & Military Press, 2006

EQUIPMENT, WEAPONS AND TECHNICAL BOOKS

Barker, A. J., *British and American Infantry Weapons of World War 2*, Arms & Armour Press, 1969

Bidwell, Shelford, and Graham, Dominick, *Fire-Power: British Army Weapons and Theories of War 1904–1945*, George Allen & Unwin, 1982

Bouchery, Jean, *The British Soldier*, Vol. 1: *Uniforms, Insignia, Equipment*, Histoire & Collections, no date

—, *The British Soldier*, Vol. 2: *Organisation, Armament, Tanks and Vehicles*, Histoire & Collections, no date

Brayley, Martin, *The British Army 1939–45*, (1) *North-West Europe*, Osprey, 2001

—, *British Web Equipment of the Two World Wars*, Crowood Press, 2005

Bruce, Robert, *German Automatic Weapons of World War II*, Crowood Press, 1996

Bull, Dr Stephen, *World War II Infantry Tactics*, Osprey, 2004

—, *World War II Street-Fighting Tactics*, Osprey, 2008

Chamberlain, Peter, and Ellis, Chris, *Tanks of the World*, Cassell, 2002

Chesneau, Roger (ed.), *Conway's All the World's Fighting Ships 1922–1946*, Conway Maritime Press, 1980

Dallies-Labourdette, Jean-Philippe, *S-Boote: German E-Boats in Action 1939–1945*, Histoire & Collections, no date

Davis, Brian L., *German Combat Uniforms of World War II*, Vol. II: Arms & Armour Press, 1985

Davies, W. J. K., *German Army Handbook 1939–1945*, Military Book Society, 1973

Enjames, Henri-Paul, *Government Issue: US Army European Theater of Operations Collector Guide*, Histoire & Collections, 2003

Falconer, Jonathan, *D-Day Operations Manual*, Haynes, 2013

Farrar-Hockley, Anthony, *Infantry Tactics 1939–1945*, Almark, 1976

Fleischer, Wolfgang, *The Illustrated Guide to German Panzers*, Schiffer, 2002

Forty, George, and Livesey, Jack, *The Complete Guide to Tanks and Armoured Fighting Vehicles*, Southwater, 2012

Gander, Terry, and Chamberlain, Peter, *Small Arms, Artillery and Special Weapons of the Third Reich*, Macdonald and Jane's, 1978

Gordon, David B., *Equipment of the WWII Tommy*, Pictorial Histories, 2004

—, *Uniforms of the WWII Tommy*, Pictorial Histories, 2005

—, *Weapons of the WWII Tommy*, Pictorial Histories, 2004

Grant, Neil, *The Bren Gun*, Osprey, 2013

Griehl, Manfred, and Dressel, Joachim, *Luftwaffe Combat Aircraft: Development, Production, Operations, 1935–1945*, Schiffer, 1994

Gunston, Bill, *Fighting Aircraft of World War II*, Salamander, 1988

Hart, S., and Hart, R., *The German Soldier in World War II*, Spellmount, 2000

Hogg, Ian V. (intro.), *The American Arsenal: The World War II Official Standard Ordnance Catalog of Small Arms, Tanks, Armored Cars, Artillery, Antiaircraft Guns, Ammunition, Grenades, Mines, etcetera*, Greenhill Books, 1996

—, *The Guns 1939–1945*, Macdonald, 1969

Kay, Antony L., and Smith, J. R., *German Aircraft of the Second World War*, Putnam, 2002

Konstan, Angus, *British Battlecruisers 1939–45*, Osprey, 2003

de Lagarde, Jean, *German Soldiers of World War II*, Histoire & Collections, no date

Lavery, Brian, *Churchill's Navy: The Ships, Men and Organisation, 1939–1945*, Conway, 2006

Lee, Cyrus A., *Soldat*, Vol. Two: *Equipping the German Army Foot Soldier in Europe 1943*, Pictorial Histories, 1988

Lepage, Jean-Denis G. G., *German Military Vehicles*, McFarland & Company, 2007

Lüdeke, Alexander, *Weapons of World War II*, Parragon, 2007

Mason, Chris, *Soldat*, Vol. Eight: *Fallschirmjäger*, Pictorial Histories, 2000

McNab, Chris, *MG 34 and MG 42 Machine Guns*, Osprey, 2012

Mundt, Richard W., and Lee, Cyrus A., *Soldat*, Vol. Six: *Equipping the Waffen-SS Panzer Divisions 1942–1945*, Pictorial Histories, 1997

Musgrave, Daniel D., *German Machineguns*, Greenhill Books, 1992

Myerscough, W., *Air Navigation Simply Explained*, Pitman & Sons Ltd, 1942

Saiz, Augustin, *Deutsche Soldaten*, Casemate, 2008

Stedman, Robert, *Kampfflieger: Bomber Crewman of the Luftwaffe 1939–45*, Osprey, 2005

Suermondt, Jan, *World War II Wehrmacht Vehicles*, Crowood Press, 2003

Sumner, Ian, and Vauvillier, François, *The French Army 1939–1945 (1)*, Osprey, 1998

Sutherland, Jonathan, *World War II Tanks and AFVs*, Airlife, 2002

Trye, Rex, *Mussolini's Soldiers*, Airlife, 1995

Vanderveen, Bart, *Historic Military Vehicles Directory*, After the Battle, 1989

Williamson, Gordon, *Gebirgsjäger*, Osprey, 2003

—, *German Mountain & Ski Troops 1939–45*, Osprey, 1996

—, *U-Boats vs Destroyer Escorts*, Osprey, 2007

Windrow, Richard, and Hawkins, Tim, *The World War II GI: US Army Uniforms 1941–45*, Crowood Press, 2003

Zaloga, Steven, *Armored Attack 1944*, Stackpole, 2011

—, *Armored Thunderbolt: The US Army Sherman in World War II*, Stackpole, 2008

—, *US Anti-Tank Artillery 1941–45*, Osprey, 2005

MEMOIRS, BIOGRAPHIES, ETC.

Adair, Allan, *A Guard's General: The Memoirs of Major General Sir Allan Adair*, Hamish Hamilton, 1986

Adam, Günter, *"Ich habe meine Pflicht erfüllt!" – Ein Junker der Waffen-SS berichtet*, Nation & Wissen, 2012

Alanbrooke, Field Marshal Lord, *War Diaries 1939–1945*, Weidenfeld & Nicolson, 2001

Alexander, Mark J., and Sparry, John, *Jump Commander*, Casement, 2012

Ambrose, Stephen E., *Band of Brothers*, Pocket Books, 2001

—, *Citizen Soldiers*, Pocket Books, 2002

—, *Eisenhower: Soldier and President*, Pocket Books, 2003

—, *The Supreme Commander: The War Years of Dwight D. Eisenhower*, Doubleday, 1970

Arnade, Charles W., *Soldier: The Memoirs of Matthew B. Ridgway*, Curtis Publishing Company, 1956

Arnold, H. H., *Global Mission*, Harper & Row, 1949

Baker, David, *Adolf Galland*, Windrow & Greene, 1996

Baldridge, Robert C., *Victory Road: The World War II Memoir of an Artilleryman in the ETO*, Merriam Press, 1995

Baumgarten, Harold, *D-Day Survivor*, Pelican, 2015

Baynes, John, *The Forgotten Victor: General Sir Richard O'Connor*, Brassey's, 1999

Below, Nicolaus von, *At Hitler's Side: The Memoirs of Hitler's Luftwaffe Adjutant*, Greenhill, 2004

Blackburn, George G., *The Guns of Normandy*, Constable, 1988

Blackburn, Richard M., *In the Company of Heroes*, Self-published, 2013

Blumenson, Martin (ed.), *The Patton Papers*, Da Capo, 1974

Bob, Hans-Ekkehard, *Betrayed Ideals: Memoirs of a Luftwaffe Fighter Ace*, Mönch, 2008

Booth, T. Michael, and Spencer, Duncan, *Paratrooper: The Life of General James M. Gavin*, Casemate, 2013

Boscawen, Robert, *Armoured Guardsman: A War Diary, June 1944–April 1945*, Pen & Sword, 2001

Bradley, Omar B., *A General's Life: An Autobiography*, Simon & Schuster, 1983

—, *A Soldier's Story*, Henry Holt, 1951

Brereton, Lewis H., *The Brereton Diaries*, William Morrow, 1946

Brett-James, Anthony, *Conversations with Montgomery*, William Kimber, 1984

Burns, Dwayne T., *Jump Into the Valley of the Shadow*, Casemate, 2006

Butcher, Harry C., *Three Years with Eisenhower: The Personal Diary of Captain Harry C. Butcher, USNR*, William Heinemann, 1946

Butler, Daniel Allen, *Field Marshal: The Life and Death of Erwin Rommel*, Casemate, 2017

Caddick-Adams, Peter, *Monty and Rommel: Parallel Lives*, Arrow Books, 2012

Chandler, Alfred D. (ed.), *The Papers of Dwight David Eisenhower: The War Years: III*, Johns Hopkins University Press, 1970

—, *The Papers of Dwight David Eisenhower: The War Years: IV*, Johns Hopkins University Press, 1970

Churchill, Winston S., *The Second World War*, Vol. VI: *Triumph and Tragedy*, Cassell, 1956

Clostermann, Pierre, *The Big Show: The Greatest Pilot's Story of World War II*, Cassell, 2004

Collins, J. Lawton, *Lightning Joe: An Autobiography*, Presidio, 1979

Collins, Michael, *Discovering My Father: The Wartime Experiences of Squadron Leader John Russell Collins DFC & Bar*, Self-published, 2012

Colville, John, *The Fringes of Power: Downing Street Diaries*, Vol. Two: *October 1941–April 1955*, Hodder & Stoughton, 1985; Sceptre, 1987

Cooper, Belton Y., *Death Traps: The Survival of an American Armored Division in World War II*, Ballantine, 1998

Cooper, Johnny, *One of the Originals*, Pan, 1991

Cooper, Robert Floyd, *Serenade to the Blue Lady: The Story of Bert Stiles*, Cypress House, 1993

Corblin, Alain (ed.), *Journal du Maquis du debarquement à la libération, Rédigé par Robert Leblanc, chef du Maquis Surcouf*, Société historique de Lisieux, 2014

Daddis, Gregory A., *Fighting in the Great Crusade*, Louisiana State University Press, 2002

Dahm, Jo, *Du oder ich: Der etwas andere Erlebnis- und Schicksalsbericht eines deutschen Fallschirmjägers während der alliierten Invasion 1944 in der Normandie*, Books on Demand, 2014

Davis, Richard G., *Carl A. Spaatz and the Air War in Europe*, Center for Air Force History, 1992

De Gaulle, General Charles, *War Memoirs: Unity 1942–1944*, Weidenfeld & Nicolson, 1956

De Guingand, Francis, *Operation Victory*, Hodder, 1960

D'Este, Carlo, *Patton: A Genius for War*, Harper Perennial, 1996

—, *Warlord: A Life of Churchill at War*, Allen Lane, 2009

Doolittle, James H. 'Jimmy', *I Could Never Be So Lucky Again*, Bantam, 1992

Douglas, Keith, *Alamein to Zem Zem*, Faber & Faber, 1992

Duboscq, Geneviève, *Dans la nuit du débarquement*, Hachette, 2004

Edgerton, David, *Britain's War Machine*, Allen Lane, 2011

—, *The Rise and Fall of the British Nation: A Twentieth-Century History*, Allen Lane, 2018

Edwards, Denis, *The Devil's Own Luck: Pegasus Bridge to the Baltic 1944–45*, Pen & Sword, 2016

Eisenhower, Dwight D., *Crusade in Europe*, William Heinemann, 1948

Engel, Gerhard, *At the Heart of the Reich: The Secret Diary of Hitler's Army Adjutant*, Greenhill, 2005

Fischer, Wolfgang, *Luftwaffe Fighter Pilot*, Greenhill, 2010

Franks, Norman, *Typhoon Attack: The Legendary British Fighters in Combat in WWII*, Stackpole, 2003

Freidel, Frank, *Franklin D. Roosevelt: A Rendezvous with Destiny*, Little, Brown & Co., 1990

Gabreski, Francis, *Gabby: A Fighter Pilot's Life*, Orion Books, 1991

Galland, Adolf, *The First and the Last*, Fontana, 1970

Gockel, Franz, *La Porte de l'Enfer*, Editions Hirle, 2004

Goodson, James, *Tumult in the Clouds*, Penguin, 2003

Gordon, Harold J., *One Man's War: A Memoir of World War II*, Apex Press, 1999

Graham, Desmond, *Keith Douglas 1920–1944*, Oxford University Press, 1974

Greenwood, Trevor, *D-Day to Victory: The Diaries of a British Tank Commander*, Simon & Schuster, 2012

Gross, Clayton Kelly, *Live Bait: WWII Memoirs of an Undefeated Fighter Ace*, Inkwater Press, 2006

Harris, Arthur, *Bomber Offensive*, Collins, 1947

Hills, Stuart, *By Tank Into Normandy*, Cassell, 2003

Holbrook, David, *Flesh Wounds*, Corgi, 1967

Holland, James (ed.), *An Englishman at War: The Wartime Diaries of Stanley Christopherson DSO, MC, TD*, Bantam Press, 2014

Horne, Alistair, *The Lonely Leader: Monty 1944–1945*, Pan Military Classics, 2013

Howard, John, and Bates, Penny, *The Pegasus Diaries: The Private Papers of Major John Howard DSO*, Pen & Sword, 2006

Howeth, T. E. B., *Monty at Close Quarters: Recollections of the Man*, Hippocrene Books, Leo Cooper, 1985

Hughes, Thomas Alexander, *Over Lord: General Pete Quesada and the Triumph of Tactical Air Power in World War II*, Free Press, 1995

Ince, David, *Brotherhood of the Skies: Wartime Experiences of a Gunnery Officer and Typhoon Pilot*, Grub Street, 2010

Irving, David, *The Rise and Fall of the Luftwaffe: The Life of Field Marshal Erhard Milch*, Weidenfeld & Nicolson, 1973

—, *The Trail of the Fox: The Life of Field Marshal Erwin Rommel*, Book Club Associates, 1977

Jary, Sydney, *18 Platoon*, Sydney Jary Limited, 1988

Jensen, Marvin, *Strike Swiftly! The 70th Tank Battalion from North Africa to Normandy to Germany*, Presidio, 1997

Jenson, Latham B., *Tin Hats, Oilskins & Seaboots: A Naval Journey, 1939–1945*, Robin Brass Studio, 2000

Johnson, Franklyn A., *One More Hill*, Bantam Books, 1983

Johnson, Margaret Ellen, *A Dance to Eternity*, Self-published, 2015

Jones, Keith, *Sixty-Four Days of a Normandy Summer*, Robert Hale, 1990

Kershaw, Ian, *Hitler: 1936–1945 – Nemesis*, Penguin, 2000

Knoke, Heinz, *I Flew for the Führer*, Cassell, 2003

Lamont, A. G. W., *Guns Above, Steam Below – In Canada's Navy of World War II*, Melrose Books, 2002

Lewin, Ronald, *Rommel as Military Commander*, Pen & Sword, 2004

Liddell Hart, B. H. (ed.), *The Rommel Papers*, Collins, 1953

Love, Robert W. Jr., and Major, John (eds), *The Year of D-Day: The 1944 Diary of Admiral Sir Bertram Ramsay, RN*, University of Hull Press, 1994

Luck, Hans von, *Panzer Commander*, Cassell, 1989

Martin, Charles Cromwell, *Battle Diary: From D-Day and Normandy to the Zuider Zee and VE*, J. Kirk Howard, 1994

Mather, Carol, *When the Grass Stops Growing*, Leo Cooper, 1997

McFarren, Peter, and Iglesias, Fadrique, *The Devil's Agent: Life, Times and Crimes of Nazi Klaus Barbie*, Xlibris, 2013

Meyer, Kurt, *Grenadiers*, Stackpole, 2005

Miller, George, *Maquis: An Englishman in the French Resistance*, Dovecote, 2013

Miller, Lee G., *The Story of Ernie Pyle*, The Viking Press, 1950

Montgomery of Alamein, Field Marshal the Viscount, *Memoirs*, Collins, 1958

Moorehead, Alan, *Eclipse*, Granta, 2000

Müller, Willi, *Vom Pionier-Bataillon in der Normandie zum Panzerjagdkommando in Sachsen*, Traditionsbuchreihe, 2017

Neil, Tom, *The Silver Spitfire: The Legendary WWII RAF Fighter Pilot in His Own Words*, Weidenfeld & Nicolson, 2013

Newton Dunn, Bill, *Big Wing: The Biography of Air Chief Marshal Sir Trafford Leigh-Mallory*, Airlife, 1992

Orange, Vincent, *Coningham: A Biography of Air Marshal Sir Arthur Coningham*, Center for Air Force History, 1992

Parton, James, *Air Force Spoken Here: Ira Eaker and the Command of the Air*, Adler & Adler, 1986

Patton, George S., *War As I Knew It*, Pyramid Books, 1966

Peyton, John, *Solly Zuckerman*, John Murray, 2001

Picot, Geoffrey, *Accidental Warrior: In the Front Line from Normandy to Victory*, Book Guild, 1993

Pimlott, John (ed.), *Rommel and His Art of War*, Greenhill Books, 2003

Pöppel, Martin, *Heaven and Hell: The War Diary of a German Paratrooper*, Spellmount, 1988

Probert, Henry, *Bomber Harris: His Life and Times*, Greenhill, 2006

Propst, Robert, *The Diary of a Combat Pilot*, Carlton Press, 1967

Pyle, Ernie, *Brave Men*, Henry Holt, 1944

—, *Here Is Your War: The Story of G.I. Joe*, World Publishing Company, 1945

Raaen, John, C. Jr., *Intact: A First-Hand Account of the D-Day Invasion from a 5th Rangers Company Commander*, Reedy Press, 2012

Raynes, Rozelle, *Maid Matelot: Adventures of a Wren Stoker in World War Two*, Castweasel Publishing, 2004

Render, David, and Tootal, Stuart, *Tank Action: An Armoured Troop Commander's War 1944–45*, Weidenfeld & Nicolson, 2016

Renouf, Tom, *Black Watch*, Abacus, 2011

Reuth, Ralf Georg, *Rommel: The End of a Legend*, Haus Books, 2008

Richards, Denis, *Portal of Hungerford*, William Heinemann, 1977

Ritgen, Helmut, *The Western Front 1944: Memoirs of a Panzer Lehr Officer*, J. J. Fedorowicz, 1995

Rosen, Richard Freiherr von, *Panzer Ace: The Memoirs of an Iron Cross Panzer Commander*, Greenhill, 2018

Rotbart, David, *A Soldier's Journal*, iBooks, 2003

Ruge, Friedrich, *Rommel in Normandy: Reminiscences*, Macdonald & Jane's, 1979

Saward, Dudley, *Bomber Harris*, Sphere, 1984

Scott, Desmond, *Typhoon Pilot*, Leo Cooper, 1982

Severloh, Hein, *WN62: A German Soldier's Memories of the Defence of Omaha Beach, Normandy, June 6, 1944*, HEK Creativ, 2011

Shockley, Orion C., *Random Chance: One Infantry Soldier's Story*, Trafford Publishing, 2007

Skinner, Revd. Leslie, *The Man Who Worked on Sundays: The Personal War Diary June 2 1944 to May 17 1945 of Revd. Leslie Skinner*, Self-published, no date

—, *Sherwood Rangers Casualty Book 1944–1945*, Self-published, 1996

Slaughter, John Robert, *Omaha Beach and Beyond: The Long March of Sgt. Bob Slaughter*, Zenith Press, 2009

Smith, Truman, *The Wrong Stuff: The Adventures and Misadventures of an 8th Air Force Aviator*, University of Oklahoma Press, 2002

Spayd, P. A., *Bayerlein: From Afrikakorps to Panzer Lehr*, Schiffer, 2003

Speidel, Hans, *Invasion 1944*, Paperback Library, 1972

Stiles, Bert, *Serenade to the Big Bird*, W. W. Norton, 1952

Stirling, John, *D-Day to VE-Day from My Tank Turret*, Self-published

Summersby, Kay, *Eisenhower Was My Boss*, Dell, 1948

Taylor, John M., *General Maxwell Taylor*, Doubleday, 1989

Tedder, Marshal of the Royal Air Force Lord, *With Prejudice*, Cassell, 1966

Tobin, James, *Ernie Pyle's War*, University of Kansas Press, 1997

Todd, Richard, *Caught in the Act: The Story of My Life*, Hutchinson, 1986

Tout, Ken, *By Tank: D to VE Days*, Hale, 2007

Turner, Richard E., *Mustang Pilot*, New English Library, 1975

Volker, Ulrich, *Hitler*, Vol. 1: *Ascent*, Bodley Head, 2016

Webster, David Kenyon, *Parachute Infantry*, Ebury Press, 2014

Williams, Charles, *The Last Great Frenchman: A Life of General de Gaulle*, J. Wiley, 1993

Wilson, George, *If You Survive: From Normandy to the Battle of the Bulge to the End of World War II*, Presidio Press, 1987

Winters, Dick, *Beyond Band of Brothers*, Berkley Caliber, 2006

Woollcombe, Robert, *Lion Rampant: The Memoirs of an Infantry Officer from D-Day to the Rhineland*, Black & White Publishing, 2014

GENERAL

Addison, Paul, and Calder, Angus (eds), *Time to Kill: The Soldier's Experience of War in the West, 1939–1945*, Pimlico, 1997

Asher, Michael, *The Regiment: The Real Story of the SAS*, Penguin Viking, 2007

Atkinson, Rick, *The Guns at Last Light: The War in Western Europe, 1944–1945*, Little, Brown & Co., 2013

Badsey, Stephen, *Battle Zone Normandy: Utah Beach*, Sutton Publishing, 2004

Badsey, Stephen, and Beam, Tim, *Battle Zone Normandy: Omaha Beach*, Sutton Publishing, 2004

Baggaley, J. R. P., *The 6th (Border) Battalion, The King's Own Scottish Borderers, 1939–1945*, Martin's Printing, 1946

Bailey, Roderick, *Forgotten Voices of the Secret War*, Ebury Press, 2008

—, *Forgotten Voices of D-Day*, Ebury Press, 2010

Baldoli, Claudia, Knapp, Andrew, and Overy, Richard (eds), *Bombing, States and Peoples in Western Europe, 1940–1945*, Continuum, 2011

Baldwin, Hanson, *Battles Lost and Won: Great Campaigns of World War 2*, Hodder & Stoughton, 1966

Ballantine, Duncan S., *U.S. Naval Logistics in the Second World War*, Naval War College Press, 1947

Barber, Neil, *The Pegasus and Orne Bridges: Their Capture, Defences and Relief on D-Day*, Pen & Sword, 2014

Barnes, Don, Crump, John, and Sutherland, Roy, *Thunderbolts of the Hell Hawks*, Barracuda Studios, 2011

Barnett, Corelli, *The Audit of War: The Illusion and Reality of Britain as a Great Power*, Papermac, 1987

Baumer, Robert W., and Reardon, Mark J., *American Iliad: The 18th Infantry Regiment in World War II*, Aberjona Press, 2004

Beevor, Antony, *D-Day: The Battle for Normandy*, Viking, 2009

Bekker, Cajus, *The Luftwaffe War Diaries*, Corgi, 1969

Bellamy, Chris, *Absolute War: Soviet Russia in the Second World War*, Pan, 2007

Bidwell, Shelford, and Graham, Dominick, *Fire-power: British Army Weapons and Theories of War 1904–1956*, George Allen & Unwin Publishers, 1982

Black, Jeremy, *Rethinking World War Two: The Conflict and Its Legacy*, Bloomsbury, 2015

Black, Robert W., *Rangers in World War II*, Ballantine, 1992

Blake, Steve, *The Pioneer Mustang Group: The 354th Fighter Group in World War II*, Schiffer, 2008

Blood, Philip W., *Hitler's Bandit Hunters: The SS and the Nazi Occupation of Europe*, Potomac Books, 2008

Bowman, Martin W., *USAAF Handbook 1939–1945*, Sutton, 2003

Buckingham, William F., *D-Day: The First 72 Hours*, Tempus Publishing 2004; History Press, 2009

Buckley, John, *British Armour in the Normandy Campaign 1944*, Cass, 2004

—, *Monty's Men: The British Army and the Liberation of Europe*, Yale University Press, 2013

Buckley, John (ed.), *The Normandy Campaign 1944: Sixty Years On*, Routledge, 2007

Burleigh, Michael, *The Third Reich: A New History*, Pan, 2001

—, *Moral Combat: A History of World War II*, Harper Press, 2011

Carafeno, James Jay, *After D-Day: Operation Cobra and the Normandy Breakout*, Stackpole, 2008

—, *GI Ingenuity: Improvisation, Technology and Winning World War II*, Stackpole, 2008

Cardozier, V. R., *The Mobilization of the United States in World War II: How the Government, Military and Industry Prepared for War*, McFarland, 1995

Carrell, Paul, *Invasion! They're Coming!*, Schiffer, 1995

Carver, Field Marshal Sir Michael (ed.), *The War Lords: Military Commanders of the Twentieth Century*, Little, Brown & Co., 1976

Chandler, David, G., and Collins, James Lawton (eds), *The D-Day Encyclopedia*, Helicon, 1994

Chant, Christopher, *Handbook of British Regiments*, Routledge, 1988

Citino, Robert M., *The Path to Blitzkrieg: Doctrine and Training in the German Army, 1920–1939*, Stackpole, 1999

—, *The Quest for Decisive Victory: From Stalemate to Blitzkrieg in Europe, 1899–1940*, University Press of Kansas, 2002

—, *The German Way of War: From the Thirty Years' War to the Third Reich*, University Press of Kansas, 2005

—, *Death of the Wehrmacht: The German Campaigns of 1942*, University Press of Kansas, 2007

—, *The Wehrmacht Retreats: Fighting a Lost War, 1943*, University Press of Kansas, 2012

Clark, Christopher, *Iron Kingdom: The Rise and Downfall of Prussia, 1600–1947*, Penguin, 2007

Clark, Lloyd, *Battle Zone Normandy: Operation EPSOM*, Sutton Publishing, 2004

—, *Battle Zone Normandy: Orne Bridgehead*, Sutton Publishing, 2004

Cobb, Matthew, *The Resistance: The French Fight Against the Nazis*, Pocket Books, 2009

Collier, Basil, *Hidden Weapons: Allied Secret or Undercover Services in World War II*, Pen & Sword, 2006

Collingham, Lizzie, *The Taste of War: World War II and the Battle for Food*, Penguin, 2012

Corum, James S., *The Luftwaffe: Creating the Operational Air War, 1918–1940*, University Press of Kansas, 1997

Crane, Conrad C., *American Airpower Strategy in World War II*, University Press of Kansas, 2016

Creveld, Martin van, *Supplying War: Logistics from Wallenstein to Patton*, Cambridge University Press, 1977

—, *Fighting Power: German and US Army Performance 1939–1945*, Greenwood Press, 1982

Cumerlege, Geoffrey, *War Report*, Oxford University Press, 1946

Daglish, Ian, *Battleground Europe: Operation Bluecoat*, Pen & Sword, 2003

Dallek, Robert, *Franklin D. Roosevelt and American Foreign Policy, 1932–1945*, Oxford University Press, 1995

Davidson, Basil, *Special Operations Europe*, Readers Union, 1980

Davis Biddle, Tami, *Rhetoric and Reality in Air Warfare*, Princeton University Press, 2002

Davis, Kenneth S., *The American Experience of War, 1939–1945*, Secker & Warburg, 1967

De Bolster, Marc, *47 Royal Marine Commando: An Inside Story 1943–1946*, Fonthill Media, 2014

D'Este, Carlo, *Decision in Normandy*, Penguin, 2004

DiNardo, R. L., *Germany and the Axis Powers: From Coalition to Collapse*, University Press of Kansas, 2005

—, *Germany's Panzer Arm in WWII*, Stackpole, 2006

—, *Mechanized Juggernaut or Military Anachronism?: Horses and the German Army of World War II*, Stackpole, 2008

Doherty, Richard, *Normandy 1944: The Road to Victory*, Spellmount, 2004

Dorr, Robert F., *Hell Hawks! The Untold Story of the American Fliers Who Savaged Hitler's Wehrmacht*, Zenith Press, 2008

Doubler, Michael D., *Busting the Bocage: American Combined Arms Operations in France, 6 June–31 July 1944*, Combat Studies Institute, 1988

—, *Closing with the Enemy: How GIs Fought the War in Europe, 1944–1945*, University Press of Kansas, 1994

Downing, David, *The Devil's Virtuoso: German Generals at War 1940–45*, New English Library, 1977

Dunning, James, *The Fighting Fourth: No. 4 Commando at War 1940–45*, The History Press, 2010

Earnshaw, James Douglas, *609 at War*, Vector, 2003

Eberle, Henrik, and Uhl, Matthias (eds), *The Hitler Book*, John Murray, 2006

Eckhertz, Holger, *D-Day Through German Eyes*, DTZ History Publications, 2015

Edgerton, David, *England and the Aeroplane*, Macmillan, 1991

—, *Warfare State: Britain, 1920–1970*, Cambridge University Press, 2006

—, *Britain's War Machine: Weapons, Resources and Experts in the Second World War*, Allen Lane, 2011

Ellis, John, *The Sharp End: The Fighting Man in World War II*, Pimlico, 1993

—, *The World War II Databook: The Essential Facts and Figures for All the Combatants*, Aurum, 1995

Elmhirst, Thomas, *Recollections*, Self-published, 1991

Elphick, Peter, *Liberty: The Ships That Won the War*, Chatham, 2001

Estes, Kenneth, *A European Anabasis*, Helion, 2015

Evans, Richard, *The Third Reich in Power*, Penguin, 2006

—, *The Third Reich at War*, Penguin, 2009

Farquharson, J. E., *The Plough and the Swastika: The NSDAP and Agriculture in Germany, 1928–45*, Sage Publications, 1976

Fennell, Jonathan, *Combat and Morale in the North African Campaign*, Cambridge University Press, 2011

Field, Jacob F., *D-Day In Numbers: The Facts Behind Operation Overlord*, Michael O'Mara Books, 2014

Fletcher, David, *The Great Tank Scandal: British Armour in the Second World War, Part I*, HMSO, 1989

Flower, Desmond, and Reeves, James (eds), *The War 1939–1945: A Documentary History*, Da Capo, 1997

Foot, M. R. D., *Resistance: European Resistance to Nazism 1949–45*, Eyre Methuen, 1976

Ford, Ken, *Battle Zone Normandy: Juno Beach*, Sutton Publishing, 2004

—, *Battle Zone Normandy: Sword Beach*, Sutton Publishing, 2004

Forfar, John, *From Omaha to the Scheldt*, 47 Royal Marine Commando Association, 2013

Forty, George, *US Army Handbook, 1939–1945*, Sutton, 1995

—, *British Army Handbook, 1939–1945*, Sutton, 1998

Fraser, David, *And We Shall Shock Them: The British Army in the Second World War*, Cassell, 1999

Frayn Turner, John, *Invasion '44*, Corgi, 1974

Freeman, Roger A., *The Mighty Eighth War Diary*, Jane's, 1986

Fritz, Stephen G., *Frontsoldaten: The German Soldier in World War II*, University Press of Kentucky, 1997

Gardiner, Juliet, *Wartime: Britain 1939–1945*, Review, 2005

Gavin, James M., and Lee, William C., *Airborne Warfare*, Washington Infantry Journal Press, 1947

Gilbert, Martin, *D-Day*, J. Wiley, 2004

Gilchrest, Donald, *The Commandos: D-Day and After*, Robert Hale, 1994

Gildea, Robert, *Fighters in the Shadows: A New History of the French Resistance*, Faber & Faber, 2015

Goerlitz, Walter, *History of the German General Staff*, Praeger, 1967

Gooderson, Ian, *Air Power at the Battlefront: Allied Close Air Support in Europe 1943–45*, Frank Cass, 1998

Graves, Donald E., *Blood and Steel: The Wehrmacht Archive – Normandy 1944*, Frontline, 2013

Grunberger, Richard, *A Social History of the Third Reich*, Phoenix, 2005

Hall, David Ian, *The Strategy for Victory: The Development of British Tactical Air Power, 1919–1943*, Praeger Security International, 2008

Handel, Michael I. (ed.), *Intelligence and Military Operations*, Frank Cass, 1990

Hansell, Haywood S. Jr., *The Air Plan That Defeated Hitler*, Arno Press, 1980

Harrison, Mark (ed.), *The Economics of World War II*, Cambridge University Press, 2000

Harrison Place, Timothy, *Military Training in the British Army, 1940–1944: From Dunkirk to D-Day*, Frank Cass, 2000

Hart, Russell A., *Clash of Arms: How the Allies Won in Normandy*, Lynne Rienner Publishers, 2001

Hart, Stephen, *Colossal Cracks: The 21st Army Group in Northwest Europe, 1944–45*, Praeger, 2000

—, *Battle Zone Normandy: Road to Falaise*, Sutton Publishing, 2004

Hastings, Max, *Armageddon: The Battle for Germany, 1944–1945*, Pan, 2005

—, *Das Reich: The March of the 2nd SS Panzer Division Through France, June 1944*, Pan, 2009

—, *All Hell Let Loose: The World at War, 1939–1945*, Harper Press, 2011

—, *The Secret War: Spies, Codes and Guerillas 1939–1945*, William Collins, 2015

—, *Overlord: D-Day and the Battle for Normandy 1944*, Pan, 2015

Havers, R. P. W., *Battle Zone Normandy: Battle for Cherbourg*, Sutton Publishing, 2004

Herman, Arthur, *Freedom's Forge: How American Business Produced Victory in World War II*, Random House, 2012

Holland, James, *Heroes: The Greatest Generation and the Second World War*, Harper Perennial, 2007

—, *The War in the West: Germany Ascendant*, Bantam Press, 2015

—, *The War in the West: The Allies Strike Back*, Bantam Press, 2017

—, *Big Week: The Greatest Air Battle of World War II*, Bantam Press, 2018

Holmes, Richard, *Firing Line*, Pimlico, 1994

House, Jonathan M., *Combined Arms Warfare in the Twentieth Century*, University Press of Kansas, 2001

Hoyt, Edwin P., *The GI's War: American Soldiers in Europe during World War II*, Cooper Square Press, 2000

Irons, Roy, *The Relentless Offensive: War and Bomber Command, 1939–1945*, Pen & Sword, 2009

Isby, David C. (ed.), *Fighting in Normandy: The German Army from D-Day to Villers-Bocage*, Greenhill, 2001

—, *Fighting the Breakout: The German Army in Normandy from Cobra to the Falaise Gap*, Frontline, 2015

—, *Fighting the Invasion: The German Army at D-Day*, Skyhorse, 2016

Jarymowycz, Roman, *Tank Tactics: From Normandy to Lorraine*, Stackpole Books, 2009

Jordan, Jonathan W., *Brothers, Rivals, Victors*, NAL Caliber, 2012

Jordan, William, *Normandy 44: D-Day and the Battle of Normandy*, Pro Libris, 2007

Jörgensen, Christer, *Rommel's Panzers*, Reference Group Brown, 2003

Keegan, John (ed.), *Churchill's Generals*, Abacus, 1991

Kemp, Anthony, *The SAS at War, 1941–1945*, Penguin, 2000

Kershaw, Ian, *Fateful Choices: Ten Decisions That Changed the World, 1940–1941*, Allen Lane, 2007

—, *The End: Hitler's Germany 1944–45*, Allen Lane, 2011

Kershaw, Robert, *D-Day: Piercing the Atlantic Wall*, Ian Allen Publishing, 2008

Keusgen, Helmut K. von, *Strongpoint WN62: Normandy 1942–1944*, Hek Creativ Verlag, 2017

Kite, Ben, *Stout Hearts: The British and Canadians in Normandy 1944*, Helion, 2014

Klein, Maury, *A Call to Arms: Mobilizing America for World War II*, Bloomsbury Press, 2013

Kohn, Richard H., and Harahan, Joseph P., *Air Superiority in World War II and Korea*, Office of Air Force History, United States Air Force, 1983

Kortenhaus, Werner, *The Combat History of the 21. Panzer Division*, Helion, 2014

Lane, Frederic C., *Ships for Victory: A History of Shipbuilding Under the U.S. Maritime Commission in World War II*, Johns Hopkins University Press, 1951

Latawski, Paul, *Battle Zone Normandy: Falaise Pocket*, Sutton Publishing, 2004

Lavery, Brian, *Hostilities Only: Training the Wartime Royal Navy*, Conway, 2004

—, *Churchill's Navy: The Ships, Men and Organisation 1939–1945*, Conway, 2006

—, *In Which They Served: The Royal Navy Officer Experience in the Second World War*, Conway, 2009

Lefèvre, Eric, *Panzers in Normandy Then and Now*, After the Battle, 1990

Levy, 'Yank', *Guerilla Warfare*, Penguin, 1941

Lewin, Ronald, *Ultra Goes to War: The Secret Story*, Penguin, 2001

—, *Rommel as Military Commander*, Pen & Sword, 2004

Lewis, Adrian R., *Omaha Beach: A Flawed Victory*, Tempus Publishing, 2004

Lewis, Jon E., *D-Day As They Saw It*, Robinson Publishing, 1994 and 2004

Liddell Hart, B. H., *The Other Side of the Hill*, Cassell, 1951

Lodieu, Didier, *Dying for Saint-Lô: Hedgerow Hell, July 1944*, Histoire & Collections, 2007

Loewenheim, Francis L., Langley, Harold D., and Jonas, Manfred (eds), *Roosevelt and Churchill: Their Secret Wartime Correspondence*, Da Capo, 1990

Lofaro, Guy, *The Sword of St. Michael: The 82nd Airborne Division in World War II*, Da Capo, 2011

Lucas, James, *German Army Handbook, 1939–1945*, Sutton, 1998

Mackenzie, William, *The Secret History of SOE Special Operations Executive 1940–1945*, St Ermin's Press, 2000

Macintyre, Ben, *Double Cross: The True Story of the D-Day Spies*, Bloomsbury Publishing, 2012

—, *SAS: Rogue Heroes*, Penguin Viking, 2016

Mallman Showell, Jak P., *Hitler's Navy*, Seaforth Publishing, 2009

Man, John, *The Penguin Atlas of D-Day and the Normandy Campaign*, Viking, 1994

Margaritis, Peter, *Crossroads at Margival: Hitler's Last Conference in France, June 17, 1944*, Self-published, 2009

Mazower, Mark, *Hitler's Empire: Nazi Rule in Occupied Europe*, Allen Lane, 2008

McFarland, Stephen L., and Phillips Newton, Wesley, *To Command the Sky: The Battle for Air Superiority Over Germany 1942–1944*, Smithsonian Institution Press, 1991

McKay, Sinclair, *The Secret Life of Bletchley Park*, Aurum, 2011

—, *The Secret Listeners: How the Y Service Intercepted the German Codes for Bletchley Park*, Aurum, 2013

McManus, John C., *Grunts: Inside the American Infantry Experience*, NAL Caliber, 2010

McNab, Chris (ed.), *German Paratroopers*, MBI, 2000

Mead, Richard, *Churchill's Lions: A Biographical Guide to the Key British Generals of World War II*, Spellmount, 2007

—, *The Men Behind Monty*, Pen & Sword, 2011

Meilinger, Colonel Phillip S., *The Paths of Heaven: The Evolution of Airpower Theory*, Air University Press, 1997

Messenger, Charles, *The Second World War in the West*, Cassell, 2001

Meyer, Hubert, *The 12th SS: The History of the Hitler Youth Panzer Division*, Vol. I, Stackpole, 2005

—, *The 12th SS: The History of the Hitler Youth Panzer Division:* Vol. II: Stackpole, 2005

Michel, Henri, *The Shadow War: Resistance in Europe 1939–45*, Andre Deutsch, 1972

Middlebrook, Martin, and Everitt, Chris, *The Bomber Command War Diaries*, Penguin, 1990

Mierzejewski, Alfred C., *The Collapse of the German War Economy, 1944–1945: Allied Air Power and the German National Railway*, University of North Carolina Press, 1988

—, *The Most Valuable Asset of the Reich: A History of the German National Railway*, Vol. 2: *1933–1945*, University of North Carolina Press, 2000

Milano, Vince, and Conner, Bruce, *Normandiefront: D-Day to St-Lô Through German Eyes*, Spellmount, 2001

Miller, Donald L., *Eighth Air Force*, Aurum, 2008

Miller, Russell, *Nothing Less Than Victory: The Oral History of D-Day*, Michael Joseph, 1993; Penguin Books, 1994

Milner, Marc, *The Battle of the Atlantic*, Tempus, 2005

—, *Stopping the Panzer: The Untold Story of D-Day*, University Press of Kansas, 2014

Milton, Giles, *D-Day: The Soldier's Story*, John Murray, 2018

Milward, Alan S., *War, Economy and Society, 1939–1945*, University of California Press, 1979

Mitcham, Samuel W., *Hitler's Legions: German Army Order of Battle World War II*, Leo Cooper, 1985

—, *Panzers in Normandy: General Hans Eberbach and the German Defense of France, 1944*, Stackpole, 2009

Monahan, Evelyn M., and Neidel-Greenlee, Rosemary, *And If I Perish: Frontline U.S. Army Nurses in World War II*, Knopf, 2003

Mortimer, Gavin, *Stirling's Men: The Inside History of the SAS in World War II*, Cassell, 2005

—, *The SAS in World War II: An Illustrated History*, Osprey, 2011

Murray, Williamson, *Luftwaffe: Strategy for Defeat*, Grafton, 1988

Murray, Williamson, and Millett, Allan R., *Military Innovation in the Interwar Period*, Cambridge University Press, 1996

—, *A War to Be Won: Fighting the Second World War*, Belknap Harvard, 2000

Napier, Stephen, *The Armoured Campaign in Normandy June–August 1944*, The History Press, 2015

Neillands, Robin, *The Battle of Normandy 1944*, Cassell, 2003

Neillands, Robin, and De Norman, Roderick, *D-Day 1944: Voices from Normandy*, Cassell Military Paperbacks, 2001; Weidenfeld & Nicolson, 1993

Neitzel, Sönke, *Tapping Hitler's Generals: Transcripts of Secret Conversations, 1942–45*, Frontline, 2007

Neitzel, Sönke, and Welzer, Harald, *Soldaten: On Fighting, Killing and Dying*, Simon & Schuster, 2012

Nielsen, Generalleutnant Andreas, *USAF Historical Studies No. 173: The German Air Forces Staff*, Arno Press, 1968

Oberkammando der Wehrmacht, *Fahrten und Flüge gegen England*, Zeitgeschichte-Verlag Berlin, 1941

O'Brien, Phillips Payson, *How the War Was Won*, Cambridge University Press, 2015

Overy, Richard, *The Bombing War: Europe 1939–1945*, Allen Lane, 2013

Overy, Richard (ed.), *The New York Times Complete World War II 1939–1945*, Black Dog & Leventhal, 2013

Pallud, Jean-Paul, *Rückmarsch!: The German Retreat from Normandy*, After the Battle, 2006

Penrose, Jane (ed.), *The D-Day Companion*, Osprey, 2004

Pons, Gregory, *9th Air Force: American Tactical Aviation in the ETO, 1942–1945*, Histoire & Collections, 2008

Pugsley, A. F., *Destroyer Man*, Wiedenfeld & Nicolson, 1957

Pugsley, Christopher, *Battle Zone Normandy: Operation Cobra*, Sutton Publishing, 2004

Ramsay, Winston G. (ed.), *D-Day Then and Now*, Vol. I, After the Battle, 1995

—, *D-Day Then and Now*, Vol. II, After the Battle, 1995

—, *Invasion Airfields Then and Now*, After the Battle, 2017

Reichmann, Günther, *The Vampire Economy: Doing Business Under Fascism*, Vanguard Press, 1939

Reynolds, Michael, *Steel Inferno: I SS Panzer Corps in Normandy*, Spellmount, 1997

—, *Sons of the Reich: II SS Panzer Corps*, Pen & Sword, 2002

—, *Eagles and Bulldogs in Normandy 1944*, Spellmount, 2003

Richards, Denis, *RAF Bomber Command in the Second World War: The Hardest Victory*, Penguin, 2001

Ritchie, Sebastian, *Industry and Air Power: The Expansion of British Aircraft Production, 1935–1941*, Routledge, 1997

—, *Arnhem: Myth and Reality*, Robert Hale, 2011

Roberts, Mary Louise, *D-Day Through French Eyes: Normandy 1944*, University of Chicago Press, 2014

Roskill, Stephen, *The Navy at War, 1939–1945*, Wordsworth Editions, 1998

Rust, Kenn C., *The Ninth Air Force in World War II*, Aero Publishers, 1970

Ryan, Cornelius, *The Longest Day: June 6, 1944*, Andre Deutsch, 2014

Saunders, Timothy, *Battleground Europe: Hill 112 – Battle of the Odon*, Leo Cooper, 2001

Schneider, Wolfgang, *Tigers in Normandy*, Pen & Sword, 2011§1

Shepherd, Ben, *A War of Nerves: Soldiers and Psychiatrists, 1904–1994*, Jonathan Cape, 2000

Shilleto, Carl, *Battleground Normandy: Utah Beach – St Mère Église, VII Corps, 82nd and 101st Airborne Divisions*, Pen & Sword, 2001

Smart, Nick, *Biographical Dictionary of British Generals of the Second World War*, Pen & Sword, 2005

Speer, Frank E., *The Debden Warbirds*, Schiffer, 1999

Spick, Mike, *Luftwaffe Fighter Aces*, Greenhill, 1996

—, *Allied Fighter Aces of World War II*, Greenhill, 1997

—, *Aces of the Reich: The Making of a Luftwaffe Fighter-Pilot*, Greenhill, 2006

Stargard, Nicholas, *The German War: A Nation Under Arms 1939–45*, Bodley Head, 2015

Stephenson, Michael, *The Last Full Measure: How Soldiers Die in Battle*, Crown, 2012

Suchenwirth, Richard, *USAF Historical Studies No. 174: Command and Leadership in the German Air Force*, Arno Press, 1969

—, *Historical Turning Points in the German Air Force War Effort*, University Press of the Pacific, 2004

—, *The Development of the German Air Forces, 1919–1939*, University Press of the Pacific, 2005

Symonds, Craig L., *Operation Neptune*, Oxford University Press, 2016

Számvéber, Norbert, *Waffen-SS Armour in Normandy*, Helion, 2012

Taylor, Daniel, *Villers-Bocage Through the Lens*, After the Battle, 1999

Terraine, John, *The Right of the Line*, Hodder & Stoughton, 1985

Tooze, Adam, *The Wages of Destruction: The Making and Breaking of the Nazi Economy*, Penguin, 2007

Trevor-Roper, H. R. (ed.), *Hitler's War Directives 1939–1945*, Pan, 1966

Trew, Simon, *Battle Zone Normandy: Gold Beach*, Sutton Publishing, 2004

Trew, Simon, and Badsey, Stephen, *Battle Zone Normandy: Battle for Caen*, Sutton Publishing, 2004

Urban, Mark, *The Tank War: The Men, The Machines, The Long Road to Victory 1939–45*, Little, Brown & Co., 2013

Van Creveld, Martin, *Fighting Power: German and US Army Performance 1939–1945*, Greenwood Press, 1982

Various, *World War II: Day by Day*, Dorling Kindersley, 2004

Vinen, Richard, *The Unfree French: Life Under the Occupation*, Penguin, 2007

Von der Porten, Edward P., *The German Navy in World War II*, Arthur Baker, 1970

Weale, Adrian, *The SS: A New History*, Abacus, 2012

Wells, Mark K., *Courage and Air Warfare: The Allied Aircrew Experience in the Second World War*, Frank Cass, 1997

Werth, Alexander, *France 1940–1955*, Robert Hale, 1956

Wheal, Donald James, and Shaw, Warren (eds), *The Penguin Dictionary of the Third Reich*, Penguin Books, 2002

Wheal, Elizabeth-Anne, and Pope, Stephen, *The Macmillan Dictionary of the Second World War*, Macmillan, 1989

White, Antonia, *BBC at War*, BBC, 1946

Whiting, Charles, *Hunters From the Sky: The German Parachute Corps, 1940–1945*, Cooper Square Press, 2001

Wood, James A. (ed.), *Army of the West*, Stackpole, 2007

Woollcombe, Robert, *All the Blue Bonnets: The History of the King's Own Scottish Borderers*, Arms & Armour Press, 1980

Wynter, Brigadier H. W., *Special Forces in the Desert War, 1940–1943*, Public Record Office War Histories, 2001

Yates, Peter, *Battle Zone Normandy: Battle for St-Lô*, Sutton Publishing, 2004

Yeide, Harry, *The Tank Killers: A History of America's World War II Tank Destroyer Force*, Spellmount, 2005

Zaloga, Steven, *D-Day Fortifications in Normandy*, Osprey, 2005

Zetterling, Niklas, *Normandy 1944: German Military Organization, Combat Power and Organizational Effectiveness*, J. J. Fedorowicz, 2000

Ziegler, Frank H., *The Story of 609 Squadron: Under the White Rose*, Crécy, 1993

Zuehlke, Mark, *Holding Juno: Canada's Heroic Defense of the D-Day Beaches, June 7–12, 1944*, Douglas & McIntyre, 2005

—, *Breakout from Juno: First Canadian Army and the Normandy Campaign, July 4–August 21, 1944*, Douglas & McIntyre, 2011

—, *Assault on Juno*, Raven Books, 2012

PAMPHLETS, JOURNALS, PERIODICALS AND MAGAZINES

After the Battle, *The Battle of the Falaise Pocket*, No. 8

—, *Normandy 1973*, No. 1

—, *Scrapyard Panther*, No. 20

Anon., 'German Army Transport', *Automobile Engineer*, October 1945

Dahlstrom, Michael P., *The Role of Airpower in the Overlord Invasion: An Effects-based Operation*, Airpower Research Institute, 2007

Hallion, Richard P., *D-Day 1944: Air Power Over the Normandy Beaches and Beyond*, Air Force History and Museums Program, 1994

O'Brien, Phillips P., 'East versus West in the Defeat of Nazi Germany', *Journal of Strategic Studies*, 23:2, 2008

Peaty, John, 'Myth, Reality and Carlo D'Este', *War Studies Journal*, Vol. 1, No. 2, Spring 1996

Widder, Werner, 'Auftragstaktik and Innere Führung: Trademarks of German Leadership', *Military Review*, September/October 2002

Zabecki, David, *Auftragstaktik*

FILMS, DVDS

The Fighting Wessex Wyverns: Their Legacy, The 43rd Wessex Association

Acknowledgements

This book has only been possible thanks to significant help from a number of people. It has been fascinating to visit several archives and I am hugely grateful to Tammy Horton at the US Air Force Historical Research Agency at Maxwell, Alabama, for all her help and for allowing me to pester her with far too many questions and requests. I am also indebted to all the wonderful people at the truly brilliant National World War II Museum in New Orleans – and specifically to Rob Citino, a true friend, as well as Jeremy Collins and Seth Paridon, who allowed me access to many of the museum's incredible oral history interviews with Normandy veterans. My thanks, too, to Sarah Kerksey, Becky Mackie and all the team in New Orleans. Thank you also to the staffs at the US Army Heritage and Education Center at Carlisle Barracks, the Bundesarchiv-Militärarchiv at Freiburg, the Liddell Hart Centre for Military History at King's College, London, the Imperial War Museum in London, the National Archives in Kew and the Mémoriale de Caen. Huge thanks as well to David Willey for all his enormous help and to all his staff at the brilliant Tank Museum, Bovington in Dorset. Thanks also to Shaun Illingworth of the Rutgers Oral History Archive for his considerable help.

A number of friends and colleagues have given me more assistance than I'm sure I deserve. In Normandy, Paul Woodadge has bent over backwards with help, advice, documents, insights and his enormous knowledge of both the campaign and the countryside over which it was fought. Professor John Buckley is a historian whom I admire enormously and who has given me much to think about. No man has done more work on the British Army in Normandy than Brigadier Ben Kite, and his book and knowledge have been invaluable. My thanks, too, to David Christopherson, son of Stanley, and a great friend. It was with David that fifteen years ago I toured Normandy and walked a quiet track on Point 103 where his father and the Sherwood Rangers had fought all those years ago. Thank you also to my great friend Trevor Chaytor-Norris and our fellow travelling companions on that trip, and to Peter Livanos and friends for two fabulous, eye-opening and highly instructive trips to Normandy. Al Murray has been a huge help and sounding board, and has pointed me in the direction of a number of works on the subject. In the US, Nicholas Moran has also been another very willing to share his immense knowledge of WWII armoured fighting vehicles and has encouraged me to think about these weapons of war in a different way. Thank you. I am also hugely grateful to Aaron Young, Freya Eden-Ellis, Jon Wood and Keith Branch, who all helped make the TV documentary *Normandy 44* back in 2014. Thanks, too, for help go to Shane Greer, Christopher Jary, Michael Dolan, Michael Wharton, Ian Holmes, Andrew Whitmarsh and his team at the D-Day Story Museum in Portsmouth, Martin Bishkek at Legasee, Daphna Rubin, Steve Hoggard, and Jonathan Ware.

Jim Clark and Jamie Meachin have become good friends and the opportunity to drive around in Jim's Sherman has added an extra experiential dimension to the research for this book. I am also hugely grateful to Tom Crawford, and especially James Shopland and Tobin Jones for all their knowledge, help and willingness to demonstrate and share their incredible collections of wartime machinery and weaponry. Several other friends have given enormous help: Simon Keeling, a brilliant meteorologist, who first alerted me to the vagaries of wartime weather forecasting. He then spent considerable time examining wartime meteorological maps and documents for the weather around the beginning of June 1944, which he then explained in painstaking detail and with immense patience. It was a reminder to me that historians do need to seek the knowledge of people beyond their own field.

Seb Cox, the Head of Air Historical Branch, has been extremely generous with his time and knowledge. Thank you, as well, to Antony Beevor for his help and advice. Paul Beaver is an expert on all matters aviation who has helped along the way, while I am also grateful to Paul Stoddart for his advice and suggestions. Two friends stand out especially: Steve Prince, Head of the Naval Historical Branch, has readily shared his enormous knowledge and I owe him for allowing me to pinch his phrases 'the freedom of poverty' and 'the constraints of wealth', for which I can claim absolutely no credit. I'm also grateful to his team in Portsmouth for all their help on naval aspects of the campaign. The second is Dr Peter Caddick-Adams, great friend, one-time neighbour, colleague and a man of immense knowledge always very happy to chew the cud, argue about Monty, and offer his services as a wise and invaluable sounding-board. Thank you, all of you.

Various others have given assistance along the way. Elisabeth Gausseron in France has helped with both research and translation, Michelle Miles and Ingo Maerker in Freiburg, Emily Brown with further French translation and Rob Schaefer in Germany has interviewed several veterans so brilliantly. Lalla Hitchings and Rachel Sykes have also helped with transcriptions, for which huge thanks, as always. Extra special thanks, however, are due to two people. The first is Laura Bailey, who has done a huge amount of photographing of documents at the National Archives in Kew and the Imperial War Museum and has been a truly enormous help. The second is Dorothee Schneider, a great friend and wonderful person, who went more than the extra mile with translations of German testimonies. Thank you so much, both of you.

Any book like this is, to a certain extent, a collaboration, and I consider myself immensely lucky to have had Brenda Updegraff to copy-edit the book. It has been a Herculean task and Brenda has done this with incredible skill and good judgement. I really am eternally grateful and simply cannot thank her enough for her phenomenal help. Enormous thanks, too, are due to all at Grove Atlantic in New York: Deb Seeger, Justina Batchelor, Morgan Entrekin and everyone who has worked on the book, but I owe especial thanks to George Gibson for all his patience, advice, wisdom and immense support. Thank you. In London, thank you to all at Bantam Press: the brilliant Phil Lord, Darcy Nicholson, Eloisa Clegg, Tom Hill and all who have helped get this book into being. Particular thanks, however, go to Bill Scott-Kerr: great friend, supporter, brilliant publisher and all-round lovely person, and to whom this book is dedicated. Thank you.

Finally, I'd like to thank Patrick Walsh for being not only a great friend but also a brilliant literary agent, advisor and advocate, and also my family, Rachel, Ned and Daisy. This book has been possible only by sacrificing many mornings, evenings and weekends, and they have been extraordinarily supportive, as always, from start to finish. Thank you.

Picture Acknowledgements

All photographs have been kindly supplied by the author except those listed below. Every effort has been made to trace copyright holders; those overlooked are invited to get in touch with the publishers.

Section 1

Page 1, bottom right
Anti-invasion beach obstacles along the Normandy coast: Helmut Grosse/ Bundesarchiv, bild: 101I-674-7773-07

Page 4, 3rd row, left
Pegasus Bridge on 7 June. On the far – Ranville – side, crashed gliders: © IWM (B5288)

Page 5, top right
Cromwells and Shermans of the 4th County of London Yeomanry heading inland from Gold Beach on 7 June: © IWM (B5251)

Page 7, top left
12. SS troops moving through the much-fought-over village of Rauray: dpa picture alliance / Alamy Stock Photo

Page 7, top right
Fallschirmjäger (paratroopers) moving by horse and cart: Zimmermann/ Bundesarchiv, bild: 101I-583-2145-31

Page 7, 2nd row
Robert Capa's photograph of German troops surrendering in Cherbourg, as witnessed and reported by Ernie Pyle on 27 June 1944: Robert Capa © International Center of Photography/Magnum Photos

Page 7, 3rd row
Churchill tanks and men of the 15th (Scottish) Division move forward through the mist and drizzle at the start of Operation EPSOM, 26 June 1944: © IWM (B5956)

Page 7, bottom left
Fontenay-le-Pesnel, the scene of vicious fighting. A knocked-out Pak 40 75mm anti-tank gun alongside its dead gunner, 25 June 1944: © IWM (B5939)

Page 7, bottom right
Shermans of the Sherwood Rangers near Rauray on 30 June 1944: © IWM (B6218)

Page 8, top left
A Panzer IV well camouflaged in the hedgerows: Reich/Bundesarchiv, bild: 101I-586-2215-34A

Section 2

Page 1, middle left
British troops awaiting a counter-attack in hastily dug trenches and foxholes between hills 112 and 113 on 16 July 1944: © IWM (B7441)

Page 3, 2nd row, left
Allied armoured units were supported by large numbers of low loaders: © IWM (B9091)

Page 6, top left
A British ammunition truck is hit and explodes during the EPSOM battle, 26 June 1944: © IWM (B6017)

Gallery of Portraits

Pages lvi–lvii
All pictures supplied by the author

Integrated Pictures

All pictures supplied by the author except where listed below:

Part IV opener; pages 408–9
Hawker Typhoon rocket attack: © IWM (CL617)

Front endpaper

Supplied by the author

Back endpaper

Courtesy of *After the Battle*

For more photographs, please visit www.griffonmerlin.com/normandy44

General Eisenhower (*left*) confers with
Generals Omar Bradley (*centre*) and
J. Lawton Collins.

Index

Men of the US 29th Infantry Division
in Weymouth, southern England,
before the invasion.

American airborne troops with French civilians.

American soldiers of the 3rd Armored
Division beside a knocked-out StuG
assault gun.

British troops take a break,
August 1944.

ABOUT THE AUTHOR

James Holland is an award-winning historian, writer and broadcaster. The author of a number of bestselling histories, including *Battle of Britain*, *Dam Busters*, *Burma '44* and, most recently, *Big Week*, he has also written nine works of historical fiction, including the Jack Tanner novels.

He is currently writing an acclaimed three-volume new history of the Second World War, *The War in the West*. He has presented – and written – many television programmes and series for the BBC, Channel 4, National Geographic, History and Discovery Channels.

He is also co-founder of the Chalke Valley History Festival and of WarGen.org, an online Second World War resource site, and presents the Chalke Valley History Hit podcast. A fellow of the Royal Historical Society, he also has a weekly podcast with Al Murray, *We Have Ways of Making You Talk: Al Murray and James Holland talk World War II*. He can be found on Twitter and Instagram as @James 1940.

For more photographs, please visit www.griffonmerlin.com/normandy44